THE
NEW TESTAMENT
AND
EARLY CHRISTIANITY

THE
NEW
TESTAMENT
AND
EARLY
CHRISTIANITY

❖

Joseph B. Tyson

Southern Methodist University

MACMILLAN PUBLISHING COMPANY
New York
COLLIER MACMILLAN PUBLISHERS
London

Macmillan Publishing Company
866 Third Avenue, New York, New York 10022

Collier Macmillan Canada, Inc.

Library of Congress Cataloging in Publication Data

Tyson, Joseph B.
    The New Testament and early Christianity.

    Bibliography: p.
    Includes index.
    1. Church history—Primitive and early church, ca.
30-600. 2. Bible. N.T.—Criticism, interpretation,
etc. 3. Jesus Christ—History of doctrines—Early
church, ca. 30-600. 4. Christian literature, Early—
History and criticism. I. Title.
BR165.T89 1984   270.   83-9378
ISBN 0-02-421890-1

ISBN   0-02-421890-1

Printing: 2 3 4 5 6 7 8   Year: 4 5 6 7 8 9 0 1 2

FOR PEGGY

❖ PREFACE ❖

THIS book is an expanded and reorganized version of *A Study of Early Christianity,* published in 1973. The title is intended to call attention to the two interrelated areas with which the book is concerned: a set of documents known as the New Testament (NT), and a movement known as early Christianity. Those who used the first version will find that the second has been entirely rewritten and reorganized, with fuller treatments of most of the topics and documents. All of the NT books are treated, and, in addition, some eighteen noncanonical texts are discussed. Outlines of the major documents are given, and updated bibliographies are included at the end of each chapter.

Despite the changes in organization, the basic concept of this edition is the same as that of the earlier book. Both were written in the conviction that the usual separation of NT studies and studies in early Christian history should be challenged. Those books that concentrate exclusively on the NT fail to do justice to the fullness of Christianity, which, in the early period, produced many more documents than those in the NT. My purpose has been to bore a small hole in the wall that separates the NT from early church history.

Like its predecessor, *The New Testament and Early Christianity* was written to serve primarily as a textbook in an introductory college or seminary course in NT or in early Christian history and literature. It is expected that students will read the primary sources in connection with the discussions here. In general, this book serves to introduce the various primary documents; it is not a substitute for them.

The Introduction, in Part One, explores, in some detail, the reasons for the present approach and discusses some of the problems in historical and literary study. Part Two presents the historical and cultural context of early Christianity and concentrates on religious life and thought in Judaism and in the Hellenistic world. Part Three treats the historical Jesus, as he may be understood by reading the Christian gospels and by studying the oral tradition that lies behind them. Part Four treats the major early Christian movements in the period 30–70 CE, and Part Five, those of the years 70–185 CE. In this last section, a number of diverse Christian groups are treated, and the emergence of early Catholic Christianity, which became the dominant movement, is traced.

With help from a grant from the publisher, I was able to consult with several scholars in the preparation of this book. I wish to thank them publicly for their expert advice, criticism, and encouragement. Harold W. Attridge, Associate Professor of NT at Perkins School of Theology, Southern Methodist University, worked closely with me, especially in the sections that deal with Gnostic Christianity. Douglas R. A. Hare, William F. Orr Professor of NT at Pittsburgh Theological Seminary, consulted with me on late Jewish Christianity, and Ellis Rivkin, Adolph S. Ochs Professor of Jewish History at Hebrew Union College—Jewish Institute of Religion, gave me expert advice on Judaism in the Hellenistic period. At an earlier time, Robert A. Kraft, Professor of Religious Studies at the University of Pennsylvania, supplied me with detailed comments on the entire first edition. I wish also to thank the following scholars, who reviewed the manuscript and offered valuable suggestions: Eldon J. Epp, Dean of Humanities and Social Sciences and Harkness Professor of Biblical Literature, Case Western Reserve University; Harry Gamble, Associate Professor of Religious Studies, University of Virginia; and Paul W. Hollenbach, chair, Religious Studies Program, Iowa State University. All of these scholars will readily recognize their contributions. Any errors, deficiencies, or misperceptions are the author's.

Joseph B. Tyson
Southern Methodist University

❖ ACKNOWLEDGMENTS ❖

The Scripture quotations in this publication are from the Revised Standard Version of the Bible, copyrighted 1946, 1952 © 1971, 1973 by the division of Christian Education of the National Council of the Churches of Christ in the United States of America and used by permission.

Sayings 3, 12, 26, 34, 37, 44, 51, 54, 77, and 114, beginning on page 205 from "The Gospel of Thomas" in THE NAG HAMMADI LIBRARY: In English, James M. Robinson, General Editor. Copyright © 1978 by E. J. Brill. Reprinted by permission of Harper & Row, Publishers, Inc.

❖ CONTENTS ❖

❖ LIST OF MAPS ❖

❖ ABBREVIATIONS ❖

BCE	Before the Common Era. Dates correspond to dates B. C.
CE	Common Era. Dates correspond to dates A. D.
NEB	*The New English Bible*
NT	The New Testament
OT	The Old Testament
RSV	The Revised Standard Version of the Bible

❖ OLD TESTAMENT AND APOCRYPHA ❖

Gen	Genesis	Ps (Pss)	Psalm (Psalms)
Exod	Exodus	Prov	Proverbs
Lev	Leviticus	Eccl	Ecclesiastes
Num	Numbers	Cant	Song of Solomon
Deut	Deuteronomy	Isa	Isaiah
Josh	Joshua	Jer	Jeremiah
Judg	Judges	Lam	Lamentations
Ruth	Ruth	Ezek	Ezekiel
1 Sam	1 Samuel	Dan	Daniel
2 Sam	2 Samuel	Hos	Hosea
1 Kgs	1 Kings	Joel	Joel
2 Kgs	2 Kings	Amos	Amos
1 Chr	1 Chronicles	Obad	Obadiah
2 Chr	2 Chronicles	Jonah	Jonah
Ezra	Ezra	Mic	Micah
Neh	Nehemiah	Nah	Nahum
Esth	Esther	Hab	Habakkuk
Job	Job	Zeph	Zephaniah
Hag	Haggai	Mal	Malachi
Zech	Zechariah	1 Macc	1 Maccabees

❖ NEW TESTAMENT ❖

Matt	Matthew	1 Tim	1 Timothy
Mark	Mark	2 Tim	2 Timothy
Luke	Luke	Titus	Titus
John	John	Phlm	Philemon
Acts	Acts of the Apostles	Heb	Hebrews
Rom	Romans	Jas	James
1 Cor	1 Corinthians	1 Pet	1 Peter
2 Cor	2 Corinthians	2 Pet	2 Peter
Gal	Galatians	1 John	1 John
Eph	Ephesians	2 John	2 John
Phil	Philippians	3 John	3 John
Col	Colossians	Jude	Jude
1 Thess	1 Thessalonians	Rev	Revelation
2 Thess	2 Thessalonians		

❖ PART ONE ❖

INTRODUCTION

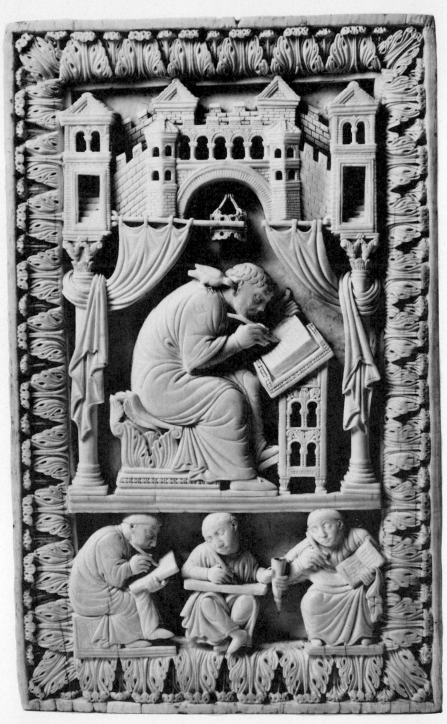

St. Gregory and the three scribes, book cover, ninth century. (Courtesy *Kunsthistorisches Museum, Vienna.*)

❖ I ❖

The Study of Early Christianity

A MODERN visitor to the archeological remains of ancient Corinth, in Greece, usually tries to imagine what life in that city might have been like. It had a fortunate setting, with access to the Gulf of Corinth and the Saronic Gulf, and we know that in the first and second centuries CE, it was a prosperous and important commercial city. One can today see the remains of ancient temples, assembly halls, theaters, baths, and shops. The temple of Apollo had been built in the sixth century BCE, with thirty-eight columns, each one twenty-four feet tall and six feet in diameter.[1] Seven of the columns remain, powerful reminders of the Greek devotion to this son of Zeus.

Near the entry to the city marketplace, or *agora,* modern archeologists have discovered a piece of white marble with an inscription that probably once identified the local Jewish synagogue. There are no other traces of a building, but it is likely that St. Paul once preached the Christian message in a synagogue that stood near the spot at which this stone was found.[2] Just north of the agora, there stands a *bema,* a platform from which city or imperial officials could address large crowds. The book of Acts reports that Paul was brought before the bema and charged with violations of Jewish law. The Roman proconsul heard the charges and dismissed the case.[3]

For the modern visitor to ancient Corinth, the visual impact of the remains of the Apollo temple is riveting. The small sign that identified a synagogue may seem insignificant to some, but it reminds us that in the middle of the first century, Paul there preached the Christian message to Corinthian citizens. A century afterward, the movement that Paul introduced had be-

[1] Cf. Jack Finegan, "Corinth," in *The Interpreter's Dictionary of the Bible* (Nashville, Tenn.: Abingdon, 1962); C. L. Thompson, "Corinth," in *The Interpreter's Dictionary of the Bible, Supplementary Volume* (Nashville, Tenn.: Abingdon, 1976).
[2] Cf. Acts 18:4.
[3] Cf. Acts 18:12–17.

come one of great vitality and variety. Its followers were to be found not only in Corinth, but all over the eastern Mediterranean area. It was beginning to attract persons of keen intellect and passionate devotion. It was destined eventually to produce monuments that would rival and supplant those that had been dedicated to Apollo and the entire Greek pantheon.

Our attention in this book will be focused on the formative events of this Christian movement and on the literature it produced. Hence, the title *The New Testament and Early Christianity* means to call attention to two foci of our study: a set of writings and the history, which also includes the thought and the social organization of the Christian movement.

To speak of the New Testament (NT) and early Christianity as two foci may suggest that it will be necessary to use two distinct methods of study: literary criticism for the writings and historical criticism for the history. The situation is a bit more complex than that, however, for there is an intimate connection between the two foci. The writings that make up the NT were produced by early Christians, and an understanding of those documents depends partially on an understanding of the historical context in which they arose. Furthermore, the NT documents do not constitute the whole of Christian writing during the period we will consider, so we cannot afford to concentrate exclusively on the NT. As we will see, it is possible to use the NT and other early Christian writings in a study of the history itself. These interrelationships suggest that our approach should be a mixture of literary and historical study. Sometimes we will look at a document with the primary purpose of understanding the message that is being communicated; at other times we will read a document for the evidence it may contain about the early Christian movement. The purpose of this chapter is primarily to explore the ways in which the NT and other writings may be used in historical study. At a later point, attention will be focused on the literary approach to the various documents.

To give a definition of Chistianity at this point would be premature and misleading. It is possible to say, however, that the primary object of our study is a movement that took various names and exhibited diverse characteristics but that came generally to be called Christianity. The surprising thing about the movement is that, in its early stages, several quite different groups could call themselves Christian. There were sometimes deep divisions and hostilities among the groups. We should not, in advance, attempt to distinguish among them by referring to one as true or orthodox and to all the rest as false or heretical. We will find that the various groups that thought of themselves as Christian can only be distinguished from one another by their leadership, their documents, or their characteristic emphases. Thus, we will in due course investigate, among others, Pauline Christianity, Jewish Christianity, and Gnostic Christianity. It is clear that out of this amalgam a unified religious movement eventually emerged, but we cannot assume that the more unified movement is identical with one of the earlier forms. Nor can we assume that there was a single thread leading from the original to the developed form. Our object of study, therefore, will be the movement called Christianity in the major forms in which it was presented in its early period.

THE BOUNDARIES OF THIS STUDY

Recent philosophers of history have pointed out that there are significant affinities between the writing of history and of fictional narrative.[4] The basic similarity is that both are written in narrative form. Aristotle defined a narrative as having a beginning, a middle, and an end. But this seemingly self-evident definition has some problematical aspects when applied to historical writing. There must be a point at which to start telling about a historical event. That starting point should introduce the context, the historical situation, the chief characters, and all aspects of the event. We should be able to proceed from the beginning of a narrative with some understanding of the ways in which things are connected and the ways in which the central events proceed from the initial ones. Similarly, the conclusion to a narrative should be the point where we can say that the central events have reached some kind of fruition. At the end, we should be able to say: "Now we understand what effects this thing had." These matters are usually clear in well-written fictional accounts, but history does not come with ready-made labels—beginning, middle, and end. To the participants it is more like a continuum. A time that may appear in a historical account as the end of an era may have seemed just like any other day to the persons who lived through it. We now can quite readily refer to the Middle Ages, but people living in those times must have had no greater sense of living in an intermediate period than those who lived at other times. When did the United States begin? We may, of course, maintain that it began when the English forces surrendered to the revolutionary colonial forces or that it began when the U. S. Constitution was adopted or when President Washington was inaugurated. But an account that started at one of these points would leave us in the dark about the beginnings of the discontent that led to the American Revolution, the oppressions that led to colonial settlements, and some of the revolutionary writings questioning absolute monarchical authority. The point is that events as they actually occur do not give the historian obvious beginnings, middles, and ends. These points depend on the subject matter the historian chooses to investigate, the thesis he or she wishes to propound, and a complex of judgments. One historian's beginning point is

---

[4] Cf. especially W. B. Gallie, *Philosophy and the Historical Understanding*, 2nd ed. (New York: Schocken, 1968).

another's end. The very structure of historical narrative depends on the historian's judgment.

Although the setting of chronological boundaries is largely a matter of judgment, such judgment should not be arbitrary. In the case of early Christianity, the judgment should be informed by reference to events that brought certain social forces into operation at the beginning and by other events that altered conditions at the end. To study early Christianity, we must devote our attention to a period of time that starts with some originating event or events and concludes with a time when one can say that there is a fundamental change. In the case of early Christianity it seems reasonable to work with both a broad and a narrow set of boundaries.

The broad set of boundaries is determined by reference to the political and social conditions that seem to make it possible for the central events in Christianity to have taken place as they did. The starting point chosen here is the beginning of the Hellenistic period—more precisely the conquest of the Near East by Alexander the Great in the fourth century BCE. The concluding point chosen is the accession of Constantine to the imperial throne of Rome in the fourth century CE.

Christianity made its appearance during a time when the political conditions were defined by historical forces initially set in motion by Alexander the Great. In the fourth century CE Christianity faced major changes because Constantine came to the throne, and he became a Christian. The formerly disfavored and frequently persecuted movement suddenly came to be tolerated and eventually favored by the greatest political power on earth—Rome. That drastic change in the political aspects of the movement inevitably produced changes in the makeup of the movement itself. The broader limits of our study are, therefore, marked by Alexander at its beginning and Constantine at its end.

The study's narrow limits are determined by reference to the movement's internal developments, and they will constitute the central focus of our study. The originating event is not difficult to find. Although we may discuss the question of the precise beginning of the institution known as the Christian church—whether with Jesus, the earliest disciples, or Paul—there is little doubt that the originating event for the Christian movement itself is somehow connected with Jesus. This is not to presuppose that he intentionally started the movement or founded a church, but only to say that the groups that thought of themselves as Christian looked to Jesus as their founder or central figure.

The end of the period, narrowly conceived, is more difficult to determine. Although most studies of this subject confine their attention to the books of the NT, this approach does not allow for a meaningful history. Such studies determine the limits of the period by theological judgments about the quality of the literature rather than by historical conditions. It may be more defensible to mark the end of the period to coincide with the writing of the latest of the NT books—that is, about 150 CE—but in this case the historian must give attention not only to the canonical literature but also to other writings by Christians of the same period. In no case can we confine ourselves to the books of the NT and claim that we are studying early Christianity.

I have opted to set the conclusion in the narrower sense at the end of the second century. By that time the chief groups that constituted the whole range of pre-Constantinian Christianity had come into existence. Near the end of the second century, a single form of Christianity began to dominate, a single universal organization began to emerge, and Christians attempted to agree on creedal statements. Anyone acquainted with Christianity in these and subsequent centuries knows that the process by which this unification was worked out went on for several centuries beyond the time of Constantine. But once the movement began to develop a procedure for discerning the differences between "true" and "false" Christianity, a new set of forces was introduced. The introduction of those forces prepared the way for the imperial state church that appeared in the time of Constantine.

We are therefore setting the broader boundaries of early Christianity as the period between Alexander and Constantine (c. 336 BCE–306 CE) and the narrower boundaries, which form our central focus, as the time between the birth of Jesus and the end of the second century CE.

THE STUDY OF DOCUMENTS

Although there are important similarities between writing fictional and historical narratives, the most striking, yet obvious, difference is that historical writers work with factors for which there must be some evidence. Fictional narrative writers are under no obligation to provide evidence that their heroes did in fact exist or acted as they are said to have acted. But historical writers are assumed to have researched the facts, characters, events, and circumstances they describe. We demand evidence that things occurred in something like the way the historian described them.

But it is not so easy to obtain convincing evidence for many of the things with which a historian must work. Nor is it clear what does in fact constitute evidence. Surely more is required than the testimony of a supposed eyewitness or a record in a book.

One major problem with which a historian must deal is the fact that the record of past events originally resided in the memory of human beings. Human memory is prior both to the record in the book and the individual's express testimony. But as a source of history it is problematical. People do not consciously remember everything that they have experienced, and there are some things that no one seems to remember. In addition, what is remembered is remembered because it has meaning to someone. Thus, a per-

Rylands Greek Pap. 457. A papyrus fragment of the Gospel of John, dating from the second century. The photograph shows both the front and back of a single leaf. (Courtesy *The John Rylands University Library, Manchester, England.*)

fectly good event may escape human memory altogether, because it did not carry any significance for the people who observed it. In general the meaning that is attached to an event outlives the memory of the event itself. Many of our attitudes are shaped by events that took place in our childhood. We may have forgotten the events, but we still have the attitudes. In the passage of time, events of a public nature gather traditional significance. Such events are initially remembered because they have significance for the participants or observers. But as time passes, the events either accrue meanings relevant for each succeeding generation, or they cease to be remembered. Moreover, the deeper in the past an event lies, the more it is subject to various interpretations. Historians usually live at a late stage in this process, so that between them and the event lie many layers of interpretation and tradition. In order to minimize their problems, historians will generally give preference to sources of information that are close to the time under study.

In the case of the study of early Christian history, the archeological evidence is relatively sparse, so the major sources of information are literary documents. The problem of the historian is largely that of working with the available texts to sort out the character of their testimony to historical events.

The early Christian writings, including the NT, have frequently been read without reference to the historical questions and hence without reference to the historical setting in which they arose. This fact testifies to the perceived value of their content and insights to large segments of the population, both Christian and non-Christian. Some modern literary critics maintain that such writings, because they are literary works, should be interpreted in dissociation from their original context. These critics define a literary work as a book that has outlived its original usefulness. John M. Ellis, a contemporary literary critic, writes: "Literary texts are defined as those that are used by the society in such a way *that the text is not taken as specifically relevant to the immediate context of its origin.*"[5] To Ellis the significance of a literary text is not dependent on its original context. Documents have originated in many different contexts and may even have served immediate and pragmatic ends. But those that outlive their immediate contexts and are treasured for their literary value are those that become literary texts. Such literary texts can and do exist in an indeterminate number of contexts, as succeeding generations read them. It is self-evident that the writings of the NT are, under this definition, literary texts and may be read without reference to their original contexts.

Because, however, we are attempting to bring together the writings and the historical phenomena, it will be essential to insist on the connection between text and context. This insistence is not to deny the validity and value of reading early Christian documents as literature, but rather to affirm that the exercise of reading them against the background of their original contexts is essential in order to understand the history that may be reflected in them and the effect that they may have originally produced on readers.

In order to understand the relation of the document to its context, the historian will ask of the literary sources such questions as: When was this document written? Where did it come from? Who wrote it? What kind of writing is it? What was the specific background of its writing, and why was it written? Do we possess the original text of the document or must the text be reconstructed? If the document is written in a language other than our own, can it be translated? To be sure, these questions involve a certain circularity, because the very context to which a text is related is known to the historian only by analyzing other texts and artifacts. These preliminary questions must, however, be addressed; and in order to answer them we must use some of the tools of literary scholarship, which will now be described in some detail.

Date

Although the study of history is more than cataloguing events and people along a time line, it cannot proceed without reference to chronology. Set-

[5] John M. Ellis, *The Theory of Literary Criticism* (Berkeley: University of California Press, 1974), p. 44.

ting documents in the time they were written is essential to evaluating them as evidence. Unless we can say something about a document's historical environment, or framework, we cannot ascertain its evidential value.

But how do we determine the date at which a document was written? In general there are two kinds of evidence: external and internal. External evidence lies outside the document under investigation. That is, some documents contain direct information about other documents, such as their authorship, place of writing, and date. So, by drawing on that external evidence, it is frequently possible to set the date of one document by a reference to it in another. Although a historian cannot simply take such information at face value, he can make inferences from it. If we want to establish a date for Document A, and we know that Document B mentions Document A, we can conclude that A was written before B. Not many documents contain such specific linear evidence. More frequently, we find that one document quotes from an earlier one or makes an allusion to something contained in it. Still more frequently, we may be able to find some way in which an earlier document has influenced a later one. All of these bits of external evidence—specific references, quotations, allusions, and influences—are helpful in settling questions of chronology.

Internal evidence is found within the document in question. The procedure used in the search for external evidence is reversed: references, quotations, allusions, and influences that can be traced to earlier writings are sought within the document. We may also look for traces of events whose dates are known. In some cases even the lack of such a trace can be an aid in chronology. If a document makes no mention of an event of crucial significance where it would be appropriate to expect some reference, it is possible to conclude that the document was written before the event. In somewhat more nebulous ways, the literary scholar and historian may try to set the time of a document by studying the relationship of its ideas to what is known about forms of thought during a specific range of periods. This kind of study is by no means precise, but we ought to be able to determine, within broad limits, the time at which a certain book was written by examining the thought forms represented in it. Not only thought forms can be examined for purposes of dating; language patterns may also throw some light on date. It is not difficult, for example, to ascertain that Chaucer's English does not come from the same period as Steinbeck's.

Once we have collected all the relevant evidence, both external and internal, for dating a document, we can infer a specific date or a range of dates for it. But it will first be necessary to set up a pair of extreme dates: the *terminus a quo* is the earliest possible date for the writing of a document; the *terminus ad quem* is the latest, the date after which the document could not possibly have been written. These extreme dates must be rigidly determined. The *terminus a quo* may be set by a reference in the document to an event of known date. The *terminus ad quem* may be set by a datable quotation from the document in question. These terminal dates must be matters of universal scholarly agreement. After the extreme dates have been set, the attempt may then be made to narrow their range by the use of less rigid procedures. In the study of early Christianity, we have no absolutely certain dates for documents, and frequently the student will meet with a range of dates of a decade, or a half century, or a century. Although absolute certainty eludes us, this process can eventually produce a chronology that will enable the historian to see the proper temporal relationships between several documents, between several events, or between documents and events.

Location

We know that Christianity during the period under discussion covered areas of Judea, Samaria, Syria, Parthia, Greece, Macedonia, North Africa, Egypt, Italy, and Gaul. Because we would expect to find some regional variations in the religious thought and practices of these areas, it is important for us to know our authors' geographical roots.

How can we determine this? Again, both internal and external evidence are used. In rare instances the author may tell us the location. The document in question may record knowledge of other documents, people, or events that are associated with a particular area. It may have linguistic, stylistic, or ideological traits that are characteristic of or similar to those of a certain region. It may share ideas with a movement known to be located in a certain part of the world. Turning to external evidence, we may find that some document tells us that our author was associated with a particular city at a certain time, or we may learn that this is a generally known fact. Or we can find out where the document was originally known by examining references or allusions to it in other writings. This information is valuable if we assume that the document was known first in its place of origin. No exactitude can be claimed for the inferences made on the basis of information of this sort, but we can determine where the cumulative weight of all such evidence falls. We might examine several alternative locations for a piece of writing and see for which one we can muster the greatest weight of evidence. In most cases, only the probable location of a document can be determined.

Authorship

Knowing an author's name is of little intrinsic value. It is a different matter, however, if we know something about an author. If, for example, we know a name and can associate it with a person who held a high administrative post in Rome or commanded a legion in Gaul, that knowledge may add significant clues to a document's meaning. Or, if we know that the author was a member of a certain philosophical school or religious group—or best of all, if we find that he wrote other books—we have discovered a great deal. With that information we are able not only to solve some chronological problems, but also to use one book as an aid in interpreting another.

How can we discover authorship? This can be done only by evaluating external and internal evidence. Success is quite illusory on this aspect of the study of early Christian literature, for we are rarely able to identify the authors of our earliest literature. The most we can hope for is to be able to identify some of the characteristics of the author or the group he represents.

A special problem plagues the efforts of historians of early Christianity, and that is the tendency toward anonymous authorship. A number of our documents contain no statements of authorship. There is no statement of authorship in the body of the gospels of Matthew, Mark, Luke, or John.[6] We suspect that there we are dealing, at least in part, with material that was not "authored" but that was traditional material—that is, material that belonged to the community and was passed down by it through the years. In these cases our efforts to identify an author will be largely frustrated.

Another problem is that of pseudonymity, a claim by one writer to be writing in the name of another, and probably more famous, author. We will see that this problem especially affects the late first- and second-century Christian literature.

Occasions and Purposes

The general historical environment of a document provides us with some knowledge of the occasion for its composition. But for some the occasion is specific because something has happened that causes an author to feel that it is necessary to write. It is helpful to know this occasion, for it frequently turns out that certain remarks in the document will be directed to it and indeed may only be understandable in that context.

More directly to the point and more difficult to determine is the author's purpose. Whereas occasion refers to the situation that prompted an author to write, the purpose is the author's intention. When we ask about purpose, we are asking what the author hoped to accomplish by writing. The relationship between the purpose of a document and its evidential value should be apparent, for we should know why an author said what he did. Such knowledge puts us one step closer to a proper evaluation of the document as evidence.

Modern literary critics have cautioned us against optimism in the effort to determine an author's intention in writing, and some have insisted fur-

---

[6] An exception may be found in John 21, which makes an attempt to identify the author of that gospel with the "beloved disciple," a character unique to John. It is thought, however, that this chapter was not originally a part of the Gospel of John. Cf. Chapter 6 here for additional information.

thermore that it is irrelevant.[7] The dissociation of author from text is a major aspect of the dissociation of context from text. Despite these judgments, it is necessary to repeat that if our interest is in early Christianity, we are dependent on texts which must be connected with their original context and author. Otherwise, there is no way to move from literature to history. Our study must make the attempt to establish an author's purpose in writing. In rare cases an author may tell us about the occasion or purpose of the writing. In most cases, however, we must resort to the usual methods of inferring these matters from an examination of the clues provided in the document itself.

Genre

An essential part of the interpretation of a text is a sense of the kind of meaning that is to be found in it, and the kind of meaning of a piece of writing is a function of genre, which means type, class, or kind of writing. As readers, we have learned to expect different kinds of meaning in different kinds of books, and so we are able to approach scientific and historical books one way and poetry and novels another. In early Christian literature we find some genres that would have been familiar to readers of Greek documents in the first two centuries: epistles (or letters), histories, apologies, and romances. We will see, however, that one of the most important types of Christian writing, the gospel, creates a special problem, because there are no exact parallels to the genre in the Greco-Roman world outside Christianity. In any event, the genre of a document is an important key to the way in which it can be understood and to the way in which it may be used in historical study. Although genre study is, strictly speaking, a literary-critical study, it is also an essential aspect of the historical use of written documents.

Text

Historians who specialize in the world of the last three hundred years usually are able to confront their evidence directly and to consult original documents. But the historian who concentrates on a more remote past is rarely so fortunate. For the study of the NT and early Christianity, there are no documents available today that are assuredly original—that is, written by the author's hand. In every known case, the original document was copied and recopied and ultimately disappeared.

---

[7] Such insistence is a cornerstone of the so-called New Criticism in literary studies. Cf. Ellis, op. cit. Cf. also I. A. Richards, *Principles of Literary Criticism* (New York: Harcourt, 1924). For an opposing view, cf. E. D. Hirsch, Jr., *Validity in Interpretation* (New Haven, Conn.: Yale U.P., 1967).

*A page from Codex Sinaiticus, fourth century. Note the marginal "corrections." (*Courtesy *The British Library, London.)*

Some of the documents relating to early Christianity were produced for public use, but none of them was produced as a museum piece. Many items, such as the letters of Paul, which were originally intended to circulate only in limited areas, were used by Christians when they met together; the letters came to be circulated widely. Although revered, those manuscripts were subject to the fortunes of repeated use. Reverence for manuscripts is no guarantee of preservation, and frequent use has a deleterious effect on them. Some of our documents were written on scrolls, whose outer edges, in time, would become worn and perhaps flake off. Some copies of those documents were later produced as codices—that is, in the form of modern books where the text appears on sequential pages. They were usually quite bulky, and repeated use would cause damage, especially to the first and last pages.

The texts of the NT and other documents relating to early Christianity were preserved for a long period without the benefit of the standardization that comes with printing. They were copied by hand for almost fourteen hundred years before they were published in printed form. Some manuscripts were produced by individuals who would copy by sight. Anyone who has ever attempted to do this will at once recognize the difficulties it presents. A copyist could easily omit a word, a phrase, or an entire line, substitute one word for another, write words in incorrect order, misspell words, or duplicate a word, a phrase, or an entire line. Some copyists, or scribes, might intentionally correct what they took to be a mistake in the manuscript they were copying. Correctors often checked new copies against older ones and noted any differences in the margins. Some people who had access to manuscripts and studied them made marginal notes, a common practice among students both ancient and modern. But when a scribe later copied a manuscript with marginal notes, he would have no way of knowing which marks were added and which had been there originally. Thus, he might transfer a note from the margin to the body of his copy. In this way a pious remark made in a marginal note by a ninth-century student could end up in a later manuscript as a saying of Jesus.

In ancient and medieval monasteries, the copying of manuscripts became well organized, but the hazards of copying were not overcome. In those institutions one monk would read from a manuscript and the others would write down what they heard. This practice perpetuated errors of the old system and added some of its own. A scribe might miss a word that had been read, or he might have heard it incorrectly. This possibility becomes a probability when we recognize that most of the documents were written in Greek and many of the monks knew only Latin. At one stage, all Greek vowels came to be pronounced with one sound, that of the Greek iota, in a phenomenon known as iotacism. The poor scribe would have a very difficult time knowing what to write down. The result is that we now have a multitude of manuscripts, all to some degree defective, and none original.

The historian has not been defeated by the lack of original manuscripts, however. It is possible to use methods and tools of textual scholarship to reconstruct the probable originals. The methods are too highly technical to be treated at length here, but we can cite a few of the basic principles used by textual scholars.

One thing that should be done with a manuscript is to date it. We should be able to ascertain the approximate time the copy was made. Because we know that letters had different shapes at different times this dating can sometimes be done by a study of calligraphy. Other possible aids are the carbon–14 or other chemical tests, which can determine the approximate age of the material on which the manuscript was written.

In general, the earlier manuscripts are to be preferred, but this is not a universal rule. Textual scholars frequently try to place the manuscripts into families and to reconstruct the originals by studying the family relationships. These relationships can be expressed in terms as shown in Figure 1.

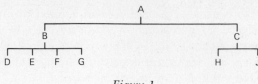

Figure 1

In this diagram, A represents the original document, which is the ancestor of all the copies but has disappeared. In this case only two copies, B and C, were made directly from the original. If we have B and C and know the precise family relationships in the group, then our job is relatively simple. We can reconstruct A by comparing B and C, and we need pay no attention to the more recent descendants, D through J. But if B or C or both are missing along with A, then B and C must be reconstructed by a close examination of their descendants. This process can be carried on down the line without limit. If we can place each manuscript within the family structure, itself a difficult task, painstaking labor should produce a fairly accurate reconstruction of each ancestor up to and including the original.

Certain implications can easily be drawn from this procedure. For one thing it is apparent that a reconstruction of the original cannot be accomplished by seeing how many manuscripts carry one reading and how many another. Let us suppose that at a certain point in our reconstruction we are not sure whether the verb should be "was" or "will be." If A originally had "was," and C copied it correctly but B did not, then five of the manuscripts in our diagram would have an incorrect reading, and only three would be correct (assuming that each descendant, D through J, copied its ancestor correctly). Under these circumstances, the majority of manuscripts would be incorrect. Another implication is that we cannot rely exclusively on the date of a manuscript. It is true that the older a manuscript is the less the chance of compounding inaccuracies and that within family groups older manuscripts are preferable, but age in no way guarantees accuracy. Indeed, we may have a relatively young manuscript with fewer errors than an older one, simply because the younger had a more accurate ancestor. It is the family relationship that provides the clue to a reconstruction of a lost original. Without some such effort, we cannot know what the original author wrote.[8]

---

[8] Modern translations of the NT and early Christian documents are based on editions of them in the original languages. The modern editions are in turn based on comparisons of manuscripts and careful textual scholarship. They represent our best efforts to reconstruct the lost originals.

Language

Many historians share the modern language of those involved in their areas of study, but scholars of the NT and early Christianity must become fully acquainted with the ancient languages of their documents. Knowing a language does not mean simply knowing word-for-word equivalencies. The scholar must be familiar with the inner workings of a language, aware of the ways in which mental concepts are reflected in it, and aware of how language can affect mental concepts. Language can be a barrier not only because of different historical environments, but because language may change with the use to which it is put. Common words may have quite different meanings in different languages. One difficulty in our particular study is the specialized nature of the language used in a religious setting. Religious language has its own technical terms, such as *heaven, angels,* and *God;* but it also uses quite common words with uncommon, though analogous, meanings. For example, terms such as *father, son,* and *kingdom* have meanings common to the general culture but special to the religious community, and it will be important to become aware of the differences.[9]

HISTORICAL EVIDENCE

All of the operations discussed here are essential and preliminary to the task of getting behind a document to the history that it reflects. To know something about the date, place, author, occasion, purpose, genre, text, and language helps us to form tentative judgments about the document, and those judgments are likely to be relevant to our study. But we are not yet able to make direct use of the material in a document.

After we have done what we can about date, place, and author we are faced with a large number of statements that may have some bearing on the historical problem. It is usually not clear, however, what that bearing is. It is helpful, at this point, to think of the statements as testimonies by the authors, some direct and some indirect. An example of a direct statement is, "In those days came John the Baptist, preaching in the wilderness of Judea" (Matt 3:1). This kind of statement purports to proclaim a factual event. An example of an indirect statement is found in the writings of Paul: "For Christ is the end of the law, that every one who has faith may be justified" (Rom 10:4). This statement does not claim to establish a historical event; rather it proclaims a theological conviction. It does not refer di-

[9] There are several good translations of the NT available today, among them the Revised Standard Version, the New English Bible, and the New American Version. For other early Christian writings, reference will be made at the appropriate points to available translations.

rectly to anything that happened in history, but it gives a principle, namely that "everyone who has faith may be justified" and the explanation for the principle, "Christ is the end of the law." In fact, however, all such statements may be regarded as testimonial. Clearly Paul is testifying to his own fervently held belief in the justification of the faithful. But Matthew is also offering testimony about John the Baptist.

The historian is not content simply with reading testimony, for he requires evidence. Remember that it is the need for evidence that defines the major difference between historical and fictional narrative. It is necessary to distinguish carefully between testimony and evidence. The difference is not so much in the character of the statements themselves as in the use to which they are put. To treat statements as testimony means simply to treat them as assertions made, directly or indirectly, by a writer of a relevant document. Such testimony may of course be believed or doubted. To treat statements as evidence means to examine them for the light they may shed on the problem at hand. R. G. Collingwood, an English philosopher, explains this point in the following quotation, in which he uses the term *scientific historian* to refer to the historian who treats statements as evidence:

> Confronted with a ready-made statement about the subject he is studying, the scientific historian never asks himself: "Is this statement true or false?" . . . The question he asks himself is: "What does this statement mean?" And this is not equivalent to the question "What did the person who made it mean by it?", although that is doubtless a question that the historian must ask and must be able to answer. It is equivalent, rather, to the question "What light is thrown on the subject in which I am interested by the fact that this person made this statement, meaning by it what he did mean?" [10]

The process we use in treating statements as evidence is largely one of asking questions and drawing inferences. To illustrate the process of inference making, Collingwood cites the analogy of the detective story. In a good detective story the hero will evaluate any statements he hears not only in terms of truth or falsity but in terms of the possible inferences they enable him to make. In a situation where an unlikely suspect in a murder case confesses to a murder, the dectective must not only decide whether the witness is telling the truth but must also ask why the person made the statement. The latter question is essential even if the person is lying. Is the person covering up for someone else? Does he suspect that his wife is the murderer, and, if so, why does he? Does he have some information he is trying to keep hidden, or to uncover indirectly? In order words, the detective does not treat a statement simply as testimony that may be either believed or doubted. He treats it as a basis of inference, as something that may have a bearing on the case. The detective must always ask himself, "What may I *infer* from the fact that this person made this statement?"

---

[10] R. G. Collingwood, *The Idea of History* (Oxford: Clarendon Press, 1946), p. 275.

The questions he asks cannot be formulated in advance. They will all spring from the basic question, "What light does this shed on this case?" His subsidiary questions will be guided by his basic one and will be related to the material with which he deals. Thus, he will probe away at the case by asking questions and drawing inferences. The historian will do the same, not with human suspects, but with documents.

The process of drawing inferences is not, however, a haphazard one. Although an indefinite number of inferences may be made in a given case, some are more adequate than others. How can we sort out the most adequate inferences from among all those that may be made?

Van A. Harvey, a contemporary American scholar of the philosophy of religion, has analyzed the process by which historical arguments in general are made.[11] He does not cite the rules of formal logic; he describes the process of historical argumentation informally because he conceives of history as a "field-encompassing field." It is not a field in itself, like mathematics and sociology, but is, rather, interested in human affairs, which are partly mathematical, partly political, partly sociological, and so forth. Because historical argumentation encompasses these fields, it uses whatever is appropriate in each field under discussion. Moreover, the form of a historical argument is not very different from any other kind of statement made in ordinary discourse, and Harvey provides a helpful analysis of it. Any assertion made, he says, can be regarded as a conclusion (C). Behind this assertion stand certain data (D). Ordinarily, the data are not cited unless someone challenges the conclusion, by asking, "What have you got to go on?" But it is also possible for someone to challenge the move from data to conclusion, and this challenge may be answered by citing certain warrants, (W). The data are the indisputable facts which call for some conclusion. The warrants are those facts which give legitimacy to the step taken between data and conclusion. Consider, for example, the following conversation:

X: I received an A on this assignment. [Conclusion]
Y: How do you know? [Request for data]
X: Because the Professor marked the assignment 95. [A datum]
Y: How do you know that this means that you made an A? [Request for warrant]
X: Because the Professor announced at the beginning of the course that a 95 is an A. [Warrant]

The mark of 95 on an assignment is a datum that calls for some conclusion. The announcement at the beginning of a course is a warrant for concluding that the 95 really means an A.

[11] Van A. Harvey, *The Historian and the Believer* (New York: Macmillan, 1966). In his analysis Harvey depends heavily on Stephen Toulmin, *The Uses of Argument* (New York: Cambridge U.P., 1958).

Moreover, says Harvey, warrants "confer *differing degrees of force on a conclusion*. They permit us not merely to assent to a claim but they justify a certain texture of assent." [12] There are some warrants that call for heavy assent and some that do not, some that seem almost certain and others that are barely possible. So Harvey suggests that before every conclusion we place a qualifier (Q), that is, one of the following words: possibly, presumably, probably, necessarily. He diagrams this situation in Figure 2.

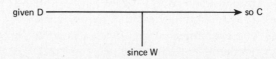

Figure 2   The Historical Agrument. (Reprinted with permission of Cambridge University Press, from The Uses of Argument *by Stephen Toulmin, 1958.)*

The diagram means that the data lead to a conclusion, which calls for a certain quality of assent, since there are warrants for the conclusion.

But there are various grounds on which an objection can be raised. Harvey calls attention to two kinds of objections: "(1) One may insist that the warrant does not apply in the particular case under discussion, that it has, for some reason, no authority, or (2) one may challenge the truth of the warrant itself." [13] In the conversation about grades, Y might make an objection of the first kind and claim that a grade of 95 on this particular assignment does not constitute an A. Or Y may say that the Professor made no announcement about grades at the beginning of the course. This would be an objection of the second kind. The first kind of objection is a rebuttal (R), which must either be conceded or rejected. In order to answer the second kind of objection, the argument must be beefed up by providing a backing (B) for the warrant, perhaps, for our imaginary conversation, a course syllabus that contained the disputed information. The complete diagram of a historical argument, as Harvey outlines it, would look like Figure 3.

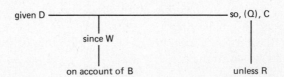

Figure 3   (Reprinted with permission of Van A. Harvey from The Historian and the Believer *by Van A. Harvey, 1966.)*

[12] Harvey op. cit., p. 53.
[13] Ibid.

Harvey illustrates the method by the use of an argument about the crucifixion of Jesus in which a rebuttal is entered: [14]

D — Jesus was crucified.
C — So Jesus was judged to have been a political enemy of Rome.
Q — Presumably.
W — Since crucifixion was reserved by the Romans for political enemies.
R — Unless, in this particular case, an exception was made to please the Jewish authorities.

In order to answer the rebuttal one would need to show that there is no ground for assuming that an exception was made in this case. If, instead of the rebuttal, we had a challenge of the truth of W, then B would be provided — that is, it would be necessary to show that contemporary documents refer to crucifixion as a penalty exercised by the Romans only for political purposes. [15]

This may appear to be a complex argument, but it is clear that it is, in form, a kind of common sense used in familiar speech. If we analyzed it closely, we would find that it draws on various patterns known in formal and informal logic, but this is not the basic point. What is basic is the principle that conclusions must have data, arguments must have warrants, and warrants must have backing. A secondary point is that assent to conclusions may be called for in varying degrees. It will be discovered that, in the case of most aspects of early Christian history, probability is our highest form of assent. The familiarity of this pattern of argument should make it useful as a description of the process of making inferences.

What we have attempted to show so far in this chapter is that, in the study of early Christianity as in the study of history in general, it is necessary to have evidence for the statements we make. Such evidence is difficult to find and evaluate, but there are documents that are relevant to our study of early Christianity. It is essential to know as much as possible about them in order to begin the process of understanding and evaluating them; therefore, we ask about date, location, authorship, occasions, purposes, genre, text, and language. When we have done this, we can begin to read them, accepting their statements as testimony, but examining them for the evidence they may contain. We do this by asking questions, making inferences, and constructing historical arguments, the forms of which are similar to patterns in ordinary discourse.

[14] Ibid.
[15] Harvey's material on the crucifixion of Jesus is used here only to illustrate the form of a historical argument. For more information about the crucifixion, see Chapter 8 here.

SOME SPECIAL PROBLEMS

Before we can move on to the study of the NT and early Christianity, there are certain problems we must face: the first, the perspective of the historian, is related to the study of history in general. Two others arise because of the special character of our object of study: the canon and the study of history, and the historical study of religious documents.

The Perspective of the Historian

Twentieth-century historiography has recognized the part played by the historian's perspective in the study of history. Every historian is a child of the age in which he or she lives. To live in this century means to be suspicious of historical explanations that rely on the efficacy of magic formulas or on a geocentric view of the universe or on any number of pre-enlightenment beliefs about the cosmos and the human role in it. This suspicion forms part of our perspective and inevitably influences the ways in which we look at the past. Our own experience provides a framework within which we shape the questions we ask of the past and evaluate the possible answers. If historical study means a rethinking of the past—that is, reading early documents and making inferences from them—does our modernity inhibit our ability to see things as they were?

Although we cannot forsake modernity and become ancient, the situation is not hopeless. For one thing, the historian who understands his or her own perspective is in a good position to understand another one. Such self-understanding is among the first goals a historian ought to set. Once we can understand our own perspective, it ceases to be a completely determinative condition of existence. The process of understanding a perspective makes it possible, at least in part, to step outside it. We can see why we act in certain ways and why we accept some things and reject others. If we can see what our own perspective is, we may be able to push it aside long enough to try on a different one.

Understanding a different perspective does not mean adopting it. For example, it is possible for a historian to understand that ancient people, and even some modern people, can accept a belief in demon possession, but it is not necessary for him to use that belief in order to explain the activities that he studies. We cannot jump out of our skins and become what we are not, but we must *imaginatively* allow ourselves to see the world from other perspectives. We do not need to become ancient Egyptians in order to understand ancient Egypt any more than a detective needs to become a criminal in order to understand the criminal mind. Empathy is essential in the imaginative process, but imaginative identification is not actual identification. Thus, a maxim for our study is: It is not necessary for the student to be an early Christian in order to study early Christianity, although he must be open to its perspective and sympathetic to the alternatives it presents.[16]

The Canon and the Study of History

During the first centuries of Christian history, the NT canon was taking shape. Eventually most Christians came to agree that the twenty-seven books that make up this canon have a degree of authority exceeding that of any other writings.[17] We will later look at this process and at the principles used in the formation of the Christian canon. It is necessary now to raise a question about the effect of canonicity on the study of early Christianity.

In general the study of early Christianity has been carried on in two distinct disciplines: the study of the NT, which concentrates on the canonical materials, and the history of Christianity, which usually starts at the end of the first century and omits a study of the NT documents. This fact is symbolized by the existence in most theological schools of two departments: the department of NT and the department of church history. This separation frequently means that a great deal of documentary evidence is either overlooked or examined only as a kind of curiosity.

It has been generally assumed that the documents of the NT, although they may not present an exhaustive picture of Christianity, do at least represent its main lines of development. But those lines are, in part, the ones acceptable to the third- and fourth-century church and not necessarily those that were viewed as the main ones in earlier centuries. After the fourth century, most noncanonical books lost whatever popularity they once had. Many, perhaps most, of them are no longer extant.[18] But some survived, and to attempt a study of early Christianity and neglect those relevant doc-

[16] This position also implies that it is not necessary for the historian to be a Christian in order to undertake this study. To be sure, it is possible that one's Christian faith makes one more likely to be sympathetic to the claims of some early Christian documents. But Christian faith does not make one immune from modern perspectives. The Christian historian has precisely the same problems that the non-Christian historian does in approaching ancient literature and history. Moreover, to suggest that only Christians can engage in this study is to close the subject to public examination. Historical arguments must make use of data, warrants, and backings that are publicly available, to the non-Christian as well as to the Christian.

[17] The word *canon* was originally a Greek word meaning a standard of measurement. It designated the ancient equivalent of a yardstick or meterstick. In Christian usage it was first applied to an approved list of biblical documents, and thus it came to be used for a standard that could measure religious belief—that is, determine the orthodoxy of beliefs. Although different standards have been used by Christians at various times, we are using the word here as equivalent to the Christian Bible, more particularly the NT, which has been one such standard. For further information about the development of the Christian canon, see Chapter XII here.

[18] Cf. E. J. Goodspeed, *A History of Early Christian Literature,* revised by Robert M. Grant (Chicago: U. of Chicago, 1966). The final chapter of this book is entitled, "The Lost Books of Early Christian Literature." It is a five-page list, by title, of the major lost documents.

uments that have survived is not a justifiable historical procedure. A historian must be willing to look at any documents that might contain clues about the subject under consideration. For the historian of early Christianity, this means including the available material that was written during the first two centuries by people who considered themselves Christians. Perhaps not all documents will be useful, but for a historian to decide in advance that the basic or sole source of information consists of a group of books canonized in a period subsequent to the time he is studying is to abdicate his position as a historian.

For these reasons, an attempt will be made here to introduce readers to several noncanonical documents as well as to those in the NT.

The Historical Study of Religious Documents

Most of the material with which we will deal is oriented toward a worshiping community and may be termed religious. This literature is not all of a kind, and it does not have a single character. When we speak of religious literature, we are speaking of various kinds of writings, with multiple purposes. Some may be liturgical, to be used formally by the community in worship services; some may be devotional, designed for use in individual prayers; and some may be homiletical, designed to exhort the faithful to greater devotion to the Lord who is the object of worship. Other such literature may be evangelistic, designed to convert the unbeliever; or it may be prophetic, attempting to give some explanation of events in time. All of these types of literature may be called religious. Our question then is: Does the fact that our literature has these purposes mean that it cannot be used in order to understand the movement it represents?

The historian's response to this question is that there is no material that can be excluded, solely on the basis of its character or purpose, from use in historical study. To put it another way, simply because an author does not intend to make straightforward historical statements does not mean that his writing cannot be used as evidence about the past. Certainly a criminal may not intend to give a straightforward account of a crime in which he was involved. But this does not keep the detective from taking his statements as evidence that might constitute a case against him. Any person may speak of his or her own guilt without so intending, and the fact that the intention was to speak on a different subject does not diminish the value of the statement.

The fact that we are sometimes dealing with material with religious intentions simply presents a special form of the historian's general task of understanding the relationship of the purpose of a document to its evidential value. But one complication should be noted before we leave this question. Although our material has certain religious intentions, it contains sections that smack of straight historical reporting. We will see that this constitutes a serious problem for those documents that seem to report facts about the life of Jesus. Namely, we have several rather long books that appear to be biographical, as well as some that relate to the earliest Christian communities and appear to be historical. What can we do with them? In general we must treat them as we do other similar documents. A good detective is not thrown off the track when his suspect goes into a long narrative that appears to be a factual report. He still asks, "Why is this person telling me this?" This must also be our attitude when we read a narrative that sounds like a historical report. We do not simply ask about its truth or falsity, although we will eventually need to determine that. First we need to know why the document records this material and treats it as it does.

The question about the relationship of religious material to historical study must be answered as follows: No relevant literature may, on the basis of its character or purpose, be excluded from use in the study of history.

Our task, then, will be to examine the literature written by early Christians, including the NT, and to question it for the evidence it may contain about the history of the movement. In doing so, it will be necessary to be aware of the differences in perspective between modern and ancient societies. In Part Two, which follows, we will devote attention to the perspectives of those societies of the ancient period that formed the immediate context for early Christianity, the Hellenistic and the Jewish.

BIBLIOGRAPHY

At the end of each chapter there are lists of books that are suggested as additional reading for students who wish to probe more deeply into selected subjects. Many titles familiar to the specialist are omitted because they require special technical or linguistic skills. The subject headings generally correspond to those in the body of the chapter, although the bibliographies also include books on additional, but related, topics.

General Introductions to the New Testament and Early Christianity

Enslin, Morton S. *Christian Beginnings*. New York: Harper & Row, Publishers, 1938, 2 volumes

Feine, Paul and J. Behm. *Introduction to the New Testament*. Rev. by W. G. Kummel. Trans. by A. J. Mattill, Jr. Nashville, Tenn.: Abingdon Press, 1966.

Goodspeed, Edgar J. *A History of Early Christian Literature*. Rev. by R. M. Grant. Chicago: University of Chicago Press, 1966.

Juel, Donald, James S. Ackerman, and Thayer S. Warshaw. *An Introduction to New Testament Literature*. Nashville: Abingdon Press, 1978.

Kee, Howard C., F. W. Young, and K. Froehlich. *Understanding the New Testament*. 3rd ed. Englewood Cliffs, N.J.: Prentice-Hall, Inc., 1973.

Koester, Helmut. *Introduction to the New Testament*. Philadelphia: Fortress Press, 1982, 2 volumes

Marxsen, Willi. *Introduction to the New Testament*. Trans. by G. Buswell. Oxford: Blackwell, 1968.

Perrin, Norman, and Dennis C. Duling. *The New Testament: An Introduction*. 2nd ed. New York: Harcourt Brace Jovanovich, Inc., 1982.

Price, James L. *Interpreting the New Testament*. 2nd ed. New York: Holt, Rinehart and Winston, 1971.

Selby, Donald J. *Introduction to the New Testament*. New York: Macmillan Publishing Co., Inc., 1971.

Spivey, Robert A., and D. M. Smith. *Anatomy of the New Testament*. 3rd ed. New York: Macmillan Publishing Co., Inc., 1982.

Weiss, Johannes. *Earliest Christianity*. Trans. by F. C. Grant. New York: Harper & Row, Publishers, 1937. 2 volumes

A general introduction treats the questions of date, location, authorship, occasion, and purpose of the early Christian writings. Most of the introductions listed here deal only with the canonical material. The Feine-Behm-Kümmel volume is usually referred to under the name of Kümmel, who thoroughly revised and updated the older work. It contains material on the development of the NT canon and the history of the text and includes comprehensive bibliographies. The book by Goodspeed concentrates on noncanonical material. The Weiss book is older than the others, but it is still valuable. It integrates the canonical and noncanonical writings with the history of Christianity to 150 CE and includes an excellent bibliography.

The Study of Documents

The books under this heading are essential aids in studying the NT and early Christianity: translations of texts, commentaries, and study tools.

TRANSLATIONS

The New English Bible (NEB)

The Revised Standard Version (RSV)

Grant, R. M. ed. *The Apostolic Fathers*. New York: Thomas Nelson Inc., 1964–68. 6 volumes

Hennecke, Edgar. *New Testament Apocrypha*. Ed. by W. Schneemelcher. Trans. by R. McL. Wilson. Philadelphia: Westminster Press, 1963, 1965. 2 volumes

Jones, Alexander, ed. *The Jerusalem Bible*. New York: Doubleday & Company, Inc., 1975.

Lake, Kirsopp. *Apostolic Fathers*. Loeb Classical Library. Cambridge, Mass: Harvard University Press, 1912, 1913. 2 volumes

Richardson, Cyril C., ed. *Early Christian Fathers*. Philadelphia: Westminster Press, 1953.

The New English Bible (NEB) and *The Revised Standard Version* (RSV) are available in a number of editions, both in paperback and hardcover. Some editions also contain the Apocrypha. The volumes edited by Grant consist of translations and commentary. Those by Hennecke and Richardson contain helpful introductions to the various documents. The book edited by Richardson is Volume I of the Library of Christian Classics. It is also available in a paperback edition published by Macmillan in 1970. The various volumes of the Loeb Classical Library contain both the Greek or Latin text and an English translation. The entire series forms a basic source for the period we are studying.

COMMENTARIES

Albright, William F., and D. N. Freedman, eds. The Anchor Bible. New York: Doubleday & Company, Inc., 1964–. 11 NT volumes published to date.

Brown, Raymond E., J. A. Fitzmyer, and R. E. Murphy, eds. *The Jerome Biblical Commentary*. Englewood Cliffs, N.J.: Prentice-Hall, Inc., 1968.

Buttrick, George A., ed. *The Interpreter's Bible*. Nashville, Tenn.: Abingdon Press, 1951–1957. 12 volumes

The Harper's New Testament Commentaries. New York: Harper & Row, Publishers, 1957–. 14 volumes published to date.

The Moffatt New Testament Commentary. New York: Harper & Row, Publishers, 1928–50. 17 volumes

A commentary traditionally contains introductory material and detailed exegetical notes on each NT document. Most present a verse-by-verse analysis of the text and are valuable for detailed research. The oldest in the group here is the Moffatt series, based on the translation of the NT by James Moffatt. The Harper series is written by a distinguished group of English and North American authors. *The Interpreter's Bible* carries the King James Version and the RSV in parallel columns, with a running exegesis printed below the translations. A commentary that concentrates on modern application of biblical teachings is printed below the exegesis. The volumes of the Anchor Bible now in print deal with the following NT documents: Matthew, Luke, John, Acts, 1 Corinthians, Ephesians, Hebrews, James, 1, 2 Peter, 1, 2, 3 John, Jude, and Revelation. Four volumes deal with the Apocrypha: 1, 2 Maccabees, 1, 2 Esdras, Wisdom of Solomon, and the Additions to Daniel, Esther, and Jeremiah. It promises to be a distinguished series. *The Jerome Biblical Commentary* is an excellent one-volume introduction and commentary by a group of Roman Catholic scholars. In addition to these commentaries, a number of similar works, which do not form parts of a series, are available. Several of these will be noted in later chapters.

STUDY TOOLS

Aharoni, Yohanan, and M. Avi-Yonah. *The Macmillan Bible Atlas*. 2nd. ed. New York: Macmillan Publishing Co., Inc., 1977.

Buttrick, George A., ed. *The Interpreter's Dictionary of the Bible*. Nashville, Tenn.: Abingdon Press, 1962, 1976. 5 volumes

Cross, F. L., and Elizabeth A. Livingstone. *The Oxford Dictionary of the Christian Church*. London: Oxford University Press, 1974.

Kittel, G., and G. Friedrich, eds. *Theological Dictionary of the New Testament*. Trans. by G. W. Bromiley. Grand Rapids, Mich.: Eerdmans, 1964–1976. 10 volumes

May, Herbert G., et al. *Oxford Bible Atlas*. London: Oxford University Press, 1962.

Morrison, Clinton. *An Analytical Concordance to the Revised Standard Version of the New Testament*. Philadelphia: Westminster Press, 1979.

Nelson's Complete Concordance of the Revised Standard Version Bible. New York: Thomas Nelson, 1978.

Van der Meer, F., and Christine Mohrmann. *Atlas of the Early Christian World*. Trans. by Mary F. Hedlund and H. H. Rowley. New York: Thomas Nelson, 1958.

Wright, G. E., and F. V. Filson. *The Westminster Historical Atlas to the Bible*. Rev. ed. Philadelphia: Westminster Press, 1956.

The dictionaries edited by Buttrick and by Cross and Livingstone will supply quick information on almost any subject related to early Christianity and its background. The fifth supplementary volume of *The Interpreter's Dictionary of the Bible* updates much of the information that is contained in the first four volumes. Concordances will help in locating a passage in the Bible if only a word or two is remembered. Morrison's breaks down each entry in terms of the actual Greek word used in the NT. The volumes edited by Kittel are detailed studies of the most important words used in the Bible and are generally helpful in spite of their use of Greek and Hebrew. Atlases will help to clarify a number of otherwise difficult points and vague geographical references. The one by F. van der Meer deals with Christianity through 600 CE and contains unique maps and excellent examples of Christian art from the period.

Historical Evidence

Bartsch, Hans W., ed. *Kerygma and Myth*. Trans. by R. H. Fuller. New York: Harper & Row, Publishers, 1961.

Collingwood, R. G. *The Idea of History*. Oxford: Clarendon Press, 1946.

Fuller, Reginald H. *The New Testament in Current Study*. New York: Charles Scribner's Sons, 1962.

Gallie, W. B. *Philosophy and the Historical Understanding*. 2nd ed. New York: Schocken Books, Inc., 1968.

Harvey, Van A. *The Historian and the Believer*. New York: Macmillan Publishing Co., Inc., 1966.

Neill, Stephen. *The Interpretation of the New Testament, 1861–1961*. London: Oxford University Press, 1964.

Collingwood, Gallie, and Harvey deal with the problems of interpreting and writing history. The volume edited by Bartsch is headed by an important essay by Rudolf Bultmann, entitled "New Testament and Mythology." It also contains several essays critical of Bultmann's position and a reply by Bultmann. Neill deals with the history of the interpretation of the NT, and Fuller pinpoints some of the major problems of interpretation confronting scholars today.

❖ PART TWO ❖

THE CONTEXT
OF EARLY CHRISTIANITY

❖ 2 ❖

The Historical Context

A HISTORIAN who intends to rethink the past must do so within a certain context. In order to approach the potential evidence relating to our subject with some sophistication, we must begin with a certain amount of information—specifically, an acquaintance with the context within which the NT was written and early Christianity developed.

Because people generally accept their own historical context, or circumstances, without question or comment—as a given, so to speak—the documents a historian consults usually contain little specific information about their authors' environments. Yet the historian is obliged to be familiar with that context because it will have had an unconscious influence on the writers of those documents. A Persian writer living in the fourth century BCE probably never addressed the fact of his historical circumstance. But the fact that he did live in that particular time and place deeply affected his attitude toward himself, his life, and his world. His attitude was affected by his own past and that of his people, as well as by the past of his neighbors, by social, political, and religious institutions, by technology and education, and above all, by the prevailing world view. Not only must the historian attempt to learn these factors, he or she must imagine being embraced by their context in studying their history.

Although Christianity began with the Jewish culture of the first century CE, it rapidly spread out into the eastern Mediterranean world. That world had had a rich and diverse heritage that affected the growth of the Christian movement and contributed to its development. As early as the middle of the first century there were missionaries who were convinced of their obligation to proclaim the message about Jesus to the world. By the second and third centuries, the overwhelming majority of Christians came from non-Jewish backgrounds. Early Christianity thus had significant contacts with Jewish, Hellenistic, and Roman cultures, and those contacts affected the movement in profound ways. In this and the next two chapters we will

33

attempt to describe those various cultural aspects that created the context in which the NT was written and the history of early Christianity occurred.

Broadly conceived, the historical context is the period between Alexander the Great and Constantine, although our chief focus will be on the first two Christian centuries. We will ask the following questions: What was going on prior to the appearance of Christianity? What cultural factors influenced life in these times? What institutions did people take for granted? What intellectual forces were at work? How did people at that time account for their world? It will be essential for us not only to have this information but also to be able to see how it could fit together into a meaningful context within which people did their working, thinking, worshiping, and writing. We must somehow be able to see how such a context could affect people then. Of course, it will also be necessary to remember that the description of this context is itself a result of the application of the kinds of procedures that were outlined in the previous chapter. Here we will examine political and social history, and in Chapters III and IV intellectual and religious aspects of the periods.

THE HELLENISTIC PERIOD (336–31 BCE)

The historical periods that provide the basic context for early Christianity are the Hellenistic period and the Roman period. Although from the point of view of broad cultural concerns we can describe the entire time between Alexander and Constantine as Hellenistic, it will be clearer if we maintain the distinction between the two periods. The dividing line between them is the establishment of the Roman Empire in 31 BCE.

Alexander the Great stood at the beginning of the Hellenistic period. His father Philip, king of Macedonia, had defeated a league of Greek cities headed by Athens and Thebes and created a political union of Greece and Macedonia. After Philip's death, Alexander fell heir to this new arrangement and ruled from 336–323 BCE. The unification of Macedonia and Greece was preparatory to a much larger task, that of freeing both those countries from the interference of the Persians, who had plagued that part of the world for two hundred years. Alexander quickly turned to that task. His defeat of Persia in 331 BCE left him in possession of the lands Persia had held; the extent of that territory still baffles the mind. Never before had so much land, containing so many people and so many diverse cultures, changed hands so rapidly. Alexander claimed control not only of Greece, Macedonia, and Asia Minor, but also of the land around the Nile, Jordan, Orontes, Tigris, Euphrates, and even the Indus rivers.

Alexander was not only a superb military leader, he was also something of a missionary. Perhaps because he had been tutored by the philosopher Aristotle, he came to recognize the values of Greek, or Hellenic, culture, and he attempted to introduce some of its aspects in the lands he conquered. He settled certain of the eastern areas with his veterans and opened others for general colonization. From these outposts it was assumed that Hellenic culture would radiate into and ultimately permeate the older cultures. But Alexander did not attempt to abolish all of the institutions and cultures of the conquered nations. In fact, much survived, and what we have after Alexander is a mixture of eastern and Hellenic culture, a mixture described by the word *Hellenistic* (meaning Greeklike).

Alexander's premature death in 323 BCE left his dream unfulfilled. Politically, the reins of government fell to his military generals. No single successor was ever strong enough to exercise political control over this whole area, and for over a century after Alexander's death the world was disrupted by almost constant struggles among his successors. In general, the Alexandrian Empire came to be divided into three parts, all with contested boundaries. Egypt was immediately claimed by Ptolemy, and his successors held it with remarkable firmness. Macedonia and Greece were subject to dispute until 279 BCE, when they came under the control of Antigonus I and thereafter by his heirs. Seleucus and his descendants claimed just about everything else — Syria, Mesopotamia, and the area around the Indus river. Judea was under Ptolemaic control until 200 BCE, when it became part of the Seleucid Empire. These empires are referred to collectively as those of the *Diadochi,* the successors. Individually we may speak of the Ptolemaic, Antigonid, and Seleucid empires. The Ptolemies enjoyed the most stable rule, and as a result, Egypt was the most profitable area for its rulers. Hellenism developed throughout these lands during the reigns of the *Diadochi,* as Greek ideas and language were introduced into the Ptolemaic and Seleucid empires and eastern ideas invaded the Antigonid.

Rome became a force in the eastern Mediterranean before the end of the third century BCE. After 240 BCE, various Greek cities organized themselves into two leagues, namely the Aetolian and Achaean. In 212 BCE, the Aetolian League allied with Rome, and in 196 BCE, the Achaean did the same. When Sparta seceded from the alliance in 148 BCE, Rome brought it back in and, in 146 BCE, declared Greece to be a Roman protectorate. In 188 BCE, Antiochus III, a successor to Seleucus, lost Asia Minor to Rome, and in the next century the Seleucids lost other holdings. The Ptolemaic Empire stood a bit longer. Julius Caesar claimed it in 48 BCE and then Antony, but finally Octavian declared it a province of Rome after the battle of Actium in 31 BCE. Thus, not by any blitzkrieg but by piecemeal military and diplomatic action, Rome could, by 31 BCE, count among its provinces most of those areas over which Alexander had held sway, as well as those lands far to the west, in Gaul, Spain, and Britain.

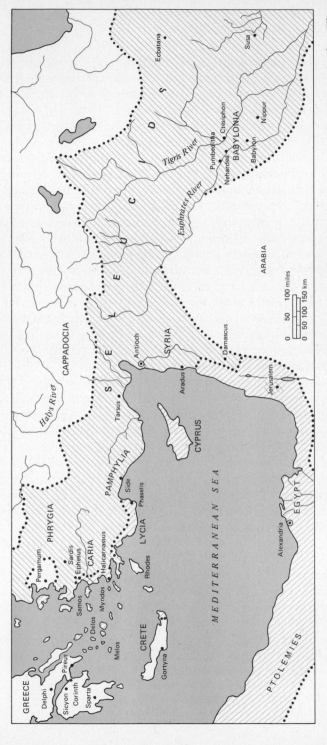

Figure 4   The Hellenistic Empires, c. 275 BCE (Adapted with permission of Macmillan Publishing Company and George Allen & Unwin, from The Macmillan Bible Atlas by Y. Aharoni and Michael Avi-Yonah. Copyright © 1964, 1966, 1968, 1977 by Carta Ltd.)

36

THE ROMAN PERIOD (31 BCE – 306 CE)

It is at the time of the annexation of Egypt by Octavian that we generally count the beginning of the Roman Empire and of the Roman period.[1] The transition from republican to imperial Rome was marked by three civil wars. The first, between Pompey and Caesar, ended in **48** BCE at the battle of Pharsalia. The victorious Caesar proclaimed himself dictator. The murder of Caesar by Brutus, Cassius, and other senators in **44** BCE marked the beginning of the second civil war. Octavian and Antony defeated Brutus and Cassius at the battle of Philippi in **42** BCE. For some years thereafter, Antony and Octavian split the Roman world between them, Antony ruling the east and Octavian the west. Antony, however, suffered defeat at the hands of the Parthians, repudiated his previous marriage with Octavian's sister, and settled in Egypt with Cleopatra VII, the Ptolemaic ruler. These actions brought about the third civil war, which concluded with Octavian defeating Antony at the battle of Actium, in Greece, in **31** BCE. Thereafter Octavian was the sole ruler of the Roman world, both east and west.

For a time it appeared that Octavian had not only rid the world of his enemies but that he had established blessed peace. A grateful Senate and citizenry bestowed on him the titles and powers that enabled him to function as emperor. He was, in fact, the creator of the Roman Empire. His most notable achievements were in the areas of political and military control. In respect to the former, he retained the earlier forms of the Roman Republic but, with the cooperation of the Senate, arranged them around his own person. He was *princeps,* or first citizen. The Senate gave him the title that became his name, *Augustus,* and thereby caused him to be regarded as semidivine. He had proconsular authority, which gave him ultimate power in the government of Spain, Gaul, Syria, and Egypt. His power as tribune carried with it the right to call the Senate into session and the right to veto any action. In **12** BCE, he was named *pontifex maximus,* chief priest of the state religion. At one point the Senate granted him an all-encompassing power to do "whatever he may deem to serve the interest of the Republic."[2]

Augustus' military control was exercised through the various Roman legions. At full strength a legion consisted of 6,000 men, although most were never full. At his death there were twenty-five legions, mostly concentrated in the provinces. This army of fewer than 150,000 men was called on to put down a number of conflicts during Augustus' reign, and it performed effectively. The emperor made two significant military decisions. First, he concluded that the extent of effective control was limited. The boundary of the empire in the west was the Rhine-Danube line, and in the east the

---

[1] In Judea, however, the Roman period begins in 63 BCE.

[2] See *Lex de Imperio Vespasiani.* Quoted by Henry S. Jones, in *Cambridge Ancient History,* ed. by S. A. Cook, F. E. Adcock, and M. P. Charlesworth (New York: Macmillan, 1934) Vol. x, p. 141.

Parthian frontier (see Figure 6, page 40). Although the Romans could probably have extended their borders, Augustus recognized that the value of any newly acquired territories to the empire was not commensurate with the problems of governing them. Augustus' second military decision was to create a standing army. He placed various legions in the frontier areas and reserved only a small contingent, the Praetorian Guard, for Rome. Each garrison was responsible for the defense of its own outpost. The arrangement was based on the assumptions that Rome's enemies were those outside the borders and that within the empire security could be guaranteed. The policy worked well in Augustus' time, so well that he could look on his reign as a time of peace. Actually, it has been observed that there was more fighting during Augustus' reign than during that of any other emperor of the first two centuries.[3] But most of that fighting was limited to border skirmishes, and the inner core of the empire was relatively secure.

MAJOR ROMAN EMPERORS

Augustus, 31 BCE-14 CE
Tiberius, 14–37 CE
Gaius, 37–41
Claudius, 41–54
Nero, 54–68
Vespasian, 69–79
Titus, 79–81
Domitian, 81–96
Nerva, 96–98
Trajan, 98–117
Hadrian, 117–138
Antoninus Pius, 138–161
Marcus Aurelius, 161–180
Commodus, 180–192
Septimus Severus, 193–211
Caracalla, 211–217
Alexander Severus, 222–235
Decius, 249–251
Diocletian, 284–305
Constantine, 306–337

Figure 5   Major Roman Emperors

No constitutional measure was devised for determining the succession of emperors. It was, however, generally assumed that an emperor should have a say in the choice of his successor and that the Senate should have the right of confirmation. The reality of the situation dictated that the army should

[3] See Stephen Benko, "The History of the Early Roman Empire," in *The Catacombs and the Colosseum,* ed. by Stephen Benko and John J. O'Rourke (Valley Forge, Pa.: Judson Press, 1971), p. 43.

also have a strong voice in such selections. In an ideal situation the three elements would agree, but this was rarely the case. Emperors would normally designate their successors from within their families or would adopt sons and heirs to succeed them. In several cases dynasties were formed. The Julio-Claudian dynasty includes the first five emperors: Augustus, Tiberius, Gaius, Claudius, and Nero (see Figure 5). Augustus had chosen his stepson Tiberius as successor, and his choice was ratified by the Senate. The Senate, however, voided the will of Tiberius on the grounds of his insanity and elected a grandson, Gaius. Nero was proclaimed emperor by the Praetorian Guard, and the Senate confirmed him. The Guard and the Senate later turned against him, but he committed suicide before he could be captured. During the civil war that followed Nero's death, three emperors served in the space of one year. But the Flavian dynasty (Vespasian, Titus, and Domitian) brought a temporary end to internal hostilities. Toward the end of Domitian's reign, however, there were several plots to overthrow him. He became increasingly suspicious and his last days were marked by tension and distrust; he was assassinated by partisans of Nerva. Nerva was not popular with the army, so he was forced to accept Trajan, who was acceptable to both army and Senate as coemperor. It was alleged that on his deathbed Trajan adopted his nephew, Hadrian, and he was proclaimed emperor by the legions in Syria and accepted by the Senate. Hadrian adopted Antoninus Pius, a senator from Gaul, who adopted Marcus Aurelius, a Spanish nephew of Hadrian's wife. In the third century, political control was usually weak, and the various military legions had increasingly larger roles in the determination of emperors. Twenty-six emperors ruled during the half century between 235 and 284 CE. In 284, Diocletian began the reforms that restored a measure of political stability to the empire, and Constantine developed an even more efficient organization. Constantine had initially been proclaimed emperor in 306 by the Roman legion in Britain, but he did not attain complete power until he had defeated all his rival claimants in 323.

For most of our period the city of Rome was at peace. The borders of the empire, however, were frequently threatened, and unsettled conditions prevailed in the frontier provinces. Parthia, in the east, was always a thorn in the side of the empire. After a number of conflicts during the rule of the Julio-Claudian dynasty, Nero had established peace on the eastern frontier. Trajan extended Roman control temporarily into Parthia, but he was compelled to withdraw. His annexation of Armenia stood up, however, until it was consciously abandoned by Hadrian. A victory over Parthia by Marcus Aurelius brought Armenia back as a client kingdom of Rome. Augustus' establishment of the imperial boundaries generally stood up. Britain was added under Claudius, and the northern frontier was pushed farther into Germany under Domitian. Trajan conquered and settled Dacia and annexed Arabia and Armenia. His reign proved to be the high point of Roman expansion, for his successor, Hadrian, followed a policy of retraction. He

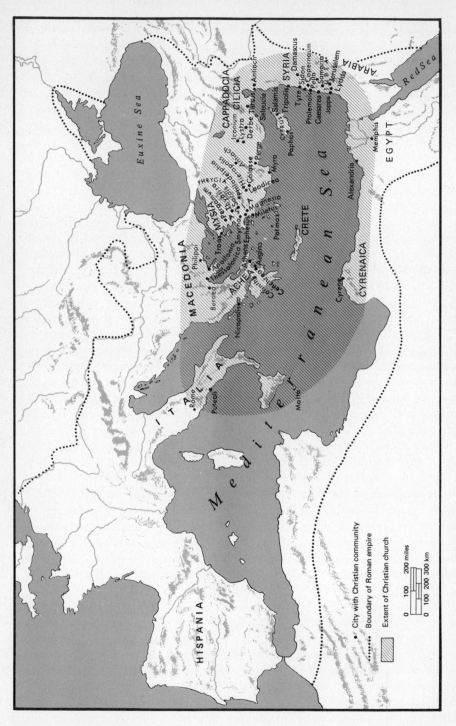

Figure 6 The Roman Empire (Adapted with permission of Macmillan Publishing Company and George Allen & Unwin, from The Macmillan Bible Atlas *by Y. Aharoni and Michael Avi-Yonah. Copyright © 1964, 1966, 1968, 1977 by Carta Ltd.)*

40

felt that the empire had overtaxed itself and needed consolidation. His wall in the north of England is a symbol of his effort simply to defend his holdings. The boundaries changed little after Hadrian's rule.

The personal character of Augustus' successors cannot be simply summarized. Some, such as Trajan, were men of judicious temperament; some, such as Hadrian, Diocletian, and Constantine, possessed remarkable talents for administration; and some, such as Nerva, had a sincere concern for public welfare. But Tiberius was thought to be insane, Gaius became a tyrannical monarch, Nero was blamed for a disastrous fire in Rome, and Domitian's reign became a debilitating witch hunt. In general, the second-century emperors are looked on as better than the first, and it is a common judgment that Marcus Aurelius was one of the best. Diocletian and Constantine must be regarded as the emperors who restored the government after the disastrous ordeals of the third century.

Jesus was born during the reign of Augustus and was executed in the time of Tiberius. Probably during the reigns of Claudius and Nero, Paul was preaching the message about Jesus. There are references to the persecution of Christians by Nero, Domitian, and Trajan, but the major attempts to eradicate the Christian movement were those of Decius and Diocletian. Diocletian considered that Christianity posed a serious threat to the efficient rule he was attempting to establish. With Constantine, the first Christian emperor, the persecutions ceased, and Christianity came to be allied with the state. Eventually it became the official religion of the Roman Empire.

SOCIAL CONDITIONS IN THE ROMAN PERIOD

Here we must briefly consider some of the more important social and economic aspects of life in the Roman period. It is essential to have at least a general idea of these aspects of culture in order to understand the response to the Christian message and the social contributions to it. In this section it seems best to concentrate on the early part of the Roman period, for it is the time that is most relevant for our study of the NT and early Christianity.

Cultural Unity

The most serious internal problem for the empire was the creation of unity among diverse nationalities. The emperors attacked the problem politically, by superimposing Roman government on top of native governments in the provinces or by recognizing client kings. In either case, the Roman presence was clear to all. Governors in the provinces were appointed by the emperor and were responsible to him. Taxation was a constant reminder of Roman authority. Armed garrisons in the provinces frequently functioned as cultural influences. The empire committed itself to maintain peace within and among provinces and to protect them from outside invasion. The guarantee of peace was, however, not always effective, for peoples such as the Parthians frequently disrupted it. Nevertheless, borders in most areas were fairly secure for the first two centuries. The price that the provinces paid for the *pax Romana* was to accept Roman political institutions and pay the taxes. It was a high price, but it was not without its benefits.

Aside from sheer political control, Rome made few incursions into the social and religious life of the provinces. Most of the native institutions continued to function as long as they did not interfere with the governing process. Language served as an important tool of unification. To be sure, native languages continued to be used within each province, but in international affairs, commerce, and literature, Greek was the language, especially in the cities. The use of Greek was not a Roman demand on the provincials; it had been a natural development during the Hellenistic period and continued on into the Roman. Latin was used in legal circles, in Italy, and in some western provinces, but it did not replace Greek until after the second century CE. The use of Greek in the provinces opened minds to the classics of Greek literature, philosophy, and religion and contributed greatly to cultural unification. Nevertheless, there was little feeling of such unity in the areas formerly controlled by the Seleucids, and there were numerous cultural conflicts. In Augustus' time, large numbers of people migrated into Italy from these eastern areas, and they generally considered Italian culture to be inferior to eastern. Cultural unity was more nearly a reality in the west than in the east, for westerners were frequently eager to think of themselves as Romans.

Social Classes[4]

The social class system among the Romans was far more definite and visible than in modern western countries. The system was not a product of the empire but was inherited from republican times; in fact it remained relatively constant in the shift from republic to empire. The basic defining criteria for social classification were birth and legal status, although under the empire wealth and talent were beginning to carry some weight. Furthermore, mobility, both upward and downward, was characteristic of the system in the first two centuries.

In the city of Rome the top class was the senatorial aristocracy. This had

[4] In the following section, the author depends heavily on John G. Gager, "Religion and Social Class in the Early Roman Empire," in Benko and O'Rourke, op. cit., pp. 99–120; John G. Gager, *Kingdom and Community* (Englewood Cliffs, N.J.: Prentice-Hall, 1975); and John E. Stambaugh, "Social Relations in the City of the Early Principate: State of Research," *SBL Seminar Papers,* **19**:75–99 (1980).

been a nobility of blood, but Augustus imposed an additional capital requirement of one million sesterces.[5] It was generally felt that a senator needed the income from this much capital in order to perform his public duties. Members of this class were permitted to wear togas with wide stripes, and so they were visibly distinguishable from persons in other classes. The most notable feature of the senatorial class during the first two centuries was the decline in its numbers. As a result of deliberate purges by the Julio-Claudian dynasty and a declining birth rate, the number of the old senatorial families shrank, until only one was left by the year 130. Consequently senatorial positions were filled from the rank below, from among persons who possessed the necessary capital. The chief source of capital for the older families was land; the newer ones engaged in commerce. Although there was, strictly speaking, no senatorial class outside Rome, there was a comparable class of nobles in each of the provinces. Seneca and other writers were very critical of the senators and attacked them for their greed, luxury, and indulgence.

The equestrian order ranked next below that of the senatorial aristocracy. The emperor could admit into the order any free-born citizen who had assets amounting to 400,000 sesterces.[6] No limit was placed on the number of families in the order, and the titles were not restricted by heredity. Provincial governors were usually drawn from this class, and many became capitalists in business and commerce and acquired considerable wealth.

Members of these two upper classes lived well, on large hereditary estates. But they contributed generously to the empire as a whole both from their possessions and their abilities.

The class of freedmen, or emancipated slaves, was perhaps the most aggressive in Rome. They owed a kind of allegiance to their former masters, and many remained in their service. Others were able to acquire significant wealth and occupy positions of power. They were to be found in commerce, banking, and government service. Those in the employ of the emperor, the imperial freedmen, managed the major administrative departments of the government, and some served as public secretaries and controlled access to the emperor. Freedwomen also formed a large part of Rome's work force. According to John Stambaugh, a contemporary American scholar, they were "shopkeepers, artisans, domestic servants, textile workers. Some, presumably among the most destitute, were prostitutes. Some were successful in commerce and became very wealthy."[7] Rome protected the rights of freedmen and freedwomen, both in their attempts to work for wages and in their assimilation to the body politic.

[5] Writing in 1971, Gager estimated the dollar value of one million sesterces to be about $50,000; cf. Gager, op. cit., "Religion and Social Class," p. 101. If this figure is correct, it should be adjusted to about $120,000 to reflect dollar values in 1983.
[6] Approximately $45,000 in 1983.
[7] Stambaugh, op. cit., p. 87.

In terms of class, the plebs ranked ahead of the freedmen, but in terms of the benefits they derived from the class structure, most must be regarded as occupying a position just above that of slaves. Although the plebs were free-born citizens, they often were poor, and many were on public relief. Those who had no marketable skills were destitute, for they were unable to compete with slaves for the least desirable jobs. Yet there is a wide range in the living standards of this class. Stambaugh describes their life-style: "The better off lived in their own houses or in relatively spacious apartments, less grand than the palazzi of the rich, but often quite comfortable. . . . The poor lived . . . in tenementlike inns and sublet rooms . . . , or else in small lofts inserted as messanines in the house-front shops."[8]

Slaves formed the bottom rung of the social ladder. Slavery was an accepted institution throughout the Mediterranean world, and the ranks were filled by Rome's conquered people. In Italy in the first part of the first century, the proportion of slaves to free people was about 2:5.[9] The problems of dehumanization and of relations between master and slave are endemic to the institution. In addition, slavery created an economic situation that restricted possibilities for a genuinely free labor market. If one looks at labor as a commodity that can be bought and sold, it is apparent that if the market is filled with cheap or free labor, there is little place for the wage earner. Thus, the price of labor was kept down by slavery, and both pleb and slave were victims. A reversal began to take place in late republican and early imperial times, however, as many masters found it too expensive to maintain large numbers of slaves. Manumissions became increasingly numerous, so much so that the government attempted to control them. Many slaves were able to build the capital given to them by their masters into an amount sufficient to buy their freedom.

Provincial foreigners below the level of the nobility were generally regarded as being outside the class system and irrelevant to it. Most were on a par with slaves because they were not Roman citizens. Roman citizenship was a birthright for children of recognized Roman marriages, and it carried with it the right to vote in certain local matters and the right to appeal an unfavorable legal decision to the emperor or his designate. Citizenship was usually granted by the emperor to native political leaders in the provinces and frequently to persons who made outstanding contributions to the empire. Such a person had all the rights of citizenship, including the right to hold a position as an equestrian, a senator, or even emperor (witness Antoninus Pius and Marcus Aurelius). Citizenship was finally granted to all free provincials by Caracalla in 212, although his motives for doing so are not clear.

[8] Ibid., p. 83.
[9] Based on estimates of Tenney Frank, *An Economic Survey of Ancient Rome* (Baltimore: Johns Hopkins, 1940), Vol. V, p. 1.

Women's rights were increasingly recognized and protected in imperial times. Free-born Roman women enjoyed the rights of citizenship. By the second century, women were not compelled to marry against their wills; the absolute authority of husband over wife had disappeared; and divorce was permitted on the request of either partner. In the early second century, Juvenal wrote about women who attempted to rival men in law, international affairs, sports, and drinking.

Education

Although the Romans did not aspire to provide universal education, schools were available for a wide range of men and women, and not exclusively for the wealthy. The form of education in the Roman period was largely a continuation of that in the Hellenistic, at least in the eastern Mediterranean region. About the goals of education, the French scholar H. I. Marrou says: "Education was not so much concerned to develop the reasoning faculty as to hand on its literary heritage of great masterpieces."[10] The major texts were the writings of the epic poets, dramatists, and orators: Homer, Virgil, Euripedes, Menander, and Demosthenes.[11] There were three levels of education: primary, secondary, and advanced. Children could start school at age seven, at the primary level, where they learned to read the classical authors and studied music and mathematics. In the secondary schools students were taught to write in the classical style. Advanced education was available for the professions of law, rhetoric, and medicine and was concluded at about age twenty. The study of philosophy was also an option at the advanced level. It involved not only a mastery of the history of philosophy but also a commitment to a particular philosophy or philosophical school. Jewish education was structurally parallel to Roman, but the curriculum consisted almost entirely of the Hebrew scriptures.[12]

Living Conditions

Shortly after the battle of Actium, Augustus established that the number of citizens in the entire empire was 4,063,000 (in 28 BCE).[13] Tenney Frank, an American classicist, used these figures to estimate that the total population of Italy, citizens and noncitizens, was 14 million.[14] This figure includes 10 million free persons and 4 million slaves. The population of the city of

[10] H. I. Marrou, *A History of Education in Antiquity,* trans. George Lamb (New York: Sheed, 1956), p. 161.
[11] See Ibid., p. 164.
[12] See John T. Townsend, "Ancient Education in the Time of the Early Roman Empire," in Benko and O'Rourke, op. cit., pp. 139–163.
[13] *Res Gestae* 8.
[14] Frank, op. cit., p. 1.

Rome has been variously estimated, but the archeologist Carcopino's calculation of about one million at the time of Augustus and 1,200,000 in the middle of the second century must be nearly right.[15] These figures may not surprise the modern reader until he or she realizes that urban transportation did not allow ancient cities to expand to a size comparable with modern ones. Consequently, the city of Rome housed a large population in a relatively small area. Although there were many private dwellings, most Romans were crowded into apartment houses. These houses were built in multiple stories to a height sometimes exceeding that of a six-story modern house. The base was frequently inadequate to support the height, and many of them collapsed. Furthermore, the wooden structures often burned. They were built close to the streets, which were crowded, twisting, and unmarked. Public latrines, which were scrupulously clean, were available, but most people carted sewage to dung heaps or turned alleyways into cesspools.

Standards of living varied considerably. Cities fared better than towns and rural areas, and Italy was more prosperous than the provinces. But even within the city of Rome, which appeared to those outside as a glamorous paradise, the situation was one of contrasts—a few millionaires and thousands of paupers. In the second century at least one third of the inhabitants lived on public charity, and many of the rest were slaves. Carcopino estimates that only about half the families in Rome could live without government aid.[16] The cost of living can only be suggested. At the end of the third century Diocletian established a freeze on wages and prices, and his list of maximum amounts gives us some idea of the living standards.[17] A farm worker, who appears to be at the bottom of the wage scale, could earn 25 denarii a day, plus maintenance.[18] Skilled laborers earned substantially more—a stonemason, for example was to be paid a maximum of 50 denarii. Diocletian allowed a maximum price of four denarii for a pint of beer and eight for a pound of beef. Thus, a farm laborer could afford to buy two pounds of beef and two pints of beer per day. Of course, wages and prices fluctuated considerably during the first three centuries CE. Both wages and prices were a great deal lower outside Italy. The government also took a large bite out of income. During the reign of Vespasian (69–79), every adult paid a poll tax and a 1 per cent sales tax. In addition there was a 5 per cent inheritance tax, a 4 per cent tax on the sale of slaves, a 5 per cent tax on manumissions, and a 2 to 5 per cent tax for port duties.[19] In addi-

---

[15] See Jerome Carcopino, *Daily Life in Ancient Rome,* ed. Henry T. Rowell, trans. E. O. Lorimer (New Haven, Conn.: Yale U. P., 1940).

[16] Ibid., p. 65.

[17] See Frank, op. cit., pp. 305–421.

[18] The value of the denarius was about forty-five cents in 1983.

[19] See John J. O'Rourke, "Roman Law and the Early Church," in Benko and O'Rourke, op. cit., p. 183.

The Three Hebrews in the Fiery Furnace, fresco, early fourth century, Catacomb of Priscilla, Rome. The painting was inspired by the OT Book of Daniel, which was probably written during the Maccabean revolt. (Courtesy *Pontifical Commission for Sacred Archives, Rome.*)

tion, many people were expected to contribute to religious institutions. Jews, for example were subject to a number of special religious dues, and after 70, Vespasian required a special poll tax from every Jew between the age of three and sixty. The NT scholar F. C. Grant estimates that for the Jewish family in the first century, a staggering 30 to 40 per cent of income went to civic and religious taxes.[20]

There was social unrest in the first two centuries but no significant reform movement. People who for one reason or another had lost their former economic or social positions—that is, those who were mobile—came closer to revolt than did the others. Small farmers felt that they were being exploited by absentee landlords, and they developed hostilities toward the cities. Others, such as the plebs, were not happy with their lot, but they felt the social disadvantages more keenly than the economic disadvantages. Freedmen were working within the system for their own betterment, and

[20] See F. C. Grant, *The Economic Background of the Gospels* (London: Oxford U. P., 1926), p. 105.

slaves, who could look forward to becoming free, felt that the system might work on their behalf. Although it had weaknesses which were to become apparent, it was at least a tolerable system for most people in the first two centuries.[21]

JUDEA IN THE HELLENISTIC PERIOD

During the Hellenistic and Roman periods Jews lived in the major urban centers throughout the eastern Mediterranean world. In general they were divided into two groups. Those who lived in the traditional areas—Judea (and later, Galilee)—were called Palestinian Jews.[22] Jews who lived outside those territories were called diaspora Jews. In many places the size of the diaspora Jewish community was quite large. In the first century CE, Jews in Egypt numbered a million and constituted about 15 per cent of the population there. Despite those large numbers, our attention is irresistibly drawn to the Palestinian Jews, especially those in Judea and its capital, Jerusalem. This part of the world holds a singular importance for us, because of Jesus and the earliest Christian communities.

Judea had been under the control of Persia for two centuries when Alexander came to power. The fact that the people of Judea enjoyed a higher degree of personal freedom under the Persians than they had under their former overlords, the Babylonians, does not alter the fact that they passionately desired political independence. But such independence was something they had not known for some time, not in fact since 587 BCE, when Judea was conquered by the Babylonians. To most Jews Alexander seemed to be a liberator when he wrested Judea from Persian control in 331 BCE. In the period of the *Diadochi*, until 200 BCE, Judea was under Ptolemaic rule. The process of Hellenization—that is, the effort to impose Hellenistic culture—was not vigorously promoted by the Ptolemies, although Ptolemy IV (221–c. 203 BCE) attempted to establish the worship of the Greek God Dionysus throughout his empire. But in 200 BCE, the Seleucid monarch, Antiochus III, annexed Judea to his cumbersome empire, and almost immediately the Jews became subject to greater Hellenizing pressure.

Antiochus IV,[23] Seleucid emperor from 175–164 BCE, was a worthy suc-

---

[21] See Clarence L. Lee, "Social Unrest and Primitive Christianity," in Benko and O'Rourke, op. cit., pp. 121–138.

[22] The name Palestine was given to this area by the Romans in 135 C.E., so it is strictly anachronistic to use the term to describe situations before that date. It is, however, customary to use it to designate Judea, Samaria, Galilee, Perea, and even Idumea for both the Hellenistic and Roman periods.

[23] It was customary for Hellenistic kings to add designating titles to their names, and Antiochus IV chose the title *Epiphanes*, meaning "revelation." He believed himself to be a revelation of Zeus, although some of his contemporaries preferred to call him *Epimanes*, or "Mad." The name is written Antiochus IV Epiphanes.

cessor to his father Antiochus III, for he intended to press the advantage of the victory of 200 BCE by invading Egypt itself. He did so in 169 and again in 168 BCE. But at this point Rome entered the picture and forced him to leave Egypt. He also had attempted to promote Hellenization in Jerusalem, as in other cities under his rule. After the first invasion of Egypt he found that there was strife in Jerusalem, the result in part of opposition to his policy, and he put down the revolt there. After he returned from the second invasion he sent an expedition to Judea to try to suppress the religious opposition to Hellenization. The Jerusalem Temple, to Jews the most sacred of all places, was captured and occupied, and the altar to the Jewish God was replaced by an altar to the Greek God Zeus Olympias. An order was issued requiring all Judeans to make sacrifices to Zeus either in their home towns or in the Temple.

In a small town near Jerusalem, an incident occurred that sparked one of the most remarkable resistance movements in Jewish history. The Seleucid authorities felt that their policy on religion would be more readily acceptable if the native Jewish leadership showed its support. One of those leaders in Modein (or Modi'in) was a Jewish priest by the name of Mattathias bar John bar Simeon bar Hasmoneus.[24] Mattathias was asked to show his public support of the Seleucid policy by making the first sacrifice to Zeus. Perhaps the Seleucids did not expect much resistance from the priests, for of all Jewish groups they had shown themselves to be the least resistant to Hellenization. According to Josephus, some of them had built a Greek gymnasium and participated in sports in Jerusalem.[25] Early in his reign Antiochus IV had entered a dispute between two priestly parties and had appointed Menelaus, of the Tobiad family, as high priest of the Jews. When Jason, of the rival Oniad family, rebelled, Antiochus put him down. The Seleucids must have felt that priests were willing to accept their demands. But Mattathias was not their man. He appeared at an altar set up to Zeus in Modein, killed the royal commissioner and a Jew who had prepared to make his sacrifice, destroyed the altar, and ran for the Judean hills, calling all loyal Jews to support him. The book I Maccabees gives a date for this incident that correlates to December 167 BCE.[26]

Mattathias was soon joined by his five sons and hundreds of fellow supporters, among them a group known as the Hasidim, who were vigorously

[24] The word *bar* is the Aramaic equivalent of the Hebrew *ben*. Both words may be translated "son of," and they are used to designate family names.

[25] Josephus, *Antiquities of the Jews* XII, 240–241. Josephus' writing constitutes one of the major literary sources for this period. His *Jewish War* was published between 75 and 81 CE, and the *Antiquities of the Jews* was published in 93 CE.

[26] 1 Maccabees, probably written before 100 BCE, is another primary source for this period. The dates used in this and the following section are based on those in Emil Schürer, *The History of the Jewish People in the Age of Jesus Christ,* rev. and ed. by Geza Vermes and Fergus Millar (Edinburgh: T & T Clark, 1973), Vol. I.

anti-Hellenistic Jews.[27] That resistance movement is known as the Hasmonean or Maccabean War. Hasmoneus was the great grandfather of Mattathias, and this became the family name for the leaders. The name Maccabeus was first given to Mattathias' son Judas; it seems to mean,"the hammerer" and was probably applied to Judas in admiration of his military ability.

THE HASMONEANS

Mattathias, 167–165 BCE
Judas, 165–161
Jonathan, 161–143
Simon, 143–135
Hyrcanus I, 135–104
Aristobulus I, 104–103
Alexander Jannaeus, 103–76
Alexandra, 76–67
Aristobulus II, 67–63
Hyrcanus II, 63–40
Antigonus, 40–37

Figure 7   The Hasmoneans

According to I Maccabees, after the initial act of resistance by Mattathias, real leadership fell to his son Judas, whose untrained troops were outnumbered, at one point, by as much as six to one.[28] However, Judas met the enemy in four instances that turned into remarkable victories for the Jews. Under his leadership, the Temple in Jerusalem was restored as the place for sacrifices to the Jewish God. I Maccabees says that the restoration occurred exactly three years after the desecration, that is, in 164 BCE. Jews commemorate this event in the annual festival of Hanukkah, which occurs in December.

Although a measure of religious freedom had been attained, it could be secured only by a comparable political independence, and this the Maccabean warriors continued to seek. Antiochus IV died in 164 BCE, but, during the reign of his son, Antiochus V, the general Lysias recaptured Jerusalem for the Seleucids. In spite of his success, he could not press his advantage, because he found it necessary to return to his capital city, Antioch, to defend it against a challenger to the throne. The next Seleucid king, Demetrius I, attempted to interfere with Jewish religion by making an appointment to the high priesthood. Judas challenged this appointment and, in 161

---

[27] See I Macc 2:42 and 7:15. The Hebrew word *Hasidim* denotes people who are loyal to Torah.
[28] I Macc 4:28–29.

BCE, defeated another Seleucid general, Nicanor. Although Josephus states that Judas assumed the role of Jewish high priest at this time, the evidence that he functioned in this capacity is weak.[29] He did, however, enter into a treaty of friendship with the Romans, in which the Jews agreed to aid the Romans in case of war and the Romans agreed to treat the Jews as their allies. Notice of this treaty was sent to the Seleucid king Demetrius I, but he acted speedily in sending another contingent into Judea in the fall of 161 BCE. In this encounter Judas himself was killed.

The leadership of the Jewish cause now fell to Judas' brother, Jonathan, leadership which he held from 161–143 BCE. Our sources are less detailed on this period, but we can gather that Jonathan was able to minimize the internal opposition that had appeared during Judas' time. Moreover, conditions in Antioch had become unsettled because succession to the Seleucid throne was constantly challenged. This not only limited opportunities for Seleucid generals to make forays into Judea, but it also meant that Jews could play some part in the succession by supporting one contestant against another. At one particular point Jonathan was able to win important concessions from rivals to the throne. Alexander Balas, son of Antiochus IV, promised to appoint Jonathan as Jewish high priest, and his rival, Demetrius I, offered to remit the tribute the Jews had previously paid, to enlarge Jewish territory, to give presents and privileges to the Temple, and to rebuild the walls of Jerusalem, which had been destroyed by Antiochus IV. Jonathan agreed to support Alexander Balas, who killed Demetrius in 150 BCE. When Balas married Cleopatra, the daughter of Ptolemy VI of Egypt, Jonathan attended, dressed in regal attire, and was seated beside the bridegroom. Jonathan's influence in the international arena continued to increase. He used his own troops to suppress anti-Seleucid revolts in Antioch, Askelon, and Gaza. He conquered Galilee for the Jews, renewed the covenant with the Romans, and may even have opened negotiations with Sparta. Eventually, however, the Seleucid king Trypho became suspicious of Jewish power and led Jonathan into a situation in which he was captured and ultimately murdered.

Simon bar Mattathias completed the work of his brother Jonathan, and Judea continued to be independent of Seleucia. In 140 BCE a popular decree proclaimed him high priest, military commander, and civil governor of the Jews, positions guaranteed by the Roman Senate. In effect Simon had become king of the Jews and head of a new Jewish dynasty. His was only the third family to rule as a native Judean monarchy. The first, that of Saul, had been overthrown after only one generation by David, whose dynasty lasted from about 1000 to 587 BCE. After that the Jewish monarchy disappeared, not to be revived until Simon, the Hasmonean, came along. The Jews of

---

[29] See Josephus, *Antiquities* XII, 414, 434. 1 Maccabees says nothing, and Josephus, *Antiquities* XX, 237, says that the high priestly office was vacant at the time in question.

Figure 8   The Kingdom of Alexander Jannaeus, 103–76 BCE. (Used with permission of Macmillan Publishing Company and George Allen & Unwin, from The Macmillan Bible Atlas *by Y. Aharoni and Michael Avi-Yonah. Copyright © 1964, 1966, 1968, 1977 by Carta Ltd.)*

Simon's time were not unaware that they had made a serious break with the past, for they knew the ancient traditions about God's promise that David's dynasty would never end, and they knew that some prophets had expected it to be restored.[30] 1 Macc 14:41 recognizes the tentative nature of Simon's leadership and high priesthood and says it is to last "until a trustworthy prophet should arise." Simon's power was nonetheless absolute and hereditary, and it was exercised to the fullest by his successors. His son Hyrcanus I built a Jewish empire such as had not been since the time of Solomon. A significant venture was his conquest of Idumea in about 125 BCE, and his forcible assimilation of these people into Jewish society.

The reigns of the later Hasmoneans were marked by family disputes. Aristobulus I, for example, had to imprison his mother in order to secure the throne for himself.[31] The reign of Alexander Jannaeus (103–76 BCE) was notable for a war with Egypt and for internal conflict. The Jewish historian, Josephus, reports that Jannaeus was once pelted by opponents at the altar of the Temple, that he crucified eight hundred Jews, and that he had to call on the Seleucid king to help him put down a general rebellion.

The early part of Alexandra's reign was fairly peaceful, but civil war between two of her sons brewed during the latter years of her life. This civil war proved to be the undoing of Jewish independence, and Rome was able to make the most of it. The war broke out in 67 BCE, between Aristobulus II and Hyrcanus II. The former was victorious that year in a battle near Jericho and settled himself on the Jewish throne. But Hyrcanus, supported by the Idumeans and the Arabians, was not yet ready to admit defeat. In 63 BCE the Roman general Pompey was advancing toward Damascus in his conquest of the east, when he was met by both contenders, who asked for his help. Pompey immediately perceived a personal advantage in the situation and attempted to pit brother against brother. He was virtually invited by Hyrcanus' supporters to conquer Jerusalem, but Aristobulus' men gathered on the Temple mount to offer resistance to his troops. After three months of siege, Pompey invaded the fortress and even entered the most sacred precincts of the Temple, but he allowed the religious services to continue without interruption. He claimed Judea for Rome, carried Aristobulus and others to Rome as prisoners, and left Hyrcanus as high priest without royal title.

---

[30] See 2 Sam 7:16.
[31] Josephus, *Antiquities* XIII, 301, says that Aristobulus was the first to use the royal title, but this seems to be only a nominal change, for Simon had effectively functioned as king decades earlier.

JUDEA IN THE ROMAN PERIOD

Although the beginning of the Roman period has been set at 31 BCE, the date of the battle of Actium, for Judea it came a few decades earlier, with Pompey's conquest in 63 BCE. That date marks the end of the independent Hasmonean royal dynasty and the end of Jewish independence. It was bound to come, for, except for Parthia, no eastern nation escaped the control of Rome. The fact that it came then rather than later and that it came under such unfortunate circumstances demonstrates the opportunisitic tactics of the Roman rulers.

The Seleucid monarchy was also over, and Pompey exercised control over the entire area through governors, who ruled from Antioch and were subject to his appointment. Julius Caesar and Cassius did the same. This was the case until 41 BCE, when Antony gained control of the east; thereafter it was Antony's men who governed the province the Romans called Syria. After the battle of Actium, Augustus continued the practice of appointing governors to Syria. Technically, Judea was a part of the province of Syria during most of the Roman period, but, in fact, it always presented a special problem.

Although the Syrian governor attempted to keep order in Judea, the historic events of those years brought together Hyrcanus II, Antipater,[32] and Julius Caesar. In 48 BCE, when Caesar moved against Pompey at the battle of Pharsalia, both Hyrcanus II and Antipater were on his side and contributed to his victory. Josephus reports that, as a reward, Caesar appointed Hyrcanus high priest and ethnarch of the Jews and appointed Antipater procurator. The word *ethnarch* means ruler. It invests its holder with political power subject only to the oversight of Caesar himself. It might or might not be granted for life, and, although usually it was nonhereditary, Caesar made an exception in the case of Hyrcanus. Procuratorship, at that point, seems to have designated a financial officer who had the duty of collecting Roman taxes. He too was directly responsible to Caesar; he did not hold his job for life, however, and the title was nonhereditary. But Antipater was one to make use of all the advantages open to him; as procurator he appointed his son Phasael governor of Jerusalem and another son, Herod, governor of Galilee. Antipater died before Antony came to power, but the two had been friends earlier, and Antony did not forget the friendship. In 41 BCE he made Phasael and Herod tetrarchs of the Jews.[33]

Things were still in a most fluid state, however, for in the year 40 BCE Jerusalem witnessed a terrifying invasion of Parthians from the east. Antony

---

[32] Antipater was an Idumean, a national group that had been assimilated into Judean society and religion in about 125 BCE.

[33] *Tetrarch* literally means a ruler of one fourth of a kingdom or province. It is not clear what effect these appointments had on Hyrcanus' political power.

had not been able to exercise control over the Parthians or to protect his holdings against them. During negotiations for peace, Phasael and Hyrcanus were both captured, but Herod fled to Rome. The victorious Parthians set up Antigonus, a son of Aristobulus II, as puppet king of Jerusalem. As it turned out, Antigonus was the last of the Hasmoneans to exercise political authority in Judea.

While in Rome, Antipater's son Herod obtained from the Senate a declaration making him king of the Jews. With the help of Antony and the governor of Syria, he fought his way back to Jerusalem, which he captured in 37 BCE. Because of his relationship to the Parthians, Antigonus was arrested by the Romans and executed at Antioch. When the dust settled in Jerusalem, the Parthians had been defeated, the Roman troops had been withdrawn, and Herod was, in both name and fact, king of the Jews and client king of the Romans. He is known as Herod the Great, and his reign lasted from 37—4 BCE.

POLITICAL CONTROL OF JUDEA

Ptolemaic Empire, 323-200 BCE
Seleucid Empire, 200-140
Hasmoneans, 140-63
Pompey, 63-48
Julius Caesar, 47-44
Cassius, 44-42
Antony, 41-40
Parthians, 40-37
Antony, 37-31
Augustus, 31 BCE-14 CE

Figure 9   Political Control of Judea

The character of Herod the Great has always been a fascinating object of study, partly but not solely because, according to Christian tradition, Jesus was born during his reign. Our sources do not allow us to picture him other than as a tyrant who knew the meaning of power politics. He was careful to retain every ounce of power due to him, brutal in executing his will, and generally insensitive to the feelings and needs of his subjects.

Throughout his reign he was fearful of any challenge to his regal right. He married, among others, Mariamme, the granddaughter of Hyrcanus II, and through her he could legitimize his reign. But her brother, Aristobulus, was drowned at Jericho, probably by assassins paid by Herod; Hyrcanus II was executed in 30 BCE, probably on a charge of conspiracy; and Mariamme herself was executed on a charge of attempted murder in 29 BCE. Alexandra, Mariamme's mother, was put to death in about 28 BCE, as were two distant male Hasmoneans, for conspiracy, a year or so later. In short, Herod left no one alive who could pretend to the throne on the ground of having Hasmonean blood.

Herod's relations with Rome demonstrate his political ability. His original appointment as king came from Antony and the Roman Senate. But when Augustus defeated Antony and established the empire, Herod was found on the winning side. In 30 BCE he met with Augustus, who confirmed his royal title and even increased his territory. He could legitimately claim the title *rex socius,* or client king, of the Romans. This was a title conferred by the emperor on a ruler of a fairly extensive territory. It was not hereditary, it did not carry with it the right to wage war without imperial consent or to conclude treaties, and it granted only a limited right to coin money. Internally, the client king had unlimited power of life and death over his subjects, an unquestioned right to impose taxes, and complete control of the police force. In general, Rome favored the policy of using native rulers in this capacity as long as they proved their ability to govern and raise taxes, and as long as they could put down rebellion. Herod worked well in this capacity. Although there are hints that some courts met for the purpose of deciding capital cases, it is clear that they were completely under Herod's control. Many of the executions in his career were carried out because of rebellions attempted against him and against Rome. In sum, whatever else may be said about Herod, he fulfilled Rome's requirements for a *rex socius:* he put down rebellion, he raised taxes, and he was loyal to Rome.

Herod physically changed the face of Judea. He is noted for his great building enterprises: temples, theaters, amphitheaters, race tracks, and for reconstructing entire cities, including Samaria, and building new cities, such as Caesarea. In Jerusalem itself he built a theater, an amphitheater, a fort, and a magnificent royal palace. Nor were his buildings confined to Judea; they were found in Arabia, Rhodes, Athens, Tyre, Sidon, and Damascus. His most magnificent enterprise, however, was the enlargement and renovation of the Jerusalem Temple. This was the Jews' second Temple, built in about 515 BCE on the site of Solomon's Temple, but the renovations Herod made were so extensive that the building was often referred to as Herod's Temple. The extent of the work can be imagined from the fact that it was begun in 20 BCE and was not completed until about 64 CE. His building enterprises demonstrate Herod's desire to bring Judea into line with the dominant culture of the world. The Hellenization that the Jews had resisted in the time of Antiochus IV came back with a vengeance.

The later years of Herod's reign were beset with family difficulties. He suspected three of his sons of conspiracy, two of whom were executed in 7 BCE and one in 4 BCE. It was a time of suspicion and intrigue, and no one was really safe. Herod died in 4 BCE, shortly after the execution of his son Antipater, leaving in a will the amazing order that, at his death, several

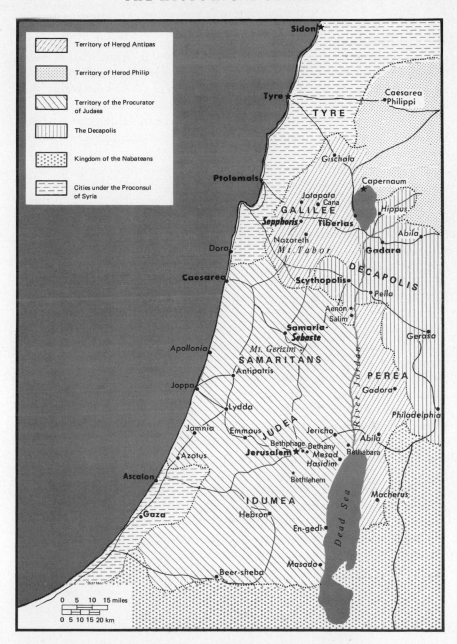

Figure 10 The Divisions of Herod's Kingdom (used with permission of Macmillan Publishing Company and George Allen & Unwin from The Macmillan Bible Atlas *by Y. Aharoni and Michael Avi-Yonah. Copyright © 1964, 1966, 1968, 1977 by Carta Ltd.)*

prominent people should be killed to ensure that there would be mourning. The order was not carried out.

For several months after Herod's death, the situation in Judea was turbulent and explosive. Two of his sons, Antipas and Archelaus, claimed to have a will of their father that gave them the royal title. Archelaus was, however, more forceful in making his claim, and he attempted to secure power immediately upon his father's death. However, a popular rebellion broke out against him, and it took his entire police force to restore temporary order.

A will of Herod the Great would carry a good deal of weight, but no one forgot that it was the Roman emperor who selected provincial rulers. Thus, Archelaus and Antipas both headed for Rome, while a third brother, Philip, held the fort at home for Archelaus. When the two brothers reached Rome, they found that other members of their family were already there. They had already requested that Augustus put Judea under direct Roman rule, but they were willing to accept Antipas if a Herodian had to be appointed. Augustus listened to all the claims and proposals but made no formal decision, although it was clear that he leaned heavily toward Archelaus. Pending a final settlement, he sent to Judea a Roman governor, Sabinus, upon whose arrival further revolts broke out, apparently directed at securing independence from Rome. These uprisings were dealt with by the use of troops assigned to the governor of Syria, who dealt brutally with the revolutionaries. Josephus says that two thousand of them were crucified. Next, another group of Jews went to Rome to request that no member of Herod's family be made king, and Philip also went to press his own claims. Finally, Augustus made his decision: Archelaus was made ethnarch of Judea, Samaria, and Idumea; Antipas was made tetrarch of Galilee and Perea; and Philip was made tetrarch of Batanea, Trachonitis, and Auranitis (see Figure 10). The extent of the territory assigned to each is misleading, but the title *ethnarch* gave Archelaus a degree of authority higher than that of his two brothers. Augustus also promised to give him the royal title if he governed well. In addition, the annual income received by the three reveals something of their responsibilities: Antipas' was double that of Philip, and Archelaus' was three times that of Antipas.

THE HERODIANS

Herod the Great, 37 BCE–4 BCE
Archelaus, 4 BCE–6 CE
Philip, 4 BCE–34 CE
Antipas, 4 BCE–39 CE
Agrippa I, 37–44 CE

Figure 11   The Herodians

The difficulty in Archelaus' territory is also reflected in the brevity of his rule. He reigned from 4 BCE to 6 CE and in the latter year a deputation of Jews complained to Augustus, who banished Archelaus and put Judea under the rule of a Roman governor.[34] Philip and Antipas seem to have had a more peaceful rule, the former retaining his position until 34 CE and the latter until 39 CE. The little we know of these two indicates that they were fairly good rulers. Philip was responsible for a good deal of building, and his loyalty to the Romans was unquestioned. His authority continued to his death. Antipas seems to be of a piece with his father so far as ambition is concerned. A few years after Philip's death, the Emperor, Gaius, turned his territory over to another Herodian, Agrippa I, and gave him the title king. Antipas felt that he should also have a royal title, and so he went to Rome to plead his case. But Agrippa's representatives opposed him; he was deposed and banished, and his territory was turned over to Agrippa.

The deposition of Archelaus in 6 CE amounted to a significant political shift. From this point on (with a brief break from 41–44 CE, when Agrippa I ruled[35]), Romans were appointed by the emperors to rule Judea, Idumea, and Samaria. In general, these governors had supreme judicial authority, but they left many matters to native courts. They had the right of capital punishment over all persons in their provinces, even over Roman citizens, who could, nevertheless, appeal the verdict. We do not know if the native courts retained their right of capital punishment, and this uncertainty creates a particular difficulty in the study of the death of Jesus. The governors also had complete financial and legislative control in their areas. Certain concessions were made for Jews because of their unique religion: in general they were not compelled to worship the emperor (except that certain emperors demanded it), but they did hold a sacrifice twice daily in the Temple "for Caesar and the Roman nation." They were not usually required to revere the image of the emperor, an act that was always odious to Jews not only because it represented foreign domination but also because the worship of images was forbidden in the Hebrew scriptures. So Roman troops in Jerusalem usually carried no image of the emperor, and Romans permitted the minting of copper coins without an image. The strangest concession was that Rome did not bring murder charges against Jews who might kill

[34] Literary sources refer to these governors as procurators. Although the term is accurate for the later ones (those from 44–66 CE) it clearly is not correct for the earlier ones. The official title for the earlier series was *prefect*. There is an inscription from Caesarea, in Samaria, that specifically identifies Pontius Pilate as prefect of Judea. See S. Safrai and M. Stern, ed., *The Jewish People in the First Century* (Assen: Van Gorcum & Co., 1974), Vol. I, p. 316. In order to minimize confusion, the technical titles will be avoided, and the nontechnical descriptive term *governor* will be used for both prefects and procurators.

[35] Agrippa I became king of Philip's territory in 37. Antipas' territory was added in 39, and Judea was added in 41. Thus, from 41 to 44 Agrippa ruled over the same territory as had Herod the Great.

Gentiles (non-Jews) within that part of the Temple that was exclusively reserved for Jews, even if the victims were Roman citizens.

THE ROMAN GOVERNORS

Coponius, 6–9 CE
Marcus Ambibulus, 9–12
Annius Rufus, 12–15
Valerius Gratus, 15–26
Pontius Pilate, 26–36
Marcellus, 36–37
Marullus, 37–41

Cuspius Fadus, 44–c. 46
Tiberius Alexander, c. 46–48
Ventidius Cumanus, 48–c. 52
Felix, c.52–60
Porcius Festus, 60–62
Albinus, 62–64
Gessius Florus, 64–66

Figure 12.   The Roman Governors.

Among the earlier governors the only one worthy of note is Pontius Pilate, who conducted the trial of Jesus. Josephus probably knows nothing about Jesus' trial, but he records several incidents involving Pilate and gives some insight into his administration. On one occasion Pilate ordered his soldiers to display the emperor's image in Jerusalem. He diverted certain Temple funds to the building of an aqueduct. He imprisoned a man who was regarded as a prophet and who gathered a crowd in Samaria by displaying objects associated with Moses; and for this Pilate was recalled to Rome. Another Jewish writer, Philo, records Agrippa I as saying that Pilate was recklessly arbitrary and that during his administration there was "corruptibility, violence, robberies, ill-treatment of people, grievances, continuous executions without even the form of a trial." [36]

The later governors (those from **44–66** CE) seemed particularly lacking in administrative skills and in understanding of their subjects. They ruled in heavy-handed fashion, attempting to suppress every sign of revolt and inadvertently creating the conditions that led to it. During those years groups of Jewish revolutionaries became more and more prominent. They represented the basic Jewish desire for independence. Many people desire to control their own political affairs, but with the Jews this desire was reinforced by their memory of recent independence under the Hasmoneans, by occasional Roman attempts to interfere with religious rites and taboos that they

---

[36] Philo, *Embassy to Gaius,* 38.

little understood, and by the distinctive nature of Jewish monotheism. Their understanding of their covenant, combined with a universal monotheism, amounted to a claim of religious sovereignty. There were two main revolutionary groups: Zealots and Sicarii. The Zealots made clear the implications of basic Jewish affirmations: "If we are God's people, God cannot be pleased by this situation in which Gentiles are our overlords. We have no king but God, and his kingdom must come." The Sicarii agreed with these convictions, but they seemed more inclined to action than to argument. A member of this group carried a *sicarius,* or short dagger, and was prepared to use it against a Roman official or against a Jew who sympathized with the Romans.

Not all Jews were prepared to go so far as the Sicarii and Zealots. Some had grown rich by collaborating with the Romans and so were not interested in opposing them. The large group in the middle seemed to be willing to wait for God to bring in his own kingdom. By 66 CE, however, the whole nation seemed ripe for rebellion. This attitude was certainly inflamed by the ineptitude and downright dishonesty of the last few governors. Josephus reports that Albinus operated by bribery and that Florus was in league with robber bands that plundered whole cities.

A view of the city of Jerusalem, showing the Dome of the Rock, center. (Courtesy *Israel Government Tourist Office, Houston, Texas.*)

The disastrous war broke out in the spring of 66, and before it was over two Romans destined for the imperial throne did battle with the Jews. Vespasian was military commander from the summer of 67 to the summer of 69, when he was proclaimed emperor. His son Titus took over in 69 and concluded the war in 74. Moreover, the historian Josephus was, for a time, commander of some Jewish forces in Galilee. The climax came in 70, with Titus' conquest of Jerusalem and the burning of the Temple, the effects of which will be noted later.

After the fall of Jerusalem, many Jews escaped to mountain areas in Judea—to Herodium, Macherus, and Masada. Masada had actually been occupied by Jewish rebels since the beginning of the war. It had a particularly fortunate location as a fortress. It rises sharply above the Judean desert near the Dead Sea and commands an unobstructed view for miles around. Recently archeologists uncovered the remains of the encampments on the top of Masada, and from the top one can see the outlines of the Roman camps far below. The rebels at Masada held out until 74, when the Roman troops were finally able to lay a siege ramp with which they approached the fortress. After much effort they broke through the wall surrounding the rebel camp. But the Jews on Masada had agreed that they would not be taken alive. They committed mass suicide the night before their enemies entered the camp. When the Romans came the next day, they found, according to Josephus, seven survivors and 960 dead.[37] The story of Masada is remembered as one of the most heroic in Jewish history and one of the most tragic, for it marks the end of the first revolt against Rome.

After the war Judea was again under the control of Roman governors. We gain the impression that, for the next several decades, it was very much devastated. Josephus says that the wall around Jerusalem "was so completely levelled to the ground as to leave future visitors to the spot no ground for believing that it [the city] had ever been inhabited."[38]

During the reign of the Roman Emperor Trajan, there was a revolt by diaspora Jews in Egypt, Cyrene, and Cyprus. The uprising began in 115 and was put down in 117. Some writers emphasize gruesome atrocities perpetrated by Jews, which may be exaggerated. But there is archeological evidence for the destruction of a number of Greek temples in Cyrene. After the suppression of the revolt on Cyprus, Jews were not allowed even to visit, let alone to live on, that island. Palestinian Jews seem not to have been involved in these revolts.

But another rebellion broke out in Judea in 132 against the Emperor Hadrian. This is counted as the second Jewish rebellion against Rome. The probable reason for it was that Hadrian had issued a ban against circumcision and had announced plans for rebuilding Jerusalem as a non-Jewish city,

[37] Josephus, *War* VII, 399–400.
[38] Josephus, *War* VII, 3.

with a temple to Jupiter on the site of the old Jewish Temple. In addition, this rebellion could claim the leadership of one who was widely regarded as the Messiah, a man called Bar Kokhba.[39] He was supported by a priest, Eleazar, and a rabbi, Aqiba. Recent archeological expeditions in the Dead Sea area have brought to light a wealth of artifacts and documents relating to this war. Among the finds are letters sent by Bar Kokhba to his generals. There are also coins minted in his name as well as coins with legends such as "Year One of the Redemption of Israel" and "Year Two of the Freedom of Israel." Despite the enthusiastic convictions of Bar Kokhba and his fellows, this revolt too failed. The leaders were captured, and Jerusalem was converted into a gentile city with temples to the Roman Jupiter and the Greek Aphrodite. After 135, the Romans drove the Jews out of Jerusalem and issued a decree forbidding them entrance into the city. Jerusalem was now named *Colonia Aelia Capitolina,* and Judea was named Palestine.

The political history of ancient Judea as a Jewish land came to an end after the Bar Kokhba rebellion. Although Jews still inhabited the province, they had no political rights. The ban against their entry into Jerusalem seems to have been upheld by subsequent Roman emperors. We know that Constantine, in the fourth century, allowed Jews to enter the city once a year. On the ninth of the Jewish month Ab, traditionally the date of the destruction of both Solomon's Temple and the second Temple, they were allowed to pray at the "Wailing Wall," the remains of the western wall of Herod's Temple. Whether this was a relaxation of previous policies or a continuation is not known.

As we will see, the political history tells only part of the story of the Jews during the Hellenistic and Roman periods. In Chapter 3 we will look at the religious and intellectual aspects of Judaism. Nevertheless, we have already seen that Judea's turbulent history, which is marked by a religiously based demand for independence from foreign control, forms a dramatic backdrop both for the appearance of new forms of Judaism and for the rise of Christianity.

BIBLIOGRAPHY

The Hellenistic and Roman Periods

Brinton, Crane, John B. Christopher, and Robert L. Woolf. *A History of Civilization.* 3rd ed. Englewood Cliffs, N. J.: Prentice-Hall, Inc., 1967. 2 volumes

Cook, S. A., F. E. Adcock, and M. P. Charlesworth, eds. *The Cambridge Ancient History.* New York: Macmillan Publishing Co., Inc., 1924–1939. 12 volumes

[39] The name *Bar Kokhba* means *son of a star* and appears to be a euphemistic Messianic designation. Recently discovered evidence shows that his real name was Simon Kosiba. See Yigael Yadin, *Bar-Kokhba: The Rediscovery of the Legendary Hero of the Last Jewish Revolt Against Imperial Rome* (London: Weidenfeld and Nicolson, 1971).

Hadas, Moses. *A History of Rome*. London: George Bell & Sons, Ltd., 1958.
Robinson, Charles A., Jr. *Ancient History*. 2nd ed. by Alan Boegehold. New York: Macmillan Publishing Co., Inc., 1967.
Rostovtzeff, M. I. *A History of the Ancient World,* trans. by J. D. Duff. Oxford: Clarendon Press, 1926, 1927. 2 volumes
Tarn, W. W., and G. T. Griffith. *Hellenistic Civilization*. 3rd ed. London: Edward Arnold & Co., 1952.

Brinton, Christopher, and Woolf is a survey of Western civilization; Robinson begins with prehistoric people and goes to 565 CE. *The Cambridge Ancient History* contains detailed studies of the Hellenistic and Roman periods, especially in Volumes 7, 9, and 10. The book by Tarn and Griffith is an excellent study of Hellenism. The book by Hadas is a collection of brief primary sources. Hadas has some additional comments, but for the most part the hsitory of Rome is told by the Roman historians themselves. Rostovtzeff's is a standard reference work.

Social Conditions in the Roman Period

Benko, Stephen, and John J. O'Rourke, eds. *The Catacombs and the Colosseum*. Valley Forge, Pa.: Judson Press, 1971.
Carcopino, Jerome. *Daily Life in Ancient Rome*. Ed. by H. T. Rowell. Trans. by E. O. Lorimer. New Haven, Conn.: Yale University Press, 1940.
Charlesworth, M. P. *The Roman Empire*. London: Oxford University Press, 1951.
Dill, Samuel. *Roman Society from Nero to Marcus Aurelius*. New York: Meridian, 1956.
Foakes-Jackson, F. J., and Kirsopp Lake, eds. *The Beginnings of Christianity*. New York: Macmillan Publishing Co., Inc., 1920–1933. 5 volumes
Frank, Tenney. *An Economic Survey of Ancient Rome*. Baltimore: The Johns Hopkins University Press, 1933–1940. 6 volumes
Grant, Frederick C. *The Economic Background of the Gospels*. London: Oxford University Press, 1926.
Grant, Robert M. *Early Christianity and Society*. New York: Harper & Row, Publishers, 1977.
Mattingly, Harold. *The Man in the Roman Street*. New York: Numismatic Review, 1947.
Rostovtzeff, M. I. *The Social and Economic History of the Roman Empire*. 2nd ed. Rev. by P. M. Fraser. Oxford: Clarendon Press, 1957. 2 volumes

Benko and O'Rourke have collected an excellent group of sociological studies relating to our period. Each essay was written by a member of the Philadelphia Seminar on Christian Origins. The books by Carcopino and Mattingly are written with scholarly care but are not pedantic. The survey by Tenney Frank, six volumes in all, is a standard reference work. Charlesworth deals with political institutions, education, and trade in the Roman Empire up to the time of Constantine. F. C. Grant analyzes the economic impact of Roman taxation and of Jewish religious observance on the Jews.

R. M. Grant studies a number of social, political, and economic matters as they affected Christians in the Roman period. Several essays in volume I of Foakes-Jackson and Lake are very useful. The paperback edition has the title *The Acts of the Apostles* (Grand Rapids, Mich.: Baker Book House, 1979). Rostovtzeff's volumes are basic for a study of social and economic conditions in the Roman period.

Judea in the Hellenistic and Roman Periods

Freyne, Sean. *Galilee from Alexander the Great to Hadrian, 323 B.C.E. to 135 C.E.* Notre Dame, Ind.: University of Notre Dame Press, 1980.

Jeremias, Joachim. *Jerusalem in the Time of Jesus*. Trans. by F. H. and C. H. Cave. Philadelphia: Fortress Press, 1969.

Mommsen, Theodor. *The Provinces of the Roman Empire*. Trans. by William P. Dickson. New York: Charles Scribner's Sons, 1887. 2 volumes

Reicke, Bo. *The New Testament Era*. Philadelphia: Fortress Press, 1968.

Rhoads, David M. *Israel in Revolution, 6–74 C.E.* Philadelphia: Fortress Press, 1976.

Safrai, S., and M. Stern, eds. *The Jewish People in the First Century*. Assen: Van Gorcum and Company, 1974, 1976. 2 volumes

Schürer, Emil. *The History of the Jewish People in the Time of Jesus Christ*. Trans. and rev. by Geza Vermes and Fergus Millar. Edinburgh: T & T Clark, 1973, 1979. 2 volumes so far published.

Tcherikover, Victor. *Hellenistic Civilization and the Jews*. Trans. by S. Applebaum. Philadelphia: Jewish Publication Society, 1959.

Yadin, Yigael. *Bar-Kokhba: The Rediscovery of the Legendary Hero of the Last Jewish Revolt Against Imperial Rome*. London: Weidenfeld and Nicholson, 1971.

———. *Masada: Herod's Fortress and the Zealots' Last Stand*. London: Weidenfeld and Nicolson, 1966.

Schürer's work, first published in 1885, has been the standard history of Judea in the Hellenistic and Roman periods. The volumes edited by Safrai and Stern are collections of essays by a number of authors on particular historical and ideological subjects. Jeremias concentrates on economic and social conditions in Jerusalem at about the time of Jesus. Rhoads has produced a brief account of the history of Judea from 6 to 74. The books by Yadin record, in readable fashion, the recent archeological discoveries relating to Masada and to Bar Kokhba. Yadin also comments on the significance of the discoveries. Although it focuses attention on Galilee, Freyne's book belongs in this group. Tcherikover challenges some of the more usual approaches to the history of Hellenistic Judaism, both in Palestine and in the Diaspora.

❖ 3 ❖

The Jewish Context

BECAUSE Christianity looks to the life and teachings of Jesus for the foundation of its own beliefs, and because Jesus was, it is universally agreed, a Jew, it is essential to understand the Jewish context in which he lived. That context is not, however, important only for understanding Jesus. Early Christian writings, both within and outside of the NT, are filled with references, quotations, and allusions to Jewish literature and reflections of its concepts and history. Indeed, the first Christians understood themselves as constituting a movement within Judaism. We will see that some basic Jewish ideas were altered by Christians, but our understanding must be informed by a knowledge of the heritage out of which those concepts arose and of the conditions that seemed to require that they be altered.

As we saw in Chapter 2, the political and social situation among Palestinian Jews was turbulent throughout much of the Hellenistic and Roman periods. Fundamental changes were occurring in the ideological sphere as well. The introduction of Hellenistic and Roman thought and institutions created new challenges for Jews both in Palestine and in the Diaspora, as some were attracted and others repelled by these new factors. Of all the historical events that we have examined, the destruction of the Jerusalem Temple in 70 CE stands out as an event of incomparable significance for Jewish life. We will, in fact, use it as a dividing line, carefully distinguishing between Judaism prior to and after 70. In addition, the geographical scattering of Jews during this period created a distinction between the character of Jewish life in the homeland and that in the Diaspora. These social factors and their effects must always be borne in mind when we study Judaism at the time of the rise of Christianity.

The focus of attention in this chapter will be on some of the basic convictions shared by Jews in that period. In the process we will also find it necessary to examine the rich diversity in Judaism in the Hellenistic and Roman periods. After a look at the basic sources of information on our subject, we will examine some of the major Jewish sects. Then we will focus attention on several of Judaism's most important concepts and institutions. The chapter will close with a brief look at Judaism in the Diaspora.

JEWISH LITERATURE

Where do we get our information about Judaism during this period? There are several major collections of literature that bear directly on the subject. In addition, two individual writers of the first Christian century must be consulted.

The earliest collection of such writings is variously named. Christians know it as the Old Testament (OT), but Jews refer to it as the Holy Scriptures, Bible, or *Tanach*. The individual books in this collection were written over a long period of time, and they have traditionally been divided into three parts: the Torah, or five books of Moses;[1] the prophets; and the writings. Not all Jews in Jesus' day recognized all three parts as having equal authority. One group, known as the Sadducees, elevated Torah above the rest, while another group, the Pharisees, regarded Torah, prophets, and some writings as sacred. Other groups probably revered still other books. The viewpoint of the Pharisees finally prevailed, and in 90 CE, all three parts were recognized as canonical.

This canonical recognition in 90 CE defined the contents of the Tanach. However, other writings remained popular and carried authority for some Jews. In Alexandria, and probably in other centers of diaspora Judaism, the canon probably included several additional books. The early Christians also included these additional books in their own Old Testament. Not until the sixteenth century were they excluded from the canon, and then only by Protestants. If one distinguishes these books from the Tanach/Old Testament, they are collectively called the *Apocrypha,* and they form our second collection of writings. Although there is no universal agreement on the actual contents of this collection, most of the documents that are usually included in it were written during the last two centuries BCE.[2]

The third collection is that of the Dead Sea Scrolls. This is the most recent set of pre-Christian Jewish writings to come to light. The story of their accidental discovery in 1947 is by now well known, and the reader

---

[1] I.e., Genesis, Exodus, Leviticus, Numbers, and Deuteronomy. The five books are frequently referred to collectively as the Pentateuch.

[2] 2 Esdras, however, was probably composed after 70 CE. Figure 14 represents the Protestant version of the Apocrypha. For a discussion of each of the books in the Apocrypha and some in the Pseudepigrapha, see Donald E. Gowan, *Bridge Between the Testaments* (Pittsburgh, Pa.: Pickwick Press, 1976), pp. 337–380.

THE ARRANGEMENT OF BOOKS IN THE HEBREW BIBLE

TORAH
  Genesis
  Exodus
  Leviticus
  Numbers
  Deuteronomy

PROPHETS
  Former Prophets
    Joshua
    Judges
    Samuel
    Kings
  Latter Prophets
    Isaiah
    Jeremiah
    Ezekiel
  The Twelve
    Hosea
    Joel
    Amos
    Obadiah
    Jonah
    Micah
    Nahum
    Habakkuk
    Zephaniah
    Haggai
    Zechariah
    Malachi

WRITINGS
  Psalms
  Job
  Proverbs
  Ruth
  Song of Solomon
  Ecclesiastes
  Lamentations
  Esther
  Daniel
  Ezra-Nehemiah
  Chronicles

Figure 13   The Arrangement of Books in the Hebrew Bible.

may consult Millar Burrows' *The Dead Sea Scrolls,*[3] for an account of it. The scrolls appear to have belonged to a group of Jews, probably the Essenes, who had established a religious community near the northwest shore of the Dead Sea in the vicinity of the modern ruins of a village by the name of Qumran. Most scholars believe that most of the scrolls were written during the last two centuries BCE, although some were probably written in the first

[3] Millar Burrows, *The Dead Sea Scrolls* (New York: Viking, 1955). See also Burrows, *More Light on the Dead Sea Scrolls* (New York: Viking, 1958).

THE BOOKS OF THE APOCRYPHA:

PROTESTANT VERSION

1 Esdras
2 Esdras
Tobit
Judith
The Rest of the Chapters of the
    Book of Esther
The Wisdom of Solomon
Ecclesiasticus, or the Wisdom of
    Jesus Son of Sirach

Baruch
A letter of Jeremiah
The Song of the Three
Daniel and Susanna
Daniel, Bel, and the Snake
The Prayer of Manasseh
1 Maccabees
2 Maccabees

Figure 14   The Books of the Apocrypha.

THE BEST KNOWN PSEUDEPIGRAPHA

Apocalypse of Baruch
Ascension of Isaiah
Assumption of Moses
2 Baruch
3 Baruch
1 Enoch
2 Enoch
Letter of Aristeas
Jubilees
Life of Adam and Eve
Lives of the Prophets
3 Maccabees
4 Maccabees
Psalms of Solomon
Rest of the Words of Baruch
Rest of the Words of Jeremiah
Sibylline Oracles
Story of Asenath
Testament of Abraham
Testament of Job
Testaments of the Twelve Patriarchs

Figure 15   The Best Known Pseudepigrapha. From Judiasm and Christian Beginnings
by Samuel Sandmel. Copyright © 1978 by Samuel Sandmel. Reprinted by permission of
Oxford University Press, Inc.

A passage from one of the Dead Sea Scrolls (IQ Isaiah 49:12). (Courtesy The Shrine of the Book, Israel Museum, Jerusalem.)

century CE. Many of the scrolls are manuscripts of Old Testament books, and every Old Testament book except Esther is represented in the collection. In addition, there are several scrolls produced especially for the Qumran community, scrolls that contain information on the beliefs and practices of the group.

A fourth collection of writings is known as the Pseudepigrapha, an indeterminate number of books produced approximately between 200 BCE and 200 CE. The word *pseudepigrapha* means false writings. These writings are false in the sense that they claim to have been written by authors who lived centuries before the time of the actual composition of the books. Some of the alleged authors are Eve, Moses, Enoch, Solomon, and Baruch. In each case it is clear that the document was not known prior to the Hellenistic or Roman period. It is equally evident that the books reflect certain aspects of the character of Judaism in the period of our chief interest. Some had marked effects on the development of early Christianity.

The Mishnah constitutes a fifth major collection of Jewish writings. We shall see later that during the Hellenistic and Roman periods, the Pharisees developed a tradition of oral law. This was a body of law that was considered, by Pharisees at least, to be equally authoritative with the five books of Moses. These laws were transmitted orally until about 200 CE, when Judah ha-Nasi collected them in his Mishnah. Thus, Judah's Mishnah is a collection of oral laws, some of which had been in circulation for centuries.[4]

Finally, brief mention must be made of certain miscellaneous bodies of literature: *Targums, Midrashim,* and Oracles. In Jewish synagogues in Palestine, it was frequently necessary to translate passages in the Tanach from Hebrew to Aramaic.[5] The translations, which were also interpretations, were originally oral but were later written down and are known as *Targums.* Some of them that are still available originated in Hellenistic and Roman times. The practice of writing explanatory and edifying commentaries on Tanach was also known in the Hellenistic and Roman periods. A few ancient commentaries, known as *Midrashim (Midrash* in the singular) are still extant. The collection known as the Sibylline Oracles[6] represents a kind of thought that is quite different from that known in the Mishnah, the *Targums,* and the *Midrashim.* All of the latter have close connections with the Tanach, particularly the Torah. The Sibylline Oracles, which probably originated among Egyptian Jews in the Hellenistic and Roman periods, seem to reflect a popular form of Judaism, a form that was interested in current prophecy and oracular utterance. These oracles must represent a larger body

---

[4] For an English translation, see Herbert Danby, *The Mishnah* (London: Oxford U.P., 1933); or Eugene J. Lipman, *The Mishnah: Oral Traditions of Judaism* (New York: Viking, 1973).
[5] Aramaic is a language related to Hebrew that was spoken in Palestine during the time of Jesus.
[6] The Sibylline Oracles are usually included in the Pseudepigrapha.

Genesis Apocryphon Scroll, one of the Dead Sea Scrolls, before it was unrolled. Fragment at upper right was removed from the back of the roll in April, 1948. Lower fragment was received loose but probably came from break on lower part. (Photo by John C. Trever.)

of Jewish and non-Jewish thought that was highly popular at the time, but about which very little is known.

In addition to these major collections, which in varying degrees came to be considered authoritative, there are two Jewish writers, Philo and Josephus, whose works are relevant for our study. Philo (c. 20 BCE–50 CE) was a leader in the Jewish community in Alexandria, Egypt; his works shed a great deal of light on diaspora Judaism. His writing manifests an attempt to resolve the intellectual conflict between Hellenism and Judaism, and he is a philosopher in his own right. His *Life of Moses* illustrates the fact that he shared the characteristic Jewish veneration for Moses but understood him largely in terms of Hellenistic values.

Josephus (c. 37–c. 110 CE) was a Palestinian Jew who was active in the rebellion against the Romans in the war of 66–74, when he was in charge of some of the Jewish forces in Galilee. From his own account we can determine that he put up a less-than-heroic struggle before surrendering. After the war he was taken to Rome, where he spent the rest of his life in the care of the Flavian family, writing for Roman readers an interpretation of the Jewish character and history.[7] His books must be read with caution, because of Josephus' distinctive position. He was a devoted adherent of the Pharisees; he was a Jew who was not sympathetic with the aims of the anti-Roman rebellion; he was a military appointee whose motives in the conduct of war were suspect; and he was a writer who intended to convince Roman nobles that Jews were an ancient and respectable people. Nevertheless, his two major works, *The Jewish War,* published between 75 and 81, and *The Antiquities of the Jews,* published in 93, are absolutely invaluable for an understanding of Palestinian Judaism during the Hellenistic and Roman periods. His apology, *Against Apion,* written in about 100, is a powerful defense of Judaism, as Josephus understood it.

FROM DIVERSITY TO UNITY

The profound effects of the destruction of the Jerusalem Temple in the year 70 can best be seen in the dramatic changes suggested by the phrase, "from diversity to unity." The phrase means that Judaism in Palestine should be understood as diverse prior to 70 and united afterward. Our information is not sufficient to allow us to make a similar claim in the case of diaspora Judaism, and it appears that the effects of the events in Palestine were not felt so dramatically in the Diaspora.

Although it is misleading to suggest that a formerly diverse culture turned overnight into a unified one, it nevertheless is important to recognize that the rebellion of 66–74 was the important turning point. We should be able

[7] The Flavian dynasty consists of Vespasian, Titus, and Domitian, Roman emperors from 69 to 96.

to understand these changes by looking at the various Jewish groups that existed before 70 and then at the situation afterward. Four groups have already been mentioned briefly—Sadducees, Pharisees, Essenes, and Zealots—but now need more detailed treatment.

Sadducees

Our information on Sadducees comes mainly from Josephus, although a few passages in the NT relate to them. In explaining Jewish sectarianism, Josephus says that Sadducees did not believe in fate. This probably means that they emphasized human freedom and ability to do what God required. He also says that Sadducees accepted only the written Torah. This does not mean that they rejected the prophets and the writings; rather it means that they accepted only the five books of Moses as having absolute authority. What the Sadducees rejected was the oral law of the Pharisees. They made a fundamental distinction between what they considered to be the divine words in the books of Moses and what they understood to be the human traditions of the Pharisees. Moreover, Josephus says that the Sadducees rejected the belief in life after death, an idea supported in several NT passages.[8] Acts 23:8 says that they also rejected belief in angels and spirits. Josephus identifies them with the aristocracy and indicates that their views were not always popular. He says that when, on rare occasions, Sadducees served in political positions, they followed the prescriptions of the Pharisees out of fear of the masses.[9] It should be remembered that Josephus was a Pharisee, so it is likely that his biases are reflected in his sketch of the Sadducees. Those biases come out clearly in another of his statements in which he compares Sadducees with Pharisees:

> The Pharisees are affectionate to each other and cultivate harmonious relations with the community. The Sadducees, on the contrary, are, even among themselves, rather boorish in their behavior, and in their intercourse with their peers are as rude as to aliens.[10]

The meaning of the name *Sadducee* is debatable, but most scholars trace its root to Zadok, the high priest during Solomon's reign. According to Ezekiel only the sons of Zadok were to minister at the altar in the Temple, and it is probable that the Sadducees originated as a party committed to that principle. Their origin appears to date from the time of the early Hasmoneans, because Josephus first mentions them in connection with Jonathan (161–143 BCE).[11] If the name does in fact indicate an insistence on

---

[8] See Matt 22:23, Mark 12:18, Luke 20:27, and Acts 23:8.
[9] Josephus, *Antiquities* XVIII, 17.
[10] Josephus, *War* II, 166, trans. H. St. J. Thackeray, Loeb Classical Library (Cambridge, Mass.: Harvard U.P., 1927), Vol. II.
[11] Josephus, *Antiquities* XIII, 171–173.

high priestly descent from Zadok, the Sadducees must have opposed the claims of the Hasmoneans to be high priests. Our sources make it clear that the Hasmoneans, although they were descended from a priestly line, were not descendants of Zadok. The basic association of the Sadducees is with the Temple and the priesthood, and it is probable that their initial opposition to the oral law sprang from their recognition that it allowed for a non-Zadokite line for the high priests.

Pharisees

Josephus attempts to show that Pharisees represent the best in Judaism, and he maintains that they had far more popular support than did the Sadducees. On the latter point he must certainly have been correct. The first notice he gives of both Sadducees and Pharisees is in connection with the Hasmonean Jonathan (161–143 BCE), but Josephus shows that Pharisees constituted a politically powerful force at the time of Hyrcanus I (135–104 BCE) and again during the reign of Alexandra (76–67 BCE). They probably originated in early Hasmonean times, no later than the time of Jonathan. The name *Pharisee* is probably derived from a Hebrew verb meaning "to separate," and it may have been given to them by their Sadducaic opponents, who accused them of separating from the authentic Mosaic tradition. In most of our literature, scribes are associated with Pharisees, and it is likely that they should be thought of as the more or less professional scholars, most of whom were part of the Pharisaic sect.

The central focus of Pharisaic thought was the twofold law, the written and the oral. Ellis Rivkin, an American Jewish scholar, has recently claimed that their concern with an oral tradition should be seen as a revolutionary act.[12] Indeed, their oral laws included both alterations of and additions to those found in the five books of Moses. Clearly they were going against a strong current in insisting that there are two bodies of law, not just one.

The oral law of the Pharisees covered ethical as well as ritualistic matters. Indeed, they recognized no distinctions between ethics and cult. Their concern with the ritual of the Temple, however, could bring them into conflict with the priesthood, which, as we have seen, was more closely associated with the Sadducees. The relationships are complex, but there is no doubt that Pharisees unhesitatingly provided prescriptions for priests and expected them to be followed. Some passages in the Mishnah indicate that priests were compelled to obey these prescriptions, whether they agreed with them or not. These passages may not accurately reflect the situation prior to 70, but there may well have been times (for example, during the reign of Alexandra) when the Pharisaic oral law governed even priestly activities.

Aside from their commitment to the twofold law, we have very little

[12] See Ellis Rivkin, *A Hidden Revolution* (Nashville, Tenn.: Abingdon, 1978).

information about the beliefs of the Pharisees. Josephus and the NT agree that they believed in the future resurrection, at least of the righteous. Josephus says that they believed in angels and in some cooperative arrangement between free will and fate. At this point, Josephus appears to be intent on explaining Pharisaic doctrines in terms the Romans, especially Stoics, would understand, but his explanation is far from clear.

The Pharisaic belief in resurrection is understood to be one of the major distinctions between them and the Sadducees. Indeed, it ought to be seen as a revolutionary departure from tradition. The idea of life after death is foreign to almost all of the OT books, some of which explicitly deny the possibility. Only in Daniel is there a clear expectation of it. In Dan 12:2–3, a resurrection of many is expected at the end of things. Some people are to be raised to everlasting reward and some to everlasting punishment. It seems likely that the concept of life after death was introduced to Jews in the course of their contact with Hellenistic culture. In any event, its adoption by Pharisees and others is a major alteration in Jewish thought. Similar ideas are to be found among Essenes and in apocalyptic thought, both of which will be treated later in this chapter. Sadducees resisted the idea on

The remains of the Qumran community. (Photo by courtesy of the Israel Department of Antiquities and Museums.)

the ground that the Torah (that is, the five books of Moses) knew nothing of any life after death.

It has been maintained that the Pharisaic party was, from a socioeconomic point of view, the party of shopkeepers and business people, whereas the Sadducees were associated with the landed aristocracy.[13] But the Pharisees also clearly had the support of the peasantry, which represented the majority of Jews in Palestine.

Essenes

Josephus treats the Essenes as the third Jewish school of philosophy. Indeed, he treats them more extensively than he does either Sadducees or Pharisees. Philo also deals with them, and the Roman writer Pliny describes one of their settlements near the Dead Sea. The location that he describes is probably the site we now know as Qumran, where archeologists have unearthed a complex of buildings that included rooms that were probably used for cooking, bathing, and dining. The Dead Sea Scrolls, which most scholars identify with the Essenes and the Qumran community, were discovered in nearby caves, where they had long been hidden. The scrolls include texts of OT books as well as documents that reflect the beliefs and practices of the community that produced them.

Philo and Josephus are in basic agreement in their description of the Essenes, whose most distinctive feature was their monastic life. Our sources say that Essenes were found in all the villages and towns, presumably throughout Palestine. But they also described the organized communities in which the members lived. Josephus says that they lived according to a fixed daily schedule of prayer, work, and common meals. The Essenes held no private property but pooled their resources and labor. Although Josephus notes that one group of Essenes engaged in marriage, both he and Philo point out that the avoidance of marriage was a distinctive Essenic characteristic. Those who did not marry adopted and trained other people's children. New members of the community were initiated after a three-year probationary period. Despite their piety, Essenes were barred from the Jerusalem Temple because, says Josephus, they performed their sacrifices by themselves, "employing a different ritual of purification."[14] In another place Josephus says that they practiced a daily rite of purification by bathing in cold water. Among their important beliefs, according to Josephus, were the immortality of the soul and the concept of the body as the soul's prison.

If the Dead Sea Scrolls are Essene documents, we are able to add to the descriptions of Josephus and Philo. Probably the most important aspect of

[13] See Louis Finkelstein, *The Pharisees: The Sociological Background of their Faith,* 3rd ed. (Philadelphia: Jewish Publication Society, 1962).
[14] Josephus, *Antiquities* XVIII, 19.

their thought, represented in the scrolls but not in Philo or Josephus, was their belief that the end of all time was at hand. Some of their practices and beliefs have affinities with early Christianity. The community is described as having had a common meal that featured the use of bread and wine, but we are not certain what, if anything, the elements signified. The scrolls also speak with reverence about a *teacher of righteousness,* an apparently historical figure whose identity cannot be determined. According to the scrolls, he was persecuted and put to death by a *wicked priest.*

The origin of this sect probably goes back to Hasmonean times, and many scholars see a connection between the Essenes and the Hasidic supporters of Mattathias.[15] In the rebellion against Rome in 66–74, some Essenes were martyred in defense of their beliefs, and at least one was a leader of Jewish military forces. Archeological evidence indicates that the Romans attacked the Qumran community during this war. As a result, the community was disbanded, and the scrolls were hidden in caves. It is reasonable to expect that further light will be thrown on the Essenes by materials yet to be published and perhaps by newly discovered texts; however, even now we are able to understand them as diverging in significant ways from both Pharisees and Sadducees.

Zealots

In using a terminology that was meaningful to his Roman readers, Josephus spoke of Sadducees, Pharisees, and Essenes as the three schools of Jewish philosophy. In distinction from these, he presents a "fourth philosophy" as an inauthentic version of Judaism. He says that it was founded by one Judas, a Galilean revolutionary, in or about the year 6 CE. The same revolutionary sentiments are to be found among Zealots and Sicarii, groups that are probably related to the one founded by Judas. In modern scholarship the term *Zealot* is generally used to designate all Jewish revolutionary groups in the first century.

Josephus' description of the fourth philosophy is brief enough to be quoted:

> This school agrees in all other respects with the opinions of the Pharisees, except that they have a passion for liberty that is almost unconquerable, since they are convinced that God alone is their leader and master. They think little of submitting to death in unusual forms and permitting vengeance to fall on kinsmen and friends if only they may avoid calling any man master. Inasmuch as most people have seen the steadfastness of their resolution amid such circumstances, I may forgo any further account. For I have no fear that anything reported of them will be considered incredible. The danger is, rather, that

---

[15] See 1 Macc 2:42 and 7:13.

report may minimize the indifference with which they accept the grinding misery of pain.[16]

Josephus was convinced that this attitude led to the unfortunate and disastrous rebellion against Rome in 66–74.

In addition to these four groups, some early Christian writers were aware of Galileans, Baptists, Genistae, Meristae, Hellenists, and Nasaraioi.[17] Philo gives a detailed description of an Essenelike group in Egypt known as *Therapeutae*.[18] We know almost nothing about these groups, but their existence reinforces the impression of diversity in first-century Judaism.

The fact of diversity should not be exaggerated, for there were many basic points on which the various groups agreed, as we will see in the following sections of this chapter. This agreement included basic theological concepts and extended to certain cultic and ethical practices. But neither must we ignore the diversity that is to be seen in the varying emphases and practices of these Jewish groups. It is a diversity that allowed for disagreement on the content of basic scriptures, to say nothing of their interpretation. It is a diversity in life-styles, political viewpoints, and belief systems.

The Situation after 70 CE

The failure of the rebellion against Rome marks a dramatic change in the nature of Judaism. We generally use the date 70 CE to designate the dividing line between two forms of Judaism, one with a high degree of diversity prior to 70 and one with a high degree of unity afterward. The Pharisaic sect was the only major group to survive the war, and the views of their leaders became normative for Jews after 70. It is no longer necessary to speak of Jewish parties in the post-70 period because, for all practical purposes, Pharisaism was equivalent to Judaism. Even today, all forms of Judaism are considered to be derived from the Pharisees.

Just before the city of Jerusalem fell in 70, Johanan ben Zakkai, a Pharisaic leader, obtained permission from the Roman general Titus to go to Jamnia and there to set up an academy for the study of the written and oral law. (See Figure 10, p. 57.) Many renowned scholars joined Johanan over the next several years, and Jamnia became the new Jerusalem. Under his leadership the academy adopted a common calendar for religious observances and dealt with questions relating to the cessation of worship in the destroyed Temple. In time some Temple practices were incorporated into

---

[16] Josephus, *Antiquities* XVIII, 23–24, trans. L. H. Feldman, Loeb Classical Library (Cambridge, Mass.: Harvard U.P., 1965), Vol. IX.
[17] See Marcel Simon, *Jewish Sects at the Time of Jesus*, trans. James H. Farley (Philadelphia: Fortress Press, 1967).
[18] See Philo, *On the Contemplative Life*.

the synagogue services. Under the leadership of Johanan's successor, Gamaliel II, the Academy at Jamnia became the recognized authority in cultic and ethical matters. In the eighties a prayer against heretics (probably including Christians) was permitted for use in the synagogues. In about 90 the question of a canon of sacred scripture, which included Torah, prophets, and writings, was discussed and for the most part standardized. It was probably Gamaliel's successor, Rabbi Akiba (who had supported Bar Kokhba in the rebellion of 132–135) who began to compile a written codification of the oral law. After 135, the Academy was moved to Galilee, where the work of codification continued. In about 200, Rabbi Judah ha-Nasi completed this process and published his Mishnah, which achieved a status tantamount to canonical authority among Jews in Palestine and Babylonia.

It was not only because Johanan ben Zakkai went to Jamnia that Pharisaism survived; there were elements in the movement itself that assured its continuation. Sadducees were too closely identified with the Temple and the sacrificial cult to survive its loss, so the destruction of the Temple eliminated their power base. The Essene community at Qumran had been largely destroyed and the group disbanded, and the Zealots had thrown all their force behind a losing war. Because Pharisees had identified with synagogues rather than exclusively with the Temple, the fall of the Temple, although a grievous calamity, was not the end of their movement. The Pharisaic development of oral tradition demonstrates their adaptability to changing situations. They do not bend to every wind, but they can interpret the word of God to be relevant in changing circumstances. Because Sadducees had committed themselves to the written word alone, they were not prepared to see its relevance to contemporary situations. After the war, the name *Pharisee* no longer appeared in Jewish literature. It did not need to because it no longer was a distinctive party. It was Judaism.

GOD AND THE COVENANT

We come now to examine a concept that is basic to Judaism, the covenant with God. It also is fundamental, although it is modified, in Christianity.

Probably the most profound and unifying idea in early Hebrew religion is the belief that God made a covenant with his chosen people, Israel. In the earliest known formulations of this concept, the God is called Yahweh, and it is implied that he is conceived as one out of many Gods. Well before Hellenistic times, however, most Jews had come to the conviction that the God of the covenant, Yahweh, was the only God. He was conceived to be the creator of the universe, the ruler of heaven and earth, and the arbiter of human destiny. This form of theological conviction is called monotheism, the belief in the existence and sovereignty of one and only one God.

The contrast between Jewish monotheism and Hellenistic and Roman polytheism is clear, and it was often noted at the time. In fact, the contrast frequently became a cause of misunderstanding and a basis for suspicion and attack. In his book *Against Apion,* Josephus probably represents a typically Jewish appraisal of Hellenistic and Roman religious viewpoints:

> They [Greek poets and legislators] represent them [the Gods] to be as numerous as they choose, born of one another and engendered in all manner of ways. They assign them different localities and habits, like animal species, some living under ground, others in the sea, the oldest of all being chained in Tartarus. Those to whom they have allotted heaven have set over them one who is nominally Father, but in reality a tyrant and despot; with the result that his wife and brother and the daughter, whom he begot from his own head, conspire against him, to arrest and imprison him, just as he himself had treated his own father.[19]

On the other side, the Roman writer Livy comments not only on Jewish monotheism, but also on the Jews' refusal to erect an image of their God:

> They do not state to which deity pertains the temple in Jerusalem, nor is any image found there, since they do not think the God partakes of any figure.[20]

An illustration of the profundity of Jewish monotheism can be seen in the use of the names for deity. The Hebrew name *Yahweh* is used in most of the earlier parts of the OT to designate the national deity, the God of the covenant. In Exodus 3 it is said to be the personal name of the God who revealed himself to Moses. But the name almost disappeared from the later literature and was generally replaced by the generic word *Elohim,* a word formerly used to designate any divine being. Long before the time of Jesus the word *Yahweh* had come to be regarded as a name that was too sacred to be pronounced. The commandment in Exod 20:7, "You shall not take the name of the Lord [*Yahweh*] your God [*Elohim*] in vain," was understood to mean that the name *Yahweh* could not be spoken. Only the high priest was allowed to speak the name, and he only once a year and in a voice too low to be heard.

In its monotheism Judaism insists on exclusive loyalty to one God, who is sovereign and who allows no images of himself. But Judaism, perhaps on a popular level and among Pharisees, also found a place for angels. Angels had been present in the earliest strands of OT literature, where they were spoken of as divine messengers.[21] With a few exceptions, these angels had no names. But in the Apocryphal books, the appearance of named angels is a commonplace, and with the names come personal functions: Gabriel is

[19] Josephus, *Against Apion* II, 240–241, trans. H. St. J. Thackeray, Loeb Classical Library (Cambridge, Mass.: Harvard U.P., 1926), Vol. I.
[20] Quoted from Menahem Stern, *Greek and Latin Authors on Jews and Judaism* (Jerusalem: Israel Academy of Sciences and Humanities, 1974), p. 330.
[21] The Hebrew word *malak* can be translated either as "angel" or "messenger."

the angel of revelation; Michael and Raphael are the champions of the Jews, etc. George Foot Moore, an American scholar of OT and Judaism, described this popular belief:

> God's will in the world was executed by a multitude of such deputies. Not only is his revelation communicated through them, not only are they his instruments in providence and history, but the realm of nature is administered by them. The movements of the heavenly bodies are regulated by an angel who is appointed over all the luminaries of heaven. There are regents of the seasons, of months, and of days, who ensure the regularity of the calendar; the sea is controlled by a mighty prince; rain and dew, frost and snow and hail, thunder and lightning, have their own presiding spirits. There are angel warders of hell and tormentors of the damned [e.g., Satan]; champions of nations and guardians of individuals, recording angels—in short, angels for everything.[22]

One may even say that the angels have wills, sometimes wills that conflict: the angel of the Jews may contend with those of other nations. Angels are wiser than humans, and they are immortal. Although we must regard this angelology as a modification of pure monotheism, it does not function as a polytheistic structure. No literature suggests that any angel is equal to God, and, although some angels operate by their own wills, God's will is never thwarted. At most, the activity of the angels is a reflection of activity on earth and a means of attributing a metaphysical dimension to history. It does not appear to detract from the worship of the one God.

Jewish thinking about God is accompanied by the idea of covenant. The basic covenant is associated with Moses and consists very simply of Yahweh's adoption of a people. The earliest written formulation of it is in Exod 20:2–3: "I am the Lord [Yahweh] your God [Elohim], who brought you out of the land of Egypt, out of the house of bondage. You shall have no other Gods [Elohim] before me." In context, these verses form a preface to the ten commandments and the first commandment of the ten. But they also express the fundamental force of the religion associated with Moses, for the covenant is the establishment of a relationship between a God and a people.

In its historical context, the covenant was not unusual, for it was only to be expected that a God would have a people. This arrangement was typical among ancient Near Eastern peoples: the God Assur had the Assyrians; Marduk had the Babylonians; Baal had the Canaanites. Because none of these cultures was monotheistic, religious relations among them were relatively tolerant. Thus, Hebrews could look on the Gods of other nations as competitors with Yahweh, perhaps inferior to him, but Gods nonetheless. But when monotheism developed, the religious relationships became totally

[22] George Foot Moore, *Judaism in the First Centuries of the Christian Era* (Cambridge, Mass.: Harvard U.P., 1927–1930), Vol. I, p. 403f.

different. Jewish monotheism means that Yahweh is the sole and universal deity and that the claims of all other nations are false claims. The Gods of other nations can no longer be looked on as competing Gods: at best their names are variants for the one God; at worst they are idols, or pseudo-Gods.

Even after monotheism became an unquestioned assumption among the Jews, the covenant was looked on as the heart of their relationship to God. It is the combination of the convenantal understanding with the affirmation of monotheism that creates the fundamental Jewish position: there is only one God, and we are his people. The practical issue that comes from this understanding is Jewish exclusivism, which determines some of the basic patterns of Jewish life and affects the conception of other nations. Exclusivism was potentially an aspect of Hebrew convenantal faith all along, but the earliest strict formulation of it came with Ezra in the fifth century BCE. At that time there was a thoroughgoing effort to eliminate all alien influences from Hebrew life. Ezra published a list of the men of Judea who had married foreigners, and he compelled them to divorce those women and send them and their children back home. The observance of the Sabbath, although it antedated Ezra, was emphasized as a visible sign of the distinction between those who are God's people and those who are not. The physical mark of circumcision also was intended to demonstrate this difference. Similarly, day-to-day activities associated with the preparation and eating of meals were governed by dietary regulations. These matters were taken very seriously in Jesus' day, and we must understand them as parts of the general effort to define the distinction between those people who were part of the covenant—Jews—and those who were not—Gentiles. Such observances gave visibility to the distinction.

By the time of Jesus, some Jews, notably Pharisees, had become willing and perhaps anxious to incorporate foreign-born people into the Jewish community. There was a standard form employed for this purpose. A Gentile who wished to become a part of the covenant people would be baptized and circumcised and then would offer a sacrifice in the Temple. Moreover, Gentiles were usually welcome to attend services in the synagogues; those who were particularly interested formed a special group called God-fearers. Nevertheless, there were certain areas in synagogues and in the Temple that were off-limits for Gentiles. And, when all is said and done, the basic exclusivism in Judaism shines through. For when a proselyte had gone through the process of baptism, circumcision, and sacrifice, he was no longer a Gentile; he had become a Jew. There was no exception to the rule that human society is formed of two groups of people—Jews and Gentiles.

The covenant also involved land. Early Hebrews understood that Yahweh, in establishing a relationship with his chosen people, also agreed to give them the land of Israel and to protect it. From time to time, and in certain Jewish groups, this thinking about God and land was interpreted in political terms. That interpretation can be seen most clearly in the so-called fourth philosophy. Those revolutionary Jews, who appeared just as Judea was coming under firm Roman control, regarded the political situation of their day as an intolerable one. They reasoned that, because the one and only God made a covenant with his people and awarded them the land of Israel, the occupation of that land by Gentiles must be resisted. Of course, not all Jews shared this view. Some were willing to wait for God to act on behalf of his people; some were able to withdraw from an active concern with politics; and some looked on the Roman occupation of Judea as punishment for corporate sin. But the Zealots, together with the other Jewish revolutionaries, felt that God required them, as their religious duty, to do all within their power to drive the oppressors out and to restore the land as the sacred land of the chosen people. Thus, for them rebellion against Rome was a sacred duty.

THE TORAH

The covenant means that God has established a special relationship with his people. He guarantees to them his protection, and he gives them a land. He also expects his people to fulfill certain obligations, some of a cultic and some of an ethical character. The word *Torah* represents the sum total of those divinely given obligations. Most readers understand that the Hebrew word *Torah* means "law," which they proceed to interpret legalistically. In fact, however, law is only one facet of the meaning of Torah and not the chief one. The basic meaning of the word is *teaching* or *direction*. It can stand for any teaching, but, when applied to God and his teaching, it effectively signifies divine revelation. Thus, Torah is the revealed teaching of God.

When we ask where this teaching may be found, we come upon one of the fundamental points of dispute in first-century Judaism. Jews generally agreed that the teaching was originally given to Moses and that it was recorded in the five books of Moses. So these books are usually called simply Torah. But Sadducees limited the concept to these written words, while the Pharisees understood Torah to include all that God had revealed to his people throughout their history. Josephus makes the distinctive interpretations of these groups clear:

> For the present I wish merely to explain that the Pharisees had passed on to the people certain laws handed down by former generations and not recorded in the Laws of Moses, for which reasons they are rejected by the Sadducaean group, who hold that only those laws should be considered valid which were

written down (in Scripture), and that those which had been handed down by former generations should not be observed.[23]

This fundamental difference between Pharisees and Sadducees surely led to observable differences in the conduct of their lives. For the Pharisees not only expressed an openness to an ongoing revelation, they also accepted a responsibility to develop oral Torah. Their concept of the distinction between written and oral Torah involved their own claims to identify the authoritative teachers who, in each generation, would determine what laws to preserve, what to modify, and what to add. In some cases the laws that Pharisaic teachers proclaimed were interpretations of written law, but in other cases they were quite new and involved whole categories that are not to be found in the five books of Moses. By contrast the Sadducees insisted that the requirements of God's covenant are to be limited to the written words in the five books of Moses. They agreed that the words required interpretation, but they did not agree to the addition of new requirements. After the year 70, to be sure, the problem became moot, because the Pharisees won the day. After the loss of that war against Rome and after the destruction of the Jerusalem Temple, the power of the Sadducees evaporated and Judaism became almost totally committed to the twofold law. It is natural, therefore, that, in our discussion of Torah, we emphasize Pharisaic and later rabbinic interpretations.

Although they were in fact innovators, Pharisees probably regarded their task as one of preserving the intent of the written Torah by updating it. They felt that the written revelation was stated in such a way that it required more specific explanation. They were aware that changing circumstances may bring about a tendency to neglect words that are cast in an ancient context. If, for example, one reads that he is not to "muzzle an ox when it treads out the grain,"[24] he may assume that the words are inapplicable if he owns no ox. But Pharisees felt that the words had eternal significance and must not be limited to simplistically literal meanings. Their oral tradition made it clear that the words were valid for persons who employed human workers as well as for those who worked animals. In this respect they could claim that they were not making new laws but were simply drawing out the relevant contemporary applications of the eternally valid written teaching.

But Pharisees did not draw a distinction between the authority of the written Torah and that of the oral. They did not regard the oral tradition as human interpretation of divine words. To them, the entire Torah, written and oral, is God's revelation of his will. A Jewish commentary on Exodus speaks of the whole tradition as sacred and affirms that it was all revealed to Moses on Sinai: "When God revealed Himself at Sinai to give the Torah

---

[23] Josephus, *Antiquities* XIII, 297, trans. Ellis Rivkin, op. cit., p. 36.
[24] Deut 25:4.

to Israel, He communicated it to Moses in order: Bible, Mishnah, Talmud, and *Haggadah.*"[25] Or there is this startling statement: "Even the question a pupil asks his teacher God told Moses at that time."[26]

In their distinction from Sadducees, Pharisees must be regarded as the more progressive group, for they attempted to make Torah applicable to their own and succeeding generations by interpreting and updating written laws and by adding entirely new regulations. On occasion they would even ignore the letter of a law that they felt went against the more basic revelation of God. The law in Exod 21:24–25 that calls for an eye to be given for an eye taken was interpreted as requiring financial compensation rather than physical retaliation. Jacob Lauterbach, a Talmudic scholar, says that the Pharisees "could not believe that these laws were ever meant to be taken literally."[27]

For the Pharisees, therefore, the Torah was a divine revelation continually being revealed. Their effort was to allow Torah to be what it should be—a perennial guide to daily life. Travers Herford, an English Rabbinic scholar, sees the impact of the Pharisaic view as a breaking of "the fetters which were cramping the religious life of the people, and [setting] its spirit free to receive fresh inspiration from God."[28] Rivkin[29] stresses the idea that Pharisees were attempting to provide for the individual an internalized means of salvation. For them, salvation did not depend on a sacrificial cult, in which the emphasis is on a system and on external action; rather, it depended on the individual's wholehearted adherence to the word of God, as revealed in the twofold Torah.

Whenever the attempt is made to apply general rules to specific situations, there is a tendency for the regulations to become extremely specific, even meticulous. Pharisees were intent on drawing out specific meanings of general rules, and they did not escape this tendency. The development of laws for the Sabbath may illustrate this. The written Torah says that the Sabbath must be kept holy and that one must avoid work on that day.[30] In the application of this principle it became necessary to define the precise limits of the Sabbath (from sundown on Friday to sundown on Saturday) and to provide a signal for its beginning and end (the blowing of a ram's horn). Moreover, because work may be defined in diverse ways, it was necessary to make its meaning more precise. If one should consider work to be

[25] *Exodus Rabbah* 47:1, in *The Midrash,* trans. S. M. Lehrman (London: Soncino Press, 1951), Vol. III, italics in original. *Exodus Rabbah* is a Jewish commentary, or Midrash, on the book of Exodus, probably originating in the ninth century. *Haggadah* refers to stories and parables in the Talmud that did not carry legal force but were used for homiletical purposes.
[26] Ibid.
[27] Jacob Lauterbach, *Rabbinic Essays* (Cincinnati: KTAV Publishing House, 1951), p. 120.
[28] R. Travers Herford, *The Pharisees* (New York: Macmillan, 1924), pp. 65f.
[29] See Rivkin, op. cit., pp. 286–311.
[30] Exod 20:8–11 and Deut 5:12–15.

anything that involves motion, only complete rigidity would be permitted on the Sabbath. The Pharisees recognized that certain human functions could not reasonably be restricted, and they attempted to make provision for them. One could, therefore, eat food that had been prepared earlier and could move about within the limits of the Sabbath boundary.[31] The Mishnah lists thirty-nine kinds of activity prohibited on the Sabbath, and one rabbi enumerated 1,521 varieties, listing thirty-nine examples for each of the Mishnaic thirty-nine. Pharisees also recognized that certain activities may be necessary in the case of imminent danger. In the Jewish war against Antiochus IV, for example, Mattathias and his supporters decided that they would defend themselves if attacked on the Sabbath. In general, anything necessary for saving a life was permitted on the Sabbath, and many such activities are listed in the literature. Although the Pharisaic procedures produced a large number of minute regulations, it must be remembered that the purpose was to allow for essential functions while maintaining the obligation to keep the Sabbath holy. Moore says, "The general principle is: The Sabbath was committed to you, not you to the Sabbath."[32]

The Pharisees were aware that people may tend to adhere to regulations in only formal ways and may thus avoid wholehearted obedience. To counter this tendency, they emphasized the absolute need for a correspondence between one's intentions and actions. The rabbinic literature makes it abundantly clear that, by itself, the most careful observance of commandments does not constitute actual obedience. In the reciting of the *Shema,* which is a required duty, it is not just the recitation that is important but the recitation with the intention to fulfill duty.[33] Even prohibited acts may escape condemnation if the perpetrator did not intend to disobey. Work that is prohibited on the Sabbath may be permitted if the worker did not intend to do the work on the Sabbath. In the trial of murder cases, the intention is of paramount importance, and accidental killing does not render a person guilty. Martin Buber, a well-known contemporary Jewish scholar, calls attention to the fact that the Pharisees were aware of the possibility of fulfilling Torah without the intention of surrendering oneself to God. Those who acted in this way were called tinged ones—"that is, those whose inwardness is a pretense."[34] Buber says further: "The project of sin and the reflecting upon it and not its execution is the real guilt."[35] He quotes a

[31] The law on the Sabbath boundary is complex, but it is usually understood to allow one to travel within an area extending about one kilometer beyond the town limit.
[32] Moore, op. cit., Vol. II, p. 31; see also Mark 2:27 and *Mekilta on Exodus,* 31:13. The *Mekilta* is a Jewish commentary on Exodus. The core of it may go back to the second century CE, and it was probably completed by the end of the fourth century.
[33] The Shema is an affirmation consisting of Deut 6:4–9 and 11:13–21 and Num 15:37–41. It begins with the words, "Hear [*Shema*], O Israel, the Lord our God, the Lord is One."
[34] Martin Buber, *Two Types of Faith,* trans. Norman P. Goldhawk (New York: Harper, 1961), p. 58.
[35] Ibid., p. 64.

Talmudic passage to this effect: "The sin for God's sake is greater than the fulfilling of a commandment not for God's sake."[36] Rivkin calls attention to the Pharisaic view about life after death, which involves a divine judgment of each individual's heart: "If one truly believed that God the Father rewarded and punished in the world to come, then one had no alternative but to peer deeply into the inner recesses of one's mind and heart, lest one be blind to what God the Father sees all too clearly. In such a system, internalization cannot be bypassed."[37]

Because, for Pharisees, the twofold Torah is the measure of the individual, there may be a tendency for some people to develop certain undesirable attitudes. The person who performs well may be boastful, whereas the one who does not may have a feeling of failure. The tendency to boast may be reinforced by a concept of merit. Such a concept is found in some Jewish writings and may lead to the feeling that one obtains eternal life by obeying certain commands. Although an obedient act gives merit to the actor, the Jew is frequently warned against obeying solely for the purpose of being rewarded. Still greater emphasis lies on the concept of corporate merit. Most passages that deal with merit do not refer to an individual's building up merit for himself but to his drawing on the merit of worthy persons of the past, present, or future. Furthermore, the Pharisees and later rabbis did not feel that a person who has completely obeyed Torah has anything of which to boast. There is a more desirable kind of person—a saint—who really rises above the Torah. This is the teaching behind the concept known as the "fence around the Torah." The Jew is advised not only to obey the commands but also to do more than Torah requires. "Sanctify thyself even in that which is permitted thee."[38] Sanctification includes not only acts, but also intentions and thoughts. The ideal saint does not disobey Torah, but this is quite incidental to his character, because he does so much more. No oral or written regulations could eliminate the boasting of an individual such as the Pharisee cited in Luke 18:9–14, but our literature shows that Pharisaism did not intentionally promote this kind of attitude.

The feeling of failure may be partially overcome by two concepts. The first is the principle that one is not required to perform every duty in the Torah. The great quantity of commands is looked on as beneficial rather than burdensome—the more commands, the more the opportunity to obey. The noted rabbinic scholar Solomon Schechter says that every Jew has many chances to obey at least one command.[39] He quotes rabbinic statements that say that a person who has accomplished one duty is as valuable as the one

---

[36] Ibid., p. 65. The Talmudic passage is *Nazir* 23.

[37] Rivkin, op. cit., p. 299.

[38] *Midrash Sifre* 95a, a Jewish commentary on Numbers and Deuteronomy, possibly dating from the second century CE.

[39] Solomon Schechter, *Aspects of Rabbinic Theology* (New York: Schocken, 1961), p. 164.

who has done all things, and that the only person who will not escape punishment is one who has not fulfilled a single duty.[40] Other statements in the
rabbinic literature say that a person is judged by the majority of his deeds.
But even these statements do not imply that God takes a mechanical approach by adding up the number of obedient and disobedient deeds. In any
case, a person who has not done all the required duties should not be regarded as an utter failure.

The second aid in avoiding the attitude of failure is the concept of repentance and forgiveness. According to Schechter, the general rabbinic rule
of repentance is "that there is nothing which can stand in the way of the
penitent, be the sin ever so great."[41] "Thus neither the quantity of sins, nor
the quality of sins, need make man hesitate to follow the Divine call to
repentance. He has only to approach, so to speak, the 'door' with the determination of repentance, and it will be widely opened for his admittance."[42]
Even here the intention is of fundamental importance. The Mishnah says:
"If a man said, 'I will sin and repent, I will sin and repent;' he will be given
no chance to repent. [If he said] 'I will sin and the Day of Atonement will
effect atonement,' then the Day of Atonement effects no atonement."[43] Just
as the intention to love God must be present for an obedient act to fulfill
Torah, just so must it be present for repentance to bring about forgiveness.

In summary, the Pharisaic understanding of Torah presents an approach
to the religious life that is definite but not mechanical. It produces a religious
system in which it is possible for a person to know precisely what God
expects and in which it is possible to do what is expected and even more
than is required. One must make every effort to do what God requires and
to do it out of love for God, not for reward, but because it is God's will. If
an individual fails to do it, she or he may repent and be forgiven, but all
must be done with sincerity. It should be kept in mind that Pharisees, unlike Sadducees, believed in life after death for the individual. This belief
underlined the importance of their concern with wholehearted obedience.
Pharisees believed that they could give definite answers to people who were
vitally concerned about their ultimate destinies.

JEWISH INSTITUTIONS

The Temple

The Temple and its rituals have roots deep in Israel's past. The original
Temple was built in the tenth century BCE by Israel's King Solomon. It was

[40] Ibid., pp. 164ff.
[41] Ibid., p. 333.
[42] Ibid., p. 326.
[43] Mishnah, *Yoma* 8:9.

The Western Wall in Jerusalem contains a portion of the second Temple. Courtesy *Israel Government Tourist Office, Houston, Texas.*)

probably regarded from the beginning as a royal shrine and so took precedence over other religious centers in Israel. In the middle of the seventh century BCE, there was a strong movement toward eliminating all other shrines to Yahweh. This was accomplished by King Josiah in 621 BCE, after a book was discovered that was thought to have been written by Moses. That book was probably a large part of what we now call Deuteronomy, which advocates the centralization of the sacrificial cult. Josiah made every effort to abolish the so-called high places, some of which had at one time been associated with Canaanite deities, and he made it illegal to perform sacrifices to Yahweh anywhere but in the Jerusalem Temple. But Solomon's Temple had been destroyed by the Babylonians in 587 BCE and many Jews exiled to Babylonia, where they formed a subculture. Even during their exile, so far as we know, they did not modify the concept that sacrifice was only permitted in the Temple in Jerusalem. Thus, they probably did not perform sacrifices in Babylonia. After the return of some Jews from Babylonia, the second Temple was built in Jerusalem, in about 515 BCE, and sacrifices were resumed. We previously observed the significance of the Temple in the war against the Seleucids and in the renovating work of Herod the Great. The Temple was finally destroyed by the Romans in 70 CE and has not been rebuilt to date. The probable site is now occupied by the Moslem shrine known as the Dome of the Rock and related buildings. A portion of the western wall, which formed the platform of the second Temple, remains; it is a place of special significance for modern Jews, not only those in Israel but from all over the world.

The primary function of the Temple was to serve as the place where the sacrificial rituals were performed. The sacrifices, of animals or grains, are required by the five books of Moses and are carefully described. Sacrifice involves the concept that the worshiper has certain obligations that can be fulfilled by presenting some possession to the divine. In Hebrew literature there are basically three forms of sacrifice. In the *thanksgiving* sacrifice, something is brought to the Temple and presented to God to express gratitude. For example, thanks for a good harvest of grain were expressed by presenting a portion of grain to God. The purpose of the *communion* sacrifice is to have fellowship with God in the form of a shared meal. In this sacrifice an animal is killed, and the blood and fat are drained and offered to God. The priests and communicants then eat the meat. The *atonement* sacrifice is performed on the Day of Atonement (*Yom Kippur*) for the forgiveness of sins. The sacrifices were presided over by priests, who were required to be in a condition of purity—that is, they could have no physical defects and could not have had recent contact with a dead person or any other source of uncleanness. Contamination from such contact could, however, be removed by certain acts of ritual purification.

The Temple was also the scene of certain special observances, most of which commemorated events in Israel's past. Passover was a reminder of that complex of events surrounding the deliverance of the Hebrew slaves from their bondage in Egypt. *Shavuot* (or Pentecost) was originally a spring harvest festival but probably also commemorated the time when Yahweh made the covenant with Moses and the Hebrew people at Mount Sinai.

Succot (or the Feast of Tabernacles), originally a fall harvest festival, also became a reminder of the nomadic period of Hebrew history, that period between the exodus from Egypt and the conquest of Canaan. *Hanukkah* (or the Festival of Lights) is a celebration that has a more recent origin, but it was observed in the Roman period and perhaps earlier. At *Hannukkah* the rededication of the Temple by Judas Maccabeus, after its capture by the Seleucids, is commemorated. These festivals drew large crowds of Jews into Jerusalem from all parts of the world. Josephus certainly exaggerated when he estimated that some three million people were in Jerusalem on Passover of 66 CE, but he probably would not have made the statement unless great crowds had swarmed into the city.[44] The international character of such a festival as Pentecost is illustrated in Acts 2:5.

The priesthood of the Temple fell into three classes: the high priesthood, the priesthood, and the Levites. The high priest was not only the head of the entire body of priests, he was regarded by most as the spiritual head of the Jewish people. It was such an important office that, in the days before the Hasmonean war, one man purchased it and another murdered for it. In pre-Hasmonean times, the practice was that the high priest must be a descendant of Zadok, high priest during the reign of King Solomon. This practice, based on the prescriptions of Ezekiel,[45] is in accord with the older provisions based on the five books of Moses, but it goes beyond them. That is, in the Mosaic books, the high priest is required to be a descendant of Eleazar, the son of Moses' brother, Aaron, and Zadok is one of Eleazar's descendants.[46] As we have seen, the Hasmoneans broke with these provisions and exercised the prerogatives of the high priesthood as well as, in some cases, the monarchy. Normally, the high priesthood was held for life. The high priest was the chief mediator between God and his people; he performed the sacrifice on the Day of Atonement and presided over judicial bodies. The second class of the priesthood was simply called the priests. These were drawn from twenty-four families, all descended from Aaron. Each family served in the Temple on two separate weeks each year, and all families were called on for the festival days. In addition to their supervision of the daily sacrifices, priests were charged with administering justice, giving medical advice, and teaching, although in Hellenistic and Roman times the authority of their teaching must have been challenged by Pharisees. The third priestly order was composed of the Levites—that is, Levitical families that were not descended from Aaron and thus not included in the order of priests. They assisted the priests and were responsible for the care of the building and its furnishings. They too served in rotation at appointed times. We have already noted that there were important ties between the various ranks of priests and the Sadducees.

[44] Josephus, *War* II, 280. In *War* VI, 425, the number is 2,700,000.
[45] See Ezek 44:15–16.
[46] See Num 3:32.

Ruins of a third-century synagogue in Capernaum. Courtesy *Israel Government Tourist Office, Houston, Texas.*)

The Synagogue

The origin of the synagogue is obscure, although it is obviously a younger institution than the Temple. Because of its character and function, many scholars look to the period of the Babylonian exile as providing the conditions under which such an institution might reasonably have originated. Less than thirty-five years before the Jews were exiled to Babylonia in 587 BCE, they had come to the conviction that sacrifices to Yahweh could be offered only in the Temple in Jerusalem, and so they had regarded the Temple as central in their religious lives. Although there was no Temple during the exile and they themselves were far from Jerusalem, these Jews managed to retain the character of a community and maintained many of their traditions. This probably would not have happened without some institution, and the synagogue would have been well suited to perform the function. It would have served as a place of assembly, for reading the scriptures, and for prayer. But there is no clear literary or archeological evidence to support the proposition that the synagogue originated in the period of the Babylonian exile. In fact, the literary evidence indicates that it originated with the Pharisees and was designed to serve their purposes exclusively. We should probably think of the origin of the synagogue in connection with the rise of the Pharisees and date it in early Hasmonean times.

If we think of the synagogue as a Pharisaic institution, its functions will be clear. It was not intended to compete with the sacrificial ritual of the Temple. Pharisees recognized that the Temple was the only place for that. They, however, emphasized the twofold law, which covered not only the sacrificial ritual but many other areas of Jewish life as well. The synagogue served largely as a place of instruction in the twofold law. Here the learned would gather to pour over the scriptures, to teach those who wanted to learn, to solve problems brought to them, and to expound in public gatherings on the meaning of Torah. Indeed, we may associate the development of Pharisaic oral tradition with the synagogue, for it is precisely under the conditions made possible by this institution that such a development could take place.

The synagogues provided other services as well. Because they were not places of sacrifice, there was no restriction on their number or location. They served as gathering places for local communities of Jews who could only seldom travel to Jerusalem. Thus, they were to be found all over the eastern Mediterranean world and in Mesopotamia—wherever Jews lived. There was even a synagogue in the precincts of the Jerusalem Temple. Many religious functions that were not specifically restricted to the Temple were carried on in the synagogues. The weekly assembly on the Sabbath day was the occasion for the reading of scripture and for prayer. In some places synagogues served as educational institutions and performed secular functions of a political and judicial nature.

Other Institutions

To the major institutions of the Jerusalem Temple and the synagogue we should add two more. One is an institution for the training of the Pharisaic leadership. Its name seems to vary in the literature, but we will call it the Academy. It probably met in Jerusalem until 70 CE but was then moved to Jamnia, under the leadership of Johanan ben Zakkai. After the Bar Kokhba war (132–135 CE), it was moved to Galilee where it continued until the time of Judah ha-Nasi, when it was moved to Babylonia. We may think of the Academy as a place for advanced, even professional, education in the twofold law. Those whose teachings were studied there were called rabbis.

The second institution had judicial functions. There is a good deal of confusion about its name as well. It is commonly called Sanhedrin, although the correct name is probably *Beth Din*.[47] It is reasonable to expect that the functions of this judicial institution would be to decide cases in accordance

[47] See Ellis Rivkin, "Beth Din, Boulé, Sanhedrin: A Tragedy of Errors," *Hebrew Union College Annual*, 46 (1975), 181–199.

with Pharisaic twofold law. But the evidence is by no means clear. It is probable that its freedom to act varied with political conditions and that during Roman times it was very limited. We will note certain special problems about the rights and duties of this body when we come to look at the trial of Jesus.

A study of the Jewish institutions of the Hellenistic and Roman periods sheds light on the impact of the destruction of the Temple and on Judaism's capacity to survive the tragedy. It was the Pharisaic institutions, most notably the synagogue, that made possible the survival of Judaism beyond 70, when the Temple was destroyed, and beyond 135, when Jews were deported from Jerusalem. If the Temple had been the only religious institution and sacrifice the only religious practice, the destruction of the Temple and the cessation of the cult would almost certainly have been the death of the entire religious system. The only thing that could have saved Judaism was something like the synagogue. Such an institution might have developed after 70 as a substitute for the Temple, but fortunately it was already an accepted, well-organized, and healthy institution; it has provided for the survival, in a modified form, of Judaism up to modern times. In addition, the existence of synagogues and other Pharisaic institutions outside Palestine meant that scattered Jewish communities could continue to function with or without the sacrificial cult. Nevertheless, the destruction of the Temple must be regarded as the end of an era for Judaism. The year 70 marks the point at which the sacrificial ritual, which had been central for centuries, gave way to a religious way of life that was dominated by Pharisaic institutions and determined by the twofold law.

MESSIANIC EXPECTATION

In some Jewish circles in the Hellenistic and Roman periods, we meet with various forms of messianic expectation. These expectations are usually encountered within the context of a form of thought known as *apocalypticism*. Apocalypticism is also associated with a type of literature, to which we will later return. In order to understand the place of messianic expectation in Judaism, it is necessary to be familiar with some aspects of apocalyptic thought, especially time and history.

In Hebraic thought, as we encounter it in the OT, the arena of human affairs is understood to be the primary sphere in which Yahweh is active. In this concept Yahweh makes himself known in those events associated with the rise and fall of kings, military conquests and defeats, and politics generally. The divine can be found mainly in these events rather than in the contemplation of nature or in individual experience. Such a concept adds a dimension of reality to the earthly course of events, a dimension that is not emphasized in all cultures. In this Hebraic understanding it is assumed that

God controls history. History is not a self-perpetuating series of events set in motion by strong individuals or by social forces. It is simply the arena in which God works. Moreover, time belongs to God. It is his to give and his to withhold. Thus, it is possible to look back to a time when God initiated the process by creating the world, and it is possible to look forward to a time when God will conclude the process. Strictly speaking, in this complex of concepts, the word *eschatology* designates the termination of historical time; this form of thought is called eschatological.

For some Jews in the Hellenistic and Roman periods, however, there was a breakdown in the confidence that God's control of history can be known. The events of most of the Hellenistic and Roman periods could surely have caused some Jews to lose confidence in history as the medium in which God acts. At least they were not able to see clear signs of that activity. So, instead of searching for divine activity within history, apocalyptists tended to look at history as the effect of events that occur elsewhere, usually in heaven, and they expected that history and time would, sooner or later, terminate. Thus, in apocalyptic thought there is a tendency to look into a suprahistorical sphere to discover the cause of historical events. Earthly history is much like a puppet show, in which the visible events on stage are controlled backstage. The apocalyptist feels that a special privilege has been given him, a privilege that enables him to see into the heavenly world; he sometimes describes the process as an opening of the veil that separates reality from history or heaven from earth. So he looks into heaven and receives an apocalypse, which means "revelation." Because both forms of thought involve an expectation of the end of historical time, the distinction between the older eschatological view of history and the apocalyptic may appear subtle, but it is important. In the older view, one looks at historical events and sees *in them* the activity of God. The apocalyptist receives a direct revelation of God's activity and uses it to interpret historical events.

With this background the general apocalyptic view can be easily understood. The present situation for the apocalyptist is one in which it is not possible to see God's activity, but God is in heaven, and his control of earthly affairs will soon be made known universally. God will intervene and conclude historical time, will abolish unrighteousness, and will create a new order in which all the world will be obedient to him.

Messianic expectation becomes a part of apocalyptic thought when there is speculation about the agent God will use in accomplishing his purposes. The word *Messiah* is a derivative of a Hebrew verb that means "to anoint." It specifically refers to the act of pouring oil on the head of a king or a high priest when he is installed in office. Anointing is equivalent to royal coronation and priestly ordination, and it signifies God's choice of king and priest. In I Sam 16:1–13, for example, Samuel is told to anoint David king of Israel. A king or a high priest who had been so anointed could be called Messiah; the title is sometimes applied to Saul, David, and other kings of

Israel and Judah. It may even be applied to a foreign king who is thought to be chosen by Yahweh for a special function, such as the Persian Cyrus in Isa 45:1. The word *Christ* is the English equivalent of the Greek *Christos,* which was used to translate the Hebrew word *Mashiach,* or Messiah. Thus, the terms Christ and Messiah are technically interchangeable.

In the Hellenistic period the word *Messiah* came to be used as a title for the agent who was expected to initiate the end of historical time. Such a usage is rare in the OT, where the word is generally used only in association with specific historical personalities. One probable exception is in Daniel, a part of which is apocalyptic. Nor do the Apocryphal books speak of an individual Messiah, although they contain many ideas associated with eschatological expectation, such as the destruction of Israel's oppressors, the glorification of Jerusalem and the Temple, the coming of Elijah, and the resurrection of the righteous dead. It is in the books of the Pseudepigrapha that widespread speculation about the Messiah is found, but in this literature we are faced with a bewildering variety. There is as yet no rigid, orthodox timetable for the coming of the Messiah. The noted Hebrew scholar Joseph Klausner, in his study of messianic expectation among the Jews, delineates certain elements that seem to be basic in the documents.[48] There are three ages: (1) the birth pangs of Messiah, (2) the Messianic Age, and (3) the Age to Come. Klausner also compiles a list of what he calls the complete messianic chain, composed of the following links: "The signs of the Messiah, the coming of Elijah, the trumpet of Messiah, the ingathering of the exiles, the reception of proselytes, the war with Gog and Magog, the Day of Judgment, the resurrection of the dead, the World to Come."[49] But this complete picture is not found in any one document; it is rather a composite formed by an analysis of the varied elements in the sources.

The documents of the Pseudepigrapha present us with a very unconsolidated picture. In some books, the Messianic Age comes suddenly, in others gradually, while in still others there is no Messianic Age at all. In the Similitudes of Enoch, the Messiah is said to have existed before the creation of the world.[50] This document describes the Messianic Age as a time when righteousness will prevail and unrighteousness will disappear. The Son of man will put down kings and the mighty, and the things of civilization will evaporate. Leviathan and Behemoth, the great beasts of primeval times, will serve as food for the righteous. Finally, the Messianic Age passes over into the Age to Come. In the Assumption of Moses, written in the early decades of the first century CE, there are descriptions of something like a Messianic Age, but there is no Messiah. In 2 Baruch, probably written toward the end

---

[48] Joseph Klausner, *The Messianic Idea in Israel,* trans. W. F. Stinespring (New York: Macmillan, 1955).
[49] Ibid., p. 385.
[50] On the date of the Similitudes of Enoch, which form part of 1 Enoch, see below, p. 100.

of the first century CE, there is a timetable of events. The end will come when the number of people to be born has been fulfilled. But before Messiah comes, there are to be twelve periods of commotions, wars, death, famine, oppression, and wickedness. Next there is to be a general judgment day on which each individual's book is opened. Then the Messianic Age will come; it will not be an endless period, but one of transition, during which the Messiah conquers Israel's enemies and establishes peace. In the Messianic Age nature becomes remarkably productive. At the end of it the Messiah is taken to heaven, and the birth pangs of the Age to Come begin. This last is an eternal age in a renewed creation. 2 Esdras has a pattern similar to that of 2 Baruch up to the end of the Messianic Age.[51] This age lasts four hundred years, and at the end of it Messiah and all survivors die. Then there is a primeval silence for seven days (or seven years), a resurrection, a day of judgment that lasts seven years, and finally the Age to Come.

Amid all of this diversity, the expected functions of the Messiah are almost constant. Where a Messiah is mentioned, his functions are to close the present age, to initiate the Messianic Age, and to preside over the Messianic Age until the final judgment. Usually he has no further part to play in bringing in the Age to Come.

When we come to efforts to define the person of Messiah, we meet still further diversity. In some passages God himself performs the messianic functions. In others, although there is a Messiah, there is no description of his person and little interest in him as an individual. In those documents that do display interest, there are some five forms that can be described for Messiah.

1. In some cases, the Messiah is a human being who is raised up by God to perform this special function. He is assumed to be a Jew, but he has no special ancestry. The historical parallel for such thought among Hebrews would be found in the period of the Judges, who were chosen by Yahweh to lead various tribes into battle against their enemies.

2. In some cases, although the Messiah is human, he has a special ancestry. A crucial passage in the Dead Sea Scrolls speaks of two such Messiahs. In the so-called *Manual of Discipline*, we have a reference to the Messiahs of Aaron and Israel.[52] Throughout this document, it is clear that the former is a descendant of Aaron and therefore a priest and that he has precedence over the other Messiah, who is the secular-political ruler.[53] The origin of this conception is not known, but it may have been suggested by the com-

[51] 2 Esdras is usually dated after 70 CE.
[52] *Manual of Discipline* 9:10–11. See also Zech 4:14, which speaks of "two anointed ones"— Joshua and Zerubbabel.
[53] See Karl Georg Kuhn, "The Two Messiahs of Aaron and Israel," in *The Scrolls and the New Testament*, ed. Krister Stendahl (New York: Harper, 1957), pp. 54–64. Kuhn finds the same idea in the Testaments of the Twelve Patriarchs and in the so-called *Zadokite Fragment*, which was discovered in 1896–1897 and is now generally regarded as an Essene document.

bination of priestly and royal functions in the Hasmonean rulers. Certainly, the importance of the priesthood in the Qumran community is compatible with the greater importance given to the priestly Messiah.

3. Another human Messiah with special ancestry is one called the Son of David. The veneration of Jews for David and his descendants is reflected in this belief, which has roots in the OT.[54] Isaiah reflected the belief in the eternality of the Davidic dynasty, and Jeremiah and Ezekiel looked forward to a restoration of the Davidic line. Haggai and Zechariah, writing about 520 BCE, actually proclaimed a Davidic descendant named Zerubbabel to be Messiah. The idea of a restored Davidic dynasty seems strong during the postexilic period, and the function of a Son of David-Messiah would be to bring back to Judea the glory once associated with the house of David. In Jesus' day this would include liberating Judea from Roman occupation and establishing the nation as an independent monarchy once again. Evidence in Josephus indicates that this was a very popular form of messianic expectation and that several persons claimed this kind of Messiahship before and after Jesus.

4. In other cases the Messiah is thought of as a resurrected figure of the past—for example, Moses. Speculation about Moses is based on Deut 18:15, which predicts the coming of a prophet like Moses. This figure would frequently be called simply the prophet.[55] Although Deuteronomy may be interpreted as a prediction of the appearance of a person who is similar to Moses, most speculation was that such a person could not be like Moses without being Moses himself. So it was expected that Moses would be raised from the dead and would return. A similar expectation revolved around the person of Elijah and was based on passages in Malachi. The situation here is not quite the same as with Moses, for the narrative in 2 Kings 2 states that Elijah did not die but was taken up to be with God in heaven. Furthermore, most apocalyptic documents that mention Elijah place him as a herald who is expected to come in order to prepare the way for the Messiah.

5. Finally, we come to the phrase, "Son of man." The phrase is common in Aramaic, where it is used in place of the singular personal pronoun or to stand for a human being. The latter usage is also found in Hebrew, in the book of Ezekiel, where the prophet himself is addressed as Son of man. The use of the phrase in connection with the events of the end begins with the apocalyptic section of Daniel, which was probably written about 165 BCE. In the seventh chapter, the author narrates a vision of the events of past, present, and future. He does this in terms of beasts that rise up out of the sea: a lion, a bear, a leopard, and a beast with ten horns. The usual interpretation is that these beasts stand for the great empires of the ancient Near East, the fourth being the Hellenistic Seleucid Empire. Then the author

---

[54] See 2 Sam 7:16, 29; 23:5; and Ps 89:3–4, 29–37.
[55] See 1 Macc 14:41.

describes, in 7:13, "one like a son of man" who comes on the clouds of heaven and establishes an everlasting kingdom. The phrase probably signifies a fifth beast, one with a human appearance. In the interpretation of the vision, which follows in Dan 7:15–27, the place of the one like a son of man is taken by "the people of the saints of the Most High" (7:27)—that is, the Jewish nation. Daniel expects this nation to be the fifth empire, one which will last forever. At this point the conception is a corporate one, and there is no attempt to make it messianic. In a later vision in Dan 9:25–26, a Messiah is mentioned whose function is to rebuild Jerusalem. But here, the author says that the Messiah will be cut off; thus, this cannot be a reference to the everlasting kingdom that was said to be established by the one like a son of man. So far as Daniel is concerned, the Messiah and the one like a son of man are different figures.

The Son-of-man figure proved to be an attractive one and reappeared in the Similitudes of Enoch—that is, in chapters 37–71 of 1 Enoch. The date of these chapters is in dispute, and they may, in fact, have originated in post-Christian times. But in them the phrase from Daniel becomes the Son of man, a figure that is clearly identified with the Messiah. He existed before the creation of the world and at the end will put down the kings of the earth; he will be a staff to the righteous and a light to the Gentiles. He will annihilate all those who mislead people, and he will be worshiped by all.[56] It is this Enochic figure that forms our fifth messianic conception. Here the Son of man is understood as supernatural and pre-existent, and he is expected to come on the clouds. Because we cannot be certain about the date of the Similitudes of Enoch, we cannot conclude that this kind of messianic conception was known in pre-Christian Judaism. We will see, however, that in the Christian gospels, the phrase "Son of man," is used as a title and probably stands for a messianic figure.

Unfortunately, it is not possible to make clear identifications between these conceptions and known Jewish groups. The double Messiah idea, with precedence going to the priestly one, may be tentatively identified with the Qumran community. But Pharisees probably had no formulated dogma on the subject, and information is lacking on the other groups. The conception of Messiah as Son of David was probably the most popular one in Jesus' day, but the other conceptions are not absent, as the early Christian writings bear evidence. The hope itself was a general one, at least in Palestine, and several would-be leaders took advantage of it.

DIASPORA JUDAISM

As was noted in Chapter 2, many Jews lived outside the traditional homeland during the Hellenistic and Roman periods. The extent of their disper-

---

[56] In 1 Enoch 71:14–17, Enoch himself is identified as the Son of man.

sion is commented on in our sources, which indicate that Jews had settled in cities all over the eastern Mediterranean as well as in Babylonia. Robert Kraft, a contemporary NT scholar, points to wide discrepancies in scholarly estimates about the number and proportion of Jews in the Diaspora, but he says, "The consensus seems to be that about two thirds of the Jews lived outside of Palestine, especially in the adjacent areas in the eastern Mediterranean." [57]

We know all too little about the social conditions of Jews in the Diaspora. There is evidence that, in some places, they were allowed to form courts to decide cases involving purely religious matters. They were frequently granted local citizenship and could sometimes participate in local politics. During the rebellions in Judea, sympathetic uprisings occurred in the Diaspora, and we have already noted the insurrection among Jews in Egypt, Cyrene, and Cyprus against Trajan in 115–117 CE.

Probably the most serious problem facing diaspora Jews was that of maintaining community identity while living in predominantly gentile communities. Their efforts were affected by an imperial ban against circumcision after 135 CE. The ban, probably effective only temporarily and locally, was enacted by Hadrian after the Bar Kokhba rebellion. To the extent that it functioned, it tended to decrease proselytism and to minimize the assimilation of Gentiles into Judaism. Under these conditions, Jews would emphasize their separateness from non-Jews. In addition, the scattered communities of Jews attempted to maintain contact with their fellows in Palestine. Diaspora Jews were expected to send financial contributions for the support of the Temple, but of course that practice ended after 70.[58] The institution of the Academy in Jamnia sparked the development of similar institutions in Babylonia and Rome. Many Babylonian scholars were trained at Jamnia or later at one of the Galilean schools. The Academy in Rome was established before the war under Hadrian, and both Johanan ben Zakkai and Gamaliel II visited there. Both these diaspora academies accepted in general the interpretive principles of Jamnia, and after 200 CE Babylonia became the major center for Jewish scholarship. Moreover, the synagogue served as a unifying institution within each diaspora community. Jews who frequented their local synagogues would hear the scriptures read and interpreted and would come to know their ancient tradition as a living force.

But diaspora Jews could not completely isolate themselves from the wider community, as we know from a study of Philo's writings. Philo, an Alexandrian Jew who wrote during the first half of the first century CE, is a direct source of information about the Jewish community in Egypt. He was, in fact, an esteemed leader among the Jews there. We cannot assume that Alexandria is a typical diaspora community or that Philo is a represen-

---

[57] Robert A. Kraft, "Judaism on the World Scene," in *The Catacombs and the Colosseum*, ed. Stephen Benko and John J. O'Rourke (Valley Forge, Pa.: Judson Press, 1971), pp. 83ff.
[58] After 70 CE, this money was sent to the Roman government in payment of the Jewish tax.

tative Jew. But we know so little about other localities that Philo's writings take on a great deal of significance. At least we can say that we know something about one community because of Philo.

It is significant that Philo could assimilate so much from gentile thought and still consider himself a Jew. His Judaism is maintained in his defense of Torah, but he does not emphasize its distinctive nature. Rather he thinks of the books of Moses as a written embodiment of the universally revealed law. He uses allegory to bring together the Jewish Scriptures and his own universalism, and he attempts to establish a rational basis for each of the Jewish laws.[59] Even the dietary regulations are so interpreted: God allows people to eat the flesh of gentle animals but forbids that of birds of prey and carnivorous mammals in order to elevate the virtue of peace. The allegorical method is, for Philo, an aid in discovering the distinction between the soul and the body of law, a distinction he also accepts as a way of understanding human nature.

In his understanding of God, Philo accepts the revelation to Moses but speaks of God in terms drawn from Greek philosophy. In this understanding he develops a system of intermediaries who stand between God and the world. The chief intermediary is called Logos, who is said to be the sum of all created beings, and yet he is not different from God himself. Philo's thought at this point is an attempt to combine general Hellenistic thought with Jewish monotheism. His is an interpretation of monotheism that may have paved the way for early Christians to think of the Messiah, who was sometimes called Logos, as uniquely related to God. Whether typical or not, Philo represents an attempt to solve a problem that must have vexed many diaspora Jews (and some Palestinian Jews): retaining their Judaism and not neglecting important aspects of the thought of their neighbors. We will see that Christians encountered similar problems.

Philo represents a manner of thought that has no counterpart in the Palestinian sects that we have examined here, and he demonstrates for us something of the diversity that is in diaspora Judaism. But diaspora Judaism surely must have been a phenomenon of still wider diversity. Apocalyptic thought finds expression in some of the Sibylline Oracles, which came out of Egyptian Judaism. Philo himself knows of a group of Jews, called Therapeutae, who lived a life of contemplation and asceticism.[60] Josephus tells us about a Jewish temple in Leontopolis, Egypt, built by a priest who fled from Jerusalem in the time of Antiochus IV.[61] The temple was served by Levitical priests, and services probably were modeled on those in Jerusalem. According to Josephus, this temple was destroyed by the Romans in 73 CE.

[59] Allegory was sometimes used by Hellenistic philosophers to interpret the Greek myths in order to make them more intellectually satisfying.
[60] See Philo, On the Contemplative Life.
[61] See Josephus, War VII, 420–436; Antiquities XIII, 62–73.

Such diversity within diaspora Judaism probably continued well after 70 CE. Standardization came more gradually outside Palestine.

We will be in a better position to appreciate the problems of diaspora Jews, as well as Palestinian Jews, after we have looked at some of the ideological aspects associated with Hellenistic and Roman culture. We turn to that task in the following chapter.

BIBLIOGRAPHY

Jewish Literature

Burrows, Millar. *The Dead Sea Scrolls*. New York: The Viking Press, Inc., 1955.
———. *More Light on the Dead Sea Scrolls*. New York: The Viking Press, Inc., 1958.
Gaster, Theodor H., ed. *The Dead Sea Scriptures in English Translation*. 2nd ed. New York: Doubleday & Company, Inc., 1976.
Gowan, Donald E. *Bridge Between the Testaments*. Pittsburgh: Pickwick Press, 1976.
Nickelsburg, G. W. E. *Jewish Literature Between the Bible and the Mishnah*. Philadelphia: Fortress Press, 1981.
Pfeiffer, Robert H. *History of New Testament Times*. New York: Harper & Row, Publishers, 1949.
Stendahl, Krister, ed. *The Scrolls and the New Testament*. New York: Harper & Row, Publishers, 1957.
Toombs, Lawrence E. *The Threshold of Christianity*. Philadelphia: Westminster Press, 1960.
Vermes, Geza. *The Dead Sea Scrolls: Qumran in Perspective*. Cleveland: William Collins & World Publishing Co., Inc., 1978.

Pfeiffer's study is a basic analysis of a wide range of Jewish literature. Gowan's book includes a treatment of the history and theology of Judaism, but its greatest strength is in its systematic analysis of apocryphal and pseudepigraphical literature. Toombs covers much the same territory. Burrows offers a vivid description of the initial Qumran discoveries and provides some translations of selected scrolls. Gaster uses other translations. The relationship between the Dead Sea Scrolls and the rise of Christianity is dealt with in a series of essays edited by Stendahl. The book by Vermes is a very competent treatment of the scrolls, the beliefs and practices of the Qumran community, and the bearing of the scrolls on biblical studies.

Jewish Sects and Institutions

Farmer, William R. *Maccabees, Zealots, and Josephus*. New York: Columbia University Press, 1956.
Finkelstein, Louis. *The Pharisees: The Sociological Background of Their Faith*. 3rd ed. Philadelphia: Jewish Publication Society of America, 1962. 2 volumes
Herford, R. Travers. *The Pharisees*. New York: Macmillan Publishing Co., Inc., 1924.

Ringgren, Helmer. *The Faith of Qumran*. Trans. by Emilie T. Sander. Philadelphia: Fortress Press, 1963.
Rivkin, Ellis. *A Hidden Revolution*. Nashville, Tenn.: Abingdon Press, 1978.
Simon, Marcel. *Jewish Sects at the Time of Jesus*. Trans. by James H. Farley. Philadelphia: Fortress Press, 1967.
Stone, Michael E. *Scriptures, Sects and Visions*. Philadelphia: Fortress Press, 1980.

These books relate to two sections of the chapter: "From Diversity to Unity" and the section on Jewish institutions. Finkelstein's, Herford's, and Rivkin's treatments of the Pharisees are generally sympathetic. Finkelstein concentrates on their socioeconomic aspects and Herford on their theology. Rivkin presents the Pharisaic movement as a conscious rebellion against priestly domination. Ringgren deals with Essenes, and Simon with the lesser-known sects. Farmer attempts to show that there was a line of continuity running from the early Hasmoneans to the Zealots. Stone calls attention to some lesser-known aspects and practices in several Jewish sects.

Jewish Thought

Davies, W. D. *Christian Origins and Judaism*. Philadelphia: Westminster Press, 1962.
Guttmann, Alexander. *Rabbinic Judaism in the Making*. Detroit: Wayne State University Press, 1970.
Moore, George Foot. *Judaism in the First Centuries of the Christian Era*. Cambridge, Mass.: Harvard University Press, 1927–1930. 3 volumes
Sandmel, Samuel. *Judaism and Christian Beginnings*. Oxford: Oxford University Press, 1978.
Schechter, Solomon. *Aspects of Rabbinic Theology*. New York: Schocken Books, Inc., 1961.

Most of these books deal with the concepts of God, covenant, and Torah, as well as with other fundamental aspects of Jewish thought in our period of interest. Although it needs updating and correction at several points, Moore's work is a valuable and comprehensive study. The books by Davies and Sandmel provide some of the needed correction. Schechter and Guttmann concentrate on Pharisaic-rabbinic elements.

Messianic Expectation

Klausner, Joseph. *The Messianic Idea in Israel*. Trans. by W. F. Stinespring. New York: Macmillan Publishing Co., Inc., 1955.
Mowinckel, Sigmund. *He That Cometh*. Trans. by G. W. Anderson. Oxford: Blackwell, 1956.

Both authors study the meaning and function of messianic expectation in Judaism during the Hellenistic and Roman periods.

Diaspora Judaism

Hengel, Martin. *Jews, Greeks and Barburians*. Trans. by John Bowden. Philadelphia: Fortress Press, 1980.

Sandmel, Samuel. *Philo's Place in Judaism*. Cincinnati: Hebrew Union College Press, 1956.

Several of the books listed under other headings here include sections on diaspora Judaism. Those that deal with it exclusively and are usable by the beginning student are rare, however. Hengel deals with the problem of Hellenism as it was faced by Jews in the homeland and in the Diaspora. Sandmel's book is an important study of the best-known writer in the Diaspora.

❖ 4 ❖

The Hellenistic Context

THE first stages in the history of early Christianity occurred within a Jewish context. These stages include the life and teachings of Jesus and the earliest preaching of his disciples. But Judaism itself was part of a larger context, for it was never isolated from contacts with and influences from the Hellenistic and Roman world. And when Christian preachers such as Paul began to present their messages in Asia Minor, Macedonia, Greece, and elsewhere, they came into immediate contact with that larger world. They had to be attuned to their audiences' religious and intellectual composition, which compelled them to present their messages in terms that would be both true to the original nucleus of faith and meaningful to the hearers. This means that the Christian message is mixed. It springs from a Jewish context and speaks to a Hellenistic one. The NT writings themselves arise in this complex situation. All of them are written in one of the languages of the larger world—Greek—and they all use concepts that are meaningful in that context. The same is true of the other early Christian writings we will examine. For us, this means that, if we are to understand the writings in their original context, we must pay significant attention both to the Jewish and to the Hellenistic areas.

As we examine this larger context, it will be good to keep in mind something of the political history that we dealt with in Chapter 2. Our concern here, however, will be to examine the religious life and thought that seems to characterize the non-Jewish culture of the eastern Mediterranean world in the Hellenistic and Roman periods. Although historically it is necessary to speak of two periods—Hellenistic and Roman—the dominant cultural elements may simply be designated by one word: *Hellenistic*. This is not to say that Roman elements played no part in the development of the intellect and religion of those periods, only that Greek and Greeklike elements dominated the culture of both periods. The purpose of this chapter, therefore, is to describe the religious aspects of Hellenistic culture in the Hellenistic and Roman periods.

Although we date the origin of Hellenistic culture with the conquests of Alexander the Great, there are some anticipations of it before his time. In classical Athens of the fifth century BCE, the Olympian religion was clearly dominant. The Gods of Olympus had been known in Greece for centuries, and Homer's writings were widely read and carefully studied. The chief Gods in the Greek pantheon then were Zeus, Apollo, and Athena, and their impressive temples could be found all over Greece. But during the fifth century the dominance of this religion began to decline, and one of the most significant characteristics of religious life in Hellenistic times was the position of the traditional religion. It did not disappear. It survived, but in an altered state, and it no longer enjoyed unchallenged dominance. The religion of Hellenistic times included new ways of worshiping old Gods, as well as new forms of religion.

There may be several reasons for this decline of dominance. A chief one was the challenge to traditional religion that came from philosophy and science in pre-Hellenistic times. In some quarters there was skepticism about the Gods and even atheism. Plato advocated a retention of traditional religion as necessary for social cohesion. But he also taught that above the Olympian deities was one more worthy of worship than they, a transcendent God who could be approached by individual contemplation. Aristotle thought of God as the prime mover, the one who causes motion but is not himself moved. Although the deity of Plato and Aristotle may sometimes be called Zeus, the concept is far from what was reflected in Homer's writings. Scientists were also beginning to talk about a kind of cosmic order, and their concepts seemed to some to make belief in traditional religion antiquated.

An event that occurred in Athens several decades before the beginning of the Hellenistic period demonstrates the interplay of forces at work at the time. In 399 BCE the philosopher Socrates was executed for crimes against the city of Athens. We know that he had been teaching about virtue, but he was accused of misleading the youth of Athens and of holding irreligious beliefs. Socrates stood within a tradition that produced a critique of religion that contributed to the decline of the Olympian deities. The reaction of the citizens of Athens was to execute the critic. In the philosophical tradition represented by Socrates, we have the attempt to establish a rational attitude toward life, and the attempt partially succeeds by contributing to the decline in confidence in the Olympian Gods. However, it does not sweep away religious feeling, and the result is that Greek religion moves progressively away from both Olympian religion and rationalism. This movement characterizes Hellenistic culture.

The decline in traditional religion had begun before the time of Alexander the Great. With his conquests we observe the introduction of certain dramatic political and social alterations that also affected Hellenistic culture. Among those changes are cosmopolitanism and individualism. Alexander felt that the culture he had known would benefit all nations, and he intended to make it a worldwide one. Ideally, the entire world would enjoy a unity of religion, intellect, and social structure. People would be citizens of the world—cosmopolitans. But cosmopolitanism was not simply the imposition of Greek culture on all the colonies that Alexander had conquered. Rather, it manifested itself in the large-scale adoption of eastern practices in the west and in the acceptance of western institutions in the east. Nevertheless, the political structures allowed people to think of themselves as citizens of the world.

Individualism was an equally important characteristic of Hellenistic culture. It had been a strong emphasis in the Greek city-states, and it became widely disseminated among the other nations of the eastern Mediterranean in Hellenistic times. Its significance is exemplified in the fact that biography became very popular, as we see in the work of Polybius, Sallust, Plutarch, Tacitus, and others. Mass movements and institutions were de-emphasized in the interpretation of history, and great events of the past were understood as the deeds of great individuals. Virgil's *Aeneid*, for example, presented the founding of Rome as an act of the brave Aeneas and attributed its present blissful state to the genius of Caesar Augustus. In Roman society, mobility was a characteristic of the early empire. Slaves could become freedmen, senators could become paupers, and much depended on individual initiative. Cosmopolitanism and individualism went hand in hand, for, as national and racial distinctions gave way, a person could be judged on the basis of individual qualities rather than social relationships.

These features brought new opportunities, but they also exacerbated significant human problems. The alteration of political structures, social-class mobility, and the movement from nationalism to cosmopolitanism tended to contribute to a certain insecurity. The relatively fluid situation in Hellenistic times meant for many the loss of an accustomed social context. As a result, people became less sure of their place in the world. The insecurity brought with it a lack of confidence in the forces that controlled human destiny. People were fearful of the unknown and generally skeptical about life after death. The changing patterns demanded new duties, and moral insecurity resulted. When we are faced with a changing moral demand and are perplexed about what is expected, we frequently feel an undefined guilt. We think that we have, somehow or other, not met the demands placed upon us. It is true that the new forces could lead the individual to feel significant. Emancipated slaves who were climbing the social ladder surely appreciated this fact. But it appears that many individuals felt isolated rather than important.

It is probable that cosmopolitanism and individualism contributed to the further decline of the traditional religion. The Olympian deities surely were exported to the eastern colonies, as Greek citizens migrated. But those citizens were not immune to the religious forces in the colonies either; in fact, they seemed to welcome them. The result was a kind of assimilation of Greek and eastern religions, a mix that significantly altered traditional religion.

In this preliminary description of the Hellenistic context, we have pointed to three interrelated phenomena and their implications: the decline of the traditional religion, cosmopolitanism, and individualism. It is now our task to examine the ways in which those factors actually worked themselves out in religious life and thought.

RELIGIOUS LIFE

A Christian missionary who had come from a Jewish background would probably have been impressed with the diversity of religious life in Hellenistic Greece and Italy. According to the author of the Acts of the Apostles, the missionary Paul began his speech at Athens with the observation, "I perceive that in every way you are very religious. For as I passed along, and observed the objects of your worship, I found also an altar with this inscription, 'To an unknown god.' "[1] The remark represents a typically Jewish response to Athenian, indeed to gentile, religion in Hellenistic times. It calls attention to the depth of piety—"You are very religious." It calls attention to the polytheistic character of religion, something that offended Jews—"The objects of your worship." It calls attention to an aspect of the actual practice of worship—an altar with an inscription. It calls attention to the practice of dedicating altars to particular Gods, even though in this case the particular God is not known—"To an unknown God."

Some of the altars that our missionary may have observed would have been dedicated to the Olympian deities. The Parthenon, the temple to Athena that crowns the Athenian acropolis, stood as a symbol of the city itself, as it does even now. Lower in the agora, or marketplace, there was (and is) a temple to Hephaistos, the God who, according to Homer, had manufactured Achilles' armor. Our missionary probably also saw the buildings dedicated to Zeus, Apollo, and Ares. If he had ventured outside Athens, to Delphi, he would have found a complex of buildings supporting the worship of Apollo. The most notable was the shrine that housed the Oracle. The Oracle had given predictive and interpretive messages to a number of important people and continued to speak in Apollo's name in the Hellenistic period. In towns all over Greece there were shrines, temples, and monuments to the Olympian Gods. And the same would be true in Italy, except that Latin names were used there. All these buildings testified to the contin-

---

[1] Acts 17:22–23.

A priestess of Isis, Capitoline Museum, Rome. Courtesy *Capitoline Museum, Rome, and Alinari/Art Resource, Inc.)*

ued power of the Olympian deities in an age in which the trend was going against them.

Our missionary who came out of a Jewish background would probably have been better prepared than we to understand what went on in the Greek temples. They were not scenes of weekly services in which people gathered together to pray, sing, and listen to scriptures and sermons. They were more like the Jewish Temple in Jerusalem, in the sense that their primary purpose was for sacrifice. Unlike the Jewish Temple, however, most of the sacrifices seem not to have been done on a scheduled basis but on individual initiative. If a person felt especially inclined to do so, he would arrange to bring a sacrifice to the temple of a particular God. A priest would be there to assist him in performing the sacrifice correctly. Some sacrifices were actually meals in which priest, worshiper, perhaps his friends and family, and the God enjoyed fellowship and food together. In addition to the sacrifices, people also brought gifts to the God at his temple. The gifts might be brought when one had a petition for the God or when one wished to express thanks for some favor. The gifts—money, jewelry, statues, and objects of art—remained in the temple or in its adjacent treasury.

In addition to the sacrifices and prayers that were done on an individual's initiative, there were special festival days for the Gods. These days would be similar to our own civic holidays. They included parades, public sacrifices, singing, dancing, games, and athletic contests—all in honor of a particular God. The festival days celebrated the harmony that was assumed to exist between the city and the God, a harmony that depended on the fulfillment of mutual duties.

We can get some sense of what a truly pious person would do from a story told about a man from Asia Minor who had brought sacrifices for the Gods every year. He brought one to Apollo at Delphi and asked the Oracle, "Who best honors the Gods?" He clearly expected the Oracle to name him, but instead she replied that one Klearchos of Methydrion was the most pious. Although he was disappointed, the inquirer traveled to Methydrion and found Klearchos, "a man who, at the proper times, every day of new moon, cleaned and garlanded the statues of Hermes and Hekate—that is domestic worship—offered incense and cakes in the sanctuaries, and took part in the yearly festivals of the gods without missing one."[2] Such must have been the ideal of Greek piety.

Another indication of the survival of traditional religion in Hellenistic times is the continued emphasis on religious practices that were tied to the home (for example, the worship of Hermes and Hekate, in the preceding reference). Worship within the family was not only important in Greece but also in Italy, where the religions of the home had an ancient history. It

---

[2] Referred to by Martin P. Nilsson, *Greek Piety*, trans. by H. J. Rose (Oxford: Clarendon Press, 1948), p. 49.

consisted in the worship of household deities, who were expected to protect the family from disaster and each member of the family from illness. These Gods were also expected to concern themselves with the economic welfare of the family. Harold R. Willoughby maintained that home religion was the original form of religion in Italy and that the heart of it survived into Hellenistic times. He wrote: "In its primitive development Roman piety was the cult of a household living in a rural environment and engaged in ritual practices intended to placate the powers on which the welfare of the family was chiefly dependent."[3] As late as the Roman period, these religions included the veneration of a small statue of the deity or deities, sacrifices of grain or meat, and certain family observances that took place at the hearth.

Although devotion to the Olympian Gods and the household deities continued, it did not dominate religious life in Hellenistic times. The expression of religious feeling becomes directed increasingly toward different forms, some of them new, many imported from the east, and others resurrected from the past: worship of heroes; magic, astrology, and the occult; mystery religions; and the imperial cult.

A hero is a semidivine being. Usually, one of his parents was thought to be human and the other divine. Or he may have been a human who had become divine at death. The worship of some heroes can be found in pre-Hellenistic times, but the practice seems to increase in the Hellenistic and Roman periods. Zeus and the other high Gods seemed unapproachable, but the heroes seemed accessible and more interested in individual human problems. So people would readily go to the shrine of a hero with their most personal concerns. They would go to ask not only for general financial aid, but also for good luck at the race track, victory in a dispute, or success in a business venture. In the main, however, the hero shrines were devoted to healing. The best-known healing shrine was that of Asclepius at Epidaurus. In popular folklore Asclepius was the son of Apollo and the human Coronis. It was believed that he had lived at Epidaurus and that during his lifetime he had cured the sick and raised the dead. To keep humans from attempting to avoid death altogether, Zeus killed Asclepius with a thunderbolt but placed him among the stars at Apollo's request. People came to Epidaurus with all sorts of diseases, and many were allegedly healed after sleeping at the shrine.[4] Similar shrines were located in Rome and other cities, where they also attracted large numbers of people. To appreciate the hero cults we must understand that the worship of the hero is precipitated by a specific purpose or a personal need. The hero is not considered to be an all-powerful or all-knowing deity.

[3] Harold R. Willoughby, *Pagan Regeneration* (Chicago: U. of Chicago, 1929), pp. 9 ff.
[4] Inscriptions found at Epidaurus record several hundred cases of the healing of various diseases and handicaps. For a translation of a few of the inscriptions, see David R. Cartlidge and David L. Dungan, *Documents for the Study of the Gospels* (Philadelphia: Fortress Press, 1980), pp. 151–153.

The growing lack of confidence in traditional religion is also indicated by the increasing attraction of the occult, magic, and astrology. Behind these phenomena there lies the conviction that we can alter our destiny, or at least anticipate the future course of events, by manipulating the exotic, using secret formulas or studying cosmic constellations. The literature of Hellenistic times is full of references to such practices. M. P. Nilsson, a classical scholar, says that the writings of Plutarch (first–second century CE) contain many "references to sorcery and magical materials, love-philtres, conjurations, the Evil Eye, amulets, magic wheels, and magical symbols, the so-called Ephesian letters."[5] Belief in demons was also widespread, and formulas for exorcising them are known. There are also abundant descriptions of sorceries, seances, and omens.

Theophrastus, who became Aristotle's successor in 323 BCE, stood within the tradition of Greek philosophy and so looked askance at some of these religious practices. In the early Hellenistic period he wrote a description of an overly superstitious person, and although it may be overdrawn, it must reflect some current practices.

Now superstition might seem to be timidity with respect to divinity, and the superstitious man one who [when he sees a bad omen] washes his hands, sprinkles himself with holy water from a shrine, and walks around all day with bay-leaf in his mouth. If a cat runs across the road, he will not go on until someone passes by or until he throws three stones across the road. If he sees a snake in his house and it is a *pareias,* [i.e., sacred to Sabazios], he calls on Sabazios; if it is the sacred kind, he installs a hero-shrine then and there. If he passes one of the "anointing stones" at a crossroads he pours olive oil from his jar, falls on his knees and worships, and then takes his leave. If a mouse gnaws into his bag of barleymeal, he goes to the soothsayer to ask what he should do; and if his response is that he should give it to the leather-worker to fix, he pays no attention to the advice, but goes off to make propitiatory sacrifices. He is constantly purifying the household on the assumption that it has come under the spell of Hecate. If owls hoot while he is walking along, he is upset and says "Mighty Athena" before going on. He is not willing to step on a grave, or approach a corpse or a woman in childbirth, on the grounds that it is better for him to avoid the pollution. On the fourth and seventh of the month he orders the domestics to boil wine while he goes out to buy myrtlewreathes, incense, and sacrificial cakes, then he comes back inside and spends the whole day putting garlands on the statues of Hermaphrodite. When he sees a dream, he goes to the dream-interpreters, to the seers, or to the specialists in bird augury, to ask them to which god or goddess he ought to pray. Every month he goes to the masters of the Orphic mysteries to be initiated, and he takes along his wife (if his wife is too busy, he takes the nurse) and his children. He is so diligent in sprinkling himself with holy water that he looks as if he has been for a dip in the sea. If he notices that one of the

---

[5] Nilsson, op. cit., p. 163. The Ephesian letters were formulas used in working magic. They consisted of six Greek words that were thought to have magical power.

Detail of a scene from the so-called Villa of the Mysteries, Pompeii. The fresco is thought to portray an act from the Dionysiac mysteries. Courtesy *Superintendenza Archeologica, Pompeii, and Alinari/Art Resource, Inc.*)

cross-road gods is garlanded with garlic, he goes off and washes his head, then calls the priestesses and bids them purify him with squill. If he sees a madman or an epileptic he shudders and spits into his breast.[6]

To this list of religious practices, we should add astrology. Persian in origin, it was widely studied and practiced in the eastern Mediterranean world in Hellenistic times. Astrology does not involve the manipulation of objects in the hope of altering fate. Rather, the belief is that our fate is determined by the position of the planets at our birth and at other crucial times in life. By practicing astrology, it was believed that one's destiny could be discovered and life made to conform to it.

[6] Theophrastus, *Character Studies*, 16, trans. by David G. Rice and John E. Stambaugh, *Sources for the Study of Greek Religion* (Missoula, Mont.: Scholars Press, 1979), pp. 158 f. Used by permission.

The mystery religions constitute the most popular form of Hellenistic religion. Shirley Jackson Case, a scholar of the NT and Christian origins, estimated the importance of these religions highly: "It would not be a mere rhetorical figure if one were to designate the religious history of the Mediterranean world in the early imperial period as the age of the mysteries."[7]

Although the religions that can be called mysteries are diverse, they share certain characteristics. The designation *mystery* indicates one of their common qualities. At the heart of these religions there are mysteries, secret lore, and practices that the devotees are pledged to keep. In general the secret is the meaning of the ritualistic practices of the religious community, but in some religions the rituals themselves are secret. This fact, of course, limits our understanding, for most of the devotees honored their pledge of secrecy, feeling that they were in possession of a reality that elevated them above other people. To be sure, several Greek and Roman writers were deeply interested in the mystery religions and wished to describe them, but they were not members of the cult. Apuleius (second century CE) is perhaps the only exception. He was once an initiate of mystery religions, and he pictured his fictional hero Lucius as one who could observe human activities undetected because he had been transformed into an ass. Lucius was finally able to obtain release through the religion of Osiris. Through this narrative Apuleius was able to give us glimpses of the mysteries.[8] In a few other cases the rituals of the religion were public, and some have been described by contemporary writers. From those descriptions we can infer the hidden meaning.

A second quality common to mystery religions is that of deification, a process by which an initiate is believed to become divine. This possibility seems to have been open to any devotee who accepted the initiatory rite; it guaranteed him the right to be worshiped by his contemporaries and granted him a blessed immortality.

Deification is closely related to the sacramental aspect of the mystery religions, for it is by a sacrament that the devotee participates in the life of the God. In most cases the sacraments were understood in highly realistic ways. Ancient sacraments were frequently associated with eating and drinking with a deity, and in some practices the concept was that of consuming the deity. This latter practice was described by Prudentius, a fourth-century Christian writer who narrated the consecration of a priest into the service of Cybele through the rite of the *taurobolium*.[9] In this sacrament the priest washed himself in the blood of a bull, covered himself thoroughly with it, and drank it. The blood of the bull was identified with divine life, and the priest who partook of it imbibed the life of the God.

[7] Shirley J. Case, *The Social Origins of Christianity* (Chicago: U. of Chicago, 1923), p. 113.
[8] See Apuleius, *The Golden Ass,* trans. by Jack Lindsay (Bloomington: Indiana U. P., 1962).
[9] Prudentius, *Peristephanon* X, 1011–1050. See the translation below, p. 119.

The idea of redemption is also common to the mystery religions. Certain practices were supposed to provide redemption from the evils of this life as well as assurance of eternal life itself (and this of a blissful quality). The distinctiveness and widespread appeal of the mystery religions probably lies in the fact that they addressed the issues of life, death, and the ultimate destiny of individuals.

The ethical value of the mysteries is by no means clear, but apparently for many the experience of initiation and sacrament reinforced their interest in nonmaterial things and even resulted in elevating the present life. Aristophanes, Cicero, and Epictetus spoke of the ethical value of these religions, but Aristotle insisted that their chief value was emotional.

Many of the mystery religions were already very old when the Hellenistic period began. They had originated in diverse locations, but in the Hellenistic period they were brought by adherents and converts to cities all over the eastern Mediterranean. After a time, they could truly be called international. The Dionysiac and Orphic religions originated in Thrace (roughly equivalent to modern Bulgaria). They were known in Greece in the fifth century BCE, and by the second and third centuries CE they were enjoying great popularity in Italy. The Eleusinian mysteries had originated in Eleusis, near Athens, and they attracted such notable adherents as the Roman emperors Hadrian, Marcus Aurelius, and Commodus. The religion of Cybele arose in Phrygia, in central Asia Minor. It was invited to Rome by the Senate in 205 BCE. Later, when it was learned that the rites included self-emasculation, the religion of Cybele was prohibited in Rome. Under Claudius (41–54 CE), however, restrictions on its practices were lifted, and in the next century it was regarded as fully legitimate. The religion of Isis originated in Egypt and became widespread in the Hellenistic period. The Roman emperor Gaius (37–41 CE) built a temple to her in Rome. The religion of Mithras came from Persia, and it became especially popular in the Roman army in the second and third centuries CE.

Each of the mystery religions involved a myth, and there were striking similarities among them. Some reflected Homeric myths, and it is probable that cultural assimilation was at work in creating similarities.[10] In the Eleusinian mystery, the myth told of the kidnaping of Demeter's daughter Persephone by Hades, in retaliation for which Demeter caused a grave famine. The Orphic religion was a reformation of an older Dionysiac cult. In it Zeus and Persephone gave birth to Dionysus, who was captured and eaten by Titans. But Athena captured Dionysus' heart and brought it to Zeus, who ate it. Then Zeus and the mortal Semele gave second birth to Dionysus. Zeus destroyed Semele by lightning but saved Dionysus. In the religion of Isis, Osiris was an Egyptian king who had been killed by Typhon. Isis

[10] For the information in this and the following paragraphs, the author is dependent mostly on Harold R. Willoughby, op. cit.

Dionysus on a Panther, mosaic, House of Masks, Delos, second century, BCE. The religion of Dionysus was a widely practiced mystery religion in Hellenistic times. Courtesy École Française d'Archéologie, Athens.)

found his body, and with help from other deities she brought him back to life and made him "Lord of the underworld and ruler of the dead." In all of these we see the dominant themes of birth, life, death, resurrection, and deification. At some points the myths gave indications of their origins in fertility cults, which revolved around the death of nature in the winter and its rebirth in the spring. Many scholars consider the seasonal rituals that dramatized these changes as constituting the original form of all the mystery religions, and they believe that the mythological formulations came along at a later time. This thesis rests on the understanding that the original human needs in the eastern Mediterranean were those that centered on raising crops. In the Hellenistic period those needs were not universally felt, and for many the problems of individual human life and destiny were the ones that needed resolution. The great international mystery religions then began to respond to those needs because they addressed the problems of birth, life, guilt, and death. Perhaps the durability of those religions was the result of their adaptability to changing circumstances and needs.

The religion of Cybele can serve as an illustration of most of the phenomena of mystery religions. Fortunately, many of the rituals of this particular religion were public, and our information about it is relatively full. Although there are several similar religions and, therefore, there is some resulting confusion, the general lines of its mythology are clear. Cybele is called the Great Mother, the mother of all Gods and humans. Her companion is Attis, a semidivine hero, who was born of a virgin and was associated with vegetation. Cybele loved Attis, who later was unfaithful to her. Out of guilt, Attis castrated himself and died. Cybele was so grieved over her loss that she restored him to life, deified him, and made him immortal. The motifs of life, death, sexuality, and seasonal change are profoundly intermixed in the myth. The association of Attis with vegetation calls to mind the death of nature in the winter and its rebirth in the spring.

The rituals of this religion are, on the one side, the dramatic presentation of the myth and, on the other, the sacramental participation of the devotee in the life of the God. There were two basic rituals; both were public and are well known. The spring festival began on March 15. On the sixteenth, a pine tree was brought into the temple of Cybele; the tree was regarded as the corpse of Attis. The next day was a day of fasting from vegetables and cereal. The climax of the spring festival came on March 24, the day of blood. The day was marked by a frenzied dance accompanied by noisy music. While dancing, people would wag their heads to the point of dizziness, lacerate their flesh, and sprinkle the Attis tree with blood. At the high point of the dance, some of the men would emasculate themselves and run through the streets, demonstrating evidence of their deed. By performing this act a young man would become a priest of Cybele and, indeed, a God. He became the counterpart of Attis, for he had done for Cybele what Attis had done. It is also possible that the new priest then thought of himself as the male counterpart of the Goddess, for he would put on feminine dress and begin to wear his hair in a female style. The resurrection of Attis was celebrated on March 25, and on March 27 the statue of Cybele was washed in a nearby river. This last act was probably thought to signify a new birth for the religious community.

The second major ritual in the religion of Cybele was that of the *taurobolium,* or bathing in the blood of the bull. This ritual could apparently be performed at any time. The bull represented the dying Attis, whose blood cleansed the bather from his past guilt and signified his entry into a new life. The idea of deification is not absent, however; the believer, in drinking the blood, is partaking of the life of the deity. The best available description of this ritual was written by Prudentius. As a Christian, Prudentius had no sympathy with this pagan rite, and his purpose in describing it was a negative one. It is a description of the ordination of a priest:

As you know, a trench is dug, and the high priest
plunges deep underground to be sanctified.
He wears a curious headband, fastens fillets for the occasion
around his temples, fixes his hair with a crown of gold,
holds up his robes of silk with a belt from Gabii [a town near Rome].
Over his head they lay a plank platform criss-cross,
fixed so that the wood is open not solid;
then they cut or bore through the floor
and make holes in the wood with an awl at several points
till it is plentifully perforated with small openings.
A large bull, with grim, shaggy features
and garlands of flowers round his neck
or entangling his horns, is escorted to the spot.
The victim's head is shimmering with gold
and the sheen of the gold leaf lends colour to his hair.
The animal destined for sacrifice is at the appointed place.
They consecrate a spear and with it pierce his breast.
A gaping wound disgorges its stream of blood,
still hot, and pours a steaming flood on the lattice
of the bridge below, flowing copiously.
Then the shower drops through the numerous paths offered
by the thousand cracks, raining a ghastly dew.
The priest in the pit below catches the drops,
puts his head underneath each one till it is stained,
till his clothes and all his body are soaked in corruption.
Yes, and he lays his head back, puts his cheeks in the stream,
sets his ears underneath, gets lips and nose in the way,
bathes his very eyes in the drops,
does not spare his mouth, wets his tongue
till he drains deep the dark blood with every pore.
When the blood is exhausted the priests drag away
the carcase, now growing stiff, from the structure of planks.
Then the high priest emerges, a grim spectacle.
He displays his dripping head, his congealed beard,
his sopping ornaments, his clothes inebriated.
He bears all the stains of this polluting rite,
filthy with the gore of the atoning victim just offered —
and everyone stands to one side, welcomes him, honours him,
just because he has been buried in a beastly pit
and washed with the wretched blood of a dead ox.[11]

In addition to these major rituals, there were certain private rites that probably included the marriage of Cybele with an emasculated priest and a ceremony of eating and drinking with the Goddess.

[11] Prudentius, *Peristephanon* X, 1011–1050. Reprinted from John Ferguson: *The Religions of the Roman Empire.* © John Ferguson 1970. Used by permission of the publisher, Cornell University Press.

Several general features of mystery religions can be abstracted from the description of this example. We must keep in mind that many of the religions were quite old. The religion of Cybele, for example, goes back to the sixth century BCE. The antiquity of the religions means that we are dealing with changing phenomena, and that the result is a mixture of Olympian myths, vegetation cults, and regenerative rituals. Nevertheless, the chief features of mystery religions in the Hellenistic period illuminate beliefs about how certain basic human needs can be satisfied. Feelings of human *guilt* played a major role in these religions. Although the nature of sin was ill defined, guilt seems to have been significant. The practice of emasculation in the religion of Cybele signified not only the act of Attis in the myth, but it probably also spoke to the devotee's attempt to expiate his own sinful acts, which were viewed as acts of infidelity to the divine mother. Those feelings of guilt moved the devotee toward the need for *regeneration*. He felt that guilt was so great he could not expiate it as he was. He needed a new birth and to become a new person. The bathing in bull's blood was the washing away of his past and the creation of a new person. Regeneration meant that the person was no longer what he had been. As a new person he had the right of *participation* in the life of the deity. He took divine life within himself as he absorbed the blood of the bull or the blood of the God. The culmination of his religious progress was *deification,* the act in which the devotee became divine. In this way he completely overcame evil and temptation to do evil. He might then be an object of worship and devotion. Because a happy immortality was essentially associated with the Gods, a man's deification was a guarantee of such *immortality*. The popularity of the mystery religions can be understood in terms of the desires they attempted to satisfy: for expiation, regeneration, participation, deification, and immortality. These desires appear to have been widely felt in the Hellenistic age, and the more successful religions spoke to them.

One more form of religion to be considered is the imperial cult—that is, emperor worship—in the Roman period. There was nothing uniquely Hellenistic about this kind of religion; rather, it had roots in ancient eastern cultures, where the worship of kings was common. But Greeks and Romans had reverence for heroes, and it was not difficult to think of rulers as heroes. Alexander the Great and his successors were usually thought of as divine, and with the establishment of the Roman Empire, the Roman imperial religion began. Willoughby has written: "It was a characteristic Roman conviction that the primary function of religion was to serve the interests of the state and that as a guaranty of political prosperity the rites of religion were potent in the extreme." [12] Technically, the Roman imperial cult did not require the worship of a living emperor, but it sometimes required citizens and subjects to make sacrifices to the emperor's "genius." Moreover,

[12] Op. cit., p. 15.

it was the prerogative of the Roman Senate to determine which emperors would be deified at death. In the first century Augustus and Claudius were deified, whereas Tiberius, Gaius, and Nero were not. In addition, there was great variance in the practice of this cult. At Rome it seems to have been treated perfunctorily; but in the eastern provinces imperial worship was serious business. Popular feelings did not always conform to senatorial proclamations, for some emperors who were not deified by the Senate were, nevertheless, worshiped. There was also some tendency to assimilate Olympian and imperial religion. In some statues, for example, Augustus is pictured as Apollo and Nero and Hadrian as Zeus.

We have already seen that Jews had serious problems with these requirements, which conflicted with their religious duties at fundamental points. We will see that Christians faced similar problems.

Because there is so much diversity among Hellenistic religions, it would be helpful to know if there is any correlation between social class and religious adherence. Unfortunately, hard information is lacking, and valid impressions are notoriously difficult to form. But there is some information relating to traditional religion and to mystery religions in the Roman period. As one might expect, traditional religion was associated with the upper classes—senators and equestrians. At the beginning of the Roman period, Augustus had all senators ordained as priests in the Olympian religions, in order to solidify the relationships between the religious and political spheres. Even so, there is evidence that some senators treated the religions with indifference or even skepticism. Some slaves, apparently under the influence of their masters, were also adherents of traditional religion.

The oriental and Greek mystery religions were introduced to Rome by foreigners, and initially they had a significant impact on the lower classes—plebs, freedmen, and some slaves. This seems to have been the case in the early years of the empire. But by the second century the mystery cults had begun to draw adherents from all ranks, even senators and emperors. John Gager, a contemporary NT scholar, gives some particulars: "For it was in the second century that the emperors Hadrian and Marcus Aurelius became initiates of the Eleusinian mysteries, that Antoninus Pius legalized the enthusiastic Phrygian cult of Cybele and that senatorial participation in non-Roman (Mithras, Dionysus) or Greco-Roman (Isis-Diana, Serapis-Jupiter) cults increased markedly."[13] Clearly, as the number of non-Roman senators increased, so grew senatorial adherence to nontraditional and foreign religions. In addition, Gager points out that there was a minimum of class consciousness in some of the mystery religions. The special appeal of the Mithraic cult to the military has already been noted.

[13] John G. Gager, "Religion and Social Class in the Early Roman Empire," in *The Catacombs and the Colosseum,* ed. Stephen Benko and John J. O'Rourke (Valley Forge, Pa.: Judson Press, 1971), p. 102.

What is known about the correlation of social class and religious adherence tends to give credence to developments we have already been able to observe. Traditional religions were declining, and the newer religious phenomena, notably mystery religions, were on the rise.

RELIGIOUS THOUGHT

We turn now to the area of religious thought. To be sure, religious life and religious thought are almost never found in isolation from one another. Those phenomena that we have already treated, such as mystery religions, were informed by concepts about divinity and human destiny, concepts that had practical consequences in the activities of the devotees. Nevertheless, religious life and religious thought can be distinguished and analyzed, and so we will now focus on the concepts about religious matters that developed, not within the religions themselves, but within the tradition of Hellenistic philosophy.

As there was a significant change in religious life in the Hellenistic period, so there was in religious thought. We have already had occasion to observe that the pre-Hellenistic philosophers played a role in the decline of traditional religion because they directly challenged the system of belief and practice; however, the leading thinkers, most notably Plato (c.428–c.348 BCE) and Aristotle (384–322 BCE), also proposed alternative religious and theological views.

In the area of religious thought, Plato has had an immeasurable influence in all of the western world, from his own time to the present. His philosophical speculations have led people to focus their attention on the immaterial as the real. In his famous "Allegory of the Cave,"[14] Plato pictured human beings as chained in a cave and situated so that they could only see one of its interior walls. Behind them is a fire, and between them and the fire, there are people walking. The walking people project shadows onto the wall of the cave, and the chained people can only see the shadows. They are not able to turn and see the source of the shadows. In the allegory Plato goes on to show that people prefer their accustomed bondage to a painful and uncertain liberation. The point of the allegory is that we, in our accustomed state, see only a vague reflection of reality, and we do not choose to be free of our illusions. The reality that Plato focused attention on was a mental world that was dissociated from sensory experience. In this kind of thought the philosopher would pay far more attention to the realm of ideas than to the realm of everyday phenomena. Thus, for Platonism, there is an identification of the real, and hence God, with the spiritual.

Aristotle also thought of God in conceptual terms. His existence, accord-

---

[14] In *The Republic* VII, 514A–521B.

ing to Aristotle, could be proven by rational argument. For example, the fact that there is motion in the universe requires a prior cause of motion—that is, a mover. We can reason back through a series of prior movers to the first mover. If this one is indeed the first cause of motion, it must be an unmoved mover. For if it is moved, there is a prior mover, and the one we called the first mover is not in fact the first. An argument similar in form was used by Aristotle to explain the relationship between cause and effect. Any occurrence can be explained as the effect of something else, which can be called its cause. For example, Aristotle might feel pain because he had been hit on the head by a flying rock. The rock was the cause, and Aristotle's pain was the effect. If someone had asked about the cause of the flying rock, the answer might have been that it was thrown by a young child. The child's act of throwing was the cause of the flying rock. The process of asking about cause and effect can be continued until one arrives at the first cause. This must be the uncaused cause—that is, the cause that is not the effect of some other cause. Otherwise, it could not be the first cause. The unmoved mover and the uncaused cause are simply partial descriptions of God.

Platonic and Aristotelian teachings define the basic character of pre-Hellenistic religious thought. We should note that the teachings are basically monotheistic; they laid a basis for rational confidence in divine existence; and they identified divine reality with the spiritual. They do not, however give people confidence for thinking of divine reality in terms of Olympian mythology, and they leave open the area of divine concern for people and their problems.

The major turn that is taken in the philosophical tradition in Hellenistic culture was toward human problems. The newer philosophies, which nevertheless had their roots in Plato and Aristotle, seem to have been attuned to the lives of individuals. They seem to have been aware of the need for guidance in perplexing times, and they exhibited a greater tendency to address the concrete questions people ask about life, death, and duty. The two leading philosophical schools in Hellenistic times were Stoicism and Epicureanism.

The founder of Stoicism was Zeno (c.335—c.263 BCE), who, in about 310 BCE, opened a school at a place called the Painted Porch (*poiklē stoa* in Greek, hence Stoicism). Other well-known Stoics were Epictetus (c.55—c. 135 CE), a freedman, and Marcus Aurelius, the Roman emperor, 161–180 CE.[15] Zeno had at one time studied Cynic philosophy, and there is an apparent relationship between the two philosophical schools. Cynicism taught that human beings are essentially products of nature and should live according to nature. The animal's mode of life should be a model for men and women. Stoics also taught that we must live according to nature, but they

---

[15] Note that Marcus Aurelius was also an initiate in the Eleusinian mysteries.

did not interpret nature in terms of animal life. Stoics, rather, understood natural life to be uniquely appropriate for human beings. When the Stoic said that we should live according to nature, he did not mean that we should take the animal as a model. He meant that there is a particular kind of life that is natural for us and that we will find happiness in accepting it with enthusiasm. To say that there is a life appropriate for humans is to say something quite positive about the universe. A Stoic would have said that the cosmos has a purpose for us. This means that there is a kind of harmony between human beings and the universe, a harmony expressed in the Greek word *Logos*. This word, which we have met in Philo, is difficult to translate. As Stoics used it, it stood for the substance that is the structure of the universe, but it was also said to be present in all people. The usual translation of Logos in Stoic writings is "reason." However, we must understand this reason in terms of a kind of harmony between the universe and us.

The Logos-harmony of universe and humanity has a very definite ethical implication: I, as a human being, have a purpose as part of the universe. The duty of each of us is to discover this purpose, which actually turns out to be our fate, and then to govern our lives in accordance with it. This ethical theory presents an interesting combination of fate and free will. Although it is clear that our destiny is set, we are called on to exercise our will in accepting it. We have the freedom either to accept destiny or reject it, but not to change it. According to Epictetus, this is where real freedom is to be found: in the freedom of the will. There are certain things that may not be within our power. For example, we may not be free to accrue and retain certain possessions, for we are limited by their availability, their present ownership, the conditions of obtaining them, and by our abilities and financial circumstances. Any one of these factors may so affect us and our possessions as to limit the freedom to have and to hold. If freedom is not present in having and holding, where is it to be found? Only in the will. We are not free to have or not to have, but we are free to will to get, or to will to avoid. We can intend getting, or we can intend not getting. Thus, Epictetus says: "That man is free, who lives as he wishes, who is proof against compulsion and hindrance and violence, whose impulses are untrammelled, who gets what he wills to get and avoids what he wills to avoid." [16]

But because we have control only over the will, we should say that the happy life is the one in which we will to get what in fact we do get, and we will to avoid what we do in fact avoid. Perhaps we should first see what we get and then will it. More accurately, we must discover the essence of what it means to be human—what is under our control and what is not. When we do this, we find that there are certain things appropriate to hu-

[16] Epictetus, *Discourses* IV, 1, trans. by P. E. Matheson, in *The Stoic and Epicurean Philosophers,* ed. Whitney J. Oates (New York: Modern Library, 1940), p. 406.

man beings. Epictetus says that among them are will and reason. To him, this means that we are intended to command (as an act of will) but to command with interest for the whole of humanity (as an act of reason). Thus, if a man finds himself to be a father, his duty is to issue commands for the benefit of the family; if he is a son, his duty is to obey the commands of the father. And when we discover what is really under our control, we are discovering only our own wills. Nothing else belongs to us—not our bodies, our souls, our children, or time.

Stoic ethics, therefore, revolve around the concept of duty, the obligation to be what we are, to discover the purpose of our lives, and to govern them in such a way that we are always in harmony with that purpose. The nobility of this ethic has usually been recognized, but it has been understood as a cold severity. We should recognize, however, that basic to Stoic ethics is a feeling of harmony between the universe and human values. Although those values do not include creature comforts, they enable us to feel at home in the universe. This emphasis is given clear expression in the *Meditations* of Marcus Aurelius. The Logos, which is the harmony between the universe and ourselves, is itself a deity; thus, there is a deity in all of us. Moreover, the presence of Logos in all of us creates a community of reason among humans, and there is a kinship between each person and the whole human race. Our place in the universe is clear: we have homes and families, and, as in all families, each person has certain duties. The Cynic philosophy must have appeared much colder in its assertion of the estrangement from the universe of characteristically human values.

The Epicurean philosophy was basically an attempt to understand nature, although, like Stoicism, it had a number of ethical implications. The founder, Epicurus (341–270 BCE), largely addressed himself to the analysis of natural phenomena, but his purpose in doing so was in large measure an ethical or even religious one. He intended to liberate people from needless superstition, and he felt that if all things could be explained there would be no need to fear the Gods. People fear Gods because they experience unexplained events and catastrophies. If people can understand that these things are not products of some whimsical or mischievous deity or the effects of displeasing the Gods, then they will be able to live their lives without fear of the unknown. Epicurus did not intend to be antireligious, and he certainly was no atheist. To him God was real but was not to be feared. On the other hand, Epicurus was no systematic theologian, for, although he attempted to bring all natural phenomena under a unified science, he did not suggest that Gods were responsible for them or that nature was the description of divine activity. In short, Gods seem to have reality but not relevance.

The world view Epicurus sets forth is scientific in the sense that it attempts to explain all phenomena from within the natural system, and it assumes consistency. It also assumes that nothing is created out of something that does not exist; thus, he understands the universe as a self-contained entity. It always was as it is now, and it is boundless. It is composed of space and bodies, and bodies are compounds of indivisible atoms. The atoms, which form the irreducible part of each body, are infinite in number and of an unlimited variety in respect to shape. They are continually in motion—falling, swerving, colliding, and recoiling. The atoms are also different from one another in texture. Some, of unsurpassable fineness, produce the sensations of sight, sound, touch, taste, and smell. Bodies formed by these atoms are similar in shape to solid bodies, but their fine texture means that they are images and not solid bodies. This distinction allows Epicurus to distinguish between a body and its image, and it allows him to account for both without introducing a second kind of nature. The same is true of the human soul. The soul is a body of very fine particles, distributed throughout the entire structure of the human body. Its primary function is sensation: it receives the sight, sound, and smell atoms, which travel at an unsurpassable rate of speed.

Epicurus' system has been called a materialistic monism. This is correct, except that we must be cautious in our understanding of these terms. The Epicurean system is a monism in the sense that all bodies are reducible to atoms. Although atoms vary in texture, shape, and speed, they do not vary in kind. This means that at its base the universe is of a single kind. It is this monism that allows the Epicurean to give a consistent explanation to all natural phenomena and to use the knowledge of them as a guide in discovering the secrets of stars and planets.[17] To say that Epicureanism is materialistic is to describe the quality that is common to the atoms. Yet this kind of description may be misleading, because it suggests that there is a "spiritual" realm that is ignored in Epicureanism, and this is not the case. It would be better to speak simply of a monism, for the qualities of the basic atom do not exclude those things we think of as spiritual.

Perhaps the major consequence of Epicurean monism is the belief in human mortality. Although nothing comes from nothing and nothing that is can become nothing, nevertheless the change from life to death is irreversible. This is so because Epicurus defines death as the deprivation of sensation. Because the soul is the seat of sensation, it is not immortal. At times, in Epicurean writing, the soul appears to be a function of various parts of the body. Lucretius, an Epicurean philosopher of the first century BCE, says that we do not experience the soul as a complete entity, nor do we experience death as the loss of a thing called soul: "For no one when dying appears to feel the soul go forth entire from his whole body or first mount up the throat and gullet, but all feel it fail in that part which lies in a particular quarter; just as they know that the senses all will suffer dissolution each in its own place."[18] Thus, we can say that death means that the ear no longer

---

[17] See especially Lucretius, *On the Nature of Things,* trans. by H. A. J. Munro, in ibid., pp. 69–219.
[18] Lucretius, *On the Nature of Things,* III, 610ff., in ibid., p. 127.

hears, the eyes no longer see, and the fingers no longer experience the sensation of touch. And in this sense, death is of no real concern. Epicurus wrote: "So long as we exist, death is not with us, but when death comes, then we do not exist. It does not then concern either the living or the dead, since for the former it is not, and the latter are no more." [19]

Great injustice has been done Epicureanism by the popular aphorism: "Eat, drink, and be merry, for tomorrow we die." It is true that death is irreversible in Epicurean thought and that the Gods do not interfere with human life in terms of rewards and punishments. It is also true that, for the Epicurean, the goal of life is well-being. But Epicurus did not advise people to pursue well-being directly. It results from a life of virtue, the chief feature of which is affection (*philia*) for other human beings, and from an absence of fear. Epicurean ethics would, then, be characterized by affection on the one side and the study of nature, which eliminates fear, on the other. A far better summary of Epicurean ethical thought is that given by Diogenes of Oenoanda, an Epicurean who lived c. 200 CE:

> *There is nothing to fear in God;*
> *There is nothing to feel in death;*
> *Evil can be endured;*
> *Good can be achieved.* [20]

Stoicism and Epicureanism were two popular philosophical schools. They had a significant impact on Hellenistic culture. Together they continued the philosophical tradition of questioning religion. Neither took the Olympian Gods seriously. Divinity could be thought of in impersonal pantheistic terms, as in Stoicism, or it could be relegated to an irrelevant position, as in Epicureanism. Ethically, the two had a joint impact in focusing attention on the inner self. Both philosophies led people away from concentrating on their outward circumstances and toward nurturing their feelings and attitudes. Both called people from fear. Stoicism assured that humans had a place in the universe; Epicureanism showed that the universe was not governed by some strange mystery. On the other hand, neither could guarantee personal immortality. Epicureanism specifically denied it; and in Stoicism, although the Logos, in which we all participate, was regarded as divine and immortal, there was no concept of the survival of a conscious self. As we have seen, it was the mystery religions that spoke to the desire for personal immortality.

Although they were dominant in Hellenistic philosophy, Stoicism and Epicureanism did not exhaust the possibilities of religious thought. There were still those who regarded themselves as Platonists, Aristotelians, and Cynics. In addition, there were Pythagoreans, who revered a semilegendary

---

[19] Epicurus, *Letter to Menoeceus,* trans. by C. Bailey, in ibid., p. 31.
[20] Quoted by Frederick C. Grant, *Roman Hellenism and the New Testament* (New York: Scribner's, 1962), p. 71.

figure of the sixth century BCE and emphasized the study of mathematics and the practice of vegetarianism. They taught that the soul was bound to a cycle of reincarnation, and they hoped for its eventual release through purification. And there were, at least by the first century CE, Hermetists, who taught methods to obtain the release of the soul, which was imprisoned in the evil body. We will see later that there were significant affinities between Hermetism and some forms of early Christianity.

The existence of Pythagoreanism and Hermetism reminds us that the line we have drawn between religious life and thought is something of an artificial one. The fact is that each of them could be regarded either as a religion or as a philosophy, for each brings together concepts and practices aimed at obtaining salvation. But, as we have seen, Epicureanism and Stoicism had their practical side, too, for they intended to help people obtain a good life. Thus, although it has been necessary to separate religious life and thought for purposes of analysis, the separation should not be regarded as total. In any event, we must give weight both to the philosophical and religious aspects of Hellenistic culture in order to understand some of the human concerns in those times.

It was stated early in this chapter that the major tendency in Hellenistic times was a movement away from traditional religion and from rational reflection on religion. We have seen that traditional religion did not die, but that its position in Hellenistic times was slipping. We have also seen that, in the area of religious thought, although the concern for reason continued, the more vital concern was with individual well-being. In addition to these changes in religious life and thought, we have observed the increased interest in the occult, magic, astrology, and the mystery religions. These features of religious life and thought seem to have been the dominant ones in the Hellenistic and Roman periods.

Hellenistic culture forms, together with Judaism, the context in which early Christianity arose. As we turn now to a study of the people and literature of the NT and early Christianity, we should be able to observe some of the relationships that exist between Hellenistic culture and Christianity. Perhaps the reader has already been able to think of some similarities, such as the Platonic conception of the reality of the spiritual or the concern for regeneration and personal immortality in the mystery religions. But these apparent similarities cannot be fully understood until we have learned a good deal more about those aspects of religious life and thought that are associated with the one who is regarded as the originator of Christianity, Jesus himself. We turn to the study of Jesus and the gospels in Part Three.

BIBLIOGRAPHY

Dodds, E. R. *The Greeks and the Irrational*. Berkeley: University of California Press, 1951.

Ferguson, John. *The Religions of the Roman Empire*. Ithaca, N.Y.: Cornell University Press, 1970.

Glover, T. R. *The Conflict of Religions in the Early Roman Empire*. London: Methuen & Co. Ltd., 1909.

Grant, Frederick C., ed. *Ancient Roman Religion*. New York: Liberal Arts Press, 1957.

———, ed. *Hellenistic Religions*. New York: Liberal Arts Press, 1953.

———. *Roman Hellenism and the New Testament*. New York: Charles Scribner's Sons, 1962.

Hadas, Moses. *Hellenistic Culture*. New York: W. W. Norton & Company, Inc., 1959.

———and Morton Smith. *Heroes and Gods*. New York: Harper & Row, Publishers, 1965.

Murray, Gilbert. *Five Stages of Greek Religion*. 3rd ed. Boston: Beacon Press, 1951.

Nilsson, Martin P. *Greek Piety*. Trans. by H. J. Rose. Oxford: Clarendon Press, 1948.

Nock, A. D. *Conversion*. Oxford: Clarendon Press, 1933.

Oates, Whitney J., ed. *The Stoic and Epicurean Philosophers*. New York: Modern Library, 1940.

Rice, David G., and John E. Stambaugh. *Sources for the Study of Greek Religion*. Missoula, Mont.: Scholars Press, 1979.

Rose, H. J. *Religion in Greece and Rome*. New York: Harper & Row, Publishers, 1959.

Willoughby, Harold R. *Pagan Regeneration*. Chicago: University of Chicago Press, 1929.

In general, authors treat religious life and thought together, although some provide an emphasis on one or the other. Two of the volumes edited by Grant, *Ancient Roman Religion* and *Hellenistic Religions,* and the book by Rice and Stambaugh contain basic primary material. The book edited by Oates contains translations of the writings of Epicurus, Epictetus, Lucretius, and Marcus Aurelius, together with introductions to each writer. The studies by Willoughby, Murray, and Rose emphasize religious life, and they are largely sympathetic treatments. Nock deals with the effects of various religions, including Christianity, on ancient people. Dodds demonstrates the dynamics in Greek culture of the interplay of rationalism and irrationalism. Nilsson's is a first-rate study of the forms and feelings in Greek religion, and he pays a good deal of attention to the role of the occult. Hadas treats religious life and thought, as well as social and political factors, in his *Hellenistic Culture.* The book by Hadas and Smith emphasizes the importance of supposed supernatural ability in the literature about Greek heroes.

It also contains translations of lives of Pythagoras, Moses, Apollonius of Tyana, and Jesus (the Gospel of Luke). Glover and Ferguson concentrate on Roman religion in the early centuries. Glover describes it from the point of view of a sophisticated Roman. Ferguson makes abundant use of ancient inscriptions and other archeological evidence. In *Roman Hellenism and the New Testament,* Grant treats religious life and thought in its relation to the NT.

PART THREE

JESUS AND THE GOSPELS

The cross of Lothar, reverse side. (Courtesy *Ann Münchow, Aachen, Germany.*)

❖ 5 ❖

The Study of Jesus
and the Gospels

HE NT begins with four gospels—Matthew, Mark, Luke, and John—which feature the life, teachings, death, and resurrection of Jesus as the originating events in Christian history. The placement of these gospels at the head of the list of canonical Christian writings indicates something about their importance for the Christians who shaped the canon. The canon itself testifies to the fundamental importance of the historical life of Jesus in Christian religious life and thought.

The importance of the life of Jesus seems manifestly clear, so much so that it might go without saying. Chronologically, Jesus came first in the history of Christianity, and so he is generally regarded as the founder of the movement. But it does not seem that the first generations of Christian believers saw things in exactly this way. They did, of course, look back to the time when Jesus had been alive among them, but they seemed to be more interested in their relationship to a Jesus who, to them, was still alive, although not in the flesh. We will see that in those decades between about 30 and 70 CE, Christian believers saw themselves as recipients of revelations, prophetic words, and oracles from the heavenly Lord. Basic to this belief was the Christian conviction that Jesus had overcome his death in his resurrection and that he would soon return to earth to exercise his dominion.

Although the gospels came first in the canon as it was finally shaped, they are not the earliest Christian documents. During the decades between 40 and 60, the apostle Paul wrote a significant number of letters dealing with Christian life and thought, but he made very little reference to the life and teachings of Jesus. The first gospel probably was not written much before 70. Between then and about 200, a large number of gospels appeared. With their appearance, there is a demonstrated interest in the Jesus of history. But the authors of the gospels did not confine themselves to the material that originated with the Jesus of history. For a variety of reasons,

133

we find in the gospels not only the words and deeds of Jesus, but also materials that had come out of the life and thought of later Christians. Even after the appearance of the gospels, Christians continued their reflection upon theological and ethical matters in their sermons, letters, teaching tracts, and other writings. So, although it is true that Jesus came first, concern with the Jesus of history did not come first in the thought of early Christians, nor did it ever come in isolation from their own experience and reflection. The German NT scholar, Günther Bornkamm, writing about the first Christian generations, put the matter succinctly: "Jesus is not in the first instance a figure of the past, but rather the risen Lord, present with his will, his power, his word."[1]

Our purpose here in studying Jesus and the gospels is fundamentally different from that of the first Christian believers in at least two major ways. In the first place, we are, in this section of the book, raising the issue of the Jesus of history. The nature of the issue must be fully understood. Our aim here is to say something about Jesus' actions and sayings in the days between his birth and his death. Ours is a biographical interest, and, so far as we can tell, the first Christians did not have a primary interest in it.

A second way in which our efforts differ from those of the first Christians is that we are committed to a critical enterprise. This means, simply, that we are searching for historical evidence. The discussion of historical evidence in Chapter 1 maintained that the historian does not simply listen to testimony but judges it and sifts it for whatever evidential value it may have. This is what must be done in the search for the Jesus of history. The first Christians, whatever questions they may have raised about history, were not fundamentally critical in their attitudes.

These differences in approach have led to some very difficult problems. They mean that the modern critical historian must rely on documents produced by persons whose aims were not to write critical biographies. The approach of the modern historian and that of the early Christians seem to be incompatible. Although it will be maintained that historical study is possible, it is necessary first to face the problems squarely. These problems relate to the nature of historical study as well as to the nature of the documents on which the historian must rely.

PROBLEMS IN THE STUDY OF JESUS AND THE GOSPELS

One of the chief problems relates to the nature of historical study, in particular the perspective of the modern scholar who studies Jesus and the gos-

[1] Günther Bornkamm, *Jesus of Nazareth,* trans. by Irene and Fraser McLuskey with James M. Robinson (New York: Harper, 1960), p. 16.

pels. The question of perspective is an especially important one there, simply because of the role that the figure of Jesus plays in modern life. Briefly stated, the problem is that, because the historian may be interested in the relevance of Jesus for modern times, there is a danger of portraying him as a "modern" person.

The NT scholar, Henry J. Cadbury, in *The Peril of Modernizing Jesus,* pointed to the large number of anachronisms in modern biographies of Jesus.[2] Many intrude into the story in inoffensive ways, but they display an amazing degree of carelessness. Cadbury cited some authors who wrote of "doctors' offices and a morgue in Jerusalem, or of a first-century house in Nazareth with a separate kitchen and private upstairs bedrooms for a family of eight or more persons."[3] He observed that those who perpetrate such gross anachronisms in reference to minor points are likely to include more subtle modernizations of major points. If they assume that Jesus' house was modern, middle class, and western, they are likely to present his words and message as agreeably modern.

The modernization of Jesus becomes an acute danger in the ideological sphere. In *The Quest of the Historical Jesus,* first published in German in 1906, Albert Schweitzer made a thorough analysis of the lives of Jesus written in German in the eighteenth and nineteenth centuries.[4] The reader of the *Quest* is impressed not only with the quantity of published material and the variety of approaches, but also with the modern character of the Jesus who is discovered by the authors. He appears in some as a social theorist and in others as a lover of nature, a romantic, or a political revolutionary. In one biography, written after the time of Schweitzer, Jesus is a top management executive.[5] Schweitzer was highly critical of research on the life of Jesus, because he felt that scholars were unable to break through their assumptions about human society, nature, and history and tended to attribute their own assumptions to Jesus. Schweitzer suspected that each writer intended to show that Jesus was relevant to modern times and that he shared the world view and social concerns of the author's day. The basic methodological fault in those biographies was the authors' failure to take seriously the historical context in which Jesus lived. Each author tended to treat him as his contemporary. Such a tendency reveals that most modern biographers are not primarily interested in history but in relevance. Presumably, if they should find Jesus to be thoroughly and unequivocally a person of his own time, they would lose interest in him. They would conclude that he had nothing to say to us, and they would find no value in historical study about him.

[2] See Henry J. Cadbury, *The Peril of Modernizing Jesus* (Naperville, Ill.: Allenson, 1962).
[3] Ibid., p. 10.
[4] See Albert Schweitzer, *The Quest of the Historical Jesus,* trans. by W. Montgomery (New York: Macmillan, 1910).
[5] See Bruce Barton, *The Man Nobody Knows* (Indianapolis, Ind.: Bobbs, 1925).

Schweitzer insisted that Jesus belonged to his own day, not to ours. Jesus is a stranger to us, and he will always remain so. To Schweitzer, Jesus held a vivid expectation about the end of history and about his own place in the events of the end time. He expected God to bring the world to an end and even attempted to force God to action. Schweitzer wrote:

> Soon after that [the appearance of John the Baptist] comes Jesus, and in the knowledge that He is the coming Son of Man lays hold of the wheel of the world to set it moving on that last revolution which is to bring all ordinary history to a close. It refuses to turn, and He throws Himself upon it. Then it does turn; and crushes Him. Instead of bringing in the eschatological conditions, He has destroyed them. The wheel rolls onward, and the mangled body of the one immeasurably great Man, who was strong enough to think of Himself as the spiritual ruler of mankind and to bend history to His purpose, is hanging upon it still. That is His victory and His reign.[6]

Schweitzer portrayed Jesus as a stranger to our day, as one whose convictions were quite contrary to our most cherished beliefs. A deluded prophet cannot be a continually relevant leader. Jesus, therefore, "comes to us as One unknown."[7]

The tendency to modernize relates to the very purpose for which the study of Jesus may be undertaken. Schweitzer maintained that a major motivation for the authors he analyzed had been to demonstrate the relevance of Jesus. Most of those associated with the endeavor were convinced that Jesus had something important to say to their own generation, and they set out to make his relevance explicit. It is probable that some such attitude is present in most historical study, for we study the past partly in order to illuminate the present. We rarely find a historian who operates from a purely antiquarian interest and produces a thoroughly irrelevant work. Surely the study of history need not be the study of the past simply for its own sake, but neither does it bring the past into the present in an immediate way. There is a kind of continuum in human affairs, a process of temporal relationships whereby a generation leaves its mark on succeeding generations. Within the continuum there are institutions that have crossed the generations, and Christianity is one of them. Anyone interested in the present age may reasonably devote attention to the contribution that Christianity has made to it, and because Christianity has a history that leads back to Jesus, the study of Jesus may form part of an effort to understand the institution and its contribution to our world. A historian who undertakes such a study must respect the boundaries of time and must not expect Jesus to embrace modern thought. The study may, indeed, include an interest in a historical process that reaches into modern times, but it does not convert an ancient person into a modern one, not even Jesus. Through a study of the historical process, it may be seen that there is a relationship between Jesus and the

---

[6] Schweitzer, op. cit., p. 370f.
[7] Ibid., p. 403.

modern world, but this relationship can only be seen by understanding Jesus' initial relationship to the first-century world.

The historian's perspective may be problematical in yet another respect. In Chapter 1 we looked at some of the ways in which world view affects historical perspective. It was stated there that a partial remedy for this trouble is to examine our own perspective and to participate imaginatively in another. This means that the historian who studies Jesus and the gospels should be aware of the ways in which we view our world and should make every effort to see the ways in which first-century people understood theirs. Such procedures always carry certain difficulties, but in the case of the study of Jesus and the gospels, the difficulties are compounded. The reason for this is that world views today include scientific considerations that were not available in the time of Jesus. Although there were a few Greek thinkers who anticipated later scientific developments, their concepts did not dominate the understanding of nature as scientific thought tends to do today. The weight that we, almost automatically, give to scientific considerations creates a wide gulf between ourselves and the objects of our study.

A scholar of the NT and early Christianity, Rudolf Bultmann, did the most to call attention to this problem.[8] He did it by talking quite directly of the presence of mythology in the NT. He did not define mythology as a set of views that go against some specific scientific discovery, for within the boundaries of scientific methodology it is possible to hold contrary views at different times. Mythology, Bultmann said, is "the use of imagery to express the other worldly in terms of this world and the divine in terms of human life, the other side in terms of this side."[9] Bultmann described the mythology of early Christianity as having a cosmological view that assumed the existence of three stories in our universe, with the earth in the center, the heaven above, and the underworld beneath. This cosmology, which Christians shared with other ancient people, is really an attempt to express certain theological concepts in physical terms, or to express other-worldly ideas in this-worldly terms. Many ancient Christians thought of life as a battleground in the struggle between the forces of good and evil. They objectified this idea by thinking of these forces as locatable in the physical world; thus, good spirits are in heaven, and evil ones in the underworld. Because ancient people thought in these terms, they could also imagine that the spirits travel back and forth and cause visible events on earth. If an inhabitant of the lower world influences us, we have a case of demon possession. The only way to get rid of such a demon is for a superior power to eradicate him, and thus we have an exorcism. If an inhabitant of the world above wishes to create an effect on earth, we have what we call a miracle.

[8] See Rudolf Bultmann, "New Testament and Mythology," in *Kerygma and Myth,* ed. H. W. Bartsch, trans. by R. H. Fuller (London: Society for the Promotion of Christian Knowledge, 1953), pp. 1–44.
[9] Ibid.p p. 10, note 2.

The problem for the modern historian is that he or she does not have the option of explaining events in terms of demon possession or miracle. Yet the historian who studies Jesus and the gospels must somehow set up a position for imaginatively reconstructing ideas that are set within a mythological context. As Bultmann says, we cannot simply adopt a world view; it is part of the inheritance we have as citizens of the world at a particular time, and the ancient view of the world, as Bultmann described it, is obsolete. His solution to this problem is that of *demythologization*. This process must not be confused with the tendency to identify and then discard mythical elements. Instead, Bultmann's proposal is that we attempt to understand the nature of myth. He says: "The real purpose of myth is not to present an objective picture of the world as it is, but to express man's understanding of himself in the world in which he lives. Myth should be interpreted not cosmologically, but anthropologically, or better still, existentially."[10] Bultmann illustrates the method by proposing existential interpretations of the crucifixion and resurrection of Jesus. We need not follow this line of thought at present, but we must understand that Bultmann is insisting on interpreting myth rather than discarding it. He means that we should ask: What does it mean that this myth is used? In the case of a report about a miracle of Jesus, it is not fruitful to ask whether it happened, or to ask what event caused people to think it happened. Rather we should ask: What kind of world is presupposed in this report? What light is shed on early Christian beliefs about Jesus by acknowledging that people reported this miracle? Thus, the historian should neither adopt nor discard the mythology of the ancient world. She or he should rather attempt to see what kind of understanding is enveloped within the mythology.

Not all of our problems relate to the historian's perspective or to mythology. Many of them relate to the nature of the sources on which the historian must draw. For one thing, we suffer from a lack of neutral or unsympathetic sources about the life of Jesus. We are unable to achieve any balance, for unsympathetic material is all but nonexistent. The Roman biographer Suetonius refers to the Christian movement but betrays no real knowledge of Jesus.[11] Tacitus states that "Christus" was sentenced to death by Pontius Pilate.[12] The Jewish historian Josephus has one incidental note in connection with the execution of James. He identifies James as "the brother of Jesus, who is called Christ."[13] Most references in Jewish rabbinic literature appear to be dependent on the Christian gospels.[14]

---

[10] Ibid., p. 10.

[11] Suetonius, *Life of Claudius* 25:4. Suetonius published his *Lives of the Caesars* in about 121 CE.

[12] Tacitus, *Annals* XV, 4. Tacitus wrote in 112–113 CE.

[13] Josephus, *Antiquities of the Jews* XX, 200. Another reference in Josephus, *Antiquities* XVIII, 63, is probably not authentic, at least in its present form.

[14] One reference that may not be dependent on Christian sources is in the Babylonian Talmud,

Even among the sympathetic writings we do not have as much relevant material as we would like. A few details about the historical Jesus may be found in incidental remarks in some of Paul's letters, but there is almost nothing in the remainder of early Christian literature outside the gospels. But we will find that some gospels are dependent on others and that the latest ones add little of historical value. The Synoptic Gospels—Matthew, Mark, and Luke—will turn out to be prime sources of information about Jesus. But there is a large amount of duplication among them, and this fact further reduces the quantity of material.

In Chapter 1 we observed that it is necessary to know several things about a document in order to judge its evidential value. We should know its date, location, authorship, and genre, the occasion that lay behind its being written, its author's purpose, the history of its textual transmission, and the language in which it was written. The information we have about the gospels will be analyzed in Chapter 6. The analysis will call attention to the fact that we do not know enough about our basic sources of information about Jesus. Ideally we would be in possession of firm information about the sources in order to make appropriate inferences from the evidence they offer, but in the case of our gospels there are few certainties. Their location is almost never a matter of record. The dating can be established only within broad limits. The authors are probably not determinable. The occasions and purposes are variously conceived. Add to this the facts that the original manuscripts are missing and that the gospels were written in an archaic language, and the historian has nearly insuperable odds against the successful completion of a study of Jesus.

The genre of the gospels is also problematical because there are no exact parallels in contemporary literature outside of Christianity. If these writings could be readily classified in terms of known genres, we would know what kind of meaning to search for in them. If they are biographies, we might expect to find a record of Jesus' teachings and the narration of actual incidents, or at least typical incidents, from his life. If they are hero tales, we would expect to find mostly a collection of miracle stories. If they are romances, we would expect travel and adventure. Actually, we find all of these in the Christian gospels, and that is the problem. The appearance in one book of teachings, miracle stories, travel narratives, a passion narrative, and an execution and resurrection is, strictly speaking, unique. There are Hellenistic writings that have some of these elements, and perhaps the closest parallel to the Christian gospels is *The Life of Apollonius of Tyana*, by Philostratus, written in the third century CE.[15]

Sanhedrin 43a. This reference says that Jesus was hanged on the eve of Passover because he practiced sorcery and led Israel astray, and that he had five disciples.

[15] See Philostratus, *The Life of Apollonius of Tyana*, trans. by F. C. Conybeare, Loeb Classical Library (Cambridge, Mass.: Harvard U. P., 1948, 1950), two volumes.

But the gospels are unlike other kinds of literature in other ways. The word itself, *euangelion,* is a Greek word that means "good news." It was often used by Christians as the object of the verb *to proclaim* and was understood by them to define the content of the Christian message. This fact itself suggests that the authors of the gospels, the *evangelists,* intended to do more than write a biography of Jesus or collect miracle stories about him. They were presenting what they conceived to be the Christian message. These authors were religious writers, and most of them wrote in the belief that the one who had been a historical human being had become the divine Lord. Although they affirmed that this Jesus had been a human being, their interest, like that of the first Christians generally, was not only in what he once had done, but also in what he was doing in their own time. Thus, there is nothing to prevent them from mixing a past word of Jesus with a later word of the Lord or with current theological interpretations. That mixing has created both a special kind of literature and special difficulties for the historian.

The gospel writers are also particularly uninterested in the psychology of Jesus. This fact should cause little surprise, because the study of psychology is not very old. But some ancient writers wrote with unusual psychological insight, and psychological questions were being asked in Greco-Roman biographies. The lack of psychologically sophisticated sources is a serious deterrent to the study of Jesus' life. We would like to know why he did certain things, what he understood about the actions of others, what he meant by what he said, and how he understood himself. But his inner consciousness is not directly dealt with in our sources. In view of the fact that the early Christians regarded him as Messiah in some sense, the question of his own messianic consciousness is an important one. Did he believe himself to be Messiah, and, if so, how did he understand the term, and what did he intend for himself? Many modern studies of Jesus have not hesitated to tackle the question of Jesus' messianic consciousness, and they have frequently offered definite answers. But they do not recognize that they are going far beyond the source material and are entering areas for which no evidence can be cited. Jesus has also been an attractive figure for professionally trained psychologists and psychiatrists. Some have found him to be paranoid, because he often spoke about his opponents. Some have called attention to his hallucinations, in which he heard a voice from heaven at his baptism and imagined that he was talking with the devil in his temptations. He had an exaggerated self-consciousness, which displayed itself at the age of twelve, when he interviewed the priests at the Temple. He had delusions of grandeur, which led him to claim an identity with God; his speech was characterized by a high degree of egocentrism; and his actions were often irrational—for example, he cursed a fig tree for not bearing fruit out of season. These psychiatric studies treat the gospel writers as if they were modern historians and biographers, and they fail to take into account the mixing of Jesus' authentic statements with those from other sources. As a result, they are unable to base their diagnoses on any kind of psychologically sophisticated observations.[16]

Finally, although we do not have all the information about the circumstances of the writing of the gospels that we would like to have, what we know leads to the probable conclusion that the first ones were written some thirty to forty years after the time of Jesus. We cannot, of course, be certain what was going on during those decades, but it is probable that the teachings of Jesus and stories about him were being circulated in oral form. If that were the case, and there seems to be no more adequate way of explaining the resulting phenomena, then we must operate on the assumption that the gospels rest directly on oral traditions about Jesus. The consequences of this assumption will be investigated in detail in Chapter 7. But, even at the outset, it should be clear that any attempt to work with a supposed oral tradition is fraught with difficulties, because there is little to prevent the mixing of authentic and inauthentic materials.

The cumulative effect of these problems is enough to make the most confident historian have second thoughts. Before we proceed to suggest ways of working through the problems, it will be good to have them all before us, stated in brief summary form:

1. The modern historian may tend to picture Jesus in a modern fashion.
2. The modern historian may not be able to understand an ancient world view.
3. There are few neutral or unsympathetic sources for the life of Jesus.
4. There is very little relevant information about the life of Jesus even in the sympathetic documents.
5. We do not know enough about the circumstances under which the primary source documents, the gospels, were written.
6. The genre of the gospels is problematical.
7. The gospel writers were not interested in the psychology of Jesus.
8. The gospels depended on oral traditions, which allowed the mixing of authentic and inauthentic material.

POSSIBILITIES IN THE STUDY OF JESUS AND THE GOSPELS

The problems that we have just listed should make it clear that a biography of Jesus is impossible. But is it possible to infer some biographical infor-

---

[16] For an analysis of several psychological studies of Jesus, see Walter E. Bundy, *The Psychic Health of Jesus* (New York: Macmillan, 1922).

mation that has a probability of being authentic? Several considerations enable us to answer this question positively.

For one thing, we can be reasonably confident that Jesus was a historical character. A generation ago some scholars were denying his existence. They were impressed with the fact that interest in the earthly life of Jesus arose at a relatively late date in the history of Christianity, and they concluded that the movement started with a theology of a divine Christ and moved toward a history of a fictitious Jesus. They bolstered their case by citing the use of miracle stories in telling the life of Jesus and the parallels with the Hellenistic hero cults.[17] Scholars today, however, are not convinced that the existence of these parallels points to the nonexistence of Jesus. In its earliest period Christianity seems to have been a faith that was oriented to the future coming of the Messiah—the one who is expected, at his coming, to bring history to a close. In view of the belief in that future event, there seems to be no adequate way to explain the invention of stories about a historical figure called Jesus. That is, if there had been no Jesus and if Christians had been living in the expectation of the coming of the Messiah, why would they have originated stories about a figure of the past whom they called Jesus?

Moreover, there are signs that the existence of Jesus as a human being was not an asset to early Christian preaching. The stories about his execution at the hands of Jewish and Roman leaders was probably a stumbling block to some Jewish and Hellenistic people who might otherwise have put credence in other aspects of the Christian proclamation. One may reasonably ask why Christians would invent problems for themselves and their message.

In addition, Christian belief in the historicity of Jesus may be found in the earliest strands of the tradition. The earliest Christian writer, Paul, assumed that Jesus was a historical reality and that he was a descendant of David.[18] Paul knew of some historical events, such as the last supper and the crucifixion, but he cautioned against an overemphasis on a human Jesus.[19] Belief in the resurrection of Jesus was present at the point of origin of the Christian movement, and what those Christians believed in was the resurrection of a human being who had been mortal, who had died, and who had been buried.[20] Their faith indicates that belief in the humanity of Jesus was to be found in the very earliest days of the Christian movement; it was not a late fiction.

We can also be confident that Jesus was a Palestinian Jew of the first half of the first century. Our documents claim that he was a Jew who had some

[17] See e.g., Arthur C. H. Drews, *The Christ Myth,* trans. by C. D. Burns (London: T. F. Unwin, 1910).
[18] Rom 1:3.
[19] See 1 Cor 2:2; 11:23–26; Gal 3:1; Phil 2:8; and 2 Cor 5:16.
[20] See 1 Cor 15:8.

connection with Galilee and Jerusalem, that he had a family, including a brother who survived him, and that he was executed under the Roman governor Pontius Pilate. In addition to these fundamental points, the written material tells of his birth at the time of the Emperor Augustus (and perhaps of King Herod the Great), his ministry at the time of Tiberius, and about his contacts with one of the sons of Herod the Great, Herod Antipas. The precise accuracy of these details may be questioned, but their presence in the gospels creates a consistent picture of Jesus as a figure of the first half of the first century. The fundamental context that appears in Christian literature must not have been a matter of the authors' choices. The authors of the gospels, most of whom wrote in Greek and probably considered themselves to be citizens of the Hellenistic world, might not have elected to present Jesus as a Jew if they had had a choice. A more universal figure would have been more attractive. In their world a Jew was generally regarded as a narrow, legalistic, antisocial person with less than universal appeal. Neither is the location of Jesus in the recent past a product of invention. Christianity was disparaged in some quarters for its newness, and the movement might have fared better if Christians could have placed Jesus several centuries earlier in time. In this light, it is interesting to see that the author of the Gospel of John seems to be sensitive to this issue; he presented a Christ who was as old as creation and who could say, "Before Abraham was, I am." [21] The synoptic authors, however, made no effort to predate Jesus.

The overwhelming evidence indicates that Christians knew they were not dealing with a mythological figure who was eternal and nonhistorical. They pointed to a historical human being, whom they knew to have existed within a certain geographical space at a particular time. This general historical connection must be correct: Jesus was a Palestinian Jew of the first century.

But only so much can be said about Jesus in this preliminary way. Any additional information must be based on a thorough search of the available material. The process of searching for authentic material about the life and teachings of Jesus cannot be fully outlined in advance but will emerge as we proceed. In general, however, it is a process of working backward from the gospels to Jesus. We will start, in Chapter 6, with an investigation of the most relevant material available, the gospels. It will be necessary to assemble information about the circumstances under which they were written, and we will need to look at the literary makeup and ideological perspective of the evangelists. In studying the gospels, it is essential to keep in mind the facts about the milieu in which they were written. Although the circumstances vary from gospel to gospel, it is true that almost all of them were written in Greek and after the first Christian generation. This means that they are likely to reflect a background that can be described as mid-

[21] John 8:58.

stream Hellenistic Christianity. It is midstream because the movement itself was significantly developed before the gospels were written. It is Hellenistic not only because the language of the gospels and presumably of the first readers was Greek, but also because the Christian movement was influenced by Hellenistic concepts and practices. Placing the gospels in time will help us shape the questions we ask and the inferences we draw, as we sift for evidence.

From the study of the gospels, we will, in Chapter 7, move back to the period that lies between them and Jesus—namely, the period in which oral traditions about Jesus were presumably in circulation. We will examine some of the consequences of the oral tradition, and, by working with what we know about those times and about the general tendencies in oral traditions, we will try to sort out the traditions that are most likely to be early and possibly authentic. In working with the oral traditions we must be sensitive to the fact that the Christian movement went through a significant cultural change during the period from 30–70. Although it is not possible to pinpoint the exact time at which the change took place, it is clear that the movement that started among Jews soon became a Hellenistic movement. The change certainly affected language, thought, and practice. This knowledge should guide the process by which we attempt to sort out the earliest oral traditions.

In Chapter 8 we come to the final and most difficult stage in the study of Jesus and the gospels. The study of oral traditions should leave us with a body of material that has some claim to authenticity—that is, it should be a body of material that may have originated with Jesus himself. But a possibility is not good enough; we prefer to have material that *probably* goes back to Jesus. How do we decide what Jesus probably did and said?

For one thing, we must employ the usual procedures for making historical judgments. Formally, we will ask questions and make inferences in the search for evidence. We should note that the historical argument, as it was discussed in Chapter 1, is an aid in arriving at conclusions, for the form of the argument reminds us that conclusions must have data and warrants and must be properly qualified.

In addition, there are certain criteria that seem to apply in the particular study at hand. Although criteria for deciding about probably authentic Jesus material have been widely discussed among NT scholars, and although several criteria have been proposed, the ones that seem best for our present state of knowledge have come out of the so-called Bultmannian school. Some were suggested by Bultmann and were developed by later scholars. Others have been recommended by later Bultmannians. The most systematic presentation may be found in the NT scholar Norman Perrin's *Rediscovering the Teaching of Jesus,* in which he offers three criteria.[22]

---

[22] See Norman Perrin, *Rediscovering the Teaching of Jesus* (New York: Harper, 1967).

Perrin's first criterion is dissimilarity; it means that "the earliest form of a saying we can reach may be regarded as authentic if it can be shown to be dissimilar to characteristic emphases both of ancient Judaism and of the early Church."[23] The assumption that lies behind this criterion is that if Jesus had *only* spoken things that were characteristic of the Judaism of his time, he would not have made the impact he did. So we must find some ways in which he departed from Judaism. But we must find ways in which his teaching differs from the early Christians, for we know that their tendency was to reflect their own thinking in their shaping of the figure of Jesus. Perrin is aware that the rigid application of this criterion is limited in scope and will not allow us to find all the authentic teaching of Jesus, but he maintains that it is a starting point and that we have no other choice. He says, "there simply is no other starting-point that takes seriously enough the radical view of the nature of the sources which the results of contemporary research are forcing upon us."[24]

Perrin's second criterion is coherence; it means that "material from the earliest strata of the tradition may be accepted as authentic if it can be shown to cohere with material established as authentic by means of the criterion of dissimilarity."[25] The third criterion, multiple attestation, means that material that, in different forms, is found in various places in the pre-gospel and gospel tradition may be regarded as authentic.

In *The New Testament: An Introduction,* published seven years later, Perrin listed a fourth criterion, which he says he had earlier assumed but had not stated explicitly.[26] It is the criterion of linguistic and environmental tests. It means that a Hebrew or an Aramaic aspect in a saying of Jesus will lend authenticity to it. Put another way, a saying that reflects an Aramaic linguistic background is more likely to come from Jesus than one that reflects a Greek background, simply because Jesus probably spoke Aramaic.

Perrin's criteria are not without their problems, some of which will be dealt with in Chapter 8. Their problems and their possibilities should, nevertheless, be borne in mind as we proceed now to work back from the gospels to the historical Jesus.

BIBLIOGRAPHY

Bartsch, H. W., ed. *Kerygma and Myth.* Trans. by R. H. Fuller. New York: Harper & Row, Publishers, 1961.

Bultmann, Rudolf. *Jesus Christ and Mythology.* New York: Charles Scribner's Sons, 1958.

[23] Ibid., p. 39.
[24] Ibid., p. 43.
[25] Ibid.
[26] Norman Perrin and Dennis C. Duling, *The New Testament: An Introduction,* 2nd ed. (New York: Harcourt, 1982), pp. 400–406. 1st ed., 1974.

Cadbury, Henry J. *The Peril of Modernizing Jesus*. Naperville, Ill.: Allenson, 1962.

Käsemann, Ernst. *Essays on New Testmanet Themes*. Trans. by W. J. Montague. Naperville, Ill.: Allenson, 1964.

Kee, Howard C. *Jesus in History*. 2nd ed. New York: Harcourt, Brace Jovanovich, 1977.

Perrin, Norman. *Rediscovering the Teaching of Jesus*. New York: Harper & Row, Publishers, 1967.

Robinson, James M. *A New Quest of the Historical Jesus*. London: Student Christian Movement Press, 1959.

Schweitzer, Albert. *The Quest of the Historical Jesus*. Trans. by W. Montgomery. New York: Macmillan Publishing Co., Inc., 1910.

The fundamental work on the historical Jesus is still Schweitzer's. His *Quest* is a critical review of the most significant biographies of Jesus written in German before 1906. All serious studies of Jesus since that time have been influenced by his work. Cadbury addresses the problem of the historian's perspective and the tendency to shape Jesus as if he were a modern person. The book edited by Bartsch contains a key essay by Bultmann on mythology and several discussions of Bultmann's views by other scholars. Bultmann's *Jesus Christ and Mythology* represents his own attempt to demythologize the gospels. After Bultmann, many scholars felt that it was no longer fruitful to pursue the study of the historical Jesus. Ernst Käsemann, however, maintained that there were still possibilities, and his book contains his 1953 lecture, which reinitiated critical studies of Jesus. Robinson's book is an American counterpart to Käsemann's lecture. Kee and Perrin give significant attention to methodology in the opening chapters of their books.

❖ 6 ❖

The Gospels

EVEN before the books called gospels were written, the term that designates them, *euangelion* in Greek, was familiar in Christian communities. It had been used in connection with the act of proclamation, and so it defined the content of Christian preaching. Only later did it come to signify a book, and the author of the Gospel of Mark seems to be the first to use the term in this capacity. He opens his book with: "The beginning of the gospel of Jesus Christ," and this was probably intended as a title. The superscription, "The Gospeal According to Mark," apparently was added later. Not all of the other evangelists used the term as Mark did. Matthew's opening is: "The book of the genealogy of Jesus Christ, the son of David, the son of Abraham." Luke has no precise title but probably thought of his document as "a narrative of the things which have been accomplished among us" (Luke 1:1). Several second-century gospels returned to Mark's model and used the term *euangelion* in their titles.

In any event, the designation *gospel* has become a convenient name to use for a particular collection of books and, hence, for a literary genre. It is a genre that is solely Christian. Technically, there are no non-Christian gospels, although there are some Hellenistic books that have significant similarities to the gospels. Gospels feature sayings of Jesus or narratives about him, and in many cases both. But in order to reflect the general use of the term in early Christian communities, we must define a gospel as a *formulation of the Christian message in terms of sayings or actions of Jesus.*[1] The definition calls attention to the twin concerns of the authors of the gospels: to proclaim the Christian message and to connect it with the life of Jesus. The evangelists are not to be thought of in the way that we think of modern

---

[1] There are, however, some second-century documents that are designated as gospels but that do not contain any stories or sayings of Jesus. Some of these documents will be treated in Chapter 11.

historical biographers. Their writing is motivated by their faith, which is, in some way, expressed in their writing. Thus, Jesus is not presented in the gospels as the human subject of a biography but as the object of Christian faith.

So far as is known, the practice of writing gospels began with the so-called Synoptic Gospels, and it continued on through the second century. During those years a large number of gospels was produced, some of which will be examined in this chapter. By the end of the second century, the process of canonization was working toward the acceptance of only four of the gospels—the three Synoptics plus John—and the elimination of all the rest. Those that were not accepted are called apocryphal gospels. Clearly, the four canonical gospels are the best known, but there are several apocryphal gospels that have survived and many others that have been recently rediscovered; it will be helpful to look at them as examples of various versions of the Christian proclamation. The procedure in this chapter will be largely a chronological one, we will look first at the Synoptic Gospels, then at John, and finally at a few of the apocryphal gospels.

It is necessary, first, however, to connect the work of this chapter with those that follow. So far as we can tell, there is a gap of several decades between the time of Jesus and the time of the first extant gospel. It is probable that the sayings and stories about Jesus were circulating in oral form during those years and that the first written account about Jesus was compiled from the traditions that had developed during those decades. In Chapter 7 we will investigate this oral period in some depth, but the probable relationship between it and the written gospels should be kept in mind as we proceed. The connection means that the writers of gospels drew, directly or indirectly, on oral traditions for their source material. In drawing on them, the writers would, of course, select some things and reject others; they would organize their material in terms of some kind of principle; and they might find it necessary, on some occasions, to offer explanatory comments. These acts of selection, organization, and explanation are usually thought of as redactional, or editorial, tasks. So, the emphasis in our study will be on such tasks; this kind of study is a form of *redaction criticism*. Because one of our interests is to work back as closely as possible toward the historical Jesus, it is appropriate that we start with the only materials we actually have, the gospels, and begin by identifying the work that the authors of these documents probably performed. That is the task of this chapter. Chapter 7 will move backward in time to the oral period, and Chapter 8 still farther back to the historical Jesus.

THE SYNOPTIC PROBLEM

The Gospels of Matthew, Mark, and Luke are called synoptic because they present an approach to Jesus that is similar in many basic respects and because they share a great deal of material. The similarities and the differences among them have attracted the attention of scholars from the earliest days. Most scholars have felt that the similarities deserved some explanation and that they could not be accounted for solely by dependence on oral traditions. The facts of similarity and difference have forced scholars to the conclusion that there is a relationship of some sort among the three. The problem of determining just what that relationship was is called the synoptic problem.

It is necessary to have a clear impression of both the similarities and the differences among the three gospels. Although some of the important facts may be discovered by the casual reader, many of the more subtle aspects of similarity and difference emerge only after several close readings, in which the reader has copies of each of the Synoptic Gospels before him or her and makes paragraph-by-paragraph, line-by-line, and word-by-word comparisons. The most helpful tool for this kind of study is a synopsis, or harmony, in which the text of the three gospels is placed in parallel columns and comparable paragraphs are placed side by side. Reliable observations about the synoptic phenomena must, of course, be based on the Greek text. The student who is able to use Greek will be in the best position to see the data, but it is possible to observe most of the phenomena with a synopsis in English translation.[2]

The Synoptic Gospels may be compared in regard to (1) compositional structure, (2) contents, (3) sequence of material, and (4) verbal agreement. In all four areas there are striking similarities and significant differences.

There is a general similarity in the compositional structure—that is, in the basic outline and in the order of large blocks of material. The table on page 150 shows the similarities and differences in the compositional structure of Matthew, Mark, and Luke.

We must not suppose that within each of the major blocks the individual narratives or teachings are given in the same words or in the same order. Nor should we imagine that the stories are always the same. In the case of the birth and resurrection narratives in Matthew and Luke (I and VII), for example, there is significant variation. Moreover, a story or a saying sometimes appears in a particular section of one gospel and in an entirely different section of another. Matthew has several extended discourses that are set in Galilee (III) and in Jerusalem (V). Luke has corresponding discourses, often with fewer sayings and located at different points in his gospel. He also has a large body of teaching material in Part IV, which forms the great central section of his gospel. Many of the sayings in Luke's central section are also present in one or another of Matthew's main discourses. But there is agreement on the basic outline and on the geographical setting of the large blocks of material. There is agreement that John the Baptist appeared on the scene somewhat in advance of Jesus, that Jesus' ministry began in

---

[2] See the bibliography at the end of the chapter for one suggestion.

MATTHEW	MARK	LUKE
I. Birth narratives and genealogy, 1–2		Birth narratives, 1–2
II. Narratives on John the Baptist, the baptism and the temptation of Jesus, 3:1–4:11	Narratives on John the Baptist, the baptism and the temptation of Jesus, 1:1–13	Narratives on John the Baptist, the baptism, the genealogy, and the temptation of Jesus, 3:1–4:13
III. Jesus in and around Galilee, 4:12–18:35	Jesus in and around Galilee, 1:14–9:50	Jesus in and around Galilee, 4:14–9:50
IV. The trip to Jerusalem, 19–20	The trip to Jerusalem, 10	The trip to Jerusalem, 9:51–19:27
V. Jesus in Jerusalem, 21–25	Jesus in Jerusalem, 11–13	Jesus in Jerusalem, 19:28–21:38
VI. The last supper, the trial, and the death of Jesus, 26–27	The last supper, the trial, and the death of Jesus, 14–15	The last supper, the trial, and the death of Jesus, 22–23
VII. Resurrection narratives, 28	Resurrection narratives, 16	Resurrection narratives, 24

Galilee, that he went to Jerusalem, and that the climactic events that brought about his death occurred in Jerusalem. We should not overlook an important distinction, however: Matthew and Luke begin with birth narratives, albeit different ones, whereas Mark has no birth or infancy stories and begins by introducing John the Baptist.

In terms of contents there is a large area of agreement among the three gospels. There is agreement in content when any two gospels, or all three gospels, have substantially the same saying or narrative. In assessing the amount of agreement in content, it is best to think in terms of small literary units called pericopes. A pericope may be a narrative (the baptism of Jesus in Matt 3:13–17, Mark 1:9–11, and Luke 3:21–22) or some form of teaching on a certain topic (the parable of the sower in Matt 13:1–9, Mark 4:1–9, and Luke 8:4–8). If we analyze each of the three gospels in terms of these literary units, we find that Matthew has a total of 223; Mark, 127; and Luke, 236 pericopes.[3] The contents can be further analyzed by separating the pericopes into five classifications.

---

[3] The calculation of the number of pericopes is taken from Joseph B. Tyson and Thomas R. W. Longstaff, *Synoptic Abstract* (Wooster, Ohio: Biblical Research Associates, 1978).

Class I. Pericopes in all three gospels. Some 86 pericopes appear in all three gospels. In this material the verbal agreements are very high in frequency, but occasionally one gospel differs from the other two and sometimes all three have different wordings.

Class II. Pericopes in Matthew and Mark. There are 16 pericopes in this class, but because Matthew and Mark also share the 86 units in Class I, these two gospels have a total of 102 pericopes in common. This amounts to about 80 percent of the pericopes in Mark and about 46 percent of the longer Matthew.

Class III. Pericopes in Mark and Luke. Only three pericopes are found in Class III, but Mark and Luke also share the 86 pericopes in Class I. The total agreement between these two gospels amounts to about 70 per cent of Mark and 38 per cent of Luke.

Class IV. Pericopes in Matthew and Luke. Some 50 pericopes, mostly teachings of Jesus, belong in this class. The total agreement between Matthew and Luke amounts to about 61 per cent of Matthew and 58 per cent of Luke.

Class V. Pericopes in only one gospel. Each gospel has some pericopes that are not found in either of the other two. Mark has only four. Matthew has about 40, including the stories of the birth of Jesus, the resurrection appearances, and many of Jesus' teachings. About 18 per cent of Matthew's pericopes are unique to that gospel. Luke has 61 pericopes that are not found in either Matthew or Mark, constituting about 26 per cent of the pericopes in Luke. They include materials on the Lukan infancy narratives, the resurrection appearances, and many of Luke's parables.[4]

For a number of reasons, the proportional amount of agreement in terms of the numbers of pericopes cannot give us a totally accurate picture of agreement in content. For one thing, pericopes are of unequal length, and sometimes they vary considerably in wording. But such comparisons, when taken together with studies of structure, sequence, and wording, afford us some valid impressions.

Not only do the synoptic writers use a good deal of the same material, they also have much of it in the same sequence. The arrangement of the individual pericopes is often exactly the same. This phenomenon is particularly important for the synoptic problem, because a substantial agreement in sequence is an almost certain sign of literary relationship. The similarity in content that we have just examined is not, by itself, proof of a direct

[4] The astute reader may notice that the figures do not quite add up. The reason for this is that there are several pericopes in each gospel that have partial or overlapping parallels in the others. These are not included in the numerations given here.

literary relationship. It is possible that all three writers were familiar with a number of stories and sayings of Jesus that had previously circulated. So it is only to be expected that they would coincide in the use of many of them. But familiarity with stories and sayings would not necessarily produce such a high degree of similarity in the sequence of the material. When we find two or more chronologically unrelated pericopes that are parallel in content and in the same order in different gospels, the conviction that there was some form of literary relationship among them is strongly suggested. The fact is that we find a large number of such cases in each pair of gospels. For example, in the span between Mark 13:1–16:8, there are 38 pericopes, 34 of which appear also in Matthew in the same sequence (see Matt 24:1– 27:61). Moreover, we find some sections of material in which all three gospels agree exactly on the sequence of pericopes.

Finally, we come to the matter of wording and can state simply that there is a substantial amount of verbal agreement among the Synoptic Gospels. The recognition of verbal agreements in comparable pericopes adds substantially to our conviction of a literary relationship among the Synoptic Gospels. Although two authors can independently agree on the use of certain materials, it is seldom that they agree to any great extent on the wording of the stories and sayings they use. But such close verbal agreement is precisely what we find in the Synoptic Gospels, agreement often extending to the common use of words, grammatical forms, and even the order of words. In a few places, there is almost complete verbatim agreement. For example, Mark 14:26 is equivalent to Matt 26:30, and Matt 6:24 is identical to Luke 16:13, except for one word out of the 28-word passage. Other pericopes with high amounts of verbal agreement are Matt 12:43–45 and Luke 11:24–26, Matt 11:20–24 and Luke 10:13–15, and Matt 28:32–36 and Mark 13:28–32.

Of course, not all passages exhibit verbal agreements of such a high order, and it is necessary to calculate the average amount of agreement between each pair of gospels. Clearly, Matthew and Mark show the closest verbal agreement. In pericopes that appear in both gospels, the rate of verbal agreement is about 50 per cent—that is, half the words are the same in the two gospels. Between Mark and Luke and between Matthew and Luke the rate is about 37 per cent.[5]

All of these comparisons—of compositional structure, content, sequence, and wording—lead to the conclusion that there is a definite relationship, probably a literary one, among the three gospels. It is extremely doubtful that the oral tradition could have provided a basis for these kinds of agreements. One of these gospels must have been written first and must have been a source for one or both of the others. But which came first, and who

---

[5] Calculations based on Tyson and Longstaff, op. cit.

copied whom? These are questions for which no totally convincing answers have yet been given.

Nineteenth-century scholarship did, however, produce a theory of synoptic literary relationships that is still held by most biblical scholars. Fundamental to the theory is the idea that Mark was the earliest of the three gospels. Some early nineteenth-century scholars had imagined a lost source from which all three writers had copied. It was frequently assumed that Mark had copied this document most faithfully, so it was called *Ur-Markus*—that is, a primitive Mark. By the end of the nineteenth century many scholars began to feel that the similarity between the hypothetical Ur-Markus and canonical Mark was so great that it was no longer necessary to speak of a hypothetical document, and they began to identify the two. Thus, to them, it seemed best to say simply that Matthew and Luke each had a copy of canonical Mark, which they independently used as a source for their longer gospels. So, the priority of Mark became one cornerstone in the solution to the synoptic problem.

In 1924 the English NT scholar B. H. Streeter[6] cited five basic reasons for accepting the priority of Mark. (1) Matthew reproduced 90 per cent of the subject matter of Mark, and Luke more than half of it, both in language nearly identical with that of Mark. (2) For any average section of common material, the majority of Mark's words are found also in Matthew or Luke, or both. (3) The relative order of Mark's material is preserved by one or both of the others. Although one or the other may rearrange some of the narratives, they almost never agree in their rearrangement. (4) Mark's language appears more primitive than that of either of the other two. (5) The distribution of material in Matthew and Luke indicates that each had Mark before him and was faced with the problem of combining Mark with material from other sources.

The priority of Mark and its use by Matthew and Luke, working independently, would explain the presence of similar material in all three gospels, in Mark and Matthew, and in Mark and Luke (Classes I, II, and III). Unique material in Mark, consisting of four pericopes, is simply material that neither Matthew nor Luke chose to use. The more extensive unique material in Matthew and Luke could be regarded as having its source either in oral traditions or in private documents used by these evangelists. In other words, pericopes in Class V cause no serious problems at this point. A problem remains, however, for comparable material in Matthew and Luke (Class IV pericopes). This material cannot be explained solely by the thesis of Markan priority. Here we have a significant amount of material in Matthew and Luke that could not have been taken from Mark because it does not appear there. Because, according to the theory, Matthew and Luke

[6] B. H. Streeter, *The Four Gospels* (London: Macmillan & Co., 1924), pp. 151–152.

worked independently of one another and neither could have copied the material from the other, an additional source must be assumed for these 50 pericopes. To explain this phenomenon, scholars assumed the existence of a hypothetical source that they called *Q,* from the German word *Quelle,* meaning *source*. This document, probably unknown to Mark, consisted mainly of teaching material and lacked the stories of Jesus' birth, death, and resurrection. The existence of Q is the other cornerstone in this solution to the synoptic problem.

Thus we have the so-called two-document hypothesis. The two documents intended are Mark and Q, which are seen to be the major sources for both Matthew and Luke. In addition, of course, it is necessary to suppose some sources behind the unique material in Matthew and Luke, but these need not be considered written documents. Figure 16 explains these relationships graphically. Here, M stands for the source of material that is found only in Matthew, and L stands for the source of material that is unique to Luke.

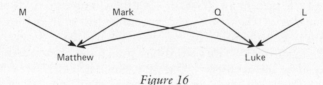

Figure 16

Although most scholars today adopt the two-document solution to the synoptic problem, it is not without its difficulties. For one thing, the dependence of the theory on a hypothetical document, Q, is something of an embarrassment, and its existence as a single document has frequently been questioned. A theory that does not depend on hypothetical sources would surely be stronger.

Moreover, the arguments for the priority of Mark, as presented by Streeter and others, are subject to question. It is not correct to say, as Streeter does in his first argument, that "Matthew reproduces 90% of the subject matter of Mark."[7] unless you already know that Mark came first. The fact that the three gospels have similar material does not in itself determine which of the three is the earliest. Streeter's second argument says that "in any average section, which occurs in the three Gospels, the majority of the actual words used by Mark are reproduced by Matthew and Luke, either alternately or both together."[8] In fact, however, there are places where the two agree with each other but disagree with Mark, and this in sections

[7] Ibid., p. 151.
[8] Ibid.

where they are allegedly using Mark. It is to be expected that two authors who use the same source will alter a word or two here and there, but it is surprising when they both make precisely the same change. Streeter's third argument on order can cut both ways. If the basic sequence is the same in two or more documents, we can assume that one has been copied. But the fact of agreement in respect to order does not in itself tell us which is the earliest of the three documents. In these three arguments, Streeter has presupposed the conclusion he intended to support, underestimated the problems with his thesis, and used a reversible argument.

Streeter's fourth argument suggests that Mark's language and grammatical usage are more primitive than those of the other two. Mark used some phrases that might have caused offense, his grammatical style is rough, and he used several Aramaic words. The Aramaic words may be a sign of an early date because the original language of the Christian oral tradition was probably Aramaic. The earliest gospel writer would, it seems, be in closer contact with oral traditions in Aramaic than would the later ones. But is a rough grammatical style necessarily an indication of primitiveness? Besides, some scholars disagree with Streeter's evaluation of Mark's grammatical style. The NT scholar William R. Farmer, for example, feels that Mark committed no more grammatical errors than did the other two evangelists. He used some Latin expressions in writing Greek, and he included some Aramaic terms, but he almost always translated them.[9]

Streeter's fifth argument states that the distribution of material in Matthew and Luke indicates that they combined Mark with other sources. In describing how they did it, Streeter says:

> Matthew's solution was to make Mark's story the framework into which non-Marcan material is fitted, on the principle of joining like to like. Luke follows the simpler method of giving Marcan and non-Marcan material in alternate blocks; except in the Passion story, where, from the nature of the case, some interweaving of sources was inevitable.[10]

Once again, we find the conclusion presupposed in the argument, for we cannot speak of Markan and non-Markan material in this way, unless we already know that Matthew and Luke used Mark.

These and other weaknesses in the two-document hypothesis have led a few scholars to reopen the question of synoptic relationships. Most notable among them is Farmer, who has proposed consideration of a theory first formulated by the eighteenth-century scholar Johann J. Griesbach.[11] This hypothesis, as Farmer explains it, maintains that Matthew was the earliest gospel, that Luke used Matthew as a source and that Mark used both Mat-

[9] William R. Farmer, *The Synoptic Problem* (New York: Macmillan, 1964), pp. 159–176.
[10] Streeter op. cit., p. 152.
[11] Farmer, op. cit.

thew and Luke. The relationships of the gospels in the Griesbach hypothesis are shown graphically in Figure 17.

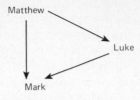

Figure 17

The Griesbach hypothesis explains the agreements between Matthew and Luke by making the simple suggestion that Luke used Matthew as a source. One should remember that these two gospels share a total of some 136 pericopes. Agreements between Mark and Matthew, and Mark and Luke are similarly explained: Mark drew on both of these gospels. The hypothesis also explains the three-way agreements: Luke took a large number of pericopes (136) from Matthew, and Mark adopted most of them (86) for his gospel. Matthew does have some unique material, but that simply means that neither Luke nor Mark used all that was available to them. Luke has some material that he did not get from Matthew, but he may have had access to oral traditions or to something like an L source. The same may be true of the material in Mark that did not come either from Matthew or Luke, but the amount of this material (four pericopes) is insignificant.

The Griesbach hypothesis has a number of advantages. It totally eliminates a need for the hypothetical Q source, which is essential for the two-document hypothesis. It maintains that Matthew and Luke share this material, because Luke copied it from Matthew. The large amount of agreement among the three occurs because Mark used both of the others. The agreements of Matthew and Luke against Mark are not problematical, for under this theory Mark is not bound to copy every word exactly.

Despite these advantages, the Griesbach hypothesis has not succeeded in overturning the general confidence of scholars in the two-document hypothesis. Those who oppose it call attention to the problems its proponents need to explain. One problematical area relates to Luke's use of Matthew. Matthew's gospel begins with a genealogy of Jesus, the story of Jesus' birth, the visit of the magi, the flight to Egypt, the story of the murder of innocent children by Herod, and Jesus' family's move to Nazareth (Matt 1–2). In the Griesbach hypothesis, Luke read these stories in Matthew, decided to begin his gospel in a similar way, rejected Matthew's stories almost altogether, and substituted others in his opening chapters. At the end of the two gospels, we meet a similar phenomenon. After Jesus' death and burial,

Matthew included reports about postresurrection appearances of Jesus, first to two women and later to the disciples (Matt 28:9–20). Luke, according to the Griesbach hypothesis, chose not to use these but did include a series of narratives in which Jesus appeared to his disciples (Luke 24:13–53). Of course, there is nothing that would compel Luke to use all of the material in Matthew, but here we find him deserting his major source at critical points. The explanation would be that Luke had sources for the birth and resurrection of Jesus that he preferred to Matthew.

A related problem has to do with the purpose of Mark. Mark has almost nothing new—that is, he has almost nothing that he did not find in either Matthew or Luke or both. So, if he had nothing new, why did he write? Perhaps he wrote to demonstrate how much agreement there is in the Christian message. If that were his purpose, it would explain his tendency to use material on which Matthew and Luke agreed. It may also explain his omission of material on which they disagreed, such as the birth and resurrection narratives. But Mark also omitted some fifty pericopes, mainly sayings of Jesus, on which Matthew and Luke agreed, so it is difficult to find a consistent principle of explanation.

Some scholars who find the Griesbach theory problematical agree with a judgment that Streeter had made in 1924. Streeter observed that, although Mark is shorter in total length, it is actually longer in a number of individual pericopes. His stories are expanded by the inclusion of relatively insignificant details that are not found in the others. Streeter was certain that Mark could not have copied Matthew, because "only a lunatic would leave out Matthew's account of the Infancy, the Sermon on the Mount, and practically all the parables, in order to get room for purely verbal expansion of what was retained."[12] Farmer, however, has drawn on the study of oral traditions to show that such verbal expansion is frequently added as stories circulate in a community. He maintains that the existence of the more detailed stories in Mark tends to confirm the theory that Mark used Matthew and Luke.

Although there are other hypotheses that attempt to solve the synoptic problem, these two—the two-document hypothesis and the Griesbach hypothesis—are the most successful. The two-document hypothesis represents the current majority view, and the Griesbach is the primary challenge to it. Clearly, work on the Synoptic Gospels will proceed on the basis of these theories, and so it is necessary to be familiar with them.

But it must be admitted that, for all its efforts, scholarship has not yet produced an unassailable solution to the synoptic problem. Because that is the case, it seems inappropriate to proceed with an examination of those gospels that relies on any one proposed solution. The current state of scholarship will be better represented if we read the gospels noting that the syn-

---

[12] Streeter, op. cit., p. 158.

optic problem is unresolved but not unresolvable. In doing so, the reader will inevitably notice similarities and differences that call for explanation. In those cases it will be helpful to examine the alternative explanations that are offered by the two leading hypotheses.

In the subsequent discussions of Matthew, Mark, and Luke, we will not assume a solution to the synoptic problem. This approach is somewhat different from the usual redaction-critical approach, which makes use of the two-document hypothesis and concentrates on the editorial changes that supposedly occurred as a writer worked with a source. For example, the writer of Matthew would be studied as he worked with Mark and Q. The approach here still asks questions of a redactional nature, but it focuses attention on the wholeness of each gospel and searches for such things as the development of themes and plots, recurring patterns, and characterizations. As occasion permits, we will also examine alternative explanations offered by the two-document and the Griesbach hypotheses, but our emphasis will be on the distinctive aspects in the composition of each of the Synoptic Gospels. We will take them up in the order in which they appear in the canon.

THE DATES OF THE SYNOPTIC GOSPELS

Before we proceed to an examination of each of the Synoptic Gospels, it is necessary to devote some preliminary attention to the question of their dates. It is obvious that their relative dates are determined by the solution to the synoptic problem. If we adopt the two-document solution to the synoptic problem, then Mark comes first, and Matthew and Luke are later and independent of one another. The hypothesis itself does not indicate which of the later two came first. In the case of the Griesbach hypothesis, the order of composition is Matthew, then Luke, and then Mark. But in neither case do we have any indication about the absolute dating of the gospels in time.

For both hypotheses, the year 70 is taken as the anchor date for the composition of the Synoptic Gospels. We know that this year was the turning point in the first Jewish war against Rome and that it was the date at which the Temple in Jerusalem was burned. We have already seen that this event had significant consequences for Jews in Palestine, and to some extent in the Diaspora. But it seems also to have had a profound effect on Christians. We know that between 30 and 70, many Christians thought of themselves as heirs of the promises to Israel. The line that marked them off from other Jews must have been a thin one, not so easy to define, and perhaps subject to change from time to time. In any event, we will find that one of the most significant problems that Christians faced in those decades was that of their own identity in relation to Jews; this was a problem both in Palestine and in the Diaspora. Christians could hardly avoid being affected by the events that affected Jews. So, to Jews and Christians alike, the events of the year 70 were world shaking.

It seems that these very events are alluded to in the Synoptic Gospels. The usual viewpoint is that the evangelists wrote with the events of 70 in mind—that they quoted words which they attributed to Jesus—using them to serve mainly as predictions after the fact. The passages on which this position is based are important enough to merit some attention.

In Matt 24, Mark 13, and Luke 21, we have a section called the synoptic apocalypse. Although the three gospels are by no means verbally identical in those passages, Mark and Matthew are very similar. At the opening of the chapter, Jesus' disciples have expressed words of admiration about the Temple, and Jesus announces: "There will not be left here one stone upon another, that will not be thrown down" (Matt 24:2 and Mark 13:2). Then Jesus speaks of battles, earthquakes, famines, and persecutions that are to precede the actual destruction; he admits that the definite time of these events is not known. In Matt 24:15 and Mark 13:14, he speaks of "the desolating sacrilege standing in the holy place" (in Mark: "the desolating sacrilege set up where it ought not to be") and says that "those who are in Judea" are to flee to the mountains when they see it. With the reference to the "desolating sacrilege," come the enigmatic words, "let the reader understand," usually printed in parentheses by modern translators. The fact that these words are placed in the context of words that Jesus spoke to his disciples is surprising, for the disciples should be addressed as hearers rather than readers. It seems almost certain that both evangelists have, for a moment, stepped out of their roles as invisible narrators in order to speak directly to their audiences. The words seem intended to attract the attention of the reader, to say that these words of Jesus are especially directed to him and call for some action on his part. It seems that Matt 24:15 and Mark 13:14 form the key to the entire synoptic apocalypse in their gospels. Most of the rest is standard apocalyptic language, probably drawn from Jewish writings. The reference to the "desolating sacrilege" is, as Matthew notes, taken from Daniel, where it probably referred to the altar to Zeus that had been set up by Antiochus IV in 167 BCE, an event that had precipitated the Maccabean revolt.[13] Perhaps Matthew and Mark wished to remind the readers of those events and to suggest that the destruction of the Temple should be seen as an analogue to the situation described in the book of Daniel and as a signal that the end has drawn near. When the reader sees these events taking place, he is to run to the mountains, as the Maccabean rebels did in 167 BCE.

In this connection, Eusebius, a Christian historian of the fourth century, refers to an oracle that had been given to the Jerusalem Christians before the Temple was destroyed, an oracle that warned them to flee from the city:

[13] See Dan 9:27, 11:31, and 12:11.

> The people of the church in Jerusalem were commanded by an oracle given
> by revelation before the war to those in the city who were worthy of it to
> depart and dwell in one of the cities of Peraea which they called Pella. To it
> those who believed on Christ migrated from Jerusalem, that when holy men
> had altogether deserted the royal capital of the Jews and the whole land of
> Judaea, the judgement of God might at last overtake them for all their crimes
> against the Christ and his Apostles, and all that generation of the wicked be
> utterly blotted out from among men.[14]

It is just possible that Matt 24:15 and Mark 13:14 reflect that same oracle,
although neither mentions the city of Pella specifically. Eusebius says that
the Christians received the oracle before the war broke out, but the synoptic
version would not call on people to leave Jerusalem until after the actual
beginning of the battles. In Matt 24:8 and Mark 13:8, the battles and earthquakes are called the "beginning of the birth-pangs." They are not to be
mistaken for the end itself, which appears to come after the destruction of
the Temple (Matt 24:29 and Mark 13:24).

The synoptic apocalypse as Luke reports it is substantially the same as
that in Matthew and Mark, but at some points it reveals more specific information, and in 21:20–24 Luke describes the Roman conquest of Jerusalem in some detail:

> But when you see Jerusalem surrounded by armies, then know that its deso-
> lation has come near. Then let those who are in Judea flee to the mountains,
> and let those who are inside the city depart, and let not those who are out in
> the country enter it; for these are days of vengeance, to fulfil all that is written.
> Alas for those who are with child and for those who give suck in those days!
> For great distress shall be upon the earth and wrath upon this people; they
> will fall by the edge of the sword, and be led captive among all nations; and
> Jerusalem will be trodden down by the Gentiles, until the times of the Gen-
> tiles are fulfilled (Luke 21:20–24).

Whether or not the words attributed to Jesus in the synoptic apocalypse
actually go back to the historical Jesus, we must reckon with the function
they seem intended to serve in the context of these gospels. The words to
the reader strongly suggest that the destruction of the Jerusalem Temple is
for them a crucial historical event that signals the approach of the end of
history. Moreover, the synoptic apocalypse seems to contain material that
comes out of an actual knowledge of the events that are being predicted.
Luke's knowledge appears to be more detailed than that of the other two,
but all of them seem to know something about the events surrounding the
year 70. Thus, the synoptic apocalypse indicates that the year 70 is the
anchor date for determining the time at which these three gospels were
written.

---

[14] Eusebius, *The Ecclesiastical History* III, 5:3, trans. by Kirsopp Lake, Loeb Classical Library
(Cambridge, Mass.: Harvard U.P., 1926).

Not all modern scholars interpret the synoptic apocalypse as an indication that the gospel writers had information about the events that took place in 70. The English NT scholar J. A. T. Robinson has, for example, questioned the basis for dating almost all of the NT documents, including the Synoptic Gospels. He is impressed with the absence of clear references to the destruction of the Temple as a past event, and he sees no compelling reason to interpret the apocalyptic material as a prediction after the fact. So he believes that all three were completed before 70; indeed, he pushes the process of composition back to the decade between 50–60 CE.[15]

Most modern scholars, however, are persuaded that the synoptic apocalypse could not have been written as it is without some awareness of the actual events that are being predicted. And so the year 70 is an anchor date for them. Using this anchor date, those who adhere to the two-document hypothesis date Mark close to 70, some before that, and some just after. Matthew comes second and may be dated in about 80. Luke, for a number of reasons, comes last and is usually dated about 80–85.

Proponents of the Griesbach hypothesis have not given much attention to the dating of the Synoptic Gospels, but Farmer, who takes Matthew's version of the synoptic apocalypse as the earliest and who interprets it as a prediction after the fact, has indicated that he believes that all three gospels were written after 70. Matthew, then, would be closest to the events in Jerusalem, then Luke, and finally Mark. He allows the possibility that Mark may have been written as late as 100–125.[16]

The question of the date of the Synoptic Gospels has, therefore, not been conclusively set. It depends on the solution to the synoptic problem and on the interpretation of the synoptic apocalypse. The present writer is inclined to agree with the majority of modern scholars in taking 70 as the anchor date, because the apocalyptic predictions seem to contain some knowledge that came out of the events of that year. In some form, of course, this material may have originated with Jesus or with a later Christian prophet. But, for the purpose of dating the gospels, the most significant question is whether the synoptic evangelists had knowledge of the actual events of the years around 70. Although we cannot be absolutely certain about such matters, it seems that they did, and so the weight of evidence points toward a date for the Synoptic Gospels in the period between 70–85. In the examination of individual gospels, the question of dates will come up again, but when it does, the relationship of dating to the synoptic problem and to the interpretation of the apocalyptic material should be borne in mind.

[15] See John A. T. Robinson, *Redating the New Testament* (Philadelphia: Westminster Press, 1976), pp. 86–117.
[16] Farmer, op. cit., p. 227.

THE GOSPEL OF MATTHEW

The earliest information about the authorship of the Gospel of Matthew comes from Papias (c. 60–130), the Christian bishop of Hierapolis in Asia Minor. Apparently Papias wrote some five volumes, entitled *Expositions on the Oracles of the Lord,* but the books have survived only in quotations by later authors. The fourth-century historian Eusebius tells us what Papias had to say about Matthew: "Matthew collected the oracles [*logia*] in the Hebrew language, and each interpreted them as best he could."[17] In speaking of oracles, Papias may have been thinking of a collection of OT texts or a collection of Jesus' sayings, or he may have meant the gospel that comes first in the NT canon. Although this gospel contains more than the words of Jesus (that is, oracles), Papias' interpreters in the second century must have assumed that it was this gospel he meant. Thus, the name Matthew was accepted as the name of the author of that book. It was assumed that Papias was affirming that Matthew was the earliest gospel and that the others interpreted, translated, or otherwise used it as a source. In addition, it was felt that the Matthew of whom Papias spoke was that disciple mentioned in Matt 9:9 and 10:3.[18] It is probable that the second-century statements about the authorship of this gospel all rest upon Papias and that the writers who quoted him selected one of several possible interpretations of the original statement. Even if theirs is the correct interpretation and Papias thought that a man named Matthew wrote this gospel, he tells us nothing further about him, and he does not clearly identify him as a disciple of Jesus. Although he speaks of a writing in Hebrew, all the earliest extant manuscripts of the Gospel of Matthew are in Greek, and the language bears little trace of being a translation. The authorship of the gospel must finally be regarded as undetermined.

We have already said that the date of Matthew, like that of Mark and Luke, is probably between 70 and 85. A more precise date depends partly on the solution to the synoptic problem. There are, however, indications that, whether he comes first or not, Matthew is writing after the year 70. In the parable of the great supper in Matt 22:1–14, we have a story that is similar to one in Luke 14:15–24. In the Lukan version a host invited some people to a banquet, and the guests declined. The host then issued a general invitation to the poor, maimed, and blind, and indeed compelled them to attend. In Matthew the host is a king who gave a wedding feast for his son. Some of the invited guests not only declined the invitation but murdered the king's servants. The king then sent troops to kill the murderers and burn their city; he then issued a general invitation, which was accepted by good and bad alike. One man who came was found to be inappropriately

---

[17] Eusebius, op. cit., III, 39:16.
[18] Matthew is also mentioned in Mark 3:18 and Luke 6:15.

dressed and was dismissed. The background for both forms of the story is probably the Jewish rejection of Jesus and the consequent Christian preaching to Gentiles. Matthew's form of the story is an allegory. The king is God, who gives a feast for his son Jesus. The Jews refuse to come, and they murder God's messengers, the prophets and apostles. God then sends troops, who defeat the Jews and burn their city. The Gentiles heed God's invitation, but not all are worthy, and some are cast out of the church.[19] If this interpretation is correct, the reference to the burning of the city must be to the destruction of Jerusalem. Matthew explains the destruction as God's punishment for the Jewish rejection of Jesus.

The *terminus a quo* for Matthew may be set in 70. Ignatius of Antioch, who wrote in about 115 CE, seems to have had an acquaintance with Matthew's birth narratives, and so 115 may be established as the *terminus ad quem*. Any attempt to narrow the limits rests largely on a solution to the synoptic problem, but most scholars date it about 80. Partly because of its apparent use by Ignatius, Matthew's location is usually understood to be Antioch, or more broadly, Syria.[20]

The placement of Matthew as the first of four gospels in the Christian canon must have been deliberate. The most casual reader should notice that there is in this gospel a deep interest in the OT and in Jewish practices. Those who shaped the canon must also have been aware of this and must have chosen Matthew as a kind of bridge between the OT and the NT, and consequently between Judaism and Christianity. Of course the author of this gospel is aware of the deep differences between Christianity and Judaism, and in fact this is one of his important themes. But he is also aware of the connections, and he is fond of pointing them out.

Like the other gospels, Matthew is a mixture of various traditions, some probably originating with Jesus but undergoing modification in the oral period. Matthew's task was to organize and edit the traditions he received, and so we should be able to understand the main thrust of his gospel by examining the ways in which he edited, or redacted, his materials. Of course we would be better able to do this if we were certain about the sources he used. Nevertheless, a close reading of this gospel can give us some impressions that can be tested. We will probably be on the right track if we concentrate our attention initially on the structure of the gospel, certain literary features, and editorial comments. With these things in mind, we may then turn to an examination of certain recurring themes that seem to govern the way Matthew has written the gospel.

The basic structure of Matthew has already been suggested in our dis-

[19] The man without a wedding garment represents a general Matthean point of view. Matthew believes that the church is now composed of both good and bad and that the separation of the two groups will not occur until the end comes. See, for example, Matt 13:47–50.
[20] See G. D. Kilpatrick, *The Origins of the Gospel According to St. Matthew* (Oxford: Oxford U.P., 1946).

cussion of the synoptic problem, but a more detailed examination is necessary now.

Birth Narratives and Genealogy, Matthew 1–2

The genealogy connects Jesus with a series of ancestors, including David and the Davidic kings of Judah, whose stories are found in the OT. Special attention is called to the structure of the genealogy, namely that it is made up of three parts, each part with fourteen generations (Matt 1:17). The birth narratives tell of the conception of Jesus by Mary and the Holy Spirit, an angelic announcement to Joseph in a dream about the birth of Jesus, Jesus' birth in Bethlehem, the visit of magi, the attempts of Herod the Great to find the child, the escape of the family to Egypt, Herod's massacre of innocent children, and the migration of Mary, Joseph, and Jesus to Galilee after Herod's death.

Narratives on John the Baptist, the Baptism and Temptation of Jesus, Matthew 3:1–4:11

John is introduced as preaching in the wilderness of Judea, and an account of his preaching is given. After Jesus is baptized in the Jordan River, he goes out to the wilderness, fasts for forty days, and is given three temptations, which he resists.

Jesus in and Around Galilee, Matthew 4:12–18:35

This long central section of Matthew's gospel contains several narratives about healings and exorcisms. There is an account of a feeding of five thousand people (14:13–21) and one of four thousand people (15:32–39); there is an account in which Jesus walks on water (14:22–33); and there is a narrative in which Jesus is transfigured—that is, his physical appearance is changed (17:1–9). In this section Jesus gathers his disciples and, on one occasion, sends them out on a mission to "the lost sheep of the house of Israel" (10:6). In one story Peter confesses his belief that Jesus is the Messiah (16:13–20), and on two occasions Jesus predicts his own death and resurrection (16:21–23 and 17:22–23). But most of the space in this section of Matthew is devoted to teaching material, which is largely arranged in topical fashion. The best known section is the Sermon on the Mount in chapters 5–7, in which we have a number of teachings about the Torah. In chapter 10, there are teachings about missions; in chapter 13, about the kingdom of God; and in chapter 18, about the regulation of community life.

The Trip to Jerusalem, Matthew 19–20

In 19:1 Matthew says that at this point Jesus left Galilee "and entered the region of Judea beyond the Jordan." This would be the eastern side of the river. In 20:17, however, Jesus is heading toward Jerusalem, and in 20:29 there is a mention of Jericho, which is on the western side of the river. The section is mostly a collection of teaching materials, but it concludes with a healing of a blind man. A third prediction of Jesus' death and resurrection is given in 20:17–19.

Jesus in Jerusalem, Matthew 21–25

Jesus' entry into Jerusalem is followed by his cleansing of the Temple and some healings in the Temple. The section includes a number of his teachings. Chapter 23 is a verbal attack by Jesus on Pharisees, and chapters 24–25 are apocalyptic.

The Last Supper, Trial, and Death of Jesus, Matthew 26–27

After the last supper, Jesus is arrested and taken before the Jewish Sanhedrin, where he is accused of blasphemy. The next morning he is taken before Pilate, the Roman governor, who, after initial resistance, agrees to have Jesus crucified. After Jesus dies, one Joseph of Arimathea takes the body for burial in a guarded tomb.

The Resurrection Narratives, Matthew 28

Two women discover the tomb of Jesus to be empty, and an angel announces Jesus' resurrection. The women then see Jesus briefly, and he repeats the angel's words about an appearance to the disciples in Galilee. In the final narrative Jesus appears to the disciples on a mountain in Galilee and gives them a commandment about missionary work among Gentiles (28:16–20).

Among the redactional features in Matthew—perhaps the most notable—is the repeated use of certain formulas. One such formula is frequently used to introduce quotations from the OT. The formula says that a certain thing occurred in order to fulfill what was spoken by the prophet, and then a quotation follows. Sometimes the name of the prophet is given. There are eleven such formulas in Matthew, all of them in editorial sections— that is , the formula is never placed on the lips of Jesus or any other character in the gospel. The words are the editor's comments on the story he is telling. Although Matthew has many OT quotations that are used without this formula, it seems to represent a deliberate effort to call the reader's attention to the connection between the life of Jesus and the OT prophets.

Another formula seems to be used to conclude major blocks of teaching material. Although the wording varies considerably, it occurs five times and each time states that Jesus has finished his teaching. It is striking that these formulas come at the end of five of the great discourses of Jesus: the Sermon on the Mount in chapters 5–7, the teachings about missions in chapter 10, the teachings about the kingdom of heaven in chapter 13, the teachings on the regulation of community life in chapter 18, and the apocalyptic discourse in chapters 24–25. Matthew may have intended the reader to be reminded of the five books of Torah. But this arrangement is not sufficiently clear to be obvious to the average reader, and we cannot be certain that he intended to suggest a parallel between Torah and the teachings of Jesus.

There is also a kind of formula that Matthew uses in general summaries of Jesus' activity. In Matt 4:23 we have: "And he went about all Galilee, teaching in their synagogues and preaching the gospel of the kingdom and healing every disease and every infirmity among the people." In 9:35 the summary goes: "And Jesus went about all the cities and villages, teaching in their synagogues and preaching the gospel of the kingdom, and healing every disease and every infirmity." The formula occurs one other time, in abbreviated form, in 13:54. One should note that Matthew, in this formula and elsewhere, speaks of "*their* synagogues." The language betrays his perspective: namely, that of a Christian who was not associated with a Jewish synagogue.

There are other literary features that could be noted, but attention to these few should be sufficient to give us some glimpses about the way this author worked. He seems interested in organizing his material so that there is a kind of topical arrangement, and he wants to give clues to the reader about that arrangement by telling him when a discourse is over and when a transition takes place. He was clearly interested in the connection between the life of Jesus and the words of the Hebrew prophets. And in his summaries he revealed his conception of the major activity of Jesus as preaching the gospel of the kingdom, teaching, and healing.

Although in content Matthew is presenting the words and deeds of Jesus, his mode of presentation indicates that his major theme is the relationship between Christianity and Judaism. The subject of Jesus' preaching is the news about the kingdom of heaven, an eschatological phenomenon into which only the righteous may enter. Jesus' function seems to be to proclaim the kingdom and, by teaching, to prepare people for its arrival. But Matthew is aware that Jesus initially proclaimed the news of the kingdom to Jews, as he preached in "their synagogues." When he sent his disciples out on a preaching campaign, he expressly confined their activities to Jews (Matt 10:6). About his own mission he says, "I was sent only to the lost sheep of the house of Israel" (15:24). Only under pressure does Jesus heal the daughter of a Canaanite woman (15:21–28) or the servant of a centurion (8:5–13). But Matthew stresses the Jewish rejection of Jesus that culminated in the trial before the Sanhedrin and the crucifixion. He seems to know that the political structures that prevailed in Jesus' day put judicial responsibility for Jesus' death in the hands of the Roman governor Pilate. But he shows Pilate to be extremely reluctant to impose the death penalty, and in one scene Pilate washes his hands, symbolically relieving himself of responsibility. That responsibility, according to Matthew, falls on the Jewish people, who shout in 27:25, "His blood be on us and on our children!" The Jewish rejection is contrasted with the confession of the Gentile centurion in 27:54: "Truly this was the son of God!" The final narrative in the gospel is one in which Jesus appears to his disciples in Galilee and says to them: "Go therefore and make disciples of all nations [Gentiles], baptizing them in the name of the Father and of the Son and of the Holy Spirit, teaching them to observe all that I have commanded you; and lo, I am with you always, to the close of the age" (28:19–20). The word translated "nations" is probably better translated "Gentiles" (the Greek permits either). It is a fitting conclusion to Matthew's Gospel. For Jesus and his disciples, the preaching mission was to Jews, but the Jews reject him and assume responsibility for his death. Now, the mission is to be to Gentiles.

But Matthew does not merely celebrate the separation between Christianity and Judaism. There is a high degree of poignancy in the realization that Matthew, more than the other canonical gospels, presents Jesus in OT and Jewish categories. In particular, the figure of Moses seems to have influenced the portrayal of Jesus. The birth of Jesus has affinities with the story of Moses: Herod's massacre of the children is reminiscent of the killing of the first-born Egyptians at the Passover; the flight to Egypt and the return recall the Egyptian period in Israel's history and the exodus under Moses' leadership. Several times Jesus teaches from a mountain, as Moses delivered the Torah from Mount Sinai, and the Sermon on the Mount includes Jesus' commentary on the Mosaic commandments. Matthew's presentation of the transfiguration seems explicitly intended to present Jesus as the new Moses.[21]

It is Moses' function as lawgiver that is most important in this regard, and in the Sermon on the Mount, Jesus is presented as lawgiver. In Matt 5–7, Jesus speaks of various Mosaic commandments and comments on them. The most important section is Matt 5:17–48, which opens with Jesus' declaration that he has come not to abolish the law but to fulfill it, and there is a condemnation of anyone who relaxes the commandments in the least. Then follows a series of six so-called antitheses. They are called antitheses because of the form in which each saying is cast. The form has four parts:

[21] See W. D. Davies, *The Sermon on the Mount* (Cambridge: Cambridge U.P., 1966), pp. 1–32.

1. "You have heard that it was said."
2. An ancient commandment.
3. "But I say to you."
4. A word of Jesus.

The apparent function of this form of statement is to contrast a word of Jesus with an ancient commandment. Three of the six antitheses include quotations from the ten commandments: You have heard that it was said, do not murder; but I say, do not be angry. You have heard, do not commit adultery; but I say, do not lust. You have heard, do not commit perjury; but I say, do not be insincere. If one should ask who it was who gave the ancient commandment, the answer would be Moses. So, apparently Matthew intended to contrast Jesus' word with that of Moses.

We have seen that the oral Torah developed in Judaism as learned teachers interpreted and commented on the written Torah. In one sense Jesus is doing here what the teachers of Torah had been doing for quite some time. One might paraphrase one of Matthew's antitheses so that Jesus says: "Moses said not to murder; I understand that to mean, do not be angry." But this paraphrase does not give full weight to the form of the antithesis. There is a contrast of some kind here. Something rests on the authority of Jesus himself. Matthew does not present Jesus as a follower of Moses nor as a Pharisaic interpreter of Torah. To Matthew, Jesus is the Messiah, and as Messiah he is here giving the authoritative interpretation of Torah. In this light his authority as lawgiver outranks that of Moses. Jesus as Messiah is the *new Moses* giving the *messianic Torah*.

But Jesus as Messiah has not come to abolish Torah but to fulfill it (Matt 5:17). That definition seems fundamental for Matthew. For him, the Torah, originally given by Moses, has been deepened and intensified by Jesus, its final interpreter. It prohibits anger, lust, and insincerity, as well as retaliation and hatred of one's enemies. The life demanded by the messianic Torah is usually designated as the higher righteousness, a degree of obedience that exceeds that of the Pharisees. It is in fact a demand for perfection (5:48).

Not only is the righteousness demanded by Jesus contrasted with that of the Pharisees, but the Pharisees themselves are condemned in no uncertain terms. The whole of chapter 23 is devoted to Jesus' attacks on them for their interpretations of Torah and for their hypocrisy. Matthew probably believed that it was Pharisees who had been the main opponents of Jesus and that it was they who had opposed his commandments and who had led the people to reject him. It is likely that Matthew's own Christian community had met opposition from Pharisees and that this fact colored his attitude. Whatever the reason, his hostility to Pharisees is clear.

Matthew's gospel is one of paradoxes. At the risk of sounding a bit too modern, we might say that Matthew had a love-hate relationship with Judaism. His love is seen in his interest in Moses and the prophets and in his belief in the eternality of Torah. His hate is seen in his attitude toward the

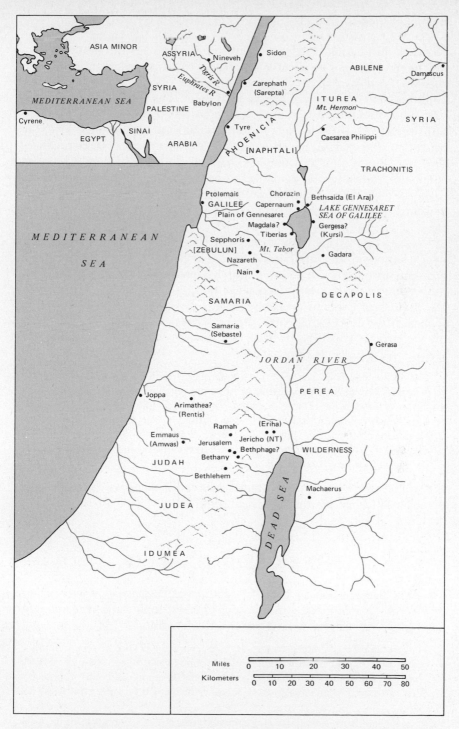

Figure 18   Palestine, the Synoptic Gospels. (Reprinted by permission of Thomas Nelson Publishers, from the book The Interpreter's Bible. *Copyright © 1949 by Thomas Nelson & Sons Publishers.)*

Pharisees, his placing of responsibility on the Jews for the death of Jesus, and for his emphasis on Gentile receptivity to Jesus' gospel. Most scholars take this paradoxical attitude to be characteristic of one who had been raised a Jew and had later accepted Jesus as Messiah. The Jewish background accounts for the author's deep interest in problems of Torah, the OT, Moses, and the meaning of Israel. His hostility to Judaism is accounted for by his belief that Jews had rejected the very one whom their scriptures predicted. This animosity is typical of one who has consciously turned away from the religion of his fellows and embraced something new. He cannot understand why his fellow Jews could refuse the new things that he sees so clearly indicated in the scriptures that he and they both acknowledge as authoritative.

What is true of the author must also be true of the congregation for which he wrote. His interests in writing must have been dictated by the problems encountered in his own church—problems of applying the Torah in the light of the higher righteousness that Jesus demanded. Matthew and his congregation should probably be regarded as Jews who had accepted Jesus as Messiah. But they must also have been committed to a mission to the Gentiles, as Jesus' last words in the gospel indicate. W. G. Kümmel, a German NT scholar, correctly states:

> The author not only lives in a Jewish-Christian tradition but also wishes to offer to his readers the message about the omnipotence of the risen Jesus, and salvation through baptism, and keeping of his commandments (28:17ff.) in a form which will reveal to them as Jewish Christians Jesus Christ as "the son of David, the son of Abraham" (1:1), whose "gospel of the kingdom will be preached throughout the whole world, as a testimony to all nations; and then the end will come" (24:14).[22]

We will see that some of the problems with which Matthew struggled come up again and again in other Christian writings.

THE GOSPEL OF MARK

The same Papias who had said that Matthew collected the sayings of Jesus in Hebrew also connected the Gospel of Mark with Peter. He claims to have gotten his material from a presbyter, who said:

> Mark became Peter's interpreter and wrote accurately all that he remembered, not, indeed, in order, of the things said or done by the Lord. For he had not heard the Lord, nor had he followed him, but later on, as I said, followed Peter, who used to give teaching as necessity demanded but not making, as it

---

[22] W. G. Kümmel, *Introduction to the New Testament*, trans. by A. J. Mattill (Nashville, Tenn.: Abingdon, 1966), p. 82.

The opening of the Gospel of Mark from the Lindisfarne Gospels, seventh century. (Courtesy *the British Library, London.*)

were, an arrangement of the Lord's oracles [*logia*], so that Mark did nothing wrong in thus writing down single points as he remembered them. For to one thing he gave attention, to leave out nothing of what he had heard and to make no false statements in them.[23]

[23] In Eusebius, op. cit., III, 39:15.

The quotation gives us some interesting information about Peter's preaching and about Mark's techniques, which will occupy our attention later. But Papias gives us no hard information about Mark; nor is it totally clear that he is describing the writing of the gospel we have. But the saying is consistent with other statements made by second-century writers, some of whom probably drew on it. Irenaeus, writing about 185, said that after the deaths of Peter and Paul, "Mark, the disciple and interpreter of Peter, also handed down to us in writing what Peter had preached."[24] The tradition that connects this gospel with a disciple of Peter is strong and consistent. But who is this Mark? The only person by this name mentioned in the NT is John Mark, who, according to Acts, accompanied Paul and Barnabas on the first missionary journey. But the statements of Papias and Irenaeus do not clearly mention this person, and there are no good reasons for drawing this conclusion. Marcus is a fairly common Roman name, and so we will have to be content with the identification of one, otherwise unknown, Mark.

If Irenaeus is right in saying that this gospel was written after the deaths of Peter and Paul, then the *terminus a quo* for it would be 62–64. The *terminus ad quem* would be the time of Papias—c. 130. We have previously seen that there are good reasons for dating Mark and the other Synoptic Gospels around the year 70. Some of those who adopt the two-document hypothesis as a solution to the synoptic problem date Mark between 66–70 because his version of the synoptic apocalypse is vague about the actual destruction of Jerusalem. They feel that he knows that the war has broken out but that he does not have the details to describe it, as does, for example, Luke. But the evidence is by no means clear, and the best that we can say is that Mark was probably written in around 70. Those who follow the Griesbach hypothesis and place Mark third in the order of composition date it much later, even in the second century.

The early traditions state that Mark was written in Italy, and most modern scholars locate it in Rome. The presence of certain Latin expressions, the tendency to explain Jewish customs, and the tendency to translate Aramaic terms probably means that Mark is writing for a Gentile audience in the western Mediterranean area. Although no conclusive evidence can be cited, we may say that Rome fits the requirements for Mark's location.

Not much can, therefore, be said about the circumstances in which the gospel was written. Authorship, date, and location are sharply debated, and no certain conclusions have been reached. We can, however, gain some insight into the thinking of the author by a close reading of his text.

As we have already observed, the basic structure of Mark is similar to that of Matthew and Luke, except at the beginning and the end. There is no birth narrative, no genealogy, and no narrative about a resurrection ap-

---

[24] Irenaeus, *Against Heresies* III, 1:1, trans. by E. R. Hardy, in *Early Christian Fathers,* ed. by Cyril C. Richardson (Philadelphia: Westminster Press, 1953).

pearance of Jesus. The basic structure and contents can be outlined in six major sections, which follow here.

Narratives on John the Baptist, the Baptism and Temptation of Jesus, Mark 1:1–13.

This section includes some of the same narratives as Matthew (and Luke), but the unit on John's preaching is much shorter. Mark also has nothing on the particulars about the temptations of Jesus.

Jesus in and Around Galilee, Mark 1:14–9:50

It is not possible to identify the exact location of all of Mark's geographical references. But he seems to use them to show that Jesus headquartered himself in Galilee but also traveled frequently "to the other side"—to locations on the eastern side of the sea of Galilee. The exorcism reported in Mark 5:1–20 occurs in Gerasa, and in the entire section from 6:45–9:1 or even 9:30, Jesus is outside Galilee—hence, presumably, in predominantly Gentile towns.

This long section includes healing stories, exorcisms, and a resuscitation, as well as teaching material. Mark announces the theme of Jesus' preaching right at the start, in 1:15: "The time is fulfilled, and the kingdom of God is at hand; repent, and believe in the gospel." Mark does not seem to group his material in a topical way, as Matthew does, but he has some blocks that appear to be made up of similar types of material. Two such blocks are the conflict stories in 2:1–3:6 and the parables in chapter 4.

Many scholars think that the confession of Peter in Mark 8:27–30 is a turning point in Mark's story. After that Jesus speaks more to the disciples than to the crowds, and he seems to be preparing them for his death. Two predictions of his death and resurrection occur in this section (8:31–33 and 9:30–32) and a third (10:32–34) in the section following. It should be observed that the anticipation of Jesus' death begins more and more to cast a dark shadow on Mark's narrative from the point of the confession of Peter on to the end of the gospel.

The Trip to Jerusalem, Mark 10

In 10:1 Mark calls specific attention to the end of Jesus' Galilean period: "And he left there and went to the region of Judea and beyond the Jordan." In Mark 10:32 Jesus is on the road to Jerusalem, and, in 10:46, he has arrived in Jericho. In this section Mark has concentrated on teaching materials, but there is a healing of a blind man in 10:46–52. The third prediction of Jesus' death and resurrection comes in 10:32–34.

Jesus in Jerusalem, Mark 11–13

Matthew and Mark are very close together in this section, except that Mark has only a trace of Jesus' attack on the Pharisees that appears in Matthew 23.

The Last Supper, Trial, and Death of Jesus, Mark 14–15

Matthew and Mark are very close together.

The Resurrection Narratives, Mark 16

Although some modern editions of Mark include more, the consensus among textual scholars is that there is no good evidence for including in Mark anything after 16:8. It is, of course, possible that Mark wrote more material and that it was later lost, but we cannot be certain about that. The material in 16:1–8 simply tells the story of the visit of three women to Jesus' tomb. Inside the tomb there is a young man who directs them to tell the disciples to go to Galilee, where they will see Jesus. But because of their fear, the women do not deliver the message. So there are no narratives about a post-resurrection appearance of Jesus. Although this is a strange, even abrupt, ending, it is possible to understand it as appropriate.

Some of Mark's literary habits can be seen in English translation. He seems to be fond of piling up phrases and joining them with the conjunction *and*. In a typical section, such as 1:16–28, for example, every major syntactical element begins with *and*. Moreover, Mark characteristically uses the adverb *immediately* to introduce a narrative. He also relies heavily on the historical present—that is, the use of a verb in the present tense to indicate past action. Unfortunately, many of these verbs have been translated in the past tense in English. These characteristics, taken together, present an almost breathless account, and they impress the reader with a sense of immediacy and urgency. Here is no leisurely narrative.

Mark also seems to be fond of including small details of fact. These generally add little to the substance of the narrative, but they add color, and they give the material a lifelike character. The paralytic who was brought to Jesus was carried "by four" persons (Mark 2:3). When a storm came up at sea, Jesus was asleep "in the stern, on the cushion" (4:38). Exorcized demons enter a herd of swine "numbering about two thousand" (5:13). Jesus sent out the disciples "two by two" (6:7). The disciples determine that it will take "two hundred denarii worth of bread" to feed the five thousand (6:37). In a trip across the sea, the disciples "had only one loaf with them in the boat" (8:14). Jesus was crucified at "the third hour" (15:25).

Because of the radically different place that is accorded to Mark in the two-document hypothesis and the Griesbach hypothesis, the understandings of Mark's compositional procedures also differ radically. For proponents of the two-document hypothesis, Mark is seen as basically drawing on the oral tradition. Some scholars think that there may have been some small collections, such as the conflict stories in 2:1–3:6, the parables in chapter 4, and the story of Jesus' trial and death in chapters 14–15, that had circulated in written form before Mark came along. But, on this hypothesis, Mark worked mainly with oral sources. For the Griesbach hypothesis, the sources for Mark are the two written documents, Matthew and Luke. His task was to conflate them—that is, to combine their accounts into a single text. The assessment of Mark's literary ability as well as the interpretation of his gospel will accordingly vary in these two fundamental approaches.

For these reasons it might seem that no discussion of themes in Mark could be engaged in except on the basis of one of the solutions to the synoptic problem. But the themes we will discuss here seem to be distinctive for Mark and integral to his gospel, whatever turns out to be the right way to conceive his compositional procedures. That is to say, if we attempt to read Mark without assuming a solution to the source problem, there are certain themes that will appear. Some understanding of those themes is necessary for appreciating Mark's contribution. We will look at four major themes: the Messianic secret, the misunderstanding of the disciples, martyrdom, and the significance of Galilee.

A German scholar, William Wrede, in 1901, was the first to call attention to the theme of the messianic secret and to the significant part it played in Mark's interpretation of the history of Jesus.[25] Mark seems to have believed that Jesus' Messiahship was not openly proclaimed until after the resurrection. Exorcised demons who proclaim Jesus to be the Messiah are commanded to be silent (Mark 1:23–25, 34; 3:11–12; 5:6, 7; and 9:20). Jesus explains that the purpose of his teaching in parables is to hide the truth from nonbelievers (4:12). The disciples are commanded to be silent about Jesus' Messiahship until after the resurrection (9:9). Wrede accounted for this phenomenon by suggesting that Mark was aware that Jesus was not in fact proclaimed to be Messiah during his lifetime. Mark felt that he was recognized as such but that Jesus himself suppressed any proclamation. Mark does not suggest why Jesus should have wanted to hide his identity; Mark simply assumes that whatever happened must have been intended.

A closely related theme in Mark is that of the misunderstanding of the disciples. As already suggested here, the confession of Peter in Mark 8:27–30 is something of a turning point. It was there that one disciple, probably speaking for the rest, recognized Jesus as Messiah. Peter's confession is met immediately by Jesus' command to silence: "And he charged them to tell no one about him" (8:30). Then Jesus predicts his death and resurrection,

---

[25] William Wrede, *The Messianic Secret,* trans. by J. C. G. Grieg (Cambridge: J. Clarke, 1971).

a prediction that Peter refuses to accept; Jesus then says to Peter, "Get behind me, Satan! For you are not on the side of God, but of men" (8:33). Although Peter has here recognized Jesus' Messiahship, he is blind to the necessity of his death and resurrection, and so he receives no commendation from Jesus, but, instead, very harsh words. It is significant that the association of disciples with Jesus began before their recognition of his identity and that, even when their recognition was expressed, it was treated as partial and possibly inadequate. Elsewhere Mark implies that the disciples have a wrong conception about the nature of Jesus. They do not understand a number of things he does and says: the stilling of the sea (4:41), the feeding of the five thousand (6:52), his attitude toward children (10:13–16), and the saying about the rich entering the kingdom (10:23). They are characteristically unable to understand parables (4:1–20 and 33–34). Above all, they do not understand the necessity of Jesus' coming suffering. Mark has Jesus speak of his death on three occasions. We have just looked at the first, in 8:31–33. In the second (9:30–32), Mark says that the disciples did not understand what Jesus said and were afraid to ask him about it. After the third (10:32–34), two of the disciples ask for special privileges in Jesus' kingdom, and they are corrected by Jesus (10:35–45). When we come to the scenes of Jesus' trial and crucifixion, the disciples are notably absent. The last we hear of them is the pitiful scene in which Peter denies any knowledge of Jesus. Thus, they are absent for the resurrection as well, and they do not receive the message to meet Jesus in Galilee.

It is difficult to know why Mark felt it necessary to emphasize the disciples' lack of understanding, unless he was trying to detract from their authority or to object to a point of view that had been identified with them. That point of view must have had something to do with an understanding of the meaning of Jesus' death. Some Christian preachers must have accepted the death of Jesus as simply an unfortunate historical fact and emphasized the resurrection as the moment of divine significance. But Mark not only emphasizes the inevitability of the death; he once refers to it as a ransom (Mark 10:45). His emphasis on the significance of Jesus' death is a creative theme, which reappears when Mark treats the theme of martyrdom. It is likely that Mark is intentionally pointing out something that he takes to be a deficiency on the part of the disciples—namely, their blindness to the necessity and redemptive significance of Jesus' suffering and death.

There are several indications in the gospel that Mark intends to speak to a situation in his own time that called for moral and physical strength on the part of Jesus' followers. Jesus is portrayed as an example to later martyrs, and the extensive attention that is given to the death of Jesus testifies to Mark's intention to speak about martyrdom. From the narrative of Peter's confession on to the crucifixion, well over half the book, the death of Jesus is discussed. It is Jesus' death and resurrection that are fundamental for this gospel, which, with some exaggeration, Martin Kähler, a nineteenth-century

German theologian, once called a passion narrative with a long introduction.[26] The emphasis on the divine necessity of Jesus' death carries with it the corollary that his followers must be prepared to meet the same fate, and Jesus' teaching makes this explicit. In Mark 8:34, Jesus defines a disciple as one who, like him, is crucified, and he condemns those who are ashamed of him. In 10:35–45, two disciples, James and John, are vying for the chief places in the kingdom, and Jesus says that it is necessary for them to "drink the cup" that he drinks—namely, the cup of martyrdom. Specific statements are included in the apocalyptic chapter (Mark 13): betrayals, arrests, trials, and persecutions for the disciples. Peter's greatest failing is his denial under stress, a particularly despicable act in times of persecution. The emphasis on martyrdom would admirably fit the situation of Christians in Rome in the sixties and later. Nero had persecuted Christians there in the early sixties, and it was then that Peter and Paul were probably executed. No Christian in Rome could feel secure during Nero's reign, and probably not for decades afterward.

When we come to the discussion of oral traditions, it will be observed that separate sayings and narratives are normally preserved without geographical notes. People who transmitted stories in oral form usually had little interest in preserving information about where Jesus was when he said or did a certain thing. Geographical notes are, however, relevant and usually necessary in a continuous narrative, and so it is usually assumed that the gospel writers added their own geographical notes, which then formed part of the structure of the gospel. Mark and Matthew turn out to be reasonably close together in respect to the geographical structure, so it is likely that one had adopted the basic structure of the other. Because we are trying to operate without a solution to the synoptic problem, we cannot say which gospel writer first used the geographical structure that is common to both. Thus, what will be observed in this regard might apply as well to Matthew as to Mark. We are treating the matter of a geographically oriented theme here, because many scholars have taken note of it in connection with Mark and because its appropriateness for Matthew is untested.

The striking geographical fact is that Mark organizes his material about two locations: Galilee and Jerusalem. Although other locations are specified, these are the two headquarters. We may generally say that the ministry of Jesus takes place in Galilee and that his death occurs in Jerusalem. Although Mark tells of only one trip that Jesus made to Jerusalem, he could have described more. He includes some indications that Jesus was familiar with the city and that he had acquaintances in nearby Bethany. These minor traces show that Mark could have presented several trips to Jerusalem, as

---

[26] Martin Kähler, *The So-Called Historical Jesus and the Historical Biblical Christ,* trans. by Carl E. Braaten (Philadelphia: Fortress Press, 1964), p. 80, note 11. Kähler actually described all the gospels in this way.

the author of the Gospel of John does. But for some reason Mark describes no other trips and places the bulk of Jesus' activity and teaching in Galilee.

In so organizing his material, Mark creates diametrically opposed images for the two locations: Galilee is the place where Jesus announces the kingdom and performs his mighty works; Jerusalem is the place of doom. The initial proclamation of the kingdom by Jesus occurs in Galilee. It is only in Galilee that exorcism takes place, and Mark understands an exorcism as the clearest demonstration of Jesus' eschatological work, for it manifests his victory over Satan (Mark 3:23–27). The eschatological significance of Galilee is further enhanced by the fact that, although Jesus' death takes place in Jerusalem, the gospel ends by pointing forward to the appearance of the risen Lord in Galilee. Jerusalem, by contrast, is the place where the great tragedy occurred: Jesus' betrayal, denial, trials, and death. The character of doom is unrelieved and, indeed, is reinforced by the predictions in chapter 13 about its abandonment and destruction. As a result, the reader comes away from Mark with a very positive impression of Galilee and a very negative one of Jerusalem.

Mark may be consciously re-evaluating the importance of the two locations. The status of Jerusalem in Jewish thought is clear, and there is evidence that some Christians shared the Jewish thinking about Jerusalem. The book of Acts, for example, paints a picture of an early Christian period in which the city had served as the seat of an apostolic group that had tremendous prestige. In fact, in Acts, Jerusalem is the original headquarters of the Christian movement.

In some Jewish writings, Galilee is looked down on, and it is frequently called "Galilee of the Gentiles." It was a place of a mixed population of Jews and Gentiles, and so it should not be unexpected that some Jewish purists would regard it as second rate. It was not far enough away from Judea to have developed a high degree of independence, and yet it was too far away to allow daily social intercourse with the Jews in Jerusalem.

Perhaps because Galilee could symbolize for Mark a degree of freedom from Judaism and a degree of openness to Gentiles, he reversed their status. He felt that God had rejected Jerusalem and chosen Galilee as the place of present and future revelation. Willi Marxsen, a contemporary German NT scholar, believes that Mark may actually be calling Christians to assemble in Galilee to await the appearance of Jesus in the conviction that he is hidden there now and is soon to be revealed.[27]

Can these themes be tied together? They all point to the death of Jesus as Mark's dominating concern. It is the death that is the secret to Jesus' Messiahship. In all the varieties of Jewish messianic expectation we have looked at, there is none that speaks of a Messiah who accomplishes the messianic tasks by suffering and dying. For Mark, however, it is precisely in

[27] Willi Marxsen, *Mark the Evangelist,* trans. by James Boyce, et al. Nashville, Tenn.: Abingdon, 1969). See also Ernst Lohmeyer, *Galiläa und Jerusalem* (Göttingen: Vandenhoeck and Ruprecht, 1936).

the suffering death of Jesus that his Messiahship can be recognized. And it is just this that the disciples do not recognize. Although Peter and probably the others are able to perceive that Jesus is Messiah, they are unable to see the necessity of his death. Therefore, they are not able to receive news of his resurrection. Their only hope is to "drink the cup" of martyrdom, that in their own deaths, the true character of Jesus will be revealed. Although Jesus' death is a ransom for many, no one is led to rejoice in it. The fact that it occurred in Jerusalem constitutes doom for the city, while the place of his expected resurrection appearance is the lowly esteemed Galilee.

Finally, the apparent awkwardness of the ending of Mark at 16:8 may be explained. There are no appearances to the disciples, because the disciples have disappeared from the narrative. Mark's rejection of them is total. But the appearance of the resurrected Messiah in Galilee is still to come, as Jesus had predicted it in 14:28, and as the young man at the tomb had said in 16:7. Perhaps Mark expected this to occur within his own lifetime, because in 9:1 he had recorded Jesus as saying, "Truly, I say to you, there are some standing here who will not taste death before they see that the kingdom of God has come with power."

THE GOSPEL OF LUKE

The Gospel of Luke and the book of Acts were almost certainly written by the same author. On this point modern scholarship and the earliest Christian testimonies about Luke are in agreement. Both of these books have prologues that reveal a self-conscious author and give us some valuable information about him and his purpose:

> Inasmuch as many have undertaken to compile a narrative of the things which have been accomplished among us, just as they were delivered to us by those who from the beginning were eyewitnesses and ministers of the word, it seemed good to me also, having followed all things closely for some time past, to write an orderly account for you, most excellent Theophilus, that you may know the truth concerning the things of which you have been informed (Luke 1:1–4).

> In the first book, O Theophilus, I have dealt with all that Jesus began to do and teach, until the day when he was taken up, after he had given commandment through the Holy Spirit to the apostles whom he had chosen (Acts 1:1–2).

We may see from the prologues that both books were addressed to a certain Theophilus and that the prologue in Acts refers to the first book.[28] The

---

[28] Theophilus is not identified in either prologue. He may have been a high-ranking government official, because Luke addresses him as "most excellent." The name means "lover of God," and the author may have intended to designate all his potential readers by the phrase.

A miniature of St. Luke from a manuscript written in gold, c. 800 CE, under the influence of Charlemagne. (Courtesy *the British Library, London.*)

brief description in Acts of the contents of the first book is a fitting description of the gospel. An analysis of the linguistic style of the two books makes common authorship a virtual certainty. The unity of the two is displayed in their overlapping. The gospel ends with a disappearance of the risen Christ (Luke 24:51), which is referred to in Acts 1:2 as "the day when he was taken up." The first narrative in Acts is a description of the ascension (Acts 1:9–11), surely an overlap with the gospel. Any evaluation of the Gospel of Luke must recognize the unity of the two books and consider the material in Acts as having a direct bearing on the meaning of the gospel.

Like the other synoptic writers, this author did not identify himself in the text. Irenaeus was the first to write about the authorship of this gospel, and he said it was written by Luke, a companion of Paul.[29] The Muratorian Canon, a Christian canonical list probably dating from about 200, refers to the author as Luke, a physician and companion of Paul, and it states that he was not an eyewitness to the things he described in the gospel. In both references the Luke in question is the one mentioned in Col 4:14, Phlm 24, and 2 Tim 4:11. Colossians and Philemon state that Luke was present with Paul when these letters were written. From the time of Irenaeus on, Christian tradition has attributed the authorship of both Luke and Acts to this companion of Paul, but many modern scholars doubt the validity of that tradition. They point out that Acts, which contains a life of Paul, is not fully consistent with what we know from Paul's letters and shows no knowledge of his literary activity or his major theological viewpoints. It is thought that a companion of Paul would have known him better and described him differently. Many other scholars, however, accept the tradition of Lukan authorship, and they point out that authorship by one such as Luke is consistent with the prologue to the gospel, which implies that the author was not an eyewitness to Jesus' life. There are also some interesting sections in Acts where the author seems to identify himself with the major participants in the story (Acts 16:10–17; 20:5–15; 21:1–18; and 27:1–28:16). These are called "we" sections, because in them the author uses the first-person pronoun instead of the usual third person. The author may have used a diary written by a participant. But if he did, he was careful to rewrite it in his own style but leave the "we" standing. Thus, some scholars conclude that the author is quoting from his own diary at these points and was actually associated with Paul on several trips. To the argument that Acts does not adequately represent Paul's life or thought, it may be said that Luke was not constantly with Paul and was writing at a time when the issues that engaged him were no longer paramount points of discussion in the church. The arguments on both sides of this issue are impressive, and it is necessary to say that the question of authorship has not been settled. Actually, it makes very little difference for our understanding or evaluation of his work.

[29] Irenaeus, op. cit., III, 1:1.

In the prologue to the gospel, he has identified himself as a Christian of the second generation, as one who consulted and studied other documents, and as one who intended to tell the story of his religion in an orderly fashion. He had a deep interest in the development of gentile Christianity. To know this much about him is to know a good deal, and the addition of a name and a limited contact with Paul means very little. We may call the author Luke, but we should not categorically identify him as the companion of Paul.

In the prologue to the gospel, Luke implies that he has consulted other documents that narrate "the things which have been accomplished among us" (Luke 1:1). Our major theories about the relationship among the Synoptic Gospels state that he not only consulted other documents but that he used them as sources. The two-document hypothesis would say that he consulted Mark and Q. The Griesbach hypothesis says he used Matthew.

Both hypotheses date Luke after the fall of Jerusalem in 70. As we have seen, his version of the synoptic apocalypse seems to be based on his knowledge of the actual circumstances of the city's fall. It is nearly impossible to set a firm *terminus ad quem* for the Lukan writings, for it is the middle of the second century before other writers begin to use them. Marcion, who came to Rome in c. 140, is said to have had an abbreviated version of Luke, and Justin, writing about a decade later, probably quoted from it. The most significant evidence relating to a *terminus ad quem* is the author's ignorance of the Pauline letters. He has no quotation from them, never mentions the fact that Paul wrote letters, and composes a number of Pauline speeches that allude to none of the chief ideas in the letters. At one point he tells about a council meeting in Jerusalem that Paul also wrote about in his letter to the Galatians.[30] But Luke must not have read Galatians, for his description is at odds with that letter at a number of significant points. This ignorance of the Pauline letters is a reason for rejecting the identification of the author as a companion of Paul. In addition, it has a bearing on the *terminus ad quem*. We will see that Paul's letters were probably collected and published in about 90. If Luke had written after that date, he almost certainly would have been aware of the letters, even if he had not known Paul personally. So, the year 90 can be set as the *terminus ad quem*. We would not err far if we set the date for Luke and Acts at c. 80–85.

The location of the author is almost impossible to determine. Eusebius puts him in Antioch, which is treated as an important Christian center in Acts.[31] Other suggestions have been made, including Alexandria, Rome, and Caesarea. The last named is the scene of a good deal of the activity in Acts, but no certainty on the subject of location is possible.

The basic structure of the Gospel of Luke is one that, by now, is familiar.

---

[30] Acts 15:1–29 and Gal 2:1–10.
[31] Eusebius, op. cit., III, 4:6.

Birth Narratives, Luke 1–2

Luke starts out as Matthew does, but his narratives are not the same. After the prologue in 1:1–4, he interweaves stories dealing with the conception and birth of John the Baptist and of Jesus. Both births are promised, and both are miraculous. John is born of aged parents, and Jesus of a virgin mother. At the births there are predictions of the magnificent things that will occur in their lives. Luke also has the story of nearby shepherds, who come to see the baby Jesus. He includes narratives about the circumcision of Jesus, the postnatal purification of Mary, and a story of Jesus' precocity as exhibited in the Temple when he was twelve years old.

Narratives on John the Baptist, the Baptism, Genealogy, and Temptation of Jesus, Luke 3:1–4:13

The narratives that introduce John the Baptist and the story of Jesus' baptism are similar to those in Matthew and Mark. Otherwise, Luke is more like Matthew in reporting John's preaching and in the story of Jesus' temptations. The Lukan genealogy, which appears in 3:23–38, bears little resemblance to Matthew's—even the grandfather of Jesus is different.

Jesus in and Around Galilee, Luke 4:14–9:50

The story of Jesus' preaching at the synagogue at Nazareth (Luke 4:16–30) opens this section and serves to alert the reader to the work of Jesus that will be described and to his rejection by his own people. Blocks of healing stories alternate with teaching materials, most of which are also found in Matthew and Mark. In 6:20–49 Jesus delivers a sermon "on a level place," and there are significant parallels to Matthew's Sermon on the Mount. Several stories familiar to readers of Matthew and Mark are included in this section, such as the stilling of the storm (8:22–25), the Gerasene demoniac (8:26–39), Jairus' daughter and the woman with a hemorrhage (8:40–56), the feeding of the five thousand (9:10–17), Peter's confession (9:18–21), and the transfiguration (9:28–36). But there is no second feeding story nor a story of Jesus' walking on the water. Luke's story of the resuscitation of the widow's son at Nain (7:11–17) is unique to this gospel. Two predictions of the death and resurrection of Jesus occur here (9:22 and 9:43b–45).

In Luke Jesus is much more closely bound to Galilee than he was in Matthew or Mark. Only the story of the Gerasene demoniac (8:26–39) takes place outside Galilee.[32] In Luke Jesus does not travel to Tyre, Sidon, or Caesarea Philippi.

---

[32] The probable location of Bethsaida, mentioned in Luke 9:10, is technically outside Galilee, but Luke does not suggest a departure from Galilee at this point. See also 10:13.

The Trip to Jerusalem, Luke 9:51–19:27

This is the long central section of Luke, which begins with words of fore-boding: "When the days drew near for him to be received up, he set his face to go to Jerusalem" (Luke 9:51). The dramatic force of this section of Luke is marked by the repeated reminders that Jesus is moving toward Je-rusalem (9:53, 13:22, 17:11, 18:31, and 19:11). Although the actual lo-cations are vaguely stated, it is Jesus' progress toward his death in Jerusalem that ties the material together. The section is almost entirely made up of teaching material, some of it similar to Matthew, much of it unique to Luke. Among the most memorable of the unique teachings in Luke are the three parables in chapter 15: the lost sheep, the lost coin, and the lost son. A third prediction of Jesus' rejection is in 17:25, and a fourth prediction of his death and resurrection appears in 18:31–34. Only four healing narra-tives are recorded in this section, and three of them are unique to Luke.[33].

Jesus in Jerusalem, Luke 19:28–21:38

Here readers of Matthew and Mark are back on more familiar ground. After the arrival in Jerusalem, Jesus enters and cleanses the Temple. Then there is a series of controversies between him and the priests. Here also is Luke's version of the synoptic apocalypse.

The Last Supper, Trial, and Death of Jesus, Luke 22–23

This material is very much like that in Matthew and Mark, but there are some significant but subtle differences in Luke's story of the trial. The most obvious difference is that Luke has no meeting of the Jewish Sanhedrin on the night before Jesus' crucifixion. He also includes a report of a hearing before Herod Antipas, a report that is not found in the other Synoptic Gospels.

The Resurrection Narratives, Luke 24

In distinction from Matthew (and Mark), all of the resurrection appearances take place in or near Jerusalem. Several women discover Jesus' tomb to be empty, and two men tell them that Jesus has been raised. In Luke 24:13–35, Jesus appears to two disciples who are traveling from Jerusalem to Em-maus, and then he appears to the other disciples in Jerusalem and departs from them at Bethany.

Luke is generally regarded as a very competent writer of Greek. Among NT writers, his literary ability is second only to that of the author of He-

---

[33] The unique ones are in Luke 13:10–17, 14:1–6, and 17:11–19.

brews. His style contrasts especially with Mark's at a number of points. He has fewer Aramaic and Latin expressions, and he almost never uses the historical present.

Charles Talbert, a contemporary NT scholar, has called attention to what he calls an architectonic pattern in Luke-Acts.[34] He means that Luke has organized his materials so that they form several series of balanced parallels. For example, the section in the Gospel of Luke on Jesus' trip to Jerusalem has a parallel in the account in Acts of Paul's last trip to Jerusalem. In each, says Talbert, there are seven references to the journey to Jerusalem, and the events that take place when the two arrive in the city are similar. Furthermore, there are parallels between the trials of Jesus and those of Paul. Talbert points out that similar patterns are to be found in Homer, Herodotus, and other Greek writers. The effect of this kind of style is to give the reader a sense of balance.

Luke has frequently been called a historian, because of his expressed purpose to write for Theophilus "an orderly account." Clearly, he means to tell what he thought that Jesus had said and done and to follow that with an account of the development of the church. These are historical concerns, but Luke undergirds his historical writing with a theological interpretation of history.

Hans Conzelmann, a German NT scholar, referred to Luke's writing as a history of salvation.[35] He said that Luke understood history to be made up of three periods: the time of Israel, the time of Jesus, and the time of the church. The time of Israel was one of the law and the prophets, and it extended to John the Baptist. Luke makes this point explicitly: "The law and the prophets were until John; since then the good news of the kingdom of God is preached, and every one enters it violently" (Luke 16:16). As the last person in the time of Israel, John is geographically separated from Jesus, and he does not preach the coming of the kingdom. He cannot, because only Jesus possesses knowledge about the kingdom. The second period is that of Jesus, which Conzelmann calls "the center of history." It is a special time of salvation, characterized by the departure of the devil at Luke 4:13 and concluded by his return at 22:3. During this period, Luke portrays the ministry of Jesus, drawing on the sources at his disposal and filling in his outline with the same kinds of materials that Mark and Matthew used. The time of Jesus includes three subdivisions. In the first, Jesus is active in Galilee, assembling the witnesses who are to convey the traditions to the later writers. During this period, Jesus also proclaims the kingdom to Israel and demands a decision about it. The second part consists of Jesus' trip to

[34] Charles H. Talbert, *Literary Patterns, Theological Themes and the Genre of Luke-Acts* (Missoula, Mont.: Scholars Press, 1974).
[35] Hans Conzelmann, *The Theology of St. Luke,* trans. by Geoffrey Buswell (New York: Harper, 1960).

Jerusalem, which consumes the entire middle section of the gospel. The death of Jesus is constantly in view here, and the whole section is intended to express the divine necessity of Jesus' suffering. The third section tells of Jesus' arrest, trial, crucifixion, resurrection, and ascension. Strictly speaking, this is a transition section, for the devil is active once again, entering into Judas to bring about his betrayal of Jesus. Jesus' death is described as a judicial murder by the Jews. It has no redemptive significance but is part of God's plan and serves as the means of Jesus' resurrection and glorification. The final period of history is that of the church, a period marked by the presence of the spirit, which comes upon Jesus' disciples in Acts 2. During this time the Lord is in heaven, and his church is on earth, preaching those things communicated to it by the eyewitnesses. The church takes over its heritage from Israel and, indeed, becomes the new Israel by virtue of its adherence to the Torah and Temple in its earliest days. The church lives amid persecution and must learn to endure it, but endurance is made possible by the expectation that the time of salvation, once known in the time of Jesus, will return. This is the message the church preaches: once again there will come a time when the devil will be inactive.

Although Luke is vitally interested in history, we should not expect him to write as a modern historian might. He is interested in the past, but his interest is not dispassionate. He looks upon the past and the present as the unfolding of the divine plan of salvation. In the final analysis, his major interest is in the church of his own time and the problems it faced in maintaining a continuity with the past and in living in the expectation of a consummation in the future. His solution to these problems is to affirm that the conditions of the past will once again manifest themselves in the future.

But Luke seems also to emphasize that the consummation is not to be in the foreseeable future. In his gospel we have little of the eschatological fevor that can be found in Matthew and Mark. To be sure, Mark, in his apocalyptic chapter, meant to put a damper on enthusiastic proclamation of an imminent end, but Luke does it even more forcefully. All three Synoptic Gospels advise their readers to beware of those who claim to be the Messiah, but Luke adds a caution about those who proclaim that the end time has arrived (Luke 21:8). According to Luke, Jesus told the parable of the pounds because some people wrongly felt the kingdom was to come immediately (Luke 19:11–27). When Pharisees ask Jesus when the kingdom will come, he answers that there will be no visible signs, and he says to the disciples: "The days are coming when you will desire to see one of the days of the Son of man, and you will not see it. And they will say to you, 'Lo, there!' or 'Lo, here!' Do not go, do not follow them" (17:22–23). Luke does retain Jesus' saying that "there are some standing here who will not taste death before they see the kingdom of God" (9:27). But the impact of the saying is almost lost among expressions of Luke's eschatological caution. Luke is unique in his emphasis on patience, a prime virtue for people waiting for a consummation that is not imminent. The expectation of a delayed fulfillment is characteristic of Luke. But, as Henry Cadbury observed, early Christian writers generally did not take an extreme position on eschatological matters; they proclaimed neither an immediate end nor a continuing history. The difference among them lies in "their skillful adjustment between these extremes as regards imminence rather than in their acceptance or rejection of apocalyptic as a whole."[36] Nevertheless, Luke moves in the direction of a delayed consummation, and this tendency forces him to take ongoing history seriously. He must treat the history of the church as part of God's entire plan of salvation, not as some brief interval before the end of time.

The concept of the history of salvation seems also to affect the way Luke treats the relationship of Jews and Gentiles. He seems to think in terms of stages and times. He limits the activity of Jesus almost entirely to Galilee and Jerusalem, and after the resurrection Jesus commands the disciples to remain in Jerusalem until they receive "power from on high" (Luke 24:49). Luke's emphasis here is a direct contrast to Mark 16:7, where the disciples are to be told to go to Galilee. Acts, in picking up where the gospel leaves off, shows us the disciples in Jerusalem for a period of time. But then the Christian message begins to spread to far distant regions in the north and the west. The geographical pattern symbolizes an ethnic pattern: the Christian message comes to the Jews first and then to the Gentiles. When the time of the Gentiles comes, the time of the Jews is over. At one point in Acts, the Christian missionaries, Paul and Barnabas, say to a crowd of Jews: "It was necessary that the word of God should be spoken first to you. Since you thrust it from you, and judge yourselves unworthy of eternal life, behold, we turn to the Gentiles."[37] Luke's own sympathies are consonant with his presentation of Paul's.

Luke also has a lively interest in classes of people who were usually objects of discrimination—the poor and women. His interest in the poor, however, is not so much out of pity for them as it is a condemnation of the self-assurance of the rich. He includes in the teaching of Jesus as much material about the duty of the rich toward the poor as he does words of assurance to the poor. He seems to adopt an equation found in contemporary Judaism and probably widely adopted by Christians in which poverty is understood to be the inevitable result of piety.

There is also a strong note of optimism pervading Luke's writings. The expectation of judgment is not absent, but the hopeful future is a distinctive emphasis in Luke. Jesus is pictured as basically kind and a doer of good deeds. God is giving and forgiving. The kingdom of God is a gift to be sought, not feared. The birth of Jesus is greeted with great joy by angels

---

[36] Henry J. Cadbury, *The Making of Luke-Acts,* 2nd ed. (London: S.P.C.K., 1958), p. 290.
[37] Acts 13:46. The same statement is made on two other occasions (Acts 18:6 and 28:28).

and pious people. At the end of the gospel the disciples are filled with joy, and they spend their time praising God in the Temple.

THE GOSPEL OF JOHN

A fourth attempt to publish the major aspects of Christian faith in terms of the ministry and teaching of Jesus is the Gospel of John, frequently called the Fourth Gospel. In certain respects the Fourth Gospel is similar to the first three. It contains some of the same material about the deeds of Jesus and concludes with a narrative of the trial, death, and resurrection. It tells of John the Baptist, a feeding of the multitude, and of a walking on the water. The story of Jesus' cleansing of the Temple is included, but it is placed earlier in John. There are a few places where the verbal similarity between Mark and John is fairly close, and some synoptic-type sayings are placed within John's larger discourses.

In spite of the similarities, most readers are overwhelmingly impressed with the contrasts between John and the synoptics. The differences are intentionally designated by our terminology, in which the word *synoptic* specifically excludes John, and by a popular habit of calling the Fourth Gospel the spiritual gospel.[38] The contrast is evident from the very beginning of the gospel. Whereas Mark begins with the ministry of John the Baptist, and Matthew and Luke with Jesus' birth, the Fourth Gospel starts with a hymn to the Logos and follows that with the Baptist's testimony to Jesus. John has no story of Jesus' birth, no narrative of the baptism, no temptation story, and no exorcisms. Most Johannine narratives have no synoptic counterparts; for example, the story of Jesus' turning water into wine and his resuscitation of Lazarus are contained only in John. Even in narratives dealing with incidents that are reported in the synoptics, John presents a different picture. At the last supper, for example, Jesus does not serve bread and wine; instead, he washes the disciples' feet. Then Jesus is arrested by Jewish and Roman authorities. He is tried by two high priests and by the Roman governor Pilate. There are differences in the location and, perhaps, the duration of Jesus' ministry. Instead of the synoptic pattern of a ministry in Galilee followed by death in Jerusalem, John places most of Jesus' ministry in Jerusalem and has him make several trips between there and Galilee. The Synoptic Gospels had mentioned only one observance of the Jewish festival of Passover, the one at Jesus' death. John has three, and he thus implies that Jesus' ministry covered more than two years.

---

[38] Clement of Alexandria, in the early third century, seems to be the first to use this expression. He says: "But that John, last of all, conscious that the outward facts had been set forth in the Gospels, was urged on by his disciples, and, divinely moved by the Spirit, composed a spiritual Gospel." In Eusebius, op. cit., VI, 14:7.

The opening of the Gospel of John, eighth century. (Courtesy *the Master and Fellows of Corpus Christi College, Cambridge.*)

The literary style in John stands in marked contrast to that in the Synoptic Gospels. Instead of brief sayings and parables of Jesus, we have several long and involved discourses. These discourses frequently employ a characteristic pattern that begins with a question addressed to Jesus. Jesus responds to the question but is misunderstood. He then corrects his questioner and launches into a long speech, which frequently seems inappropriate to the original subject. Through the discourses he employs words that have both obvious meanings and deeper significance. Often, a miracle story is used as a point of departure for a long discourse, but the connection between them is not obvious.

The subjects of the discourses are also different. In the Synoptic Gospels, Jesus speaks of the kingdom, repentance, and the Torah; but in John, he speaks of eternal life, the contrast of true and false, light and dark, good and evil, and believing and not believing. He frequently speaks of his unique relationship with God.

The resemblances and contrasts between John and the synoptics raise the question of their relationship. The use of Matthew is not seriously entertained by many scholars, but some think that John probably used Mark and may have used Luke. The English NT scholar C. K. Barrett, for example, thinks that John's use of Mark is indicated by the fact that both gospels have a sequence of ten events.[39] But the ten events are not found in a single continuous section in either gospel; they are interrupted by material that is not common to them. Four of the ten are found in the narrative of Jesus' trial and death, where there are substantial similarities. In the others, however, the verbal and formal differences outweigh any similarities. If John knew Mark's gospel, he used very little from it. At most, it was a springboard from which he moved to the development of non-Markan stories and discourses. The evidence is lacking to show, with any degree of probability, that John made use of Mark or the other Synoptic Gospels.

John, therefore, seems to be drawing on a tradition independent of the Synoptic Gospels. This may have been an oral tradition—perhaps a variant of those that underlay Matthew, Mark, and Luke. But there are some signs that John worked, at least in part, with written documents. There are a number of rough spots in the gospel that seem to be caused by the attempt to put together some documents that contained contrary geographical and chronological notes. Those notes probably stood in written documents that John used, and, as a result, there are certain geographical and chronological difficulties in the gospel as it now stands. In John 5, for example, Jesus is in Jerusalem, and in chapter 6, he is in Galilee, but no trip has been described. In John 14:31 Jesus invites his disciples to depart, but the departure does not occur until 18:1. There is also an inconsistency in the enumeration of Jesus' deeds. In John 7:21 Jesus claims that he has performed only one Sabbath miracle, but John had recorded others. John 2:21 calls the miracle at Cana the first sign, but 2:23 speaks of signs in the plural. In 4:45 there is a reference to all that Jesus had done, but 4:54 says he had only accomplished two signs. Such enumeration appears also to be the work

[39] C. K. Barrett, *The Gospel According to St. John* (London: S.P.C.K., 1955), pp. 34–45.

of editors, who must have compiled certain written materials that the author of the Fourth Gospel then put together.

To know that John used written sources is not to know what sources he might have used. Bultmann suggested three major sources.[40] One is the passion narrative—the story of Jesus' trial and death. This is a hypothetical, nonsynoptic source. A second is a collection of signs that partially overlapped the synoptic miracle stories and included the gathering of the disciples, the miracle at Cana, the story of the Samaritan woman, the healing of the ruler's son, the feeding of the multitude, the walking on water, the healing of the man who had been ill for thirty-eight years, the healing of the man born blind, and the raising of Lazarus from the dead. The third source was a collection of discourses that included the prologue, a discourse with Nicodemus, and discourses on water, testimony, bread, and the good shepherd. It concluded with the long speech in John 14–16 and Jesus' prayer in chapter 17. This means that almost all of the long discourses of Jesus are from a single source. Of course, the evangelist rearranged and assimilated his sources and sprinkled them with his own comments. It should be borne in mind that all three are hypothetical sources. There is no concrete evidence for their existence.

It is not likely that we can identify the author of the Fourth Gospel. Irenaeus (c. 185) first recorded the tradition to the effect that the gospel was the composition of John bar Zebedee, a disciple of Jesus.[41] It is, however, difficult to accept this testimony for several reasons. The son of Zebedee would have been an eyewitness to Jesus' history, but an eyewitness would not be so dependent on written sources as the author of the Fourth Gospel seems to have been. Neither John, nor his brother James, nor their father Zebedee are even mentioned in the Fourth Gospel, except in chapter 21, which appears to have been added some time after the gospel itself was made public. The synoptic narratives that have John as a participant are missing from the Fourth Gospel. Although John bar Zebedee is, according to the Synoptic Gospels, from Galilee, the Fourth Gospel has no special interest in that area. Moreover, the world of thought in which the gospel moves seems far removed from the world of a Galilean fisherman.

The earliest known attempt to identify the author is in John 21, a late addition to the gospel. The unknown writer of this chapter claims, in effect, that the first twenty chapters were written by the "beloved disciple." The beloved disciple is the nameless person who figures in three Johannine narratives: he was present at the last supper; he received Jesus' mother at the

[40] Rudolf Bultmann, *The Gospel of John,* trans. by G. R. Beasley-Murray, et al. (Philadelphia: Westminster Press, 1971). An excellent analysis of Bultmann's work can be found in D. Moody Smith, *The Composition and Order of the Fourth Gospel* (New Haven: Yale U.P., 1965). See also Robert T. Fortna, *The Gospel of Signs* (Cambridge: Cambridge U.P., 1970).
[41] Irenaeus, op. cit., III, 1:2.

crucifixion; and he, with Peter, discovered the empty tomb.[42] He is never named in John 1–20 and is not designated as the author. Nor does chapter 21 give him a name. If he is not an ideal figure, he must be either one of the unnamed disciples in 21:2 or else one of the sons of Zebedee. It is not clear that the author of John 21 thought the evangelist was John bar Zebedee, but if he did not, we are in no positioin to give a name to the beloved disciple.

We cannot agree that the author of the Fourth Gospel was John bar Zebedee, and the testimony about the beloved disciple is not determinative. The tradition recorded by Irenaeus probably reflects an older interpretation of John 21, in which the beloved disciple is identified as John bar Zebedee, who therefore is acknowledged as the author of the Fourth Gospel. In the final analysis, although modern scholarship has produced a number of elaborate and fascinating theories about the authorship of this gospel, some of them supporting Irenaeus' identification, there is no certainty on this matter.

In 1935 a small fragment turned up in Egypt that has been identified as a part of the Gospel of John. Although minute, its significance is great. The fragment is almost certainly not the original, but it probably is a very early copy of the gospel. It was produced in the middle of the second century and, thus, sets for us a *terminus ad quem* for the gospel at c. 130. The determination of the *terminus a quo* depends on the author's awareness of a certain Jewish practice. There is evidence that Jews in some places began to exclude Christians from synagogues in c. 85. The author of the Fourth Gospel seems to know of this practice and is probably making an allusion to it in John 9:22 and 16:2. The likely terminal dates for this gospel are, therefore, 85–130; most scholars date it to 90–100.

As we will see, the author of this gospel is knowledgeable about a number of diverse religious and philosophical concepts. There are at last two locations in which one could come in contact with those currents of thought: Ephesus, in Asia Minor, and Alexandria, in Egypt. A good case can be made for either city, but it may be important that ancient testimony favors Ephesus. Most modern scholars also favor Ephesus as the location for the Fourth Gospel.

The outline of the Gospel of John is not so clear as that of the Synoptic Gospels. This is so because of the different geographical structure in John and because of the ways in which the author has handled the narrative and discourse material. Nevertheless, it should be helpful for the reader to keep a kind of general outline in mind as he or she reads.

---

[42] John 13:23, 19:26, and 20:2. According to Bultmann's source analysis, all three of these notes are from the hand of the evangelist.

The Prologue, John 1:1–18

John introduces the Logos and announces that it became flesh in the person of Jesus. This section is discussed more fully subsequently.

John the Baptist, John 1:19–51

John is introduced in the prologue, but here he is treated more extensively. The main purpose of this section appears to be to deny that John claimed to be the Messiah and to affirm that he believed Jesus to be the Lamb of God and the Messiah. Through John's testimony, some of his own disciples begin to follow Jesus, and then others gather around him.

Jesus in Galilee, Samaria, and Judea, John 2:1–12:11

After the miracle at the wedding feast at Cana in Galilee (John 2:1–11), we find Jesus in Jerusalem cleansing the Temple (2:12–22). Other miraculous signs are contained in this section: the Samaritan woman (4:1–26), the healing of the ruler's son (4:43–54), the man who had been ill for thirty-eight years (5:1–18), the feeding of the multitude (6:1–15), walking on water (6:16–24), the man born blind (9:1–41), and the raising of Lazarus (11:1–57). Discourses are intermixed with these narratives and sometimes connected with them. For example, the teaching of Jesus about the bread of life (6:25–71) follows the feeding of the multitude. At the end of this section (12:1–11), Jesus is in Bethany, ready to enter Jerusalem for Passover.

Jesus in Jerusalem, John 12:12–17:26

A supper is mentioned in 13:1–20, but the narrative actually describes a ceremony in which Jesus washed the feet of his disciples. In chapters 14–16 Jesus gives a long farewell speech to his disciples, and in chapter 17 he prays for them and for the believers.

Jesus' Trial and Death, John 18–19

There are formal similarities between John's narrative and that in the synoptics, but there are also significant differences in content. After Jesus' arrest, he is taken first to Annas, the father-in-law of the high priest, then to Caiaphas, the high priest, and finally to Pilate. Although Pilate pronounces Jesus innocent, he finally gives in to pressure from the Jews and hands him to them for crucifixion.

The Resurrection Narratives, John 20–21

In chapter 20 the empty tomb is discovered by Mary Magdalene, but Peter and then the beloved disciple are the first to enter it. There are three post-resurrection appearances: the first to Mary Magdalene in the cemetery; the second to all the disciples except Thomas; and the third, a week later, to all the disciples including Thomas. All these appearances seem to be located in Jerusalem. In chapter 21 Jesus appears to some of the disciples at the Sea of Tiberias in Galilee. The identification of the beloved disciple as the author is in John 21:24.

If the original ending of the gospel was at John 20:30–31, as is generally thought, we have a clear statement of the author's purpose:

> Now Jesus did many other signs in the presence of the disciples, which are not written in this book; but these are written that you may believe that Jesus is the Christ, the Son of God, and that believing you may have life in his name (John 20:30–31).

But even without this statement, we would know that the author's purpose was to convince the reader of Jesus' divine sonship. The overriding concern that shows through this gospel is a concern with *Christology*—that is, the meaning of the nature and function of Jesus the Christ.

The prologue (John 1:1–18) announces the concern with Christology before Jesus or any of the other characters are even introduced. It is likely that the prologue draws on a pre-Johannine hymn to the Logos, which the author connected with Jesus. He also added some notes on John the Baptist (1:6–8 and 15), apparently in order to explain to the reader that the Baptist was only a witness to the real Logos. Although Logos is customarily translated as word, its meaning in the context of John's prologue is by no means clear. Logos was used by Stoics to designate a divine element present in all people. Philo used it as a mediator between God and humans and as a translation of the Hebrew word for *wisdom* (*hochmah*), a personal agent of God in the creation of the world.[43] It is probably this last that is intended by John, for the prologue appears to be a creation story. The evangelist uses this hymn to picture Jesus as the divine being whose existence antedates the world itself. He was present with God, dwelt with God, and was divine. All things were created through him. Light was present with Logos and overcame the darkness of precreation chaos. The Logos became flesh and lived among us. Finally, the author gives the name of Jesus Christ as the name of the fleshly Logos. His function is to reveal God.

The prologue clearly affirms a belief in the pre-existence of Christ. Before there was a fleshly appearance in the person of Jesus, the Logos was in

---

[43] See also Prov 8:22–31.

existence with God. The idea of pre-existence is confirmed in other parts of the gospel as well. In one of his discourses Jesus says, "Truly, truly, I say to you, before Abraham was, I am" (John 8:58). He claims to be one with the father—that is, in perfect union with God. He claims to have been sent by God, and he talks about a return to the father. Thus, there is a pre-existence and a postexistence, and the time of the fleshly Jesus is only a small part of the entire time of the Christ, who is actually nontemporal.

The prologue also announces that the function of Jesus Christ is to reveal God. There is a logical progression in three widely separated statements: "No one has ever seen God" (John 1:18); "Not that anyone has seen the Father except him who is from God" (6:46); "He who has seen me has seen the Father" (14:9). Jesus reveals the Father by revealing himself, through the miraculous signs and through his discourses. The signs seem intended to reveal something about Jesus: his power to provide wine from water, his supernatural knowledge of the life of the Samaritan woman, and his ability to give life to the four-day-old corpse of Lazarus. The discourses also are pointed inward. In chapter 6 Jesus claims to be the bread of life, and he proclaims, "He who eats my flesh and drinks my blood has eternal life, and I will raise him up at the last day" (6:54). In other discourses he claims to be the light, the water of life, the resurrection, the shepherd, the door of the sheep, and the way to eternal life.

The prologue also affirms that the Logos became flesh (John 1:14). On the face of it, this statement expresses a belief in the true humanity of Jesus. To say that the Logos became flesh is to express a kind of incarnational Christology. There is a conjunction between the pre-existent, divine Logos and the human being known as Jesus of Nazareth. Just what that connection was is not explored directly in the Fourth Gospel, but it is appropriate at this point to make some observations about it.

We will see that a significant form of Christological thinking that crops up in early Christian writings is *Docetism*. Docetism is a form of thought that proceeds from the assumption that Christ is divine, but it refuses to admit that there can be any real connection between divinity and humanity. That is, a divine being does not become a human being, in whole or in part. It may appear to do so, but the appearance is an illusion. Docetic Christians were, thus, people who believed that Jesus was divine but not human.

John's prologue shows little sympathy with Docetism. It affirms the reality of the flesh and, hence, of the humanity of Jesus. This nondocetic motif is to be found at other points as well. Jesus showed human emotions: for example, he wept at the death of Lazarus (John 11:35), he was violent in driving the money changers from the Temple (2:14–15), and at the crucifixion he became thirsty (19:28). In 19:17 a point is made of the fact that Jesus carried his own cross to the place of crucifixion. In the Synoptic Gospels, one Simon of Cyrene carried the cross part of the way, and this apparently served as evidence for some Docetists to claim that an exchange had taken place and that it was Simon who was crucified and not Jesus.[44] But the Fourth Gospel leaves no doubt that Jesus was really executed. Finally, the fleshly nature of the resurrected body is affirmed in the episode in which Thomas is challenged to touch the wounds in Jesus' hands and side (20:26–29).

With all of the notes in the Fourth Gospel about the human, fleshly nature of Jesus, the divine nature is not blocked out. Indeed, the purpose of the flesh is to aid people to see his divinity, for that is what he reveals. The prologue in John 1:14 says: "And the word [Logos] became flesh and dwelt among us, full of grace and truth; we have beheld his glory, glory as of the only Son from the Father." Glory is traditionally an aspect of divinity, and so that which flesh makes it possible to see is not the human, but the divine, nature of the Logos. The flesh is real, but it is only the means by which humans are able to see the true glory of God's son.

The Christology of the Fourth Gospel, in summary, contains the following elements: (1) the pre-existence and postexistence of the divine Logos; (2) the incarnation of the Logos in Jesus, who is both human and divine; and (3) the function of Jesus to reveal God by revealing himself. John's Christology is not docetic, but it comes closer to it than some other writings that we will examine. For example, a Christology that talks about a nondivine, solely human Jesus would be further from Docetism than John. John's is a Christology that turns attention away from the human and, hence, away from the actual history of Jesus. His gospel, to a higher degree than the synoptics, is less a narrative about what Jesus did and said than a meditation on the meaning of the revelation to be found in him.

Christological concerns dominate the Fourth Gospel. But there are two additional aspects that merit brief attention. One is the paucity of eschatological expectation. It is not totally absent. At one point (John 5:28–29) there is an allusion to a future general resurrection and judgment, but judgment is usually interpreted as a present phenomenon, and the idea of a future resurrection is partially corrected on the spot: "Truly, truly, I say to you, the hour is coming, *and now is,* when the dead will hear the voice of the Son of God, and those who hear will live" (5:25). Aside from these questionable verses, there is no idea of a future resurrection, and there are no predictions of destruction. Some persons may not expect death, but not because the end of time comes first. Such people bypass death in their transition from life to life. There is no final judgment, for judgment is present now. In John 14:3 Jesus speaks of his coming again in a way that could cause the reader to think of his coming as the apocalyptic Son of man. But none of the functions traditionally associated with the Son of man are described. In John, Jesus returns to receive the disciples. He also promises to

---

[44] See Irenaeus, op. cit., I, 24:4.

send them the *Paraclete*.[45] The Paraclete is a substitute for Jesus after his return to the Father, and it seems to be an equivalent to the Spirit. It functions to aid the believers' understanding, to guarantee authenticity in the community, to intercede for the believers, and to be their advocate; it is the champion of the community of believers. But this is no eschatological promise, for it was fulfilled on the day of the resurrection. On the evening of that day, Jesus was present with his disciples. He spoke to them and then, "He breathed on them, and said to them, 'Receive the Holy Spirit' " (20:22).[46] Jesus gives the spirit in the act of breathing. In sum, almost all of Jesus' promises about the future have already been fulfilled. Except for the promise to return and receive the disciples, there is no unfulfilled promise, no eschatological threat, no destruction to come, no future resurrection, and no final judgment.

The second important aspect of the Fourth Gospel is the attitude toward Judaism. There are significant signs of a Jewish background in the gospel, and some material of the evangelist's composition indicates an acquaintance with Jewish ideas and procedures. The English NT scholar C. H. Dodd was impressed with this quality. He wrote, "The Fourth Evangelist, even more definitely than the Synoptics, is developing his doctrine of the person and work of Jesus with conscious reference to Jewish messianic belief."[47] Over against this, however, there is a good deal of hostility toward Jews in the gospel. Jesus' opponents are usually styled simply as Jews. It is rare that the author specifically mentions Pharisees, Sadducees, or individuals. Most scholars account for this paradoxical attitude by suggesting that there was a proximity between the evangelist and a Jewish synagogue.[48] Some people were probably being excluded from the synagogue because of their beliefs about Jesus. Other Jews, represented in the gospel by Nicodemus, secretly held the belief and remained within the synagogue. In his own Christology, the author of the Fourth Gospel understood Jesus to be the Messiah of Jewish expectation, but more than that, to be the glorified divine being who had come to earth and returned to heaven. The influence of the local synagogue may have given to John an acquaintance with Jewish ways, but the practice of excluding Christians created deep hostility between his community and the Jews of his city.

There is evidence that the Fourth Gospel was not well received by all Christians in the second century. We know of one group, called Alogoi,

---

[45] *Paraclete* is translated as "counselor" in the RSV and as "advocate" in the NEB.

[46] In both Hebrew and Greek, the words for *spirit* and *breath* are from the same root. The same is true in English: compare *spirit* and *respiration*.

[47] C. H. Dodd, *The Interpretation of the Fourth Gospel* (Cambridge: Cambridge U.P., 1953), p. 92.

[48] See J. Louis Martyn, *History and Theology in the Fourth Gospel*, 2nd ed. (Nashville, Tenn.: Abingdon, 1979), and Raymond E. Brown, *The Community of the Beloved Disciple* (New York: Paulist Press, 1979).

that objected to the treatment of Logos in the gospel and believed that it was written by a Gnostic Christian, Cerinthus. But, as we have seen, it seems to have been widely accepted by the time of Irenaeus. In the third and subsequent centuries, it had a tremendous impact on the Christian movement. People felt that it complemented the other gospels and went directly to the heart of the matter to present the real meaning of the Christ. The author must have had something like this in mind as he wrote. He was not so interested in matters of historical fact as he was in affirming that in Jesus Christ we have a direct revelation of God.

The Fourth Gospel is the chief document to be considered in studying a version of early Christianity called Johannine Christianity, which will be discussed in Chapter 11. In that discussion, we will return to this gospel with additional questions about the nature of this kind of religious thought, its relationship to Hellenistic and Jewish thought, and its place within the spectrum of early Christianity.

APOCRYPHAL GOSPELS

The four gospels already treated here have received a place of importance in Christianity that is rivaled by no other books. But it has not always been the case that these four were universally regarded by Christians as the only authentic gospels. During the second and third centuries, scores of other gospels were produced. Each one was revered at least by some Christian group, and in that time it was not at all clear that Matthew, Mark, Luke, and John would eventually achieve the position they finally did. The non-canonical books form a diverse lot, and, in fact, they have usually not been thought of as a collection. In general, they are called apocryphal gospels, and that designation means that they were not recognized in the Christian canon, the NT. We will examine the process of canonization in a later chapter, but here we will treat a few of the gospels that did not receive a place in the canon.

Space permits treatment of only a few of the apocryphal gospels of the second century. Some of them would be inappropriate here in any case. A number of books that bear the title *gospel* do not in fact make reference to things said or done by Jesus. The fact that they call themselves gospels, while treating widely diverse themes unconnected with the historical life of Jesus, testifies to the elasticity of the term in the second century. Some of the gospels of this sort will be treated in Chapter 11. Here, in a section on Jesus and the gospels, we will treat only those that purport to narrate something about the historical Jesus, and, to be sure, we can only treat a few of those. These apocryphal gospels are like the canonical gospels in the sense that both proclaim the Christian message through the deeds and sayings of Jesus. But one notable contrast between them is that the apocryphal gospels have more specialized interests than the canonical. They each highlight a certain portion or aspect of Jesus' history, such as his family, his childhood, his resurrection, or his teachings. Each of the gospels treated subsequently has a special interest in one of those aspects of Jesus' life.

The Book of James [49]

The church never canonized but was nevertheless deeply affected by the Book of James. We know it now from one third-century Greek manuscript and from several later translations. It has influenced popular Christian piety almost as much as the canonical gospels have.

The Book of James is properly called a protogospel, for it deals with events prior to the beginning of the other gospels and ends with the birth of Jesus. In it Joachim and Anna are introduced as a childless couple. For this reason, Joachim was not allowed to make a sacrifice in the Jerusalem Temple. He went into the wilderness to fast for forty days and forty nights, and his wife Anna, thinking him dead, went into her garden to pray. An angel appeared to her and promised that she would conceive, and Anna vowed to dedicate the child to God. The child was called Mary, and at three she was taken to the Temple to be brought up by the priests. When she was twelve, the widower Joseph, an old man with sons, was chosen to be her husband. But Joseph acted only as Mary's guardian, considering her to be sacred and preserving her virginal state. But Mary became pregnant, and Joseph was afraid that his neglect had allowed an adulterer to seduce her. So the priests gave both of them a trial by bitter water, a trial they survived. In response to the census decree of Augustus, they went to Bethlehem, Joseph's home town, and Jesus was born there in a cave.

The author draws heavily on the infancy narratives of Matthew and Luke, quoting large segments of them. The book may have been known by Justin in the second century, and so it could be dated between 100 and 150. In any case, it was known in the third century, so could not be written later than 200.

At the end of the book, the author identifies himself as James. There are several bearers of this name mentioned in the Synoptic Gospels—one is a son of Zebedee and one of Alphaeus. Another is called the brother of Jesus in Matt 13:55 and Mark 6:3, both of which mention other brothers by name and refer to unnamed sisters. In Acts James is frequently referred to as the brother of the Lord. It is probable that the actual author intended to imply that James, the brother of Jesus, wrote the document. This James would have been an eyewitness to the events described, so authorship by

---

[49] The title in the text itself is "Nativity of Mary. Apocalypse of James." It is also sometimes called the Protevangelium of James—that is, the protogospel of James—as well as the Book of James.

Giotto, The Presentation of the Virgin in the Temple, *Scrovegni Chapel, Padua. The painting was inspired by the Book of James.* (Courtesy *Civic Museum, Padua and Alinari/Art Resource Inc.*)

him would guarantee the authenticity of the story. The sons of Joseph are mentioned in the story, but it should be noted that their names are not given. If we are to understand that the brother is intended as the author, it is important to note the implication that he is actually a half brother, a son of Joseph but not of Mary. In any event, the date of the document precludes actual authorship by anyone who was alive at Jesus' birth. The author probably was a gentile Christian of the second century.

The book appears to be a unified composition, based on the birth stories in Matthew and Luke. It is a single story told meaningfully and in chronological order. It is probably the product of pious speculation on the birth of Jesus and on his family. Three basic features in the narrative may indicate the author's purpose.

In the first place, the major emphasis is on Mary herself. Her miraculous birth and upbringing in the Temple are reminiscent of the story of Samuel in the OT. Her virginity is especially cared for by the priests and by Joseph. The author emphasizes the distance between Mary and Joseph. When Joseph sets out for the census in Bethlehem, he debates with himself whether to register her as his wife or his daughter, for she is in fact neither. The perpetual virginity of Mary is strongly implied in the document. Here we have an elaboration of the synoptic infancy narratives in the direction of the elevation of celibacy. Thus, the focus of attention subtly shifts from Jesus to Mary, and the reader is called on to agree that the life most pleasing to God is the celibate life.

A second feature is the claim that Mary is of Davidic ancestry.[50] The traditions embodied in Matthew and Luke had created a certain problem at this point, for they asserted both that Jesus was virgin born and a descendant of David, and they traced his relationship to David through Joseph. They assume that Joseph was of Davidic lineage, but they never claim it for Mary. The problem is: if Joseph is not Jesus' father in fact, how can Jesus be a descendant of David? The author of the Book of James must have been aware of this problem, and he deftly solved it by saying that Mary was a descendant of David. In this way, Jesus can be both Davidic and virgin born.

A third feature is similar. Matthew and Luke had affirmed the virginity of Mary, but they referred also to brothers of Jesus.[51] Jesus is called the firstborn son but never the only child of Mary. As we have seen, James was frequently called the brother of the Lord. The author of the Book of James is not so much interested in the birth of Jesus as he is in the virginity of Mary, so he accounts for the older brothers as sons of the widowed Joseph.

The purpose of the author must have been threefold: (1) to glorify Mary, (2) to emphasize the value of celibacy, and (3) to solve some problems in the traditions represented in Matthew and Luke.

The Book of James was never canonized, but some aspects of it have been widely accepted. The names of Mary's parents, given for the first time in this book, are usually agreed to be Joachim and Anna. The perpetual virginity of Mary was taught by church fathers from the fifth century on. The idea that Jesus had half brothers, however, was generally rejected after the fourth century, when James and the others were understood to be cousins. Although the book was condemned in the medieval period, the Immaculate Conception of Mary, a teaching that is related to traditions in the Book of James, was proclaimed to be a dogma for Roman Catholics in 1854.

The Infancy Gospel of Thomas

The canonical gospels are almost silent on the childhood of Jesus. Luke (2:41–52) contains one narrative about a conversation between the learned teachers of the Temple and the twelve-year-old Jesus, but that is the extent

[50] Book of James 10:1.
[51] Matt 13:46–47; 13:55; Luke 8:19–20.

of it. The Infancy Gospel of Thomas attempts to fill this gap by narrating a number of incidents involving Jesus between the ages of five and twelve. He made clay sparrows on the Sabbath, and they flew away when he clapped his hands. A child who hit Jesus on the shoulder died immediately. On one occasion, several children were playing together in the upper story of a house. One of them fell to the ground and died, and Jesus was blamed. So Jesus revived the child, who confessed that his death was an accident. When Joseph, a carpenter, cut a board too short, Jesus stretched it to its proper length. When he was sent to school to learn the alphabet, he refused to hear about the second letter until his teacher had fully explained the first. Then Jesus himself explained *alpha* to his exasperated and dumbfounded teacher. The Infancy Gospel concludes with the Lukan story of Jesus in the Temple.

The Infancy Gospel of Thomas fits into the same time period as the Book of James. Its dependence on Luke places it in the second century. Irenaeus alludes to it in c. 185, so a date around 150 would seem appropriate.[52]

The putative author is Thomas, probably the disciple who is listed with the others in the Synoptic Gospels and to whom a special postresurrection appearance was granted, according to John 20:26–29. The Infancy Gospel seems to have no relationship to the Coptic Gospel of Thomas, to be discussed subsequently. The actual author of the Infancy Gospel is not known.

In character, the Infancy Gospel appears to be a collection of popular legends, many of which may have circulated orally. If so, they must have originated in a gentile environment, because they contain no knowledge of Jewish practices except those that could be learned from the canonical gospels. The prodigious childhood of Jesus is looked on as an anticipation of his later miracles and teaching. In the teaching material, which is minimal, there is a leaning toward Gnosticism, which will be treated in Chapter 11. Jesus' allegorical interpretation of the letter *alpha,* for example, is similar to many Gnostic speculations. The church did not canonize this gospel, but its popularity is demonstrated by the fact that it was translated into several languages and appeared in a number of collections in the ancient period.

The Gospel of Peter

Near the end of the second century, Serapion, bishop of Antioch, referred to a gospel in use at the church of Rhossus, a coastal town near Antioch.[53] It was called the Gospel According to Peter. At first the bishop saw no harm in its use, although he was sure that Peter had not written it. But on closer examination he concluded that it must not be used because of its docetic connections. Although some later writers referred to a Gospel of Peter, no one quoted from it. Thus, nothing was known of its contents

---

[52] Irenaeus, op. cit., I, 7:1.
[53] In Eusebius, op. cit., VI, 12:2–6.

A silver plaque showing the apostle Peter carrying a cross on a staff. Found near Antioch, Syria, and dating from the sixth century. (Courtesy the Metropolitan Museum of Art, Fletcher Fund, 1950.)

until 1886, when a fragment of the gospel was discovered in Upper Egypt. The manuscript was in Greek and was produced in the eighth or ninth century CE.

The most notable feature in the fragment is the description of the resurrection itself, something totally missing in the canonical gospels. It begins with the Matthean story of Pilate's washing his hands at the trial of Jesus (Matt 27:24) and continues with Jesus' crucifixion, burial, and resurrection. On the Saturday night after the crucifixion, the soldiers guarding Jesus' tomb saw the heavens open and two men descend to enter the tomb. A few moments later they saw three men come out—two whose heads reached heaven and one even taller. They were followed by a cross. A voice from heaven asked if Jesus had preached to the dead, and a voice from the cross answered, "Yes." Then another man descended from heaven and entered the tomb. The scene was set for the discovery of the empty tomb by the women on Sunday morning, and that episode is described in Markan terms.

Bishop Serapion was certainly correct in suspecting the authorship of this document. The author made use of all four canonical gospels and so could hardly have lived during the apostolic period. In addition, although the gospel claimed to be by Peter, the central event of the resurrection took place in front of soldiers, who agreed to tell no one what they saw. There is no suggestion that Peter was present at the tomb when this event took place; rather, the gospel implies that he was fishing. Once again, we have an unknown author. The document should probably be assigned to the middle of the second century, because the church at Rhossus was using it a few decades later. The identification with Rhossus suggests a Syrian location for the author.

Although Serapion judged that the gospel should no longer be read in the church, it is not easy to identify the cause of his objections. But there are some traces in the extant fragment that may have had docetic overtones. For example, during the crucifixion, Jesus held his peace "as if he felt no pain."[54] The gospel does not explicitly say that Jesus died; rather we have, "he was taken up."[55] Just before that, he cried out, "My power, O power, thou hast forsaken me!"[56] Taken together, these statements might have been intended to suggest the unreality of Jesus' humanity and, hence, of his death. They imply that he felt no pain and did not die. The power that forsook him would be identified as the divine Christ, which left the body at that moment. Although it is possible to interpret these remarks in other ways, it is likely that in this gospel we are in touch with a version of Christianity that subtly undermined convictions about the real humanity of Jesus and at the same time satisfied popular curiosities about his resurrection.

[54] Gospel of Peter, verse 10, trans. by Christian Maurer, in Edgar Hennecke, *New Testament Apocrypha*, ed. by W. Schneemelcher, trans. by R. McL. Wilson (Philadelphia: Westminster Press, 1963), Vol. I.
[55] Ibid., verse 19.
[56] Ibid.; see Matt 27:46 and Mark 15:34.

The Coptic Gospel of Thomas [57]

In 1945 a remarkable discovery of several manuscripts, containing fifty-two documents, was made near the town of Nag Hammadi in Egypt. Although the manuscripts were written in the Coptic language, they had been translated from Greek originals, most of which have been lost. The manuscripts themselves were probably produced in the fourth century CE, but some of the Greek originals would be much older. Among the texts were several that had the word gospel in their titles. The Gospel of Truth and the Gospel of Philip, although they are Christian documents, were not written in the form of the traditional gospels—that is, they are not stories about or sayings of Jesus. But the Coptic Gospel of Thomas consists of 114 sayings of Jesus, and may, thus, be compared with the canonical gospels.

Scholars had long known of the existence of a gospel under the name of Thomas. The third-century Christian writer Hippolytus had transmitted one saying from it,[58] and several sayings are contained in the Oxyrynchus papyri, which had been discovered in 1897. But until the Nag Hammadi discovery, we did not know that these sayings had come from the Gospel of Thomas. These tantalizing bits of information can now be put together, and we can see just what the Gospel of Thomas looked like.

The gospel consists entirely of sayings of Jesus. There is no narrative framework except the general introduction, which states: "These are the secret sayings which the living Jesus spoke and which Didymos Judas Thomas wrote down." All the sayings are addressed to disciples, individually or collectively, some in response to their questions. Although a pattern can be discerned within a short series of sayings, no overall structure is apparent. The sayings take the form of parables, proverbs, and short exhortations. Some sayings appear to have been taken from other apocryphal gospels, but most have no known parallels. But in both form and content, many sayings are similar to those in the Synoptic Gospels and may be drawn directly from them. Consider, for example, the following sayings:

> Jesus said, "You see the mote in your brother's eye but you do not see the beam in your own eye. When you cast the beam out of your own eye, then you will see clearly to cast the mote from your brother's eye." [59]

> Jesus said, "A city being built on a high mountain and fortified cannot fall, nor can it be hidden." [60]

[57] This document is frequently called simply The Gospel of Thomas. The title used here is intended to distinguish it from the Infancy Gospel of Thomas.
[58] Hippolytus, *Refutation of All Heresies*, V, 7:20.
[59] Coptic Gospel of Thomas, Saying 26, trans. by Thomas O. Lambdin, in *The Nag Hammadi Library in English*, ed. by James M. Robinson (New York: Harper, 1977). Cf. Matt 7:3–5 and Luke 6:41–42.
[60] Ibid., Saying 32; cf. Matt 5:14.

Jesus said, "If a blind man leads a blind man, they will both fall into a pit."[61]

Jesus said, "Whoever blasphemes against the Father will be forgiven, and whoever blasphemes against the Son will be forgiven, but whoever blasphemes against the Holy Spirit will not be forgiven either on earth or in heaven."[62]

Jesus said, "Blessed are the poor, for yours is the Kingdom of Heaven."[63]

In a comparison of sayings in Coptic Thomas and in the synoptics, Hugh Montefiore, an English theologian, has concluded that, although many parables in Thomas depend on the synoptics, others have come from an independent source. Montefiore writes: "Occasionally this source seems to be superior [to that on which the synoptics drew], especially inasmuch as it seems to be free from apocalyptic imagery, allegorical interpretation, and generalizing conclusions."[64] One implication of this discovery is that, if we are looking for historically authentic words of Jesus, we cannot afford to overlook the Coptic Gospel of Thomas.

The teachings in the gospel are said to be the secret sayings of Jesus recorded by Thomas. Even so, Thomas does not reveal all that Jesus said, even to the other disciples.[65] The disciples here are understood as an elite group, and the message of Jesus is intended for a limited number. Many sayings relate to the kingdom of God, but the kingdom is not understood as something to come in future time; it is to be found in the present. This means that some effort is called for on the part of the disciples, but the effort is largely a matter of self-knowledge. The kingdom is a present spiritual phenomenon to be found within the disciples.

Jesus said, "If those who lead you say to you, 'See, the Kingdom is in the sky,' then the birds of the sky will precede you. If they say to you, 'It is in the sea,' then the fish will precede you. Rather, the Kingdom is inside of you, and it is outside of you. When you come to know yourselves, then you will become known, and you will realize that it is you who are the sons of the living Father."[66]

The resurrection of the dead is no eschatological occurrence of the future but an event of the past:

His disciples said to Him, "When will the repose of the dead come about, and when will the new world come?" He said to them, "What you look forward to has already come, but you do not recognize it."[67]

---

[61] Ibid., Saying 34; cf. Matt 15:14 and Luke 6:39.
[62] Ibid., Saying 44; cf. Matt 12:31 and Mark 3:28–29.
[63] Ibid., Saying 54; cf. Luke 6:20 and Matt 5:3.
[64] Hugh Montefiore and H. E. W. Turner, *Thomas and the Evangelists* (Naperville, Ill.: Allenson, 1962), p. 78.
[65] See Coptic Gospel of Thomas, Saying 13.
[66] Ibid., Saying 3, trans. by Lambdin, op. cit.
[67] Ibid., Saying 51.

In some sayings the kingdom is equated with Jesus, and there is a kind of incorporation of the disciples with Jesus. There is also a degree of pantheism in one saying:

> Jesus said, "It is I who am the light which is above them all. It is I who am the All. From Me did the All come forth, and unto Me did the All extend. Split a piece of wood and I am there. Lift up a stone, and you will find Me there." [68]

Jesus is the Light and the All; he is one with the Father. But not everyone can see him for what he is. Some may mistake him for a human being:

> Salome said: "Who are you, man; as if you were from someone special you have come up on my couch and eaten from my table?" Jesus said to her, "I am He who exists from the Undivided. I was given some of the things of My father." [69]

In this passage, Salome has apparently mistaken Jesus for a human being, and Jesus has corrected her.

The method by which we attain to the kingdom is, in Greek, *gnosis*, which means knowing oneself and knowing God. Gnosis is the key word in Gnosticism, which will be discussed in Chapter 11. We will see that there are several contacts with the Coptic Gospel of Thomas. In this gospel, self-knowledge is the means of salvation. There are few moral duties. Above all, we must despise all things material and abhor sex. The ideal is a unisex, which means the abolition of the male-female dichotomy. One saying may reveal a degree of antifeminism:

> Simon Peter said to them, "Let Mary leave us, for women are not worthy of Life."
> Jesus said, "I myself shall lead her in order to make her male, so that she too may become a living spirit resembling you males. For every woman who will make herself male will enter the Kingdom of Heaven." [70]

Because allegorical interpretations abound in most of the Nag Hammadi texts, it is likely that the surface meaning of this saying is not to be trusted. Male seems to stand for the spiritual and female for the physical, so that the meaning is that a physical person who becomes spiritual will enter the kingdom of heaven. Even so, the use of the female to symbolize the physical is itself a form of antifeminism. In another saying, the ideal state is symbolized by nudity:

> His disciples said, "When will You become revealed to us and when shall we see You?"

---

[68] Ibid., Saying 77.
[69] Ibid., Saying 61, trans. by Harry Attridge, "Greek Equivalents of Two Coptic Phrases," *Bulletin of the American School of Papyrologists,* 18:27–32 (1981).
[70] Ibid., Saying 114, trans. by Lambdin, op. cit.

> Jesus said, "When you disrobe without being ashamed and take up your garments and place them under your feet like little children and tread on them, then [will you see] the Son of the Living One, and you will not be afraid."[71]

Although the plain meaning of this saying is that we should become nude, the garments probably refer to the human body. The meaning would be that we should strip off our bodies and become pure spirits, so the purely spiritual person is the ideal.

The Coptic Gospel of Thomas is a mixture of secret sayings about self-knowledge and inwardness. It brings together mysticism, pantheism, Docetism, and antimaterialism. And yet, as R. M. Grant notes, this gospel should have a strong attraction for people of the twentieth century. He writes:

> Thomas is silent about sin and forgiveness. He records no miracles or, indeed, deeds of Jesus. There are no embarrassing stories about demons and the exorcism of demons. The kingdom of God is almost entirely inward, unrelated to time or history. One need not love his enemies. . . . Self-knowledge is all-important.[72]

The date for this gospel has usually been set about 150, but in fact it could have been written almost any time in the second century. The probably erroneous attribution to Thomas is interesting. He is here referred to as Didymos Judas Thomas. Both Didymos and Thomas mean twin, the former from Greek and the latter from Aramaic, and so we may read the name as Jude, "the twin." In the Gospel of John, Thomas is called by the Greek Didymos, but the author does not say whose twin he was. Matthew, Mark, and the letter of Jude call attention to a brother of Jesus by the name of Jude or Judas. In another Nag Hammadi document and in the third-century Acts of Thomas, the identification of Thomas as Jesus' twin brother is explicit. These traditions evidently rest on the assumption that Jude and Thomas were names for the same person, namely, the twin brother of Jesus. He is, thus, highly regarded in the Coptic Gospel of Thomas. The only competitor is James, identified in some documents as a brother of Jesus. Here he is proclaimed to be the leader of the community after the departure of Jesus. In one saying we have:

> The disciples said to Jesus, "We know that You will depart from us. Who is to be our leader?"
> Jesus said to them, "Wherever you are, you are to go to James the righteous, for whose sake heaven and earth came into being."[73]

We have come to the end of our survey of some of the Christian gospels that tell of the deeds and sayings of Jesus. Here we must be reminded that

[71] Ibid., Saying 37.
[72] R. M. Grant and D. N. Freedman, *The Secret Sayings of Jesus* (New York: Doubleday, 1960), p. 112f.
[73] Coptic Gospel of Thomas, Saying 12, trans. by Lambdin, op. cit.

these documents contain a mixture of material, some drawn from tradition and some added by the authors. Our survey has concentrated on some of the major themes in each of the gospels, themes that probably affected the editing of the traditional material. We must also be reminded that there is a gap between the life of Jesus and the earliest extant gospel, a gap of about forty years. It is during this period that the tradition about Jesus was developing orally, and it is ultimately on this tradition that our gospels drew. For these reasons, it is important to know what that oral period in Christian history was like, and we turn to an investigation of that subject in the next chapter.

BIBLIOGRAPHY

The Synoptic Problem

Butler, B. C. *The Originality of St. Matthew.* Cambridge: Cambridge University Press, 1951.

Farmer, W. R. *The Synoptic Problem.* New York: Macmillan Publishing Co., Inc., 1964.

Parker, Pierson. *The Gospel Before Mark.* Chicago: University of Chicago Press, 1953.

Streeter, B. H. *The Four Gospels.* London: Macmillan & Company Ltd., 1924.

Throckmorton, Burton H., ed. *Gospel Parallels,* 4th ed. New York: Thomas Nelson Inc., 1979.

The most widely accepted solution to the synoptic problem, the two-document hypothesis, is presented in classic form by Streeter. Farmer's book analyzes the historical development of the two-document hypothesis and presents an argument for the Griesbach. Butler argues for the priority of Matthew, and Parker presents the case for the existence of a hypothetical source for both Matthew and Mark. Throckmorton's synopsis in English is a basic tool for comparing the three gospels side-by-side.

The Gospel of Matthew

Bornkamm, Günther, G. Barth, and H. J. Held. *Tradition and Interpretation in Matthew.* Trans. by Percy Scott. Philadelphia: Westminster Press, 1963.

Davies, W. D. *The Sermon on the Mount.* Cambridge: Cambridge University Press, 1966.

———. *The Setting of the Sermon on the Mount.* Cambridge: Cambridge University Press, 1964.

Stendahl, Krister. *The School of St. Matthew and Its Use of the Old Testament.* 2nd ed. Philadelphia: Fortress Press, 1968.

The volume by Bornkamm, Barth, and Held consists of a series of redaction-critical essays on Matthew's eschatology, legal theory, and interpretation of the miracle stories. Davies, in *The Setting of the Sermon on the Mount,* analyzes the various settings through which the material in Matthew 5–7 passed, and he treats its relationship to Judaism and to Jewish messianic expectation. Davies' *Sermon on the Mount* is an abridged version of *The Setting of the Sermon on the Mount*. Stendahl looks at Matthew as the product of a school, rather than the composition of a single author or editor.

The Gospel of Mark

Burkill, T. A. *Mysterious Revelation*. Ithaca, N. Y.: Cornell University Press, 1963.
Kee, Howard C. *Community of the New Age: Studies in Mark's Gospel*. Philadelphia: Westminster Press, 1977.
Kelber, Werner. *Mark's Story of Jesus*. Philadelphia: Fortress Press, 1979.
Marxsen, Willi. *Mark the Evangelist*. Trans. by James Boyce et al. Nashville, Tenn.: Abingdon Press, 1969.
Nineham, D. E. *St. Mark*. Westminster Pelican Commentaries. Philadelphia: Westminster Press, 1978.

Burkill concentrates on Mark's treatment of secrecy. Kee attempts to look behind the gospel to see the social aspects of the author's community. Kelber takes the blindness of the disciples as the major theme in Mark and traces it back to Mark's intention. Marxsen's book consists of four essays that attempt to discover the intention and point of view of Mark. Nineham's is a traditional commentary, and he includes a helpful section on oral tradition.

The Gospel of Luke

Cadbury, Henry. *The Making of Luke-Acts,* 2nd ed. London: Society for the Promotion of Christian Knowledge, 1958.
Conzelmann, Hans. *The Theology of St. Luke*. Trans. by Geoffrey Buswell. New York: Harper & Row, Publishers, 1960.
Talbert, 'C. H. *Literary Patterns, Theological Themes and the Genre of Luke-Acts*. Society of Biblical Literature Monograph Series 20. Missoula, Mont.: Scholars Press, 1974.

Cadbury's analysis of the author of Luke-Acts, his materials, methods, personality, and purpose, is a classic study. Conzelmann's was the first redaction study of Luke-Acts. Talbert concentrates on some important literary aspects of these books.

The Gospel of John

Brown, Raymond E. *The Community of the Beloved Disciple*. New York: Paulist Press, 1979.
Bultmann, Rudolf. *The Gospel of John*. Trans. by G. R. Beasley-Murray et al. Philadelphia: Westminster Press, 1971.

Dodd, C. H. *The Interpretation of the Fourth Gospel*. Cambridge: Cambridge University Press, 1953.

Käsemann, Ernst. *The Testament of Jesus*. Trans. by Gerhard Krodel. Philadelphia: Fortress Press, 1968.

Martyn, J. Louis. *History and Theology in the Fourth Gospel*. 2nd ed. Nashville, Tenn.: Abingdon Press, 1979.

Smith, D. Moody. *The Composition and Order of the Fourth Gospel*. New Haven, Conn.: Yale University Press, 1965.

Bultmann's commentary on John first appeared in 1941 in German. This is the first English translation. Smith's book is a critical analysis of Bultmann's treatment of the Fourth Gospel. The Dodd commentary is difficult for the student who does not read Greek, but the sections on the Hellenistic religious and philosophical background of John are invaluable. Brown and Martyn approach the gospel differently, but they both see the background of John in the dialogues between the synagogue and the emerging church. Käsemann emphasizes the Gnostic qualities of the author in his analysis of John 17.

Apocryphal Gospels

Grant, Robert M., and D. N. Freedman. *The Secret Sayings of Jesus*. New York: Doubleday & Company, Inc., 1960.

Hennecke, Edgar. *New Testament Apocrypha*. Ed. by W. Schneemelcher. Trans. by R. McL. Wilson. Philadephia: Westminster Press, 1963, 1965. 2 volumes.

Montefiore, Hugh, and H. E. W. Turner. *Thomas and the Evangelists*. Naperville, Ill.: Allenson, 1962.

Robinson, James M., ed. *The Nag Hammadi Library in English*. New York: Harper & Row, Publishers, 1977.

The two-volume edition by Hennecke includes translations of all the apocryphal gospels treated in this chapter. In addition there are many more gospels and other writings included. The book edited by Robinson is a translation of all the Nag Hammadi texts, including the Coptic Gospel of Thomas. The translation was the work of the Coptic Gnostic Library Project of the Institute for Antiquity and Christianity. The books by Grant and Freedman and by Montefiore and Turner are studies of the Coptic Gospel of Thomas.

❖ 7 ❖

Oral Traditions

I F there is a connection between the gospels and Jesus, that connection runs through a period in which the sayings of Jesus and stories about him circulated almost entirely in oral forms. Because there is good reason for dating the earliest gospel in or near 70 CE, and because the crucifixion of Jesus can be dated in about 30 CE, there is a gap between Jesus and the gospels of about forty years. During that period there was undoubtedly a great deal of activity in various Christian communities. The primary evidence for such activity is found in the letters of Paul, which were probably written in the 50s. In those letters, Paul alluded to a few sayings of Jesus, and he showed definite awareness of the last supper, the crucifixion, the burial, and several resurrection appearances.[1] But Paul's letters are the sole surviving literary documents written by Christians in the pregospel period, and they do not contain sufficient material about Jesus to form a connection between him and the gospels.

The connection between Jesus and the gospels should be understood as an oral one. In general, it is thought that the memory of Jesus' words and deeds was kept alive by oral communication from 30–70. Of course, oral communication did not cease in 70, but when the period of gospel-producing activity began, the situation was changed.

The supposition about an oral period in the history of Christianity is not merely that. Some writers of the late first and early second centuries have left us some indications of it. There seems to be a distinction made in the prologue to the Gospel of Luke between those who write narratives and those who transmit traditions:

> Inasmuch as many have undertaken to compile a narrative of the things which
> have been accomplished among us, just as they were delivered to us by those

---

[1] See 1 Cor 11:23–26 and 15:3–8.

212

who from the beginning were eyewitnesses and ministers of the word, it seemed good for me also . . . to write an orderly account . . . (Luke 1:1–3).

The reference to those who compiled narratives seems to be a reference to people who produced written documents. But their information came, says Luke, from eyewitnesses and ministers of the word, who delivered material. The implication is that the delivery was oral. More explicit is the remark of Papias about the writing of the Gospel of Mark. Papias' remark was quoted in the previous chapter, but it bears repeating here:

> Mark became Peter's interpreter and wrote accurately all that he remembered, not, indeed, in order, of the things said or done by the Lord. For he had not heard the Lord, nor had he followed him, but later on, as I said, followed Peter, who used to give teaching as necessity demanded but not making, as it were, an arrangement of the Lord's oracles, so that Mark did nothing wrong in thus writing down single points as he remembered them. For to one thing he gave attention, to leave out nothing of what he had heard and to make no false statements in them.[2]

We may understand the reference to Peter's activity as oral and Mark's as literary. Luke and Papias give us adequate grounds for the conviction that there was an oral period, and Papias includes some helpful remarks about its character.

The initial reaction to an oral tradition may be despair, for it is not immediately clear how it should be treated. It seems inaccessible. Nevertheless, the study of oral traditions is generally one of the tasks of historical research, for oral materials almost always lie at the base of the historian's quest. An event is preserved in memory and oral discourse before it is committed to writing. Historians, therefore, have found it possible to study oral processes. In the first place, it is possible to learn a great deal about an oral period by studying the characteristics of the oral traditions that are close to our own time. There are living oral traditions still available in some cultures, and, in our own, some materials, such as fairy tales, nursery rhymes, folk songs, and folk tales, were not collected and written down until the nineteenth century. By studying these living and recent traditions, we can become aware of tendencies at work in the transmission of oral materials. Second, in the case of the Christian oral tradition, we have in the gospels a deposit that was left behind. The gospels represent an accessible stage in the transmission of materials about Jesus, and it should be possible to work back from them to the earlier stages. Third, we must use historical imagination. This is not a device to fill the gaps between certainties; rather, it should function as a methodological tool for discriminating between the probable and the merely possible.

[2] In Eusebius, *The Ecclesiastical History* III, 39:15, trans. by Kirsopp Lake, Loeb Classical Library (Cambridge, Mass.: Harvard U.P., 1926).

CHARACTERISTICS OF ORAL TRADITIONS

If we ask what usually happens to material preserved orally, and in particular what happened to the material about Jesus, several observations can be made.

(1) *A great deal of information about Jesus was not preserved in the oral tradition.*

No person or group of persons can remember everything, and most of what is remembered never comes to expression. What may come to expression is the significant moment or the meaningful pronouncement. The gospels conform to this thesis, because they contain almost no details about the interesting externals of Jesus' life: the kind of education he had, his possible association with a partisan group, where he stayed when he traveled away from home, how often he traveled, what he looked like. Many of Luke's eyewitnesses would have known the answers to these questions, but the information is not found in the gospels. Such information about Jesus must not have circulated widely in the oral period, because it was not regarded as significant. We may reasonably assume that the oral tradition retained only a minimal amount of the information about Jesus and that most of the facts about his life are forever lost.

(2) *The material that was preserved in oral form was retained because it was regarded as significant.*

Ultimately, historical investigation must deal with the nature of human memory. In Chapter 1 it was observed that people tend to remember those things that have significance—that is, those incidents that serve as signals of a reality that seems to be more than the incident itself. The signal of reality may be a glimpse into the character of another person, an insight into the meaning of one's own life, an understanding of the way things work, or a flash of awareness about the meaning of good and evil. Quite incidental things may serve as vehicles for such insights. Long years after the event, a mature person may remember a certain Christmas morning as a particularly bright day, on which as a child she received some special gift from her parents. She may remember the gift, those who gave it, the wrapping, the Christmas tree, the house decorations, and any number of other details. And when she thinks of this incident, she finds that her memory is surrounded by feelings of affection, joy, and pleasure. She remembers because the incident serves as a signal of the meaning of human love. In general, human beings tend to remember subjectively significant events and to forget those that seem to lack significance. But we must go a step further to say that such significance is not inherent in the event itself. It is a product of the interplay between the event and the persons involved, and this means that an event that is remembered is an event that has been interpreted. The disciples of Jesus probably were witnesses to any number of occurrences that carried little significance for them; however, what they remembered and brought to expression was what they interpreted as having significance.

(3) *The oral tradition could contain diverse interpretations.*

From time to time we are able to see the presence of an interpretative element by examining the deposit of the oral tradition. When the Christian gospels include two or more versions of the same incident, the interpretative elements are sometimes not difficult to isolate. Jesus' saying about the sign of Jonah is a case in point. In Mark 8:11–12 Jesus, in response to a Pharisaic question, categorically refuses to cite a sign of his authority. In Matt 16:4 he says simply that the sign of Jonah is the only sign to be given to that generation. In Luke 11:29–32, we have the same saying with an interpretation in which the sign is Jonah's preaching of repentance. People "repented at the preaching of Jonah, and behold, something greater than Jonah is here" (Luke 11:32). In Matt 12, the statement reappears with the interpretation about repentance. But in between the saying and this interpretation, Matthew has sandwiched an additional explanation that interprets the sign as the burial of Jesus: "For as Jonah was three days and three nights in the belly of the whale, so will the Son of man be three days and three nights in the heart of the earth" (Matt 12:40). This must mean that a saying has reached the synoptic writers in several forms: (1) one in which there is no sign, (2) one in which there is a sign but no interpretation, (3) one in which the sign is understood as repentance, and (4) one in which the sign is understood as Jesus' burial and implied resurrection. The various forms of the saying may stem from different oral traditions, in each of which the saying was significant but in each of which there was a different interpretation. In this case it is likely that Jesus once cited the sign of Jonah but did so without an explicit interpretation, so that various listeners preserved the saying in the light of the significance it had for them.

(4) *The oral tradition could confuse the original words of Jesus with the interpretations.*

The saying about the sign of Jonah illustrates this possibility. Here an original statement of Jesus, subject to diverse understandings, has picked up different interpretations that finally became part of the saying itself. Once the interpretation became attached to the saying, it would be difficult to distinguish between the original saying and the interpretation. Thus, the explanation came to be attributed to Jesus himself. This must have been the case when Matthew wrote. Aware of several forms of the Jonah-saying, the evangelist concluded that Jesus said all of them. So he recorded the original saying and the interpretations with no attempt at discrimination.

(5) *The oral tradition was carried on in the contexts of preaching, teaching, debates, worship, and prophecy.*

It is a truism to say that the oral tradition was preserved and transmitted by the primitive Christian communities, but it is a meaningful one. It implies that the tradition was largely a product of Christian reflection and activity and that the various activities provided the contexts for the transmission of oral material. One of those activities was preaching. Preaching is denoted by the Greek word *kerygma,* which literally means the act of proclamation. C. H. Dodd, an English NT scholar, and others have been able to find an outline of the main features of this proclamation. Dodd investigated the letters of Paul and the speeches in Acts to determine the basic framework of the kerygma, which he defined as "the public proclamation of Christianity to the non-Christian world."[3] The most primitive recoverable form of the kerygma seems to be as follows:

1. The age of fulfillment has dawned.
2. "This has taken place through the ministry, death and resurrection of Jesus, of which a brief account is given, with proof from the Scriptures that all took place through 'the determinate counsel and foreknowledge of God.' "[4]
3. Jesus has been exalted as Messiah.
4. "The Holy Spirit in the Church is the sign of Christ's present power and glory."[5]
5. "The Messianic Age will shortly reach its consummation in the return of Christ."[6]
6. Repent and receive salvation.

Although the primary purpose of apostolic preaching was not to convey information about Jesus, such information would be given indirectly. The kerygma would be punctuated throughout by illustrative material drawn from the OT and other Jewish writings, from Jewish folklore and oral traditions, as well as from the apostolic memory of Jesus' life and teachings.

The sermon was not the only context in which oral traditions survived. In the early period, Christians were frequently engaged in debates with Jews, and, in the course of such debates, material from the life of Jesus would be cited. The Christian communities would also provide teaching for those initiates who needed ethical instruction. In their worship the communities developed a cult with an emphasis on baptism and a meal, and material about Jesus was cited in their hymns and liturgy. Finally, the early communities included people called prophets, who spoke in the name of the

---

[3] C. H. Dodd, *The Apostolic Preaching and Its Developments* (London: Holder and Stoughton, 1936), p. 7.
[4] Ibid., p. 39.
[5] Ibid., p. 42.
[6] Ibid.

risen Lord. Although such prophets may not have been eyewitnesses to Jesus' life, their words would come into the tradition as the words of Jesus. All of these activities provided the contexts for the preservation and transmission of the stories and sayings of Jesus: preaching, teaching, debates, worship, and prophecy.

(6) *No connected account of the life of Jesus was preserved in the oral tradition.*

The contexts in which the material about Jesus circulated were not such as to produce and preserve a consecutive account of Jesus' life. If the material about Jesus was preserved in oral traditions through preaching and teaching, then it was preserved in bits and pieces, not in sequential narratives. Papias was aware of this when he said that Mark did not write down the life of Jesus in order, because Peter taught as necessity demanded. Peter would probably support his own teaching by referring to sayings of Jesus and, hence, Mark would in time have built up a supply of such sayings, but they would not be in any particular order. Thus, Papias implies that Mark's account is accurate in respect to content but not in respect to order. The various contexts of transmission would bring to light a large number of sayings and stories of Jesus but would neither put them in order nor provide chronological or geographical notes, which might serve a biographer. We may be assured, therefore, that no connected account of the life of Jesus was preserved in the traditions that lie behind the gospels.

(7) *The contexts in which the material was used affected the meanings.*

The fact that the materials about Jesus were used in the service of various Christian activities means that only what served those functions was retained and that the context affected the meaning. We are faced again with the probable disappearance of some remembered, but no longer useful, material. In addition, the interpretative force of the context must be considered. We are familiar with the possibility of using a quotation out of context. A public official who makes a statement in one context intends thereby to convey a certain meaning. But supporters or opponents may use the statement in a different context in order to attribute a quite different meaning to it. That this happened to sayings of Jesus is illustrated in the Synoptic Gospels. Both Matt 5:25–26 and Luke 12:58–59 have a saying of Jesus about going to court. Although the saying is substantially the same in both gospels, the context in Luke compels an eschatological understanding of it. The meaning in Luke is that because the end of all things is near, one should make friends *now* with one's accuser. Matthew, however, places the saying in a group of moral prohibitions, where it is an expansion of a saying on hatred. In Matthew the meaning is: Do not hate your brother and, above all, do not allow hatred to come to the level of legal proceedings, because you may lose your case, and it will be disastrous for you. The Lukan version speaks of the urgency of settling disputes, whereas the Matthean gives us a bit of prudential legal advice. It is possible that the gospel writers provided the contexts for the saying, but it is more likely that the oral tradition did so. It is probable that the saying was used in preaching, where the eschatological emphasis determined its meaning, and that it was also used in teaching, where prudence was emphasized.

(8) *Some sayings and stories used in oral traditions may have had sources other than Jesus.*

A statement made by a revered Christian in the act of preaching, or a story used in debates or teaching, or a prophetic pronouncement, may later have been accepted as a word of Jesus. In the course of the development of oral tradition, it becomes increasingly difficult to retain an awareness of the originator of a saying. Although our age, in its emphasis on printed and recorded information, differs substantially in this respect, the difficulty can still be illustrated. We no longer know who originally said: "A stitch in time saves nine," "A cat has nine lives," "Where there is smoke, there is fire," or "Make love, not war." It is notoriously difficult, if not impossible, to trace the origin of such popular sayings. The Christian gospels contain a number of sayings that are also found in rabbinic literature, and it is possible that some of them came into the Christian oral tradition from Jewish sources. Hellenistic folklore may have provided another source for the oral tradition. Prophetic pronouncements would have caused great difficulty, because they were introduced as sayings of the Lord. Although this did not originally mean sayings of the historical Jesus, the distinction was not always maintained.

(9) *The Semitic linguistic and cultural environment of the oral tradition was modified by the Hellenistic.*

Some time during the four decades between Jesus and the gospels, Palestinian Christians began a successful missionary movement among Gentiles. By the time the gospels were written, most Christians were probably Gentiles living in a non-Jewish environment. The language of the oral tradition consequently shifted from Hebrew or Aramaic to Greek, and Hellenistic thought forms and images began to dominate the language. More and more, the tradition could draw on Hellenistic sources for use in preaching and teaching. Of course, the oral tradition did not lose its Semitic background, but it did expand into Hellenism, and it used stories and sayings familiar in that world. A simple illustration of the adaptation to the Greek language may be seen in a saying of Jesus recorded in Matt 5:18: "For truly, I say to you, till heaven and earth pass away, not an iota, not a dot, will pass from the law until all is accomplished." The saying refers to the durability of the Jewish Torah, but the component parts of the Torah are spoken of in terms meaningful to those who know Greek. The *iota* is a Greek letter, and the *dot* is a breathing or accent mark used in written Greek. The saying as it stands would have perplexed a Semitic person, although a similar Aramaic saying may once have existed.

(10) *The oral tradition probably made use of a limited number of forms.*

Historians frequently use oral sources to supplement their information. A biographer, for example, may need to consult a number of individuals who can provide information about a subject. He or she will listen to an oral narration and judge its quality in terms of its evidential value and its correspondence with other information. The material in the gospels, however, has come not from a number of individual sources, but from oral tradition, and the characteristics of oral tradition are not those of individual oral sources. An oral tradition has become the property of a group, and it has a history. Oral tradition is that unwritten material that has been delivered from one generation to another. The author of Luke was fully aware of this and claimed to follow the things "that were delivered to us." In oral tradition, stories and sayings are seemingly not the conscious creations of individuals; they become forged by constant oral repetition and are unconsciously and spontaneously developed by a community. Frequent oral repetition requires the development of certain patterns or forms. The repeated use of the forms aids the memory and the use of stories and sayings in the community. The number of such forms is limited, as Kendrick Grobel, a scholar of the NT, has observed: "A given folk at a given time is likely to use a limited number of types of unit, into one or another of which by an instinctive mnemonic economy it pours the content of each particular tradition."[7] One key to understanding oral tradition consists in an analysis of the forms with which the tradition operated.

We turn next to such an analysis of the forms that were probably used in the Christian oral tradition.

FORMS OF THE ORAL TRADITION

The study of forms, or form criticism, has been found to be very useful in dealing with oral traditions. Hermann Gunkel, a German OT scholar, was the first to apply the study of forms to OT materials. The first detailed treatments of forms in early Christianity were made by Rudolf Bultmann and Martin Dibelius, both writing in about 1920.[8] They began their study with the Synoptic Gospels and discovered that a number of primitive patterns underlie the written documents. The patterns can be analyzed in such a way that secondary elements are separated from the primary saying or

---

[7] Kendrick Grobel, "Form Criticism," in *The Interpreter's Dictionary of the Bible,* ed. G. A. Buttrick (Nashville, Tenn.: Abingdon, 1962), Vol. II, p. 320.
[8] See the bibliography at the end of this chapter for references.

Jesus Teaching Among the Apostles, fresco, early fourth century, Catacomb of Domitilla, Rome. (Courtesy *Pontifical Commission for Sacred Archives, Rome.*)

story. When the original form for a story is found, it is then possible to make a judgment about the context (or *Sitz im Leben,* setting in life) in which that form of the story first circulated.

The methods of the original NT form critics have been further sharpened by later practitioners of the art. Although Dibelius and Bultmann were skeptical of the possibility of working back from the oral tradition to Jesus, other scholars have been more positive about the veridical quality of the Christian oral tradition. For example, Vincent Taylor, in 1933, followed the main lines of Bultmann's analysis but found much less reason to doubt the accuracy of the tradition.

Form critical studies concentrate on the Synoptic Gospels almost exclusively, although some attention is now being given to the Coptic Gospel of Thomas. The reason for this concentration is that these gospels seem closer to the oral tradition than do John and the rest of the apocryphal gospels. This is not to say that the Synoptic Gospels have retained pure oral forms.

The assumption that form critics make is that sayings of Jesus and stories about him achieved certain forms *and then* picked up secondary elements as they circulated in the oral period. By the time they were used by Matthew, Mark, and Luke, they already had been altered from the original forms. But at least these gospels can be broken down into small units or pericopes, which can be further analyzed. The Gospel of John, as we have seen, does not easily lend itself to this kind of treatment. Its long discourses and miracle signs seem farther removed from the oral tradition than do the synoptics. A similar literary style is found in many of the apocryphal gospels. Moreover, their dependence on the canonical gospels essentially disqualifies them from form-critical analysis. The Coptic Gospel of Thomas, however, is a possible candidate, because it is made up of small teaching units that, in some form, could have circulated in the oral period.

Dibelius, Bultmann, and Taylor have provided a basic way to classify the forms of the oral tradition. Their systems are not precisely the same, nor is their terminology. But there is enough similarity that we can draw on all three in discussing the classifications. We will use a terminology that draws on Taylor and Bultmann, and much of the description of the various forms will depend on Bultmann's analyses.

The basic system of classification divides the material into two main categories: discourse material and narrative material. The discourse material is subdivided into sayings, parables, and pronouncement stories; the narrative material is made up of miracle stories and stories about Jesus.

Sayings

Sayings attributed to Jesus probably circulated widely in the oral period. They may have been used in almost any context, where they would have served to support ideas presented in Christian preaching, teaching, or debates. Essentially, these sayings had a free-floating existence, and they must have been quoted by preachers and teachers without any particular explanations or accompanying narratives. Many such sayings now appear in the gospels with little or no narrative framework. They are often introduced simply with the words, "Jesus said," without any notes about when or where the words were spoken or to whom they were spoken. Nothing is said about the circumstances that elicited the words or their effect on the audience. Some have been grouped together in the gospels to form longer discourses of Jesus. These sayings are simply that—sayings.

Bultmann discussed four basic types of sayings: logia, prophetic and apocalyptic sayings, legal sayings and community rules, and I-sayings. The logia are mostly proverbs, such as the following: "For out of the abundance of the heart the mouth speaks" (Matt 12:34 and Luke 6:45). "Let the day's own trouble be sufficient for the day" (Matt 6:34); "For the laborer deserves his food" (Matt 10:10 and Luke 10:7); "What therefore God has joined together, let not man put asunder" (Matt 19:6 and Mark 10:9); "Leave the dead to bury their own dead" (Matt 8:22 and Luke 9:60). By the time the logia reached the synoptic authors, some were expanded by the addition of explanations or combined with similar sayings and illustrations. The main contents of the logia consist of "observations on life, rules of prudence and popular morality, sometimes a product of humor or scepticism, full now of sober, popular morality, and now of naif egoism."[9] Some logia breathe the atmosphere of popular piety and are concerned with such things as the sovereignty of God, retributive righteousness in world affairs, trust in God's providence, and the efficacy of prayer. Most of these motifs and many similar sayings are found in rabbinic literature, and many of them probably came out of the Jewish oral tradition. Bultmann says that Palestinian Christians probably introduced these sayings out of the lore of folk wisdom, and the words were soon attributed to Jesus. But the possibility that Jesus himself used proverbs from Jewish traditions seems equally strong.

The prophetic and apocalyptic sayings are those concerned with the imminence of the kingdom of God and with the effects of its coming. They include the individual sayings in the synoptic apocalypse in Mark 13 and parallels, the beatitudes in Matt 5:3–12 and Luke 6:20–26, woes on the rich, woes on the scribes and Pharisees, and other admonitions. Many of the sayings have been taken over from Jewish traditions. The individual sayings in the synoptic apocalypse, for example, appear to be Christianized forms of Jewish apocalyptic sayings. This group also includes a number of prophetic sayings, which probably originated with revered Christian prophets. Bultmann observed, "The Church drew no distinction between such utterances by Christian prophets and the sayings of Jesus in the tradition, for the reason that even the dominical sayings in the tradition were not the pronouncements of a past authority, but sayings of the risen Lord, who is always a contemporary for the Church."[10]

The legal sayings and community rules include certain comments on the Torah, such as those in Matt 5:17–48, and certain rules on prayer and church discipline. These materials are not so old as the other sayings, and most have come out of Jewish tradition or Christian preaching.

A fourth category of sayings is called the I-sayings—that is, those in which Jesus makes some pronouncement about himself. In them Jesus appears as an eschatological prophet, Messiah, and judge of the world. According to Bultmann, they appeared relatively late in the oral period and were mainly products of Christian prophets in the Hellenistic Christian communities.

The result of Bultmann's analysis of the sayings is that we have in this

[9] Rudolf Bultmann, *The History of the Synoptic Tradition*, trans. by John Marsh (New York: Harper, 1963), p. 104.
[10] Ibid., p. 127ff.

group a mixture of possibly authentic and original sayings of Jesus, sayings that Jesus or some later Christian introduced from Jewish sources, and sayings that were introduced into the tradition by Christian preachers, teachers, or prophets. Although Bultmann was skeptical about the possibility of finding authentic sayings of Jesus, Taylor was much more confident. Taylor believed that Bultmann had overemphasized the creative power of the Christian communities. He agreed that Christians would modify and adopt Jesus' sayings, but he insisted that the sayings had to be there first.

Parables

Many of the sayings attributed to Jesus made use of vivid metaphors, such as, "No one puts new wine into old wineskins" (Mark 2:22 and parallels); "If a kingdom is divided against itself, that kingdom cannot stand" (Mark 3:24 and parallels); and "Can a blind man lead a blind man?" (Luke 6:39; cf. Matt 15:14). The meaning of these statements depends on an understanding of the comparison that is implied in the metaphor.

A parable is a metaphor told as a story. It "gives as its picture not a typical condition or a typical recurrent event, but some interesting particular situation."[11] The parable is a specific form in the oral tradition but there are variations in the parable pattern. Many begin with an introductory question, such as, "What is the kingdom of God like?" or with a formula of comparison, such as, "The kingdom of God is like this." A story is then told with marked brevity. There are few characters or groups and never more than three. In some cases a group consists of several persons, but in these cases only one person speaks for the group. The characters are denoted very simply, as kings, workers, publicans, fathers, and the like, and they are described only in terms of their action or speech within the story. A single course of action is described with economy of language. At the conclusion of the story, the hearer's judgment is implicitly or explicitly called for on the point of the story. Some parables have a concluding application introduced by the words, "Truly I say to you," or simply, "Thus." Others end with no explicit application.

No one parable can demonstrate all of these characteristics, but we will examine two for illustrative purposes. The brief parable in Matt 18:12–14 (cf. Luke 15:3–7) begins with a question: "What do you think?" Then comes a narrative about a man who has a hundred sheep, loses one, and rejoices when it is found. The character of the shepherd, his location, and his family are all ignored in the narrative. No other characters enter. There is no description of the search. At the conclusion the point is made, "So it is not the will of my Father who is in heaven that one of these little ones should perish" (Matt 18:14). The story is told to establish this one point.

[11] Ibid., p. 174.

No other application is called for, although readers may be interested in subsidiary questions.

The parable of the laborers in the vineyard in Matt 20:1–16 has an introductory formula: "For the kingdom of heaven is like a householder who went out early in the morning to hire laborers for his vineyard" (Matt 20:1). Then follows the story in which the householder employs people for various lengths of time and then pays all of them the same wages. The ones who had worked all day grumbled, but the householder explains that he has cheated no one. He has paid those who worked all day the contracted wages, and he has been generous to the rest. He claims that he can do what he will with what he has. The brevity of style is notable. Although many individuals are involved in the story, they are treated as groups, and there are only three speaking parts. The application in 20:16 probably did not originally belong to this parable, because it makes a point rather different from that in the parable itself. In the parable the kingdom of heaven is being compared to the situation in the story. Some people come in early and some late, but all receive the same reward. This is not the same as saying that "the last will be first, and the first last" (20:16). In the parable, both first and last become the same. Those who have come into the kingdom first have no advantage over the latecomers.

One of the fundamental insights in modern scholarship on parables is that a parable has one and only one point. Such a thesis seems eminently reasonable when we recognize that parables were originally used in oral situations, frequently situations of crisis or tension. Whether spoken by Jesus or by some later Christian, they were used to support a concept that the speaker was making. If they did not support that point, they did not work. As we think about parables, subsidiary questions may well come to mind. This is more likely to happen in reading and rereading a parable than in hearing it once in the context of a sermon. In the parable about the householder and the workers, for example, we may question the wisdom and the moral propriety of the employer's action in treating workers without due consideration for the quantity of their work. But this is a subsidiary matter that should not receive primary attention if we are interested in the original meaning of the parable. The interpreter of a parable should look for one clear and relevant point and only one.

Many of the parables in the Synoptic Gospels must have come from Jewish traditions, for similar parables are found in rabbinic literature. Some may have originated with Jesus, but it is extremely difficult to be certain on this point, because many were altered during the history of the oral period. They were frequently provided with introductions, conclusions, and applications. Sometimes two or more were grouped together. Explanations were added, and in some cases the explanation turned the parable into an allegory. When the gospel writers found the parables, they already may have contained secondary features, which were then included in the written compilations. The parable of the great supper in Matt 22:1–10 was given an allegorical expansion in 22:11–14. The parable of the sower in Mark 4:1–9 acquired a detailed interpretation in 4:13–20. Bultmann felt that, by the time of the Synoptic Gospels, the changes in the parables were so extensive that, *"The original meaning of many similitudes* [parables] *has become irrecoverable* in the course of the tradition." [12] He felt that the only ones that might go back to Jesus were those that expressed a distinctive eschatological temper and that lacked any features characteristic of Jewish piety or Christian thought. Once again, Taylor was not so negative.

Pronouncement Stories

A pronouncement story is a saying with a narrative introduction. [13] As such it is generally classified with sayings and parables, but it actually uses both discursive and narrative elements. The narrative introduction gives only the information needed to understand the pronouncement of Jesus, which comes at the conclusion. The narrative is generally marked by an absence of detail. There are almost no references to time or place. Most of the participants are representatives of a group (a scribe, a Pharisee, a disciple), and individual characteristics are either not given or are given indirectly by reference to something done or said. The action is generally initiated when someone poses a question to Jesus or makes some objection. The chief interest is in the saying or pronouncement of Jesus, which forms the conclusion to the pronouncement story. The saying is probably the most nearly original part. In the course of preaching, teaching, and debates, the saying picked up the explanatory narrative. Further details, such as more elaborate descriptions of the situation or the participants, were sometimes added at an even later time.

Bultmann subdivided the pronouncement stories into three types: controversial, scholastic, and biographical. The general pattern for a controversial story is found in the following:

> And as he sat at table in his house, many tax collectors and sinners were sitting with Jesus and his disciples; for there were many who followed him. And the scribes of the Pharisees, when they saw that he was eating with sinners and tax collectors, said to his disciples, "Why does he eat with tax collectors and sinners?" And when Jesus heard it, he said to them, "Those who are well have no need of a physician, but those who are sick; I came not to call the righteous, but sinners" (Mark 2:15–17; cf. Matt 9:10–13 and Luke 5:29–32).

The narrative element provides only the information that is needed to understand the story: Jesus is at home eating with his disciples and with tax

---

[12] Ibid., p. 199. (Italics Bultmann's)

[13] Pronouncement Story is Taylor's designation for this category. Dibelius calls them paradigms and Bultmann, apophthegms.

collectors and sinners. The scribes of the Pharisees observe this and question the disciples about it. Their question constitutes an objection to Jesus and therefore initiates a controversy. But the controversy concludes with Jesus' pronouncement, "Those who are well have no need of a physician, but those who are sick; I came not to call the righteous, but sinners" (Mark 2:17). The secondary nature of the narrative portion may be seen here, because there is not a tight fit between the pronouncement and the narrative. The pronouncement relates to the work of a physician, whereas the narrative pictures Jesus as a host. The scribes question the disciples, but Jesus answers. We are not told how the scribes found out about the meal or how they were able to observe what was happening. We can assume that the narrative came into the tradition to clothe the pronouncement with an interpretation. Once narrative and pronouncement came together, the pronouncement story circulated as a unit.

Another pronouncement story of the controversial type deals with the question of the Sabbath:

> One sabbath he was going through the grainfields; and as they made their way his disciples began to pluck heads of grain. And the Pharisees said to him, "Look, why are they doing what is not lawful on the sabbath?" And he said to them, "Have you never read what David did, when he was in need and was hungry, he and those who were with him: how he entered the house of God, when Abiathar was high priest, and ate the bread of the Presence, which it is not lawful for any but the priests to eat, and also gave it to those who were with him?" And he said to them, "The sabbath was made for man, not man for the sabbath; so the Son of man is lord even of the sabbath" (Mark 2:23–28; cf. Matt 12:1–8 and Luke 6:1–5).

Notice again the sparse details in the narrative section. The question the Pharisees ask is an objection to the action of the disciples, and Jesus responds to the objection in the pronouncement, "The sabbath was made for man, not man for the sabbath; so the Son of man is lord even of the sabbath" (Mark 2:27–28). There is here an additional section, namely a reference to an action of David, which seems intended to provide justification for Jesus' pronouncement.

Bultmann thought that, although the central saying in a controversy story may go back to Jesus, the narrative section originated "in the discussions the Church had with its opponents, and as certainly, within itself, on questions of law."[14] The dialogues are imaginary constructions of debates between Jesus and opponents. In the earlier stages of the tradition, the opponents were not named, but there was an active tendency in the later stages to use scribes and Pharisees in these roles. In reference to the historical authenticity of these stories, Bultmann says, "The individual controversy dialogues may not be historical reports of particular incidents in the life of

[14] Bultmann, op. cit., p. 41.

Jesus, but the general character of his life is rightly portrayed in them, on the basis of historical recollection." [15]

The scholastic type of pronouncement story differs from the controversial only in the respect that the topics of the scholastic type are matters on which Christians needed instruction. There may be traces of controversy in the narrative section, as there is in the following example:

> And they sent to him some of the Pharisees and some of the Herodians, to entrap him in his talk. And they came and said to him, "Teacher, we know that you are true, and care for no man; for you do not regard the position of men, but truly teach the way of God. Is it lawful to pay taxes to Caesar, or not? Should we pay them, or should we not?" But knowing their hypocrisy, he said to them, "Why put me to the test? Bring me a coin, and let me look at it." And they brought one. And he said to them, "Whose likeness and inscription is this?" They said to him, "Caesar's." Jesus said to them, "Render to Caesar the things that are Caesar's, and to God the things that are God's." And they were amazed at him (Mark 12:13–17; cf. Matt 22:15–22 and Luke 20:20–26).

Here again we have a brief narrative, a dialogue, and a pronouncement of Jesus, in this case, on the payment of Roman taxes.

The biographical stories are somewhat more varied in form and include such stories as the calling of the disciples, the blessing of the children, and Jesus' rejection in Nazareth. The pericope in Mark 3:31–35, however, seems to be in the classic form of the pronouncement story:

> And his mother and his brothers came; and standing outside they sent to him and called him. And a crowd was sitting about him; and they said to him, "Your mother and your brothers are outside, asking for you." And he replied, "Who are my mother and my brothers?" And looking around on those who sat about him, he said, "Here are my mother and brothers! Whoever does the will of God is my brother, and sister, and mother" (Mark 3:31–35; cf. Matt 12:46–50 and Luke 8:19–21).

Most form critics agree that, in all three types of pronouncement stories, the pronouncement that comes at the end of the story is not only the heart of it but also the oldest part of it. If any part of a pronouncement story goes back to Jesus, it is the pronouncement itself. Christian preachers, teachers, and debaters may have provided the introductory narrative in order to interpret the saying, but at least some of the sayings probably came from Jesus.

Miracle Stories

We come now to the narrative material about Jesus. A large number of narratives in the Synoptic Gospels are told in the form of miracle stories.

[15] Ibid., p. 50.

These can easily be spotted on the basis of content, but they also have a particular form. There are two basic types of miracle stories found in the gospels: healing miracles and nature miracles. The former include the curing of diseases, the exorcism of demons, and the resuscitation of the dead. Nature miracles are those performed on inanimate objects.

In the usual form of the healing miracle, the story begins with a description of the illness and sometimes includes a statement on its duration, its dreadful and dangerous character, and the ineffective efforts of former physicians to heal the patient. In the performance of the miracle, all attention is focused on Jesus, and the person being cured is of little significance. The miracles frequently work in an automatic fashion and without the agency of Jesus' will. A woman with a hemorrhage, for example, was cured by touching Jesus' garment without his prior knowledge (Mark 5:25–34, Matt 9:20–22, and Luke 8:43–48). In a few cases the healing takes place when Jesus himself is at some distance from the patient (for example, Matt 8:5–13 and Luke 7:1–10). The healings that Jesus performs generally take place by means of a gesture, a touch, a word (sometimes imcomprehensible or foreign), a name, or by a threat to the sickness or the demon. Then follow certain features that demonstrate the successful result of the miracle: a lame person walks, a blind person describes what he sees, or an exorcised demon creates a disturbance. The story concludes with the dismissal of the healed person and a report of the crowd's response.

There are very few nature miracles in the Synoptic Gospels. Taylor counts only five and Bultmann six. These stories do not have a consistent form. In general, Jesus encounters some problem that he solves by controlling the elements. In Mark 4:35–41 (cf. Matt 8:23–27 and Luke 8:22–25), Jesus and his disciples are in a boat on a lake when a storm begins and threatens to capsize it. Jesus is awakened from his sleep, he commands the storm to cease, and the disciples are filled with awe. Most of the nature miracles probably came out of a general lore of folk stories. Bultmann cites a number of parallels to the walking on water in several traditions, including one in which a disciple walks across water to the Buddha. Some of the stories may have arisen within the Christian tradition, where they were first told as resurrection narratives. The conception of the risen Lord presiding at a messianic banquet may have become a story of a miraculous feeding (Mark 6:32–44 and 8:1–10 and parallels). Other nature miracles may have been fashioned out of sayings or parables. The parable of the fig tree in Luke 13:6–9 probably became the story of the cursing of the fig tree in Mark 11:12–14 and Matt 21:18–19, where it is told as a nature miracle. We cannot, of course, be certain that historical incidents do not underlie the nature miracles, but that is another study that will engage our attention later.

The form of both healing and nature miracles was altered to some extent by the oral tradition in two particulars: there was a tendency to increase the miraculous element, and there was a tendency to develop an interest in the secondary participants of the stories. When the narratives reach a literary stage, it is possible to trace the continuation of these tendencies. The miracles in the later gospels are often more stupendous than those in the earlier. The same is true of the interests in secondary characters. Characters who are barely mentioned in the earlier gospels are given names and detailed treatment in the later ones. This tendency is at work even in the canonical gospels. For example, in Mark 14:47, at the arrest of Jesus, an unnamed person cuts off an ear of the high priest's slave. In John the story is more specific, as details and names are added: in John 18:10 it is Peter who cuts off the right ear of the slave, whose name is given as Malchus.

Stories About Jesus

Stories about Jesus are those stories about the events of Jesus' life that function as religious or edifying narratives. It is possible that some of the stories embody authentic historical recollections, but their chief value lies in their suitability for Christian preaching and teaching, which was the probable context for most of them. The various narratives about Jesus' trial and execution, the stories of the discovery of the empty tomb, and the various postresurrection appearances of Jesus are included in this category. Several stories about Jesus' birth probably circulated in the oral period and were later grouped in larger narratives by Matthew and by Luke, or by traditions lying behind them. The stories of Jesus' baptism, temptation, and transfiguration are also included here.

These stories are quite varied in terms of content and form. In fact, it is not possible to find formal elements that are consistently applied in all the stories in this category. The most that can be said is that the stories are marked by a conciseness of style and an economy of characterization. Bultmann felt that the stories consistently presented Jesus in terms of messianic ideas and that, because messianic expectation was a Jewish phenomenon, the stories arose among Christians with a Jewish background. The stories about Jesus do not treat his life as a pattern of devotion, and there is little interest in his life in the historical sense, because he is believed to be the Messiah. Thus, the stories tell of evidences of his Messiahship and his messianic activity. Incidents from his life are not, strictly speaking, presented as models for believers to copy.

With form critical studies such as those by Bultmann, Dibelius, and Taylor in mind, we may more fully appreciate the work of the gospel writers. The connection they had with Jesus was through the oral tradition. This means that they had access to materials that had circulated orally, some over several decades. In the process of transmission, the various sayings, parables, pronouncement stories, miracle stories, and stories about Jesus were altered, as they picked up explanatory or edifying additions. The task of the gospel writers seemingly was not to separate the original forms from secondary additions, but to organize the available materials into meaningful narratives. Because the oral tradition provided no consecutive account of the life of Jesus, one would have to be composed. This composition would provide the basic structure of the gospel. For example, Mark chose to begin his gospel with the materials about John the Baptist, Jesus' baptism, and his temptation. Then he situated Jesus in Galilee and located various miracle stories and much of the discourse material there and in adjacent territories. Then he grouped the stories of Jesus' passion at the end, while painting Jerusalem in dark, gloomy colors. He placed no healing miracles in this section. Those decisions were permitted by the oral tradition but were not dictated by it.

Not only did the evangelists have to make basic decisions about the compositional structure of their gospels, they had a number of decisions to make about the treatment of the individual pericopes. They had to select some pericopes and reject others; they had to decide on the proportion of discourse and narrative material; and they had to locate the individual pericopes within the gospel structure. For some of the materials, they needed to write introductions, conclusions, and explanatory notes, and they needed to provide the appropriate geographical and chronological settings. Finally, they needed to write occasional transitions and summaries, so that the reader could follow the narrative.

Perhaps it is now clearer than before that our modern goal, the historical Jesus, was not shared by the evangelists. Their goal was to present the Jesus who had become known through the early Christian oral tradition. Our goal is discovering the more elusive figure of someone who pre-existed the Christian oral tradition. Our method, therefore, is one that works back from the gospels, and it is essentially made up of the following three stages:

1. *From the gospels to the late oral tradition.* In starting with the gospels, we must first recognize the contribution of the evangelists in providing a basic structure for their writings and in making innumerable editorial decisions. By doing that we should ideally be able to reconstruct the materials the gospel writers had at their disposal.

2. *From the late oral tradition to the early oral tradition.* We recognize that the materials the evangelists had did not arrive on their doorsteps in their original forms. Thus, the task of separating secondary additions from original forms is necessary for us, in the effort to uncover the oral tradition at an early stage. The result of these efforts should be a collection of sayings, parables, pronouncement stories, miracle stories, and stories about Jesus in the forms in which they originally circulated in the contexts of preaching, teaching, debates, worship, and prophecy.

3. *From the early oral tradition to the historical Jesus.* The procedures and criteria for making judgments at this stage were introduced in Chapter 5 and will be discussed more extensively in Chapter 8.

Clearly, each stage in this process requires informed judgment. This practice is an art, not a science, which means that equally good scholars will sometimes come to completely different conclusions. That fact does not, however, invalidate the method, and it is probably more important to become aware of the ways in which scholars work than to know what their conclusions are.

In Chapter 8 we will attempt to apply these principles to some selected aspects of the life and teachings of Jesus.

BIBLIOGRAPHY

Bultmann, Rudolf. *The History of the Synoptic Tradition*. Trans. by John Marsh. New York: Harper & Row, Publishers, 1963.

Dibelius, Martin. *From Tradition to Gospel*. Trans. by B. L. Woolf. New York: Charles Scribner's Sons, 1935.

———. *The Message of Jesus Christ*. Trans. by F. C. Grant. New York: Charles Scribner's Sons, 1939.

Dodd, C. H. *The Apostolic Preaching and Its Developments*. London: Holder and Stoughton, 1936.

Gerhardsson, Birger. *Memory and Manuscript*. 2nd ed. Uppsala and Lund: C.W.K. Gleerup, 1964.

———. *Tradition and Transmission in Early Christianity*. Lund: C.W.K. Gleerup, 1964.

Koch, Klaus. *The Growth of the Biblical Tradition*. Trans. by S. M. Cupitt. New York: Charles Scribner's Sons, 1969.

Montgomery, R. M., and W. R. Stegner. *Auxiliary Studies in the Bible: Forms in the Gospels: I. The Pronouncement Story*. Nashville, Tenn.: Abingdon Press, 1970.

Stegner, W. R. *An Introduction to the Parables through Programmed Instruction*. Washington, D.C.: University Press of America, 1977.

Taylor, Vincent. *The Formation of the Gospel Tradition*. 2nd ed. London: Macmillan & Company Ltd., 1935.

The books by Bultmann, Dibelius, and Taylor are fundamental to the study of oral forms in early Christianity. Although English translations of Bultmann and Dibelius did not appear until much later, their work in German came out around 1920. The first German edition of Dibelius' *From Tradition to Gospel* was published in 1919, and Bultmann's *History of the Synoptic Tradition* came out in 1921. Dibelius' *Message of Jesus Christ* catalogues the synoptic pericopes in terms of the categories he had formulated. Taylor's book is based on lectures he had delivered at the University of Leeds in 1932. It is a serious critique of Bultmann and Dibelius from a conservative English point of view. The works by the Scandinavian scholar

Birger Gerhardsson present an approach to the oral period that runs counter to traditional form criticism. Gehardsson thinks that there was significant effort to memorize Jesus' words and that great care was taken to preserve and transmit them with exactitude. Although his point of view has not been widely accepted among NT scholars, it is deserving of serious attention. The book by Dodd has been very influential. In it he attempts to identify the earliest Christian kerygma. Klaus Koch, treating both OT and NT, reviews and updates form criticism. The publication by Montgomery and Stegner and the one by Stegner alone are programmed instructional materials on the pronouncement stories and parables. Use of this material should help the student to deal with form-critical methods and should facilitate the ability to distinguish between primary and secondary elements in oral materials.

❖ 8 ❖

Jesus

OUR study of the gospels and of oral traditions has shown that there are severe limits to the study of the historical Jesus. One of the most regrettable restrictions is that we are not able to give a connected account of the life of Jesus. Because the chronological structures of the gospels are largely provided by their writers, and oral traditions, by their nature, do not retain chronological sequences, we have no dependable basis for a connected account of Jesus' life. Except in the most obvious of situations (the order of birth, childhood, ministry, and death), it is not possible to say anything about the sequence of events. Consequently, we cannot really talk about the matter of development in Jesus' life—that is, how his thinking may have changed from an earlier to a later period. Another restriction is that we cannot say much about those circumstances that we usually expect to be treated, such as Jesus' physical appearance or his economic situation. Neither the gospels nor the oral traditions display much interest in these matters. Finally, the question of Jesus' intentionality is essentially hidden from us. There are a few statements in the gospels that allegedly express Jesus' purpose, such as, "Think not that I have come to abolish the law and the prophets; I have come not to abolish them but to fulfil them" (Matt 5:17). Such statements, of course, need to be examined in the light of the chief motifs in the gospels as well as in the history of the oral traditions. But it can be stated at the outset that whatever statements Jesus may have made about his intention have come through several layers of interpretation. They do not come to us with sufficient directness that we are able to make confident statements about Jesus' intention or self-understanding. Such a question as, "Did Jesus think of himself as Messiah?" simply cannot be answered as a historical question.

Although there are serious restrictions to the study of the historical Jesus, it is nevertheless possible to make certain qualified judgments about his life and teachings. Previous chapters contain some suggestions about how this kind of study may proceed, and it should be helpful to bring these suggestions together at this point.

The study of the historical Jesus inevitably begins with the gospels, and the first step in the study is the attempt to identify the work of the gospel writers. Editorial comments, basic literary organization, themes, and motifs need to be identified, and their effect on the narrative needs to be assessed. This study is called redaction criticism, and some of its results were given in Chapter 6.

Behind the gospels lies a period in which the material about Jesus circulated in oral form. The oral tradition had a history, in which the stories and sayings of Jesus were altered in the process of transmission. The history needs to be studied in the effort to isolate the earliest forms of the oral tradition. This study is called form criticism, which was treated in Chapter 7.

In Chapter 7 reference was made to the primitive Christian kerygma. The kerygma was the content of the earliest Christian preaching, or proclamation, about Jesus. Of course, knowledge about what the earliest Christians were preaching is not identical with knowledge about the actual life and teachings of Jesus. But such knowledge does put us in touch with Christian activity at a very early date. Thus, any traditions we find to be in conformity with the primitive kerygma are probably older than traditions that are not in conformity with it. Actually, C. H. Dodd, who isolated the kerygma, found two forms of it: a Jerusalem form and a Pauline form.[1] The former, he claimed, represents the Christian proclamation as it was given in Jerusalem in the very earliest decades of Christian history, in the 30s and 40s, and it is found mainly in the speeches of Peter in the first several chapters of Acts. The Pauline form shared most aspects with the Jerusalem form but contained some distinctive traits that represented the theology of Paul. The Jerusalem kerygma, according to Dodd, proclaimed that in Jesus the last day had dawned and that, at his resurrection, he had become the messianic head of the new Israel. It pointed to the Holy Spirit in the church as the sign of Jesus' continued power and glory, and it proclaimed his imminent return. It included a brief mention of the ministry of Jesus, his Davidic descent, his death, and his resurrection. It closed with an appeal for repentance. The fullest account of Jesus' ministry is given within a speech of Peter as reported in Acts 10:34–43. Here we are told that the ministry of Jesus began in Galilee after that of John the Baptist, that Jesus went about doing good and healing, and that he was hanged on a tree and raised on the third day. Statements in the kerygma about historical matters may act as controls in form-critical study.

In Chapter 5 we examined certain criteria for making judgments about the historical Jesus. Reference was made there to four criteria for deciding

---

[1] Cf. C. H. Dodd, *The Apostolic Preaching and its Developments* (London: Holder and Stoughton, 1936).

about probably authentic material. The criterion of dissimilarity means that we look for early traditions that are not similar to characteristic emphases in ancient Judaism or early Christianity. The second, the criterion of coherence, means that we may add to the dissimilar traditions any others that are early and in basic agreement with them. The criterion of multiple attestation requires us to look for material that circulated in various forms and appeared in different layers of gospel tradition. The fourth criterion gives precedence to material that contains Semitic linguistic or environmental traces. There will be a few occasions on which one or more of these criteria can be fruitfully employed.

Finally, we must call attention to the material in Chapter 1 on historical evidence and the nature of historical argumentation. We should keep the distinction between testimony and evidence constantly in mind. We must also be aware of the process of drawing inferences, asking questions, demanding data, examining warrants, and using qualifiers. Although the study of Jesus requires specialized knowledge about oral traditions, gospels, social and political history, and religious life, it does not require departure from the usual methods of studying history. In the various sections of this chapter, both specialized and general considerations will be used in the effort to reach the historical Jesus.

Because we are not able to give a connected account of the life of Jesus, trace his development, describe his personality, or discuss his intention, we must satisfy ourselves with examining other selected topics. No attempt will be made to be exhaustive, but the more important aspects of Jesus' probable history will be treated: his birth, teachings, miracles, trial, and resurrection.

THE BIRTH OF JESUS

Accurate historical information about the birth of someone who lived in antiquity is usually very difficult to obtain. Such information was not considered important unless the person had achieved notoriety, and by then it was frequently too late to rescue it. As a general rule, the death dates of esteemed leaders were observed in the ancient world because their birth dates were unknown. But Hellenistic authors did not hesitate to include birth stories in their biographies. Frequently those stories contained references to auspicious and miraculous events accompanying the births of famous persons. Diogenes Laertius, for example, refers to a story about the virgin birth of Plato. Plutarch says that, prior to the birth of Alexander the Great, Alexander's father had refrained from intercourse with his wife Olympias because a snake had wound itself around her body. The snake was said to be Zeus, so that Alexander was the son of Olympias and Zeus.[2]

---

[2] For a translation of these and other Hellenistic birth stories, cf. David R. Cartlidge and David L. Dungan, *Documents for the Study of the Gospels* (Philadelphia: Fortress Press, 1980), pp. 129–136.

Hellenistic writers also usually included genealogical notes with their birth stories. The purpose of such notes appears to be to show the illustrious nature of the child's family.

Among the gospels, only Matthew and Luke have substantial material about the birth of Jesus (Matt 1:1–2:23 and Luke 1:1–2:52 and 3:23–38).[3] In form, they are similar to Hellenistic biographies, for both have accounts of a miraculous birth, and both have genealogies of Jesus. The opening chapters of both gospels are devoted entirely to nativity material, most of it quite familiar. What many casual readers fail to notice, however, is that the stories and the genealogies in the two gospels are not the same. Whatever may have been the common source or sources on which Matthew and Luke depended, they had no common source for the opening chapters.

Matthew begins with a genealogy that shows Jesus' descent from David. He starts with Abraham, includes David and the kings of Judah, and concludes with Jacob, the father of Joseph, "the husband of Mary, of whom Jesus was born, who is called Christ" (Matt 1:16). Then Matthew narrates the circumstances preceding and surrounding the birth. Joseph has discovered that his contracted bride, Mary, is pregnant, and he has decided not to go through with the marriage. But an angel appears to him in a dream and tells him that Mary has conceived by the Holy Spirit and will give birth to a son who is to be named Jesus.[4] The angel further explains that the birth will fulfill the prophecy of Isa 7:14, which Matthew quotes: "Behold a virgin shall conceive and bear a son, and his name shall be called Emmanuel" (Matt 1:23). Joseph is obedient to the angelic message, and Jesus is born in Bethlehem during the reign of King Herod the Great. Later on, wise men from the East observe a star, and they come to search for the one they believe to be the newborn king of the Jews. They find the child in a house, presumably in Bethlehem, and present him with gifts of gold, frankincense, and myrrh. Afterward, Joseph has another angelic visitation, in which he is warned to take the family to Egypt in order to protect Jesus from the wrath of Herod, who orders the death of all male children born in Bethlehem within the previous two years. When Herod dies, Joseph receives a third vision, in which he is told to return, but to Galilee rather than Judea, for fear of Herod's son and successor in Judea, Archelaus.

Luke interweaves the story of Jesus' birth with one about the birth of John the Baptist. John's parents were Zechariah, a priest, and Elizabeth, also a member of a priestly family. An angel, Gabriel, announces the birth of John to Zechariah even before conception takes place. Zechariah is dubious because he and his wife are both very old, so as punishment for his

---

[3] The Book of James contains an account of the birth of Jesus, but nothing that would be new to readers of Matthew and Luke. It focuses attention on the life of Mary and Joseph prior to Jesus' birth.

[4] The name is a transliteration of the Hebrew or Aramaic *Joshua* and means "Yah[weh] saves," or "will save."

doubts he is stricken with muteness. When Elizabeth is six months pregnant, Gabriel visits her kinswoman Mary, in Galilee, and announces that she too will conceive and that she will give birth to a son by the Holy Spirit. Mary is described as "a virgin betrothed to a man whose name was Joseph, of the house of David" (Luke 1:27). Luke next tells of the birth of John and his naming, which releases Zechariah from the spell of muteness. Toward the end of Mary's pregnancy, it becomes necessary for her to go with Joseph to Bethlehem, to be counted in the census decreed by the Emperor Augustus. Luke specifies that this survey was made while Quirinius was governor of Syria. So Mary gives birth to Jesus in Bethlehem and lays him in a manger. Nearby shepherds are sent by an angel to visit the newborn child. Luke concludes the nativity story with the circumcision and naming of Jesus, his presentation in the Temple, the testimony of Simeon and Anna, and the return of the family to Nazareth. After the story of Jesus in the Temple at the age of twelve, the recounting of the preaching of John the Baptist, and the narrative about Jesus' baptism, Luke gives the genealogy of Jesus. His ancestry is traced through Joseph, son of Heli, back through David and Abraham to "Adam, the son of God" (Luke 3:38).

We should not overlook or minimize the similarities between the accounts in Matthew and Luke. Both name Mary and Joseph as the parents of Jesus. Both speak of Mary as Joseph's betrothed, and both speak of Joseph as a descendant of David. Both have Bethlehem as the place of birth. In both there are angelic announcements, and in both Mary conceives by the Holy Spirit, and, thus, Jesus is born of a virgin. In both narratives there are visitors who come after they have seen auspicious signs. In both stories the family settles in Galilee after the birth. In both genealogies there is an expression of some hesitancy, either about Joseph's paternity or about the entire list of Jesus' ancestors (Matt 1:16 and Luke 3:23).

But neither should the similarities obscure the differences between Matthew and Luke. The visit of the wise men in Matthew cannot be equated with the visit of shepherds in Luke. Luke has nothing like Matthew's story about the massacre of the children by Herod the Great or the trip of the family of Jesus to Egypt. Matthew has nothing similar to the Lukan stories about Jesus' circumcision or Mary's postnatal purification. Luke's story of the precocious Jesus at twelve is also unique to that gospel.

The date of Jesus' birth is not precisely given in either gospel, but Matthew clearly places it before the death of King Herod the Great. In terms of our present calendar, Herod died in 4 BCE, so according to Matthew, Jesus could not have been born after that date. Luke is more vague on the date of birth. He says that John's father, Zechariah, was a priest during the reign of "Herod, king of Judea" (Luke 1:5)—that is, presumably Herod the Great. But he also says that the census for which Mary and Joseph traveled to Bethlehem occurred "when Quirinius was governor of Syria" (2:2). Such a census is reported by Josephus and dated, in terms of our calendar, in

6 CE. The taxation that followed from it resulted in a rebellion led by one Judas of Galilee.[5] But it is by no means certain that Luke knew the exact date of the census under Quirinius, and there are places in his gospel that imply a somewhat earlier date for Jesus' birth. In 3:1–2 Luke has an elaborate statement about the date at which John the Baptist made his first public appearance. He puts it in the fifteenth year of the Roman Emperor Tiberius, and he lists those who were ruling in various areas at that time. The fifteenth year of Tiberius would be about 29 CE. Then, in introducing Jesus' genealogy, he says that Jesus was about thirty years old when he began his ministry (3:23). Luke's lack of precision in this statement prevents a definite conclusion, but he implies that Jesus' ministry began after John's, hence after 29 CE. If Jesus was about thirty at this time, his date of birth would be about I BCE. In any case, Matthew and Luke are using different traditions and calculations about the date of Jesus' birth, and we have possibilities ranging from before 4 BCE to as late as 6 CE.

The two genealogies are remarkably dissimilar and must have originated quite independently. They both trace the ancestry through Joseph to David and thence to Abraham (to Adam in Luke). In the generations between Abraham and David, several almost identical names, familiar from OT genealogies, appear in both lists. But between David and Joseph there is no possibility of harmonization. Two or three names appear in both but in different locations. Zerubbabel is the eleventh generation from Jesus in Matthew and the twentieth in Luke. Shealtiel is the twelfth in Matthew and the twenty-first in Luke. Luke's Matthat may be the same as Matthew's Matthan. But from David to Joseph no other names appear in both genealogies.

Perhaps the oral traditions behind these two gospels can be discovered by looking for the editorial material in them. Matthew has arranged his material in line with his motif of Jesus as the new Moses. The motif is suggested by the flight to Egypt and the return, which calls to mind the period of Hebrew slavery in Egypt and the Exodus. Matthew makes the theme explicit by quoting Hos 11:1, "Out of Egypt have I called my son" (Matt 2:15). The massacre of the children also calls to mind the killing of firstborn Egyptians at the time of Moses. Subsidiary themes in Matthew are the angelic visits to Joseph and the fulfillment of prophecy. Luke's story is characterized by a parallelism between the births of John the Baptist and Jesus and by his citation of the testimony of human witnesses. He includes two hymns, which were probably of Jewish origin (Luke 1:46–55 and 68–79). Luke also shows a tendency to include, within the hymns and speeches, predictions of the future work of John the Baptist and Jesus.

When the editorial material has been isolated, we are left with two stories about Jesus, both of which state that he was born of the virgin Mary, and

[5] Josephus, *Antiquities* XVII, 355; XVIII, 1–4, 26; cf. *War* VII, 253.

The youthful Christ, fourth-century statuette, Museo Nazionale delle Terme, Rome.
(Courtesy *Alinari Art Resource, Inc.*)

two genealogies, both of which claim that Jesus was descended from David. Strictly speaking, the stories and the genealogies are not consistent with one another. In presenting the virginal conception of Jesus, the stories eliminate Joseph as the actual father of Jesus. But the genealogies connect Jesus with David through Joseph. It is worth observing that similar problematical combinations are sometimes found in Hellenistic biographies. Diogenes Laertius told of Plato's virgin birth, but he also gave a paternal genealogy. The same is true in Plutarch's life of Alexander the Great.

The inconsistency between the stories and the genealogies suggests that they probably arose separately in the Christian oral tradition. The story about Jesus is, according to form critics, one of the forms used in oral traditions, so there is no reason to doubt that stories about his birth circulated in the pregospel period. They probably circulated in several forms, but at the heart of them there was a claim about Jesus' virginal conception. This claim embodies a belief that Jesus is son of God in the same way that birth stories were used to show that Plato was the son of Apollo, and Alexander the son of Zeus. Clearly, consideration of an OT scripture, such as Isa 7:14 in the Greek version, could also have given rise to the belief in Jesus' virgin birth. Although the Hebrew version of this text does not speak of a virgin birth, the Greek does, and it is in its Greek form that Matthew quotes it.[6] In any event, there is no problem in assuming that oral forms of virgin birth stories lay behind the gospel accounts.

Genealogy is not a form listed for the Christian oral tradition, and it is not likely that the particular genealogies in Matthew and Luke circulated in oral form in the period between Jesus and the gospels. It is known, however, that some Jewish families made serious attempts to preserve their family records, particularly priestly families. In addition, there was concern in Jewish apocalyptic circles for tracing the ancestry of the Messiah.[7] Different messianic concepts, of course, required different genealogies, but one popular concept was that of Messiah as son of David. If Christians believed Jesus to be Messiah—and they did—and if they understood Messiah as son of David—and at least some did—they might very well have applied a Davidic genealogy to him, or their reflections on his Messiahship may have led to the composition of one or more genealogies.

Concern for the ancestry of the Messiah is found in an interesting pericope that appears in all three of the Synoptic Gospels (Matt 22:41–46, Mark 12:35–37, and Luke 20:41–44). In this pericope Jesus asks, "How can the scribes say that the Christ is the son of David?" (Mark 12:35). Then

---

[6] The RSV translation of Isa 7:14 follows the Hebrew: "Behold, a young woman shall conceive and bear a son, and shall call his name Immanuel." Drawing on the Greek version of this verse, the editors have printed "virgin" in the margin as an alternative translation to "young woman."

[7] Cf. Marshall D. Johnson, *The Purpose of the Biblical Genealogies* (Cambridge: Cambridge U.P., 1969).

after quoting Ps 110:1, he says: "David himself calls him Lord; so how is he his son?" (Mark 12:37). Bultmann has suggested that this saying may have arisen at a time when there was some tension between belief in Jesus as Lord and belief in him as son of David. He also has said that it represents a feeling that the conception of Jesus as son of David maintains a tie with Judaism that should be broken.[8] The pericope was shaped so that the objection to the Messiah's Davidic ancestry was placed on the lips of Jesus. Its existence within the tradition demonstrates that Christians did not unanimously embrace the concept of the Davidic-type Messiah. Probably, however, objection to it would only arise after it had been embraced by some substantial portion of the Christian community.

The primitive kerygma shows that belief in Jesus as descended from David was standard in the earliest decades of Christian history. It is found both in the Jerusalem form of the kerygma (Acts 2:30–31) and the Pauline form (Rom 1:3). Dodd has observed that it was not a matter of vital importance for Paul.[9] It formed, rather, a part of the pre-Pauline tradition about Jesus that Paul accepted, and it served to authenticate the belief in Jesus' Messiahship.

These considerations lead to the probable conclusion that belief in Jesus as son of David was a very early Christian tradition. As such it probably gave rise to the genealogies we now find in Matthew and Luke. It is not possible to say when stories of Jesus' virgin birth arose, but they probably accompanied the emergence of beliefs about Jesus that de-emphasized his Jewish connections. Such beliefs, by their very nature, would be later than those that accepted his Jewish connections.

What finally can be said about the birth of Jesus as a historical phenomenon? Because of its probable early date, the tradition of Jesus' Davidic ancestry is a serious candidate for authentic history. Some details of the virgin birth stories, such as date of birth and names of parents, despite the inconsistencies, present nothing impossible or unlikely. But the stories themselves probably emerged at a relatively late date in the history of the oral tradition. We may reasonably ask, however, if Jesus was in fact a descendant of David? Certainly it is not unlikely that he was. Many Jews in Jesus' day probably were descended from David. But in the case of Jesus, the statement about his descent comes only within the context of religious belief. The statement about his ancestry, as we find it in the kerygma and in the genealogies, is not presented as a simple fact of history. It is a religious statement—a way of affirming belief in Jesus as Messiah. It does not pass the test of dissimilarity, because it simply represents early Christian belief; it is not distinct from it. We may say, then, that Jesus' Davidic ancestry, although not unlikely, is also not certain.

[8] Cf. Rudolf Bultmann, *The History of the Synoptic Tradition*, trans. by John Marsh (New York: Harper, 1963), pp. 136ff.
[9] Dodd, op. cit., pp. 21f.

In short, our search for authentic information about the birth of Jesus has been nearly fruitless. The character of the material gives us no sure way to decide, one way or the other, about Jesus' ancestry or about the manner of his birth.

THE TEACHINGS OF JESUS

The very forms in which the teachings of Jesus were preserved may predispose one in favor of their historical authenticity. Sayings and parables are words allegedly spoken by Jesus, whereas stories about Jesus and miracle stories can represent him only indirectly. Because Jesus, according to the gospels, did not tell stories about himself, at best the form of a story may go back to a disciple. By contrast, the sayings and parables may represent, in translation, the very words that Jesus spoke, or at least something close to them.

The primitive kerygma did not include a specific statement about Jesus' teaching, but the Synoptic Gospels, John, and Coptic Thomas present abundant examples of it. It is contained in sayings, parables, and pronouncement stories, found in all three Synoptic Gospels and in the Coptic Gospel of Thomas. Some are logia, which contained typical wisdom sayings and probably circulated widely but were not originally connected with Jesus. Some are prophetic sayings, which came into the tradition as revealed sayings of the risen Lord. A number of pronouncement stories probably arose in the context of debates between Christians and Jews about the Torah or about some legal point. As a consequence, not all of the teaching material in the Synoptic Gospels and Coptic Thomas was contained in the earliest oral tradition. As we have already seen, the Gospel of John presents

A second or third-century sarcophagus showing the figure of the good shepherd in the center. (Courtesy *Vatican Museum.*)

the teachings of Jesus in the form of long and involved discourses that have little relationship to the forms of the oral tradition. Thus, most of the material in John probably did not circulate in the earlier oral period.

The canonical gospels do not present the teachings of Jesus in neat units, as Matthew and Luke do for the birth material. The teachings are scattered through several sections of the gospels and mixed with miracle stories and stories about Jesus. Because this is the case, it is more appropriate to treat the teaching in topical fashion, rather than in terms of its sequence in the gospels. As is the case with all of the material in the gospels, the redactional work of the evangelists has affected the teaching material. But it is difficult to generalize about this effect, and it seems better to comment on redactional alterations in connection with particular pericopes as we examine them.

Fortunately, it is possible to treat the teachings of Jesus in topical fashion. The topic that seems to dominate all of the teachings and to give them coherence is the kingdom of God. Although the concept is almost totally absent from the Fourth Gospel, the term *kingdom of God* (or kingdom of heaven in Matthew) dominates the teachings in the synoptics. It is used in sayings, parables, and pronouncement stories, so there is multiple attestation for it. Although we cannot assume that all of the teachings about the kingdom that we find in the gospels are identical with those that were preserved and transmitted in the oral tradition, it is likely that teachings about the kingdom circulated in oral form in the earliest period of Christian history. There are several factors that can be cited as data for this conclusion.

First, we know from both the Jerusalem and the Pauline forms of the kerygma that primitive Christianity had a strong eschatological orientation. In their preaching, Christians proclaimed that the age of fulfillment had dawned, that Jesus had been exalted as Messiah, and that he would soon return. In the synoptic teachings of Jesus, the kingdom of God is presented as an eschatological phenomenon, and it is intimately connected with early Christian messianic expectation. The affirmation that Jesus proclaimed the kingdom, together with belief in his resurrection, may have served as a basis for messianic beliefs. The fact of messianic expectation points to an early tradition about Jesus as proclaimer of the kingdom.

Second, the teaching about the kingdom of God is similar to contemporary Jewish apocalyptic and messianic expectations. To be sure, Jews were not in agreement on messianism, nor did they all regard it as important. But the teaching on the kingdom represents a basic form of apocalyptic hope. The age of the Messiah is the age in which God manifests his righteousness, and the phrase "kingdom of God" rightly reflects its meaning. The imminence of its coming and its initiation by the Messiah are consistent with Jewish thought, and the eschatological concept that is embedded within it is basically Jewish. Because the earliest traditions about Jesus were linked to Jewish teachings, and because the teaching about the kingdom is consistent with that background, it is probable that the earliest Christian traditions included sayings on the kingdom.[10]

Third, the teaching on the kingdom is central to the other teachings in the gospels. In an editorial sentence Mark summarizes Jesus' teaching as a proclamation of the kingdom: "Now after John was arrested, Jesus came into Galilee, preaching the gospel of God, and saying, 'The time is fulfilled, and the kingdom of God is at hand; repent, and believe in the gospel' " (Mark 1:14–15; cf. Matt 4:17). But this does not seem to be Mark's idea only, for the kingdom teaching is vitally related to other areas of Jesus' teaching, namely the ethical teachings and the teachings on Torah. The ethical teachings tell what the present situation demands in terms of getting ready for the kingdom. The teachings on Torah show that the imminence of the kingdom demands a different understanding of God's will. There is a coherence in Jesus' teaching that points to the centrality of the teachings about the kingdom. For this reason, the kingdom teachings appear to belong to the oldest layer of Christian tradition.

It is therefore probable that primitive Christians presented Jesus as the one who proclaimed the coming of the kingdom and that this was a major aspect of their message. Two related questions, however, need to be faced. The first is: Did the early traditions contain any indication about the time at which the kingdom would come? The second is: Did the traditions say that Jesus' proclamation involved a particular demand on the part of his hearers? The second question will require an examination of the ethical teachings and the teachings on Torah.

As for the first question, it is clear that the kingdom was presented as a future event. The future aspect of the kingdom is represented in a number of sayings, some of which speak about the Son of man:

> For as the lightning comes from the east and shines as far as the west, so will be the coming of the Son of man (Matt 24:27; cf. Luke 17:24).

> When they persecute you in one town, flee to the next; for truly, I say to you, you will not have gone through all the towns of Israel, before the Son of man comes (Matt 10:23).

> For whoever is ashamed of me and of my words in this adulterous and sinful generation, of him will the Son of man also be ashamed, when he comes in the glory of his Father with the holy angels (Mark 8:38; cf. Luke 9:26).

[10] The criterion of dissimilarity would reject teachings that are so close to Jewish apocalyptic literature. But the criterion of dissimilarity is to be used in the search for authentic material about the historical Jesus, whereas we are here looking for early Christian traditions. Nevertheless, there appears to be a problem, for if similarity is a criterion for early traditions, will we end up with traditions that are dissimilar and therefore candidates for authenticity? Such problems as these point to the limited usefulness of the criterion of dissimilarity.

Truly, I say to you, there are some standing here who will not taste death before they see the Son of man coming in his kingdom (Matt 16:28; cf. Mark 9:1 and Luke 9:27).

Truly, I say to you, I shall not drink again of the fruit of the vine until that day when I drink it new in the kingdom of God (Mark 14:25; cf. Matt 26:29 and Luke 22:18).

Although the traditional understanding of the future coming of the Son of man, which was held in primitive Christianity, is here attributed to Jesus, the identification of Jesus with the Son of man is not made. Here the Son of man appears to be a figure independent of Jesus, and the sayings reflect a belief that Jesus himself expected the future appearance of the Son of man. In the parables in which Jesus is ostensibly describing the kingdom, he does so in terms of a time of imminent judgment. A good example is the parable of the wheat and weeds in Matt 13:24–30. A man planted wheat, but his enemy came along and sowed weeds among the wheat. When the workers asked the owner if the weeds should be pulled up, he replied that they should wait until harvest time. In the parable, the harvest is the kingdom, for that is the time of judgment, the time when God will separate the worthy from the unworthy. Similar sayings point to the kingdom as a future event.[11]

However, some sayings in the gospels suggest that the kingdom is not simply expected as a future event but is experienced as a present phenomenon. One such saying is found in Matt 13:16–17 and in Luke 10:24. It is a saying in which Jesus blesses those who hear what people of the past had longed to hear. It may belong to the earliest tradition, but even if it does, it does not imply that Jesus' hearers have experienced the kingdom itself.

In another saying we have a clearer allusion to the kingdom as present. Luke 11:20 has "But if it is by the finger of God that I cast out demons, then the kingdom of God has come upon you." The parallel in Matt 12:28 reads, "But if it is by the Spirit of God that I cast out demons, then the kingdom of God has come upon you." In both it is found in a pronouncement story that describes a controversy between Jesus and some people who thought he had used the power of Beelzebul to cast out demons. Jesus counters their argument by offering two alternatives. If he is using the power of Beelzebul, he is using it against that prince of demons, and his divided kingdom is soon to fall. If, on the other hand, he is using the power of God, then God's kingdom has come. A subsidiary question is also raised about exorcisms performed by other Jews. Mark 3:23–26 has something similar, but it is a purer pronouncement story. Here Jesus answers the accusation of his opponents by pointing to a ridiculous implication in their argument—namely, that it makes Satan a rebel against himself. The form

[11] Cf., for example, Matt 13:47–50.

of the pronouncement story in Matthew and Luke shows signs of development from something like the Markan form. It introduces an irrelevant question and presents the alternative of Jesus' using the power of God, which is not essential to the original objection. Mark's narrative raises and meets the objection forcefully, simply, and directly, whereas the Matthew/Luke form serves only to confuse the issue. Thus, on form-critical grounds, it appears that the statement in Matt 12:28 and Luke 11:20, about the presence of the kingdom, is secondary and did not belong to the Beelzebul story in its more primitive form. It may have circulated independently as a saying.

Luke 17:21 is a direct statement about the presence of the kingdom: "The kingdom of God is in the midst of you." [12] Luke uses this saying in the context of a larger section that is designed to de-emphasize eschatological expectation. It serves as a warning against expecting visible signs of the kingdom. In the following verses, Jesus goes on to say that the disciples must not be misled when people call them to see signs of the kingdom. The Son of man will indeed come, and his coming will be as visible as a flash of lightning. But first the Son of man must endure suffering and be rejected by the current generation. The passage appears to come from a relatively late period. It reflects a time when people were citing visible signs for the kingdom. The reference to rejection by the current generation reflects the Christian community's experience some years after the time of Jesus. The use of the phrase "Son of man" to express both the experience of Jesus' suffering and the expected eschatological appearance creates some confusion. And the conflict between the idea of the kingdom as present, in 17:21, and as future, in 17:25–37, creates ambiguity about the meaning of the saying. These verses probably did not belong to the earliest tradition but arose later and were used by Luke to play down eschatological expectation.

There remain a few sayings in the Coptic Gospel of Thomas in which the kingdom seems to be understood as a present experience, for example:

> Rather, the Kingdom is inside of you, and it is outside of you. [13]

> His disciples said to Him, "When will the repose of the dead come about, and when will the new world come?"
> He said to them, "What you look forward to has already come, but you do not recognize it." [14]

These sayings actually do not treat the kingdom as an event at all. It is rather the reality in which the person with gnosis stands, and the concept is heavily individualized. The future coming of the kingdom is rejected, to

---

[12] Note the variant translation in RSV: "The kingdom of God is within you."
[13] Coptic Gospel of Thomas, Saying 3, trans. by Thomas O. Lambdin, in *The Nag Hammadi Library in English,* ed. by James M. Robinson (New York: Harper, 1977).
[14] Ibid., Saying 51.

be sure, but it is no longer thought of as an age—present or future. The gnosticizing tendency has removed both the societal and temporal aspects of the kingdom, and it seems to run counter to the eschatological emphasis in primitive Christianity.

It is probable that the earliest traditions did not present the kingdom as a present phenomenon. They spoke of it entirely as a future event but made no effort to define the time of its coming with any precision. The best we can say is that they proclaimed the kingdom as an event of the very near future and probably expected it within a generation (Matt 16:28, Mark 9:1, and Luke 9:27). Jesus was understood as the one who proclaimed the kingdom, so he might have been compared with those OT prophets who had predicted eschatological events. But he was distinguished from them by the understanding that his appearance was not merely the prediction of the kingdom, but the announcement that it was beginning to appear. The kingdom of God is an event of the future, but it is a future that is virtually present. The relation of dawn to sunrise is analogous to this conception. At dawn we may say that sunrise is yet to come, but dawn is an assurance that it is close at hand. So Jesus announces the kingdom in the way that dawn announces sunrise. The kingdom was, in the early traditions, proclaimed as an event belonging to the near and assured future.

The second question we need to pose is this: Did the early traditions say that Jesus' proclamation involved a particular demand to be met by his hearers? Several possibilities present themselves, and the demands of the kingdom have been interpreted in various ways. If the kingdom is coming, perhaps people ought to pitch in and help construct those conditions that will hasten its arrival. This might include a certain kind of social action, which arranges political conditions in such a way as to exhibit the principles of the kingdom. Or it may mean that people should begin to live by the rules of the kingdom and that when enough people begin to live so, the kingdom will have arrived. But these ideas are not even suggested by the texts preserved in the gospels. On the contrary, we have an implied condemnation of human effort in Matt 11:12 and an assurance that the kingdom is God's gift in Luke 12:32.

But the texts do present Jesus as making certain demands. Mark's summary statement says that Jesus' proclamation of the kingdom was followed by a demand for repentance (Mark 1:14–15). This demand is part of the fabric of the synoptic presentation of Jesus' teachings. It is intimately related to the proclamation of the kingdom, for if the kingdom means judgment, the proclamation implies a demand for repentance. We must be careful to note that repentance does not affect the coming of the end. One does not hasten the coming of the kingdom by repenting or delay it by refusing to repent. The kingdom simply comes automatically, just as a seed planted in the ground grows into a plant (Mark 4:26–29). The coming of the kingdom is proclaimed as a fact, and repentance is presented as the appropriate response to the impending fact. The urgency of the need for repentance is sounded in a number of sayings. There is neither time to regret what is past or to dispose of it in the usual way. "No one who puts his hand to the plow and looks back is fit for the kingdom of God" (Luke 9:62). "Follow me, and leave the dead to bury their own dead" (Matt 8:22; cf. Luke 9:60). The intimate connection of the demand for repentance with the proclamation of the kingdom suggests that both are to be found among the early traditions.

The repentance demanded by the impending kingdom involves a radical decision. The kingdom means the end of all usual values, so we must decide between the values of the present and those of the future. Present values are generally understood in terms of material possessions. So the demand means that we must not store up earthly treasures or try to hold on to wealth (Matt 6:19–21). A camel can go through a needle's eye with greater ease than a rich person can go into the kingdom (Matt 19:24 and parallels).[15] On any scale of values, however, the kingdom is worth the sacrifice. A merchant who deals in fine pearls and finds one of very special value sells everything in order to purchase it (Matt 13:45–46). Someone who finds a treasure in a field sacrifices everything in order to purchase the field (Matt 13:44). The point in these sayings is not that one makes a prudential calculation of values and tries to obtain a good bargain but that the kingdom is worth any sacrifice. Repentance, therefore, means a rejection of those things associated with life as usual and an acceptance of the kingdom. It is not simply material possessions that must be rejected, but anything that hinders a full acceptance of the kingdom. It may be necessary for some to cut off a hand or pluck out an eye (Mark 9:43 and 47).

Repentance means not only turning away from something, but also turning toward something; in this case it means obedience to the demand of God. The gospels include a number of teachings on this subject. Many of them are found in pronouncement stories that tell of conflicts between Jesus and Jewish leaders, and they deal with questions about Torah and its applications. In most of these stories Jesus displays a fairly liberal attitude about the application of Torah. Several of the stories make the point that regulations about the observance of Sabbath are secondary to considerations of human need (Matt 12:1–8 and 12:9–14 and parallels; Luke 13:10–17). In these stories, Jesus maintains that the healing of human beings has an importance that surpasses any regulations about work on the Sabbath day. In rabbinic legislation the importance of healing on the Sabbath was rec-

---

[15] The interpretation that "needle's eye" is the name of a Jerusalem gate is without foundation. There is more merit to the suggestion that the original wording of the verse read "rope" for "camel," because the two words are similar in Greek. But the intention of the saying is to say that it is humanly impossible for a rich person to be saved. Jesus says in Matt 19:26 that this is only possible by divine action. The reading "camel" gives the hyperbolic meaning that seems to be required here.

ognized but was carefully restricted. In other sayings in the Synoptic Gospels, Jesus severely attacks Pharisees for failing to distinguish between the more and the less important elements in Torah, for "straining out a gnat and swallowing a camel" (Matt 23:24). He attacks the hypocrisy of Pharisees and challenges their regulations on purification (Mark 7:1–23, Matt 23:25–26, and Luke 11:37–41).

But there are some sayings in which Jesus seems much more conservative about the Torah. Matthew has most of them in passages that are unique to that gospel. A particularly striking collection of such sayings is found in Matt 5:17–19:

> Think not that I have come to abolish the law and the prophets; I have come not to abolish them but to fulfil them. For truly, I say to you, till heaven and earth pass away, not an iota, not a dot, will pass from the law until all is accomplished. Whoever then relaxes one of the least of these commandments and teaches men so, shall be called least in the kingdom of heaven; but he who does them and teaches them shall be called great in the kingdom of heaven.

Although the sayings here support a peculiarly Matthean emphasis, it is not likely that Matthew composed the passage. The stress on the continued authority of Torah is probably to be found among Palestinian Christians in the pregospel period. But there are traces in the sayings that suggest that they do not belong to the most primitive layer of oral tradition. The tone of the sayings reflects a community that has begun to settle down in the world. The urgency of eschatological expectation is blunted in the clauses, "till heaven and earth pass away" and "until all is accomplished." The ranking of people within the kingdom is inconsistent with the sayings we have just examined, where the demand for repentance would exclude talk about the least and greatest in the kingdom. In addition, there is a reactionary tone in the passage condemning the person who sets aside the law's demands and teaches others to do the same. It seems clear that some Christian group is being censured in this saying, possibly a group under the influence of Pauline theology.

Matthew not only has the teachings that seem critical of the application of Torah and sayings that uphold it, but he has some unique material that appears to challenge the authority of Torah in a radical fashion. In our treatment of Matthew in Chapter 6, we noticed his employment of the theme of Jesus as the new Moses. One aspect of that theme was found in a set of antitheses in Matt 5:21–48. Matthew seems to have used the form of the antithesis in order to call attention to the contrast between the word of Moses and the word of Jesus. There are six antitheses, three of which deal with prohibitions in the Ten Commandments. Here the contrast is not that Jesus allows what Moses prohibited, but that Jesus sharpens and extends the Mosaic prohibitions. Moses said not to murder; Jesus says not to be angry. Moses said not to commit adultery; Jesus says not to be lustful. Moses said not to commit perjury; Jesus says not to be insincere. The point of the antitheses is that the will of God cannot be limited to the prohibition of specified acts. Prohibitions against murder, adultery, and perjury allow a person to interpret duty toward God in a restricted sense. One may say, "This is what I owe to God, and not a cent more." But in the antitheses the demand of God is interpreted in the most inclusive sense possible; it prohibits the inward attitudes that lead to external acts of disobedience. God demands nothing less than the entire person, in attitudes and actions. This interpretation implies a radical criticism of legal applications of Torah, for it understands God's demand in terms with which law cannot deal. Law and courts can control murder, adultery, and perjury, but not anger, lust, or insincerity.

In a number of parables and sayings, Jesus proclaims the demand of God for love. "You shall love your neighbor as yourself" (Matt 22:39 and parallels). One must love the enemy and forgive without limit (Matt 18:21–22). The demand for love concentrates on our attitude and intention, but the matter cannot be left there. The parable of the Good Samaritan (Luke 10:29–37) defines the working of love as the unlimited helpful response to a fellow human being in need. The teaching makes no effort to list precisely appropriate responses to particular situations, but it gives examples of such responses. The notable characteristic in the examples is the lack of measurement. A Samaritan does what he thinks is helpful but stands ready to do more if needed. A father of a derelict but returned son greets him with a celebration without worrying about punishment or equal treatment for a son who caused no trouble (Luke 15:11–32). One who is asked for a coat gives two, and one who is asked to go one mile goes two (Matt 5:41 and Luke 6:29). Even here the point is not simply a demand for doing something extra. The teachings do not call for a simply literal performance of the demand, after which one can grudgingly say, "I have gone the second mile." The point is that the response is not to be measured. Love simply has no limit.

Thus, on the question of the attitude toward Torah, the situation is complex. In some teachings Jesus takes a liberal attitude toward the application of Torah, and in others he seems to uphold it firmly. We have some sayings that involve a radically negative attitude toward Torah, and some that interpret the demand of God in ways that are far removed from legal formulations. Which of these positions seems to be the earliest? It is not possible to answer this question with certainty, but perhaps we can explain the reason for the complexity. If Jesus had first been pictured as one who taught that unmeasured love for persons in need was the essence of God's demand, then some Christians might have felt that he had, by implication, challenged Torah, and others might have felt that he had fulfilled it. A demand of the sort we find in many of Jesus' parables could impress people in different ways. Some might feel that he was simply giving examples of what Torah required, in haggadic fashion, and some might say that he was challenging the very applicability of Torah to daily life. This teaching about love, although not ambiguous in itself, may lead to ambiguity on the question of Torah. We do know that there were vigorous discussions about Torah in the first several decades of Christian history, and we will examine them in a later chapter. It is possible to understand how Christians could take sides on this matter if the most primitive traditions about Jesus' teaching had allowed for some ambiguity.

We may reasonably conclude, therefore, that the earliest Christian traditions pictured Jesus as one who proclaimed the future coming of the kingdom of God and demanded that persons repent. The proclamation was understood as requiring renunciation of life as usual and radical obedience to the will of God—that is, love of one's neighbor. Love was understood as an unmeasured response to a human being in need and a renunciation of such indulgences as anger, lust, and insincerity. These demands did not settle the question of Torah as the will of God.

In the case of these teachings about the kingdom of God, the need for repentance, and the demand for unmeasured love, it is probable that the earliest Christian traditions have authentically portrayed Jesus. The first Christians lived in an eschatological climate that was pervaded by an expectation of the kingdom. They also practiced a kind of sharing of possessions, which exemplifies a tendency to de-emphasize life as usual. Their very activity points to something or someone who gave impetus to this way of living. We could not explain the tradition or the life of early Christians without pointing to an authoritative figure who did in fact proclaim the kingdom. If Jesus did not proclaim the kingdom, someone else did, and the burden of proof is on the one who claims that it was not Jesus.

It has been proposed that the chief criterion for establishing authentic information about the historical Jesus is the criterion of dissimilarity. This criterion means that we can be the most confident of those early traditions that are dissimilar both to aspects of contemporary Judaism and of early Christianity. Something that is dissimilar to early Christianity either conflicts with basic Christian convictions or fails to confirm them. Something dissimilar to Judaism at Jesus' time challenges important and widely shared Jewish convictions or, at least, does not merely duplicate Jewish teaching. There is much in the teaching about the kingdom that is similar both to Judaism and early Christianity. But there is one related aspect that seems to meet the criterion of dissimilarity, and that is the teaching of Jesus about himself. In brief, the teaching falls short of embracing claims of being Son of man or Messiah, and, hence, differs with claims made by early Christians; and Jesus' teachings imply a personal authority that seems inappropriate in terms of contemporary Judaism. Both points need explanation.

According to Christian oral traditions, Jesus' teaching about the kingdom of God included the expectation about an appearance of the Son of man. As we have seen, the Son of man played a significant messianic role in some Jewish apocalyptic writings. Similarly, in Jesus' teachings, the Son of man is the initiator of the kingdom, and his advent is still in the future. Although Christians later identified Jesus with the Son of man, the early oral traditions did not make that identification; the distinction between the two was preserved up to the time of the Synoptic Gospels. To be sure, there are some points of confusion in the synoptics, because the phrase is used there in more than one way. There are, for example, some places where the Son of man has no eschatological connotations, as in predictions of Jesus' coming suffering (Mark 8:31, 9:31, and 10:33 and parallels). But the striking fact is that where the phrase is used in an eschatological sense, Jesus himself is not identified with the Son of man. The most natural reading of these passages is that Jesus expected the coming of the Son of man but did not identify himself with this figure. In this respect the teaching of Jesus differs from that of early Christianity.

In respect to the use of the title Messiah, or Christ, there is also a dissimilarity between the teaching of Jesus and early Christianity. Although the motif of the messianic secret probably originated with Mark, its existence points to the probability that Jesus did not in fact claim to be Messiah. If it had been known that Jesus had clearly presented himself as Messiah, such a claim could hardly have disappeared from the tradition. But in Mark, Jesus does not claim Messiahship until his trial, when he responds positively to the question of the high priest. The priest asks, "Are you the Christ?" and Jesus answers, "I am; and you will see the Son of man sitting at the right hand of Power, and coming with the clouds of heaven" (Mark 14:62). For Mark, Jesus' claim about himself is only given here at the last moment, so to speak. Matthew and Luke, however, are reluctant to include a claim by Jesus even at this point. Matthew has Jesus reply ambiguously to the high priest's question: "You have said so" (Matt 26:64). Luke has: "If I tell you, you will not believe; and if I ask you, you will not answer" (Luke 22:67–68). To the question, "Are you the Son of God?" Jesus ambiguously responds, in Luke, "You say that I am" (Luke 22:70). These gospels produce an overwhelming impression that, although Christians were convinced that Jesus was Messiah, he was not remembered as having taught this about himself. In respect to the claims of Jesus about himself, there is dissimilarity between him and early Christianity.

The dissimilarity between contemporary Judaism and the teachings of Jesus is more subtle and implicit. The early Christian oral traditions do not maintain that Jesus claimed to be the Son of man or Messiah, but they leave no doubt that he presented himself with authority. That he did so is implied by his proclamation of the kingdom and his demand for repentance and obedience. In his teachings he presented neither credentials nor evidence. He claimed neither special training nor esoteric knowledge. He approached his hearers simply with the words, "I say to you." The effect of this forceful implication of authority is summarized by Mark, "And they were astonished at his teaching, for he taught them as one who had authority, and not as the scribes" (Mark 1:22; cf. Matt 7:28 and Luke 4:31). Jesus' authority is also implied in Matthew's antitheses, where it is contrasted with the teaching of Moses. It is represented in a characteristic word that precedes a number of the sayings. This is the word *Amen*, which is translated as "verily," "truly," or "I tell you this." Many modern scholars feel that *Amen* was a characteristic word that Jesus used to preface his teachings. It is a Semitic word frequently found at the conclusion of a clause, where it serves to indicate one's agreement with the preceding proposition. There are no parallels in rabbinic literature to the use of the word at the beginning of a saying. So perhaps Jesus himself used the word in such a way that it would imply a claim of authority.[16] Of course, Jews in Jesus' day recognized authoritative teachers, but they required some credentials. Jesus, by contrast, appears to have had none. In this respect, the teaching of Jesus is dissimilar to contemporary Judaism.

The criterion of coherence allows us to include teachings that are coherent with those established by the criterion of dissimilarity, and the criterion of multiple attestation means that we can have confidence in traditions that appear in several forms or sources. The teaching of Jesus about the kingdom, as we have previously analyzed it, meets these criteria: it is coherent with the teaching about himself, and it is found in several forms of the oral tradition. It also makes use of Semitic concepts and terminology and so meets the fourth criterion.

From a study of the teachings of Jesus we may come to the highly probable conclusion that Jesus proclaimed the imminence of the kingdom, urgently demanded repentance, and interpreted the will of God in terms of unmeasured love toward humans in need. He did this without claims about his own person, but nevertheless with an impressive degree of authority. On these points, we are probably close to the historical Jesus.

THE MIRACLES OF JESUS

Miracle stories are found in all three Synoptic Gospels, the Gospel of John, and the Infancy Gospel of Thomas. Many of the miracle stories in the Synoptic Gospels are found in all three, and only a few are unique to a particular gospel. Proponents of the two-document hypothesis point to the pauc-

---

[16] Cf. Ernst Käsemann, "The Problem of the Historical Jesus," in *Essays on New Testament Themes*, trans. by W. J. Montague (Naperville, Ill.: Allenson, 1964), pp. 15–47. Here Käsemann wrote that Jesus' use of *Amen* and his claim to operate by the spirit mean that he looked on himself as "the instrument of the living Spirit of God, which Judaism expected to be the gift of the End" (p. 42).

The raising of Jairus' daughter, fourth-century ivory casket from the Church of Santa Giulia, Brescia, Italy. (Courtesy *Civico Museo d'Arte e Storia, Brescia.*)

ity of miracle stories in Q. The only one is the healing of the son of the centurion (Matt 8:5–10 and Luke 7:1–10). John and the Infancy Gospel of Thomas have several miracle stories that were not derived from synoptic accounts. Christian stories treat nature miracles, healings, exorcisms, and resuscitations.

In the study of a miracle story, form critics have shown that we must work back from the written narrative to the earliest recoverable form of the story. The first step is to discover the editorial materials in the narrative—namely, the additions that the gospel writer made to a story he found elsewhere. These materials would connect the story with the narrative as a whole and might include geographical notes. The second step is to discover secondary additions—that is, elements that made their way into the narrative in the course of tradition but did not originally belong to the story. The form critic will be on the lookout for a number of things: a description of action that detracts from the main line of action, a novelistic treatment that shows a particular interest in some character, a detail that might pose an inconsistency with the main line of action, and material of an expository nature—that is, that makes some application of the story to a more general situation or tries to draw a moral from it. Study of the development of oral traditions shows that these kinds of elements generally are added to a miracle story in the course of its oral transmission.

This suggests that the oldest recoverable form of a miracle story will probably be brief and simple. We have some miracle stories in the Synoptic Gospels that seem to be close to the primitive form. One of the simplest is found in Matt 9:32–34. This exorcism narrative contains a few editorial materials, such as the connecting phrase, "as they were going away," in verse 32. Matthew has also probably added the words in verse 33 that express the astonishment of the crowds, and verse 34 seems intended to remind the reader about the opposition of the Pharisees to Jesus and to anticipate the Beelzebul controversy, which Matthew will describe in 12:22–30. Notice the simplicity of the rest. The oldest recoverable form of this story is printed here without brackets. The phrases that are probably the result of Matthew's editorial activity are bracketed.

[As they were going away,] behold, a dumb demoniac was brought to him. And when the demon had been cast out, the dumb man spoke; and the crowds marveled, [saying, "Never was anything like this seen in Israel." But the Pharisees said, "He casts out demons by the prince of demons.] (Matt 9:32–34).

By contrast, notice the complex exorcism account in Mark 5:1–20 and parallels. This narrative probably includes some secondary features, such as the transfer of the demons to the swine in verses 10–13, which detracts from the main line of action; the reaction of the crowd in verses 14–17, which introduces an additional line of action; and the sequel in verses 18–20, which concentrates attention on the cured demoniac and his subsequent history.

After we have identified the editorial and secondary features, the next step in the analysis of a miracle story is to look for the situation that may have given rise to the original form. Clues may be supplied by similar stories from the same period. It is possible that stories from Hellenistic or Jewish sources were modified and used in the Christian tradition. We know that miracle stories were attributed to a number of people and circulated widely in the Hellenistic period. There were professional exorcists and healers, such as Asclepius, as well as teachers, Roman emperors, and Jewish rabbis, who performed occasional miracles. A special class of Hellenistic miracle workers consisted of people called *divine men*. They were thought to be superhuman, and their prime occupation was to work miracles for the benefit of human beings. In contemporary accounts we find stories of healings at a distance, healings of the lame, the blind, and the paralyzed, and resurrections from the dead. Bultmann cited a probable parallel to the still-ing of the storm (Mark 4:35–41 and parallels) in rabbinic literature from about 350 CE. Notice also the parallels with the OT story of Jonah.

> A Jewish child went on a voyage in a heathen ship. When a storm brought the ship into danger, all the heathen called on their gods and when that proved useless, finally urged the Jewish child to call on his God. When the child prayed, the storm ceased and the heathen paid respectful admiration.[17]

The parallels show that Christians may have imported miracle stories from other traditions. But in a more significant way they illustrate the kind of world in which the stories were circulating, and they give us some insight into the general situation that may have prompted them. After all why did Christians tell miracle stories about Jesus? To answer that they told the stories because they happened begs the question. Because similar stories were told of Asclepius, rabbis, teachers, and emperors, the answer must be that they thought of Jesus as somehow comparable with the great persons of the age. It seems that miracle stories were told in order to demonstrate a person's status. Each age has its own measure of importance. Among early Hebrews it was expressed in terms of a long life, and the maxim was that the best people live the longest. In some cultures, ancestry or intelligence are expressions of importance. Political power is nearly always a measure of importance. In our age, wealth is a demonstration of importance. In the Hellenistic period, one criterion was the ability to work miracles. We must keep in mind the fact that most Hellenistic people had neither the ability nor the inclination to make sharp distinctions between the possible and the impossible. To many of them, healings, exorcisms, and resuscitations were not, strictly speaking, impossible. They were, of course, extraordinary, and so were used as indications of a person's extraordinary importance. When Christians told miracle stories about Jesus, they were affirming his importance.

But did the earliest oral traditions claim that Jesus worked miracles? The kerygma, as found in Acts 10:38, says that "he healed all that were oppressed by the devil." This sentence may refer to general healings or exorcisms or both, for oppression by the devil may designate either demon possession or illness (it was generally understood that evil and illness were connected). On the other hand, form critics think that most of the miracle stories originated among Greek-speaking Christians and so were not part of the very earliest traditions. Bultmann was convinced, however, that some miracle stories were told in the earliest days. He found two groups that seemed to have originated in the early oral period in Palestine. One group contains miracle stories that were actually transmitted in the form of pronouncement stories. The fact that the stories were not told as miracle stories but were embedded within a form that was used to transmit the words of

---

[17] Bultmann, op. cit., p. 234f.

Jesus argues for their early origin. This group includes the Beelzebul controversy in Matt 12:22–30, a Sabbath healing in Mark 3:1–5, the exorcism
of a demon from a Syro-Phoenician woman's daughter in Mark 7:24–30,
and the healing of a centurion's son in Capernaum in Matt 8:5–13.[18] The
second group consists of three miracle stories that have parallels in rabbinic
literature or contain clear Palestinian traces. The three are the stilling of the
storm (Mark 4:35–41), the feeding stories (Mark 6:34–44 and 8:1–9),
and the healing of a leper (Mark 1:40–45).[19] To be sure, this is a relatively
short list, for most of the miracle stories came out of a Greek-speaking and,
hence, later context. Yet they are sufficient to show that the earliest traditions contained narratives about Jesus as healer and exorcist and claimed
that he had power over nature.

These claims about Jesus' miraculous power were not merely reports of
historical events. They embodied a designation of Jesus' status as Messiah.
In Jewish apocalyptic thought, the Messianic Age was expected to be one
in which righteousness dominates unrighteousness and, hence, health dominates illness. The resurrection of the dead and a revolution of nature were
expected. In the apocalyptic literature these miraculous happenings are signs
that the Messianic Age is here, and, in some, they are functions of the
Messiah. So Christians, who were convinced of Jesus' messianic status, associated miraculous events with him. He raised the dead, dominated evil
demons, and had power over nature. His healings demonstrated his righteous power.

But did Jesus actually perform healings and nature miracles? We, as
twentieth-century people, cannot easily conclude that he did. Too much
stands in the way of such an inference. We cannot approach the question
of miracles without facing a number of problems. To be sure, we are in no
position to say that we know all the rules whereby changes in nature and
human beings take place. But we do know some things. We may be called
on at any time to revise our understanding of natural regularities, but we
are cautious about doing so and demand documented evidence provided
under controlled conditions. We have nothing like this kind of evidence in
the early Christian oral traditions. Instead, we have unscientific reports preserved by pre-Enlightenment people. People who are not disposed to see
nature as regular do not require what scientists require. The scientific, skeptical attitude was not present among early Christians, so they did not produce anything resembling documented proof. In view of this situation, we
cannot simply conclude that the tradition about miracles is historically accurate.

The inevitable conclusion seems to be that the miracle tradition has no
historical basis. But before we come to this conclusion, it is necessary to

[18] Ibid., p. 239. Relevant parallels in the other Synoptic Gospels are included in each case.
[19] Ibid., p. 240.

consider an objection. In the ancient world, ill health and demon possession were frequently related to moral evil. If Jesus proclaimed the kingdom and authoritatively demanded repentance, and if his demand was met by a positive response, as it must frequently have been, many people would have understood his effect as an overcoming of evil. Such positive responses to Jesus might sometimes have shown themselves visibly. A mentally ill person who made a positive response to Jesus might very well have found a reorientation for his life that would result in a kind of mental peace. This possibility is most easily demonstrated by reference to the exorcisms. Although most of us do not talk about demon possession, we must not assume that there is no reality reflected in the term. We are familiar with the symptoms associated in the ancient world with demon possession, and in most cases demoniacs displayed symptoms with which modern psychology is familiar. Witness, for example, Mark's description of the demoniac at Gerasa (Mark 5:1–20). He lived alone among the tombs. People had tried to bring him under control but had failed. He cried out and cut himself with stones. The information that Mark gives is not sufficient to provide the basis for a full diagnosis, but it is enough to suggest that some kind of mental illness was involved. The tradition of exorcism might well reflect the fact that Jesus' proclamation met with a positive response. The relationship between Jesus' battle against evil and his healings is beautifully expressed in the kerygmatic formula: Jesus "went about doing good and healing all that were oppressed by the devil" (Acts 10:38).

Here we can only assent to a conclusion as being possible. It is historically possible that Jesus had a positive effect on people that resulted in a visible improvement of their psychological or physical states. A fact such as this may partially account for the rise of a tradition about Jesus as miracle worker. Nevertheless, it is probable that conviction about his messianic status is the chief support for this tradition.

THE TRIAL OF JESUS

Our written sources agree that Jesus' death was the result of a judicial verdict and that he was crucified. Paul reflects the tradition at a number of points, and Tacitus, the Roman historian, refers to it.[20] The Synoptic Gospels present detailed narratives of the trial, the Gospel of John has a long section on it, and a fragmentary account from the Gospel of Peter has been preserved. The contents of these narratives should be kept in mind.

Matthew and Mark have similar reports of the trial. Matthew has a few additional items, the place of which may be seen more clearly if we analyze Mark first. Mark's account runs from 14:43–15:15. In it, Jesus is arrested

[20] Cf. 1 Cor 2:2, Gal 3:1, Phil 2:8, and Tacitus, *Annals* 15:4.

Scenes from the passion of Jesus, showing the arrest of Jesus and Peter's denial in the upper panel and, in the lower panel, the testimony of false witnesses and Pilate washing his hands. A fourth-century ivory casket from the Church of Santa Giulia, Brescia, Italy. (Courtesy Civico Museo d'Arte e Storia, Brescia.)

at night and taken before the high priest, chief priests, elders, and scribes. In Mark 14:55 this body, called the Sanhedrin, or court, hears testimony that Jesus once threatened to destroy and rebuild the Temple, but Mark says that the witnesses did not agree, and he calls the testimony false. The high priest then questions Jesus directly: "Are you the Christ, the Son of the Blessed?" (Mark 14:61). Jesus answers: "I am, and you will see the Son of man sitting at the right hand of Power, and coming with the clouds of heaven" (14:62). The high priest regards this as a self-incriminating confession and charges Jesus with blasphemy. The other members of the Sanhedrin agree, and they unanimously call for Jesus' execution. Mark tells the story of Peter's denial of Jesus as an event that occurs simultaneously with the Sanhedrin trial. The following morning Jesus is taken before the Roman governor, Pontius Pilate, who asks him, "Are you the King of the Jews?" (15:2). Jesus replies, "You have said so" (15:2), but he makes no defense. Mark then tells of a customary Passover amnesty, in which the governor releases one prisoner. Pilate offers to release either Jesus or Barabbas, a rebel and murderer. The crowd chooses Barabbas and insists on the crucifixion of Jesus. The story ends with these words: "So Pilate, wishing to satisfy the crowd, released for them Barabbas; and having scourged Jesus, he delivered him to be crucified" (15:15).

Matthew's account of the trial (26:47–27:26) is nearly identical with Mark's, but there are some subtle differences. For one thing, Jesus' answer to the high priest's question is more ambiguous in Matthew than in Mark—"You have said so" (Matt 26:64). Matthew has three narratives that are not found in Mark or Luke: the story of the death of Judas (27:3–10), the warning of Pilate's wife to have nothing to do with the innocent Jesus (27:19), and the story of Pilate's symbolic gesture of washing his hands of responsibility for Jesus' death (27:24).

The framework of Luke's narrative (22:47–23:25) is comparable with that in Matthew and Mark, but there are significant differences. Luke has no night meeting of the Sanhedrin but one the morning following Jesus' arrest. The court does not examine witnesses but questions Jesus directly. He is asked if he is Messiah and Son of God, and he gives evasive answers to both questions. Afterward the Sanhedrin takes Jesus to Pilate and brings three charges against him: perverting the nation, opposing the payment of Roman taxes, and claiming to be a king (Luke 23:2). Pilate is initially reluctant to hear the case, and, when he finds that Jesus is a Galilean, he sends him to be examined by Herod (Herod Antipas, tetrarch of Galilee). The examination seems inconclusive, and Jesus is returned to Pilate, who reaffirms his verdict of innocence. Then Luke tells of the crowd's demand for the release of Barabbas and for the crucifixion of Jesus and of Pilate's capitulation to the demand.

The account in the Gospel of John (18:1–19:16) presents interesting similarities and differences. Here Judas procures a band of soldiers and officers from the priests and Pharisees. Jesus surrenders to them, saying, "I am he" (John 18:5), upon which they all fall to the ground. He is taken to the high priest's father-in-law, Annas, who questions him about his disciples and his teaching and sends him to the high priest Caiaphas, who sends him on to Pilate. Pilate calls for the accusation, to which "they" reply that Jesus is an evildoer. Pilate tells them to judge him by their own law, but "the Jews" answer that they are calling for the death penalty but cannot execute such a punishment.[21] Pilate then questions Jesus directly, and we have the following dialogue (18:33–38):

PILATE: Are you the king of the Jews?

JESUS: Do you say this of your own accord or is this my accusation?

PILATE: Am I a Jew? This is the charge against you drawn up by your own people. What have you done?

JESUS: You say that I am a king. This is my purpose. Everyone who is of the truth hears my voice.

PILATE: What is truth?

[21] It is uncertain whether Jewish legal bodies had the right to use the death penalty at this time.

Pilate then goes out to the Jews, declares Jesus innocent, and offers to release him in accordance with the Passover amnesty. But the crowd calls for
Barabbas, whom John describes as a robber. After he allows Jesus to be
beaten, mockingly dressed in royal purple, and crowned with thorns, Pilate
again declares that Jesus is innocent. The chief priests and officers call for
crucifixion, and Pilate offers to turn Jesus over to them. The Jews, however,
tell him that their law demands capital punishment. Pilate again questions
Jesus and again tries to release him, but the Jews insist that it would be
disloyal to Caesar to release one who claims to be a king. Finally, Pilate
orders Jesus to be crucified.

The surviving fragment of the Gospel of Peter begins with the statement
that none of the Jews washed their hands, nor did Herod or any of his
judges. There must have been a story, borrowed from Matthew, about Pilate's hand washing, which immediately preceded this. The fragment goes
on to say that Herod gave the order for Jesus' execution.

In order to work back from these accounts to the earliest traditions, we
must first try to identify the editorial additions, some of which form parts
of certain motifs to be found in the gospels. One such motif is a tendency
to place major responsibility for Jesus' execution on the Jews rather than on
the Romans. All the gospels have this tendency. In Mark and Matthew, the
Jewish Sanhedrin conducts the initial trial and acts as prosecutor before
Pilate. Although, strictly speaking, Luke does not describe a Sanhedrin trial,
he does have that body initiate the proceedings. In all the canonical gospels,
when the Jews are given a chance to release Jesus, they call for Barabbas. In
Matthew Pilate washes his hands as a symbolic act, declaring that he has no
responsibility in the proceedings. He says, "I am innocent of this man's
blood; see to it yourselves" (Matt 27:24). By contrast, the people in atten-
dance accept responsibility not only for themselves but also for their descendants: "His blood be on us and on our children!" (Matt 27:25). The
Gospel of John goes to great lengths to show the guilt of the Jews. Pilate
repeatedly declares Jesus' innocence and attempts to release him. The Jews,
however, insist that their law requires Jesus' execution, and they threaten to
charge Pilate with insubordination if he refuses to crucify him. The Gospel
of Peter has Pilate wash his hands and claims that it was Herod (presumably
Herod Antipas) who ordered the crucifixion.

Another tendency in the gospels is to insist on the innocence of Jesus.
Mark calls attention to disagreement among the witnesses against him and
expressly declares their testimony false. Matthew describes Judas' suicide as
an act of remorse at the realization that he had betrayed an innocent man.
In the midst of the Roman trial in Matthew, Pilate's wife warns him to
have nothing to do with this innocent man. In Luke, Pilate and Herod both
declare Jesus to be innocent, and in John, Pilate makes repeated declarations
to this effect. On specific charges listed in Luke, the evangelist has shown
Jesus to be innocent. In Luke 23:2 Jesus is accused of opposing payment

of Roman taxes, but in Luke 20:25, when he was questioned about taxes, he said, "Then render to Caesar the things that are Caesar's, and to God the things that are God's" (cf. Matt 22:21 and Mark 12:17). Luke also says that Jesus was accused of claiming to be Christ, a king. But Luke has not included any such claims by Jesus in his gospel.

Another tendency that is discernible in the gospels is to call attention to scriptural predictions about Jesus' suffering and death. The motif of prophetic and scriptural fulfillment is notable throughout Matthew and plays a role in the report of the trial in that gospel. Matthew expressly calls attention to prophetic fulfillment in connection with Jesus' arrest (Matt 26:54 and 56) and in the story of the purchase of the potter's field (27:9–10). Peter's denial (26:69–75) is a fulfillment of Jesus' own prediction (26:34). Luke has few explicit OT references in the trial narratives, but in chapter 24 the risen Jesus interprets the scriptures to his disciples so that they are able to understand the divine necessity of his suffering and death (cf. Luke 24:26–27 and 45–46). Moreover, scriptural passages probably influenced the narratives in subtle ways. For example, the silence of Jesus before Pilate may have been inferred from reading an OT scripture such as Isa 53:7, where Yahweh's suffering servant is pictured as silent in the face of oppression. This verse is specifically applied to Jesus in Acts 8:26–40. The hearing before Herod in Luke 22:6–12 may have been influenced by Ps 2:2, "The kings of the earth set themselves, and the rulers take counsel together, against the Lord and his anointed." In Acts 4:25–28, Luke himself calls attention to this OT scripture and its connection with Jesus' trial.

The presence of these various motifs in the gospels has produced many of the difficulties in the narratives of the trial. The Sanhedrin trial in Matthew and Mark seems to be highly irregular. This point is difficult to evaluate, because the rules of procedure for the Sanhedrin are found only in a tractate in the Mishnah, which was not codified in present form until about 200 CE. Thus, these rules may not have been known at the time of the composition of the gospels and may not have been in effect at the time of Jesus' trial. But much that is in the Mishnah does go back to the first century, so it is reasonable to compare the accounts in our gospels with the Mishnaic tractate. There are some sixteen points at which the Matthew/Mark account varies from the Mishnaic rules.[22] The Mishnah, for example, forbade a night meeting of the Sanhedrin. It did not allow a verdict of guilt to be given, in capital cases, on the same day that the trial began. It forbade a unanimous vote for conviction.[23] Matthew and Mark, by contrast, describe a night meeting in which Jesus is unanimously convicted within a matter of hours.

[22] An analysis of the Mishnaic rules and their application to the Gospel of Mark may be found in Herbert Danby, "The Bearing of the Rabbinical Criminal Codes on the Jewish Trial Narratives in the Gospels," *Journal of Theological Studies,* **21**:51–76 (1920).
[23] Cf. Mishnah, Sanhedrin 4:1.

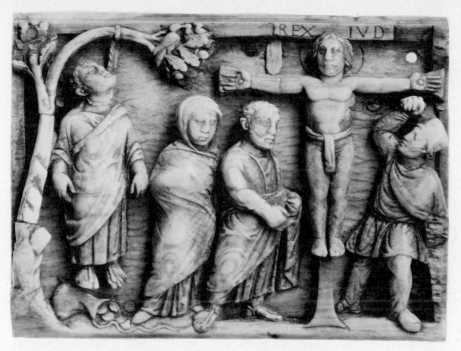

An ivory casket from c. 420 CE, showing the death of Judas by hanging and Jesus on the cross. (Courtesy *the Trustees of the British Museum, London.*)

The problems in the narratives are not confined to the variances from Mishnaic regulations. They impress themselves on any attentive reader of the gospels. In Mark, for example, the Jewish court convicts Jesus of blasphemy but makes no effort to carry out the usual penalty for blasphemy, namely, stoning. Instead, they take him to Pilate and charge him with the Roman crime of royal pretension, the usual penalty for which is crucifixion. In John the Jews demand Jesus' execution on the basis first of Jewish law, then later on the basis of Roman law. The fact of a Passover amnesty cannot be verified in contemporary non-Christian records and is brought into the narratives in a peculiar way.[24] Although Pilate tries to use it as a device for securing Jesus' release, he presents as an alternative a person who is already convicted of sedition, that is, a person on an entirely different legal footing. Add to this the picture of Pilate acting totally under pressure from subject peoples. He is presented as convinced of Jesus' innocence and anxious for his release, as holding the powers of life and death in his hands, but

---

[24] A defense of the amnesty narrative is given by Charles B. Chavel, "The Releasing of a Prisoner on the Eve of Passover in Ancient Jerusalem," *Journal of Biblical Literature,* **60**:273–275 (1941).

as succumbing to the insistence of the people he governed, even though they offered no evidence for their charges. The tendency of the gospel writers to place major responsibility for Jesus' death on the Jews has probably created most of the difficulties in the narratives about the trial.

In the case of the synoptic trial narratives, source criticism has played a significant role. Some proponents of the two-document hypothesis have called attention to certain differences between the Gospel of Luke and the other two. These scholars maintain that Luke used Mark as one source for his trial narrative but that he had a second source, which he preferred to Mark at a number of points.[25] Evidence for a second source is found in Luke's change from a night meeting of the Sanhedrin to a morning session and in his addition of a hearing under Herod. Moreover, Luke alone omits the charge of blasphemy and records specific political charges. Although the theory of a special Lukan trial source arose among proponents of the two-document hypothesis, it would work as well with the Griesbach theory. Because Matthew and Mark are so nearly identical in their trial narratives, the case for a special source could be made on the assumption that Luke used either Matthew or Mark. In either case, if Luke had a special source, it included the following data: Jesus was arrested at night and held until the next morning, when the Sanhedrin examined him; at the conclusion of the examination, he was taken to Pilate and charged with political crimes—perverting the Jewish nation (presumably against Rome), opposing the payment of Roman taxes, and claiming to be messianic king; and Pilate sent Jesus to Herod, who questioned him and returned him to the Roman governor. These items, then, were combined by Luke with his other source, either Mark or Matthew.

Not all scholars are convinced that Luke had a separate source for the trial. Bultmann, for example, believed that the other writers used Mark but felt free to add, delete, and modify items at will. He maintained, however, that Mark had a *"primitive narrative* which told very briefly of the arrest, the condemnation by the Sanhedrin and Pilate, the journey to the cross, the crucifixion, and death."[26] This brief narrative of Jesus' condemnation was enlarged by the addition of separate stories that told of the proceedings before the Sanhedrin and Pilate.

Thus far we have looked at the accounts of Jesus' trial in the gospels and have found that certain motifs that were employed by the evangelists have affected their reports. We have seen that there is a possibility that there were at least two separate sources used in the gospels: one like the narrative in Matthew/Mark and another that contained some unique Lukan elements.

Is it possible now to move back from the gospels to the oral period and

---

[25] Cf., e.g., Vincent Taylor, *The Passion Narrative of St. Luke,* ed. by Owen E. Evans (Cambridge: Cambridge U.P., 1972).

[26] Bultmann, op. cit., p. 279. (Italics Bultmann's)

to find elements that probably were present in the earliest traditions? Admittedly we are in hazardous territory, where form criticism is of little help. Bultmann was probably right in suggesting that the earliest traditions contained no detailed narratives of the legal proceedings against Jesus. But the study of forms does not tell us specifically what those traditions included, or probably included. All we can do at this point is to speculate about the items that seem indispensable to any traditions about Jesus' death. This speculation should take into account evidence that might come from the gospels as well as from the early Christian kerygma and from the letters of Paul.

One item that would appear to be indispensable to Christian traditions about the death of Jesus is a statement that he was crucified. The tradition that Jesus was executed by hanging on a tree or cross appears in early kerygmatic formulations (cf. Acts 2:23 and 10:39) and in the letters of Paul (1 Cor 2:2, Gal 3:1, and Phil 2:8). The Roman historian Tacitus does not specifically refer to crucifixion, but he says that the founder of the Christian movement was put to death by Pontius Pilate.[27] Paul does not expressly refer to Pilate, but Acts 2:23 refers to crucifixion "by the hands of lawless men," which in context probably means Gentiles—people without Torah. Pilate is named explicitly in Peter's speeches in Acts 3:13 and (with Herod) 4:27. It is almost certain that the earliest Christian oral traditions maintained that Jesus had died by being crucified, and it is probable that Pilate was mentioned in connection with the execution.

Another element that surely seems to be a part of the early tradition is the claim of Jewish responsibility in the death of Jesus. Such a motif is emphasized in the gospels, but it is also found in earlier material. In Acts 2:23 Peter charges that the Jews crucified and killed Jesus "by the hands of lawless men." The implication is that Jews bear the major responsibility and that they used Gentiles as accessories. In 1 Thess 2:14–15 Paul makes no mention of Gentiles but says that Jews "killed both the Lord Jesus and the prophets."

No other points can, with equal certainty, be assumed to have circulated in the earliest period, for neither the Jerusalem nor the Pauline kerygma gives us additional information. It is not likely that the early traditions said anything about the charges against Jesus, the grounds of the charges, or the legal proceedings. All we can say, with conviction, is that the first Christians believed that Jesus had been crucified and that the Jews had something to do with it.

The actual facts surrounding the death of Jesus are so thickly clouded over by tradition and by gospel accounts that we cannot expect easily to sort them out. Yet there are some minimal bits of information that carry the conviction of authenticity.

[27] Tacitus, loc. cit.

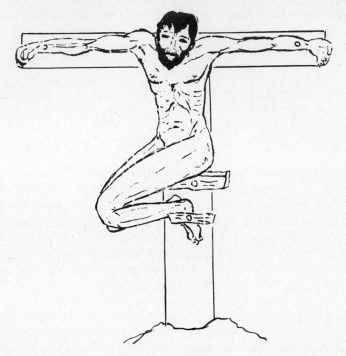

Figure 19   A sketch of a crucifixion position based on analysis of a skeleton found in the ancient cemetery at Givat Hamivtan in N.E. Jerusalem. The skeleton is about 2,000 years old. (Copyright 1971 Time Inc. All rights reserved. Reprinted by permission from TIME.)

First, it is almost certain that Jesus was crucified. Crucifixion was an ignominious death, a punishment that was used as an effective deterrent. It was carried out in public, and frequently large numbers of people were crucified at the same time. The victim was lashed to a stake, sometimes with a crossbeam, and sometimes a spike was driven through one or more of the limbs. The victim would die slowly, and usually there was bloodshed. The contemporary NT scholar Martin Hengel calls crucifixion "an utterly offensive affair, 'obscene' in the original sense of the word."[28] Hengel shows that it was regarded in this way by Greeks, Romans, barbarians, and Jews. He also shows that, in Roman times, it was used mostly for slaves, rebellious foreigners, and hardened criminals.

The criterion of dissimilarity, which has had limited usefulness up to now, proves fruitful at this point. The crucifixion of Jesus was harmful to the

---

[28] Martin Hengel, *Crucifixion in the Ancient World and the Folly of the Message of the Cross,* trans. by John Bowden (Philadelphia: Fortress Press, 1977), p. 22.

Christian message, and it goes counter to Jewish apocalyptic expectation. These points require some elucidation.

The death of Jesus by crucifixion was essentially a problem for early Christian preachers. Paul must be reflecting common experience when he says that the word of the cross is "folly" (1 Cor 1:18), and when he says that it is "a stumblingblock to Jews and folly to Gentiles" (1 Cor 1:23). Hengel's study has shown that most people in the first century would associate crucifixion with slavery and extreme humiliation. Except for Jesus, he finds no cases where one becomes a revered martyr by being crucified. He writes: "An alleged son of god who could not help himself at the time of his deepest need (Mark 15:31), and who rather required his followers to take up the cross, was hardly an attraction to the lower classes of Roman and Greek society."[29] But neither was he attractive to upper classes: "That this crucified Jew, Jesus Christ, could truly be a divine being sent to earth, God's Son, the Lord of all and the coming judge of the world, must inevitably have been thought by any educated man to be utter 'madness' and presumptuousness."[30] In short, Christians did not claim that Jesus was crucified in order to complement or confirm their message about him or to make it more palatable, and this fact argues for the historicity of the death of Jesus by crucifixion.

But perhaps Christians proclaimed Jesus to have been crucified because that was somehow connected to Jewish expectations. The first Christians believed in the messianic exaltation of Jesus, and clearly their concept of the Messiah originated in Jewish apocalyptic circles. Although we find there a number of variations in the descriptions of the expected person and work of the Messiah, we search in vain for one that describes a Messiah who accomplishes his purpose by dying. We will see that the belief in the redemptive significance of the death of Jesus arose in Christianity out of speculation about his death. But such theology does not reflect contemporary Jewish belief.[31] On the contrary, Christians believed in Jesus' Messiahship in spite of the death, not because of any previous Jewish expectations. In this sense, the death of Jesus, especially death by crucifixion, constitutes a dissimilarity with both Judaism and early Christianity, and it may be regarded as one of the best established facts in the first century.

Second, Jesus was probably crucified under Roman authority. We know that crucifixion had been used by Jewish rulers in Hasmonean times, for Alexander Jannaeus once crucified eight hundred of his subjects, according to Josephus. But Josephus does not record any crucifixions after Herod the Great became king. Hengel thinks that it ceased as a Jewish practice from

---

[29] Ibid., p. 61f.
[30] Ibid., p. 83.
[31] Although Christians interpreted the death of Jesus as a fulfillment of such passages as Isa 52:13–53:12, Jews at that time did not interpret them as messianic predictions.

that time and that the rabbinic interpretation of Deut 21:23 prevented its use by Jews.[32] There we have these words:

> And if a man has committed a crime punishable by death and he is put to death, and you hang him on a tree, his body shall not remain all night upon the tree, but you shall bury him the same day, for a hanged man is accursed by God; you shall not defile your land which the Lord your God gives you for an inheritance (Deut 21:22–23).

By contrast we know that crucifixion was used extensively by the Romans, especially for foreigners in occupied territories. Furthermore, the gospels themselves provide evidence on this point. Although the evangelists intended to place major responsibility on the Jews, they were unable to show that Jews controlled Jesus' execution. In all the gospels it is the Roman governor who gives the final verdict and orders the crucifixion. After the death of Jesus, Joseph of Arimathea requests the body from the Roman governor (Matt 27:58 and parallels), and, in Matthew, chief priests and Pharisees request Pilate to place a guard at Jesus' tomb (Matt 27:62–66). These traces show that the gospel writers were unable to avoid giving the impression that the Romans were in control at the trial and the crucifixion. The evidence we have points to the almost certain conclusion that Jesus was crucified under Roman authority.

Third, it is probable that Jesus was crucified on orders from the Roman governor Pontius Pilate. Although Pilate was not mentioned by name in the letters of Paul, he was named in a Petrine speech in Acts and in the writing of Tacitus. Besides, if the broad lines of Jesus' chronology, as implied in Christian writings, are reasonably correct, then Pontius Pilate, governor of Judea from 26–36, was the supreme representative of the Roman emperor in Judea at the time of the crucifixion and the appropriate person to give the orders. Pilate had a reputation for the tyrannical treatment of his subjects. Philo quoted a contemporary, Herod Agrippa I, as saying that he was recklessly arbitrary. He said that Pilate's greatest fear was that his conduct would be exposed, and he described his governorship as marked by "the briberies, the insults, the robberies, the outrages and wanton injuries, the executions without trial constantly repeated, the ceaseless and supremely grievous cruelty."[33] Josephus reports that, at the beginning of his rule, Pilate had his garrison soldiers enter Jerusalem by night, carrying staffs with the emperor's image. To protest the act, citizens stormed his citadel at Caesarea. Pilate kept them out for six days, and when they were finally admitted, they found themselves surrounded by soldiers with drawn swords. It was only when the people daringly bared their necks to the swords that

---

[32] Hengel, op. cit., p. 85.
[33] Philo, *The Embassy to Gaius,* 302, trans. by F. H. Colson, Loeb Classical Library (Cambridge, Mass.: Harvard U.P., 1962), Vol. X.

Pilate relented.[34] Josephus also reports that Pilate misdirected Temple funds in order to build an aqueduct and that he violently crushed all opposition to his plans.[35] In other words, Pilate was known to be a harsh, arbitrary, and insensitive ruler, who would probably deal swiftly with a person he suspected of criminal activity. The gospels, which picture Pilate as weak and vacillating, have probably altered his portrait in the interests of shifting blame away from him and toward the Jews.

Fourth, it is probable that Jesus was crucified for alleged political crimes. Crucifixion was frequently used by Romans for crimes such as rebellion or sedition, and its use implies some such accusation in the case of Jesus. The gospels seem to imply that Jesus was accused of royal pretension. This charge appears implicitly in all the gospels and explicitly in Luke and John. The gospels also imply that the reason for the charge was a confusion of Messiahship with royal power. We have seen that there are no grounds for saying that Jesus claimed to be Messiah, or that he claimed any other title for himself. So it is not likely that he was actually accused of claiming to be a king. It is more likely that the charge of royal pretension was an inference that came out of later Christian belief that Jesus was Messiah. But we have also seen that Jesus proclaimed the kingdom of God and did so authoritatively. Kingdom is a political term, and a proclamation such as that made by Jesus would, in some quarters, seem politically dangerous. Only a few decades later Jewish Zealots were proclaiming the kingdom of God, and there was no uncertainty about the political dimensions of their preaching. Roman governors frequently dealt with suspected Jewish revolutionists, and they dealt with them harshly. Jesus was probably regarded as a revolutionist because of his preaching of the kingdom of God.

Fifth, Jewish opposition may have played a role in the death of Jesus. The part that Jews may have played is difficult to determine. They may have had nothing to do with it, but in that case it is difficult to account for the early rise of the tradition about their complicity. Of course, in the period between Jesus and the gospels hostility between Jews and Christians exacerbated the situation, and charges became increasingly heated. But even in the early days, we have the picture of Jews such as Peter charging their fellow Jews with the murder of Jesus. It is difficult to avoid the conclusion that there was a Jewish involvement in Jesus' death.

We can only guess at the nature of that involvement. We know that, in some places, a Roman governor used an existing native court in his administration of justice. For example, after the Roman conquest of Egypt, native courts there were allowed to judge minor civil cases involving such things as loans and contracts. In major criminal cases, especially in cases of political crimes, the native court was charged with gathering evidence against the

---

[34] Josephus, *Antiquities* XVIII, 55–59; *War* II, 169–174.
[35] *Antiquities* XVIII, 60–62; *War* II, 175–177.

accused and preparing a case for the governor's judgment. In the presentation of the case, the native court, or its presiding officer, acted in the capacity of a prosecuting attorney.[36] If the judicial structure in Judea was analogous to that in Egypt, it is likely that the Jewish Sanhedrin, a native court in Judea, played a similar role. It was probably used by Roman governors to aid them in keeping order and even in investigating cases. Under those circumstances, it is not unreasonable to conclude that the Sanhedrin had some part to play in Jesus' trial, perhaps in preparing the case for Pilate. Luke has probably come closer to describing that role correctly than has Matthew, Mark, John, or Peter.

In any event, we must be careful to see things in the proper perspective. Roman responsibility for Jesus' death is clear and unquestionable. He was convicted of violating Roman law, probably because he was suspected of political agitation against the government, and he was crucified on orders from Pontius Pilate. The role of the Jewish Sanhedrin in the proceedings is at best secondary.

THE RESURRECTION OF JESUS

The place of the resurrection faith in early Christianity is beyond question: it is at the heart of the movement in its earliest days. Belief in it is reflected in the earliest identifiable forms of the kerygma and in nearly every Christian document of the first two centuries. It is not certain, however, what was contained in the earliest traditions about the resurrection. All four of the canonical gospels end with narratives about Jesus' resurrection, but do the narratives actually point back to early traditions, and if so, can we define their contents? Our investigation necessarily begins with a careful reading of the material in all four canonical gospels and in the apocryphal Gospel of Peter.

The story in the Gospel of Mark (16:1–8) is the briefest one we have. It tells of the visit of Mary Magdalene, Mary the mother of James, and Salome to the tomb of Jesus on the Sunday after the crucifixion. They find it unsealed. Inside there is a young man in a white robe, who proclaims that Jesus has risen and will meet the disciples in Galilee, as he has previously said he would (cf. 14:28). At the point that is usually considered to be the earliest preserved ending of the gospel (16:8), the women flee from the tomb in terror and say nothing to anyone.

In Matthew's account (28:1–20), Mary Magdalene and one other woman, called the other Mary, go to the tomb. They find it unsealed as a result of

---

[36] Evidence is found in the Oxyrynchus papyri. Cf A. S. Hunt and C. C. Edgar, eds., *Select Papyri,* Loeb Classical Library (Cambridge, Mass.: Harvard U.P., 1934), Vol. II, pp. 172–225.

Gero's crucifix, c. 970 CE, in the cathedral at Cologne. (Courtesy P. Dr. W. Schulten, Cologne.)

an earthquake, and they meet an angel sitting outside the tomb. The angel proclaims Jesus' resurrection, invites the women to see the empty tomb, and announces a coming appearance of Jesus in Galilee. So far, the main lines of the story are similar to Mark's account. But from here on, Matthew's material differs from that in both of the other Synoptic Gospels. As the women leave the tomb, Jesus himself appears and repeats the angel's message about going to Galilee. Matthew then includes a paragraph explaining the unbelief of the Jews. He claims that the Jewish priests bribed the tomb guards to say that Jesus' disciples had stolen the body. In Matthew's final scene, Jesus appears to the disciples on a mountain in Galilee and commissions them to baptize and teach.

Luke's resurrection stories are found in 24:1–53, to which must be added Acts 1:1–11. His account of the empty tomb is similar to that in Mark and Matthew, but there are differences in detail. Mary Magdalene, Joanna, Mary the mother of James, and other women go to the tomb to find it open and empty except for two men, who announce Jesus' resurrection. The women hasten to return to the city and to report the news to the disciples. Then follows a narrative about Cleopas and another disciple who are traveling from Jerusalem to Emmaus. Along the way, the resurrected Jesus joins them, but they do not recognize him until he sits down to eat with them. The two return immediately to Jerusalem and meet the other disciples, who proclaim that Jesus has appeared to Simon. Jesus himself then appears to all of them and demonstrates his physical reality by inviting them to touch him and by eating a piece of fish. He gives the disciples a missionary command and orders them to remain in Jerusalem until they have received power from the spirit. He then departs from them at Bethany.

The first several verses in Acts overlap with the ending of the Gospel of Luke. Here we find that there is a period of forty days between the resurrection and the ascension. During this time Jesus preaches about the kingdom of God and repeats his command that the disciples should remain in Jerusalem until they have received power. Then he is lifted up and taken away in a cloud, after he gives the disciples a final missionary command. After the ascension, two men in white robes (cf. Luke 24:4) promise that Jesus will return in the same manner in which he left. In Acts the ascension apparently was from the Mount of Olives (cf. Acts 1:12).

As we have previously seen, the Gospel of John has two narratives of the resurrection (20:1–30 and 21:1–25), apparently composed by different authors. We will treat each separately. In John 20 Mary Magdalene alone discovers the unsealed tomb. Instead of entering, however, she reports the discovery to Simon Peter and the beloved disciple. After a race to the tomb, won by the beloved disciple, Peter enters first and finds only the grave clothes. After their departure Mary Magdalene looks inside the tomb and sees two angels; subsequently Jesus himself appears to her. Later the same day he appears to all the disciples except Thomas, and a week later, to the whole group, including Thomas. Thomas' faith arises only when he is invited to touch the wounded body of Jesus.

In John 21 we have another appearance of Jesus, this time in Galilee. Seven disciples are present: Simon Peter, Thomas, Nathaniel, the sons of Zebedee, and two others. Jesus appears to them as they are fishing on the Sea of Tiberias and directs them to a large catch.[37] When they come ashore, he and they eat breakfast together, and Jesus gives a missionary charge to Simon Peter. The chapter closes with an attempt to identify the author of the Gospel of John.

Only in the Gospel of Peter do we have a description of the actual resurrection, and even here the scene is set outside the tomb. Two men come down from heaven, enter the tomb, and escort Jesus outside. Then another man descends from heaven, enters and remains in the tomb. This man proclaims Jesus' resurrection to Mary Magdalene and the other women, who come on Sunday. He says that the risen Jesus has "gone thither whence he was sent,"[38] and the gospel reports the frightened flight of the women.

There are essentially four kinds of stories in the various documents. The discovery of the empty tomb, in all documents; stories of postresurrection appearances, in Matthew, Luke, and John; the ascension of Jesus, in Luke-Acts; and the story of the process of resurrection, in Peter. The story of the ascension may represent a special Lukan motif, and the story of the process of resurrection appears to be a product of late pious reflection. It may, therefore, be fruitful to bracket these narratives and concentrate on the various versions of the discovery of the empty tomb and of the postresurrection appearances of Jesus.

The story of the discovery of the empty tomb appears in all of our documents. Moreover, there is a higher degree of similarity in the various accounts of this story than in the stories of the appearances of Jesus. Undoubtedly, the use of one gospel by another has affected this similarity. If Matthew and Luke independently used Mark, they used and edited his story of the empty tomb. If the Griesbach theory is correct, Luke used Matthew's version, and Mark produced his account with both of the other stories before him. Whichever view is correct, we must note both the similarities and the differences in these accounts as well as those in the stories in John and Peter. Among the similarities, we should observe that the time of the discovery is set very early on the first day of the week—Sunday. The setting, of course, is at Jesus' tomb, as required by the terms of the story. Perhaps of greatest importance is the fact that Mary Magdalene is expressly mentioned in all the stories. She is mentioned either alone or with unnamed women, or she is named first in a group of named women. Thus, a constant in all the versions of this story is that the discovery of the empty tomb was

---

[37] John 21:1–8 may be a variant of the narrative found in Luke 5:1–11.
[38] Gospel of Peter, verse 56.

by Mary Magdalene. And if other persons were present, they were all women. Furthermore, in all versions of the story there is a mysterious messenger present, either in or just outside the tomb. The messenger speaks to Mary Magdalene and the other women, if present. Finally, in most versions, the messenger gives some information about the present whereabouts of the risen Jesus. Sometimes there is an accompanying prediction that Jesus will meet the women or the disciples at a certain location. Thus, the empty tomb accounts are in basic formal agreement on the time and setting, the characters involved, the presence of a mysterious messenger, and a message about the present whereabouts of Jesus.

Despite the formal similarities, there are several differences in the details of the stories. The number and names of the women who accompanied Mary Magdalene to the tomb are not the same. The person of the mysterious messenger varies: in Mark a young man sits inside the tomb, in Matthew an angel sits outside, in Luke two young men are inside, in John 20 there are two angels, and in Peter it is the man who had descended from heaven. The differences in the story in John 20 are compounded by the presence there of Peter and the beloved disciple, who saw the grave clothes inside the tomb. After they left, Mary Magdalene looked inside the tomb, where she saw and heard the angels. Then the risen Christ appeared to her and gave her the message about his whereabouts: "I am ascending to my Father and your Father, to my God and your God" (John 20:17). The contents of the message vary in the other gospels as well. In Matthew and Mark, Galilee is the place designated for the disciples to meet the risen Jesus. In Luke the mysterious messengers actually say nothing about the whereabouts of Jesus, but he himself, in later appearances, orders the disciples to remain in Jerusalem (Luke 24:49 and Acts 1:4). John and Peter are vague on the whereabouts of Jesus. Finally, we can observe differences in the reaction of the women who go to the tomb. In Mark and Peter they flee, in Mark without saying anything to anyone. In the other gospels they report to the disciples.

In the accounts of the postresurrection appearances of Jesus, there are fewer formal similarities. In general it is thought that the stories in the Synoptic Gospels are independent of one another. Under the two-document hypothesis, Matthew and Luke drew on their own sources, because Mark had no accounts of postresurrection appearances. Under the Griesbach theory, Luke substituted his special material for Matthew's, and Mark used neither because they were so very different.[39] However, among the documents with such stories—Matthew, Luke, and John—there are similarities, if not literary relationships. In general, the postresurrection appearance of

---

[39] Mark 16:9–20 (if an original part of Mark) may be regarded as a conflation of postresurrection appearance narratives from Matthew and Luke. Cf. William R. Farmer, *The Last Twelve Verses of Mark* (Cambridge: Cambridge U.P., 1974).

Jesus is described as having both visual and auditory elements. The physical aspects of these narratives are notable. In Matt 28:9 the women take hold of Jesus' feet; in Luke 24:30 Jesus eats with two disciples at Emmaus; in Luke 24:39 Jesus calls attention to his hands and feet and says, "A spirit has not flesh and bones as you see that I have"; in Luke 24:42–43 Jesus eats a piece of broiled fish in the sight of the disciples; in John 20:26–29 Jesus invites Thomas to touch his hands and side; and in John 21:9–14 Jesus and the disciples dine together on bread and fish. In these stories it is as if Jesus has come back to life in the very same body that had died. The appearance stories are also similar in that they all contain missionary orders given by the risen Jesus. We will return to this point subsequently.

But the appearance narratives differ in respect to locations, duration, and persons present. In the matter of location, Luke and John 20 set all the appearances in Jerusalem, whereas Matthew and John 21 have them in Galilee.[40] A particular problem revolves around the nature of the appearances, especially in Luke, John 20, and John 21. In all three Jesus appears and disappears suddenly, as if out of nowhere, despite the physical nature of the resurrection body. A still more serious question is that about the witnesses to the appearances. In Matthew Jesus appears briefly to the two women at the tomb, then to the disciples in Galilee. In Luke the two disciples going to Emmaus are accompanied by Jesus, but they do not recognize him until he departs. When they report to the other disciples, they are told that Jesus has already appeared to Simon, and then he appears to all of them. In John 20 there are appearances to Mary Magdalene, to all the disciples except Thomas, and then to all of them with Thomas. In John 21 the appearance is to seven of the disciples. On the matter of duration, Matthew gives no indication of time, but enough time has to elapse for the disciples to travel from Jerusalem to Galilee. Luke's major appearances occur on one day, except perhaps the one at Bethany (Luke 24:50–53). If that narrative is a duplicate of the ascension story in Acts 1:6–11, Luke must place it some forty days after Easter (see Acts 1:3). John 20 has the appearances extend over a period of one week.

Many of the variations in these narratives are the result of the influence of motifs at work in the gospels. The location of the appearances is largely the result of individual motifs. Luke's use of Jerusalem in the history of salvation probably accounts for his setting the appearances in and around that city. John's motive is not so clear, but he has tended to emphasize Jesus' connection with Jerusalem throughout his gospel. Mark's preference for Galilee over Jerusalem was noted in Chapter 6. For him Galilee is the place for the anticipated appearance of the resurrected Jesus. The duration and sequence of the appearances are also the work of the evangelists. Luke,

---

[40] In 28:9–10 Matthew locates an appearance of Jesus to the women at the tomb, but in it Jesus points to Galilee.

for example, extends the duration of the appearances to forty days, and he thinks of this period as a time in which Jesus explains, by use of scriptural interpretation, the necessity of his suffering and death. During this time, the disciples are being prepared for their work, which is to be described in Acts. The work of the evangelists is probably also to be found in the sequence of appearances, especially in the statements about the first appearance. In Matthew the first appearance was to two women at the tomb. Luke's first description is to two disciples at Emmaus, but he reports that the first appearance was to Simon, presumably Peter. In John 20 Mary Magdalene is the first to see the risen Jesus. In this version the author has taken away Mary's priority in entering the tomb—that belonged to Peter—but has given her priority in the appearance tradition.

If we concentrate on the common elements in the various accounts, we may be in touch with pregospel traditions. We may presume that, in the pregospel period, various stories of the discovery of the empty tomb and of the postresurrection appearances of Jesus circulated, but without notations of location, sequence, or duration, and probably with little detail. Undoubtedly, the empty-tomb narratives were associated with women, primarily Mary Magdalene, and the appearance narratives were associated mainly with the male disciples.

Is it possible to speculate about the nature of resurrection faith in the earliest days of Christian history? We know that belief in Jesus' resurrection was an element in the Jerusalem kerygma. It is referred to in Peter's speeches in Acts 2:24, 3:15, and 4:10, but in each case all we have is the simple statement that God raised Jesus from the dead. In Acts 3:15, however, Peter calls himself and the other disciples witnesses to the resurrection, possibly implying an appearance. In the fullest Petrine statement, in Acts 10:40–42, there is a clear reference to a postresurrection appearance, but there are also traces of Lukan redaction and a back reference to a story in Luke 24:36–43.

The Pauline kerygma is far fuller, and it will require more detailed investigation. Of course we know that Paul believed in Jesus' resurrection, but in 1 Cor 15:3–8, he gives some of the bases for his belief. In this chapter of his letter, Paul is laying the groundwork for belief in the resurrection of Christians, and he goes on to explain the nature of this expected resurrection. It is, he says, to be in a spiritual body—that is, a nature that is corporal but different from the physical body. Before Paul gets into this explanation, to which we will return in Chapter 10, he reminds his readers about what he calls the terms of the gospel he has preached. It is these terms that give him confidence in life after death, and he is careful to say that the terms were communicated to him by early believers. In other words, in these verses Paul claims that he is duplicating early Christian tradition. If he is right, the terms would represent Christian beliefs at least in the 40s and possibly earlier. The passage goes as follows:

For I delivered to you as of first importance what I also received, that Christ died for our sins in accordance with the scriptures, that he was buried, that he was raised on the third day in accordance with the scriptures, and that he appeared to Cephas, then to the twelve. Then he appeared to more than five hundred brethren at one time, most of whom are still alive, though some have fallen asleep. Then he appeared to James, then to all the apostles. Last of all, as to one untimely born, he appeared also to me (1 Cor 15:3–8).

We note immediately that the setting in time seems to conform with that in our other sources—"on the third day" corresponds to the Sunday after the crucifixion. In our other sources, however, this is a reference to the time at which the tomb was discovered to be empty. Paul, however, makes no explicit reference to an empty tomb. His is a catalogue of postresurrection appearances, the first to Cephas—that is, Simon Peter. Here we have a tradition that agrees with Luke 24:34. The sequence of appearances in Paul's catalogue seems deliberate, as does the reference to his own experience as the last of all. It is remarkable, however, that the list includes appearances that are not described or alluded to elsewhere (to the five hundred, to James, and to all the apostles). It is no less remarkable that Paul makes no reference to an appearance to Mary Magdalene or other women and no reference to the discovery of an empty tomb. If Paul knew of any such traditions, he did not mention them.

In view of the material in the Pauline kerygma, it is necessary to say that evidence for early traditions about postresurrection appearances of Jesus is stronger than for empty tomb traditions. The Jerusalem form of the kerygma, as represented in the speeches of Peter, also shows no awareness of the discovery of the empty tomb. Traditions about the empty tomb surely antedate the gospels, but evidence is lacking to show conclusively that they are among the earliest Christian traditions.

Historical study of the resurrection narratives just about reaches its limit at this point. It is not possible to proceed with a historical proof or disproof about Jesus' resurrection from the dead. It simply cannot be treated as an object of historical investigation. The resurrection of the dead to everlasting life is not, after all, a matter of history. Although belief in it is a historical phenomenon, such belief always points beyond history. The resurrection of Jesus can no more be proven by historical method than can the existence of God. Moreover, the material on which we must depend presents the resurrection of Jesus only as an inference. Except for the scanty narrative in the Gospel of Peter, nowhere can we find an attempt to describe the resurrection as an event. No character in any narrative is able to offer eyewitness testimony about it, to convey the process by which Jesus came back to life, and thus to verify the historical factuality of the resurrection. It is always and only an inference based on the experience of an appearance of Jesus or the discovery of an empty tomb or the hearing of a message of angels. Although such an inference may have seemed entirely justified in the experience of a first-century Christian, it is not the same for the modern historian.

Although it is not possible to verify or deny Jesus' resurrection, it is possible to search for the meaning of the resurrection faith. We need to understand what Christians meant when they told stories of Jesus' post-resurrection appearances and stories of the discovery of his empty tomb.

Stories of the empty tomb seem designed to verify the factuality of the resurrection. It is possible to raise questions about the psychological states of persons who claimed to have seen Jesus alive after his death. But the emptiness of the tomb is purported to be a fact, not an experience. Either it was empty, or it was not. It should have been possible to verify that, and if it turned out to have been empty, that would have been a fact calling for some explanation. Christians must have been aware that alternative explanations were possible. Matthew refers to one in 28:11–15.

But the stories seem to be designed to do more than this. The emptiness of the tomb is basically a mystery. A sense of mystery frequently surrounds death and burial places, and in our stories that sense is heightened by the presence of the mysterious messenger(s). The empty tomb stories also include a promise: that Jesus will appear. Mystery and expectation were probably uppermost in the minds of those who circulated the stories.

The meaning of the appearance narratives, in their earliest recoverable forms, seems to be threefold: they constitute divine revelation, they embody a missionary command, and they call attention to the communion of the believer with Jesus.

The meaning of the postresurrection appearances of Jesus as revelations can be seen in the verbs used in the various versions of the early traditions. The choice of verbs in the gospels seems in this case not to be purely an option of the evangelists. There is a consistency among the gospels as well as agreement with the Pauline kerygma. The most frequently used verb in the gospel narratives is a form of the Greek *horan*. This is only one of several verbs that express visual perception. But *horan* can also refer to an intellectual exercise or to a spiritual perception. It is similar to the English *to see*, which has the same kind of ambivalence. If I say that I saw my friend this morning, it is clear that I am referring to a visual experience. But if I say that I see what you mean, I intend to express the fact that I understand. In addition, the verb *horan* is used in the Greek translation of the OT as a technical term to express the receiving of a revelation. When we read in Isa 40:5 that people will see the glory of God, we think of a revelation from God, which may or may not contain visual perception. The variable meaning of the verb should guard us against a hasty decision to understand the resurrection narratives as limited to visual experiences. They seem to signify something closer to spiritual perception or the receiving of a relevation.

The same verb appears in the Pauline version in 1 Cor 15:3–8. Here it is used in the passive, and may be translated: "Jesus was seen," "Jesus allowed himself to be seen," "Jesus appeared," "Jesus showed himself," or "Jesus was revealed."[41] To the traditional catalogue of appearances, Paul adds the one to himself, and he is careful to use the same verb to designate both his own experience and those of Cephas, James, and the others. He believes that whatever happened to them also happened to him. Thus, he points to his experience, which he also refers to in Gal 1:11–17. In the Galatians passage he reminds his readers that he once had been a persecutor of the church but that he became a missionary to the Gentiles when God *revealed* his Son to him. The passages are parallel in substance, although the wording and context differ. The most notable point is the change of verbs, from *horan* in 1 Cor 15:8 to *apokalyptein* ("to reveal") in Gal 1:16. The fact that Paul could use either verb to designate his experience is of the highest significance. It means that he thought of his experience as a revelation from God himself. Because the verb *horan* had frequently been associated with revelation, it is fair to suppose that Paul intended to emphasize the idea of revelation in 1 Corinthians as well as in Galatians. Thus, in 1 Corinthians, Paul is saying: Jesus was revealed to Cephas, to the twelve, to the five hundred, to James, to the apostles, and last of all to me.

The major importance of this study of verbs is to show that the post-resurrection appearances of Jesus were understood to be revelations of God, not simply visual experiences. But their meaning is probably still more specific. In Jewish apocalyptic thought, one of the chief functions of Messiah is to raise the dead. To be sure, the miracle stories in which Jesus resuscitated dead people may have been told in order to show his messianic power. But his own resurrection would be a demonstration, par excellence, of Jesus' Messiahship. Paul clearly recognized that Jesus' resurrection was a confirmation of the resurrection to come. He maintained that Jesus Christ was "the first fruits of those who have fallen asleep" (1 Cor 15:20). The post-resurrection appearances, therefore, are revelations, specifically revelations of Jesus as Messiah.

Another aspect of the meaning of the postresurrection appearances of Jesus is that those who received them also received certain commands. Paul says in Gal 1:15–16 that, as a result of his experience, he became a missionary to the Gentiles. In 1 Cor 9:1 he connects his mission to the Corinthians with his having seen the Lord. The association of an appearance with a missionary function is not unique to Paul, for it appears in other versions of the tradition. In Matthew, Jesus' Galilean appearance issues in a command for the disciples to baptize and teach (Matt 28:16–20). The climactic appearance in Luke is accompanied by a command to proclaim forgiveness (Luke 24:24–49). In John 20:21–23 the risen Jesus sends out the disciples and gives them power to forgive sins. In John 21:15–19 the appearance is

---

[41] Cf. Willi Marxsen, *The Resurrection of Jesus of Nazareth*, trans. by Margaret Kohl (Philadelphia: Fortress Press, 1970), p. 98.

accompanied by the command to Peter to tend Jesus' sheep. The Jerusalem kerygma in Acts 10:42–43 also couples the appearance with Jesus' command to proclaim him as judge of living and dead. In almost all references to a postresurrection appearance of Jesus, there is a missionary command, the fulfillment of which serves as the consequence of the experience. This fact points to a basic meaning in the appearance tradition. If we should ask what the appearances meant to those who experienced them, the answer would be that they felt appointed to preach. The functional meaning of the appearance is a conviction about the significance of Jesus and his message. This is true of the Pauline kerygma the Jerusalem kerygma, and the appearance narratives in the gospels.

A third meaning associated with the appearance traditions is that of the communion of the believer with Jesus. This meaning does not come out explicitly in all the versions, but it is sufficiently pervasive to be notable. Matthew states it most explicitly: in the appearance to the disciples in Galilee, Jesus promises, "I am with you always to the close of the age" (Matt 28:20). Luke 24:36–43 and John 21:9–14 have some interesting narratives in which the risen Jesus shares a meal with his disciples (see also Acts 10:41). In Luke's story of the trip to Emmaus, Jesus remains incognito until he shares a meal with the two disciples (Luke 24:13–35). On one level, these accounts serve to interpret the resurrected body of Jesus as physical. But on another level it should be observed that the act of eating is not simply a physical act, but frequently a social act. The sharing of a meal is one of the most basic forms of social intercourse, or communion. All three Synoptic Gospels demonstrate a recognition of this fact when they include narratives about Jesus' last supper with his disciples. They also record his interpretation of wine as his blood and bread as his body. We know from Paul's letters that Christians in his day observed a meal in memory of Jesus. Paul's words about the supper (1 Cor 11:23–25), which form part of the Pauline kerygma, are remarkably similar to the synoptic accounts, and for him the bread and wine stand for the body and blood of Jesus. It is likely that, from a very early date, Christians periodically held a cultic meal in which they felt themselves to be in communion with the risen Lord. Prototypes for that experience would be found not only in the last supper but also in those meals that the risen Jesus shared with his disciples. Thus, we may understand communion as a third meaning associated with the postsurrection appearance tradition.

There is, therefore, a complex of meanings associated with the stories of Jesus' resurrection. The empty tomb stories swing between the hard rock of alleged fact and an aura of mystery and expectation. The appearance stories seem intended to proclaim Jesus as the Messiah now revealed to those whom he also has appointed to preach. With them and with all believers he remains in communion.

The information we have gleaned from this study of Jesus is, indeed, minimal. Historically, the most reliable area that we have investigated is his teachings. He authoritatively proclaimed the imminence of the kingdom of God and demanded repentance. Although he approached his contemporaries with authority, he probably did not claim any particular title or status. We may also conclude that he was crucified, probably on orders from Pontius Pilate and probably for suspected violation of Roman law, namely political agitation.

Perhaps certain implications can be drawn from this meager information and our conclusions amplified. But we probably will never have enough information to write a biography of Jesus. We probably will always lack those vital pieces of data on his intention, on what he thought of himself, and on what he really meant by his words and deeds. At best we end up with a few impressions about him, impressions that are lacking in internal connection and rational consistency. This is the case because when we have reached back as far as we can, we have only begun to understand something about the effect that Jesus produced on some of his contemporaries. This should not disillusion the historically minded, for a person is never a part of history except as she or he affects other people. History knows of no such thing as a person in total isolation from other people. In the third century the Christian hermit St. Antony lived alone and made every effort to avoid contact with other people. He was only partially successful, because people were attracted to the very isolation he embraced and copied his way of life. From him began a stream of ascetic monasticism that formed a significant tradition in the western world. The irony of St. Antony is that if he had been completely successful, we would never have heard of him. To say that history knows of no one totally in isolation from other people does not mean that the historian is interested only in a person's effect on others. In many cases intentions and effects are quite different things, so the historian is interested in both and in the relation between them. But we recognize that in some cases the intention cannot be recovered. The life of Jesus is one of those cases. We do not know his intention. We know only that he impressed many of his contemporaries as the one who authoritatively proclaimed the coming of God's kingdom and, with like authority, demanded repentance.

BIBLIOGRAPHY

General Treatments of the Historical Jesus

Anderson, Hugh, ed. *Jesus*. Englewood Cliffs, N.J.: Prentice-Hall, Inc., 1967.
Barrett, C. K. *Jesus and the Gospel Tradition*. Philadelphia: Fortress Press, 1968.
Betz, Otto. *What Do We Know about Jesus?* Philadelphia: Westminster Press, 1968.

Bornkamm, Günther. *Jesus of Nazareth*. Trans. by Irene and Fraser McLuskey. New York: Harper & Row, Publishers, 1960.

Brandon, S. G. F. *Jesus and the Zealots*. New York: Charles Scribner's Sons, 1967.

Braun, Herbert. *Jesus of Nazareth: The Man and his Times*. Trans. by E. R. Kalin. Philadelphia: Fortress Press, 1979.

Bundy, Walter E. *The Psychic Health of Jesus*. New York: Macmillan Publishing Co., Inc., 1922.

Cadbury, Henry J. *The Eclipse of the Historical Jesus*. Harverford, Pa.: Pendle Hill, 1963.

———. *Jesus: What Manner of Man?* New York: Macmillan Publishing Co., Inc., 1947.

Cullmann, Oscar. *Jesus and the Revolutionaries*. Trans. by Gareth Putnam. New York: Harper & Row, Publishers, 1970.

Kee, Howard C. *Jesus in History*. 2nd ed. New York: Harcourt, Brace Jovanovich, 1977.

Klausner, Joseph. *Jesus of Nazareth*. Trans. by Herbert Danby. New York: Macmillan Publishing Co., Inc., 1925.

Meyer, Ben F. *The Aims of Jesus*. London: S.C.M. Press, 1979.

Reumann, John H. *Jesus in the Church's Gospels*. Philadelphia: Fortress Press, 1968.

Vermes, Geza. *Jesus the Jew*. London: William Collins, 1973.

Most of these books treat several aspects of the life of Jesus, although some concentrate on a single topic. Betz and Braun have produced elementary but sound texts. Hugh Anderson's book is a collection of readings that exemplify various historical and contemporary positions in regard to the study of Jesus. Cadbury's books are well-written and nontechnical attempts to say something positive about the historical Jesus. The problem of finding the historical Jesus through the faith of the Christian evangelists is dealt with by Barrett, Kee, and Reumann. Bornkamm's book represents the first serious attempt by a German scholar to work within a Bultmannian framework and yet to produce something positive about the historical Jesus. Brandon has taken the political dimensions of the gospel narratives seriously, and he takes the position that Jesus was, in fact, a Zealot. Cullmann attempts to counter this claim. The book by Klausner and the more recent study by Vermes concentrate on the Jewish aspects of Jesus' life and teachings. Bundy's book is a review of psychological studies of Jesus, a popular endeavor made in the early part of this century. For books that concentrate on methodological problems relating to the study of Jesus, see the bibliography at the end of Chapter 5.

The Birth of Jesus

Brown, Raymond E. *The Birth of the Messiah*. New York: Doubleday & Company, Inc., 1977.

Daniélou, Jean. *The Infancy Narratives*. Trans. by Rosemary Sheed. New York: Herder and Herder, 1968.

Brown's is a masterful study of the birth narratives in Matthew and Luke. It is, in effect, a thorough (570 pages) commentary on the opening chapters of these gospels. Daniélou makes an interesting attempt to find the historical basis of the birth narratives.

The Teachings of Jesus

Bultmann, Rudolf. *Jesus and the Word*. Trans. by Louise P. Smith and Ermine Huntress. New York: Charles Scribner's Sons, 1934.

Dodd, C. H. *The Parables of the Kingdom*. Rev. ed. New York: Charles Scribner's Sons, 1961.

Higgins, A. J. B. *Jesus and the Son of Man*. Philadelphia: Fortress Press, 1964.

Jeremias, Joachim. *Rediscovering the Parables*. Trans. by S. H. Hooke and Frank Clarke. New York: Charles Scribner's Sons, 1966.

Otto, Rudolf. *The Kingdom of God and the Son of Man*. Trans. by F. V. Filson and B. L. Woolf. Grand Rapids, Mich.: Zondervan, 1938.

Perrin, Norman. *Jesus and the Language of the Kingdom*. Philadelphia: Fortress Press, 1976.

————. *The Kingdom of God in the Teaching of Jesus*. Philadelphia: Westminster Press, 1963.

————. *Rediscovering the Teaching of Jesus*. New York: Harper & Row, Publishers, 1967.

Tödt, H. E. *The Son of Man in the Synoptic Tradition*. Trans. by Dorothea M. Barton. Philadelphia: Westminster Press, 1965.

Via, Dan O. *The Parables*. Philadelphia: Fortress Press, 1967.

Wilder, Amos N. *Eschatology and Ethics in the Teaching of Jesus*. Rev. ed. New York: Harper & Row, Publishers, 1950.

Jesus and the Word presents those aspects of Jesus' teaching that Bultmann thought were historically accurate. He examined teachings on the kingdom, ethics, and the nature of God. Rudolf Otto's book is a classic study of selected aspects of Jesus' teaching. He examined the kingdom and the Son of man against a Jewish background and as used by Jesus. He maintained that Jesus was convinced that he was the instrument of the kingdom's power. Perrin concentrated on the kingdom as Jesus' theme in all three of the books listed here. In *Rediscovering the Teaching of Jesus,* he made a systematic effort to apply the criteria of dissimilarity, coherence, and multiple attestation. In *Jesus and the Language of the Kingdom,* he emphasized the symbolic value of Jesus' language. Wilder's is a valuable study of two major aspects of Jesus' teaching—eschatology and ethics—and the relationship between them. The meaning of Son of man remains a serious problem in the study of the gospels and Jesus' teachings. Both Higgins and Tödt agree that the identification of Jesus with the apocalyptic Son of man was the work of early Christians and not a claim of Jesus. Dodd, Jeremias, and Via concentrate on the parable as a specific form of teaching. Dodd believed that the parables of the kingdom represented Jesus' interpretation of his own ministry. That interpretation involved a realized eschatology—that is, the conviction that the kingdom had come in Jesus' own work. Jeremias is particularly strong in relating the parables to Palestinian customs and society. Via feels that many of the parables in the Gospels show signs of literary composition rather than of oral transmission.

The Trial of Jesus

Catchpole, David R. *The Trial of Jesus*. Leiden: Brill, 1971.
Hengel, Martin. *Crucifixion in the Ancient World and the Folly of the Message of the Cross*. Trans. by John Bowden. Philadelphia: Fortress Press, 1977.
Winter, Paul. *On the Trial of Jesus*. Berlin: Walter de Gruyter, 1961.

The studies by Winter and Catchpole come to opposite conclusions; both are highly competent and somewhat technical. Winter emphasizes the political aspects of Jesus' trial, whereas Catchpole concludes that it was the religious aspects, namely Jesus' claim to divine sonship, that constituted the case against him. Hengel does not write about the trial of Jesus itself, but he gives some exceedingly valuable information about the use of crucifixion in the ancient world.

The Resurrection of Jesus

Fuller, Reginald H. *The Formation of the Resurrection Narratives*. 2nd ed. Philadelphia: Fortress Press, 1980.
Marxsen, Willi. *The Resurrection of Jesus of Nazareth*. Trans. by Margaret Kohl. Philadelphia: Fortress Press, 1970.
Perrin, Norman. *The Resurrection According to Matthew, Mark, and Luke*. Philadelphia: Fortress Press, 1977.

Fuller and Marxsen attempt a full history-of-traditions approach to the resurrection of Jesus—that is, a study that traces the history of the rise and development of the Easter traditions and their use in the gospels. Marxsen concludes that the belief in Jesus' resurrection begins when "someone discovers in a miraculous way that Jesus evokes faith even after his death" (p. 138). Perrin limited his study to the meaning of the resurrection narratives in the Synoptic Gospels.

PART FOUR

CHRISTIANITY FROM 30-70 CE

❖ 9 ❖

Early Jewish Christianity

FOR a number of reasons the historical transition from the life of Jesus to the earliest Christian communities is far from clear. We can legitimately assume that Jesus, in his lifetime, attracted both adherents and opponents, but our source material does not clearly describe the process by which his adherents became believing Christians. Nor do the earliest gospels leave us with the clear impression that Jesus intended to establish a community that would be organized and perpetuated in later times. On the contrary, the eschatological element in Jesus' teaching does not suggest long-term expectations about a surviving community. However, the gospels do maintain that Jesus attracted disciples, and some of them recorded his last words to them. As we have seen, those words include missionary directions. Especially in Matthew, Jesus' last words required his followers to proclaim the gospel and to baptize—that is, to gather believers together into some form of community. Undoubtedly, some of Jesus' own adherents, or disciples, felt themselves committed to some kind of missionary preaching, and it is largely because of their work that Jesus was remembered and belief in him was institutionalized. Modern sociological studies of earliest Christianity have shown that the movement was led by wandering charismatic preachers.[1] These followers of Jesus felt compelled to give up their homes, family, and possessions. Their separation from society and their rootlessness were, in effect, protests against social structures and criticisms of economic systems. Their charisma, of course, added to their authority, and their work resulted in the establishment of local communities of believers. Nevertheless, although communities of Jesus' believers were established, there is great uncertainty about their historical details. The uncertainty extends to their dates of origin and the locations of the first communities, the sequence

---

[1] Cf., e.g., Gerd Theissen, *Sociology of Early Palestinian Christianity,* trans. by John Bowden (Philadelphia: Fortress Press, 1978).

The Breaking of Bread, third-century fresco from the Catacomb of Priscilla, Rome. (Courtesy *Pontifical Commission for Sacred Archives, Rome.*)

of events, the people involved, the belief systems, and the organization.

One thing that is clear is that the history of early Christianity was marked not only by vital growth, but also by lively diversity. Throughout the first two centuries, Christians are to be found in different groups, with diverse viewpoints and practices. In this chapter and in Chapter 10, we will be looking at two varieties of Christianity, both found in the period from 30–70—namely, early Jewish Christianity and Pauline Christianity. These two forms are not totally different from one another, but they are distinct, and so it is necessary to be aware of their agreements and their disagreements. They largely overlapped in time, although Pauline Christianity did not come on the scene until after 40.

The year 70 marks a time of dramatic change in Judaism and in early Christianity. After 70 we are able to see an increasing proliferation of Christian groups. The earlier forms continued, but not unchanged, and newer ones began to make their appearance. In Chapter 11 we will investigate the varieties of Christianity in the period after 70.

The purpose in this chapter is to investigate one of the varieties of Christianity in the period from the time of Jesus to the destruction of the Jewish Temple. We call it early Jewish Christianity, to distinguish it from a form of Christianity to be found in the second century, late Jewish Christianity, which has certain affinities with the earlier but is also sufficiently different to require separate treatment. The word *Jewish* in this phrase indicates the religious and social orientation of the believers—that is, early Jewish Christians were, essentially, Jews who, in the period leading up to 70, associated themselves with adherents of Jesus. This should be taken only as a minimal working definition, on the basis of which we may begin to investigate the chief characteristics of those people. Before we can do that, however, we must analyze our sources of information about this form of Christianity.

The problem of sources for early Jewish Christianity is notorious. The only known Christian documents from the period 30–70 were written by Paul. In Chapter 10 we will examine the date and sequence of Paul's letters in greater detail. Here we need only anticipate the fact that they were written between c. 40 and c. 60. Paul, of course, was identified with a variety of Christianity other than the one we are examining here, and he was largely involved in issues relating to his own newly founded churches. Nevertheless, we cannot afford to ignore the potential value of the letters. Paul writes with some knowledge about early Jewish Christianity and, from time to time, refers to items of belief and practice that had been associated with the movement before he came into it. For example, in 1 Cor 15, he includes a traditional list of witnesses to Jesus' resurrection and, in 1 Cor 11, he refers to material about Jesus' last supper with the disciples. Paul claims that these are items of information he received from those who had been Christians before he became one. In Gal 1–2 he describes some of the contacts he had with Peter and other early leaders. Because Paul was in a position to know something about early Jewish Christianity and was frequently careful to distinguish between his own views and those of others, his letters are valuable sources for understanding this variety of Christianity.

We have already seen that the early Christian kerygma was useful as a guide in sorting out authentic material about Jesus. It will be of similar value in studying early Jewish Christianity. The kerygma, especially in its so-called Jerusalem form, may serve as a basic indicator of early Jewish Christian preaching.[2]

Although, so far as we know, no Christian documents other than the letters of Paul were written between 30 and 70, the book of Acts, especially chapters 1–12, contains narratives about early Jewish Christianity. In order to evaluate it as a potential source, it will be necessary here to examine this book with some care.

THE ACTS OF THE APOSTLES

We have already examined the evidence about the authorship and date of the Acts of the Apostles and have concluded that it was written in about

[2] Cf. C. H. Dodd, *The Apostolic Preaching and its Developments* (London: Holder and Stoughton, 1936).

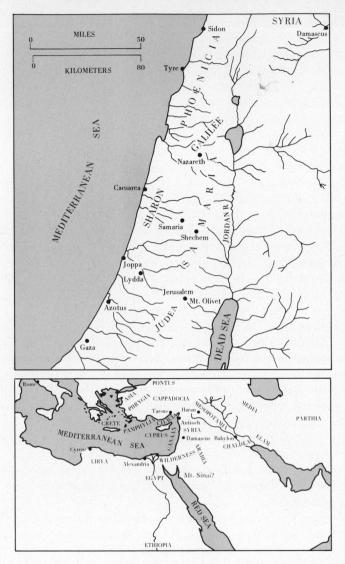

Figure 20   The Book of Acts (Reprinted by permission of Thomas Nelson publishers, from the book The Interpreter's Bible. *Copyright © 1949 by Thomas Nelson & Sons Publishers.)*

80–85 by the same author who wrote the Gospel of Luke. As far as we know, this joining of a gospel with a sequel is unique in Christian literature, and it raises questions about Luke's intentions.

At first glance the book of Acts appears to be a straightforward history of the Christian movement from the time of Jesus to the time of Paul's arrival in Rome. It is, however, a history that is dominated by a certain religious conception. In the analysis of Luke in Chapter 6, we saw that, according to Conzelmann, Luke thought of the history of the world as the history of salvation and that he divided that history into three periods: the period of Israel, the period of Jesus, and the period of the church.[3] The book of Acts, thus, is Luke's description of the third period in the history of salvation, the period of the church.

Charles H. Talbert has attempted to be somewhat more precise about the genre of Acts.[4] He refers to it as a succession narrative. As the gospel was intended to give what Luke regarded as the authentic stories and teachings of Jesus, so Acts was intended to tell the reader the story of Jesus' authorized successors. Talbert understands that the increasing diversity within the Christian movement posed serious problems for Luke and for the community for which he wrote. If there are several groups of Christians, one varying from the other and all making rival claims, it becomes important to identify those teachers who were authorized by Jesus himself to carry on his message. The book of Acts does this by giving the list of authentic successors in 1:13, by narrating the dramatic fashion by which they were empowered to teach (2:1–13), and by tracing their subsequent journeys. A successor to Judas had to be selected under divine direction (1:23–26), and when a new successor, Saul/Paul, came on the scene, he too had to be shown to have been selected by divine appointment (9:1–9). Talbert compares Acts to *The Lives of Eminent Philosophers,* written by Diogenes Laertius in the third century CE. In his preface Diogenes listed several schools of philosophy and then listed the philosophers who belonged to each. Together with the lives of the 82 philosophers, he sometimes listed the most important pupils of a given philosopher and the names of the persons who succeeded them. Both Diogenes and Luke were concerned to identify authentic successors. But they did so in rather different ways, for Diogenes did not write anything resembling the stories in Acts about the successors.

The book of Acts has sometimes been called an apology—that is, a defense of Christianity directed to Roman authorities. Under this interpretation, Theophilus, to whom both Luke and Acts are addressed (Luke 1:3 and Acts 1:1), is understood to be a Roman official who is investigating the movement. Acts is notable for its high regard for Roman justice. At every opportunity the author calls attention to the favorable attitude of Romans toward Christian leaders and frequently contrasts it with the treatment those leaders received from the Jews. For example, Paul, who is designated as a Roman citizen, is mobbed by Jews in Jerusalem and rescued by the

---

[3] Cf. Hans Conzelmann, *The Theology of St. Luke,* trans. by Geoffrey Buswell (New York: Harper, 1960).

[4] *Literary Patterns, Theological Themes and the Genre of Luke-Acts* (Missoula, Mont.: Scholars Press, 1974).

Roman tribune (21:30–36). Later, some Jews plot to ambush Paul, but the Romans spirit him away for his own protection (22:12–35). The Jewish high priest and his spokesman appear before the Roman governor Felix to accuse Paul, but the governor adjourns the court (24:1–27). The same Felix would have freed Paul except for his desire not to offend the Jews (24:27). This is just the kind of defense, or apology, one might give to a Roman official. The purpose is not to curry favor but to show that Rome has nothing to fear from Christians and that Christians have hitherto been regarded as innocent by Roman officials.

It is, therefore, difficult to fit Acts strictly within a single literary genre, for it is partly a religious history, partly a succession narrative, and partly an apology. To emphasize one aspect of the writing and de-emphasize others may cause a reader to overlook something important. Luke probably had an apologetic intention, as well as an intention to write a succession narrative. But what seems most important is his emphasis on history and his conviction that God is working out a plan of salvation within the arena of human events. For Luke, the book of Acts must have been intended as the final chapter in the history of salvation.

Because Luke probably used written sources for his gospel, we would expect him to do the same for Acts. But no such material has survived. It is likely that he put together the traditions of various localities, especially of Jerusalem and Antioch, and added to them a number of speeches of his own composition. The "we" sections may rest on personal recollection, perhaps his own.[5] Some of these sections deal with sea voyages, and the information in the last two chapters of Acts betrays such extensive technical knowledge about and interest in sailing that we may say that the author of these chapters was a seaman.

As a history of the period the church, Acts begins where the Gospel of Luke leaves off. The time of Jesus is concluded with the ascension, and the last period is initiated by the descent of the spirit at Pentecost. Luke offers a vivid description of the latter event, in which the disciples' ability to speak in foreign languages is pictured as the outward manifestation of the spirit (2:1–13). Just before the ascension Jesus gives certain orders to the disciples, and the words suggest the outline for the remainder of the book. He tells them to remain in Jerusalem until they receive the spirit and then to become his witnesses, first in Jerusalem, then in Judea and Samaria, and finally to the end of the earth (Acts 1:8). The words suggest a gradual spreading of the Christian message from its origin in Jerusalem. The rest of the book of Acts generally follows this geographical scheme. We can get a

---

[5] Cf. Chapter 6 in this textbook. The "we" sections are those in which the narration takes place in the first person. They consist of the following sections of Acts: 16:10–17, 20:5–15, 21:1–18, and 27:1–28:16.

grasp of the contents of the book by using the following largely geographical outline.

Christians in Jerusalem, Acts 1:3–8:3

After the prologue in 1:1–2 we have Jesus' last words and the narratives of his ascension, the selection of a replacement for Judas, and the coming of the spirit at Pentecost. Then the apostles begin their witnessing in Jerusalem. Most of the attention in these chapters is focused on Peter, who seems to be the leader of the community. He speaks for the group on several occasions and exercises the power of healing. The congregation of Christians meets in a portion of the Jewish Temple and observes Jewish customs, but it is opposed by the priests. The community also shares its resources, and internal friction develops between a group of Hellenistic Christians and one of Hebrew Christians.[6] Stephen, who, with six others, is appointed to solve the problems between the groups, is executed by the Jews, and a period of persecution follows, which causes Christians to be scattered throughout Judea and Samaria.

Christians in Judea and Samaria, Acts 8:4–12:25

Although some of the action in this section takes place in Damascus (9:1–25) and Antioch (11:19–30)—that is, in Syria—most of the narratives are set in Judea and Samaria. Philip, apparently an associate of Stephen, works in Samaria, where he converts Simon, a magician; in Gaza he converts an Ethiopian government official. The conversion of Paul occurs on the road to Damascus. Peter goes out into Judea and Samaria, where he converts the first Gentile, Cornelius.[7] Before he meets Cornelius, however, Peter receives a vision that convinces him that there is no distinction between permitted and nonpermitted foods. A voice from heaven effectively proclaims the end of dietary regulations, and Peter is told that he may eat and talk with a Gentile, which he does. Even so, Peter has to defend this drastic change before the other apostles, who finally agree that "to the Gentiles also God has granted repentance unto life" (11:18). Other Gentiles are brought into

---

[6] The identity of the two groups is not clear. But because Luke has not yet told of the entry of any Gentiles into the Christian movement, he must think of them as two groups of Jewish Christians. Most scholars think that Hebrews here means Jewish Christians who spoke Hebrew or Aramaic and that Hellenistic Christians means Jewish Christians who spoke Greek. However, some feel that the terms represent theological distinctions—that is, that Hebrews adhered more closely to Torah than Hellenists did. Cf., e.g., Marcel Simon, St. Stephen and the Hellenists in the Primitive Church (London: Longmans, Green and Co., 1958, and Walter Schmithals, Paul and James, trans. by Dorothea M. Barton (London: SCM Press, 1965).

[7] Apparently the Ethiopian official whom Philip converted in 8:26–40 was considered by Luke to be a Jew.

the community at Antioch. The section closes with a note about the death of James, who was one of the apostles, the story of the imprisonment and miraculous escape of Peter from a prison in Jerusalem, and the story of the death of Herod Agrippa I, who had killed James and persecuted Peter.

Christians in Gentile Lands, Acts 13:1–21:6

The interest now shifts to Paul and his missionary journeys in gentile territories. He goes out first with Barnabas on a tour of Asia Minor (13:1–14:28). They speak first in Jewish synagogues, but after opposition from Jews, they decide to go to the Gentiles. Both success and violence meet them in every town. When they return to Antioch, they find that a group of Judean Christians is insisting that gentile converts be circumcised. The Antiochean church decides to raise a question with the apostles about the necessity of circumcision, and Paul and Barnabas are sent to a council in Jerusalem (15:1–29). At the session it is decided that Gentile Christians must avoid sexual immorality and obey three of the dietary regulations: they must avoid meat offered to idols, blood, and strangled things (15:20 and 29).[8] Circumcision is not included among the requirements. The way has been prepared for the admission of uncircumcised Gentiles into the Christian community. After the council meeting Paul launches out still farther to Macedonia (Philippi and Thessalonica), Greece (Athens and Corinth), and Asia (Ephesus). At one point Luke notes that "all the residents of Asia heard the word of the Lord, both Jews and Greeks" (19:10). At the end of the section, Paul has made a farewell speech to the Ephesian elders and is heading for Jerusalem.

The Trials of Paul, Acts 21:7–26:32

We are back now in Judea and Samaria. After Paul returns to Jerusalem, he meets with James, the brother of Jesus, and then goes through a purification ritual in the Temple. Some Asian Jews spread the story that Paul took a Gentile into the Temple and Paul is almost killed by a mob; he is arrested and protected by the Roman tribune. He then undergoes a series of four trials. The first is before the Sanhedrin in Jerusalem, where he is supported by Pharisees, but attacked by others. The Roman tribune finally has Paul spirited away to Caesarea, where his second trial is conducted before the Roman governor Felix. The third trial is before Felix' successor, Festus, during which Paul appeals to the Roman emperor. The fourth trial is before Herod Agrippa II. All of the trials end inconclusively, but after the fourth,

---

[8] The direction to abstain from blood has sometimes been interpreted as a prohibition against murder. However, the context makes it far more likely that it is one of the dietary regulations. Consumption of blood was prohibited in Lev 3:17 and Deut 12:16 and 23:25.

Agrippa says to Festus, "This man could have been set free if he had not appealed to Caesar" (26:32). So preparations are made to send Paul for his final trial before the emperor in Rome. There is a strong suggestion of divine necessity in this section, and the description is reminiscent of Luke's portrayal of Jesus' trials.

Paul's Voyage to Rome, Acts 27:1–28:31

In the last two chapters of Acts we have a detailed description of the voyage to Rome, including an exciting story of a shipwreck. When Paul finally arrives in Rome, he is assigned to a private lodging with military escort; he preaches in Rome for two full years "quite openly and unhindered" (28:31).

Geography appears to be a significant aspect in Luke's composition of Acts. He is interested in the progressive spread of Christianity from Jerusalem to Judea, Samaria, Syria, Asia Minor, Macedonia, Greece, and finally to Rome. Jerusalem and Rome form two foci for his attention in Acts. But Jerusalem is the pivot for Luke-Acts as a whole, for Jesus brought the gospel to it, the apostles received the spirit there, and from there the gospel spread to the rest of the world. Rome is the goal, for that is where the gospel is headed, and there the book ends. When Paul has reached Rome, Christianity has spread to "the end of the earth" (1:8). Geography also seems to suggest ideology, for Luke is not simply interested in the spread of the gospel but in its progressive independence from Judaism. Paul is important to him not simply as a missionary but as the one who established a movement that became independent of Judaism. Although he is the hero of Acts from chapter 13 to the end, and although his arrival in Rome is the culmination of the book, Paul is not the first to bring Christianity to the capital. Italian Christians meet Paul's boat when he arrives at the port of Puteoli. The gospel has actually outrun the hero. Nor is Paul the first to admit Gentiles into the Christian movement; that honor belongs to Peter. Paul's importance for Luke is indicated in his last recorded words, which repeat an affirmation made twice before and are directed to the Jews in Rome: "Let it be known to you then that this salvation of God has been sent to the Gentiles; they will listen" (28:28).[9] Luke's geographical structure, thus, indicates his interest in the spread of Christianity and an even deeper interest in its growing independence from Judaism.

Looking back from his vantage point in 80–85 CE, Luke sees that there is a gulf between Judaism and Christianity, but he is aware that it had not always been so. He shows that the first Christians had been Jews. According to his account, they met in the Temple and remained faithful to Jewish traditions. Although he believes that the efforts to incorporate un-

[9] Cf. also Acts 13:46 and 18:6.

circumcised Gentiles into the Christian movement are directed by God, he still maintains that Jews have a certain priority. As Luke tells the story, when Paul begins his missionary work in a town, he usually goes into the Jewish synagogue, where he has some success. After he has been rejected by some Jews, sometimes violently, Paul then carries his message to Gentiles. This pattern is frequently repeated in Acts and forms a paradigm for the entire history of Christianity in the period covered by Acts. According to the model that Luke used, the Christian movement began among Jews but was rejected by most of them. Then it came to Gentiles and was accepted by them in large numbers.

According to Luke's presentation, Jews who did not accept the Christian message were rejected by God. Paul speaks words of rejection in three key passages in Acts. In 13:46 he and Barnabas say, "It was necessary that the word of God should be spoken first to you. Since you thrust it from you and judge yourselves unworthy of eternal life, behold, we turn to the Gentiles." In 18:6, Paul says, "Your blood be upon your heads! I am innocent. From now on I will go to the Gentiles." Paul's last words in Acts reiterate this theme: "Let it be known to you then that this salvation of God has been sent to the Gentiles; they will listen" (28:28). In these announcements we have not only a contrast between the receptivity of Gentiles and the rejection of Jews, but the theme that Jews have cut themselves off from God's promises, even though they were the first to hear the preaching. For Luke, God has rejected the Jews as his covenant people, and Christians have become the people of God.

Although he conceives of the divine rejection of the Jews, Luke is aware of the role played by the early Jewish Christians. He knows that those people were Jewish converts and that they continued to adhere devoutly to Jewish practices. He seems proud to report that in Jerusalem the Christian community was attractive to some Pharisees and priests and that the apostles were held in high regard by their fellow Jews. Thus, we have in the first several chapters of Acts a positive portrayal of early Jewish Christianity. But Luke's sympathies are with Pauline Christianity, as he pictures it. In that picture it is through the efforts of Paul that large numbers of Gentiles are introduced to the Christian message. To be sure, the apostles seem to concur with Paul that roadblocks should not be placed in the way of Gentiles. But Paul is the one who is valiantly led by the spirit to preach to them. In short, Luke seems to have respect for the early Jewish Christians, but their time is simply the first chapter in the period of the church. When Gentiles accept the Christian message and when Paul comes on the scene, it is as if that first chapter is over. For Luke the devotion of the early Jewish Christians should be remembered with reverence, but the character of that group by no means limits the character of future Christian groups.

Although the apostles are part of early Jewish Christianity, they form a distinct group. They are Jesus' successors and, as such, they are lifted above the ordinary believers. They are identified with early Jewish Christianity, but they cooperate in the gentile ministry and fully support Paul. The apostles are twelve in number, and this number must remain constant. At the death of Judas, Matthias is chosen to bring the group to its full strength. The title *apostle* is restricted to those twelve. Only once is it given to others, namely to Paul and Barnabas (Acts 14:14). Although he gives us no explicit information on the organization of any Christian community, Luke understands that the apostles occupy a dominant position for the body of Christians everywhere. It is they who must decide if circumcision is required for Gentiles. It is on the authority of the apostles that requirements are set for Gentile Christians. If we look for individual leaders, Peter appears to occupy the chief position until his arrest in chapter 12. After that he does not disappear, but leadership is exercised by James, who is not counted among the twelve and is not called an apostle. At the meeting of apostles and elders with Paul and Barnabas described in chapter 15, James himself makes the final decision. When Paul returns to Jerusalem for the last time, in chapter 21, it is James who suggests that he should perform a ritual of purification. Luke has assigned a special position to the apostles and to James as well. They are the successors of Jesus.

A particular problem adheres to the ending of Acts. Readers are frequently puzzled by the fact that Luke does not state what finally happened to Paul. This appears to be a problem, because at least half of the book has Paul as the hero, and his journey to Rome is described in minute detail. But at the end he is awaiting trial and preaching. Several suggestions have been made to account for this apparent difficulty: that the original ending of the book, which described Paul's fate, has been lost; that Luke intended to write a third volume, in which he would describe Paul's fate, but failed to do so; and that Luke wrote before the outcome of Paul's trial at Rome was known. A fourth and more convincing suggestion is that the book ends precisely where the author intended and that the present ending is perfectly appropriate to the overall structure of the book. Proponents of this position point out that a narrative about Paul's death or about his later activities would be an anticlimax for Acts. Despite the attention that was paid to Paul, Luke was not writing his biography. He is, rather, telling the story of the period of the church, which, in his own conception, constituted the last period in the history of salvation. The importance of Paul is that he carried the gospel to the capital of the world and made Christianity independent of Judaism. His fate is secondary to the fact that he preached the gospel in Rome, "quite openly and unhindered" (Acts 28:31).

What may be said about the value of Acts as a source for early Jewish Christianity? The relationship of Acts to early Jewish Christianity is similar to the relationship of the first gospels to Jesus. The separation in time is nearly the same, and the attitudes of the authors toward their subjects are comparable. These observations suggest that Acts, like the gospels, must be used with great care, if we are interested in the actual history of early Jewish Christianity. In addition, we have some written materials that are closer in time to the historical situation than Acts is—that is, the letters of Paul. To be sure, the letters must also be used with caution, because Paul was not on the scene in the very earliest days and his views did not totally duplicate those of the early Jewish Christians. Still, the letters are invaluable for the study at hand, and they have a kind of priority to Acts. Moreover, the Jerusalem kerygma has a similar kind of priority, although the situation with it is complex. C. H. Dodd has found the Jerusalem form of the kerygma embedded in Acts, specifically in the speeches of Peter in the first several chapters. He did not deny that Luke shaped the speeches, but he thought that the main points within them represented Christian preaching in the earliest days.[10]

These observations suggest a basic principle for studying early Jewish Christianity—namely, that we look for points on which Paul, the kerygma, and Acts agree. It will be at those points that we will have the highest degree of confidence in our sources. In addition, it will, as usual, be necessary to engage in the use of historical imagination.

In Chapter 10 we will examine Acts as a source for Paul's career. At this point, however, we turn to a discussion of the character of early Jewish Christianity.

THE CHARACTER OF EARLY JEWISH CHRISTIANITY

All of our sources point to the central importance of eschatological conviction in early Jewish Christianity. Despite his own apparent feeling that the end of things was not imminent, Luke emphasized the fervent expectation that must have existed in the earliest Christian communities. We will see that Paul similarly caught the fervor of this early expectation. The Jerusalem kerygma included a proclamation that the final age of history had begun in the ministry, death, and resurrection of Jesus, who had become exalted as Messiah. History, it said, would soon reach its consummation at his return. The preachers further proclaimed that the spirit in the church was a signal of the Messiah's present power and glory but that there was still time for repentance before the end. The very earliest community must have been made up of those who were convinced of the imminent end of history.

Closely connected with eschatological conviction is the resurrection faith. Here again our sources agree that the genesis of Christianity was the belief that Jesus had been raised from the dead. In Chapter 8, where we had occasion to examine the possible meaning of the resurrection faith, we found

[10] Cf. Dodd, op. cit.

The city of Jerusalem, showing the Jaffa Gate in the foreground, the site of the Temple in the center, and the Mount of Olives in the background. (Courtesy Israel Government Tourist Office, Houston, Texas)

a complex of meanings, in which Jesus' resurrection was understood as revelation, as a command to preach, and as a confirmation of his communion with the believers. In that chapter an analysis was given of Paul's catalogue of postresurrection appearances in 1 Cor 15:3–8, as well as of the material in the gospels and in Acts 1. An illuminating variation on some of the same themes is found in a speech of Peter in Acts 2.

Although the speech in Acts 2:14–36 is Luke's composition, it seems to contain a kernel of non-Lukan primitive material. In fact, Dodd found elements of the Jerusalem kerygma embedded in this speech. The scene is Jerusalem at Pentecost (Shavuot). The followers of Jesus are gathered together, and suddenly they begin to speak in tongues.[11] The phenomenon, called glossolalia, causes a great uproar, and Peter attempts to explain it to the crowd. He does so by quoting from the OT prophet Joel (2:28–32), who had predicted ecstatic phenomena on the last days. Peter claims that the fact of glossolalia demonstrates that the end is imminent. Then he goes on to proclaim the resurrection of Jesus, and he quotes an OT prediction of it (Ps 16:8–11). He announces: "This Jesus God raised up, and of that we all are witnesses. Being therefore exalted at the right hand of God, and having received from the Father the promise of the Holy Spirit, he has poured out this which you see and hear" (Acts 2:32–33). Then Peter concludes with these words: "Let all the house of Israel therefore know assuredly that God has made him both Lord and Christ, this Jesus whom you crucified" (2:36). Peter is saying that the phenomenon of glossolalia is precisely what Joel had predicted. It had been made possible by the risen Jesus. Although there are Lukan elements in the composition of this speech, there appear to be some basic primitive elements as well. In respect to the eschatological conviction in it, it contrasts with Luke's own views, so far as these can be determined. Nor is the speech consistent with Luke's presentation of Jesus' resurrection, in which the empty tomb and physical postresurrection appearances are cited as evidence. In Peter's speech the evidence for Jesus' resurrection is the activity of his followers.

This speech of Peter illustrates the connection between the eschatological climate and the resurrection faith. The followers of Jesus came to the conviction that the last days were upon them and that they could expect to see visions and experience ecstatic phenomena. They must have understood the eschatological hope in terms of a Messianic Age, one aspect of which was to be the resurrection of the righteous. They came to believe that this resurrection was represented by the resurrection of Jesus himself; it was the first act in the concluding period of history and an anticipatory confirmation of the life to come. They focused on Jesus as their hope for the future and refused to believe that his defeat in death was God's last word. They knew that he had been killed by lawless people, but they were convinced that God had exalted him. Once this conviction was established, ecstatic phenomena and reports of appearances would confirm their faith. It is not possible to

---

[11] The phenomenon of glossolalia is also dealt with in 1 Cor 14, where it appears to be ecstatic speech of an unknown tongue. Luke, however, probably understands it as the ability to speak an actual human language that is foreign to the speaker.

describe fully the origin or nature of their convictions, but the belief in Jesus' resurrection and the belief in the imminent end of history seem to go hand in hand.

The connection between eschatological conviction and resurrection faith suggests an affinity with certain Jewish movements of the Hellenistic period, namely those associated with apocalypticism. Although eschatological thought is found in other Jewish movements, the emphasis on the imminence of the end and the tendency to observe signs of the end are associated with apocalyptic Judaism. We would not go far wrong if we were to understand that many, if not most, Jews who became adherents of Christianity in its earliest days had already been influenced by apocalyptic thought. For them, the figure of Jesus could become the focal point of their speculations about the end of history.

Apocalyptic Judaism also provided for them a way of understanding the person and function of Jesus. To express their convictions about him, the followers of Jesus found the concept of the Messiah, or Christ, which had had a significant history in several versions of apocalyptic thought. In the speech in Acts 2, Peter concluded by saying: "God has made him both Lord and Christ, this Jesus whom you crucified" (Acts 2:36). These words, taken within the context of the speech as a whole, imply that Messiahship was granted to Jesus at the resurrection. Before the resurrection he is referred to in strictly human terms. He is called a man (2:22), through whom God performed mighty works. His human mortality is also affirmed in the speech (2:23). In general, the early Jewish Christians seem not to raise questions about the humanity of Jesus. His humanity was part of the given situation, neither questioned nor treated as problematical. Nor do they think of his human life as, strictly speaking, messianic. It is attested by "mighty works and wonders and signs" (2:22), and the attestation anticipates his coming Messiahship. But Jesus does not actually become the Messiah until the resurrection. This concept is usually referred to as a form of adoptionistic Christology. It is a Christology—a kind of speculation about the Christ— that maintains that God did not send Jesus as the Christ from heaven but adopted him or designated him as such at the resurrection. Even so, the early preachers were sure that the whole complex of events occurred in accordance with God's plan and foreknowledge (2:23). The point to be emphasized in early Jewish Christian Christology is that God did not send a divine being to earth as the Messiah but selected a human. Other varieties of early Christianity will present significant alternatives to this Christology.

Although the term *Messiah* was readily available for Christian use, it was not an unambiguous term. We have seen in our analysis of Jewish apocalyptic literature that there were several interpretations of the person of the expected Messiah. It is, consequently, erroneous to concentrate on any one interpretation as the orthodox Jewish view. Similarly, it is not possible to be very precise about early Jewish Christian views. We may reasonably as-

Sarcophagus showing a baptismal scene, third century, National Museum, Rome. (Courtesy *Soprintendenza Archeologica, Rome.*)

sume that they thought of Jesus as "Son of David," but there is no evidence that they pressed the political implications of this conception—that is, they did not preach the restoration of the monarchy to Israel. There is no direct evidence that they used the expression "Son of man," but they seemed to be waiting for Jesus' return in the manner that was expected of this figure—

on the clouds of heaven. The evidence only allows us to say that the early Jewish Christians believed that Jesus had become the Messiah and would soon return to earth in power to initiate the Messianic Age. To prepare themselves for the coming end, they demanded that their hearers repent.

Several practices and beliefs in the early Jewish Christian communities deserve our attention. Luke has said that they practiced a sharing of possessions, and this may be historically correct. Those who could do so donated money for the support of those who were not able to work. The author of 2 Thessalonians also alludes to this practice when he decrees that anyone who does not work shall not eat (2 Thess 3:10). This is an unenforceable decree unless the community controls the food supply, and it could do so if the sharing of possessions were practiced. Baptism was used as a rite of initiation in the primitive period. It may have arisen in imitation of a practice in the sect originated by John the Baptist, and it was associated with repentance. A community meal was probably observed among the early Jewish Christians as a continuation of the fellowship that was begun in Jesus' lifetime, or in observance of the communion that was associated with his resurrection. Paul indicates that the usual pattern consisted of breaking bread, then a full meal, and then drinking wine (1 Cor 11:23–26). In most other respects early Jewish Christians were probably indistinguishable from their fellow Jews. They were monotheists and accepted the God of Moses as the one God. They accepted Hebrew scriptures and felt that they stood in a continuum with Israelite history. They accepted Jewish institutions, probably participated in worship at the Jewish Temple, and represented themselves as the Israel of the latter days. They felt that the initial stages of the eschatological collection of Israel had begun with them.

The leadership of the early Jewish Christian community is far from clear. The city of Jerusalem seems to be the focal point for them, although communities soon arose in Damascus and Antioch, in Syria. Our sources sometimes speak of leadership by the twelve apostles or disciples. It is frequently stated today that the idea of the twelve is a legendary conception of later times, although Paul was aware of it (cf. 1 Cor 15:5). The group of twelve is supposed to be representative of all Israel, which was originally made up of twelve tribes. That there probably was no formal group of twelve disciples who attached themselves to the historical Jesus is shown by the fact that the gospel writers differ widely in their lists of those who were in it. The term *apostle* designates certain leaders. It is impossible to determine how many people bore the title, but Peter certainly did, and Paul at least claimed it for himself (cf. Gal 1:1 and 1 Cor 9:1 et al.). The word denotes persons who have been commissioned for a specific task, and most of them are described as traveling to make an initial proclamation of the gospel in foreign countries. According to Paul, apostles held positions of prime authority in the church, ranking ahead of prophets, teachers, miracle workers, and healers (1 Cor 12:28). In reference to the leadership of the community in Jerusalem, he speaks of three "pillar" apostles, namely Peter, John bar Zebedee, and James, the Lord's brother (Gal 2:9; cf. Gal 1:19). The synoptic writers also have a group of three intimates of Jesus, but they have James bar Zebedee rather than the Lord's brother. Paul is more dependable at this point, and his "pillar" apostles probably represent the top group of early Jewish Christians. If one is to point to a single leader, it would be either Peter or James. Luke implies that Peter was the first leader of the community in Jerusalem and that James later took over. Paul says that on his first visit to Jerusalem three years after his conversion, he saw Peter and James (Gal 1:18–20). At his visit fourteen years later, the "pillars" are in charge, and they recognize Peter as apostle to Jews and Paul and Barnabas as apostles to Gentiles (Gal 2:1–10). A certain time later, Paul meets Peter in Antioch and accuses him of acting hypocritically in response to criticism from Jews and other persons who came from James (Gal 2:11–14). The picture is by no means clear, but it is likely that James held a very high position in the community from the beginning. Although Paul made his first Jerusalem trip to see Peter, he could not leave without paying his respects to James. By the time of his second trip, James' position was firmly established. Leadership by James is perfectly consistent with the thinking of early Jewish Christians. They are anxiously awaiting the appearance of the Messiah, and it is appropriate that his nearest relative should be his vice-regent until he comes.

According to both Paul and Acts, the city of Jerusalem was the focal point for early Jewish Christians. The community there seems to exercise a kind of hegemony over Christians in other locations. The influence of the Jerusalem leaders was felt as far north as Antioch (Gal 2:11–14). Paul felt it necessary to present his gospel for approval to the Jerusalem leaders (Gal 2:2). Although the pillars did not deem it necessary to require the circumcision of Gentile Christians, they requested Paul to take up a collection (Gal 2:10). The funds were probably necessary to enable the Jerusalem community to exist in a precarious and volatile environment. Paul was eager to raise the money, because he was interested in the survival of the community in Jerusalem, and he made special efforts to take the collection and present it personally. Another indication of the dominance of the Jerusalem leaders may be seen in their approval of the Gentile mission undertaken by Paul and Barnabas (Gal 2:9).

There is little in the book of Acts to indicate that there were any serious internal problems among the early Jewish Christians. Luke probably de-emphasized them intentionally. But in a few places we may see some hints about problems relating to the admission of Gentiles into fellowship with Jewish Christians.

In Acts the incident about the admission of the first Gentile receives a great deal of attention. Most of chapters 10 and 11 are devoted to this incident. Cornelius, according to Acts, was a devout Gentile and a resident of

Caesarea who was highly regarded by Jews. One afternoon he had a vision in which he was directed by an angel to send for Peter in Joppa. The next day at about noon Peter had a vision in which a large sheet, with all kinds of animals, reptiles, and birds, appeared to be coming down out of heaven. We are to understand that the sheet contained animals that are, according to the Hebrew scriptures, not to be eaten. Peter also heard a voice commanding him to kill and eat the animals, but he refused, claiming that he had never violated the dietary regulations. But the voice came a second and a third time, and Peter was told, "What God has cleansed, you must not call common" (10:15). Immediately after this, the delegates from Cornelius arrived, and the next day Peter set off for Caesarea with them. When Peter and Cornelius met, they told each other about their respective visions, and Peter preached about Jesus, after which the spirit descended and the Gentiles spoke in tongues, as had the original apostles in Acts 2. Peter then decided that they could all be baptized. But when Peter got back to Jerusalem, he was criticized by the "circumcision party" (11:2) for visiting with and eating with Gentiles.[12] So Peter retold the entire story, and everybody fully agreed, and they said, "Then to the Gentiles also God has granted repentance unto life" (11:18).

The story of Cornelius and Peter is clearly important for Luke. It not only signifies the first admission of a Gentile into fellowship with the early Jewish Christians, but it also calls attention to some attendant problems. Significantly, the central feature of the story is a vision in which dietary regulations are effectively abolished. Peter is pictured as a Jewish Christian who has never violated the dietary laws given in the Hebrew scriptures, and who is reluctant to surrender them. The point that Luke seems to stress is that the early Jewish Christians, here represented by Peter, obeyed the food laws and only departed from them as a result of a vision and a direct command from God. The words from heaven, "What God has cleansed, you must not call common" (10:15), signify the abolition of Jewish dietary regulations and open the way for the admission of Gentiles into Christian fellowship. Note also that Peter was criticized by some Jewish Christians for fraternizing and eating with Gentiles.

It would be misleading to say that Luke intends the reader to understand that only the Jewish food laws stood in the way of the admission of Gentiles into Christian fellowship. Cornelius also must hear the gospel and receive the spirit before he is baptized. Luke elsewhere shows that circumcision was also a controversial issue. But the food laws play an important role in the narrative. Moreover, Luke elsewhere indicates that the dietary regulations are not totally abolished for Gentile Christians. In Acts 15, in the meeting of the apostles with Paul and Barnabas, James decides that circumcision is

---

[12] Luke apparently uses the phrase "circumcision party" to designate those who opposed any relaxation of regulations for Gentile Christians.

not to be required for Gentiles but that they must refrain from blood—that is, from eating meat with blood, from eating meat from animals that have been sacrificed to idols, and from eating meat from animals that have been strangled. These are rules that form part of the Jewish dietary regulations. The picture we get in Acts is that there were some problems attendant on the admission of Gentiles and that among those problems was the place of the dietary regulations.

Paul, of course, does not address himself to the problems of early Jewish Christians prior to the time of his own entry on the scene. Nor can we here go into detail on his treatment of the issues that engaged his attention at a somewhat later time. But we will see that he found it necessary to deal with problems not unlike those treated in Acts. He will stress the issue of circumcision and will maintain that Gentile Christians must not be required to undergo the rite. In 1 Corinthians he will also face the question of eating food offered to idols. Evidently the questions of circumcision and of at least some food laws were still contested in Paul's day. We will, in the following chapter, see how Paul dealt with them.

When we put Luke and Paul together and allow for the fact that they were writing at different times, a high degree of agreement emerges. Although we cannot be certain of all the circumstances or the history of those early times, it appears probable that the admission of Gentiles was a major and controversial issue among the early Jewish Christians. Historically, it seems likely that it should be. Because the first Christians had been Jews and still thought of themselves as such, it probably was not patently obvious to them that non-Jews should also hear the gospel message. If any of them maintained that they should, then others would probably raise questions about the relationship of Gentiles to the Jewish Torah: Should they be circumcised? Must they adhere to the dietary regulations? May we eat with them? These would be terribly important questions for people who took their Jewish roots seriously. In fact, however, they constitute only the most visible problems relating to Torah observance. They point to the more fundamental question about the continued validity of Torah for Christians, a problem that consumed a great deal of Paul's attention and to which he devoted some of his most serious thought.

Our earlier examination of the teachings of Jesus increases the likelihood that the place of Torah was contested in early Jewish Christianity. We saw in Chapter 8 that the earliest layer of oral tradition consisted of Jesus' teaching about God's demand for love. We also saw that those teachings did not directly address the question of Torah and that, in consequence, an ambiguous situation resulted. In that situation some must have felt that Jesus had abolished Torah, whereas others, with equal conviction, felt that he intended for it to remain as fundamental to the lives of his followers. In this situation partisans on both sides could cite words of Jesus, as the gospel writers did later. Thus, it seems highly probable that early Jewish Christians were divided on the admission of Gentiles and on the attendant problems of their possible admission, because they had no uncontested understanding of the authority of Torah.

The place of Torah was surely not the only problem that might affect a missionary movement among Gentiles. Some of the basic convictions held by early Jewish Christians would be difficult to express to a non-Jewish audience. We have seen that early Jewish Christians readily adopted the title *Christ* to express their beliefs about the status of Jesus as well as their eschatological convictions. Most Jews probably had little trouble understanding what early Jewish Christians meant when they called Jesus the Messiah, or the Christ. But one could not presume that Gentiles would understand it. If one is to speak meaningfully to Gentiles, it is necessary either to give them a full education in the meaning of messianic expectation or to find some term or terms that are equivalent. The second alternative appears more efficient, but there is no term that would mean to Gentiles precisely what Messiah would mean to Jews. There are, however, two terms that may serve to suggest something of the value that early Jewish Christians saw in Jesus. These terms are *Son of God,* and *Lord.*

The term *Son of God* was familiar in the Hellenistic period as a designation for the divine and semidivine descendants of Zeus and as a title for emperors. Although the term came to be used for Jesus, its use surely did not mean that Jesus was thought of as a son of Zeus, but it meant that the term was a near equivalent to Messiah. The case is comparable to one in which Americans draw on their own experience to express the significance of a British monarch. There is no American equivalent, for the term *president* does not carry the same weight or express the same complex of meaning and feeling. But it is the closest term available. Similarly, Son of God approximates early Jewish Christian beliefs. The two terms, *Messiah* and *Son of God,* may produce similar reverential feelings, if not the same meaning. In time the use of the latter term will produce additional changes in meaning, for later Christians will analyze the phrase on its own merits, without respect to any relation to the title *Messiah.* In doing so, they will raise questions about the humanity and divinity of Jesus, the relationship of the two, the metaphysical nature of Jesus, and his relationship to God.

The Greek word *kyrios,* which we translate "Lord," was familiar in the Hellenistic period, when Caesar was addressed as *kyrios,* as was the central deity in religious cults. It was also known in Greek-speaking Jewish circles, where it was used to designate God himself. In early Christianity we find the practice of calling on the name of the Lord Jesus in prayer, exorcism in Jesus' name, and cultic veneration of the Lord in worship.[13] Here again we

---

[13] It is possible that early Jewish Christian communities also thought of Jesus as Lord. Luke used both terms, *Christ* and *Lord,* in Peter's speech in Acts 2:36. In 1 Cor 16:22 Paul refers to a liturgical phrase in Aramaic, *Maranatha,* that means "Come, O Lord." The German NT

may point to a rough equivalency in terms of value, but not in meaning, for Messiah is one whose future appearance is expected, and kyrios usually signifies a deity present in a worshiping community. Paul will adopt the idea of Jesus as Lord, and it will be further elaborated in John and Hebrews, but it was used in the pre-Pauline period as well. Thus, it is a consequence of the need to present Jesus to non-Jews that a multiplication of titles develops. Although these titles—Son of God, Lord, and Christ—are not exact equivalents, they served to express similar beliefs about Jesus' status.

Thus, early Jewish Christianity appears to be a movement that began among a group of Jews for whom Jesus had activated certain apocalyptic expectations. These people, probably led by charismatic preachers, saw Jesus as God's Messiah, and they believed that he had been raised from the dead. They established the movement in a number of localities, but Jerusalem continued to be looked on as a kind of headquarters. Eventually, some of them began to admit Gentiles into their fellowship, but not without facing problems about the meaning of Torah and not without encountering problems of communication.

We have no way of knowing how long early Jewish Christian communities existed as such. We will find a group of Jewish Christians in the second century, but they seem distinct from the earlier group, despite their claims. We will examine them in Chapter 11. Now, however, we must turn our attention to one Jewish Christian, Paul, who inherited a good deal from the earlier movement but also developed a significant alternative to it.

BIBLIOGRAPHY

General Studies of Early Christian History and Thought

Bauer, Walter. *Orthodoxy and Heresy in Earliest Christianity*. Ed. by R. A. Kraft and G. Krodel. Philadelphia: Fortress Press, 1971.

Bousset, Wilhelm. *Kyrios Christos,* Trans. by John E. Steely. Nashville, Tenn.: Abingdon Press, 1970.

Bultmann, Rudolf. *Theology of the New Trstament*. Trans. by Kendrick Grobel. New York: Charles Scribner's Sons, 1951, 1955. 2 volumes

Kee, Howard C. *Christian Origins in Sociological Perspective: Methods and Resources*. Philadelphia: Westminster Press, 1980.

Kelly, J. N. D. *Early Christian Doctrines*. Rev ed. New York: Harper & Row, Publishers, 1978.

Lietzmann, Hans. *The Beginnings of the Christian Church*. Trans. by B. L. Woolf. New York: Meridian Books, 1949.

scholar W. Bousset, however, argued that the idea of Jesus as Lord was originally Gentile and that Aramaic-speaking Christians picked it up from them. See his *Kyrios Christos,* trans. by John E. Steely (Nashville, Tenn.: Abingdon, 1970), pp. 119–152.

Theissen, Gerd. *Sociology of Early Palestinian Christianity*. Trans. by John Bowden. Philadelphia: Fortress Press, 1978.

Many of these books deal with the history of Christianity in the first and the second centuries and, thus, will be helpful for the material to be covered in Chapters 11–12 of this book. In addition, many of the general introductions listed in the bibliography for Chapter 1 will also be useful. Bousset, Bultmann, and Kelly concentrate on theological developments, whereas Lietzmann integrates theological and historical elements. Bousset's *Kyrios Christos* has been influential since its initial publication in German in 1913. Bauer emphasizes the varieties of early Christianity and organizes his material around the main locations of Christian groups. Theissen and Kee will introduce the reader to sociological studies and to methods that have only recently begun to be applied to the history of early Christianity.

The Acts of the Apostles

Barrett, C. K. *Luke the Historian in Recent Study*. London: Epworth Press, 1961.
Cadbury, Henry J. *The Making of Luke-Acts*, 2nd ed. London: Society for the Promotion of Christian Knowledge, 1958.
Conzelmann, Hans. *The Theology of St. Luke*. Trans. by Geoffrey Buswell. New York: Harper & Row, Publishers, 1960.
Hengel, Martin. *Acts and the History of Earliest Christianity*. Trans. by John Bowden. Philadelphia: Fortress Press, 1980.
Jervell, Jacob. *Luke and the People of God*. Minneapolis, Minn.: Augsburg Press, 1972.
O'Neill, J. C. *The Theology of Acts*. London: Society for the Promotion of Christian Knowledge, 1961.
Talbert, Charles H. *Literary Patterns, Theological Themes and the Genre of Luke-Acts*. Society of Biblical Literature Monograph Series 20. Missoula, Mont.: Scholars Press, 1974.

Barrett reviews the research on the author of Acts and classifies him as a "primitive catholic." Cadbury and Conzelmann, listed here and in the bibliography for Luke, are indispensable for any serious study of Luke-Acts. O'Neill's is an excellent introduction to Acts. The author treats such subjects as the date of the book, its structure, and its main themes. Jervell addresses himself to problems associated with the relationship of Jews and Christians in Acts. Talbert maintains that Acts is a succession narrative that was written in order to identify the authentic successors of Jesus. Hengel takes seriously what he understands as the claim of Luke—that is, to write a historical narrative. He intends to find the historical reality that underlies the book of Acts.

Early Jewish Christianity

Caird, G. B. *The Apostolic Age*. London: Duckworth Press, 1955.

Cullmann, Oscar. *Peter: Disciple, Apostle, Martyr*. Trans. by F. V. Filson. New York: Living Age Books, 1958.

Dodd, C. H. *The Apostolic Preaching and its Developments*. London: Holder and Stoughton, 1936.

Longnecker, Richard N. *The Christology of Early Jewish Christianity*. Grand Rapids, Mich.: Baker Book House, 1970.

Nock, Arthur D. *Early Gentile Christianity and Its Hellenistic Background*. New York: Harper & Row, Publishers, 1964.

Schmithals, Walter. *The Office of Apostle in the Early Church*. Trans. by John E. Steely. Nashville, Tenn.: Abingdon Press, 1969.

———. *Paul and James*. Studies in Biblical Theology 46. London: SCM Press, 1965.

Streeter, B. H. *The Primitive Church*. New York: Macmillan Publishing Co., Inc., 1929

Dodd's book is fundamental in the study of the earliest form of Christian preaching. Cullmann's is an interesting study of the traditions and history of Peter. Nock concentrates on the origin of Gentile Christianity in the pre-Pauline period. Caird and Streeter are more comprehensive. Longnecker and Schmithals treat specific theological and institutional problems connected with early Jewish Christianity. See also the books by Bousset, Bultmann, and Lietzmann listed under "General Studies of Early Christian History and Thought," on p. 308f.

❖ IO ❖

Pauline Christianity

ACCORDING to all the documents we possess, the single most influential Christian in the period 30–70 CE was Paul. Despite the fact that, before he had associated with the movement, early Jewish Christians had probably concluded that Gentiles could be admitted into Christian fellowship, he is known as the apostle to the Gentiles. He traveled extensively throughout eastern Mediterranean lands, preached the Christian gospel, and kept up a lively correspondence. Indeed, it is the correspondence itself that assures his significance for later generations, for in his letters we are able to see the ways in which he worked out his basic convictions. Moreover, his letters constitute the earliest extant Christian literature, and they are invaluable historical documents.

THE LIFE OF PAUL

Paul's letters are, by definition, primary sources for the study of his life. But before we examine them, it is necessary to return briefly to the book of Acts, which is, though secondary, an important source for Pauline studies.

We have already seen that Paul was the hero of the book of Acts. Chapters 13–28 are completely devoted to narratives about his travels and adventures. Even earlier in the book, Luke carefully introduced Paul and told the story of his conversion. The reader first meets him in Acts 7:58–8:3, where it is said that he was in agreement with those who executed Stephen and, indeed, assisted those who killed him.[1] In Acts 9:1–19 Luke tells the story of Paul's conversion. He was on the way to Damascus to arrest some

---

[1] In the earlier references in Acts, the name Saul is used: Acts 7:58–8:3; 9:1–19; 9:22, 24; 11:25, 30; 12:25; and 13:1, 2, 9. At 13:9 Luke introduces the name Paul and uses it in all of the following narratives. The name Saul is not used in the NT outside of Acts. Paul appears to be a Latin name and Saul an Aramaic name.

Christians when he saw a blinding light and heard the voice of Jesus. Paul was then led on into Damascus, where a Christian named Ananias cured him of blindness. Thereafter, Paul preached about Jesus.[2]

The book of Acts has a few biographical details about Paul. According to this account, he was a Jew who had been born in Tarsus (21:39 and 22:3). He was brought up in Jerusalem, where he studied under Gamaliel (22:3), and he considered himself a Pharisee (23:6). He had Roman citizenship as a privilege of birth (22:25–28). Of these biographical details, only his Judaism and Pharisaism are mentioned in his own letters. Luke, however, is not interested in Paul's preconversion life but in his life as a Christian, which he narrates in detail in Acts 13–28.

Because we have already examined chapters 13–28 as part of the structure of Acts, it is necessary now to make only a few observations about this material.[3] Luke organizes most of Paul's Christian career in terms of three missionary journeys. The first trip (Acts 13:1–14:28) takes Paul and his party to Cyprus and to central Asia Minor (including visits to the cities of Perga in Pamphylia, Antioch in Pisidia, Iconium, Lystra, and Derbe in Lycaonia). The second (15:36–18:22) is a far more extensive trip and includes visits to Derbe and Lystra but has Paul move on to western Asia Minor (Troas and Ephesus), Macedonia (Philippi, Thessalonica, and Beroea), and Greece (Athens and Corinth). On the third trip (18:23–21:6) Paul returns to many of the places he visited on the second, but most of his time is spent in Ephesus. Between these trips Paul returns to the East. After the first he reports to Antioch and then is dispatched to Jerusalem for a conference with the apostles. After the second he returns to Antioch, but the narrative of the third trip begins without pause. After the third trip Paul goes to Jerusalem, where he is captured and undergoes the series of trials reported in 21:7–26:32.

Luke's arrangement indicates to the reader that Paul is somehow responsible to Christian leaders in the East, especially in Jerusalem. These leaders seem to exercise a kind of restraining force on him, periodically pulling him back toward his point of origin. After the third trip James advises Paul to perform a ritual of purification, and Paul readily takes the advice. This story stands as a symbol that Paul is both geographically and theologically responsible to the Christian community in Jerusalem.

Despite the impression given by the periodic returns, most of the emphasis in the narratives is on the heroic success that Paul, under the guidance of God's spirit, has in gentile lands. The reader captures a sense of adventure and excitement as Paul travels farther and farther away from Jerusalem, proclaims the Christian gospel to increasingly larger crowds of people, and meets with success after success. Clearly, the thrust of Paul's

---

[2] The story of Paul's conversion is told twice more in Acts, cf. 22:4–16 and 26:10–18.
[3] Cf. Chapter 9 in this book.

travels is toward the West. It is on the second trip that he crosses the Aegean and opens the mission to what was traditionally thought of as the West. Luke has marked the significance of this crossing by telling about a vision of Paul (16:6–10). In the vision a Macedonian appears to Paul and invites him to come to his country. In response to the vision Paul and his party leave Asia Minor for Macedonia and Greece. On the third trip we read of Paul's still more extensive travel plans. While he is in Ephesus he announces that he intends to travel through Macedonia and Greece, return to Jerusalem, and then go to Rome (19:21–22). From that point on it becomes increasingly clear that Paul is under a divine necessity to go to Rome. This motif is underscored by an appearance of the Lord to Paul in 23:11 and by the report of an angel's visit in 27:23–24. At the end of the book Paul is in Rome, preaching the gospel openly and unhindered.

But in Acts Paul's missionary work is not an unmitigated success. There is opposition, misunderstanding, imprisonment, and persecution. In telling the story of Paul's visits to individual localities, Luke frequently employs a particular narrative pattern. It serves him as a kind of formula. Paul enters a city and goes immediately to the local synagogue, where he preaches and meets a positive response from some Jews and some Gentiles. However, a reaction comes from some unresponsive Jews, and Paul leaves the synagogue and preaches exclusively to Gentiles, among whom he has great success. In some narratives the opposing Jews stir up crowds against Paul, and he is either imprisoned or forced to move on to another locality.[4] This pattern represents in microcosm Luke's conception of Paul's significance as well as his conception of the relationship of Judaism and Christianity. To him Paul's significance is that he established the independence of Christianity over against Judaism. Luke wants to make clear that this independence was the result of Jewish opposition to Paul and his message, not the result of Paul's animosity or rejection of Jews. Indeed, Jewish opposition is not total, and Paul's attitude to them is always amicable. Nevertheless, the independence of Christianity is inevitable, as Paul three times announces that he will hereafter go to Gentiles (13:46, 18:6, and 28:28).

If we had only the book of Acts as a source for Pauline studies, our understanding would be grossly deficient. This is so not because Luke presents a basically erroneous account, but because he leaves out so much of importance. Fortunately, we are able to read about Paul from his own hand and, hence, to correct and amplify the account in Acts.

The letters, of course, are valuable mainly for understanding the thought of Paul, and we will presently examine them for this purpose. Some of them contain autobiographical traces that enable us to ascertain some of the basic facts of Paul's life. According to them we learn that Paul was a Jew, specifically a Pharisee, and that he exhibited an unusual degree of zeal for the

---

4 Cf. e.g., Acts 14:1–7, 17:1–9, 17:10–15, 18:1–17, and 19:8–20.

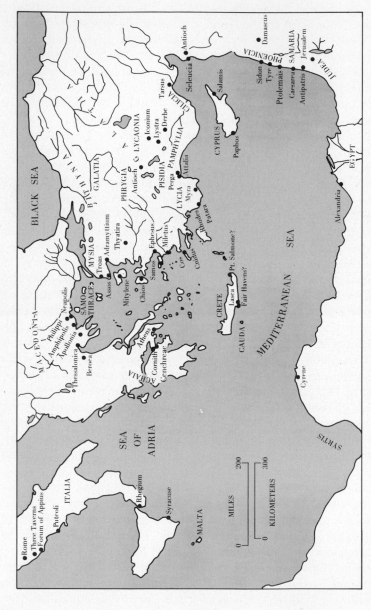

Figure 21   The Travels of Paul in the Book of Acts (Reprinted by permission of Thomas Nelson Publishers, from the book The Interpreter's Bible. Copyright © 1949 by Thomas Nelson & Sons Publishers).

Torah (Phil 3:5–6 and Gal 1:14). His dedication to Judiasm led him to become a persecutor of the emerging Christian movement (Phil 3:6 and Gal 1:13). It is probable that he was in the act of persecuting Christians when he felt that he had received a revelation from the Christ. To him this revelation meant that he was to preach Christ among the Gentiles. He went into Arabia and then returned to Damascus and Jerusalem (Gal 1:17–18). In Jerusalem he was known only by reputation, as a former enemy of the church who was preaching the faith he had once tried to destroy. On this visit to Jerusalem, Paul became acquainted with Cephas (that is, Peter), and with James, but he met none of the other Christians (Gal 1:18–20). Still, he felt himself obliged to preach to Gentiles, and out of response to his revelatory experience he spent the next fourteen years preaching and establishing churches in gentile territories. He made a second trip to Jerusalem and conferred with James, Peter, and John on the question of the treatment of Gentiles in the Church (Gal 2:1). The chief question was whether such persons should be required to be circumcised, and on this issue Paul stoutly affirmed the negative. His position apparently prevailed, and he was asked to collect money for the poor in Jerusalem. He spent the next few years collecting that money and preaching. Paul never lists the places he visited, but we learn from individual letters about Thessalonica, Corinth, Galatia, and Philippi, among others. When Paul completed the collection, he planned to return to Jerusalem for the third time. We have no autobiographical material on Paul's life after this point. He mentions a number of imprisonments, and it is likely that Acts is correct in reporting that he was arrested in Jerusalem and was then sent to Rome for an imperial trial. A letter known as 1 Clement says that he became a martyr.[5] Late second-century tradition affirms that he and Peter were both executed in Rome at the same time.[6]

Although the letters and Acts are not fully consistent on Paul's life, they confirm one another at a number of points. For example, Luke knows that Paul was a missionary to the Gentiles, that he was opposed to the circumcision of Gentile Christians, and that some Jewish Christians opposed him. He knows that he brought a collection of money to the Christians in Jerusalem. He is correct on some of the localities that Paul visited—Thessalonica, Philippi, Corinth, and Ephesus. He knows that he attended a conference in Jerusalem that dealt with the circumcision issue. He knows that Paul intended to go to Rome. We can be completely confident that we are in possession of accurate information about Paul on these points.

The actual chronology of Paul's life is almost impossible to determine. Luke connects Paul's visit to Corinth, on the second trip, with the arrival there of the Roman Governor Gallio (Acts 18:12). We know from an inscription at Delphi that Gallio came to Corinth between 51 and 53. If Acts

[5] 1 Clement 5:4–6.
[6] Irenaeus, *Against Heresies* III, 1:1 Eusebius, *The Ecclesiastical History* II, 25:8.

is correct about this connection, as most scholars think, the period 51–53 establishes a hinge date for Paul's chronology. The NT scholar John Knox accepted the Gallio connection but drew mainly on Paul's letters for his chronology of Paul.[7] Knox argued convincingly that Paul's conversion occurred in 34–35 and that his first visit to Jerusalem as a Christian took place between 37 and 40. His long period of activity in Galatia, Macedonia, and Greece occurred in the period 40–51, and his second visit to Jerusalem, the visit for the conference, was in 51. According to this scheme Paul made additional trips to Asia Minor and Greece, preaching and collecting money for the poor, in 51–53, at which time he met Gallio in Corinth. He returned to Jerusalem in 53–54, where he was arrested. The tradition that he died in Rome under Nero in the early 60s is probably correct. Although we cannot here go into the detailed support that Knox offers for his chronology, his method appears to be sound and his arguments convincing.

THE LETTERS OF PAUL

Luke never mentioned the fact that Paul wrote letters. But because Paul was an itinerant missionary, it is entirely appropriate that he would attempt to maintain contact with communities of Christian believers by this means. His letters were written for specific purposes, and they were addressed to situations in the local Christian communities. Sometimes we can learn from his letters that in those communities there were deep conflicts, misunderstandings, and opposition to Paul and his message, as well as honest questions about social practices.

The historical value of these letters cannot be overestimated. Although there are certain disadvantages in using letters as historical sources, the advantages far outweigh them. The major disadvantage lies in the fact that a letter is written against a background that is shared by author and recipient but that is no longer available to a modern reader. A noted scholar of early Christianity, Kirsopp Lake, long ago noted that "the writer of a letter assumes the knowledge of a whole series of facts, which are, as he is quite aware, equally familiar to his correspondent and to himself. But as time goes on this knowledge is gradually forgotten and what was originally quite plain becomes difficult and obscure."[8] On the positive side, a letter tends to be more candid than other forms of literature. Because a letter is addressed to a defined audience, an author may make little effort to hide facts that he would be reticent to reveal to a wider public. The modern student of Paul is privy to a good deal of information that might never have appeared if Paul had written only treatises and no letters.

---

[7] John Knox, *Chapters in a Life of Paul* (Nashville, Tenn: Abingdon, 1950).
[8] Kirsopp Lake, *The Earlier Epistles of St. Paul* (London: Rivingtons, 1919), p. vii.

The NT canon contains a number of letters that claim to be written by Paul. There is scholarly consensus that Paul did in fact write 1 Thessalonians, Galatians, 1, 2 Corinthians, Romans, Philippians, and Philemon. Opinion is divided on 2 Thessalonians and Colossians, but they will be treated in this chapter. Most scholars agree that Paul himself did not write Ephesians, 1, 2 Timothy, and Titus; we will examine them in Chapter 11.

1 Thessalonians

Almost all scholars agree that 1 Thessalonians is the earliest of Paul's letters and, thus, the oldest piece of Christian literature available to us. Behind the writing of this letter lies a visit that Paul, and probably Silvanus and Timothy, paid to that Macedonian city, where they established a church. They had come from Philippi, also in Macedonia, where they had been "shamefully treated" (2:2). In Thessalonica they preached "in the face of great opposition" (2:2), and their word was received "in much affliction" (1:6). It is not possible to document the nature of the trouble these itinerant preachers met in Philippi and Thessalonica, but it is probable that they were greeted with a good deal of hostility, if not violence. The book of Acts says that Paul and Silas (probably the same as Silvanus) spent three weeks in Thessalonica and preached there in a Jewish synagogue. Although some Jews embraced their preaching, most opposed them and caused an uproar, which brought the missionaries to the attention of the city fathers. Acts concludes the narrative by saying that Paul and Silas were spirited away before they could be arrested. Luke's treatment here appears to be governed by his pattern of initial Jewish acceptance followed by rejection. In 1 Thessalonians, no Jewish opposition is mentioned, nor does the letter indicate that Paul's primary contacts were with Jews. On the contrary, it says that the converts were those who "turned to God from idols, to serve a living and true God" (1:9). Such language would signify conversions from paganism not Judaism. It also appears that Paul and his companions spent more than three weeks in Thessalonica. Although no specific period of time is mentioned in the letter, the impression of duration is stronger than that of speed. Paul says that they worked night and day so as not to burden their hosts. He speaks of treating the believers as children, exhorting and encouraging them and treating them with gentleness. In all probability the mission to Thessalonica was one of months rather than weeks and was marked by hostility from some Gentiles and acceptance by others.

After Paul and his companions left Thessalonica and went to Athens, Paul desired to see his converts again. He apparently made plans, at least on two occasions, to return, but he was prevented from doing so. When he "could bear it no longer" (3:1), he sent Timothy to see if they had remained faithful to the newly embraced religion. The lapse of time between the departure from Thessalonica and Timothy's departure from Athens is spoken of as a short time (2:17). The letter 1 Thessalonians was written when Timothy rejoined Paul, bringing news that the converts had indeed remained steadfast even in the face of persecution.

Most scholars call attention to a kind of conformity between this letter and Acts, and they maintain that 1 Thessalonians was written in about the year 51. In narrating the second missionary journey, Luke traces Paul's geographical movements from Philippi to Athens in general conformity with those given in the letter. So, if we employ Acts in the task of dating 1 Thessalonians, we would say that Paul was in Corinth at the time the letter was written, and, as we have seen, he was there from 51–53. Knox has shown, however, that nothing in the letter itself would force us to accept this date. He is convinced that the letter was written during Paul's earlier period of activity—between 40–51—when he first visited Thessalonica. Knox suggests that it could have been written shortly after 40.[9] Certainty is elusive on this matter, but it is almost certain that, whether written in the early 40s or the early 50s, 1 Thessalonians is Paul's earliest extant letter.

The letter, jointly written by Paul, Silvanus, and Timothy, was primarily intended to express joy over the news that Timothy had brought from Thessalonica. But it is apparent that Timothy had also brought word about some problems that had to be faced. There was, it seems, a need for a sexual ethic, probably brought to light by cases of adultery or promiscuity among Christians (1 Thess 4:1–12). In addition, probably because some among them had died, the Thessalonians needed an understanding of life after death (4:13–18). Finally, they needed a clarification of the Christian future expectation (5:1–11). It looks as if Paul had preached to them that the end of history was imminent and that, as a result, some of the converts had begun to believe that that end was already upon them. Some of them may have quit work in the exuberance of their faith, so that Paul called on the leaders to "admonish the idlers" (5:14). The letter, therefore, had a twofold purpose: to congratulate the Thessalonian Christians on their steadfastness and to address problems related to sex, death, and the future. It closes with the request that it be read to all the Christians in Thessalonica.

2 Thessalonians

From time to time the authenticity of 2 Thessalonians has been seriously questioned. Scholars who doubt that Paul wrote this letter cite two main reasons for their suspicion. In the first place, the bulk of the letter seems too much like the first, so much so that some call it a slavish imitation of 1 Thessalonians.[10] The same themes are found in both letters, but the second

---

[9] Cf. Knox, op. cit., pp. 85–86.
[10] Cf., e.g., Morton S. Enslin, *The Literature of the Christian Movement* (New York: Harper, 1938), p. 242.

lacks the warmth of the first. It is difficult to imagine Paul copying himself, and it is possible that a later writer used 1 Thessalonians as a model for a letter that he wrote in Paul's name. The second ground for suspicion lies in the apparently different eschatological expectations presented in the two letters. The first letter had said that the day of the Lord would come without warning, "like a thief in the night" (1 Thess 5:2), but the second insists that "the man of lawlessness" must precede the coming of the Lord and that something is now restraining him (2 Thess 2:1–12). The passage in 2 Thessalonians says directly that signs will accompany the appearance of the lawless one and that one of the signs will occur in the Temple, presumably the Temple in Jerusalem (2 Thess 2:4).

But these objections to authenticity can be answered. The similarities between the two letters should not be unexpected if both were written by the same person within a brief period of time. The formality and lack of warmth in the second letter may be the result of the gravity of the problems and of news of the continued persecution of believers. As for the different eschatological expectations, we can observe the same kind of inconsistency in Jewish apocalyptic writings, where we read both that the end comes suddenly and that it is preceded by signs. In some of these writings it is difficult to tell whether the period of lawlessness is the initial stage of the end or a sign of the end.[11] Paul's basic point is that the end has not come because the first stage has not occurred. The appearance of "the man of lawlessness" is not a warning that the end *will* come, but a signal that it *is* here. The concept is not, strictly speaking, inconsistent with the idea that the day of the Lord comes without warning.

In addition, there are positive reasons for regarding 2 Thessalonians as a genuine letter by Paul. In the first place, it includes a reference to Paul's earlier visit to Thessalonica. In speaking of "the man of lawlessness," the author says, "Do you not remember that when I was still with you I told you this?" (2 Thess 2:5). It would be unbelievably daring for an imposter to make such a statement to people who were in a position to refute it. Second, there is a probable reference to fraudulent letters in 2:2. A person writing a fraudulent letter would not be likely to call attention to fraud. But the remark is natural from a person who had already been embarrassed by letters written over his signature by imposters. Finally, the letter is signed with the conscious intention to validate it as genuine (3:17). This would be a bold stroke indeed if the letter is not by Paul, but a natural one for a person who had had trouble before. Although there are difficulties, it seems probable that Paul did write 2 Thessalonians not long after he had written 1 Thessalonians.

The occasion for the letter, if genuine, is sufficiently clear: 1 Thessalonians had probably been sent by a messenger, who returned to Paul with

11 Cf., e. g., 2 Esdras 5:1–13.

additional information about the Christian community in that city. In this way Paul learned of continued persecution in the church and of the existence of extreme eschatological expectations. The latter troubled him. He may have felt partially responsible, because he had initially preached the return of the Lord and had dealt with eschatological matters in 1 Thess 4:13–5:11. It is also possible that some fraudulent letters had circulated in Thessalonica and had proclaimed that the end had arrived. Whatever be the cause, some Christians in Thessalonica were saying that the day of the Lord had already come. Some of those people had quit work as a result of their zealous belief, and they were drawing on the contributions of working Christians. Paul wrote 2 Thessalonians to correct those errors and to assure the readers that the day of the Lord had not yet come. He ordered that those who had quit work must not be fed (3:10). The gravity of those problems for Paul is displayed toward the end of the letter, where he advises that those who do not go back to work should be avoided (3:14–15).

Galatians

In our discussion of early Jewish Christianity, we found that the issue of admitting Gentiles into Christian fellowship was a serious problem in the early years. We saw that the question of the place of Jewish dietary regulations was one problem that stood in the way of the admission of Gentiles. In Paul's letter to the Galatians, we find that circumcision was also a serious issue and that the battles were vigorously fought.

The location of the letter to the Galatians within the general chronology of Paul's life is far from certain. We know that it was written after he had paid his second visit to Jerusalem, because he refers to both visits in the letter (Gal 1:18 and 2:1). A report of the second visit forms a significant part of this letter. This is the visit during which Paul and Barnabas met with Peter, James, and John in order to come to some agreement about the admission requirements for Gentiles. Obviously, Paul could not have written the letter to the Galatians before the meeting took place. Knox dates the visit in 51, and if he is correct, it is the earliest possible date for the writing of the letter.[12] It could, of course, have been written a few years later.

The churches to which the letter is addressed are in central Asia Minor, but doubt persists about their specific location. Before 25 BCE the term *Galatians* referred to people who lived in north-central Asia Minor. But after that date Augustus organized the Roman province of Galatia, which then included south-central Asia Minor as well—that is, the towns of Iconium, Lystra, and Derbe. According to Acts these towns were among those that Paul visited. The book of Acts does not include narratives about visits

[12] Cf. Knox, op. cit., p. 85.

to north-central Asia Minor, although 16:6 may refer to such a trip. We cannot be certain about the specific destination of this letter, because Paul includes only the general address: "To the churches of Galatia" (1:2). Whether he had traveled both in the North and South, or only to one region, we will probably never know.

This letter is extremely important because it contains so much autobiographical information. It is here that Paul acknowledges that he had earlier persecuted the church but had become an adherent of the Christian movement and had begun to consider himself as apostle to the Gentiles. He says that after his conversion to Christianity he went to Arabia and then to Damascus. He tells of his two trips to Jerusalem and says that they were separated by fourteen years. There is a great deal of interest in his description of the second visit (2:1–10) because of its similarities and differences with the narrative of Acts 15:1–29. It is almost certain that both passages describe the same event. The participants are the same—Paul, Barnabas, Peter, and James—and the issue is the same—admission requirements for Gentiles.[13] But there are differences. Acts has the visit as Paul's third visit to Jerusalem, and Galatians has it as the second. In Acts the result of the meeting is a decision to impose certain restrictions on Gentiles (Acts 15:20 and 29), but Galatians refers to none of these. According to Paul the only requirement was to "remember the poor" (Gal 2:10). Despite the differences it seems altogether probable that Acts and Galatians are presenting two accounts of the same incident, and we can be reasonably confident that the participants did, in fact, agree that circumcision was not to be a requirement for Gentile Christians.

The letter reflects a situation in which the issues of circumcision and perhaps dietary regulations were matters of harsh disagreement. There were probably personal attacks on Paul. In the letter he feels it necessary to defend himself, to affirm solemnly that he is telling the truth (1:20), and to claim that he is not trying to please anybody (1:10). He feels that he has become an enemy to the people to whom he had formerly preached (4:16), and he vigorously attacks his opponents (5:10). In view of the fact that the issue is circumcision, his words in 5:12 have an unusually harsh tone: "I wish those who unsettle you would mutilate themselves!" Clearly Galatians is a letter written in the midst of a controversy about which Paul felt very deeply.

The trouble probably dates back to the earliest days of the Galatian churches. Galatia must have been invaded by a number of Christian preachers, some of whom required the use of circumcision as a rite of initiation. They probably reasoned that, because it, along with baptism and sacrifice, was required for Jewish proselytes, it would necessarily be required for Gen-

---

[13] Paul mentions two persons who were not mentioned in Acts, Titus (Gal 2:1) and John (Gal 2:9).

tiles who believed in Jesus. But others, such as Paul, did not require it, and as converts of various missionary preachers mixed with each other, circumcision became a hotly debated issue. Eventually there was probably some confusion about Paul's position and that of the Jerusalem apostles, and some of Paul's own converts accepted circumcision.

Paul's purpose in writing the letter to the Galatians is to affirm that circumcision must not be required for Gentile Christians. He explains that he had not required it, and he shows that the Jerusalem apostles did not add it to his gospel. He claims that he was recognized as apostle to the Gentiles, just as Peter was apostle to the circumcised (Gal 1:8–9). He also deals briefly with the issue of dietary regulations and even shows that Peter and Barnabas were once in the wrong on this issue (2:11–21). But Paul does not stop with a formal solution to the problem. He attempts to show by argument and by scriptural interpretation that in Christ one is freed from Torah. He uses an allegorical interpretation of Genesis to show that Christians are sons of Abraham through his free-born wife rather than through his slave wife (4:21–31). Paul's fundamental position is altogether clear in this letter, but his general attitude toward Torah constitutes a problem to which we will reutrn later.

1 Corinthians

In writing to the Galatians, Paul said that he and the Jerusalem leaders had agreed to raise funds from Gentile Christians for the poor, presumably the poor Christians in Jerusalem (Gal 2:10). In his letters to Corinth and Rome, he shows that he is in the process of collecting this money. In 1 Cor 16:1–4 he gives detailed instructions on the collection and transmission of the funds. Each person is to make a contribution each Sunday that, on Paul's arrival in Corinth, will be sent to Jerusalem. Designated envoys will carry it, perhaps accompanying Paul, to Jerusalem. Paul's treatment of the details about the collection serves as an indication of the date of this letter, which can be placed after Galatians and before 2 Corinthians and dated in about 51–52.

Although the NT contains two letters from Paul to Corinth, this is not all he wrote to that city. We will see that 2 Corinthians probably consists of at least two letters. Moreover, Paul wrote at least one letter to Corinth before he wrote 1 Corinthians. In 1 Cor 5:9 he refers to a previous letter, but that one is now probably lost.[14] Paul probably received additional information about situations in Corinth after he had written this lost letter. He received this information from two sources: a letter from some of the Christian leaders in Corinth (7:1) and an oral report from the people of

---

[14] Some scholars identify 2 Cor 6:14–7:1 as a fragment of the letter referred to in 1 Cor 5:9.

Chloe (1:11).[15] The reports brought to Paul's attention a number of problems in the church, such as dissensions, problems of sexual morality and dietary regulations, perplexity about worship practices, the place of women, spiritual gifts, and the resurrection of Christians. To address these problems, Paul wrote 1 Corinthians from Ephesus and sent Timothy to deliver it to Corinth. At the end of the letter he mentions his plans. He intends to remain in Ephesus until Pentecost. After that he expects to go to Macedonia and then down to Corinth, where he plans to spend some significant period of time (16:5–9). As in 2 Thessalonians and Galatians, so here Paul adds some words in his own handwriting (16:21).

The nature of the problems at Corinth is complex. In reading 1 Corinthians and trying to reconstruct the situation that lies behind Paul's words, we gain the impression of a Christian community that is deeply divided on a number of ethical and cultic issues. There appear to be divisions about sexual issues. Some Christians are associating with prostitutes (1 Cor 6:15), and at least one man is sleeping with his stepmother (5:1). But other Christians seem to have advocated total celibacy and to have regarded both sex and marriage as immoral (7:1–40). There were divisions about certain dietary regulations, specifically about the question of eating food that had been sacrificed to idols—that is, to Gods other than the Jewish and Christian God (8:1–13 and 10:23–11:1). Some felt the practice of eating such food was harmless and, thus, optional; others were convinced that it was not permissible to eat it. There seem to have been divisions about the place of spiritual gifts in the church, especially that of the glossolalia, or speaking in tongues (chapters 12–14). Some apparently felt it was the major, if not the only, demonstration of one's receiving the spirit of God, but others were not so certain about its place and use. Excess must have characterized some of the services of worship, for Paul notes that their observance of the Lord's Supper sometimes ended in drunkenness (11:17–34). Although he does not specify the positions that each group took, Paul was clearly aware of the fact of division at Corinth. He names three and perhaps four groups, each designated by a name to which each subscribed. One of the major pieces of information Paul received from Chloe's people was that of internal quarrels. Paul says: "What I mean is that each one of you says, 'I belong to Paul,' or 'I belong to Apollos,' or 'I belong to Cephas,' or 'I belong to Christ'" (1:12). These names are probably party labels, but unfortunately it is not possible to connect the labels with particular positions. Nevertheless, we have enough information to draw a credible picture of the Christian community at Corinth at the time of this letter. It was a community that was deeply divided and consequently confused on a number of fundamental issues.

[15] The people of Chloe are otherwise unidentified, but the phrase suggests that they were her associates or agents, not members of her family.

The source of the difficulty probably is to be found in the earlier history of the Corinthian community. Like Galatia, Corinth probably had seen a number of itinerant Christian missionaries come and go. We know that Paul was one, and the letter shows that Apollos was another, and Peter probably a third.[16] Who established the "Christ" party is not known. It is likely that the early missionaries emphasized different things in their preaching and even presented quite different versions of the gospel. The foundational visits by several different missionaries probably issued in the establishment of various Christian groups in the city.

Several modern scholars believe that one of the groups in Corinth had been influenced by certain concepts that may be associated with Gnostic Christianity. Although Gnostic Christianity is generally regarded to be a second-century variety, there may well have been certain aspects of the movement that made their appearance at a much earlier date.[17] Willi Marxsen finds several characteristically Gnostic features in the Corinthian church, such as the esteem for knowledge, possession of the spirit, ethical freedom, and a denial of a future resurrection.[18] If this is the case, we have in 1 Corinthians a record of the first confrontation between Gnostic and Pauline Christianity.

Yet another factor may help to explain the situation in Corinth. It is likely that Paul himself had given different signals at different times. In a painstaking analysis of 1 Corinthians, John Hurd has attempted to reconstruct the main lines of Paul's initial preaching in Corinth, the lost letter, and the letter from the Corinthian Christians to Paul.[19] He suggests that Paul's original preaching had allowed for a good deal of ethical freedom, but that after he left Corinth, he found it necessary to reach an agreement with the Jerusalem apostles that involved more restriction than he would have liked (cf. Gal 2:1–10 and Acts 15:1–29). In the lost letter he attempted to communicate those restrictions, presenting them as his own. The Corinthians replied, expressing confusion over the new information and accusing Paul of inconsistency. Paul then wrote 1 Corinthians, in which he attempted to justify the restrictions and maintain his consistency.

All of these factors show that, for various reasons, the Christian community was divided and perplexed. Thus, the problem that Paul faced in writing 1 Corinthians was that of creating unity in a situation where none had previously existed. We should, therefore, not be surprised to find that he will attempt to occupy the middle ground in these arguments, partially agreeing with all sides. His main concern and stress in the letter are on the

---

[16] Cf. Acts 18:24–28 on Apollos.

[17] Cf. Chapter 11, "Gnostic Christianity."

[18] Cf. Willi Marxsen, *Introduction to the New Testament,* trans. by G. Buswell (Philadelphia: Fortress Press, 1968), pp. 74–76; Walter Schmithals, *Gnosticism in Corinth,* trans. by John E. Steely (Nashville, Tenn.: Abingdon, 1971).

[19] Cf. John C. Hurd, *The Origin of I Corinthians* (New York: Seabury, 1965).

unity of the church and the legitimate role that all members play. On the question of spiritual gifts, he says, "Now there are varieties of gifts, but the same Spirit; and there are varieties of service, but the same Lord" (1 Cor 12:4–5). He stresses the unity of the church in saying, "Now you are the body of Christ and individually members of it" (12:27).

Although Paul's concern for unity is the controlling factor in his response to the Corinthian situation, he gives serious attention to each of the problems that had been raised. 1 Corinthians is, therefore, an extremely valuable source of information about Paul's views on a wide variety of subjects. In our treatment of the character of Pauline Christianity later in this chapter, we will draw heavily on this letter.

2 Corinthians

The unity of 2 Corinthians has been seriously questioned by almost every writer on the subject. Although most scholars think that Paul wrote almost all of 2 Corinthians, they contend that it is made up of two or more letters, written at different times and probably now misarranged. One indication that we have here several misarranged letters is that there is confusion in regard to Paul's travel plans. At the end of 1 Corinthians he had said that he would not leave Ephesus for Corinth until after Pentecost (1 Cor 16:8). In 2 Cor 1:16 and 2:1 it is apparent that a planned trip has been canceled because Paul was sure that it would have increased animosity. But in 2 Cor 9:3–5 he speaks of coming to Corinth to receive the offering for Jerusalem. In 2 Cor 12:14 and 13:1 he speaks of a third visit to Corinth, during which he intends to deal severely with his opponents. The comment on the visit in 9:3–5 carries no note of hostility, whereas the animosity in 12:14 and 13:1 is plain. Another indication that we have more than one letter here is the tonal change within 2 Corinthians. Chapters 1–9 are, on the whole, conciliatory and seem to have been written after some serious controversy involving the personal relations between Paul and the Corinthians had been resolved. But chapters 10–13 seem to have been written during the midst of such a controversy. In these chapters Paul is contentious and altogether hostile.

A partial solution to these problems is to rearrange 2 Corinthians, so that chapters 10–13 come before chapters 1–9. In this way the hostile letter comes before the conciliatory letter. In fact, there may be a reference to 2 Cor 10–13 in 2 Cor 2:3–4, 9, and 7:8. Here Paul refers to a letter written with tears, which caused grief to the recipients. 2 Cor 10–13 surely seems to be that kind of letter. This rearrangement does not, however, resolve the difficulties with Paul's travel plans, so some scholars subdivide chapters 1–9 into several more letters. In any event, the probable date for the letters that now constitute 2 Corinthians is 52–53.

The problem around which 2 Cor 10–13 revolves is probably basically personal. Paul's defense here is almost altogether personal, and it indicates that he has been charged with being humble when present and bold when absent, with boasting, and with showing favoritism. He has been compared unfavorably with Jewish Christian apostles and has apparently been accused of not speaking in Christ. In writing this letter, probably from Ephesus, he threatens to come to Corinth for the third time and deal severely with his opponents. Apparently, the second visit, which Paul describes as painful (2:1), was the one that had been promised in 1 Cor 16:8. Paul also seems to allude, in 2 Cor 13:1, to a pending trial. He speaks of "passing the test" and seems to prepare for a trial by reminding the readers that "any charge must be sustained by the evidence of two or three witnesses" (13:1). This is an allusion to Deut 19:15, and it suggests that the Jewish Torah was accepted in Corinth for basic procedure in this trial. Unfortunately, Paul is vague on the charges to be examined, and we cannot even be certain that he is the one to be tried.

If 2 Cor 1–9 is a single letter, and that is by no means certain, it appears to have been written after Paul had received word about the Corinthian response to 2 Cor 10–13. That letter had been taken to Corinth by Titus. Some time later, when the two met again in Macedonia (2:13 and 7:5–6), Paul received news that most of the Corinthians were still zealous for him and wished to see him again. One of the leaders of the opposition to Paul had been censured by the community, and Paul found it necessary to ask them to forgive his former enemy (2:5–11). The chapters indicate that Paul had not yet made his third trip to Corinth, the one he threatened to make in 2 Cor 12:14 and 13:1. Nor does he plan such a trip in the immediate future. Rather, he will send Titus once more to receive the collection for the poor in Jerusalem (9:1–5). When that has been done, Paul will finally return to Corinth (9:5).

The personal character of these letters and the emotional feeling that Paul poured into them limit their usefulness to us, because they tell us so little about the related issues and circumstances. They do, however, show us Paul as a lively human being. He was a person whose presence brought about controversy, a person who did not shrink from a fight. He could express high emotion and deep fondness. He could sometimes be hostile and at other times conciliatory. He had a capacity for anger and love. He must have been the kind of person who could make lasting enemies and loyal friends.

Romans

The last Pauline letter to be related to the offering for the Jerusalem poor is the letter to the Romans.[20] It was probably written in 53–54. The occa-

---

[20] One ninth-century manuscript of this letter lacks the word *Rome* in 1:7 and 1:15, but this must be regarded as an error of omission, for all other manuscripts have Rome as the letter's

sion for the letter is stated in some detail in Rom 15:22–29. This passage indicates that Paul has for some time planned a trip to Rome and that now he expects to stop by there on the way to Spain. He must, however, first go to Jerusalem to deliver the offering, the collection of which is now complete. Then he will go to Rome.[21] The general background of the letter is sufficiently clear: Paul had been through serious controversies with the Corinthians, but they were settled amicably. He has fulfilled his obligation to Jerusalem, although he has some apprehension about his pending reception there (Rom 15:30–33). He has fulfilled his mission in the East, preaching "from Jerusalem and as far round as Illyricum" (15:19). He has looked forward to visiting Rome for many years and is now planning for wider areas of work, even in Spain (15:23, 24, and 28). It is in this relatively peaceful but expectant situation that Paul writes this letter to a church he has not previously visited.

At first glance, the purpose of the letter seems to be threefold: to establish relations with Christians in Rome, to acquaint them with his travel plans, and to ask for their help on the projected trip to Spain. But the letter does much more than meet those needs, for in it Paul gives a more complete and systematic statement of his theology than he does in any of his other letters. This was probably not necessary, and a much briefer note would have been sufficient, unless he had another purpose in mind. It has been suggested by some scholars that Paul was in such urgent need for travel funds that he felt it necessary to explain his thinking as fully as possible.[22] Other scholars feel that he wished to allay the kind of misunderstanding he had encountered in Galatia and Corinth.[23] Others believe that Paul was preoccupied with his pending return to Jerusalem, and still others suggest that he had heard of controversies within the Roman church and that he wrote

destination. Two other facts raise a question about the integrity of the letter. A doxology, which sounds like the conclusion, appears in different places in the various manuscripts. Most modern editions of Romans place the doxology at 16:25–27. Although some scholars feel that the variable position of the doxology means that the letter has been expanded by later copyists, it is equally possible that Paul wrote all sixteen chapters and that later copyists abbreviated it. A second problem revolves around the nature of chapter 16, which contains greetings to twenty-five persons and two families. This appears incredible in a letter addressed to a place where Paul is a stranger, and some scholars suggest that chapter 16 was originally addressed elsewhere (that is, Ephesus) and was attached to Romans by mistake. Nevertheless, it is not impossible that Paul knew this number of people in Rome. He certainly would wish to cite all his acquaintances there if he intended to establish good relations with the church. Cf. Harry Gamble, Jr., *The Textual History of the Letter to the Romans* (Grand Rapids, Mich.: Eerdmans, 1977).

[21] References in the Corinthian and Roman correspondence give a fairly complete account of the process of raising the money. The Corinthian correspondence (1 Cor 16:3; 2 Cor 8:6 and 9:1–5) indicates that Paul wished to culminate the collection in Corinth and carry it from there to Jerusalem. 2 Cor 9:1–5 implies that Paul is just about ready to come to Corinth for that purpose. Rom 15 reveals that the task of collecting has been completed.

[22] Cf. E. F. Scott, *Paul's Epistle to the Romans* (London: S.C.M. Press, 1947).

[23] Cf. John Knox, in *The Interpreter's Bible* (Nashville, Tenn.: Abingdon, 1951–1957), Vol. IX, pp. 358–363.

in order to aid their resolution.[24] However, it is most likely that the reason for the letter lies within Paul himself. He seems to be conscious of a turning point in his life. He has completed a number of things and now intends to begin work in a totally new region. He has preached his gospel in the East; now he expects to preach it in the West. This is indicated by the fact that in Romans he deals with a number of topics that he had already covered in other letters. He must have intended this letter to be a summary and restatement of his basic thinking and also an introduction to Pauline Christianity for the Christians at Rome.[25]

This letter will be our major source of information about Paul's views on Torah and its relevance for the Christian life. Although he had dealt vigorously with the matter of circumcision in Galatians, here in Romans he treats questions about the value of Torah as a whole. He writes about the dominance of sin over every human life, and he claims that God has dealt with the problem of sin through the death and resurrection of the Christ. He also includes three chapters (Rom 9-11) on the Jewish people and their relationship to Christianity. He is aware that, although some Jews responded positively to the Christian message, most did not. For Paul this fact opened the way for the mission to the Gentiles, which was largely successful. But Paul insists that God has not rejected the Jews (11:1), and he holds out the expectation that in the future they will be included among the believers (11:12 and 25-26). Paul also treats some problems that had been dealt with in other letters: the use of spiritual gifts, eating food offered to idols, and allegiance to the ruling powers. Although it covers some old territory, the letter to the Romans should be regarded as the most important of Paul's letters, for in it he deals with topics more systematically and with a cooler deliberation than he does elsewhere. It probably represents Pauline Christianity at its best; we will draw on it extensively in the latter part of this chapter.

Colossians, Philemon, and Philippians

Three letters of Paul were written while he was in prison: Colossians, Philemon, and Philippians. Our knowledge of his life is not full enough to allow us to specify the number, duration, dates, or locations of those imprisonments. He speaks of them in the plural without giving locations (2 Cor 6:5 and 11:23). The book of Acts describes imprisonments in Jerusalem, Caesarea, and Rome (Acts 21:27-28:31). But many scholars feel that Paul himself referred to an imprisonment in Ephesus (1 Cor 15:32). Because the material does not present a clear or precise picture of the impris-

---

[24] Cf. Lake, op. cit., pp. 379-418.
[25] Cf. Günther Bornkamm, "The Letter to the Romans as Paul's Last Will and Testament," *Australian Biblical Review,* 11:2-14 (1963).

onments, we must be content to say only that these three letters were written from prison but that the locations and dates are unknown.

Colossians and Philemon were probably written at about the same time. Both letters were sent jointly by Paul and Timothy. Some of the people who are said to be with Paul when he wrote Colossians are also mentioned in Philemon—Aristarchus, Mark, Epaphras, Luke, and Demas (Col 4:10–14 and Phlm 23–24).

Substantial doubt persists among scholars about the authorship of Colossians. There are some unusual expressions in the letter, the style is unusual when compared with the other Pauline letters, and some of the concepts are arguably un-Pauline. In terms of style and ideology, there is a relationship between Colossians and Ephesians, which was almost certainly not written by Paul. But most modern scholars accept Colossians as a genuine letter of Paul, while recognizing that its genuineness is not so firmly established as that of the letters we have previously examined. Perhaps it is best to say that doubts about the authenticity of Colossians have not been convincing.

Colossae was a town about 160 kilometers west of Ephesus. The church there had been founded by a man named Epaphras. Paul himself had not been there, but he mentions two people at nearby Laodicea who know him—Nympha (4:15) and Archippus (4:17). He also refers to a letter from Laodicea and directs that the Christians in the two towns exchange letters (4:16).

The precise situation that lies behind the letter to the Colossians is obscure, but there are signs of controversy within the community. Perhaps some itinerant Christian missionaries had visited the area and had taught some doctrines that were strange to Paul. He makes reference, for example, to self-abasement, angel worship (2:18), and possibly worship of cosmic forces (1:8 and 2:15). However, other teachings would not have been unfamiliar to Paul. The missionaries must have taught that Christians must adhere to Jewish dietary regulations, the Jewish calendar (2:16), circumcision (2:11), and other aspects of the Torah (2:21). In most respects these are familiar opponents, similar to those Paul had attacked in Galatians. In other respects, however, their teachings bear resemblances to Gnostic Christian views that we find in the second century. It is possible that the itinerant missionaries were also teaching a kind of Christology that Paul found offensive, because that topic is stressed in Colossians. Paul's major Christological assertion here is that in Christ "the whole fulness of deity dwells bodily" (2:9). Christ is described as "the firstborn of all creation" (1:15). We will return to these passages in our examination of Pauline Christology.

Philemon is actually addressed to three people—Philemon, Apphia, and Archippus—and to a church that meets in the house of one of them. In Colossians Paul had mentioned some correspondence with Laodicea, and, although no precise destination is given in the letter to Philemon, it is plausible to think that it was sent to Laodicea. Archippus, for example, seems to be associated with Laodicea in Col 4:16.

The letter to Philemon is mainly concerned with the fate of a slave named Onesimus, who had been with Paul during his imprisonment, and who was mentioned in Col 4:9. Although Paul seems inclined to keep Onesimus with him and hints that he would like to have him returned, he sends him back to his owner—that is, either Philemon, Apphia, or Archippus—and promises to pay anything the slave might owe. It is probable that Onesimus had left Laodicea without permission, for Paul appeals to the master that he be taken back and treated with kindness. The question of his freedom is not raised.

The letter to the Philippians was probably originally composed as three letters, all sent from Paul while he was in prison. In the letter as it stands, there are abrupt changes of topic and tone and some confusing statements about Paul's associate Epaphroditus. The complete story of the three letters to Philippi goes something like this: After Paul's imprisonment he received a gift from the Christians in Philippi, delivered by one Epaphroditus. Paul sent a note of thanks for it, namely Phil 4:10–23. Later on, Epaphroditus, who remained with Paul, fell ill, and when word about his sickness reached Philippi, there was grave concern. Paul heard about their concern but also about some opposition to him at Philippi, and he wrote Philippians 1–2. He later sent Timothy, who wrote back about further difficulties, and Paul responded with Phil 3:1–4:9 to try to deal with those problems. There is no indication in any of the letters of Paul's precise location at the times of writing.

In Philippians 1–2, the second letter, Paul seems unsure about his future prospects. On the one hand he hopes to be released from prison, but on the other hand he expresses a willingness to die. Indeed, he expresses a preference for death: "My desire is to depart and be with Christ, for that is far better" (1:23). He says this despite a recognition that there is work remaining for him to do, so he concludes:

> But to remain in the flesh is more necessary on your account. Convinced of this, I know that I shall remain and continue with you all, for your progress and joy in the faith, so that in me you may have ample cause to glory in Christ Jesus, because of my coming to you again (Phil 1:24–26).

A dominant theme in Philippians 1–2 is humility: "Do nothing from selfishness or conceit, but in humility count others better than yourselves" (2:3). Paul finds the compelling model for humility in Jesus himself, who emptied himself of divine status and took the form of a servant. "And being found in human form he humbled himself and became obedient unto death, even death on a cross" (2:8). Although this material occurs in the context of advice about humility, it is thought that Phil 2:6–11 was an early Christian hymn that Paul appropriately quoted. The passage is also important for a study of Pauline Christology.

There is a more hostile tone in Phil 3:1–4:9, the third letter, than in chapters 1–2. Undoubtedly Paul is here attacking some who have opposed his message. Apparently itinerant missionaries have appeared in Philippi as they had in Galatia and Corinth. However, Paul's attacks do not give us a clear picture of the opponents' beliefs. Seemingly they require circumcision, but they also possess certain characteristics that we find in later Gnostic Christianity.

Phil 3:1–4:9 is exceptionally valuable to us because it contains an auto-biographical section. In 3:4–7 Paul describes himself as a Pharisaic Jew, who had been circumcised, who had been blameless under the law, and who had persecuted Christians. He cites his Jewishness as a possible source of pride, but he considers it worthless when compared with "the surpassing worth of knowing Christ Jesus my Lord" (3:8).

As we have seen in the preceding analyses, there is substantial uncertainty about the genuineness of two letters that are usually attributed to Paul—2 Thessalonians and Colossians. There is also doubt about the integrity of 2 Corinthians and Philippians. Moreover, the dates of all the letters are uncertain. Nevertheless, with the exception of the so-called prison letters—Colossians, Philemon, and Philippians—we can be reasonably certain about the order in which the letters were written. Although caution should be exercised in associating a particular document with a precise date, we can arrange the letters in sequence and group them in two periods, as follows:

A. In the period 40–51
   1 Thessalonians
   2 Thessalonians

B. In the period 51–54
   Galatians
   1 Corinthians
   2 Corinthians 10–13
   2 Corinthians 1–9
   Romans

The letters from prison almost certainly belong in the period 51–54 or later, but it is not possible to fit them precisely into the sequence here.

THE CHARACTER OF
PAULINE CHRISTIANITY

We turn now from the analysis of the individual letters to a study of the major elements in Paul's theology. His letters show that he was aware of various forms of the Christian message. In his own proclamation he shared some convictions with early Jewish Christians, and he displayed a need to conform to tradition whenever he could. However, he was motivated by concerns that led him to depart from tradition in significant ways. The most notable departure was in his attitude toward the Torah and its place in the Christian life, and we will examine that topic in some detail. Three foundational concepts seem to affect Paul's thought: monotheism, universalism, and grace. Monotheism was itself a fundamental Jewish conviction, and Paul never questioned it. Nor did he question the belief that the Christian message was intended for all persons. Because there is one God, there is one Christ and one gospel, and the gospel has universal applicability. With Paul the distinctive barriers between Jew and Gentile, between slave and free, and between man and woman are, for the most part, ignored. At heart Paul is a monotheistic universalist. The third basis of his thought is the concept of grace, which focuses attention on the part God plays in human salvation and virtually ignores the human part. People are never pictured as deserving good treatment from God, for they are never in a position to deserve anything but condemnation. God's good action, therefore, is a gift, a gracious act, a totally undeserved way of treating human beings. With these basic concepts in mind, we will now examine Paul's thought on several interrelated topics: eschatology, the Torah, ethics, Christology, and the church.

Eschatology

Paul shared with early Jewish Christians a basic eschatological conviction. The implications of such a conviction are frequently treated in his letters. Moreover, in some of the letters eschatological conviction has a dominating force, whereas in others it moves to the background.

In the Thessalonian correspondence Paul's expression is vivid, and he expects to live until the end. In 1 Thessalonians, he attempts to answer a question about the death of Christians. The question is not literally preserved in Paul's letter, but it can be reconstructed as follows: "Although you have promised that we will be present when Jesus returns, some among us have died. What happens to these people?" The question itself demonstrates the dominating force of Paul's eschatological thought. When he first preached in Thessalonica, he must have felt so strongly about the end that it never occurred to him that death might come to some of his converts. Nor would he have provided them with teaching that might have prepared them to accept death. Eschatological hope was surely stressed in Paul's previous preaching in Thessalonica. But when some, or even one, among the converts died, a serious question arose, and Paul answered it in 1 Thessalonians and in some detail. He said that Christians will be raised from the dead because Jesus was. We who are still alive when Jesus returns will join the resurrected Christians preparatory to meeting the Lord in the air. The resurrection will occur at the end and is limited to Christians. Paul gives no specific date for the resurrection or for the return of the Lord. It comes, he says, "like a thief in the night" (1 Thess 5:2), and the Christian must always be prepared. There is no hint of a long delay; Paul confidently proclaims its imminence and assumes that it will occur in his own lifetime. It is notable, however, that he probably had not expected even a brief delay until the question about the dead came to his attention.

In 2 Thessalonians Paul finds it necessary to put a damper on some overly enthusiastic people who believe that the end has already arrived. It appears that fraudulent letters have come to Thessalonica announcing the dawning of the day of the Lord. The letters were probably accepted at face value by some in the community. In 2 Thessalonians Paul says that the day of the Lord cannot have come because its initial signs have not yet occurred. Before the final day arrives there must be a rebellion and a revelation of Christ's enemy, the "man of lawlessness." These events cannot yet occur, because something is restraining the lawless one, although his secret power is already at work and is soon to be revealed. Although this line of thought is not totally inconsistent with that in 1 Thessalonians, it represents a variation in Paul's thought. Now some events must occur before the Lord returns, events that had not been mentioned in 1 Thessalonians. Paul does, however, assure the people in Thessalonica that he is telling them nothing new. Moreover, his own hope is still vivid, and he expects to be alive at the end.

A more detailed description of the events of the last day is included in 1 Cor 15. There Paul describes the transformation that will occur for all Christians, living and dead. When the last trumpet sounds, the living will be changed within the twinkling of an eye. The mortal body will become an immortal, imperishable one. At the same time, the Christian dead will be raised in spiritual bodies. This new resurrection body is unique—imperishable, glorified, and powerful. To Paul it was perfectly obvious that a person should have a spiritual body at the resurrection, for he could point to all sorts of bodies, each one appropriate to some creature—beast, bird, fish, sun, moon, star. By *spiritual body*, he does not mean an invisible, incorporeal soul, but a human form that is not subject to change, corruption, illness, or death. Paul does not speak of immortality in the Platonic or Stoic sense—that is, he does not suppose that each of us has an undying, invisible, immaterial element, such as a soul. Neither did he think of the resurrection of the same body that died. His thought is somewhere between. There is continuity between the dying one and the rising one, but not identity. There is resurrection in a body, but it is a spiritual body. Although this is a more detailed statement than the one in 1 Thessalonians, it is consistent with the eschatological concept that we find there. There is no suggestion of postponement, and Paul still expects to be alive at the end.

Elsewhere in 1 Corinthians Paul makes certain suggestions about sex and marriage in the light of the impending end. He says that the status quo should be maintained because the time is so short. Unmarried people should remain celibate, and married people should not seek to get divorces (1 Cor 7:26–29). These ethical pronouncements depend on a firm conviction about the ending of things in the near future.

In all of these letters—1, 2 Thessalonians, and 1 Corinthians—Paul's eschatological expectation plays a significant role, dominating his thought in the first two letters. In other places, however, it is not so prominent. In Philippians he expresses a doubt about staying alive until the end, and he says that he prefers to die and be with Christ (Phil 1:23). This expression seems peculiar when we compare it with what he had said in the other letters. In Philippians death is not something to be overcome by a general resurrection at the time of the Lord's coming. It is rather a means by which one may instantly go to Christ. In other places Paul implies a realized eschatology—that is, a termination that has already occurred. In 2 Cor 3:18 he says that believers are already transfigured into the Lord's likeness. In 2 Cor 5:17 he says, "Therefore, if any one is in Christ, he is a new creation; the old has passed away, behold, the new has come." In Romans, although he still regards the resurrection as future, Paul feels that the Christian has begun to embark on a new life in the spirit. He has been united with Christ in baptism and can expect to be raised as he was (Rom 6:1–11). Meanwhile he lives in the spirit, dead to sin and law. In Col 3:1–4 Paul seems to take one more step. He there maintains that the Christian has been raised to live with Christ but that his life is now hidden. It will be made visible when Christ himself returns.

Although no precision is possible on the dates of Paul's letters, the distinction in eschatological thought generally conforms to that between the earlier and the later letters. Thus, in his earlier letters, especially 1, 2 Thessalonians, he identified the resurrection of the dead and the transformation of the living with the future day of the Lord. He expected that event within his own lifetime. In some of the later letters he expressed doubt about his endurance, de-emphasized the future general resurrection, and spoke of a transformation at baptism. The day of the Lord seems to be a good deal farther off and less important than it did in the earlier letters. As time wore on, Paul played down eschatological hope, probabably because he recognized that the day had not come as soon as he had expected.

The Torah

In our examination of early Jewish Christianity, we saw that certain aspects of Torah observance had come to be problematical in the first decades of Christian history. In particular, the observance of dietary regulations and circumcision inhibited and probably delayed the admission of Gentiles into Christian fellowship. Paul clearly recognized the impact of those matters not only in regard to social intercourse between Jews and Gentiles, but also in regard to the theological meaning of Torah itself. In his treatment of those problems, Paul made his most distinctive contribution. Thus, the treatment of Torah lies at the heart of Pauline Christianity.

Paul's letter to the Galatians exhibits the vigor and passion with which he could deal with problems of Torah observance. He wrote that letter because some Christians had been demanding that his converts in Asia Minor become circumcised. It also looks as if some significant group had challenged Paul's position as an apostle. In the very salutation of the letter, he launches into a vigorous defense of his apostleship: "Paul an apostle—not from men nor through man, but through Jesus Christ and God the Father, who raised him from the dead" (Gal 1:1). He then accuses his converts of turning away from the gospel. His language is so vehement in the opening of the letter that we suspect that he is reacting to some personal charges. It also appears that Paul had been accused of being overly dependent on the Jerusalem apostles. He takes special pains to outline in detail his relations with this group—namely, with James, Peter, and John. The central event in his relationship with them occurred in a meeting held in Jerusalem. At the meeting certain people (Paul calls them false brethren) insisted that all Christians must be circumcised. Paul and Barnabas opposed this group and introduced an uncircumcised Greek convert, Titus, as a test case. In his own account Paul carried the day: the "pillars" authenticated his apostleship to the Gentiles and agreed "that we should go to the Gentiles and they to the circumcised" (Gal 2:9).

Because Paul wrote his letters in Greek, he did not use the Hebrew word *Torah*. To express the concept of Torah, he, along with other Hellenistic Jews, used the Greek word *nomos*. Nomos is not an exact equivalent, however, for it basically means standard, principle, custom, system, or law. We usually translate it as law, but we should remember that the chief meaning of Torah is the revealed teaching of God. In most of the places where Paul uses nomos, he is really speaking of the Mosaic Torah, or God's Torah, as contained in the Hebrew scriptures. Thus, we are permitted to think of Torah in most of the Pauline passages in which we find the Greek word *nomos* or the English word *law*.

In most passages Paul speaks very positively about Torah: "So the law is holy, and the commandment is holy and just and good" (Rom 7:12). But in some cases he speaks of it in a highly pejorative way: "For all who rely on works of the law are under a curse" (Gal 3:10). The difference seems to depend on the various ways in which Paul thinks of Torah, or on the various relationships in which Torah stands. There are four relationships: Torah and God, Torah and Sin, Torah and humanity, and Torah and Christ. We will examine each of these in some depth.

TORAH AND GOD

In its relationship to God Torah is good. Paul is convinced that God gave Torah, which is embodied in scripture, as his authentic demand and that he intended it to lead to righteousness and life. The revelation of Torah is a gracious act on God's part, and it defines what God wills and what he opposes. Its authority is unquestioned. The point is simple enough: God gave the Torah, and he expected us to follow it. Paul's understanding of the intention of God is clearly expressed in Rom 2:13: "For it is not the hearers of the law who are righteous before God, but the doers of the law who will be justified."

But Paul makes it clear that there are some things that God never intended, even if they seem to be commanded in scripture. These are called works of law. The phrase is subject to various interpretations but probably is meant to refer specifically to those acts that signify the conditions of Jewish existence. The works of law are primarily circumcision, dietary regulations, and the observance of the holy days. Paul is able to separate them from God's Torah. To him they are opposed to the divine will, because they are marks of exclusivism. They are ethnic practices that may cause Jews to feel they have a relationship with God that is superior to that of other people. But the idea of a special relationship is intolerable for Paul, partly because he believes a new age has been inaugurated with Christ and partly because he is motivated by basic concepts of monotheism and universalism. To Paul, God is God of both Jews and Gentiles, so marks of exclusivism cannot be in accord with his will. Those works of law are not to be generalized, as if Paul were condemning all so-called good works. He, in fact, speaks positively about good works, but negatively about those particular works that distinguish the Jew. He is quite clear on this point: "By works of the law shall no one be justified" (Gal 2:16). "For all who rely on works of the law are under a curse" (Gal 3:10). Paul takes pains to show that the scriptures do not mandate the observance of circumcision as a requirement for justification. In Rom 4 he shows that Abraham, the ancestor of all the Hebrew people, was accepted by God even though he had not yet been circumcised. According to Paul's interpretation of Genesis, circumcision came later as a seal of God's acceptance of Abraham, not as a condition for it. In summary, God gave Torah, which is holy and good, but circumcision, dietary regulations, and the calendar form no part of the divine will.

TORAH AND SIN

To understand the relationship of Torah and Sin, we must first comprehend Paul's use of the word *Sin*. He seems to think of it on two levels. On one level it is an entity that stands outside the empirical world and dominates human beings. Paul does not personalize the concept, so it would be improper to think of a devil. Nevertheless, it is, in our terms, a mythological power that we may designate as Sin—that is, with a capital letter. All people stand under the power of Sin. Paul speaks of Sin reigning and having dominion; he thinks of being in slavery to Sin and being freed from Sin. Sin works all kinds of desire in people; it dies and rises again; it deceives and kills and causes us to produce what we do not intend. It is allied with death, so that its slave inevitably dies. On the other level, Paul thinks of sin (lower case) as disobedience or transgression, a human act made necessary by the domination of Sin. Sin controls human beings, so all are sinners who have fallen short of God's intention (cf. Rom 3:23).

Torah enters this picture in an unexpected way. It has been established that God gave Torah as his authentic will. It, therefore, is a definition of those acts that God requires and those that he forbids. It is the definition of disobedience or sin. Except in the case of works of law, Paul does not question Torah's accuracy and dependability as a measure of sin. It comes from God, and it is absolutely correct. But because it defines sin, it actually comes under the control of Sin. It comes to us not simply as definer of sin but as agent of Sin. As a result, we are able to say, "I would not have known Sin if it had not been for Torah" (cf. Rom 7:7). This good Torah has been used by the demonic power to effect the reign of Sin in the world, and the evidence is that we disobey Torah when we hear it. This does not mean that we begin to commit forbidden acts only when we hear the Torah or that it would not have occurred to us to disobey if we had not heard the command. For example, Torah says that a man is not to desire his neighbor's wife. However, a man can in fact desire his neighbor's wife whether or not he has heard the commandment. Without the commandment he has no way to evaluate himself. He has a kind of ignorant innocence. With Torah, however, he is able to evaluate himself, and he can only evaluate himself as sinner—that is, as under the power of Sin—because he still desires his neighbor's wife. Torah has brought about the knowledge of Sin but has not diminished its power. Although God intended Torah to produce righteousness and life, it does not do so because this world is dominated by Sin. Even God's Torah is subject to be used by Sin.

TORAH AND HUMANITY

According to Paul, human beings attempt to exist in a situation in which they are dominated by Sin. Paul does not hesitate to cite the evidence for this situation. He finds it in disobedience to Torah as well as in reliance on circumcision. The Gentile disobeys the common rules that all human beings acknowledge. The Jew is, if anything, more guilty, because he boasts in his status and produces a pseudorighteousness by misunderstanding Torah, as if it included works of law. It is clear that in this situation Torah is no real help. It is God's measure of humanity, and when it measures it finds all to be controlled by Sin. In a profound passage in Rom 7:7–8:4, Paul explores the meaning of existence under Torah. He finds that there is a deep rift between one's intention to live under Torah and the result of that intention. Although the passage is written in the first person, it is not simply an autobiographical passage, but one that seems intended to express the plight of any person who faces Torah. Imagine that any person is speaking in these words, although Paul chose to use personal language: "I discover that I do not produce what I intend to produce. I intend life, but death results, because I am dominated by Sin and my actions are not my own. In this relationship, Torah designates an existential situation which is without hope. Torah produces the wrath of God upon me. It does so invariably and unavoidably, because it demands that I be righteous, although I am flesh—that is, under the domination of Sin. I, therefore, find myself trapped. I cannot escape the trap by saying that Torah is invalid or somehow inadequate or by denying my guilt. The trap is inescapable, and Torah always brings with it God's condemnation. God really speaks in his Torah, but when he speaks he says, 'You are a sinner, and you must die.' I can only respond, who will deliver me from this body of death?"

TORAH AND CHRIST

Existence in Christ is an alternative to attempted existence under the domination of Sin. Life in Christ is marked by righteousness, guiltlessness, and freedom from Sin. Paul sometimes presents Torah and Christ in opposition to each other, but in most cases he affirms a profound harmony between them. In what is probably his fundamental statement on the whole issue, he presents Christ as the end of Torah (Rom 10:4). Here *end* has eschatological connotations and suggests the possibility of a new mode of existence that was inaugurated by Christ. But it also means fulfillment—that is, Christ is the fulfillment of Torah. As Torah was God's first word, Christ is his second, but the second fulfills the first and was implicit in it. In Christ God presents the ultimate meaning of Torah, for Christ is what Torah was all about. It was possible, thus, to understand it before the appearance of Jesus, but it is in the death of Jesus that the meaning becomes explicit.

Here we have arrived at perhaps the most difficult point in Pauline Christianity. How can the death of the Christ be the fulfillment of Torah? We cannot get at this without entering into the mythological world that Paul took for granted. Sin dominates humanity, controls God's Torah, and leads inexorably to death. Jesus, who is not dominated by Sin, nevertheless, is condemned and dies. But at this point God intervenes and raises him from the dead. This act breaks the power of Sin, for death is not the ultimate fate of Jesus the Christ. Although he is condemned, his condemnation is ineffective. Sin now is powerless, for without the threat of death it is empty. Torah now can have its intended result; it can produce life, not because a person lives under Torah, but because he or she lives in Christ. In the death and resurrection of Jesus the Christ, God has not condemned human beings, as he did under Torah; instead he has condemned Sin. Sin is dead, and we can live.

Paul uses a number of terms to express this new relationship, among them justification, reconciliation, and redemption. These terms point to the same thing but are intended to illuminate the situation by different analogies. Justification is a legal term that refers to a verdict of not guilty. Reconciliation stands for the restoration of a broken friendship. Redemption means the recovery of lost property, animate or inanimate. The situation for believers can be described by any of the three terms: a guilty person is pronounced not guilty; friends have become reconciled; the alienated have been recovered. In all the terms the emphasis is on the gracious act of God, never on the merits of the human subjects. Paul's fundamental concept of God's grace is at work in his use of these words.

Of the four relationships, that between Torah and Christ is the most important for Paul, for it represents the solution to the human problem. The relationship to God expresses God's intention that is unrealized in Torah. The relationship to Sin and to humanity turns out to be temporary. The relationship to Christ is the ultimate and permanent one, the final act of God in his defeat of Sin. Christ is, therefore, both the termination of ineffective Torah and the fulfillment of God's intention in Torah. The news that Paul felt required to proclaim was that God has now made available a new life in Christ, one that is not bound by Torah observance but nevertheless fulfills it.

Ethics

The ethical implications of Paul's semimythological analysis of Torah are not easy to see. His conviction centers in the belief that a situational change has taken place. The new situation means that we can live in Christ. Anyone who does not recognize the new possibility is doomed to exist under the domination of Sin and death. In the new situation, however, we can live in faith. The content of faith can be interpreted mythologically, as belief that God has defeated Sin, or existentially, as our understanding of the self as free of guilt. There is no sense in which human effort carries weight in this system, but we must make a choice between living under Sin and living in Christ. One who lives in Christ lives in faith and in the spirit. The spirit is the representative of the Lord to the Christian, and it functions as an ethical guide both for the community and for the individual Christian. Under its leadership believers work out the meaning of freedom from Sin as they live out their lives.

Pauline Christianity is, therefore, characterized by a rarity of hard and fast ethical rules. The specifically required duties are those that express love to the brothers and helpfulness to the group. Nevertheless, Paul can be quite clear that leadership by the spirit produces a certain style of life that we may call eschatological life. This is a life marked by "love, joy, peace, patience, kindness, goodness, faithfulness, gentleness, self-control" (Gal 5:22 – 23). Similarly, Paul does not hesitate to list the acts and qualities that do not belong to the eschatological life: "fornication, impurity, licentiousness, idolatry, sorcery, enmity, strife, jealousy, anger, selfishness, dissension, party spirit, envy, drunkenness, carousing, and the like" (Gal 5:19–21).[26] For the most part, the separate items are drawn from traditional Hellenistic and Jewish lists of commonly acknowledged virtues and vices. Paul intends to provide a representation of required and restricted matters, not an exhaustive list of duties and prohibitions. The virtues are typical of the behavior that characterizes eschatological life.

On a few points Paul cannot escape from giving specific ethical advice. In fact, it appears that when he wrote 1 Corinthians several acute problems were developing. We have already observed that a good deal of perplexity formed the background for this letter. Paul's converts in Corinth were seriously confused on a number of points. One problem that came to the surface was that of meat offered to idols.[27] The background of the problem lies in the widespread Hellenistic practice of making previously sacrificed meat available for ritualistic meals in a temple and for purchase on the open market. Consumption of such food by Jews was forbidden in the Mishnah, but avoidance of it had probably been observed for a long time before 200 CE.[28] The principle would be that consuming this food brought one into contact with idolatry. We should also remember that, according to Acts, the apostles had included the eating of meat offered to idols among the things prohibited to Gentile Christians (Acts 15:29). If there actually were such a prohibition for Christians, or if there were Jewish Christians at Corinth, we can understand that there would have been serious objections to eating the food. Whatever may have been the cause, the Corinthians were confused on this issue, and they presented the problem to Paul. Some argued that because there is only one real God, the question of eating sacrificed meat is irrelevant and that Christians should be free to eat it if they wish. Others, however, were not so sure.

Paul approached the problem of sacrificed meat by agreeing with those who said that there is but one God. If this is the case, it follows that meat offered to a so-called God is in no way different from other meat. A false God can neither sanctify nor pollute anything. But Paul goes on to say that the Christian's actions must be governed by the recognition that some are unsure. Although Paul disagrees with those who oppose eating sacrificed meat, he shows amazing respect for them. He calls them weak, but he requires the strong Christians to respect their weakness. His counsel is that strong Christians should forgo their right to eat meat if their eating causes the moral downfall of a weaker brother. Although this advice appears to move in the direction of regulation, upon closer examination it turns out to be an application of the basic Christian ethic, love of the brothers. Eating

[26] Similar lists are found in Rom 1:29–31, 1 Cor 5:11, and 6:9–10.
[27] Cf. 1 Cor 8:1–13 and 10:23–11:1. Cf. also Rom 14:13–23.
[28] Cf. Mishnah, *Abodah Zara* 2:3.

sacrificed meat is, in Pauline Christianity, not strictly forbidden. Rather, the Christian is called on to avoid contempt for the weak and to have consideration for those with whom one disagrees.

In Corinth there were also some problems of relations between the sexes.[29] Paul had heard reports of promiscuous sexual activity among the believers in Corinth, but he also knew that some Christians there stood opposed to sex and to marriage.

In dealing with sexual questions, Paul initially agreed that "it is well for a man not to touch a woman" (1 Cor 7:1). He also agreed that, if a man has made a compact with a virgin and intends to preserve her in that state, he does well (1 Cor 7:37). But, says Paul, if this man finds that he cannot restrain himself, he does no wrong in getting married and engaging in sex. Marriage is a permissible means of avoiding immorality, and in a strictly monogamous marriage sex has its proper place. In this relationship a man's body belongs to his wife and his wife's to him. Except for periods of abstinence mutually agreed on for the purpose of praying, a husband and wife should not deny each other their sexual rights. On the relative value of celibacy and marriage, Paul clearly prefers the former. At one point he expresses a desire that everyone should follow his own example and remain unmarried. He knows, however, that this is impossible, and he is cautious to avoid downgrading the marital state. Some persons do not have the gift of celibacy, and they do not disobey God if they marry. Paul has only one substantively negative objection to marriage, and that is a practical one. The married man is forced by his position into a concern for worldly things, because he must devote himself to the wife. The unmarried man is able to devote himself completely to God, but the husband finds his loyalty divided. In spite of his preference for celibacy and his objection to marriage, Paul feels that the institution must be protected. Marriage is not dissoluble by divorce except in the case of a Christian's marriage to a non-Christian, and only then if the latter finds the situation intolerable. In one respect, Paul's treatment here is similar to that of the sacrificed meat. He is able to express and defend his point of view, but in the end he shows no disrespect for persons he regards as weak.

When he dealt with sacrificed meat, Paul based his argument partly on his monotheism. But what is the basis for his preference for celibacy? It is difficult to find anything in Judaism that would account for it, and his statements about divided loyalty sound too much like attempted rationalizations. It is probable that we have here a matter of personal attitude rather than profound theological or ethical thought. His preference for celibacy has affected Pauline Christianity profoundly, but it does not depend on deep religious or ethical convictions. At one point, however, Paul's theological views are clear. His eschatological convictions led him to say that the status quo

[29] Cf. 1 Cor 7:1–40.

should be maintained: the unmarried should remain unmarried, and the married should remain married; because the time is so short, we should not make a big issue out of the matter of marriage and celibacy. The latter is preferable, but neither is wrong. More than likely, Paul's eschatological expectation also led him into a generally conservative attitude on social issues. In the letter to Philemon, he did not question the institution of slavery. In Rom 13:1–7 he expressed only a positive appreciation for political governments. Because he felt the time was short, he gave no serious attention to reforming the structures of human society.

In 1 Corinthians Paul wrote an exalted analysis of the core of his ethics. In other places he said that the whole Torah is summed up in the maxim: "You shall love your neighbor as yourself" (Rom 13:9).[30] In 1 Cor 13, he wrote about the meaning of this love. The chapter is frequently interpreted in isolation, but it can be properly understood only in context. In chapter 12 Paul introduces certain questions about spiritual gifts. He and his converts believe that the spirit let its presence be known in the community by granting certain abilities, many of them ecstatic. So Paul discusses the gifts in the light of their benefit to the community. He seems to be aware of two problems. The first is that of distinguishing between the spirits—that is, testing them. This must have been an acute problem in a community that tried to rely on spiritual guidance for its ethical life. How do people know if the gifts they have received are those from God's spirit or from some other? Or, what attitude can one take toward the spiritual claims of someone else? It would seem easy for anyone to claim the backing of the spirit for any position that might be taken. Paul lays down two principles for testing: one who lays a curse on Jesus is not led by the spirit, and one who says that Jesus is Lord is. Our sophisticated age may find these tests inadequate, for they appear to ignore the possibility of dishonesty. But Paul would take it for granted that a person's curse or confession is dictated by a spirit and that only the spirit of the one God can cause a person to confess Jesus as Lord.

The second problem about spiritual gifts is that they bring about dissension. Because the gifts come in a variety of forms, it is possible to compare them. Recipients of various kinds of gifts can claim positions of authority on the basis of them. In order to solve this problem, Paul does three things. First, he asserts that the community needs all of the spiritual gifts. Just as the human body needs hands, feet, and head and cannot function without a harmonious cooperation of all parts, just so the church needs all the spiritual gifts. Second, Paul lays down a list of gifts, ranked in order of importance, and he encourages the readers to seek the higher gifts. He says, "And God has appointed in the church first apostles, second prophets, third teachers, then workers of miracles, then healers, helpers, administrators,

---

[30] Cf. Gal 5:14.

speakers in various kinds of tongues" (1 Cor 12:28). Third, Paul commends to them "a still more excellent way" (1 Cor 12:31).

In 1 Cor 13 Paul presents love as the "still more excellent way," and he contrasts love to the spiritual gifts. Although a person may speak ecstatically "in the tongues of men and of angels" (1 Cor 13:1), without love he or she produces only meaningless sounds. One may have the gift of prophecy or faith, but without love he is nothing. Even acts of self-sacrifice are meaningless without love. The trouble with the gift of prophecy is that it is partial and will evaporate with the appearance of ultimate truth. Prophecy can only be a matter of seeing "in a mirror dimly" (1 Cor 13:12), but in the future, Christians may expect to see things as they really are. Paul compares spiritual gifts, such as prophecy and glossolalia, with the behavior and speech of a child. They are meaningful for a while, but they must be put aside as a person approaches maturity. In contrast to the temporary nature of the other gifts, love is permanent. A definition of the practices that love accomplishes is not a definition of love, but it is as close as Paul gets. In the following passage, we are at the center of the Pauline ethic:

> Love is patient and kind; love is not jealous or boastful; it is not arrogant or rude. Love does not insist on its own way; it is not irritable or resentful; it does not rejoice at wrong, but rejoices in the right. Love bears all things, believes all things, hopes all things, endures all things (1 Cor 13:4–7).

Even the catalogue of love's functions does not become a list of regulations for the Christian life. Paul does not mean that if a person lives in love, he or she qualifies as a Christian. The case is rather the other way around. Because God has accomplished in Christ the justification of sinners, it is possible to live in Christ, under the guidance of the spirit, and to live in love. Paul is not perfectly consistent on ethical matters. His personal tastes and his varying eschatological expectations sometimes enter the scene. But in the main his ethical pronouncements avoid concrete rules. In general, the life-style of the Christian is to be governed by love of others. The Christian should live in the faith that he or she has died in respect to Sin and is able now to live righteously, in the joyful expectation that the end, the time of salvation, is coming soon.

Christology

Paul's Christology is related to his interpretation of Torah. As the fulfillment of Torah, the death of Christ is also the defeat of Sin. The believer lives in Christ—that is, he or she experiences a mode of existence that means freedom, righteousness, and life. Paul uses a number of terms to express his understanding of Jesus. He frequently uses the word *Christ* (that is, Messiah), but for him this is more a proper name than a title. He is more likely to say, "Jesus Christ" or "Christ Jesus" than "Jesus the Christ." The historical life of Jesus seems to have held little interest for him. He makes very few references to things that Jesus said or did. In 2 Cor 5:16 he says that he intends no longer to know Jesus in a fleshly way. He concentrates his attention on the eschatological dimension of Christ. He speaks of Christ as the Wisdom of God in 1 Cor 1:24 and 30, in verses that remind one of the Wisdom of God in Proverbs 8. He also presents Jesus as the second Adam, the originator of a new creation and a new humanity (Rom 5:12–19). Paul's most characteristic Christological expression is Lord, but he surely was not the first to use that term for Jesus.

Although he expresses little interest in the historical life of Jesus, Paul never displays any doubt about his humanity. He also believes that Christ existed with God prior to his life on earth and that he exists now with God awaiting his return. The fullest expression of Paul's Christological thought is found in Phil 2:6–11, a hymnlike expression that he was probably quoting. Although it probably is not a passage of his own original composition, it seems to represent his thought adequately. It starts with the pre-existence of Christ Jesus. He was in the form of God, but he did not "count equality with God a thing to be grasped" (Phil 2:6). He emptied himself of the divine nature and became human. In the human life he was humble and obedient to the point of death. But God raised him up and bestowed on him the title, Lord, the highest status in heaven and earth (see Figure 22).

In Philippians, Paul uses the quotation within a larger admonition to humility. He feels that it gives his readers the supreme example of humility, which is seen in Jesus' giving up of his divine form. Two points in the quotation need further elaboration. First, nothing is said about the precise relationship between Christ and God, but it is clear that Christ is subordinate. In this light it is possible to say that when Christ gave up his divine form, he did not expect to regain it. In fact, if he did expect it, he would lose his force as an example of humility. The giving up would be a form of condescension at best or posturing at worst. But the giving up must be genuine if it is meaningful. No one receives an example of humility from a

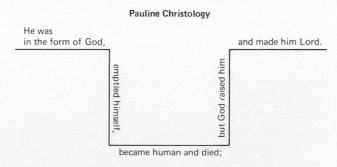

Pauline Christology

He was
in the form of God,   and made him Lord.

emptied himself,   but God raised him

became human and died;

Figure 22   Pauline Christology

rich person who pretends to be poor for a time, but only from one who permanently gives away what he has. Second, the human life must be completely human. To Paul both the life and death of Jesus are real. So when he became human, Christ became mortal, and only after death did God intervene and exalt him to the status of Lord. It is implied that God intervened because of the humble and obedient quality of Jesus' life. The intervention has given a cosmic dimension to the death, but the fact remains that God has not interfered with the purely human working out of Jesus' life. For Paul the humanity is not only unquestioned, it is devoid of any nonhuman quality. He never refers to a miraculous birth or to Jesus' performance of miracles.

In Colossians the pre-existent state of Christ is described more fully than in Philippians. It is claimed that he was "the firstborn of all creation" (Col 1:15) and that he is the one through whom all else was created. There is also a reference to the present existence of Christ as "seated at the right hand of God" (Col. 3:1) and to his expected return. These points are not dissimilar to the Christological statements in Philippians. But there is no mention of any act by which the Christ emptied himself of the form of God and became human. On the contrary, it is implied in Colossians that he was permanently filled with divinity—"for in him all the fulness of God was pleased to dwell" (Col 1:19); "for in him the whole fulness of deity dwells bodily" (Col 2:9). There is a reference to the death and the cross, but the chief impression one gets from reading Colossians is that the author conceives of the Christ as the permanent "image of the invisible God" (Col 1:15). Indeed, the Christological expressions add to the suspicion about the genuineness of this letter, and we are probably well-advised to regard Phil 2:6–11 as the more fundamental statement.

The Church

Paul's understanding of the church is related to his other concepts. In eschatological terms the church is composed of those persons who expect the return of the Christ. In relation to Paul's understanding of Torah, the church is the community of those whom God has justified through the death of Jesus. Ethically the church is composed of those who are led by the spirit. Christologically the church exists under the Lord, Jesus Christ. None of these relationships demands that the church have regulations and organization. However, as a matter of practical necessity, groups develop structure or they evaporate. So, even in Pauline Christianity there is minimal organization in the church.

Paul frequently speaks of the individual Christian as the person in Christ. This conception borders on the mystical and reflects a belief in a kind of incorporation of believer in the object of faith. It also relates to Paul's concept of Torah, for the person in Christ is the one whose existence is determined by the word of God in Christ rather than the word in Torah. Existence in Christ is marked by righteousness, guiltlessness, and freedom from Sin, and it is possible because Christ is God's second word. When Paul writes about the corporate life of those in Christ, he is thinking of the church. It is in this vein that he speaks of the church as the body of Christ. Because the community of those who find their existence in Christ manifests itself as Christ himself, the church is a kind of earthly counterpart to the heavenly Christ. At the same time, because of Paul's eschatological convictions, the church is a community in waiting, not one of permanent duration but one whose existence is soon to expire.

Paul emphasizes the unity of the church as Christ's body. He seems to proceed on the conviction that the one church manifests itself in the various localities. The church is primary, and the local groups are secondary. The importance of unity is signified by the agreement worked out in Jerusalem between Paul and the pillar apostles. In describing this meeting, Paul says that he had received a revelation that told him to go to Jerusalem. But he also says that he needed to know if his missionary work was going to be in vain (Gal 2:2). His meaning is not altogether clear, but the need for unity between the Pauline churches and the early Jewish Christian churches probably played a part in his concern. In his treatment of the question of a head covering for women, he chides the Corinthian church for differing from the others (1 Cor 11:16). The need for unity and mutual dependence within local churches is also stressed in Paul's letters.

The churches that Paul established probably met in private homes. The homeowner would be looked on as convenor and in some cases may have become an authoritative leader of the church. But Paul himself continued to have a high degree of authority over those churches. The people felt it perfectly natural to ask him about ethical and doctrinal matters, and he did not hesitate to give answers. He insisted that he was an apostle, and in listing the gifts of the spirit he gave priority to apostleship. He assumed that the traveling apostle was the symbol of authority in the church. The local churches, however, must soon have developed an independent stability. At first the leadership would have been charismatic, but as time passed it must have become more formal. Only once in Paul's letters is there a reference to those leaders by title. In Phil 1:1 Paul addresses himself to the bishops and deacons. This may mean that by the time this letter was written churches had become more formalized, or that the Philippian church arrived at a point of organized development earlier than the others did. But there is no description of the functions of these officers, and the titles may be intended in an untechnical sense. In any case, it is clear that Paul himself paid little attention to the process of selection of church officers or to a definition of their rights and duties.

There are certain corporate practices associated with Pauline Christianity. Ecstatic utterance seems to be a frequently practiced manifestation of the spirit. Baptism was used as the rite of initiation, just as it probably had been used in pre-Pauline times. With Paul, however, it took on significance as a symbol of the believer's dying in respect to Sin and rising to a new life in Christ. It was also an anticipation of the resurrection to come:

> Do you not know that all of us who have been baptized into Christ Jesus were baptized into his death? We were buried therefore with him by baptism into death, so that as Christ was raised from the dead by the glory of the Father, we too might walk in newness of life (Rom 6:3–4).

Baptism is, thus, the passage from one form of existence to another and a guarantee of the life to come. The Pauline churches also celebrated the Eucharist, which Paul understood as the repeated proclamation of Jesus' death. It consisted of eating bread and drinking from the cup. For some in Corinth it had become an occasion for gluttony and drunkenness, a fact that Paul deplored. He required that those at Corinth test themselves before they participate in the meal, for one must not desecrate the body and blood of the Lord. In the main the Eucharist is, for Pauline Christianity, a memorial of Jesus' death, not a means of union with him.

The place of women in Paul's churches constitutes a complex and disturbing issue. In 1 Corinthians, amid his regulations on glossolalia, he says, "As in all the churches of the saints, the women should keep silence in the churches. For they are not permitted to speak, but should be subordinate, as even the law says" (1 Cor 14:33–34). The context of these words suggests that Paul is thinking of glossolalia and that he means that women are not allowed to speak in tongues. But there are some suggestions here of a more generalized prohibition, for he adds that women should ask their husbands to explain anything they do not understand. He also appeals to the Torah in defense of the subordination of women, but he neither alludes to nor quotes a specific passage from the Hebrew Scriptures. Some scholars think that 1 Cor 14:33b–36 was added by a later editor of Paul's letters. It seems to be contradictory to 1 Cor 11:5, which allows women to pray and prophesy. The passage also conforms closely with 1 Tim 2:11–12, which is almost certainly non-Pauline. If it were written by Paul, it stands in sharp contrast to his more noble proclamations about the equality of men and women in Christ (Gal 3:28).

1 Cor 11:2–16 also appears to put some restrictions on the religious practices of women. Here Paul presents a complex argument to show that women must cover their heads when engaged in prayer or prophecy. In the passage he also talks about the necessity for women to wear long hair and for men to wear their hair short. Surely his thought is socially conditioned, but he alludes to scripture to support his contention that "woman is the glory of man" (1 Cor 11:7). His interpretation of the creation story in Genesis 2 is that "man was not made from woman, but woman from man. Neither was man created for woman, but woman for man" (1 Cor 11:8–

9). Thus, Paul thinks that the requirement for a woman to have long hair and to cover her head while praying is part of the order of creation and that it harmonizes with the divine will. Similarly, the more general subordination of women appears to be a theological matter. There is little point in making apologies for Paul's remarks here except to understand him as a person who did not always look critically at social conditions. Regrettably, he did not consistently adhere to the implications of his own proclamation: "There is neither Jew nor Greek, there is neither slave nor free, there is neither male nor female; for you are all one in Christ Jesus" (Gal 3:28).

We probably know more about Pauline Christianity than about any of the other varieties because it is represented in a significant body of literature written by Paul himself. We will see that it continued to exist within Christian communities and was modified by later leaders, some of whom wrote in Paul's name. Throughout the history of Christianity people have turned to Paul's letters, and most have been attracted by what he said about the depth of human disobedience and about the power of God's grace to save believers from the domination of Sin and death.

Pauline and early Jewish Christianity do not constitute the only Christian groups in the period from 30–70. Paul's letters indicate that diverse missionary movements were going on during this period. His letter to Rome shows that a Christian church had already been established in that city. There were probably missionary movements in other areas as well, but we have no direct literary or archeological evidence about them. Unfortunately, knowledge about other forms of Christianity in those first years is simply not available. We must, however, remember that the Christian movement in its first four decades was both lively and diverse.

BIBLIOGRAPHY

The Life and Letters of Paul

Bornkamm, Günther. *Paul*. Trans by D. M. G. Stalker. New York: Harper & Row, Publishers, 1971.

Buck, Charles, and Greer Taylor. *Saint Paul: A Study in the Development of His Thought*. New York: Charles Scribner's Sons, 1969.

Knox, John. *Chapters in a Life of Paul*. Nashville, Tenn.: Abingdon Press, 1950.

Meeks, Wayne A., ed. *The Writings of St. Paul*. New York: W. W. Norton & Company, Inc., 1972.

All of the books listed here include sections on Paul's thought. In each of them there are chapters on his life or analyses of the letters, and sometimes both. Knox was one of the first to attempt to reconstruct the chronology of Paul's life on the basis of the letters alone. Buck and Taylor carried the process a bit further and attempted to solve the problem of chronology by analyzing the course of the apostle's thought. Bornkamm, similarly, drew mainly on the letters in his treatment of Paul's life and thought. The book edited by Meeks contains brief notes on each of the letters and reprints of some classical essays on Paul. In addition to these books the commentaries in the bibliography for Chapter 1 include treatments of the Pauline writings. For books on Acts, see the bibliography for Chapter 9.

The Character of Pauline Christianity

Enslin, Morton S. *The Ethics of Paul*. Nashville, Tenn.: Abingdon Press, 1957.

Fitzmyer, Joseph A. *Pauline Theology: A Brief Sketch*. Englewood Cliffs, N.J.: Prentice-Hall, Inc., 1967.

Furnish, Victor P. *The Moral Teaching of Paul: Selected Essays*. Nashville, Tenn.: Abingdon Press, 1979.

———. *Theology and Ethics in Paul*. Nashville, Tenn.: Abingdon Press, 1968.

Käsemann, Ernst. *Perspectives on Paul*. Trans. by Margaret Kohl. Philadelphia: Fortress Press, 1971.

Keck, Leander E. *Paul and His Letters*. Philadelphia: Fortress Press, 1979.

Sanders, E. P. *Paul and Palestinian Judaism*. Philadelphia: Fortress Press, 1977.

Sandmel, Samuel. *The Genius of Paul*. New York: Farrar, Strauss & Giroux, Inc., 1958.

Schoeps, Hans J. *Paul: The Theology of the Apostle in the Light of Jewish Religious History*. Trans. by Harold Knight. Philadelphia: Westminster Press, 1961.

Stendahl, Krister. *Paul Among Jews and Gentiles*. Philadelphia: Fortress Press, 1976.

Wiles, M. F. *The Divine Apostle*. Cambridge: Cambridge University Press, 1967.

The relationship of Pauline Christianity to first-century Judaism is treated in the books by Sanders, Schoeps, and Stendahl. Sanders' study is probably the most comprehensive treatment of the points at issue between Paul and Palestinian Judaism. Sandmel's book is an appreciative study of Paul from the point of view of a modern Jewish scholar. Käsemann, Fitzmyer, and Keck treat Paul's thought in general. These books were produced by experts for a nonexpert audience. The books by Enslin and Furnish concentrate on Pauline ethics. In *The Moral Teaching of Paul,* Furnish deals with several issues that are of interest to contemporary Christians—sex, homosexuality, women in the church, and Christians and the governing authorities. Wiles studied the influence and treatment of Paul by Christian writers in the second and subsequent centuries. See also Bultmann's *Theology of the New Testament,* listed in the bibliography for Chapter 9.

❖ PART FIVE ❖

CHRISTIANITY FROM 70–185 CE

❖ II ❖

Increasing Diversity

THE year 70 was a critical one for Palestinian Judaism. It marked the time at which the leaders began to search for fixed points for Jewish life and thought. After that year Jewish diversity began to give way to demands for unity. We have seen that rabbinic Judaism was the result of those efforts that began to become effective after 70. In Christianity something like an opposite effect occurred. Although there had been no unity in the period from 30–70, the time after 70 was one of increasing diversity.

There are three factors that may be cited to explain, at least partially, the increasing diversity in Christianity after 70. First, the fall of Judea to the Romans seemed to mean, for some Christians, the loss of a significant connection. For many Christian groups there was a growing tendency to move farther and farther from Judaism and to neglect altogether the heritage that had been so highly valued in early Jewish and Pauline Christianity. There was also a growing tendency to define Christianity in distinction from and in opposition to Judaism and, in some circles, to condemn the Jewish people for their rejection of Jesus. The increasing distance between Christianity and Judaism, although not experienced in all varieties of Christianity, brought with it the possibility of increased diversity. In Marcionite Christianity, for example, the Jewish heritage was displaced, and the character of Christianity was, accordingly, altered.

Second, the spread and growth of the Christian movement partially accounts for the increasing diversity. In the period from 70–185, Christian groups were established in most of the lands surrounding the Mediterranean Sea—North Africa, Egypt, Palestine, Syria, Asia Minor, Macedonia, Greece, Italy, and Gaul. The large variety of peoples and cultures represented in these areas means that the forms of Christianity also varied.

Third, the year 70 marks the transition from the first to the second generation of Christians. By that year most of the leaders from the first generation had died, and new leaders had emerged. The second generation was

353

deprived of living links with the historical Jesus. After 70 there probably were no disciples who could recite stories or sayings of Jesus from their own recollections of him. The eyewitness period was over, and with the disappearance of the eyewitnesses came the weakening of a control factor. No one could any longer serve to check the accuracy of reports of Jesus or about early apostolic beliefs; hence, increasing diversity was almost inevitable.

All of these factors meant a loss of control, and the result was that Christianity was free to develop in a large number of ways. In this chapter we will examine some of the diverse ways in which the development occurred. We will look first at two groups that developed from Pauline and early Jewish Christianity. Late Pauline Christianity is represented in some documents that were written pseudonymously in Paul's name. Those who wrote in Paul's name must have considered themselves to be his followers, and they probably felt that they were carrying on his work and maintaining his form of Christian faith. Late Jewish Christianity has many affinities with that form we examined in Chapter 9, but it too exhibits some alterations and developments. We will look next at a form of Christianity represented in the Gospel of John and the letters of John, namely Johannine Christianity. We will look finally at Gnostic and Marcionite Christianity, two forms that seemed to their opponents to present very formidable threats.

In Chapter 12 we will observe the rise and development of early Catholic Christianity, a form that attempted to steer a middle course between the extreme varieties and that finally dominated the Christian movement after the end of the second century. The rise of early Catholic Christianity may be seen as a search for unity. This search was motivated not only by the fact of increasing diversity, but also by violent persecution from the non-Christian public. The very survival of the Christian movement was threatened by those attacks, which were all the more successful against a fragmented Christian movement. In Chapter 12 we also will examine the history of the oppression of Christians in the Roman period and the Christian responses to that persecution. We will then turn to an analysis of early Catholic Christianity.

We have far more literature for this period than we did for the period from 30–70. Indeed, it appears that when Christians recognized that the eyewitness period was over, they began to write large quantities of material. The Christian gospels now make their appearance, partly to make up for the lack of eyewitness accounts. But Christians not only wrote gospels, but letters, teaching tracts, apocalypses, martyrologies, and sermons. Almost all of the NT documents were written in this period, but they form only a small part of the books written by early Christians. The documents illustrate the increasing diversity and the search for unity in this period; thus, we will analyze many of them in the course of this chapter and the next.

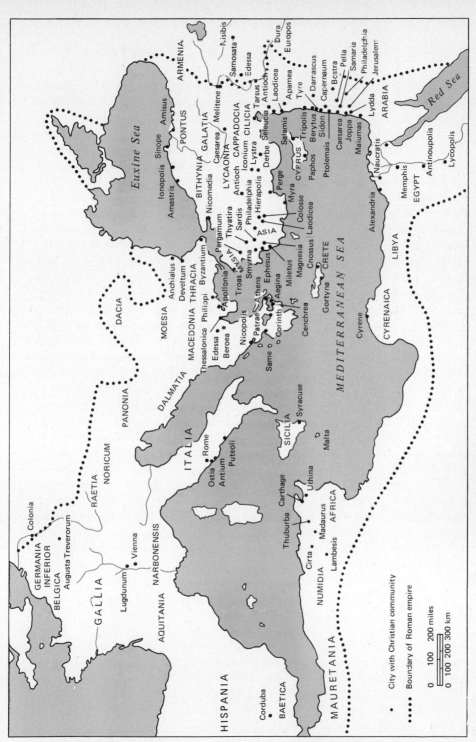

Figure 23 The Church in the Second Century. (Adapted with permission of Macmillan Publishing Company and George Allen & Unwin, from The Macmillan Bible Atlas by Y. Aharoni and Michael Avi-Yonah. Copyright © 1964, 1966, 1968, 1977 by Carta Ltd.)

LATE PAULINE CHRISTIANITY

The figure of Paul continued to be attractive in the late first and the second centuries. His popularity did not, however, guarantee that he would be understood. It meant that his name would be used to lend authenticity to views of later thinkers, whether or not such thinking was consonant with the historical Paul. In short, the available evidence leads to the probable conclusion that certain documents were produced after Paul's death and attributed to him. Those who produced the documents were, to be sure, claiming the authority of Paul, and they probably felt, rightly or wrongly, that they were carrying on the Pauline tradition. The phenomenon of pseudonymity (claiming false authorship) was neither unusual nor dishonorable in the ancient world, and it is possible that our writer or writers intended no deception in writing in Paul's name. D. E. Nineham, an English NT scholar, offers an interesting parallel from the area of Hellenistic philosophy: "The Neo-Platonist Iamblichus praises the Pythagoreans for ascribing their work to their master; in this way, he thinks, they renounced all praise for themselves and turned everything to the honour and glory of their masters."[1] Plato similarly presented many of his own concepts through the mouth of Socrates. It is not difficult to imagine that a later Pauline Christian did much the same.

A major problem in dealing with the phenomenon of late Pauline Christianity is that the documentary evidence is not altogether clear. Because the documents under consideration claim Pauline authorship, the burden of proof is on the one who doubts the claim. In Chapter 10 we examined two letters in which Pauline authorship was claimed—2 Thessalonians and Colossians—and saw that scholarship is divided on the issue of the actual author. We felt inclined to accept them as Pauline. There are four additional letters in the NT that bear the name of Paul—Ephesians, 1, 2 Timothy, and Titus. The majority of scholars today doubt that Paul wrote these four letters, but even here there is no universal scholarly agreement. In analyzing the documents we will attempt to show that they were not written by Paul but were produced by one or more later writers and published in his name. Sometimes these letters are described as Deutero-(second) Pauline letters.

Ephesians

Although Ephesians was known by some Christian writers in the early second century and was generally accepted as Pauline, the majority of scholars today doubt that Paul wrote it. There are four main reasons for the doubt. First, no indication of a specific background, occasion, or purpose is included in Ephesians. The genuine letters of Paul were written in response

---

[1] D. E. Nineham, in *Studies in Ephesians,* ed. by F. C. Cross (London: A. R. Mowbray, 1956), p. 22, note 1.

to specific occasions and for certain purposes. They included definite notices of Paul's relationship to the recipients, but Ephesians has none of this. In fact, a number of early manuscripts of the document do not even mention Ephesus as the destination of the letter. Several attempts have been made to account for this omission, including the attractive suggestion that Ephesians was intended as a circular letter. This hypothesis, first set forth by the Anglican Archbishop James Ussher in 1654, maintains that a blank was included in Eph 1:1 and that the person who delivered copies of the letter could fill it in as appropriate. E. J. Goodspeed and other NT scholars have suggested that the author of Ephesians also collected the other Pauline letters and intended his to be a covering letter or introduction to the entire collection.[2] However we may account for those manuscripts that omit the address, we can be almost certain that the author of Ephesians did not have a specific location in mind when he wrote. The generalized character of this letter contrasts with the specific and local character of Paul's genuine letters. Second, the Ephesian letter is an expansion of Colossians. It is true that it also contains allusions to passages in other Pauline letters, but the similarities in content and style between Ephesians and Colossians are far greater than between any two of the genuine letters of Paul. Third, in Ephesians several characteristic Pauline words are used without their Pauline meanings. For example, the word *mystery* is used three times, with meanings that are strange to Paul (Eph 1:9, 3:3–4, and 5:32). Fourth, some key ideas in Ephesians are at variance with expressions in the genuine letters. In 1 Cor 3:11 Paul emphatically stated that Jesus Christ is the only foundation of the church, but Eph 2:20 makes the apostles and prophets the foundation and Christ the cornerstone. In 1 Cor 7 Paul displayed little appreciation for matrimony, but in Eph 5 marriage is treated positively, and it stands as a symbol of the union of Christ and church. The German NT scholar W. G. Kümmel is probably correct in saying that "the theology of Ephesians makes the Pauline composition of the Epistle completely impossible."[3]

Although we may not be able to explain fully how this document was written, it is safe to assume that its author counted himself as a disciple of Paul. Goodspeed's suggestion that Ephesians was written to introduce the entire collection of Paul's letters is an attractive one. The work of collecting the letters was no easy task, for it would not be immediately obvious to the recipients of a single Pauline letter that Paul had written others. Nor would they immediately know where to look for additional letters. A clue could have been provided by a reference in Colossians to the letter from Laodicea (Col 4:16).[4] At least this note referred to an additional letter and

---

[2] Cf. Edgar J. Goodspeed, *The Meaning of Ephesians* (Chicago: U. of Chicago, 1933).

[3] Paul Feine and J. Behm, *Introduction to the New Testament*, rev. by W. G. Kümmel, trans. A. J. Mattill (Nashville, Tenn.: Abingdon, 1966), p. 254.

[4] A problem with this theory is that the letter to Laodicea was not in the collection, unless the letter to Philemon is the letter intended by the reference in Col 4:16. This view was

named the location of the addressees. A resident of Colossae may have become intrigued by this reference and have begun the long search for other Pauline letters in the places associated with the great apostle. After bringing the letters together, he may have written a covering letter, our Ephesians, which he modeled on the letter he knew best, namely Colossians. In doing so he could not avoid interjecting his own point of view, which was not consistent with that of Paul at every point. Goodspeed believed that the collection of letters was made in about 90, a satisfactory date for the writing of Ephesians.

In Ephesians we find a number of emphases that were characteristic of Paul. The divine will has operated in the selection of Christian believers, and salvation is by grace. The church is said to be the body of Christ, and there is a plea for unity among believers. Many Pauline ethical principles reappear, such as the emphasis on humility and patience.

But there are some sections of Ephesians that do not sound quite like Paul. Paul's historical situation was such that he had to speak with bitter disappointment about the Jewish rejection of the preaching about Jesus. He looked forward to a time in which Jews would accept Jesus, but he could not say that that time had arrived. However, in Ephesians there is a celebration of the unity of Jews and Gentiles in the Christian church. The author recalls that Gentiles had once been separated from Christ and "alienated from the commonwealth of Israel, and strangers to the covenants of promise, having no hope and without God in the world" (Eph 2:12). But the author claims that now Jews and Gentiles have been made one in Christ. He implies that gentile believers have been assimilated into the Jewish people.

A good deal of space in Ephesians is devoted to household duties (Eph 5:21–6:9). Directions are given to husbands, wives, children, and slaves. The directions appear to be based on a hierarchical understanding of family relationships. There is a chain of command that runs from the husband down, so wives are commanded to be subject to husbands, to obey them, and to respect them. Children, similarly, are told to obey their parents, and slaves are required to obey their masters, although not as "men-pleasers." But the obligations also work in the other direction. Husbands are to love wives, fathers are not to provoke children, and masters are to treat slaves with kindness. The model for the relationship of husbands and wives is the relationship between Christ and the church:

> For the husband is the head of the wife as Christ is the head of the church, his body, and is himself its Savior. As the church is subject to Christ, so let wives also be subject in everything to their husbands. Husbands, love your wives, as Christ loved the church and gave himself up for her (Eph 5:23–25).

maintained by Goodspeed, op. cit., and by John Knox, *Philemon Among the Letters of Paul*, rev. ed. (Nashville, Tenn.: Abingdon, 1959).

The combination of Pauline and non-Pauline elements in Ephesians probably means that this document is from the pen of an unknown disciple of Paul. It stands within the tradition that found its origin in Paul, but it expresses a more developed stage of the tradition.

1, 2 Timothy and Titus

1, 2 Timothy and Titus are usually grouped together and called pastoral letters. The word *pastoral* indicates that a significant aspect of their content is devoted to prescriptions for pastors and officers in the churches. Qualifications for deacons, presbyters, and bishops are given in some detail, but the last two terms seem interchangeable, and the functions appear to be the same. The probable situation is that the bishop is one of the presbyters, probably a first among equals. The attention paid to these officers constitutes a significant aspect of the non-Pauline character of the pastoral letters. In the unquestioned letters of Paul, little attention was paid to church officers. Paul had referred to bishops and deacons in Phil 1:1, but he included no descriptions of their qualifications or functions. We may translate these words in Phil 1:1 in the nontechnical sense of "overseers" and "servants." By contrast, the pastoral letters treat bishops, presbyters, and deacons as special officers of the church. In addition, the author understands Timothy to be in charge of the church at Ephesus and Titus of that in Crete. Both are pictured as subject to Paul, who grants them authority to appoint presbyters or bishops. Thus, the historical situation required for these letters is not that of Paul's lifetime. The letters must have been written at a later time, when the various churches were becoming stabilized and were creating suitable and lasting organizations. No longer does the vivid eschatological perspective dominate Christian thought and life. The pastoral letters come from a time when Christians were beginning to adjust to an indeterminate extension of historical time.

Another aspect of the pastoral letters is their attack on unacceptable interpretations of Christianity. It has long been recognized that the kind of thought under attack here is similar to Gnostic Christianity, which will be treated subsequently. There are warnings about myths and genealogies, which may be those of the Gnostics (1 Tim 1:4 and 4:7, 2 Tim 4:4, and Titus 1:14). The heretics of the pastoral letters also forbid marriage and the eating of certain foods (1 Tim 4:3). In addition, there may be a direct reference to a book by Marcion, a second-century leader. In 1 Tim 6:20–21 Timothy is warned to beware of the "contradictions [in Greek, *antitheses*] of what is falsely called knowledge [in Greek, *gnosis*]." We know from other sources that Marcion wrote a book entitled *The Antitheses,* and that he was sometimes regarded as a Gnostic.[5] Resistance to objectionable ideas, what-

[5] Cf. Tertullian, *Against Marcion* I, 19; IV: I.

ever their source, is very important to the author of the pastoral letters. He must have been keenly aware of the threats that increasing diversity posed to the survival of the Christian movement.

Not only is Paul's name used in the addresses, but the pose of Pauline authorship is carried through all three pastoral letters. Personal details are given, and the names of Paul's erstwhile companions are sprinkled through-out.[6] Although most modern scholars reject Pauline authorship because of the post-Pauline conceptions and practices alluded to, it is evident that the author intended readers to believe that Paul wrote the letters. He imagines that Paul has gone through his trial at Rome and has survived. He has engaged in additional travels in the eastern Mediterranean and is now facing a new trial. The probable reason for the author's procedure is that he wishes to invoke the authority of Paul in strengthening the hands of leaders in the churches of Ephesus and Crete. We may assume that the letters were made available to those leaders, who felt themselves to be the successors of Timothy and Titus. They would be able to say that Paul granted authority to Timothy and Titus and thus to their successors.

It is difficult, if not impossible, to arrive at a satisfactory date for the pastoral letters. They could not have been written before the collection of Paul's letters was made in around 90, for they show familiarity with several letters in the collection, including Ephesians. Moreover, they must have been written at a time when the authority of Paul was widely acknowledged among Christians in the eastern Mediterranean. Many scholars tend to date them toward the middle of the second century because of the possible references to Gnostic Christianity, but there may well have been certain Gnostic ideas much earlier. If we could be assured that the reference to the "Antitheses" in 1 Tim 6:20 is to a book by Marcion, we could confidently date the letters in the mid-second century. Unfortunately, other interpretations are possible, for the author of the pastoral letters may simply have been thinking of the contradictions between what he took to be true and what he understood to be false Christianity. Or he may have been thinking of the self-contradictory teaching of his opponents. It may be possible to date the letters on the basis of the kind of church organization represented in them. We will see in Chapter 12 that the letters of Ignatius, written between 98–117, assume the existence of a monarchical episcopate—that is, a system in which a single bishop holds supreme authority in the churches of a city and the surrounding region. The pastoral letters seem to represent a somewhat less formal structure, with a bishop presiding over a group of presbyters. Caution must be exercised, however, for we cannot assume that church organization developed uniformly in every place. It is more likely that some

---

[6] Some scholars feel that a few genuine fragments of Paul's correspondence can be found in the pastoral letters. See, e.g., P. N. Harrison, *The Problem of the Pastoral Epistles* (London: Oxford U.P. 1921).

cities had a monarchical episcopate while others had a group of presbyters. In view of the complexity the best we can do is to date the pastoral letters some time after 90. The latest possible date would be c. 185, when Irenaeus quotes from them. Although there are some resemblances between the pastoral letters and some writings from earlier in the second century, Irenaeus is the first writer whose quotations from the letters are beyond doubt.

The Character of Late Pauline Christianity

Ephesians and the pastoral letters are not sufficiently similar to give us a distinct impression of a unified late Pauline movement. They probably are not from the pen of the same author, and they probably represent different times and places. Through Ephesians we see a community of converts from Judaism and from the Hellenistic religions, living in harmony. In the pastoral letters we see a community that had no significant interest in eschatological considerations but rather was gearing itself up for continued existence in the world and for resistance to forms of Christian thought that seemed to be deviant. In both Ephesians and the pastoral letters, there is an emphasis on order—within the church, at home, and in the community at large. Peace, harmony, and tranquility appear to be prized virtues. What we see in these documents need not be thought of as illegitimate developments, but they clearly are not characteristic of Paul himself. We miss here Paul's profound theological struggles with problems of eschatology, sin, and Torah. Instead we find a community that is beginning to settle down in the world.

LATE JEWISH CHRISTIANITY

As the name implies, late Jewish Christianity is closely related to early Jewish Christianity, which was treated in Chapter 9. It is not to be regarded as a new phenomenon, for those who represented it were keenly conscious of their continuity with the earliest Christian groups. Nevertheless, it is not to be equated with the earlier form, because it represents a more developed stage of religious thought and life. We have no precise definition of late Jewish Christianity from first- and second-century authors. Different writers use different names, such as Ebionites, Nazoreans, and Elkesaites. These may have been distinctive names of different groups, or they may be locally variant designations for late Jewish Christians. We know little about the subtle distinctions between the groups, but it is possible to describe the main lines of late Jewish Christian thought.

The origin of late Jewish Christianity is most appropriately found in the religion of the Christians in Jerusalem in the period between 30–70. As we have seen, this early community was led by the three apostles, Peter, James,

Christian Baptistry at Dura-Europos, overall view. The chapel was built about 232 CE and is the oldest known Christian meeting house. (Courtesy Yale University Art Gallery, Dura-Europos Collection.)

and John; among them James, who was known as the Lord's brother, probably became the chief leader. The death of James, in about 62, and the approach of war with Rome threatened the existence of this Christian group. The fourth-century historian Eusebius referred to an oracle that led the Christians to abandon Jerusalem just before the war broke out in 66 and to flee to Pella, in Perea.[7] The legend that probably lies behind Eusebius' report is undoubtedly an exaggeration, but it must reflect the presence in Pella of late Jewish Christians, who traced their origins to Jerusalem. Eusebius also reports that, after the fall of Jerusalem in 70, Simeon bar Clopas, James' cousin, was selected to succeed James as leader, but it is not clear whether this decision was made in Jerusalem or elsewhere.[8] Between the two Jewish rebellions against Rome—between 70 and 135—there seems to have been a late Jewish Christian presence in Jerusalem. Eusebius lists fifteen persons who were, in succession, leaders of the church in Jerusalem, beginning with James and Simeon and coming up to the second rebellion.[9]

[7] Eusebius, *The Ecclesiastical History* III, 5:3.
[8] Ibid., III, 11.
[9] Ibid., IV, 5.

Eusebius adds that all these were Jews. During this period there was a good deal of hostility between Jews and Christians, and some late Jewish Christians were probably being excluded from synagogues. Roman officials also saw those Christians as potential threats, and Eusebius reports that Simeon bar Clopas was executed during the reign of Trajan.[10] After 135 late Jewish Christianity in Jerusalem ceased, and a flourishing gentile church probably took its place in the city. But late Jewish Christianity continued in other locations in the eastern Mediterranean for several centuries, perhaps to the time of Mohammed in the seventh century.

The literature on which we may draw for an understanding of this movement is minimal, and not much of it comes directly from late Jewish Christian writers. One NT document, the letter of James, may possibly come out of a late Jewish Christian background. Some gospels—the Gospel of the Ebionites, the Gospel according to the Hebrews, and the Gospel according to the Nazoreans—are known to us only by quotations from other writers. In addition, the third- and fourth-century pseudo-Clementine writings, *Clementine Homilies* and *Recognitions of Clement,* contain some late Jewish Christian material. Finally, Symmachus' translation of the OT into Greek, done late in the second century, is helpful, because the translator may have been a late Jewish Christian. We will examine the letter of James and the Gospel of the Ebionites in greater detail.

The Letter of James

Although this document has traditionally been called a letter, the only letter forms in it are the address, in which the author is identified as James and the recipients are called the "twelve tribes in the dispersion," and the one-word salutation, "Greeting" (Jas 1:1). In the body of the letter there is no reference to a specific occasion to which the letter might be a response and there are no personal details. In form it is more like a sermon, but it was apparently intended for widespread publication among Christians in the Hellenistic world. Christian writers may have adopted the practice of writing such general letters from Greek and Hellenistic philosophers. J. H. Ropes, an American NT scholar, cites examples from Isocrates, Aristotle, and Epicurus, who wrote treatises intended for an indefinite number of audiences.[11]

The author is identified only as "James, a servant of God and of the Lord Jesus Christ" (Jas 1:1). He implies that he is a teacher (3:1). James, or Jacob in its Hebrew form, is a common Jewish name. We know of several

---

[10] Ibid., III, 32:3–6.
[11] J. H. Ropes, *A Critical and Exegetical Commentary on the Epistle of St. James,* International Critical Commentary (New York: Scribner's, 1916), p. 7. Cf. also Abraham J. Malherbe, *The Cynic Epistles* (Missoula, Mont.: Scholars Press, 1977), and Harold W. Attridge, *First Century Cynicism in the Epistles of Heraclitus* (Missoula, Mont.: Scholars Press, 1976).

early Jewish Christians who bore it. The best-known is the one known as the Lord's brother, who came to be the chief leader in the early Jewish Christian community; however, the author of the letter of James does not identify himself with this figure. The actual author appears to be a second-century Christian, who is otherwise unknown. His writing style is marked by the use of some elements associated with the Greek diatribe, such as a dialogue with an imaginary interlocutor, a series of brief questions and answers, and the use of paradox, irony, imperatives, comparisons, figures of speech, and examples from famous individuals.[12] He also uses some elements of Semitic style, which reveal a probable Jewish background.

The letter of James was probably written in the second century. Several indications of such a date may be mentioned. For one thing, it appears to come from a time well after that of Paul. Although the author makes no explicit reference to Paul, he attempts to combat an amoral form of Christianity that appears to be an interpretation of some of the Pauline letters. This doctrine apparently taught that Paul's emphasis on faith excluded the necessity of good works—that is, that faith is all that is required for salvation. The author of James, however, vigorously attacked the separation of faith and works and taught that both are necessary for the Christian life (Jas 2:14–26). He maintained that faith without works is dead and that faith is brought to life and demonstrated only in certain moral activities. The doctrine James opposed probably did not arise until some time after Paul himself had died, and the letter of James could hardly have been written before 70. Other indications suggest an even later date. The letter of James contains probable allusions to the Synoptic Gospels and to Paul's letters, so a date before 90 would be out of the question. It is not possible to be so definite on a *terminus ad quem,* and almost any date in the second century is possible. No satisfactory location for the author has been determined.

The letter of James has usually been characterized as a late Jewish-Christian writing because of its use of the OT and of Jewish wisdom literature. Many scholars, however, observe that there is no indication of loyalty to the Jewish people and nothing on Sabbath observance, dietary regulations, or circumcision. Many have also noticed the absence of specifically Christian ideas; for example, there are only two references to Jesus Christ. The ethical teachings include love of the neighbor as the fulfillment of the "royal law" (Jas 2:8). The author stresses the need for patience, humility, and service to the oppressed. He speaks with considerable force on the necessity of ethical principles, on control of one's desire and control of the tongue, and against discrimination in favor of the rich. Although there is nothing distinctively Christian here, there is no reason to classify it as a non-Christian document. Nothing in it is inconsistent with the ethical teachings in the Christian gospels and elsewhere, and it includes an eschatological expecta-

---

12 Ropes, op. cit., pp. 6–18.

tion that is characteristic of some Christian documents. As for the late Jewish-Christian character of James, it is true that it lacks many of the elements we should expect and represents no systematically partisan approach. However, there is in it one theme that makes it lean toward late Jewish Christianity—namely, the understanding of Torah as constituting the basic character of Christianity. In Jas 1:25 Christianity is looked on as the perfect law, which makes us free. In 2:8 the rule of neighbor love is called the "royal law." In 2:10–11 the author accepts the principle that breaking one part of the law makes a person guilty of breaking all of it, and it is clear that he means the Torah, for illustrative quotations from the ten commandments follow. In 4:11–12 he says that the one who speaks evil against a brother really does so against the law. The author contrasts keeping the law with judging it and condemns the latter. To be sure, there is no polemic against other forms of Christianity nor any partisanship. This letter lacks some of the distinctive concepts and emphases that we associate with late Jewish Christianity. Nevertheless, the letter of James is best seen as coming out of that side of Christianity that continued to revere the Torah and to use it, together with the teachings of Jesus, as the basic ethic of Christianity.

The Gospel of the Ebionites

The fathers of the church frequently referred to gospels used by late Jewish Christians, variously titled. There is a good deal of confusion in the references and citations, but it now appears that there were at least three distinct late Jewish-Christian gospels—the Gospel of the Ebionites, the Gospel of the Hebrews, and the Gospel of the Nazoreans. Unfortunately, no manuscript of any of the three has turned up. It is possible, however, to judge something about their contents and character from citations in the fathers. Our sole authority for the Gospel of the Ebionites is Epiphanius, a fourth-century bishop of Salamis, who said that this gospel was used by a sect called Ebionites (in Hebew, "the poor") and that it was a falsification and abridgment of Matthew.[13] It was probably written in the middle of the second century. It claims that the disciple Matthew is the author, and the Ebionites may have combined it with the canonical Matthew.

In the fragments that Epiphanius cites we have narratives about the call of the disciples and the baptism of Jesus, as well as a few of Jesus' sayings. In the description of the baptism, it is stated that the Holy Spirit entered into Jesus in the form of a dove descending from heaven. It was in that moment that the heavenly voice said, "Thou art my beloved Son, in thee I am well pleased. And again: I have this day begotten thee."[14] Here the

---

[13] Epiphanius, *Refutation of All Heresies* XXX, 13:2–3.
[14] Ibid., XXX, 13:7f., trans. by P. Vielhauer, in Edgar Hennecke, *New Testament Apocrypha,* ed. by W. Schneemelcher, trans. by R. McL. Wilson (Philadelphia: Westminster Press, 1963), Vol. I.

baptism is not a symbolic act of the human Jesus. It is the actual adoption of Jesus by God. Epiphanius also says that Jewish-Christian gospels deny that Christ was human, and they reject the belief that he was begotten of God. He is conceived to be an archangel, a creature of God rather than his son. Strong emphasis is also placed on the vegetarianism of John the Baptist and Jesus and on Jesus' mission to abolish sacrifices. These principles were important for some late Jewish-Christian groups.

The Character of Late Jewish Christianity

Despite the paucity of literature, we are able to take note of some general characteristics of late Jewish Christianity. Adherents of this movement were devout monotheists; they revered the OT, they practiced circumcision, and they saw a continuity between Moses and Jesus and between Jesus and themselves. They insisted that James was the first head of the church, and they expressed deep hostility toward Paul. In the pseudo-Clementine literature, Paul is referred to as the enemy of Christianity. Peter contests his claim to be an apostle and insists that Paul lacks the prime qualification for apostleship, namely acquaintance with the historical Jesus. Although there were significant controversies surrounding the historical Paul, it appears that hostility toward him hardened in late Jewish Christianity. It probably grew as late Jewish Christians felt more and more isolated from other Christian groups, which were largely composed of Gentiles and were more sympathetic to Paul. As late Jewish Christians looked back on the early history of the Christian movement, they came to feel that Paul was responsible for all the troubles. The hostility they felt toward other Christian groups came to be focused on the one who, according to them, began the process of separation.

In many areas late Jewish Christians shared ideas with other groups of the time, but their Christology and their interpretation of Torah are distinctive. In their Christology they looked on Jesus as the prophet like Moses, who was predicted in Deut 18:15–18. Although some accepted the belief that Jesus had been born of the virgin Mary, they did not believe that this granted to him a special divine status. Despite Epiphanius' comments, the prevailing belief seems to have been that Jesus' earthly life was purely human. According to some documents he committed no conscious sins but was not without unwitting sins. As the second Moses he fulfilled and purified Mosaic institutions, including the Torah. To emphasize his continuity with Israelite history, they thought of him as one in a line of bearers of revelation. The glory of God passed from one bearer to the next in a line that started with Adam and went through Enoch, Noah, Abraham, Isaac, Jacob, and Moses, to Jesus, the final bearer of revelation. His messianic designation came at his baptism, when the descent of the dove symbolized God's adoption of him. They believed also in his resurrection and his future return as Messiah. Because the earthly life was characterized by humility and suffering, he must return in conquest. Although his messianic designation came at the baptism, he was not expected to function as Messiah until his return. In most respects the Christology of late Jewish Christianity is similar to that of their earlier counterparts. Jesus was a human being upon whom the spirit of God descended; he will return in power as Messiah. He was not a God who came to earth.

To late Jewish Christians the Torah was still of paramount importance, but they felt that Jesus had made some drastic modifications in it. The major change was the elimination of the sacrificial cult and the ritual of the Jerusalem Temple. The sacrificial slaughter of animals was abominable to them. In this light they held distinctive interpretations of the OT. They objected to the idea of the Israelite monarchy, severely criticized David and Solomon, and did not look upon Jesus as son of David. They rejected all the prophets except the bearers of revelation already mentioned. They rejected certain OT passages—namely those that spoke of God anthropomorphically and those that reported immoral acts by OT worthies. Late Jewish Christians felt themselves relieved of the sacrificial laws, but they put correspondingly greater emphasis on other regulations. They shared with other Christian groups a refusal to eat meat with blood and meat from an animal that had been sacrificed to an idol. They put a high value on poverty and personal ritual purity. Late Jewish Christianity did not direct itself toward a deep analysis of the meaning of Torah such as we find in Paul, and it did not question the status of Torah as the word of God. As people of Jewish background, late Jewish Christians retained and even intensified some matters from Torah that related to their personal lives. However, as Christians they were convinced that Jesus had made significant changes in the content of Torah. He had not abolished it but fulfilled it by relieving his followers of some parts and intensifying others. H. J. Schoeps, a student of Jewish Christianity, writes:

> The really creative contribution of the Ebionites [late Jewish Christians] to religion lay in their internalization of the Old Testament law. On the one hand they wanted to purge it of falsification, and so they abbreviated and lightened it; on the other hand, they wanted to augment it and make it more difficult by intensifying that which was essential.[15]

With some justification late Jewish Christians claimed to retain without change the earliest beliefs and forms of Christianity. It is not correct to say that they made no changes, but we need to take seriously their claim of continuity with the original Christians. At the same time, their religion came more and more to be identified with a particular ethos and was less and less

---

[15] H. J. Schoeps, *Jewish Christianity,* trans. D. R. A. Hare (Philadelphia: Fortress Press, 1969), p. 76.

appealing to Christians from a gentile background. Late Jewish Christianity was finally relegated to a position of interesting but irrelevant antiquity.

JOHANNINE CHRISTIANITY

A third variety of Christianity takes its name from the traditional author of the Fourth Gospel and of three NT letters. These documents are referred to collectively as the Johannine literature.[16] The existence of a Johannine movement is attested to only indirectly in our documents, and we know nothing concrete about the life or career of the anonymous founder. Nevertheless, there are distinctive concepts associated with the Johannine literature and indications that there was a group that originated and developed in the period from 70–185. Because the Gospel of John has already been treated in Chapter 6, it remains only for us to look now at the three letters.

1, 2, 3 John

Although these three documents have traditionally been attributed to John, they do not actually claim to have been written by anyone with that name. 1 John was probably not written as a letter, and no writer is mentioned in it by name. 2 and 3 John are genuine pieces of correspondence, but the writer calls himself "the elder." The three documents are called Johannine because a tradition developed among early Christians to the effect that one person wrote all three letters as well as the Fourth Gospel and that this person was John bar Zebedee, a disciple of Jesus.

Modern scholars have answered the question of authorship in various ways. Most do not think the author was John bar Zebedee. If there is little reason to think that this disciple wrote the Fourth Gospel, there is even less reason to think he wrote the letters. But some scholars do think that one person wrote the letters and the gospel, although they do not think that person was John bar Zebedee. They point to the similarity in language and literary style that runs through all four documents, as well as the similar themes and theological conceptions. Other scholars, however, emphasize the ideological differences that seem to preclude the possibility of common authorship. Probably the dominant scholarly position is that there are two authors represented in the Johannine literature, one who wrote the gospel, and another who wrote the three letters.

In the final analysis the author of the letters is anonymous. He identifies

[16] The Revelation of John is sometimes included as Johannine literature. However, the author of Revelation is almost certainly not the same as the author either of the Fourth Gospel or the letters of John.

himself in 2 and 3 John as the elder, or presbyter. Presbyter may mean simply the old man, or it may be a technical title for an officer in a church. Eusebius, the fourth-century historian, has a confused account, drawn from Papias, about a presbyter at Ephesus named John.[17] In this account, presbyters appear to be successors to the apostles—that is, they seem to belong to the generation after the apostles. The evidence in 2 and 3 John suggests that the presbyter who wrote these letters was regarded as having a high degree of authority within a Christian church and perhaps among a group of churches. He is able to address others and give them directions, simply by using his title "the elder." He assumes that his readers know who he is and that they accept his authority. Perhaps the author was that very presbyter of Ephesus, named John, about whom Eusebius informs us. If that is so, and if there were some confusion between the presbyter John and the disciple John, we might have an explanation of the early tradition of Johannine authorship. But that is only an interesting and speculative possibility. We are on safer ground simply to say that these documents were written by someone known to his fellows as the elder.

Although it does not seem likely that the gospel and the letters were written by the same individual, there is a relationship between them. Raymond Brown, a contemporary NT scholar, suggests that the letters were written after the gospel by a presbyter who accepted its authority but felt that it needed interpretation.[18] It needed interpretation because others were using it to support ideas with which the presbyter disagreed. Brown feels that both the presbyter and his opponents regarded the Fourth Gospel highly but disagreed on its meaning. The presbyter, therefore, undertook to explain the gospel and in doing so imitated its style and language. Thus, Brown can convincingly speak of a Johannine school of writers.

In Brown's scheme, the letters were written after the gospel, and he dates them c. 100. The first writer to refer to 1 John was Polycarp, writing between 115 and 135.[19] References to 2 and 3 John are scarce until the end of the second century. If, however, one author wrote all three, a date of c. 100 would be appropriate.

The author of 1 John has in mind an interpretation of Christianity that he believes is dangerously false and that has already caused division in some communities. Some people have already left the author's group, possibly forming new Christian groups on the basis of their theology. The most significant feature of their theology is a docetic Christology—that is, a denial of the real humanity of the Christ. This idea frequently formed a part of Gnostic Christianity in the second century. It is based on the assumption that human flesh is essentially evil and could not have been present in the

---

[17] Cf. Eusebius, op. cit., III, 39. Papias was bishop of Hierapolis in Asia Minor until c. 130.
[18] Cf. Raymond E. Brown, *The Community of the Beloved Disciple* (New York: Paulist Press, 1979), pp. 93–144.
[19] Cf. Polycarp, *Letter to the Philippians* 7. On Polycarp, see Chapter 12 in this textbook.

Christ. It assumes that the Christ did truly appear on earth and appeared to be human. But to Docetism the human appearance was deceptive.[20] The disciples of Jesus saw something they thought was human, but their eyes deceived them. Docetic Christology maintains that the Christ was a thoroughly divine, spiritual being. Against this form of thought, the author of 1 John sets forth his own version of Christianity, with belief in the true humanity of Jesus, who had come in the flesh. He insisted on the identification of the man Jesus with the Christ. In addition, the author affirmed that love of the brethren is essential. His aim was to unify the community in belief and in brotherly love.

The purpose of 2 John is much the same. It is a genuine letter written to a church ("the elect lady and her children," 2 John 1) by the presbyter. The author warns the readers that some people are preaching a docetic Christology and that such persons are not to be received in the church.

3 John was written to a man named Gaius, who supported some people who had been sent out by the presbyter. Gaius has, however, had opposition from Diotrephes, who refused to welcome the presbyter's representatives and who put their supporters out of the church. The presbyter threatened to intervene personally in the case and to challenge the authority of Diotrephes. It is tempting to speculate on the issues at stake in this incident. Some have suggested that there is a conflict between two different kinds of church organization, perhaps between that with an itinerant, charismatic leadership and that with a more fixed structure. But the short note does not make things very clear to us. Kümmel has said about all that can be said: "We can think of a conflict between a fixed ecclesiastical organization and an earlier, freer charismatic situation. . . . Yet it is not clear that 'the elder' represents the freer charismatic situation."[21]

The Character of Johannine Christianity

The major source for our understanding of Johannine Christianity is the Gospel of John. The letters may be understood as representing a slightly later form of the same movement. In order to distinguish these two documents, the name *John* will be used to refer to the author of the Fourth Gospel, and the author of the letters will be called the presbyter.

In Chapter 6 we saw that John was more interested in the suprahuman nature of Christ than in the history of Jesus. We also saw that, although the author cannot be described as docetic, he is closer to Docetism than most of the other NT writers—for example, Paul and the synoptic evangelists. The problems that probably lie behind 1 John demonstrate that the

---

[20] The word *Docetism* is derived from the Greek verb *Dokein* which means "to think, suppose, believe." It emphasizes the disciples' erroneous supposition that they saw a fleshly thing when they saw Jesus.
[21] Feine and Behm, op. cit., p. 314.

Fourth Gospel could have been interpreted in docetic fashion. The presbyter, writing perhaps only a decade after John, found it necessary to deal with a group that embraced Docetism and at the same time acknowledged the authority of the Fourth Gospel. The emphasis on the suprahuman nature of Christ in this gospel must have led some followers to interpret it in docetic fashion.

The interest in the suprahuman is part of a general Johannine tendency to emphasize the spiritual at the expense of the physical, the nontemporal in opposition to the historical. John uses the gospel as a vehicle of communication, so he describes a number of things that appear to be historical events. But when we look closely we find that Jesus' teachings in this gospel are usually not teachings about God but revelations of God. His deeds are not the visible events of ordinary life; neither are they done out of kindness or even power. They are, rather, symbols of truth for those who have the eyes to see it. The real nucleus of Johannine Christianity is a preference for a truth revealed to the intellect in nonhistorical terms. John cannot agree with Paul that the meaning of life is to be found in a single historical event, even the death of Jesus. Nor can he believe that it matters whether Jesus was a Galilean, a Jew, or whatever. To John there is eternal truth in this religion, and such truth cannot be identified with historical events, although it may be found within them. John surely finds a large number of sympathizers in the twentieth century among people who find it difficult to believe that an event that occurred hundreds of years ago can have any significance now. Such people are far more ready to accept an idea that seems to have eternal validity. It is possible to illustrate this dehistoricizing tendency by re-examining John's Christology and by looking at his understanding of the church.

The subject of Johannine Christology was introduced in Chapter 6, in connection with the treatment of the prologue to the Fourth Gospel (John 1:1–18). We saw there that John affirmed belief in the pre-existence of the Christ as Logos and in his incarnation in human flesh. John also showed that, in his death and resurrection, the Christ returned to the Father. The incarnation is real and fleshly, but flesh appears to be a means of communication rather than a genuine participation in human nature. In Jesus' flesh human beings are able to see the divine nature of the Christ. The basic elements of Pauline Christology are present in John's three stages: the eternally existent Logos, the incarnate Logos, and the return of the Logos to its proper realm. But the dramatic force of Paul's Christology is missing. Instead of a Christological picture with sudden breaks and alterations of direction, the Johannine is one of continuous and rather gentle flow from one stage to another (Figure 24). Christ is an eternally divine being, present with God at the creation, appearing on earth as an incarnated but still divine being, and now eternally present with God and in the church.

The idea of the Logos may have been drawn from Hellenistic concep-

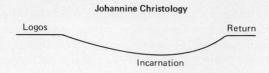

Figure 24   Johannine Christology

tions of Logos as an intermediary through whom the world was created. Such a concept is, for example, to be found in the writings of Philo. The conception of pre-existence was already present in Pauline Christianity, and Jesus' return to the Father is related to earlier Christian speculation. In his description of the incarnate Logos, John uses some older conceptions but is not limited to them. He speaks of Jesus as the Christ, but he does not think of him in eschatological terms. One of his characters calls him the King of Israel (John 1:49), an acceptable but not very significant title for John. He is also called Rabbi (John 1:38, 49; 3:2, 26, and 6:25), but John probably understood this title in a nontechnical sense. Various characters in the gospel address Jesus by the title Lord, and it has the customary meaning found in earlier forms of Christianity. John's favorite title is Son of God. By affirming the divine sonship of Jesus, the author means to say that in him we have a public revelation of reality, a thoroughly dependable communication from God himself. In him, and only in him, is real life possible. His words are trustworthy, and his promises are sure. According to John it is essential to believe that Jesus is the Son of God, although not all people have the ability to do so. But those who have seen Jesus and really discerned who he is have seen the Father. John also uses the term Son of man in reference to the incarnate Logos. But this term has no eschatological significance for him. His understanding of the title is similar to that found in the Hermetic literature. This material is from the second and third centuries CE, but it is probable that some of it goes back much earlier and may have been available to John. It includes a series of revelations by Hermes Trismegistus, a supposed sage of ancient Egypt, who became the God Thoth. One of the revealed characters is the heavenly man, who had been sent to earth by Thoth, and who knew where he had come from and where he was headed. He was divine and immortal.[22] John pictured Jesus as this kind of divine man, who had been sent by God to earth, knew his origin and destiny, and possessed unity with God. It seems clear that John had become acquainted with the Son of man title from earlier Christianity, but he was not disposed to understand it eschatologically. He was, however, familiar with a heavenly

---

[22] For a good analysis of Hermeticism and its possible influence on the Fourth Gospel, cf. C. H. Dodd, *The Interpretation of the Fourth Gospel* (Cambridge: Cambridge U.P., 1953), pp. 10–53.

man teaching like that in Hermeticism, and he used that teaching to interpret the title.

The titles do not tell the whole story. John probably also used a model for his life of Jesus, perhaps one drawn from Stoicism. Jesus, in the Fourth Gospel, does come off as a kind of ideal Stoic. There is no conflict between his will and his fate; he is completely self-possessed; he has no temptations; he is unaffected by popularity; and he moves with divine necessity.

Thus we have a nearly ahistorical Christology. Even the picture of the earthly segment concentrates on mythological and theological conceptions rather than on historical events. This Christology must be understood in context. It is a skillful blending of Christian, Platonic, Stoic, and Hermetic elements, and it constitutes an approach to the best religious thought of the day. John took the value of Jesus and put it in terms that were meaningful for his culture. As we have seen, every Christian generation tends to see Jesus in terms of its own highest ideals. To John these ideals took the form of the Stoic man, the Hermetic heavenly man, and the philosophers' Logos. Because these represented the highest ideals of his place and time, John would not picture Jesus in a way that would make him less meaningful to people of morality and intellect. For the same reason he played down the historical. A form of Christianity that goes a step further in the same direction is Gnostic Christianity, which usually includes docetic Christology. It seems that some of John's followers felt positively disposed toward docetic Christology, and John may be thought of as opening the way for the fuller development of Gnostic Christianity. But the presbyter attempted to counter these developments by condemning those Christians who denied that the Christ had come in the flesh. When we consider both the Fourth Gospel and the letters of John, it becomes clear that Johannine Christianity does not embrace a docetic Christology, although it emphasizes ahistorical and suprahuman aspects of the Christ.

Another area in which the dehistoricizing tendency of Johannine Christianity is apparent is in the teaching about the church. To John, the church is made up of persons who have been united with Christ. Such people are said to have life, or eternal life. This conception is similar to Paul's idea of life in Christ, but it has more of the quality of mystic absorption. The believers are joined to Christ as branches are to the vine. This life is eternal in the sense that it is both unending and unchangeable. In this conception death is meaningless, for one can enter into union with Christ now and continue unchanged in that relationship beyond death. Such a person does not die but passes from life to life (cf. John 8:51). The extent to which the believer is united with Christ is the extent to which he or she is separated from the world. John considers the world to be a place of evil, so Christians must separate themselves from it. This motif is present in chapter 17, where Jesus says, "I am not praying for the world but for those whom thou hast given me, for they are thine" (John 17:9). The disciples, who represent the

Christian at this point, are spoken of as strangers in the world, and the world is alienated from God and Christ. It knows neither God nor Christ nor the Christian.

The individual Christian is not left alone to find union with Christ, for there is a sense in which the church itself is united with Christ. There is no explicit persecution language in the Johannine literature, but there is a deep feeling for the estrangement between church and world. This feeling is frequently associated with sectarianism.[23] Anyone familiar with small sects of fairly recent origin knows that a certain kind of psychology often goes along with the movement. It is one that maintains the correctness of the small group and the error of the world as a whole. The sect may present its message to the world outside, but it attempts to maintain its distance, feeling that its integrity and purity depend on its separateness. For John, the church finds itself in union with the heavenly Christ, and this lifts the group and its members above the plane of ordinary existence. The sectarian character of the Fourth Gospel opens still another door to Gnostic Christianity. We will see that one of the fundamental assumptions of the Gnostics is the evil nature of the world.

1 John shares the feeling of separation between the church and the world: "The reason why the world does not know us is that it did not know him" (1 John 3:1). In 2 and 3 John the sectarian character does not come through; instead we see an emphasis on order within the church, an emphasis that is frequently found among sects after their first generation. In those letters the presbyter addresses members of distant churches as his children. He sends out delegates, and he is in a position to receive reports on churches supposedly under his care. He sets himself forth as the judge of truth and doctrine; he puts his testimony on the side of truth; and he is certain that his personal intervention in a dispute will turn the tide. These churches may still have felt a separation from the world, but now they have turned their attention to problems of church order.

The church expresses its union with Christ through the sacraments. But the Fourth Gospel has no record of a sacramental institution. The last supper, which served as an institution of the Eucharist in the Synoptic Gospels, is replaced by a foot-washing ceremony in John (John 13:1–17). Despite this absence there is a significant amount of material dealing with the sacramental meaning of water, bread, and wine. At Cana, Jesus turns water into wine (2:1–11). When Nicodemus complains that a mature person cannot re-enter his mother's womb to be born again, Jesus replies that one must be reborn from water and spirit (3:5). The water must be that of baptism and may have been suggested by the bag of waters in which the fetus develops. In conversation with the Samaritan woman, Jesus claims the ability

---

[23] Cf. Ernst Käsemann, *The Testament of Jesus,* trans. Gerhard Krodel (Philadelphia: Fortress Press, 1968), pp. 56–73.

to supply her with water sufficient for her entire life (4:7–15). The foot-washing ceremony is a type of baptism (13:1–17). At the crucifixion, sol-diers pierce Jesus' side, and out pour water and blood (19:34). In the dis-course in chapter 15, Jesus speaks of himself as the vine and of his disciples as the branches. It is no accident that the figure is that of the vineyard. Chapter 6 contains the most extensive treatment of the sacraments. It be-gins with a narrative about the feeding of the multitude. In the interpreta-tive commentary which follows, Jesus affirms that it is necessary to partake of his body and blood in order to have eternal life. He claims to be the bread of life. He has come down from heaven as the manna descended during the time of Moses. Then Jesus says that the bread he gives is his own flesh. His body is real bread, his blood is real drink, and it is absolutely essential to partake of his body and blood. The long discourse draws to a close with Jesus saying, "It is the spirit that gives life, the flesh is of no avail" (6:63). Despite the importance of the material elements, it is the spirit that stands behind the sacraments and authenticates them. The lan-guage of the Fourth Gospel reminds one of the Hellenistic mystery reli-gions, which emphasize the sacrament as a means of participation in deity. John is able to say that the union of a believer with the Lord is made secure in the sacraments. At the same time, he intends to guard against highly materialistic interpretations of the sacraments by having the spirit be the guarantor of their efficacy.

The importance of the spirit in the Fourth Gospel led Clement of Alex-andria to call it the gospel of the spirit.[24] This is an accurate generalization because the author de-emphasizes historical, fleshly, and earthly phenom-ena. His Christology does not depend heavily on the life of Jesus of Naza-reth. The believer does not find revelation in a series of historical events but in his own union with Christ. The church is not intended to create a Chris-tian world but is to understand itself as separated from the world. Although the teaching was used in connection with sacraments, it is appropriate to the whole of Johannine Christianity: "It is the spirit that gives life, the flesh is of no avail" (John 6:63).

GNOSTIC CHRISTIANITY

Popular religious systems describe human beings in meaningful terms. They tell people who they are, why they are here, what is expected of them, and where they are headed. Religion is not only speculation about God; it is also an expression of deep feelings about the nature and context of human existence. The more meaningful religious expressions are those to which people can make positive responses. They are meaningful if a person can

---

[24] Quoted in Eusebius, op. cit., VI, 14:7.

listen to the assertions and say, "Yes, those statements adequately describe me." Generally optimistic people may not respond to a religious system that tells them they are in a hopelessly depraved situation, and socially deprived persons may reject a religion that tells them that all is right with the world. Gnostic Christianity appealed to large numbers of people in the Hellenistic period because it seemed to address them where they were with a message of hopeful change.

The immense popularity of Gnostic Christianity, especially in the second century, is attested to by the vast attention that was given to it by those who opposed it. We find references to Gnosticlike concepts and systems in most second-century Christian writings. By the end of the century writers such as Irenaeus found it necessary to deal systematically with Gnostic (and Marcionite) Christianity and to attempt to refute its basic concepts. Irenaeus recognized the formidable threat that this form of thought posed to his own religious system. To him it was a demonic perversion of true Christianity that had led large numbers of people astray. He and others knew that it had to be opposed tooth and nail. Indeed, we will see that it was mainly the battle with Gnostic (and Marcionite) Christianity that shaped early Catholic Christianity. The battle, although not violent, was not easy. It probably was the major phenomenon in second-century Christian history.

Gnosticism is a modern term that is used in a variety of ways. Sometimes it is used to designate a world view that is found in Hellenistic culture generally. At other times it is used to designate certain specific and identifiable systems of thought. Such systems generally share some mythological speculations and basic attitudes about the nature of God, the world, and human beings.[25] Both uses of the term have merit, for the Gnostic systems would not have been appealing unless the culture as a whole found them compatible. Here, however, we intend to use the term in the more specific sense, rather than to refer to general attitudes shared in the culture as a whole.

Actually, we know Gnosticism primarily as a variety of Christianity. This variety is associated mainly with the systems of Valentinus, Ptolemy, Basilides, and others, who were active in the mid-second century. Many modern scholars are convinced, however, that it arose prior to and independently of Christianity. The Hermetic literature, for example, is often thought to include non-Christian Gnostic texts. In other Gnostic documents the Christian elements are not integral to the basic thought and were probably added to a previously developed system.[26] Although the full-blown Gnostic Chris-

---

[25] For a discussion of the problems of defining Gnosticism, cf. Ugo Bianchi, *Le Origini dello Gnosticismo: Texts and Discussions of the Colloquium of Messina, 1966* (Leiden: E. J. Brill, 1970).

[26] For example, one Nag Hammadi tractate, The Sophia of Jesus Christ, appears to be a Christiain version of another tractate, Eugnostos the Blessed, which has no Christian affinities. Cf. James M. Robinson, ed. *The Nag Hammadi Library* (New York: Harper, 1977), pp. 206–228.

tian systems probably did not develop until the second century, some Gnostic ideas may have been known even as early as Paul's time. However, the precise time at which non-Christian Gnosticism arose is unknown. In its second-century Christian forms it appears to combine Jewish, Greek, Hellenistic, and oriental influences. Some documents use OT texts, and others have affinities with Jewish apocalyptic literature. Some scholars suggest that the origin of non-Christian Gnosticism is to be found among apocalyptically inclined Jews who had suffered a series of disappointments when their expectations were not fulfilled.[27] But Gnosticism also has positive and closer affinities with Greek philosophy and oriental mythology. Whatever the origin, many second-century Christians found Gnosticism attractive and utilized Gnostic elements to produce a number of conceptual systems.

The name is a form of the Greek word *gnosis,* which we translate as knowledge. The Gnostic feels that he has been granted knowledge, which is a means of salvation. But gnosis is not to be confused with learning. It does not result from a process of study that is gradually built up by reading books, listening to lectures, and having discussions with scholars. The definition of knowledge as learning rests on the assumption that human beings have within them the ability to arrive at understanding. For reasons that will soon become apparent, Gnostic Christians were convinced that people could not achieve knowledge without divine aid. Gnosis comes from outside. It cannot be taught; it must be revealed. For this reason gnosis is usually secret and retained within the community of Gnostics.

Irenaeus and the other opponents of Gnostic Christianity have, until recently, been the only sources of information about Gnostic movements. Their information was, to be sure, biased and selective, but it has been useful. Fortunately, we now have a large treasure of material that bears on the subject. Some Coptic Gnostic documents were discovered in 1896, but fifty-two additional documents in the Coptic language were found in 1945 at Nag Hammadi, Egypt. We looked at one of those documents, the Coptic Gospel of Thomas, in Chapter 6. Because it is not possible to describe the contents of all the other documents in this library, we will look at two representative texts—the Gospel of Mary, found in 1896, and the Gospel of Truth, from Nag Hammadi.[28] Although these documents are called gospels, they bear little literary resemblance to those that were analyzed in Chapter 6; it seems more appropriate to treat them as examples of Gnostic Christian thought than as possible sources for the life of Jesus. After we have examined these two Gnostic documents, we will look at Irenaeus' description of one Gnostic system.

[27] Cf. R. M. Grant, *Gnosticism and Early Christianity,* 2nd ed. (New York: Columbia U.P., 1966).
[28] For translations of these documents, cf. Robinson, op. cit., pp. 37–49 and 471–474.

The Gospel of Mary

The Gospel of Mary begins with the final words of Jesus as he departs from the disciples. He charges them to preach the gospel of the kingdom. But the disciples are concerned about this task, and they ask, "If they did not spare him, how will they spare us?"[29] Then Mary, presumably Mary Magdalene, gives them words of encouragement, and Peter asks her to tell them the secret words that Jesus taught her. She replies by narrating a vision in which the soul ascends from earth to heaven and overcomes opposing powers. When Mary finishes speaking, Andrew and Peter express disbelief, and Peter says, "Did he really speak privately with a woman (and) not openly to us? Are we to turn about and all listen to her? Did he prefer her to us?"[30] Levi, however, objects to Peter's hot temper and counsels the group to believe Mary; he claims that Jesus loved her more than he did the other disciples.

This short text is interesting for several reasons. It is unusual because it makes a woman the center of attention. There appears to be a condemnation of the attitude that Peter represents because Levi describes him as "contending against the woman like the adversaries."[31] But there is more here than male-female contrasts. Mary represents the Gnostic, who has received a secret revelation from the Lord. As such, she stands opposed to the disciples, especially Peter, to whom Jesus only spoke openly. Gnostic Christians frequently emphasized an esoteric tradition in contrast to a public tradition, and they claimed to be in possession of secret gnosis. Such texts as the Gospel of Mary would explain why Peter and other disciples did not pass on vital information. They did not do so because they refused to believe and accept it when it was communicated to them.

The Gospel of Truth

The Gospel of Truth is one of the more important tractates among those discovered at Nag Hammadi. Irenaeus said that a book by this title had been written by Valentinus, and he claimed that it was totally different from the documents he called the gospels of the apostles.[32] The tractate from Nag Hammadi is sometimes thought to be the very book that Irenaeus mentioned. If that is the case, it is notable that it contains nothing like the complex speculations that Irenaeus attributed to Valentinus and his disciples. We know very little about Valentinus himself. He probably came from Egypt originally, but he resided in Rome from c. 135–165. He was excom-

[29] The Gospel of Mary 9:10–12, trans. by George W. MacRae and R. McL. Wilson, in Robinson, op. cit.
[30] Ibid., 17:18–22.
[31] Ibid., 18:9–10.
[32] Cf. Irenaeus, *Against Heresies* III, 11:9.

municated by the church there because of his alleged heresy. Some of his followers set up schools of their own, and we know of Valentinianism mainly through them. It is likely that the Gospel of Truth comes from the Valentinian circle rather than from Valentinus himself and dates from about 150.

Irenaeus was quite correct in saying that the Gospel of Truth was not like other gospels. It contains no narratives and no sayings of Jesus. From first to last it is an essay, or a meditative homily. It is exceedingly difficult to find a principle of organization or structure. Connections between topics are vague, and it is difficult to identify the topics that are treated.

Because of the apparently unsystematic nature of this text, it is difficult to identify the leading ideas. Nevertheless, there are some points that come through with a reasonable degree of clarity. Theologically most of the attention is directed toward the Father, who surely is the chief divine being. The Son is the revelation of the Father, and he is identified as Jesus Christ. There is also mention of the Holy Spirit, but little attention is directed toward it. Some remarks are made about the creation of the world, in which the act of creation appears to be the result of error. Clearly the material elements are regarded to be deficient, and the homily contrasts the deficiency of matter with the perfection, or fullness, of the divine realm, which is called the pleroma. It is possible that this text speaks about the creation of the world by a lesser, fallen, God, here called the All. As a result of the creative process, human beings are in a state of oblivion, but there is an expected salvation. Salvation is an overcoming of oblivion by knowledge (gnosis) of the Father, which is revealed by the Son, and it results in participation in the pleroma. The nature and position of some other beings, called Aeons, are unclear. They seem to be suprahuman, but they also seem to need revelation, just as humans do. There also are hints of predestinarian thought and indications that only some humans will be saved.

Such seems to be the basic ideology represented in the Gospel of Truth, but some additional matters deserve comment. At one point there is a reference to Jesus' parable of the lost sheep.[33] The parable is summarized and then given a numerological interpretation. Moreover, there is a set of ethical maxims that remind the reader of some of the synoptic teachings of Jesus. Finally, there are several references to the suffering and death of Jesus, and none of them seems to have docetic overtones. We will see below that, according to Irenaeus, some of Valentinus' disciples moved deeply into the world of mythological speculation, docetic interpretation, and amoral life style. If the Gospel of Truth is a composition of a member of the Valentinian school, it is evident that some members of the school were farther removed from the other Christian groups than others.

[33] Cf. The Gospel of Truth 31:35–32:34; cf. Matt 18:12–14 and Luke 15.3–7.

Irenaeus' Description of Gnostic Christianity

We will treat Irenaeus in Chapter 12 as one of the major early Catholic writers. He must be introduced here, however, because a large area of his thought was forged in opposition to Gnostic Christianity and because his writings include detailed descriptions of Gnostic thought. These descriptions, although biased, are fundamental sources for our understanding of Gnostic Christianity.

Irenaeus was probably born and raised in Asia Minor, but he moved to Gaul and became a presbyter in Lyons. He carried some correspondence from there to Rome and, upon returning to Lyons in 177, found that his bishop had been killed in a recent persecution and that he had been selected as the new bishop. In about 185 Irenaeus wrote a five-volume work entitled *A Refutation and Overthrow of Pseudo-Gnosis,* usually referred to as *Against Heresies.*

In the first book of *Against Heresies,* Irenaeus describes the Gnostic system of the disciples of Ptolemy, who was a disciple of Valentinus.[34] This scheme is usually thought of as Valentinian, but it should be noted that it is removed from Valentinus himself by two generations of disciples.

The system is a complex description of creation and redemption. The creation myth begins with the existence of a God named Depth. The name indicates the importance of certain qualities of the divine—namely, profundity, unknowability, eternality, and limitlessness. Depth symbolizes deity in its most profound and inscrutable sense. But Depth has other qualities, which are personified. He is paired with Silence, another symbol of the incommunicable character of deity. Depth and Silence give birth to two additional Gods, Mind and Truth. These in turn produce Logos and Life. Altogether there are fifteen pairs of Gods, or Aeons, the last being Theletos (Desired) and Sophia (Wisdom). These thirty Aeons make up what is called the pleroma or Fullness, the sum total of all divinity and goodness. Each pair is composed of a male and a female. Depth, Mind, Logos, and Theletos are male, and the others are their female consorts. Together they give birth to the succeeding Aeons.

Within the pleroma there are certain gradations. The distance between Depth, the highest, and Sophia, the lowest, is emphasized. Mind is the only one who can know Depth, but all the others desire this knowledge. Sophia desired it to such an extent that she forsook Theletos and had to be restrained by a personification called Limit, a kind of guardian of Depth and the pleroma. Limit restored her to her proper place in the pleroma but the unfulfilled desire that she had expressed became independent of her. This personified desire was thrown out of the pleroma and is afterward called Achamoth.[35] Disturbed by the crisis caused by Sophia, the other Aeons

---

[34] Cf. Irenaeus, op cit., I, 1–8. For a thorough and clear analysis of this material, cf. Hans Jonas, *The Gnostic Religion,* 2nd ed. (Boston: Beacon, 1963), pp. 174–205.

[35] *Achamoth* is Hebrew for wisdom, so it is the equivalent of the Greek *Sophia.*

prayed to Depth, who gave birth to two more Aeons, Christ and Holy Spirit. Their duties were to restore order in the pleroma and to begin the recovery of the fallen Achamoth. When the original order of the pleroma was established, all the Aeons together produced the God Jesus, who was not paired with a female.

The scene now shifts to the region outside the pleroma, at present inhabited only by Achamoth. Christ stretches outside the pleroma in order to acquaint Achamoth with her separation from deity and to awaken her desire for restoration. In her frustration she expresses grief, fear, shock, and ignorance. Those negative expressions become independent of her and become sources for the material elements. But Achamoth also turns toward the pleroma in an act of conversion. In response the divine Jesus comes to be her consort and grant to her gnosis, which frees her from her negative passions. In her joy she produces spirit, which continues to exist in the lower world. She also produces soul and forms it into a being called the Demiurge. He is characterized by ignorance, which Achamoth can use to obtain her will. Demiurge then creates the seven planetary spheres and the earth. He also creates human beings by imprisoning spirit within soul and combining them with the material elements. Thus, a human being is made up of a divine spirit, a soul, and a material body.

The work of human salvation is largely carried out by Jesus and Christ, and for it the restoration of Achamoth serves as a model. The Aeons, Jesus and Christ, descended on the earthly Jesus at his baptism and left him before his death. In this system the earthly Jesus was only the vehicle for the saving work of the divine Jesus and Christ. He was completely human, and he died, but his death is irrelevant to salvation. Salvation comes when the divine Jesus and Christ impart gnosis to spirits in human beings. Not all people will be saved, because in some the spiritual element is minimal or missing. When the work of Jesus and Christ has been completed, the released spirits and Achamoth re-enter the pleroma. The divine sparks have finally returned home.

Irenaeus not only describes the system of Ptolemy's disciples, but he also tells us something about the Gnostic interpretation of the NT. It appears to be mainly a numerological interpretation. For example, Luke 3:23 says that Jesus was about thirty years old when he began his ministry. The reason he did not appear in public for this period of time was that he was setting forth the mystery of the thirty Aeons. One of the subdivisions of the Aeons is a group of twelve Gods, symbolized in the NT by the twelve disciples and by Jesus' age when he debated in the Temple (Luke 2:42). Moreover, the woman whom Jesus healed of a hemorrhage had been ill for twelve years (Matt 9:20–22 and parallels), and Jairus' daughter, whom Jesus raised, was twelve years old (Mark 5:35–43 and parallels). As Sophia was the last member in the group of twelve, so was Judas the last of the twelve disciples of Jesus.

If Irenaeus' description is not trustworthy in every detail, it at least illustrates the ways in which Gnostic Christians were perceived by informed, though unsympathetic, persons.

The Character of Gnostic Christianity

In the second century there was a bewildering array of Gnostic-Christian groups, and it is difficult to generalize about them. They are so diverse that some do not even use the concept of gnosis. Irenaeus bemoaned the fact that each day one of them came up with something new.[36] The diversity prevents us from doing full justice to all the groups that might be called Gnostic, so we shall concentrate on some distinctive characteristics that appear to be widespread.

In general, Gnostic Christians are regarded as polytheists. The sense in which they were must be carefully understood. In the Valentinian system, for example, the Aeons are thought of as to some degree independent of one another. Yet they are all born of Depth and Silence. The figure of the family and birth is appropriate in calling attention to the tension between unity and independence. At conception, a mother and her son are so intimately connected that the son is a completely dependent and indistinct part of the mother. At birth, the son is distinct, and his independence begins and grows gradually. The developing family undergoes a process in which indistinct persons become distinct and dependent persons become independent. Throughout the process, the family exists in a state of tension between unity and independence. The same is the case in the Gnostic pleroma. As the deity gives expression to one of his qualities, that quality becomes a distinct entity. It is true that there are thirty deities in the pleroma, but they are all projections of the original God. In any event, this system does not reflect what had traditionally been meant by Jews and Christians when they emphasized belief in one God. By strict definition, Gnostics were not monotheists even if they believed in one divine family.

In the typically Gnostic teaching about creation, there is a very negative attitude toward the world. The universe is not created by the high God but by a lesser being, sometimes called the Demiurge, who also governs the created order.[37] The universe is structured in such a way that people are imprisoned within it. The earth is surrounded by the planetary spheres and the sphere of the so-called fixed stars. The Demiurge has placed rulers, or Archons, over each of the spheres, and they serve to separate the universe and humans from the divine realm. The rule of the Demiurge and Archons is called Fate, a force that alienated people from a freedom that is rightly theirs.[38] The well-known philosopher Hans Jonas described the Gnostic

---

[36] Cf. Irenaeus, op. cit., I, 18:1.
[37] "Demiurge" is the designation for the creator of the world in Plato's *Timaeus*.
[38] Cf. Chapter 4 in this book for the concept of fate in astrology and in Stoicism.

universe as "a vast prison whose innermost dungeon is the earth, the scene of man's life."[39] Many Hellenistic thinkers would agree. Indeed, the idea of the human body as a prison is found in some very old Greek documents.

People find themselves to be residents here and subject to Fate, but they are essentially strangers to this world. Strictly speaking, we are composed of three parts: body, soul, and spirit. Spirit is a portion of the divine that fell from the upper world. In order to imprison it, the Demiurge or the Archons created bodies and souls and made them subject to the rule of Fate. The usual state of the imprisoned spirit is sleep, but it may be awakened through gnosis and informed about its true condition. Humans, thus, consist of a mixture of the divine and the demonic. When the awakened spirit discovers that it does not belong here, a deep dissatisfaction results. People become lonely, alienated, and frustrated in their worldly and bodily imprisonment.

Salvation comes by way of a messenger from the divine region, who comes secretly through the stellar and planetary spheres to bring gnosis to human beings. After death, the Gnostic, having received gnosis and being free of the material body, begins a journey through the spheres. At this point, the Gnostic is still a spirit surrounded by a soul. The soul is understood to be a covering around the spirit, and at each sphere a layer of the covering is removed. At the end the spirit is totally free and is finally reunited with the divine substance. Salvation has a twofold significance for the Gnostic. It is release from demonic bondage and absorption into divinity.

In Gnostic Christianity the savior is usually conceived of in docetic fashion as pure spirit. Otherwise he would be imprisoned in soul and body as we are, and a fellow prisoner could not execute our escape. If it seemed to Jesus' disciples that he was human, this was the result either of intentional deception by the Demiurge or of the disciples' inability to ascertain the presence of pure spirit. Whatever the disciples felt, Gnostics were sure that the divine Christ was not composed of soul and body, that he was not born in human fashion, and that he did not die. To be sure, in the system described by Irenaeus, there is a human Jesus, but he is only the vehicle by which the divine Jesus and Christ operate.

Ethics appears to be a matter of secondary importance in Gnostic Christianity because it involves the relation of humans to the created world. The Gnostic was able to adopt either of two opposing life styles—either ascetic or libertine. If a person exists as a spirit imprisoned in a soul and a body, it stands to reason that he or she ought to have as little as possible to do with the prison. The spirit should practice a kind of dominance over the other components in order to prepare itself for its release. This way leads to asceticism, and the practicing Gnostic would avoid contact with the world as much as possible. He would be unmarried and celibate and he would prac-

[39] Jonas, op. cit., p. 43.

tice fasting and perhaps poverty. But, on the same premises, it is possible to regard the body and the soul as ethically irrelevant. Nothing is to be gained by disciplining the body and soul, for the spirit is eventually to lose them anyway. Moreover, some Gnostics felt that they should demonstrate their disdain for the Demiurge and his system of governance by abusing the body and material things. This way leads to libertinism, which permits unrestrained indulgence in sex, food, drink, and wealth. According to their opponents, both asceticism and libertinism were to be found among Gnostic Christians. It is likely, however, that charges about Gnostic libertinism are mostly forms of polemical slander and that Gnostics leaned heavily toward asceticism.

Another characteristic aspect of Gnostic Christianity was the use of myth. To be sure, the tendency to employ mythical expression was part of the cultural equipment of the day. To most Hellenistic people myth was a narrative description of the nonhistorical world, which was thought to be at least as real as the historical. Not only was mythology fundamental to pre-Hellenistic and Hellenistic religion, but it also played a role in Judaism and in other varieties of Christianity. A conception of a pre-existent divine being, for example, lies behind the prologue of the Gospel of John (John 1:1–18) and the Christological hymn in Paul's letter to the Philippians (Phil 2:5–11). The Gnostic myths differ from those in other varieties of Christianity only in their complexity and in their degree of importance. Gnostic myths frequently consist of an almost innumerable cast of characters, and they occupy a position of greater importance than do those in the other versions. What appears to be peripheral in, say, Pauline Christianity is central in Gnostic Christianity.

There is no one right way to read Gnostic myths, which probably served a number of functions among Christian Gnostics. Some of them probably were read as explanations of the existence of the natural world, and others satisfied curiosity about human psychology. The Valentinian myth that Irenaeus described may be read most fruitfully as referring to the human situation, as Gnostic Christians understood it. In the myth of the fall of Sophia, for example, something parallel to the human situation can be seen. Gnostics emphasized the inner conflict that people frequently feel. Many people recognize that they are part of the world in which they live, but they do not always feel content in it. They are torn between desires for material things and guilt at succumbing to desires. They have aspirations that are unfulfilled because of physical and moral incapacities. They feel that the observable world must not be all there is and that somehow they are related to, but separated from, that other world beyond this one. The myth of Sophia, who has impossible desires, may be seen as a symbol of the human attempt to rise to higher levels and to leave behind the material prison. The myth is able to speak to frustrated people and tell them that they are essentially aliens and prisoners and that there is a savior, Jesus, who has come, or will come, to release them and lead them back home. It can show that what is impossible for us is possible through the work of Jesus. It can teach that human frustration will finally disappear because we will achieve authentic selfhood and will become pure spirits, free of soul and body. To many people in the second century, mythology imparted a high degree of authority to Gnostic teaching. Without it, such teaching could be regarded simply as one more human opinion. To the opponents, such as Irenaeus, that is precisely what it was. But to Gnostic Christians, the myth provided a grounding in the very structure of reality.

Although they represented a wide diversity of thought, Gnostic Christians, taken as a whole, had distinct advantages over other Christian groups. They could think in terms that did not require strict monotheistic belief and, thus, would appeal to many who had been associated with Hellenistic religions. They could use a popular form of expression, namely myth, to explain human frustration and to offer hope for future salvation. They could explain the apparently evil nature of the world. Above all, they felt little obligation to connect their theology with historical events, such as the life of Jesus. His life and teachings were either irrelevant or they served as mysterious revelations of Gnostic mythology. His death was not a saving event but an illusion. Opponents, such as Irenaeus, fully recognized that the ahistorical aspects of Gnostic Christianity were appealing to many people. But they also believed that Gnostics omitted something that was absolutely fundamental in Christian faith: recognition of the theological importance of certain historical events.

MARCIONITE CHRISTIANITY

There are important affinities between Gnostic and Marcionite Christianity, so much so that the latter is frequently considered to be a Gnostic movement. But there are also fundamental differences that tend to distinguish the two. Marcionite Christianity had a negative attitude toward the created order and its creator, but it did not have a complex mythology, such as we associate with Gnosticism. Irenaeus and the other opponents felt that Marcionite Christianity was an extremely dangerous sect, and they gave it a great deal of attention. Irenaeus was afraid that the teachings of the group would pull away many people from the "true" faith.

Marcion, the founder, was a wealthy shipowner from Pontus, in Asia Minor. Hippolytus reports that his father, a Christian bishop, had excommunicated him because of his immorality.[40] He came to Rome in about 140 and joined the church there but was excommunicated a few years later. He spent the remaining years of his life (until c. 160) organizing churches

[40] Quoted in Epiphanius, op. cit., XLII.

all over the Roman Empire. His writings have completely disappeared, except for quotations and summaries used by opponents in their attacks on him.

Fundamental to Marcion's thought is the idea of two Gods—one the creator, the other the savior. The two Gods are totally unlike each other and hostile to each other. There is no genealogical relationship between them as there is between Depth and Demiurge in the Valentinian system. The creator God is characterized by pettiness, and he rules the world by retributive, vindictive justice. He is known in nature and through the OT. His creation of the world is described in Genesis, and he gave the Torah to his chosen people, the Jews. The other God is one of saving love, revealed for the first time by Jesus. The God whom Jesus addressed as Father has nothing to do with the OT God, and his function is to save us from the creator's rule. He does so out of his freely given grace, for the people he saves are not fallen spirits who belonged to him, but creatures of the lesser God. The loving God saves them by adopting them as his own. Marcion's Christology was docetic. The Christ was not a product of the creator God and, hence, was not truly human. He came directly from the loving God in the fifteenth year of the Roman emperor Tiberius (29 CE) and assumed an apparently human body. His death was the price paid to the creator for our salvation. We receive this salvation in faith, not by gnosis.

Marcion's inspiration came from Paul. He was deeply impressed with Paul's contrast of Torah and Christ, but he did not see the underlying unity between them that Paul did. To him the revelation in Christ was completely new, in no way anticipated in the OT.[41] Thus, he made Paul's letters (including Ephesians but excluding the pastoral letters, which he either did not know or did not accept) the basic canon for his churches. He included with them the Gospel of Luke in a form lacking any suggestion of connection between Jesus and the OT God. The OT was totally discarded as the work of the creator, whose pettiness and inconsistency it revealed. To our knowledge, Marcion's canon, consisting only of Luke and Paul, was the first attempt to form a body of authoritative Christian Scripture. His canon, his organizing ability, and his demand for strict asceticism created a strong group of churches parallel to but distinct from the other groups of Christians.

Despite Hippolytus' claims, Marcion was known as a profoundly ethical person and a practicing ascetic. His theology probably came out of a deep concern for the religious life. The nineteenth-century scholar Adolf Harnack's estimate rings true:

> [Marcion] had in general nothing to do with principles, but with living beings whose power he felt, and . . . what he ultimately saw in the Gospel was not

---

[41] Marcion agreed that the OT had predicted the coming of a Messiah, but he maintained that those predictions were not fulfilled in Jesus. According to him, the Messiah is yet to come from the creator God, but his coming is totally irrelevant to the God of love.

an explanation of the world, but redemption from the world,—redemption from a world which even in the best that it can offer has nothing that can reach the height of the blessing bestowed in Christ.[42]

Marcion's effort to establish a religion separated from its Jewish background, with its own scriptures, its own organization, and a rigid ethic, was appealing to many, but challenging and threatening to most Christian groups. Probably the most radical aspect of his religious thought was the separation of Christian faith from the OT and from Judaism. In this respect Marcionite Christianity was an extreme movement in early Christianity. The range of Christian variety in the period from 70–185 can be seen by placing late Jewish Christianity at one end of the spectrum and Marcionite at the other. Late Jewish Christians intended to hold fast to the Jewish connections, and Marcionite Christians intended to sever any relationships between Christianity and Judaism. Marcionite Christianity not only had the potential for creating a rootless variety of Christianity, but also the possibility for injecting into it a heavy dose of anti-Judaism.

In this chapter it has been necessary to concentrate on the major early Christian groups and on their distinctive emphases. This examination can suggest, but not fully describe, the variety of Christianity in the period from 70–185. The names of those early Christian groups—late Pauline, Johannine, Gnostic, and the like—are, in the final analysis, only academic and modern at that, for those Christians probably did not call themselves by those names. The important point is that in the period from 70–185 there was great diversity in Christianity.

BIBLIOGRAPHY

Late Pauline Christianity

Cross, F. C., ed. *Studies in Ephesians*. London: A. R. Mowbray, 1956.

Dibelius, Martin, and Hans Conzelmann. *The Pastoral Epistles*. Trans. by Philip Buttolph and Adela Yarbro. Hermeneia Commentaries. Philadelphia: Fortress Press, 1972.

Goodspeed, Edgar J. *The Meaning of Ephesians*. Chicago: University of Chicago Press, 1933.

In *The Meaning of Ephesians,* Goodspeed lays out his theory about the collection of Paul's letters and the place of Ephesians in that process. Cross includes a number of diverse interpretations of Ephesians written by several scholars. The book by Dibelius and Conzelmann is a traditional commentary on the three letters. It was originally published in German in 1955 but did not appear in English until 1972.

[42] Adolf Harnack, *History of Dogma,* trans. Neil Buchanan (Boston: Little, Brown, 1905), Vol. I, p. 270.

Late Jewish Christianity

Brandon, S. G. F. *The Fall of Jerusalem and the Christian Church.* 2nd ed. London: Society for the Promotion of Christian Knowledge, 1957.

Daniélou, Jean. *The Theology of Jewish Christianity.* Trans. by John A. Baker. London: Darton, Longman and Todd, 1964.

Dibelius, Martin. *James.* Rev. by Heinrich Greeven. Trans. by Michael A. Williams. Hermeneia Commentaries. Philadelphia: Fortress Press, 1976.

Hennecke, Edgar. *New Testament Apocrypha.* Ed. by W. Schneemelcher. Trans. by R. McL. Wilson. Philadelphia: Westminster Press, 1963, 1965. 2 volumes

Schoeps, Hans J. *Jewish Christianity.* Trans. by D. R. A. Hare. Philadelphia: Fortress Press, 1969.

Schonfield, Hugh J. *A History of Jewish Christianity.* London: Gerald Duckworth & Co. Ltd., 1936.

Volume I of Hennecke's *New Testament Apocrypha* includes an introduction and translation of the remaining fragments of the Gospel of the Ebionites, as well as other Jewish-Christian gospels. Dibelius' is a commentary on the letter of James. Brandon's book centers on a specific historical incident but contains a good deal of material on both early and late Jewish Christianity as well as on Paul. Schoeps is a helpful, nontechnical introduction to the subject. The most comprehensive study of late Jewish-Christian theology is that by Daniélou, who, however, has a rather broad definition of the phenomenon.

Johannine Christianity

Brown, Raymond E. *The Community of the Beloved Disciple.* New York: Paulist Press, 1979.

Bultmann, Rudolf. *The Johannine Epistles.* Trans. by R. Philip O'Hara et al. Hermeneia Commentaries. Philadelphia: Fortress Press, 1973.

———. *Theology of the New Testament.* Trans. by Kendrick Grobel. New York: Charles Scribner's Sons, 1951, 1955. 2 volumes

Dodd, C. H. *The Interpretation of the Fourth Gospel.* Cambridge: Cambridge University Press, 1953.

The books by Brown and Dodd were listed in the bibliography for Chapter 6, but they are relevant here as well. Brown has a section on the Johannine epistles and on their relationship to the Fourth Gospel. Dodd deals with the relationship of Johannine Christianity to the Hermetic literature and Gnosticism, as well as to other contemporary forms of thought. Bultmann's *Johannine Epistles* is a commentary on the three letters. His *Theology of the New Testament* has a section on "The Theology of the Gospel of John and the Johannine Epistles" in Volume II.

Gnostic and Marcionite Christianity

Blackman, E. C. *Marcion and his Influence*. London: S.P.C.K., 1948.

Grant, Robert M. *Gnosticism and Early Christianity*. 2nd ed. New York: Harper & Row, Publishers, 1966.

Grobel, Kendrick. *The Gospel of Truth*. Nashville, Tenn.: Abingdon Press, 1960.

Jonas, Hans. *The Gnostic Religion*. 2nd ed. Boston: Beacon Press, 1963.

Knox, John. *Marcion and the New Testament*. Chicago: University of Chicago Press, 1942.

Pagels, Elaine. *The Gnostic Gospels*. New York: Random House, Inc., 1979.

Richardson, Cyril C., ed. *Early Christian Fathers*. Library of Christian Classics, Volume I. Philadelphia: Westminster Press, 1953.

Roberts, Alexander, and James Donaldson, eds. *The Ante-Nicene Fathers*. Grand Rapids, Mich.: Eerdmans, 1885. 10 volumes

Robinson, James M., ed. *The Nag Hammadi Library in English*. New York: Harper & Row, Publishers, 1977.

Wilson, R. McL. *Gnosis and the New Testament*. Philadelphia: Fortress Press, 1968.

———. *The Gospel of Philip*. London: A. R. Mowbray, 1962.

Most scholars treat Gnostic and Marcionite Christianity together, although they recognize the differences between them. The major collection of Coptic Gnostic literature is that edited by James M. Robinson. It includes the Gospel of Mary and the Gospel of Truth. Grobel's *Gospel of Truth* and Wilson's *Gospel of Philip* are translations and commentaries on these two documents from Nag Hammadi. *The Ante-Nicene Fathers,* Volume I, contains a translation of the complete text of Irenaeus' *Against Heresies*. Richardson has a selection of the most important parts. The studies by Grant, Jonas, and Wilson, as well as the provocative book by Pagels, are all highly competent. In *Marcion and the New Testament,* Knox explores the influence that Marcion had on the development of the NT canon. Blackman's is a more general and more cautious approach to Marcion.

❖ 12 ❖

Persecution and the Rise
of Early Catholic Christianity

E ARLY Catholic Christianity was not just one more type of Christianity with distinctive emphases and teachings. It was more than that:
it was a conscious attempt to unify Christian doctrine and thus diminish diversity. To those who spoke for this movement, the diversity of
groups such as late Jewish and Marcionite Christianity represented perver-
sions of the Christian message. Their existence was a challenge to Christian
unity. But diversity also seemed to represent weakness. The weakness became apparent in the conflicts between Christians and the non-Christian
public. Some of the conflicts were marked by violence, and it was in the
crucible of violent persecution that early Catholic Christianity arose. By the
end of the second century, however, it had become the dominant form of
Christianity.

CHRISTIANS AND PERSECUTION

From the very beginning of the movement, Christians occasionally met violent responses from the non-Christian public. In his letters Paul confessed
that he himself had been a persecutor of Christians in Judea. He is probably
representative of a group of deeply religious Jews who felt that the preaching about Jesus was theologically dangerous. He knew that Christians in
Judea had suffered persecution from Jews, but he also knew of a community
in Thessalonica that had been oppressed in some way by Gentiles. He wrote
to them: "For you, brethren, became imitators of the churches of God in
Christ Jesus which are in Judea; for you suffered the same things from your
own countrymen as they did from the Jews" (1 Thess 2:14). Paul also refers
to his own suffering from Jewish authorities. He says that he was punished
by them on five occasions (2 Cor 11:24). But clearly not all of Paul's
troubles came from Jews, for he wrote of other beatings as well as imprisonments. In his catalogue of labors in service to Christ, he included "danger

390

The flagellation of Aelia Afanasis, 270–280 CE Catacomb of Praetextatus, Rome.
(Courtesy *Pontifical Commission for Sacred Archives, Rome.*)

from my own people, [and] danger from Gentiles" (2 Cor 11:26). Although we cannot be certain about the location of the prison (or prisons) from which he wrote some of his letters, a reference in Phil 1:13 shows that it probably was guarded by Roman troops and hence was under imperial jurisdiction. If Paul writes about oppression and imprisonment, he writes even more about problems internal to the churches. Problems of factionalism and dissension seemed to have bothered him more than problems arising out of conflict with the non-Christian community. The image of the community at Corinth, for example, is one of vigorous Christian activity, not seriously impeded by external threats.

The author of the book of Acts also knew that Christians were persecuted. He told of the martyrdom of Stephen, the persecution that led to the scattering of Christians from Jerusalem, the execution of the apostle James, and the persecuting activity of Paul. He emphasized the Jewish opposition that caused the Christian Paul trouble everywhere he went, and he described the trials of Paul as initiated by false charges made by Jews. In Luke's pattern of things, Jews are the persecutors of Christians, and Roman officials are their protectors.

Paul's account is probably more dependable than Luke's at those points where they differ. His letters indicate that Christians were sometimes persecuted by Jews and sometimes by Gentiles and that Christians suffered in Judea as well as in other parts of the Roman Empire. The indications are that persecutions broke out from time to time in various locations. There are no signs this early of any sustained attempts to exterminate Christians or of any policies that would have impeded their activities. The individual communities were probably at peace most of the time.

The persecution under the emperor Nero that occurred in c. 62 is no exception to this rule. Although it occurred at the instigation of the emperor and in Rome, and although many Christians were cruelly tortured and killed, there are no signs of a systematic policy to exterminate Christians. Our earliest and most complete reference to the incident is from the pen of the Roman historian Tacitus, writing in c. 112. Tacitus tells about the great fire in Rome, which many people blamed on Nero. He says that the emperor, in order to direct attention from himself, pointed to the Christians in Rome as the culprits. Tacitus clearly does not believe that the Christians were guilty, although he describes them as "a class hated for their abominations." Tacitus also describes the methods of punishment:

> Besides being put to death they were made to serve as objects of amusement; they were clad in the hides of beasts and torn to death by dogs; others were crucified, others set on fire to serve to illuminate the night when daylight failed. Nero had thrown open his grounds for the display, and was putting on a show in the circus, where he mingled with the people in the dress of a charioteer or drove about in his chariot. All this gave rise to a feeling of pity, even towards men whose guilt merited the most exemplary punishment; for it was felt that they were being destroyed not for the public good but to gratify the cruelty of an individual.[1]

Tacitus was probably right. This persecution, cruel as it was, was not the result of a public policy. Once Nero felt vindicated, there appears to have been no repetition of such an outburst.

The persecution under Domitian (81-96) must have been more terrifying. The technical requirements of the imperial cult must have created difficulties for Christians almost from the beginning. As long as they were not distinguished from Jews, they probably were not forced to bring the required sacrifices for the Roman emperor. Romans generally recognized that Jewish monotheism prevented their participation in the cult. But once a distinction between Christians and Jews was recognized, it was not obvious that Christians should enjoy the same exemptions as Jews. Even so, we know of no occasions before the time of Domitian on which Christians were punished for failure to participate in the cult. Apparently Domitian required worship of himself during his lifetime, technically a departure from traditional practice. Evidence about a persecution under Domitian comes from Chriatian sources, particularly the Revelation of John, which will be treated subsequently.

Both the persecution under Nero and that under Domitian could be regarded as precipitated by the personal idiocyncracies of the two emperors.

---

[1] Tacitus, Annals 15:44, in Henry Bettenson, *Documents of the Christian Church*, 2nd ed. (London: Oxford U.P., 1963), p. 2.

Head of Domitian, Capitoline Museum, Rome. (Courtesy *Capitoline Museum, Rome, and Alinari/Art Resource Inc.*)

Morever, there were specific violations that could be cited in these two cases: arson and failure to participate in the imperial cult. After the turn of the century, we know of a number of persecutions in various localities. Ignatius, for example, was carried from Antioch to Rome during the reign of Trajan (98–117). As he traveled toward Rome, he wrote a series of letters, which we will examine. In the letters he does not explain the reason for his perse- cution, and we have no record of it from the authorities. We do, however, have a remarkable pair of letters exchanged by the emperor Trajan and one of his governors in Asia Minor. The letters were probably written in c. 112. Pliny the Younger, governor of Bithynia, wrote to Trajan asking for an imperial policy about Christians in his territory. He described his own method of dealing with those who had been accused of being Christians. He said that he asked them three times if they were Christians, and if they persistently answered that they were, he sentenced them to death. If, how- ever, they denied it, worshiped the traditional Gods, worshiped the em- peror's image, and cursed Christ, he set them free. Apparently there had been a series of accusations, some anonymous, and many false. Still the Christian religion is regarded as a problem, for Pliny says that the temples to the other Gods have been, until recently, deserted.

Trajan's reply to Pliny is brief enough to be quoted in full:

> You have taken the right line, my dear Pliny, in examining the cases of those denounced to you as Christians, for no hard and fast rule can be laid down, of universal application. They are not to be sought out; if they are informed against, and the charge is proved, they are to be punished, with this reserva- tion—that if any one denies that he is a Christian, and actually proves it, that is by worshipping our gods, he shall be pardoned as a result of his recantation, however suspect he may have been with respect to the past. Pamphlets pub- lished anonymously should carry no weight in any charge whatsoever. They constitute a very bad precedent, and are also out of keeping with this age.[2]

The judicious and restrained language of the emperor does not hide the fact that he allows Christians to be persecuted for being Christians. No other criminal charge needs to be brought. The fact is that it is illegal to be a Christian. Trajan may have been repeating a policy that had been in effect before his own time, but his letter is the earliest extant evidence of the illegal status of Christianity under Roman policy.

It is probable that Trajan's policy, or one similar to it, was effective throughout the second century. Some Christian writings during this period display an awareness of governmental policies, but many more simply de- scribe incidents of persecution. We will now examine some of the Christian literature that appears to have been written during times of oppression. Then we will look at the various responses Christians made to persecution.

---

[2] Pliny, Epistles 10:97, in ibid., p. 4. Eusebius, *The Ecclesiastical History* III, 33:1–3, summa- rizes the correspondence and notes the effect on Christians.

1 Peter

1 Peter is written in the name of "Peter, an apostle of Jesus Christ" (1 Pet 1:1), but it is also signed by Silvanus (5:12). This may mean that the letter was dictated by Peter and written by Silvanus, who had served also as the co-author of some of the Pauline letters. Others believe that Peter dictated the main lines of the letter and Silvanus shared in its composition.[3] Still others deny that Peter had anything to do with the letter.

The addressees are in Asia Minor. They are called "exiles of the Dispersion" (1:1), a phrase suggesting that the recipients were Jews or thought of themselves as such. Those outside the addressed group are called Gentiles (2:12 and 4:3). The language may express a self-identification of these Christian groups as Jewish. But it does not require us to believe that they had come out of a Jewish background, for some Gentile-Christian groups signified their adoption into the people of God by using Jewish terminology. The letter does not give us sufficient information to identify the character or location of the addressed group.

Nor is the situation clear. Some parts of the letter imply that life is going on in a relatively undisturbed fashion. In passages that remind one of Ephesians, there is advice for slaves to be submissive to masters and wives to husbands. The general view is that all persons must be submissive to those who govern them. This view extends to governmental authorities: "Be subject for the Lord's sake to every human institution, whether it be to the emperor as supreme, or to governors as sent by him to punish those who do wrong and to praise those who do right" (2:13–14). Later the readers are told: "Honor all men. Love the brotherhood. Fear God. Honor the emperor" (2:17). Those counsels suggest that there are in Asia Minor communities of Christians who enjoy relative peace in clearly understood social structures.

But there are also some words in this letter that suggest that Christians are facing an unsettled situation, one in which they will be required to suffer. The author says that unjust punishment merits God's approval and that willing acceptance of it constitutes an imitation of Christ. One should not be surprised "at the fiery ordeal which comes upon you to prove you" (4:12). This should be a cause of rejoicing, because it will give the believer the chance to follow the example of Christ. Although little detail is given about any persecution, the author is aware that people may be charged with being Christians. "But let none of you suffer as a murderer, or a thief, or a wrongdoer, or a mischief-maker; yet if one suffers as a Christian, let him not be ashamed, but under that name let him glorify God" (4:15–16). These words remind us of the legal situation implied in the letters of Pliny and Trajan.

---

[3] Cf. e.g., Archibald M. Hunter, in *The Interpreter's Bible* (Nashville, Tenn.: Abingdon, 1957), Vol. XII, pp. 77–80.

Although some scholars think that two separate letters have been combined in 1 Peter, it probably is not necessary to come to this conclusion. The author knows that the addressed communities are facing a "fiery ordeal." Yet he counsels that all should obey the emperor, even if he punishes Christians unjustly. For this author the probably unrealized ideal of the Christian life is an orderly social structure, and obedience to the authorities is requisite. The entire letter probably reflects the time of Trajan, when obstinate confession of one's Christian belief was taken to be a crime against the state. This author probably wishes to make sure that Christians are not persecuted as murderers or thieves but as Christians, and he wants them to defend themselves with gentleness and reverence, always remembering that they are subject to the emperor and his governors.[4]

Thus, the most likely occasion for the letter is the time of Trajan, when imperial policy toward Christians was worked out in correspondence between the emperor and Pliny. It should therefore be dated during Trajan's reign, 98–117, but the actual author is anonymous. The fact that he chose to write in Peter's name suggests that he may have been a second-generation follower of the great apostle.

The Letters of Ignatius

Some time during the reign of Trajan (98–117), Ignatius, the bishop of Antioch, in Syria, was arrested and taken to Rome to be thrown to the wild beasts in the Colosseum. On the trip he was escorted by ten Roman soldiers, who did little to make his trip comfortable. They traveled mainly by land, coming through Asia Minor and stopping at Philadelphia, Smyrna, and Troas. From Troas they crossed to Philippi and finally Rome (see Figure 23, p. 355). Despite his condition, Ignatius was allowed to have contact with Christians in the cities where the party stopped overnight. In Smyrna he was met by a delegation headed by four bishops representing their constituency: Polycarp of Smyrna, Onesimus of Ephesus, Damas of Magnesia, and Polybius of Tralles. Before he left Smyrna, Ignatius wrote letters to the congregations in Ephesus, Magnesia, and Tralles, thanking each for its encouragement and addressing himself to certain ecclesiastical problems that the bishops must have brought to his attention. From Smyrna he also wrote to the Christians at Rome, asking them not to interfere with his impending martyrdom. From Troas he wrote three more letters: one to Philadelphia, where he had stopped on the way to Smyrna; one to Smyrna; and one to bishop Polycarp. Thanks to Polycarp all seven letters were preserved. They all must have been written within a relatively brief period of time, but we can date them no more precisely than in the time of Trajan.[5]

[4] Cf John Knox, "Pliny and I Peter," *Journal of Biblical Literature,* 72: 187–189 (1953).
[5] On the date of Ignatius, cf. Eusebius, op. cit., III, 22. Eusebius lists Ignatius as the second bishop of Antioch.

Ignatius' desire for martyrdom is probably the most interesting theme in the letters. He feels that the martyr is the only true disciple of Jesus. His thought is largely bound up with a mystical conception of the unity of the believer with Christ. To Ignatius the believer must imitate Christ not only by adhering to the ethical teachings of Jesus, but also by living and dying as he did. Genuine discipleship to Christ is demonstrated by sharing his passion. For this reason Ignatius writes to the Romans to dissuade them from making any attempts to defend or rescue him, for that would frustrate his efforts to be a true disciple. He can foresee himself pleading with the beasts in the Colosseum and provoking them if they avoid him out of fear. He writes, "I am the wheat of God and I am ground by the teeth of wild beasts so that I may be found the pure bread of Christ."[6]

A secondary theme in the letters is Ignatius' insistence on good order and unity in the church. The key to both is the bishop. In every letter except that to Rome, he speaks of the respect and obedience that is owed to the bishop. This is to be granted even if the bishop is young, as is Damas of Magnesia. The bishop presides in God's place, and nothing may be done without his approval. "Wherever the bishop appears, the whole congregation is to be present, just as wherever Jesus Christ is, there is the whole church."[7] "He who does anything without the bishop's knowledge worships the devil."[8] These letters clearly present the picture of the bishop as the single chief officer in a particular community. The arrangement is called the monarchical episcopate. It is also clear that the bishop is associated with a group of presbyters and assisted by deacons. Ignatius compares the relative position of the three orders in his letter to Magnesia: "Be eager to do everything in God's harmony, with the bishop presiding in the place of God and the presbytery in the place of the council of the apostles and the deacons, most sweet to me, entrusted with the service of Jesus Christ."[9] Although he carefully deals with the authority of church leaders, Ignatius does not enlighten us on the method by which they were selected.

Ignatius is also concerned with divergent forms of Christianity. He warns the Magnesians and Philadelphians to beware of "Judaism." By this term he probably means to designate neither the Jewish religion nor Jewish Christianity, but the adoption of certain Judaistic practices by Gentile Christians. One such practice was the observance of the Sabbath day instead of Sunday, or the Lord's day. A more serious danger was posed by Docetism, and Ignatius describes it explicitly. He takes the denial of Jesus' humanity as a perversion of truth and calls on Christians to believe in the death of Jesus

---

[6] Ignatius, Letter to the Romans 4:1, trans. by Robert M. Grant, *The Apostolic Fathers* (Nashville, Tenn.: Nelson, 1966), Vol. IV.

[7] Ignatius, Letter to the Smyrneans 8:2, trans by Grant, op. cit.

[8] Ibid., 9:1.

[9] Ignatius, Letter to the Magnesians 6:1, trans. by Grant, op. cit. Cf. Letter to the Trallians 3:1, ibid.

in spite of docetic denials. The denial of the reality of Jesus' passion seems to Ignatius the most serious error made by Docetists. To him, belief in Jesus' death is not solely a belief in its redemptive quality but, more fundamentally, confidence that it really occurred.

Unfortunately we know nothing of the circumstances that led to Ignatius' arrest. There are some indications in the letters that other Syrians had already become martyrs in Rome and that still others were in the same circumstances as Ignatius. By the time he reached Troas, he received word that the church in Syria was at peace, and he asked the Philadelphians and Smyrneans to send delegates to Antioch to give them aid and encouragement. We lose sight of Ignatius after he left Troas, and we can only assume that he met the fate he so fervently desired.

A remarkable sense of solidarity is implied in the correspondence of Ignatius. Christians in Asia Minor have met with a transient prisoner from a distant country and have been called on to send delegates back to Syria. Ignatius could write to Rome on the assumption that Christians there, whom he had never met, will want to come to his aid. He called on Polycarp to write to the other churches in cities where he expected to visit. A significant network of communication seems to present itself at this point, a fact we might not have expected at such an early date and at a time when travel was not without difficulty and danger. Despite the fragmentation that we continue to note, a deep sense of solidarity seems to have been developing among some Christian communities in the early second century.

Polycarp's Letter to the Philippians

Polycarp, bishop of Smyrna, was Ignatius' host and a recipient of one of his letters. Ignatius had requested Polycarp to appoint a delegate to go to Antioch to help that church celebrate its return to peace. Polycarp had also received a request from the church at Philippi to forward a letter of theirs to Syria and to send them copies of Ignatius' letters. In his letter to Philippi, Polycarp agrees to the first request and sends along copies of the Ignatian correspondence. He specifically remarks that this includes the letters he has received (presumably the letter to Smyrna and the one to himself) "and any others which we possess."[10]

Polycarp must, therefore, be the one who collected Ignatius' letters. He continued as bishop of Smyrna until his martyrdom at the age of 86 in 155 or 156. Many years later Irenaeus recalled meeting him, and Eusebius says he went to Rome shortly before his death to confer with Anicetus, the Roman bishop.[11] In addition, Irenaeus notes that Polycarp converted many

---

[10] Polycarp to the Philippians 13:2, trans. by William R. Schoedel, *The Apostolic Fathers* (Nashville, Tenn.: Nelson, 1967), Vol. V.

[11] Cf. Eusebius, op. cit., IV, 14:1; V, 24:16. Irenaeus, *Against Heresies* III, 3:3, numbers Anicetus as the tenth bishop of Rome.

heretics at Rome and met Marcion, whom he called the firstborn of Satan.[12]

P. N. Harrison claimed that Polycarp wrote two letters to Philippi and that they were assimilated into the one we now have.[13] The earlier letter consists of chapters 13–14. In it Polycarp states his willingness to accede to the request of his correspondents, and he forwards to them copies of Ignatius' letters. He also inquires about any information they may have about Ignatius and his fate. Ignatius had passed through Philippi after he left Asia Minor, and Polycarp assumes that the Philippians will be the first to receive news about him. This letter must have been written within weeks after Ignatius passed through. The second letter, consisting of chapters 1–12, was written some decades later (c. 135). In it, Polycarp looks on Ignatius as having joined the ranks of the martyrs. Harrison has solved a peculiar difficulty by dividing the letter into two, for Polycarp could hardly speak of Ignatius as a martyr in the same letter in which he inquired about his fate. As Harrison says, "One does not include in a list of glorious dead the name of a man as to whose fate one is *in the same letter* asking for information, and who, for all that one knows, may be still alive."[14]

If Harrison is right, the purpose of the earlier letter would have been to respond to the Philippians' request and to find out about Polycarp's friend and colleague. It should be dated during Trajan's reign (98–117). The occasion for the later letter seems to have been some crisis in the Philippian church involving one of the presbyters, Valens, who was excommunicated, apparently for some financial problems. In it Polycarp also alludes to the dangers of a heresy that denies the reality of Jesus' flesh, denies the testimony of the cross, perverts the sayings of the Lord, and denies resurrection and judgment. Harrison identifies the heretic in question as Marcion.[15] He feels it significant that Polycarp calls his heretic "the first-born of Satan," the same phrase that, according to Irenaeus, Polycarp used in meeting Marcion.[16] Although Harrison's thesis is attractive at this point, Polycarp's language seems more likely to point to a series of heretical points of view to which he is opposed rather than to a single individual who is guilty of all these errors. Some of the heretics are Docetists, similar to those Ignatius attacked. Nevertheless, Harrison is probably close to the truth when he dates Polycarp's second letter in Hadrian's time—c. 135.

---

[12] Cf. Irenacus, op. cit., III, 3:4.
[13] P. N. Harrison, Polycarp's *Two Epistles to the Philippians* (Cambridge: Cambridge U.P., 1936).
[14] Ibid., p. 152. Italics Harrison's.
[15] Harrison believes that the meeting took place before Marcion had arrived at his theory of two Gods.
[16] Cf. Polycarp, op. cit., 7:1.

The Martyrdom of Polycarp

The document that tells the story of Polycarp's death is the first in a long line of Christian martyrologies. In form it is a letter from the Christians at Smyrna to those in Philomelium, also in Asia Minor, and sent at the latter's request. The author, identified as Marcion (certainly not Polycarp's "first-born of Satan"), requests that the letter be forwarded to Christians elsewhere. It may have actually circulated as a letter, but the clear purpose of the document is to tell the story of Polycarp, the eighty-six-year-old bishop of Smyrna and Christian martyr. The document probably rests on an eyewitness account and so was written shortly after Polycarp's death in 155 or 156. By telling the story of this great saint, it was hoped that the courage of others in similar situations would be bolstered.

As the narrative opens it is clear that a persecution is in progress. Some Christians had already been tortured by flagellation, and some were killed by wild beasts or by being burned. For some time Polycarp had hidden from the authorities, but he was found, tried, and burned. A vivid, though partially miraculous, account of the burning is included in the narrative. The author also tells of the gathering of the martyr's bones, and we read that the day of Polycarp's martyrdom was observed as a special day in the church at Smyrna. This is the earliest reference in extant Christian literature to reverence for relics and memorials. The significance of Polycarp and his martyrdom is indicated by inclusion of the exact date and time of his death— 2 PM on February 22. The year would be 155 or 156.

The document does not allude to any specific reason for the persecution, but there are indications that something like Trajan's policy was being put into effect. It appears that people were being charged with being Christians and that they could have escaped punishment by denying Christ, making a sacrifice, and swearing by the "Genius of Caesar." One Quintus, a Phrygian Christian, had escaped in that way. Polycarp had been given a chance to recant his beliefs, but he refused and met his punishment.

As in Ignatius, so here, we find the fundamental concept that the martyr is following the example of Jesus.

Persecution in Gaul

Eusebius, the fourth-century church historian, quotes extensively from a letter sent by Christians in Gaul to those in Asia Minor and to the Roman bishop, Eleutherus.[17] He dates the letter during the reign of Marcus Aurelius (161–180); it narrates events of the year 177 or 178, in the cities of Lyons and Vienne, in the valley of the Rhone River. The letter is probably an eyewitness account of an atrocious persecution of Christians. Christians

---

[17] Cf. Eusebius, op. cit., V, 1–4.

were suspected of eating children and of having incestuous relationships. Such rumors, once started, were substantiated by non-Christian slaves, who fearfully testified against their masters. The author of the letter categorically denies the charges and expresses outrage that anyone would do such things. Nevertheless, several people were killed on the charge of being Christians, for the emperor had decreed that Christians should be tortured to death unless they denied their religion. Those who were Roman citizens were beheaded; others were thrown to wild beasts or roasted in an iron chair. Here we have a brutal development of Trajan's policy: Christians are not only given the chance to recant; they are induced to do so by being cruelly tortured.

Although the martyrs were put to death on the charge of being Christians, it appears that it was suspicion about their practices that gave rise to the persecution. The citizens of Lyons and Vienne were probably not trying to get rid of Christianity because they were hostile to its basic theological tenets, but because they suspected its adherents of vile practices.

Some time after these events, Irenaeus, the author of five books against heresies, became the bishop of Lyons.

CHRISTIAN RESPONSES TO PERSECUTION

Christian responses to persecution include the writing of martyrologies, narratives about incidents of oppression, and letters of encouragement. In addition, Christians produced two kinds of literary responses: apocalypses and apologies.

We saw in Chapter 3 that apocalyptic thought had been present in some Jewish circles in the Hellenistic and Roman periods. Jewish apocalypses had usually come out of situations of despair, in which righteous Jews found it difficult to discern the hand of God. They expressed a firm conviction that God's control of the world will soon be made known to all and that in that time the righteous will be vindicated. It was in this context that messianic expectation arose in Jewish thought.

When apocalyptic thought manifested itself in literary form, the result was a specific genre, the apocalypse, with definite literary characteristics. The apocalypse is filled with angels, devils, and animal figures. In many there is a definite schedule of events. Sometimes the apocalyptic writer looks back in time to describe the schedule, but usually he looks forward to see a plan, which he describes. With the schedule there is an assigned duration for each historical period. Heaven may be pictured as a contest between God and the devil, with earth the battlefield, but the contest has a predetermined battle plan and outcome.

The author of an apocalypse feels himself to be especially endowed with the ability to see reality, but he usually has assistance from an angel, who interprets what he sees. His communication with heaven takes place through dreams, visions, and trips, and he is easily and quickly transported from place to place. His literary product records the dreams and visions, and he includes with them a good deal of animal symbolism and allegorical interpretation. In many cases the author uses pseudonymity, and he frequently antedates his book by setting himself back in time. He speculates in numbers and sets the time for events in semiveiled language.

The literary style makes the apocalypse a particularly difficult book for the modern reader or for anyone who does not share the apocalyptic world view. We must assume, however, that apocalypses contained meaningful messages for the oppressed, and we can be assured that they contain a good deal of information about the religious life of their times. We will examine one Christian apocalypse here: the Revelation of John.

If apocalypses were directed to the persecuted, apologies were directed to the persecutors. The apocalypses were intended to convince Christians that they were on the side of right and ultimate victory. The apologies were written to defend Christianity against misunderstanding and false charges. The apologists were not regretfully acknowledging an error and asking for forgiveness; they were acting as advocates for the faith. They tried to present Christianity in the best possible light and to show that the state had nothing to fear from it. Christianity was widely misunderstood by Roman officials and by the general populace. It seemed to be like Judaism but also seemed novel. It challenged all other religions. It upset economic patterns and social relationships. It admitted women and slaves, but its meetings were open only to members. It spoke of a kingdom to come. It revered a criminal. The Christian apologists attempted to explain these difficulties to Roman authorities and to show that the teachings of their religion were compatible with the best thought of the culture.

The literary form of the apology had a time-honored history, dating back to the Apology of Socrates by Plato. The customary approach was to take the charges, explore their meaning, and demonstrate their erroneous nature. Their style was characterized by clarity of exposition and interesting detail. Many were replete with quotations from poets and philosophers. They generally concentrated on one major point and gave slight attention to one or two minor matters. A concluding appeal summed up the argument. It takes a learned person to be an apologist. The writer must write in a clear, forceful, and appealing style and must be familiar with a wide range of literary allusions. He must be aware of the basic ideas and motivating forces of his opponents and must know what in his defendant will appeal to them.

It is notable that second-century Christianity could produce so many apologies, including one by Aristides, an Oration to the Greeks by Tatian, three books addressed to Autolycus by Theophilus, and the anonymous Epistle to Diognetus. The chief principles, methods, and viewpoints of the apologists will be illustrated here by reference to two apologies, one by Justin and one by Athenagoras.

The Revelation of John

The only full apocalypse in the NT is that called the Revelation, or Apocalypse, of John. The Muratorian canon, which probably represented the accepted list of NT books in the church at Rome in c. 200, included it. But questions were raised about it from several quarters, and Eusebius said that one could take it or leave it.[18] It was, however, included in the generally accepted list of Athanasius in 367.[19]

The Revelation of John begins with seven letters addressed to churches in western Asia Minor (chapters 1–3). The bulk of the book (chapters 4–18) is a series of visions, which appear to describe the time of the author. In the last several chapters (chapters 19–22), there are visions of the end of all things and a description of a new creation.

Unlike many apocalypses, this one is neither pseudonymous nor antedated. It claims to be written by a prophet named John, who had been exiled to the island of Patmos during a persecution of Christians. Justin claimed that it was written by one of the apostles, but the author calls himself a prophet rather than an apostle, and he speaks of the twelve as a group in the past.[20] The seven letters to the churches, which are included in Rev 1–3, suggest that the author was a Christian of some influence in western Asia Minor, and his acquaintance with the apocalyptic tradition indicates that he may have come from a Jewish background. Differences in diction, vocabulary, style, and phraseology demonstrate that he was not the author of either the Fourth Gospel or the Johannine letters.

Irenaeus said that the Revelation of John was written "toward the end of Domitian's reign [81–96]."[21] The internal evidence suggests the same period. It is evident that the historical situation that prompted the book was a persecution of Christians, brought about by their refusal to obey an order to conform to the imperial cult. At least one well-known man, Antipas of Pergamum, has been killed, and John has been exiled to Patmos. The book refers to divine claims made by the ruler and to marks, or symbols, that were required to be worn by his subjects. The imperial cult, rooted in the worship of the Goddess Roma, began with the posthumous worship of Julius Caesar. It arose more or less spontaneously among people who found

---

[18] Cf. ibid, III, 25:2.
[19] For Athanasius' letter, cf. Edgar Hennecke, *New Testament Apocrypha,* ed. by W. Schneemelcher and trans. by R. McL. Wilson (Philadelphia: Westminster Press, 1963), Vol. I, pp. 59–60.
[20] Cf. Justin, *Dialogue with Trypho* 81:4.
[21] Irenaeus, op. cit., V, 30:3.

A parchment painting illustrating the Book of Revelation, from a fourteenth-century German manuscript ("The Apocalypse"; folio 23, verso). (Courtesy the Metropolitan Museum of Art, The Cloisters Collection, 1968.)

in imperial power the chief expression of divine power. To most the cult was simply a demonstration of patriotism and gratitude for the peace and security the empire afforded. Augustus attempted to discourage it, and the Roman Senate later restricted it to a select group of deceased emperors. But it was difficult to control an emperor who recognized the political utility of the cult. There is evidence that Domitian was such an emperor and that he practiced religious persecution.[22] In addition, there are certain allusions in Revelation that point to Domitian. The author speaks of a series of rulers and identifies his own time as that of the "sixth." Domitian was not the sixth Roman emperor, but he was the sixth to be declared divine.[23] Moreover, in Rev 6:6 there is a possible allusion to an imperial edict on Asian vineyards. In 92 Domitian ordered that half the vineyards in Asia Minor be plowed under in order to protect the price of Italian wine. The various internal evidences indicate that Irenaeus was right and that Revelation was written toward the end of Domitian's reign—that is c. 95–96.

Most of the literary features associated with apocalypses are present in Revelation. The author describes his vision as a revelation of what is about to happen. After the seven letters (chapters 1–3) he narrates a series of visions, the first of which features a scroll containing a schedule of events. Only the Christ, described as a lamb, is able to open the scroll. The events to come include famines, rebellions, wars, pestilences, and conflagrations. The devil, or Satan, is described as a dragon, who has an earthly counterpart, a beast, that probably represents the Roman Empire. The central section of the book is largely descriptive of the time of the author. With chapter 19, however, there begins a chronological sequence that projects into the future. Christ appears as head of an army, conquers the beast, and throws him into a lake of fire. Satan is bound and thrown into a bottomless pit for a millennium (one thousand years). During this period the Christian martyrs come back to life and reign with Christ. At the end of the millennium Satan is released, and he, with the help of the nations, makes war on Christ and on the saints. But Satan and his allies are finally defeated and thrown into the lake of fire. Then earth and sky disappear, and all the dead are raised for judgment, the standard for which is the book of life. All those whose names are not recorded therein are thrown into the fiery lake. In the final scenes we have the creation of a new heaven, a new earth, and a new Jerusalem. God is eternally and immediately present in the new creation, and there is no pain, sorrow, or mourning. The new Jerusalem is characterized by order, beauty, riches, and righteousness.

---

[22] Cf. Eusebius, op. cit., III, 17; Dio Cassius, *Roman History* 67:14. For an analysis of the relevant literature on Domitian's enforcement of the imperial cult, cf. Donald McFayden, "The Occasion of the Domitianic Persecution," *American Journal of Theology* **24**: 46–66 (1920).

[23] The first five were Julius Caesar, Augustus, Claudius, Vespasian, and Titus. Cf. Martin Rist, in *The Interpreter's Bible* (Nashville, Tenn.: Abingdon, 1957), Vol. XII, p. 495.

The Revelation of John has been the object of a wide diversity of interpretation. Many today understand it as intended for a modern audience and attempt to interpret its symbols as twentieth-century figures and events. It is inevitable that some Christians will see their own time reflected and anticipated in a book that is regarded as sacred, and Revelation's obscurity lends itself to this tendency. Modern readers should, however, keep in mind the fact that the book was written for people living at the end of the first century. Those Christians were facing persecution and needed encouragement to endure. They would not have found it if John of Patmos had been speaking over their heads to us. Nor is it likely that they would have preserved a book that was virtually meaningless to them. Any interpretation must be controlled by this fact.

The First Apology of Justin

Justin, called the Martyr, was born in Samaria of Gentile parents. He had a passing acquaintance with Stoics, Peripatetics, and Pythagoreans, and he was deeply attracted to Platonic philosophy. In about 130 he met a Christian who exposed him to the writings of the OT prophets. Impressed with the correspondence between those writings and the life of Jesus, he became a Christian convert. Eusebius lists a number of his writings, most of which have been lost.[24] His *First Apology* and his *Dialogue with Trypho* have, however, come down to us in late manuscripts. The former is his defense of Christianity addressed to Roman authorities; the latter is a debate with a Jew. Both are characterized by an irenic spirit and seek to convince by persuasion without depreciating the opponent. The *First Apology* was written in Rome in c. 155 and the *Dialogue* a few years later. There is a so-called *Second Apology* that is attributed to Justin, but there is substantial doubt that he was the actual author of this document. At some time between 163 and 167, Justin was executed for refusing to make the imperial sacrifice.

The *First Apology* is addressed to Antoninus Pius, Roman emperor from 138–161. It begins by calling on the emperor to investigate the charges brought against Christians and not to persecute them simply for the name. Justin's work reflects the fact that Trajan's policy to allow the persecution of Christians was still being followed in the time of Antoninus Pius. Justin admits that some Christians may have been guilty of criminal activities, but he insists that not all Christians are criminals. If all philosophers do not say the same thing, then all Christians are not alike. Those who have committed crimes should be charged with them, but it should not be illegal simply to be a Christian. In fact, says Justin, Christianity opposes those activities that harm the state. It teaches its adherents to pay taxes and to pray for the emperor. Christians have such a high sexual standard that some in their

---

[24] Cf. Eusebius, op. cit., IV, 18.

sixties and seventies are still virgins. Because they are taught that God judges all persons on the basis of their virtue or vice, Christians are the emperor's best helpers in securing order.

A different way to state the fundamental charge against Christians is to accuse them of refusal to worship the traditional Gods. To Roman authorities this refusal was tantamount to atheism. Justin admits that Christians neglect the worship of the demons and the sons of Zeus. Nor do they make sacrifices to any God, because they believe that the one true God has no need of offerings. But to Justin, Christians are not atheists. They refuse to worship the demons and Zeus because of their immorality, but they worship the one true God.

Justin also objects to the charge that Christianity is novel and strange. Throughout his *First Apology* he makes comparisons between Christianity and other religions and philosophies. He asks why Christians are singled out for persecution, if they believe something like what is believed by others?

> When we say that all things have been ordered and made by God we appear to offer the teaching of Plato—in speaking of a coming destruction by fire that of the Stoics; in declaring that the souls of the unrighteous will be punished after death, still remaining in conscious existence, and those of the virtuous, delivered from punishments, will enjoy happiness, we seem to agree with [various] poets and philosophers; in declaring that men ought not to worship the works of their hands we are saying the same things as the comedian Menander and others who have said this, for they declared that the Fashioner is greater than what he has formed.[25]

Justin compares the virgin birth of Jesus with the births of the sons of Zeus, his healings with those of Asclepius, and his ascension with those of deceased emperors. In making these comparisons Justin does not intend to question the superiority of Christianity to other religions. Rather, he believes that similarities are present because the other religions have imitated Christianity and the philosophies have been given a partial truth.

The key to the relationship of Christianity to the other religions and philosophies is Justin's understanding of Logos. He believes that Logos is in every person, but this presence does not grant divinity to humans. It acts, rather, as the means of the revelation of truth, given to the OT prophets and to the Greek philosophers. Thus, Christianity is not to be regarded as some strange new thing. It was preached even by Moses, to whom the Logos was revealed, and by Plato, who learned from Moses. The relationship that Justin sees between Moses, Plato, and Christ does not rest on any historical connections. Justin's purpose is to point to the unity of truth. In a reference to Plato's *Timaeus,* he says that the Son of God was placed X-

[25] Justin, *First Apology* 20, trans. by E. R. Hardy, in Cyril C. Richardson, ed., *Early Christian Fathers,* Library of Christian Classics, I (Philadelphia: Westminster Press, 1953).

wise in the universe—that is, in the shape of a cross. Plato got this from Moses, who protected the people from snakes by a cross, and both Moses and Plato were speaking of the crucifixion of Jesus. The Logos, then, is the source of truth for Moses, the prophets, the philosophers, and for Christianity. Christianity has the fullness of truth, because the Logos has appeared in the man Christ Jesus. The evidence for the truth resident in the incarnation is the remarkable correspondence between the OT prophets and the life of Jesus. Some of the prophets spoke five thousand years before the time of Jesus but correctly predicted the things he would do. The Logos revealed those things in advance, so that they would be believed when they occurred.

In the concluding chapters Justin gives a description of Christian worship in order to show its inoffensive nature, and he ends with a letter of Hadrian, which he takes to be helpful to the Christian cause.

The most notable features of Justin's thought are his understanding of Logos and his accommodation to Greek and Hellenistic philosophy. The Logos is that of which "every race of man partakes."[26] But the Logos was also born, taught, and crucified; it died and ascended. Although other religions have imitated Christianity, they have nothing like the crucifixion. Justin's accommodation to philosophy may be deceptive. Although he finds much of value in Platonism and Stoicism, he makes it abundantly clear that whatever truth they have is revealed by the Logos. The essential difference between the philosophies and Christianity is that the former have a knowledge that is the result of human conjecture and an incomplete divine revelation, whereas the latter is altogether the product of divine revelation.

The Apology of Athenagoras

Athenagoras seems even more at home in Greek and Hellenistic philosophy than Justin. In his *Apology* he quotes extensively from the philosophers, as well as from the Greek poets and dramatists. He knows the *Iliad,* the *Odyssey,* and the writings of Hesiod and Herodotus. He is acquainted with religious life among the Greeks and their religious traditions.

Apart from the evidence about Athenagoras' cultural level, which is contained in the *Apology,* we know nothing about his life. The *Apology* is addressed to the emperors Marcus Aurelius and Commodus, and so it may be dated in 176–177.

Athenagoras sets out to answer three charges: that Christians are atheists, that they practice incest, and that they are cannibals.[27] In fact, however, he pays very little attention to the last two charges. It is the charge of atheism

---

[26] Ibid., 46.
[27] Note that similar charges were made against Christians in Gaul at about the same time. Cf. Eusebius, op. cit., V, 1:14.

that he wishes to address, and he does so vigorously. He defends Christians by affirming their monotheism, and he shows that Plato, Aristotle, and the Stoics were also monotheists. He claims that "all philosophers, then, even if unwillingly, reach complete agreement about the unity of God when they come to inquire into the first principles of the universe." [28] He next turns to his own proof for monotheism and then engages in a counterattack against traditional religion. He claims that the Olympian deities were immoral and not worthy of devotion. He speculates that the names may have originally designated material substances and that the Gods may have originally been human. In all this Athenagoras stands in the tradition of pre-Hellenistic and Hellenistic philosophy.

Athenagoras has a few quotations from the ethical teachings of Jesus. He also writes something about the relationship of the one God to the Logos, which is the Son of God. But he tells us nothing about the life or death of Jesus. There is no emphasis on OT prophecy, no proclamation about the redemptive significance of Jesus' death, and no eschatology. Although the *Apology* may not be a full expression of Athenagoras' religious thought, it is clear that he could write a fairly lengthy document without these characteristically Christian items and still think of himself as a Christian.

Athenagoras should be considered as an example of the Christian philosopher. His mode of argument and his literary references show that his world was that of the cultured Hellenistic thinker. With him and with Justin we may observe a growing alliance between Christianity and second-century forms of Platonic-Stoic philosophy. The alliance served as a useful device for communicating the Christian message to the Greco-Roman intellectual. In the third century and later, it came to play a leading role in the development of Christian theology.

We do not know if Justin and Athenagoras achieved their immediate purpose of defending Christians against persecution. Unfortunately, Justin's writing did not save him from martyrdom in the time of the Stoic philosopher-emperor Marcus Aurelius. But the apologists produced a significant long-term effect by fostering lines of communication that proved to be of immense value in the centuries to come.

THE RISE OF EARLY CATHOLIC CHRISTIANITY

In the third century the variant Christian groups were either eliminated or assimilated into a larger synthesis. The synthesis is known as Catholic Christianity. But Catholic Christianity did not simply burst on the scene as a novel phenomenon or even as an ad hoc attempt at elimination and assim-

---

[28] Athenagoras, *Apology* 7, in Richardson, op. cit.

ilation. It had been prepared for by an earlier tradition, to which we may give the name early Catholic.

Apocalyptic writers and, to a more significant extent, apologists contributed to the rise of early Catholic Christianity. So did many of the other writers we have previously considered, although probably in unintended ways. The writers we will consider here seem to have been keenly aware of the problems that faced Christians in the period 70-185, and they appear to be in basic agreement on what to do about the problems.

Early Catholic Christianity was a conscious attempt to unify Christian doctrine and to diminish diversity. The process of unification was, however, exceedingly complex. It required the talents of persons who were willing to address themselves to several issues and to fight on several fronts. On one of the fronts were the so-called heretics, whose views must be discredited. Moreover, the relationship between Judaism and Christianity, which involved the Christian understanding of the OT, constituted an issue that raised the question of the definition of Christianity itself. In addition, life within the Christian group was a matter of concern, for the community required a strong organization and the members needed ethical guidance. All of these activities had to be pursued with full awareness that there were enemies outside as well as inside the church. Subsequently, we will examine these three major concerns as they were treated in contemporary documents. Then we will see how they came together to contribute to the character of early Catholic Christianity.

Antiheretical Writings

The word *heresy* is derived from a Greek word meaning "choice." It had been used to designate the particular teachings of philosophical schools, and it denoted the opinions that each one had chosen. Christian writers began to use the term and soon gave it a pejorative significance. To them it indicated that a person had chosen a human opinion and rejected divine revelation. In this sense heresy has an evil significance, and the heretic is considered to be evil.

Antiheretical literature arose to deal with those who were teaching divergent opinions, and the writers usually looked on their opponents as evil. Probably most Christian groups looked on others as heretical, and it is something of an historical accident that most of the extant literature represents only one side of an argument. It is reasonable to assume that there were arguments, charges, and countercharges among Christian movements for several decades. A Gnostic would claim that other forms of Christianity were deficient in knowledge. A late Jewish Christian would feel that the church had largely diverged from its heritage. The antiheretical writings that are to be associated with early Catholic Christianity make the claim that problems in Christian faith are caused by rebellious acts of choice in matters of belief. They will insist that the basis for authentic faith is a particular historical revelation.

Almost all of the writers who had told us about persecution also showed us that they were aware of heresy. Ignatius was surely conscious of the problems, as was the author of 1 Peter. Even the author of the Revelation of John was disturbed about divergent views in the churches of Asia Minor. But the three writers who are treated here concentrated almost their entire attention on heresy. We will look at three examples of the antiheretical literature: Jude, 2 Peter, and Irenaeus.

JUDE

This little letter claims to be the composition of a brother of James. This may be the James who was known as the brother of Jesus, and if so, the author of Jude is claiming also to be a brother of Jesus. A Jude, or Judas, was named as one of four brothers of Jesus in Matt 13:55 and Mark 6:3. The same person may have been intended as the author of the Coptic Gospel of Thomas.[29] We know nothing more about him except that, according to Eusebius, Hegessipus reported an interview between the emperor Domitian and two of Jude's grandsons.[30] The emperor decided that these two unlearned farmers were harmless, and they lived on into the reign of Trajan.

Despite the probable claim that is made, it is not likely that this letter was actually written by a brother of James and Jesus, or by anyone in the first Christian generation. The author speaks of that generation as a past time and of the apostles of Jesus as belonging to an earlier period. He says that the apostles warned about the later time: "But you must remember, beloved, the predictions of the apostles of our Lord Jesus Christ; they said to you, 'In the last time there will be scoffers, following their own ungodly passions'" (Jude 17–18). Jude saw that those apostolic predictions were being fulfilled in his own time. Once again, we have an anonymous document from the period 70–185. Because of its relations to 2 Peter, it should probably be dated c. 140.

The purpose of the letter of Jude is to warn the faithful about certain people within the church whose ideas and actions were perverting Christianity. Jude's attack on these people is strictly ad hominem: they are licentious and immoral; they do not respect present or past authority; they revile what they do not understand; and they cause divisions in the church. The recipients of the letter are advised to hold on to their faith, to convince and save some of the heretics, and to have a fearful mercy on others. There is no legitimate way to identify the theological point of view of the persons under attack, but the letter illustrates something about the problems of heresy. Differences in belief and practice were taken seriously because they

---

[29] Cf. Chapter 6 in this book.
[30] Cf. Eusebius, op. cit., III, 20:1–7.

caused division in the Christian community. Whatever the issues may have been, Jude was convinced that the division was deplorable and must be overcome.

2 PETER

One of the most impressive aspects of Christian faith in the period between 30 and 70 was the eschatological conviction. This conviction included an expectation of the Parousia—that is, the belief that Christ would return in judgment and victory. The heretics who are attacked in 2 Peter have abandoned this expectation. They say, "Where is the promise of his coming? For ever since the fathers fell asleep, all things have continued as they were from the beginning of creation" (2 Pet 3:4).

Doubt about the Parousia could have appeared at any time in the first or second centuries, but the expression of it here is a signal that 2 Peter is a relatively late document. The question in 2 Pet 3:4 seems to reflect the passing of a long period of time. The expression about the fathers who have "fallen asleep" probably refers to the first generation of Christians, which by the time of this letter is long past. But there are other signs of a late date for 2 Peter. The bulk of chapter 2 is dependent on the letter of Jude. There is a specific reference to 1 Peter in 2 Pet 3:1. The author of 2 Peter is aware of Paul's letters and of misinterpretations of them (2 Pet 3:15–16). As in Jude there is a reference to the apostles as living deep in the past. All these bits of internal evidence suggest that 2 Peter is a relatively late document that was not written by the apostle Peter. The external evidence tends to confirm this judgment. 2 Peter appears to be unknown to the authors of all second-century documents that are still extant. The first writer to mention it was Origen, in the middle of the third century, and he doubted that the apostle Peter actually wrote it.[31] A date of c. 150 is usually given for 2 Peter in view of its relationships with other Christian literature, the absence of citations from second-century authors, and its possible allusions to Gnostic Christianity.

Like Jude, this letter attacks a form of Christianity considered by the author to be heretical. Much of the argument is familiar: the heretics are licentious and immoral. In addition, there is a reference to "cleverly devised myths" (2 Pet 1:16), which may be an allusion to Gnostic mythology. The most distinctive aspect of the heretical thought is an agnosticism in regard to the Parousia. The author answers that doubt by asserting that our time is not God's time. "With the Lord one day is as a thousand years, and a thousand years as one day" (2 Pet 3:8). But the author also assures the readers that the heavens and the earth will be dissolved by fire and that "the day of the Lord will come like a thief" (2 Pet 3:10). 2 Peter is more specific than Jude about the viewpoints of the heretics, but, even so, it is

---

[31] Origen, *Commentary on John*, 5:3.

not possible for us to be certain about their identity. The reference to "cleverly devised myths" may be to Gnostic systems, such as those associated with Valentinus. But certainty on this score is not possible.

IRENAEUS

Of the three writers treated here, Irenaeus is by far the most explicit in dealing with heretical movements. He was introduced in Chapter 11, where we examined his description of one Gnostic system. It will be recalled that he was born in Asia Minor and moved to Gaul, where he became bishop of Lyons in 177. He says that when he was a boy he knew Polycarp, the bishop of Smyrna who had met Ignatius and who also became a revered martyr. At one point in his life, Irenaeus carried some correspondence from Lyons to Rome. Perhaps he carried the letter about persecution in Gaul to the Roman bishop Eleutherus. It was in that persecution that Irenaeus' predecessor on the bishop's seat at Lyons was killed. Thus, Irenaeus did not carry on his work in ignorance of persecution. But he is mainly remembered for his five-volume work *Against Heresies,* written in c. 185, in which he dealt most extensively with Gnostic and Marcionite Christianity.

Irenaeus had a strongly pastoral intent in writing, and he was disturbed at the damage done to the simple Christian by the heresies. To him the heresies were wrong chiefly because they denied monotheism. They set up a multitude of deities, attributed the work of creation to a lesser God, and separated redemption from creation. This is the fundamental error, because, for Irenaeus, there is but one God, who created the world and spoke his redemptive word in Jesus the Christ.

How does Irenaeus know that his opponents are wrong? For one thing, they use spurious scriptures, such as the Infancy Gospel of Thomas and the Gospel of Truth. Some of them confine themselves to one gospel, as Marcion did, who used a "mutilated" copy of Luke. When they comment on the scriptures, they misinterpret them and read fanciful speculations into them. In addition, their teaching is irrational, for polytheism cannot be defended by reason. They make Jesus superfluous, because they derive their systems from the Greek philosophers and mix them up in strange ways. They claim to have a secret tradition from Jesus, known only to themselves, but they are inconsistent with one another, and they all say different things. By contrast, monotheism may be rationally defended and is based on the consistent teaching of OT and NT alike. It has been taught publicly by Jesus, the apostles, and all the churches. It is a more ancient teaching than that of Valentinus or Marcion.

Irenaeus believed that true Christianity was to be found in the church. But a number of complexities immediately arise with that definition, because there were churches that held to Marcionite teaching, and there were Christians who were Valentinians. A definition of *church,* was needed, and

Irenaeus provided one. He defined the church by three factors, which together guarantee its possession of the truth.

1. The church is guided by the rule of faith, a creedal statement that is, according to Irenaeus, taught in all churches, whether in Spain, Gaul, Italy, or Asia Minor. This creed, which Irenaeus quoted, may actually have been used in many churches:

> Now the Church, although scattered over the whole civilized world to the end of the earth, received from the apostles and their disciples its faith in one God, the Father Almighty, who made the heaven, and the earth, and the seas, and all that is in them, and in one Christ Jesus, the Son of God, who was made flesh for our salvation, and in the Holy Spirit, who through the prophets proclaimed the dispensations of God.[32]

Irenaeus believed that this rule was delivered by the apostles to the church. The church, therefore, has received and continues to preserve the revealed tradition expressed in the rule of faith.

2. The churches were established by the apostles, who also chose their successors. Irenaeus could point to an unbroken succession of bishops in the churches and, as an illustration, listed the bishops in the church at Rome, from Linus to the then current Eleutherus. He chose the Roman church because of its age and pre-eminence. In that way he guaranteed the authenticity of the rule of faith and guarded against the notion of secret traditions. If Jesus had conveyed secret teachings to the apostles, they would have delivered them to their successors, and the apostolic church, not the heretical groups, would then have possessed them. But the apostles did not deliver secrets; they delivered the rule of faith, which is known in all true churches.

3. The church has the apostolic writings. The OT contains the word of Christ by anticipation, but the apostles were eyewitnesses to the incarnation and vehicles for the transmission of Jesus' teachings. But because many books claimed apostolic authorship, a definition of *scripture* was needed and Irenaeus contributed significantly to it. He maintained that there are four gospels, no more and no less. Matthew and John were written by apostles, Mark and Luke by disciples of apostles. Irenaeus also relied on the authority of Paul and quoted from every document now in the NT except Philemon, 3 John, and perhaps Jude.

In citing the authority of the rule of faith, apostolic succession, and the apostolic writings, Irenaeus was probably following the traditional practices of many, but by no means all, churches. The demands of his historical situation and his response to them have made him a figure of crucial significance for early Christianity. He saw the problem of diversity and the need for authority. The honest but simple Christian who is anxious about his salvation needs only to depend on the church, its rule of faith, its bishops,

---

[32] Irenaeus, op. cit., I, 10:1, trans. by E. R. Hardy, in Richardson, op. cit.

and its scriptures. They have authority because the rule of faith is the content of apostolic teaching, because the leaders of the church stand in an unbroken succession from the apostles, and because the scriptures were written by the apostles or by their disciples. With these tools Irenaeus built the foundation for early Catholic Christianity, a foundation that served well for the erection, in succeeding centuries, of a formidable edifice.

Christianity, Judaism, and the Old Testament

Christianity originated within a Jewish matrix, and its fundamental forms and beliefs had been intially shaped under the influence of the Hebrew Scriptures and Jewish religious thought. Thus, it was inevitable that Christians would define themselves in relationship to Jews. We saw that in the period from 30–70 Paul and his opponents engaged in sharp controversy over the validity of Torah for Christians. We also saw that early Jewish Christians faced problems with Jewish dietary regulations. Even in those early decades, Christians were defining the relationship between the two groups.

In the period from 70–185, the question of the relationship between Judaism and Christianity was answered in exceedingly diverse ways. Late Jewish Christians emphasized the continuity between the two, and Marcion totally severed the relationship. In both, Christianity was being defined in relation to Judaism, but the definitions were extreme; neither was to become normative for early Catholic Christians because both were treated as heretical. What was needed was a definition with careful nuances; the documents we will consider now provide such statements, although they turn out to be different from one another. Other writers—such as, Justin—had also given attention to these matters. In every case, what was at stake was not only the relationship of two living religions but the meaning of the OT for Christians. The problem of the OT for early Catholics was that it had been the sacred scripture for Jews but now had to be understood as authoritative for Christians. Thus, the Christian interpretation of the OT was at the heart of the matter.

THE EPISTLE TO THE HEBREWS
The relationship between Judaism and Christianity is not the only concern of the author of Hebrews; indeed, it is probably not his main concern. He seems to know nothing about Judaism as a living religion, but he does know a great deal about the religion of the OT. It is in his treatment of the relationship of the OT to Christ that we can understand implications about the relationship between Judaism and Christianity.

Although this document is called an epistle, there are few signs that it actually was composed as such. There is no address or salutation, but there is an epistolary-type conclusion. Chapter 13 has several moral injuctions, a doxology, a farewell, a reference to Timothy, and a note about the author's travel plans. But the basic document reads more like a sermon than a letter. It contains references appropriate to oral communication and exhortations to a listening rather than a reading audience.[33] It is possible that we have in Hebrews a sermon that was initially preached and then circulated to a distant congregation.

The author is deeply disturbed by a kind of apathy among Christians. His church has faced opposition before and may need to again. In citing the courage of Christians in the first blush of enthusiasm, he raises a question about the preparedness of his contemporaries. He fears that they may not remain faithful and may fall away from the true religion; he challenges them by cataloguing the faithful heroes of the past. That he anticipates bloody persecution is indicated in a threatening word: "In your struggle against sin you have not yet resisted to the point of shedding your blood" (Heb 12:4). The implication is that martyrdom may be necessary in the future. The author, therefore, is probably associated with a church that had passed through a persecution in the previous generation and is now facing another. Such a situation did in fact exist in Rome in the late first century. That church was attacked by Nero in the sixties and by Domitian in the nineties. Clement of Rome first cited Hebrews in c. 95, and his knowledge of it suggests that it was connected with Rome.[34] Hebrews was probably a sermon delivered in Rome during the latter part of the reign of Domitian, c. 90–95.

The title is fairly early but no part of the original document. There is no internal evidence that the author was addressing Hebrew people, or Jews, or Jewish Christians. The title must have been the result of speculation by people who were impressed with the weighty OT material contained in the document and by the contrasts between Judaism and Christianity. Actually, the sermon appears to be addressed to Gentile Christians who were in danger of falling away from their faith.

The author is anonymous, but Christian writers began speculating about him very early. In the East, Hebrews was accepted as Pauline, but western writers were not so sure. Clement of Alexandria (c. 150–c. 215) thought that Paul wrote it in Hebrew and that Luke translated it.[35] Not until the fourth century did the western churches accept it as Pauline. Almost all modern scholars deny Pauline authorship to it on the grounds that it does not claim it, its ideas are different from Paul's, and its date is too late. Speculations continue, however, and authorship by Barnabas, Apollos, Priscilla, or Aquila is frequently proposed. Interesting as these suggestions are, they do not remove the anonymous character of this work.

---

[33] References to the act of speaking may be found in Heb 2:5, 5:11, 6:9, 8:1, and 9:5. A listening audience seems to be addressed in Heb 5:11, 6:9, 10:25 and 32, and 12:4–5. In Heb 11:32 the speaker refers to a lack of time to cover the subject.

[34] Cf. I Clement 17:1 and 36:2–5.

[35] Cf. Eusebius, op. cit., VI, 14:2–3.

Although we may not know the name, we are able to describe the author with a high degree of exactitude. He is a Christian of the second generation. He is acquainted with the OT, and his principles of interpretation are, on the whole, those of Philo, the Alexandrian Jew. His basic philosophy is Platonic; his literary style is the best Greek in the NT. He knows about Judaism from the OT, but not from firsthand experience. He is an intelligent and skillful Gentile-Christian writer, deeply influenced by the OT, Plato, and Philo.

The framework of Platonic thought is fundamental to our author's understanding of the relationship between Judaism and Christianity. He accepts Plato's distinction between the world of ideas and that of shadowy phenomena. The latter contains visible objects, which are imperfect copies of those real entities found only in the world of ideas. He believes, moreover, that Jesus has brought about a direct revelation of reality, a reality that is imperfectly revealed in the OT and, hence, only partially perceived in Judaism.

Central to the relationship between Judaism and Christianity is the concept of sacrifice, with the supporting institutions of the priesthood and the Temple. The author of Hebrews states that sacrifice is necessary for the forgiveness of sins. But the practice of sacrifice in Judaism is only an imperfect realization of this concept, because Jews sacrifice animals in a temporary sanctuary. They have a succession of priests who sin and must sacrifice for themselves and who die and must be replaced. Christians, however, have a direct, real, and permanent sacrifice. Instead of the repeated sacrifice of animals, they have the one sacrifice of the Son of God. Instead of a temporary tabernacle, Jesus has entered the heavenly sanctuary, which is permanent and real. Instead of sacrifice by priests, Christians have Jesus as the one high priest. In his function as high priest, Jesus is the one mediator between us and God, for he is both human and divine. As a human being, he committed no sins, but he knew both humanity and temptation. As divine, he is able to bring about total forgiveness.

Jesus' dual nature means that he is the mediator, but it is necessary for the author to qualify Jesus as priest in another way. He knows that Jesus was not a Levite, so he cannot associate him with the Levitical priesthood, the legitimate line of Jewish priests. He affirms, however, that Jesus is a priest of the Melchizedek order. Melchizedek was described in Genesis 14 as a priest to whom Abraham paid a tithe. He was without ancestry or progeny, but his temporal priority to Levi proves to our author that his priesthood is superior to the Levitical. Jesus is the only other member of that priesthood, and he is the true high priest; the Levites are imperfect copies. Thus, Jesus, as both priest and sacrificial victim, has performed the ultimate and perfect sacrifice, and there is no need for repetitions.

In his own context the author of Hebrews must have intended his sermon to combat lethargy in his church. He elevates his listeners by claiming that their religion is the one reality in a world of imitations. Perhaps he drew the contrast between Christianity and Judaism mainly to inspire the congregation, but the contrast itself is provocative. He does not speak negatively about Judaism, for he regards it as a product of God's revelation. However, it is an imperfect product of a partial revelation, whereas Christianity is in touch with God himslf. This theme is announced in the opening lines:

> In many and various ways God spoke of old to our fathers by the prophets; but in these last days he has spoken to us by a Son, whom he appointed the heir of all things, through whom also he created the world (Heb 1:1–2).

In addition, we must note the tendency of this author to ignore contemporary Judaism and to concentrate exclusively on the OT. This tendency probably implies that he thought of the partial revelation to the Hebrew people as a thing of the past. The full revelation in Christ makes any alternative religion, including Judaism, passé.

THE EPISTLE OF BARNABAS

In the Epistle of Barnabas, as in the letter to the Hebrews, the author is not exclusively concerned with the relationship of Christianity and Judaism. At the end of Barnabas there is a section that deals with Christian ethics, in which the "way of light" is contrasted with the "way of darkness." This section is quite similar to a section of a document that will be treated subsequently here, the Didache. It is likely that both versions of this "two ways" teaching are based on an older Jewish or Christian source. This kind of ethical instruction comes to be associated with baptism, in preparation for which the initiate was taught the way to follow and the way to avoid. The last section in Barnabas may originally have been part of a baptismal ritual.

Despite the interest in ethical teachings, the bulk of the Epistle of Barnabas lays out an interpretation of the OT and of Judaism. The author affirms that Christians have been given the divine covenant that Jews never accepted. He attacks the view that God's covenant belongs to both Christians and Jews. To him the sin of the Jews is total, and they are not to be regarded as God's people. He explicitly condemns Jewish sacrifices, as well as the practice of circumcision, the Sabbath, and the dietary regulations. Yet he holds firmly to the authority of the OT. He maintains that Moses and the prophets taught the things of God well, but that the people of Israel never rightly understood them. What is required for understanding is gnosis, which appears to involve an allegorical understanding of the Hebrew Scriptures. For example, the OT prohibition against eating swine is really a prohibition against associating with people who are like pigs. The requirement of circumcision does not refer to a cutting of the foreskin, but to the ear that has been opened to hear the word of God and to the heart that believes. The author of Barnabas also employs a typological interpretation of the OT. In this method the interpreter attempts to find evidences for the work of Christ in the OT. Persons, events, and practices in the OT are understood to be models, or types, of Christ. In Genesis 17, for example, Abraham circumcised 318 men. This is not to be understood, says Barnabas, as a fleshly circumcision but as an anticipation of Jesus' death on the cross, because the 18 is the numerical equivalent of JE (for Jesus) and the 300 = T, the shape of the cross. His basic attitude toward the OT is expressed in these words: "See how appropriately Moses legislated! But how could they [the Jews] perceive or undersand these things? But since we [Christians] rightly understand the commandments, we are speaking as the Lord desired."[36]

Although this document is called an epistle, it probably did not circulate as one. It has certain formal characteristics of a letter—namely, a salutation, a benediction, and a few artificially personal words—but the body of the document reads more like a sermon or a teaching tract. External sources retain little information about the author or about the circumstances under which he wrote. The textual history indicates that it was first known in Alexandria, so it may have been written there. The author is aware of the destruction of the Jerusalem Temple in 70 and appears to allude to the construction in Jerusalem of a new temple. This may be an allusion to Roman plans to build a temple of Jupiter on the site of the Jewish Temple. The threat to build the Roman temple was a cause of the Jewish rebellion in 132–135. If the statements in Barnabas are allusions to this planned construction, a date after 132 would be appropriate for the writing of this document; however, the statements are not sufficiently clear to enable us to date it confidently.

It is also difficult to comment on the character of the author, who is essentially anonymous. He certainly is hostile to a Judaism that observes circumcision and dietary regulations, but he has a deep reverence for the OT. He is aware of the Jewish use of the scriptures, and he works hard to employ an alternative method of interpretation. For him Christianity is independent of Judaism, and Christians are the only people of God. The author's use of gnosis and related terms may indicate that he was influenced by Gnostic Christianity, but the document was not suspected of Gnosticism in early Christian history. It was widely accepted and considered to be in the mainstream of early Catholic Christianity.

A Sermon of Melito of Sardis

According to Eusebius, Melito, bishop of Sardis, was one of the most prolific writers in the ancient church. He lists some twenty of his works, in-

---

[36] Epistle of Barnabas 10:11e–12a, trans. by Robert A. Kraft, *The Apostolic Fathers* (Nashville, Tenn.: Nelson, 1965), Vol. III.

cluding a sermon dated to 167–168.[37] Only fragments of his works survive, but in 1940 an almost complete manuscript of the sermon came to light. In 1958 an even earlier copy appeared, dating from the third century and entitled *On the Passover*.

Melito was involved in a second-century controversy that deeply disturbed relations between Asian and western churches. The former observed the crucifixion of Jesus to coincide with Passover as calculated by the Jewish calendar—namely, on the fourteenth of the Jewish month of Nisan. Christians in Asia Minor were referred to as Quartodecemians, or fourteenthers. In the West it was customary to observe the crucifixion on the Friday following the first day of Passover—that is, on Good Friday. Melito followed the Asian practice, and his sermon is a contribution to the discussion. Although he does not discuss the date of the crucifixion directly, he treats the subject of Jesus' suffering in such a way as to identify it with the observance of Passover.[38]

The sermon begins with a review of the scripture for the day, namely the Passover narrative from the book of Exodus. Melito vividly describes the escape of the Hebrew people and the slaughter of the Egyptians. He then interprets the passage. The Passover holds a dual significance for him. It is both a Jewish institution commemorating a historical event and a type, or model, of the sacrifice of Christ. Melito accepted Christ as pre-existent and active in the history of Israel. Working on this assumption, he finds it possible to discern pre-Jesus examples of Christ's work, examples that are consistent with the deeds of Jesus. He states his own principle: "So the people became the pattern of the Church, and the Law the writing of a parable, and the Church the reservoir of the truth."[39] Melito applies typological interpretation to the Passover narrative and explains that the slaying of the lamb means that Christ suffers for us. The Hebrew sons were spared from plague by the mark of lamb's blood on the doors. The Christian is spared from destruction by the death of Christ. But it is not only in the lamb that Christ's suffering is seen:

> If you wish to see the mystery of the Lord, look at Abel who was slain like him, at Isaac who was bound like him, at Joseph who was sold like him, at the prophets who in like manner suffered for Christ's sake.[40]

The Christ, therefore, appeared in all of these forms and came finally as a man born of a virgin.

---

[37] Cf. Eusebius, op. cit., IV, 26:2.

[38] Paul, in 1 Cor 5:7, seems to express the view that Jesus' crucifixion occurred at the time the Passover lambs were being killed. John 19:14 agrees with Paul, but the synoptic chronology does not.

[39] Melito, *On the Passover* 40, trans. by Campbell Bonner, *The Homily on the Passion by Melito Bishop of Sardis* (Philadelphia: U. of Pa., 1940).

[40] Ibid., 59.

In the latter half of the sermon, Melito turns his attention to the Jews, whom he makes responsible for the death of Jesus. He acknowledges that the suffering of the Christ was foreordained by God, but he believes that the Jews could have avoided guilt in the matter. They could have washed their hands of guilt as did Pilate; they could have pleaded with God to let him die by the hands of the Gentiles; but they crucified him. As a result, the Passover of the Jews is a bitter feast, and they must eat bitter herbs.

With Hebrews, Barnabas, and Melito, Christian independence from Judaism is recognized, although in different ways. In all three we see the tendency to appropriate the OT for exclusively Christian use. Such appropriation required authors to employ something other than literal interpretations. But those authors managed to avoid the extremes of Marcionite Christianity, by maintaining the full authority of the OT and affirming that only Christians really understood it. Explicitly or implicitly, their interpretations put the question of Christian identification in sharp focus. Christianity could no longer be seen as a form of Judaism. The anti-Judaic consequences of this conception are forcibly expressed in Barnabas and Melito. They seemed unable to think of the independence of Christianity without picturing Jews as sinful people whom God had rejected.

Ethical and Ecclesiastical Teachings

Almost no early Christian writing is without ethical teaching. Paul, in his letters, characteristically included teachings about Christian action and duty. The ethical teaching of Jesus formed a large part of many gospels. Barnabas included a long section of the two ways—the way of light and the way of darkness. Instruction in church organization, although not so prevalent as ethical teaching, is not absent. Paul dealt with problems of factionalism in Corinth and Galatia, and he referred to bishops and deacons in Phil 1:1. In late Pauline Christianity concern about church order becomes far more noticeable, as the pastoral letters show. Ignatius also displayed as much concern for the authority of the bishop as he did for his approaching martyrdom. The documents that will be examined here now indicate that order in the churches and ethical instruction were becoming ever more important in early Catholic Christianity.

1 CLEMENT

Near the end of the first century, the Christian church at Rome addressed a letter to the church at Corinth. It was occasioned by a controversy in Corinth over that Church's leadership. Certain younger members had apparently challenged the leaders and had taken over control of the church. Although this was probably more than a simple power struggle, we have no way to determine the issues that may have been involved; nor do we know how word got to Rome about the incident.

Although the letter is known as 1 Clement, it was actually written in the name of the church in Rome. The identification of the author as Clement is not found in the text but is in the traditional titles. The letter was well known to second-century Christian writers, some of whom identified Clement as the author. According to Irenaeus, Peter appointed Linus as the first bishop of Rome, and Linus was succeeded by Anencletus and then by Clement.[41] Eusebius, who identified him with the Clement mentioned in Phil 4:3, said that his episcopacy began in the twelfth year of Domitian's reign—92–93—and ended in the third year of Trajan's—100–101.[42] The Shepherd of Hermas, a second-century writing, mentions Clement as a kind of foreign secretary for the church at Rome.[43]

The external witnesses tend to date 1 Clement to c. 95. The internal evidence confirms the date. The author looks back to the time of the apostles and recognizes that some of the leaders appointed by them are dead. He says that some of the members of the church in Rome have been in it from youth to old age. Corinth is called an ancient church. The persecution in which Peter and Paul died is well in the past. But the author is living in the generation after the apostles, for he says that some of their appointees are still alive. It is probable that he speaks of a persecution under Domitian as his own historical context. He apologizes to the Corinthians for not writing sooner, saying that, "It is because of a series of misfortunes and accidents that suddenly came upon us, beloved, that we have in our view been rather slow in turning our attention to the matters in dispute among you."[44] In several places he speaks of current imprisonments of Christians and of potential dangers. The prayer at the end of the letter includes the petition, "And deliver us from those who hate us without a cause."[45] In spite of all this, the author upholds the virtue of obedience to the rulers. A date of 95 for 1 Clement would satisfy all known conditions.

The chief purpose of the letter is to resolve the problem of rebellion in the Corinthian church. It seems to be addressed to those who were holding power in Corinth, and Clement appeals to them to return the church to its former situation. He does not regard the ringleaders of the rebellion as non-Christians or as heretics, and he seems to be unaware of any ideological issues. His appeal is from Christian to Christian, and he expects the Corinthian rebels to understand order as a Christian virtue.

To Clement the gravity of rebellion lies in the fact that the leaders who were overthrown were appointed by the apostles, or stood in succession from them, and governed with the consent of the whole church. Here for

[41] Cf. Irenaeus, op. cit., III, 3:3.
[42] Cf. Eusebius, op. cit., III, 15; III, 34.
[43] Cf. Shepherd of Hermas 8:3.
[44] 1 Clement 1:1, trans. by Robert M. Grant and Holt H. Graham, *The Apostolic Fathers* (Nashville, Tenn.: Nelson, 1965), Vol. II.
[45] Ibid., 60:3.

the first time we have an explicit formulation of the doctrine of apostolic succession. This doctrine affirms that the only legitimate leader in a church is one who is able to trace his line of succession back to one of the apostles. Clement understands that church unity depends on clear lines of authority. But he also believes that church order conforms to the divine will. He alludes to OT models of the divine appointment of descendants of Aaron as priests. About apostolic succession he says:

> And our apostles knew through our Lord Jesus Christ that there would be strife over the title of bishop. So for this reason, because they had been given full foreknowledge, they appointed those mentioned above and afterward added the stipulation that if these should die, other approved men should succeed to their ministry. Those therefore who were appointed by them or afterward by other reputable men with the consent of the whole Church, who in humility have ministered to the flock of Christ blamelessly, quietly, and unselfishly, and who have long been approved by all—these men we consider are being unjustly removed from their ministry.[46]

A significant implication of Clement's letter revolves around the assumed relationships between the churches of Rome and Corinth. It appears that, even at this early date, the church at Rome felt responsible for maintaining order in other places. Not only does Clement write to Corinth in the name of the church, he also sends ambassadors to mediate between the opposing groups and to restore peace. He writes without apology for interfering, as if such were his acknowledged right. There is no other evidence that Corinth naturally looked to Rome for leadership or that Rome had yet maintained a position of supremacy over others. It is more likely that the letter arose out of a genuine concern and that Clement saw his authority as based on moral right rather than ecclesiastical position. The tone of the letter is that of one who sees a fellow Christian acting in error and who thus speaks with the conviction of being in the right. Witness the statement near the end of the letter: "For you will give us joy and gladness if you prove obedient to what we have written through the Holy Spirit and desist from wanton, jealous anger in accordance with the plea for peace and harmony which we have made in this letter".[47]

A large part of the letter is devoted to ethical instruction. But it is ethical instruction that appears to the author to be appropriate to the situation at hand. It emphasizes the virtues of patience, sobriety, self-discipline, and humility. It warns against arrogance, jealousy, and disobedience to God's commands. The importance of order probably lies behind the positive attitude toward the state, which Clement holds despite the references to persecution. He even treats the Roman army as an example of the kind of order that should prevail among Christians.

---

[46] Ibid., 44:1–30.
[47] Ibid., 63:2.

The author quotes abundantly from the OT, and he also knows some Pauline writings and the letter to the Hebrews. Stoic thought also appears to be an influence on Clement, for he establishes the need for order partly on the basis of the concept of natural law. He uses natural law to prove the validity of belief in the resurrection. But he also supports this belief by referring to the legend of the phoenix, which appears to have been widely known and believed at this time.

THE DIDACHE

The Greek word *didache* means teaching, and the full title of this Greek document is "The Lord's Teaching to the Heathen by the Twelve Apostles." It, and a companion known as the *Doctrina,* in Latin, were discovered in the nineteenth century. They both probably came from an original source in Greek, for the first half of the Didache is about the same as the *Doctrina*. The *Doctrina* is probably a Latin translation of the Greek original, and the Greek Didache is a copy. The Epistle of Barnabas has much of the same material, and some of it also appears in the fourth-century document *The Apostolic Church Order*.

The shared material appears in the first section of the Didache. It consists of ethical instruction about two ways, which sets forth a comprehensive body of teaching. The way of life includes loving God and the neighbor and following the ten commandments. The Christian is told not to get angry, because that leads to murder, and not to lie, because that leads to theft. He is also commanded to share freely with the needy. The way of death is the neglect of the commandments:

> But the Way of Death is this: First of all, it is wicked and full of cursing—murderers, adulteries, lusts, sexual promiscuities, thefts, idolatries, magic arts, sorceries, robberies, false testimonies, hypocrisies, duplicities, guile, conceit, malice, stubbornness, greediness, foul speech, jealousy, arrogance, pride, boastfulness.[48]

The two-ways section ends with these words: "For if you can bear the whole yoke of the Lord, you will be perfect; but if you cannot, do what you can."[49]

The second section of the Didache is devoted to a set of instructions about church order and ritual. It includes regulations about diet, fasting, prayer, the performance of baptism and the Eucharist, the election of bishops and deacons, and the treatment of itinerant teachers, prophets, and apostles. In some of these teachings there is a moderate tone. In regard to food, the Christian is advised to do what he is able, so long as he eats no meat that has been sacrificed to an idol. Baptism should be done in cold

[48] Didache 5:1, trans. by Kraft, op. cit.
[49] Ibid., 6:2.

running water, but it may be done in warm still water. If an adequate body of water is not available, pouring is permitted. Other teachings seem to allow for no deviation. Fasting is to be observed on Wednesdays and Fridays because "the hypocrites" do it on Mondays and Thursdays. The Lord's prayer (from Matt 6:9–13) is to be used three times a day. There is a prescribed form for the Eucharist, which is to be observed each Sunday and is only open to the baptized. The cup of wine is given first, with the words:

> *We thank you, our Father, for the holy vine of David your servant,*
> > *which you have made known to us through Jesus your Servant.*
> *Glory to you forever!* [50]

As the bread is distributed, the following prayer is used:

> *We thank you, our Father, for the life and knowledge*
> > *which you have made known to us through Jesus your Servant.*
> *Glory to you forever!*
> *Just as this loaf previously was scattered on the mountains, and when*
> > *it was gathered together it became a unity,*
> *So may your Church be gathered together from the ends of the earth*
> > *into your kingdom.*
> *For glory and power are yours forever, through Jesus Christ!* [51]

A final prayer concludes the observance.

We have already seen that itinerant preachers and prophets sometimes caused problems in Christian communities. The Didache shows that the problems continued, for it spells out ways in which a commuity can tell the difference between a true and a false prophet or apostle. A false one will remain in a community for three days or more and will request money. "And every prophet who, in the spirit, orders a table to be spread shall not eat therefrom; but if he does, he is a false prophet." [52] But a prophet who settles in a community and continues a ministry there may have his meals provided. The permanent leaders are the bishops and deacons, who seem to be appointed by the community. There is here no reference to the doctrine of apostolic succession.

The anonymity of the Didache is not a particular disadvantage for the interpreter because it is a community document. The two-ways section was probably read at baptisms, and the other regulations formed a kind of church manual. It probably came out of Syria and may be dated in the mid-second century. It shows acquaintance with the Synoptic Gospels, especially Matthew. It was quoted in some early third-century documents. The Greek two-ways source, which it used, probably dates from the early second century. It came close to being canonized and was highly revered in early Catholic Christianity.

[50] Ibid., 9:2.
[51] Ibid., 9:3–4.
[52] Ibid., 11:9.

The Didache affords us a good look at Christian life and practices at a time of transition. Itinerant preachers were still to be found, but the sedentary Christian communities to which the Didache was addressed were in need of institutional regulations. From the point of view of these churches, the charismatic itinerants were beginning to be thought of as representatives of an era that was passing out of existence.

THE CHARACTER OF EARLY CATHOLIC CHRISTIANITY

The literature we have just examined illustrates some of the concerns and issues that Christians had in the period 70–185. It also illustrates the character of early Catholic Christianity, which should be seen mostly as an attempt to achieve unity.

The ethical teachings and ritual practices in the Didache and 1 Clement became basic in early Catholic Christianity. The uses and interpretations of the OT in Hebrews, Barnabas, and Melito also became widely adopted. But of all the writers we have examined, Irenaeus is the most self-conscious exponent of early Catholic Christianity. More than any other single document, his writing exemplifies the attempt to create a form for the Christian faith with definite and clear limits. To him the church must rest on a definite creed, the authority of the apostolically appointed bishops, and a limited canon of sacred writings. Those three formal elements became the building blocks for early Catholic Christianity, giving it a controlling organization and a means for distinguishing true and false expressions of faith. Irenaeus is our best guide to an understanding of early Catholic Christianity, for he represented it and was a crucial figure in its development. He represented a viewpoint that was probably dominant in his own region, and he stood at a point from which he could look back to diversity and ahead to unity.

The factors that influenced the development of early Catholic Christianity should now be reasonably familiar. It is possible to point to three of them. The first was the perceived delay of Jesus' Parousia. The vivid eschatological expectation of the earliest Christians finally had to give way, and we have already seen the effects of the delay in some of Paul's letters. Late Jewish Christianity retained a belief in the second coming but did not expect its immediate fulfillment. Johannine and Gnostic Christianity substituted or emphasized a belief in some form of eternal life for the individual rather than a cataclysmic end to history. The problems of waning enthusiasm are treated in 2 Peter. Early Catholic Christians adapted to the delay by retaining in their creed a statement of the second coming but at the same time giving attention to the structure of a continuing Christian commu-

The Enthroned Christ, mosaic dating from before 547 CE, Church of San Vitale, Ravenna, Italy. (Courtesy Basilica di S. Vitale, Ravenna, and Alinari/Art Resource, Inc.)

nity, with a definite church order and specific ethical teachings. They probably expected nothing to happen in the immediate future. The church finally came to emphasize the immortality of individual Christians and to de-emphasize the corporate resurrection on the last day. By the fourth century Eusebius was able to characterize Papias as somewhat stupid for his materialistic eschatological expectations.[53]

A second factor in the development of early Catholic Christianity was the very fact of diversity. A movement that had once embraced a wide freedom in the expression of faith began to ask if such diversity were not dissolving the very meaning of the movement. Can Christianity mean anything if it includes both late Jewish Christians and Gnostic Christians? The situation is complicated by the fact that the diverse groups were making religious claims. When we proclaim a religious doctrine, we are not simply giving an opinion, which can be discussed, analyzed, and finally accepted or rejected. We believe that we are uttering an absolute truth, and we are demanding acceptance and allegiance from our listeners. When two or more competing claims are made in the name of one religious system, mutual rejection is more likely to result than mutual acceptance. To solve the problem, we may call for a dissolution of the movement into independent groups or plead for unity amid a tolerable diversity. Early Catholic Christianity pursued a third alternative. It intended to create a united church, but it did so by attempting to identify the heart of Christianity and by proclaiming the core doctrines over against the diverse claims of competing groups. Its proponents did this not simply in order to preserve meaningfulness for the word *Christian,* but in order to remain faithful to what they believed they had found in Jesus the Christ.

A third factor influencing early Catholic Christianity was the threat from outside. The apologists, who attempted to answer the challenges of Roman authority, knew that they had to produce an image of Christianity that was acceptable to the government officials. Thus, it turned out that Christianity had to be understood as excluding some people who claimed to be Christians. Justin deplored the fact that Christians did not all believe the same things and live the same way. He called on Rome to differentiate between various Christians and to punish only those who committed actual crimes. In affirming that Christianity is not a crime, he implied that the true Christian is not a criminal, an implication that Athenagoras made explicit. This means that not all who claim the name are really Christians. Oppression and persecution taught the church that it needed a visible unity, for it was recognized that a divided church could not long stand.

Irenaeus had made clear the formal elements in early Catholic Christian-

---

[53] Cf. Eusebius, op. cit., III, 39:12. It should be noted, however, that Montanist Christianity, which held to a vivid eschatological belief, continued to be popular into the third century. It attracted such a notable Christian leader as Tertullian.

ity—namely, a definite creed, the authority of the bishops, and a canon of scripture. In insisting on particular forms, he also had in mind the preservation of certain emphases and beliefs, for form without content is meaningless. A further analysis of Irenaeus' forms should give us some insight into the interests and beliefs of early Catholic Christianity. We therefore ask: Why did early Catholic Christianity, as illustrated by Irenaeus, insist on these formal elements?

The creed, or rule of faith, that Irenaeus cited gives explicit notice of the things he feels Christians must hold to.[54] To him it expresses the faith of the apostles and of the universal church. The claim of universality must not be taken lightly. It is probable that the creed was recited in a significant number of churches, and, if so, we can say that early Catholic Christianity had achieved a degree of unity before Irenaeus. The creed expresses belief in one God, who is the creator, one Christ, the Son of God, who was made flesh, and the Holy Spirit, who inspired the prophets to foretell every event of Jesus' life. It concludes with a recitation of the events of Jesus' life and death. It emphasizes monotheism, the historicity and humanity of Jesus the martyr, creation as the work of one God, and the inspiration of the prophets.

The authority of the bishop was a particularly important safeguard for faith. We saw that Ignatius and Clement insisted on this, as did Irenaeus. Irenaeus accepted the doctrine of apostolic succession, that was first made explicit in 1 Clement. The doctrine guards the episcopacy against false claimants, for the bishop must stand in a line of succession from the apostles. The form implies two major emphases in early Catholic thought. In the first place there is an implicit emphasis on historical continuity. Irenaeus believes that the faith he holds is in conformity with that of the apostles and the first Christians. Whether or not he is correct is debatable, but the fact that he makes the claim indicates that he is interested in the historical manifestation of faith. On this point he may be contrasted with the Gnostics and with Marcion. Gnostics did not insist on apostolic authority for their doctrines and usually de-emphasized the importance of historical contact with Jesus. They taught that gnosis comes to a person quite independently of previous historical events. Marcion revered Paul, but he was quite sure that the other apostles understood nothing of the message that Jesus taught. Irenaeus, in his argument against the secret doctrines of the Gnostics, insisted on the historical visibility of the revelation in the Christ and the continuity in the transmission of the revelation. It was primarily in reaction against Gnostic disparagement and esoteric claims that Irenaeus adopted the doctrine of apostolic succession, and it is apparent that historical continuity is important to him. In the second place, apostolic succession implies an emphasis on the historical Jesus. What gives authority to the apostles is the

[54] Cf. Irenaeus, op. cit., I, 10:1.

fact that they had been with Jesus. Irenaeus makes his own stand clear in his polemic against Docetism. Those who accepted a docetic Christology found it necessary to say that the apostles were deceived and that their testimony should be dismissed. Irenaeus correspondingly emphasized the disciples' contact with a genuinely human, flesh-and-blood Jesus, who is nonetheless the Son of God. In both of these emphases the early Catholic respect for history is apparent.

In this connection it is necessary to comment on Irenaeus' appraisal of the church in Rome. He uses this church as an illustration of the doctrine of apostolic succession, and he lists the first twelve bishops, starting with Linus, who was appointed by Peter and Paul. He justifies giving only one succession list by saying that it would take too long to give them all. But he justifies his choice of Rome by saying that it is the oldest and best-known church and that it was established by the two "most glorious apostles Peter and Paul." He adds, "For every church must be in harmony with this Church because of its outstanding pre-eminence."[55] Irenaeus does not draw any additional implications from these statements, but he lays a basis for others to do so. He does not claim that the Roman bishop is supreme over other bishops. But his words will allow that claim to be made, and it will be made in subsequent centuries.

The canon of sacred writings was for Irenaeus the third guarantee of the faith. Earlier, his opponent Marcion had shaped a canon consisting of Luke and Paul. Perhaps Irenaeus was aware of the strength that this canon provided for Marcionite Christians. He surely saw the danger of the particular one that Marcion used. Irenaeus was also aware of the plethora of gospels, letters, apocalypses, and other Christian writings that had appeared and of the confusion and havoc that had resulted. His response was to say that there is a limited number of books that contain the authoritative word of God. All doctrines must be measured by these books. That is the meaning of canon.

Irenaeus' canon was made up of two major divisions: the OT and the NT. The inclusion of the OT, probably with the so-called Apocrypha, was in direct contrast to Marcion's canon. It is in line with the treatments in Hebrews, Barnabas, Melito, and Justin, all of whom regarded the OT as sacred. At various places in his book Irenaeus alludes to specific reasons for including the OT in the Christian canon. In the first place, it taught monotheism. Irenaeus was convinced that the first Christians were monotheistic. He was equally convinced that Valentinian Gnosticism taught polytheism, because it spoke of Gods in the plural. He also felt that true Christianity was opposed to Marcionite belief in two Gods and that the OT provided a means to counter this teaching. In the second place, the OT taught that the world was created by one God. Monotheism and a positive attitude toward

55 Ibid., III, 3:2, trans. by Hardy, op. cit.

creation go together. Against the background of some form of dualism or polytheism, one can be wholly negative about the world, as Gnostics were. Irenaeus knew that the OT would counter Gnostics and Marcionites on this score. The third reason for the retention of the OT was the belief that the prophets had foretold the coming of Christ and his church. This too is an anti-Marcionite reaction, for Marcion said that the prophets were inspired by the creator-God, not by the father of Jesus Christ. Irenaeus' interest in history is again visible. For him the Christ did not suddenly appear on the scene; he was anticipated and announced ahead of time, and he fulfilled the expectations of the ancient prophets, who devoted themselves to the one God. In retaining the OT, Irenaeus emphasizes the continuity between Christianity and Hebrew religion.

Irenaeus imparted a shape to the NT section of the canon that has remained essentially the same up to our own time. His insistence on four gospels almost certainly represents current tradition in the regions that he knows. Even the order that he used—Matthew, Mark, Luke, John—remained normative. His justification for the number four may appear to be ill-founded, but it represents his sense that the concept of four gospels harmonizes with the fundamental structure of the world:

> The Gospels could not possibly be either more of less in number than they are. Since there are four zones of the world in which we live, and four principal winds, while the Church is spread over all the earth, and the pillar and foundation of the Church is the gospel, and the Spirit of life, it fittingly has four pillars, everywhere breathing out incorruption and revivifying men.[56]

Irenaeus is by no means so explicit about the other books of the NT, but it is possible to discover which ones had canonical authority by studying his references and quotations. One reconstruction of Irenaeus' NT is shown in Figure 25 (p. 432). Only the order of the gospels appears to be sacrosanct. The other books have no particular arrangement. In this figure the question marks indicate a degree of uncertainty about the status of certain documents.

In this list is should be noted that all of the documents from Romans through Titus are judged by Irenaeus to be letters of Paul, including all those we have designated as late Pauline. The other letters were thought to have been written by other apostles. The last two books on the list are Christian apocalypses, at least in form. The Shepherd of Hermas is a Christian teaching tract that was written in the form of an apocalypse. Incidentally, it appears in the Muratorian canon, with a note that it is not to be read in church but may be read privately.[57]

Irenaeus emphasizes the apostolic origin of the NT documents. Therefore he is able to correlate the apostolic appointment of church leaders with

---

[56] Ibid., III, 11:8.
[57] For the Muratorian canon, cf. Hennecke, op. cit., pp. 42–45.

IRENAEUS' NT CANON

Matthew
Mark
Luke
John
Acts of the Apostles
Romans
1, 2 Corinthians
Galatians
Ephesians
Philippians
Colossians
1, 2 Thessalonians
1, 2 Timothy
Titus
Hebrews?
James?
1 Peter
1 John
2, 3 John?
The Revelation of John
The Shepherd of Hermas?

Figure 25   Irenaeus' NT canon

the apostolic origin of the church's canon. However, Irenaeus was probably in error about the origin of some of the NT documents, and he was aware of many others that contained claims about apostolic authorship. He must, therefore, have had additional considerations that influenced his choices. Some rejected writings were excluded because they were associated with rejected groups, but that is probably not the case with all of them. Although the situation is far from clear, William Farmer has recently called attention to the emphasis on martyrdom that may be found in the canonical documents.[58] Farmer reminds us that Irenaeus worked in an atmosphere of persecution, that his community in Gaul had recently gone through horrifying events, and that Irenaeus' predecessor as bishop had been executed. In this situation martyrdom inevitably receives a great deal of attention, and consequently a community under threat of persecution would find documents about martyrdom to be most meaningful. Farmer suggests that it was the prevalence of persecution that underlay Irenaeus' canonical choices. He writes:

And his [Irenaeus'] New Testament embraced the scriptures of the martyrs. The gospels reminded all Christians of the martyrdom of Jesus. The epistles reminded them of the martyrdom of the apostles. Acts reminded them of the

[58] Cf. William R. Farmer, *Jesus and the Gospel* (Philadelphia: Fortress Press, 1982), pp. 178–259.

martyrdom of Stephen. The Revelation of John reminded them of the martyrdom of the saints. Virtually the whole of what Irenaeus championed as New Testament scripture reminded the church of the central role of martyrdom in the life of God's people.[59]

If Farmer is right, Irenaeus had practical as well as ideological reasons for elevating Matthew, Mark, Luke, and John to canonical status. Those gospels, more clearly than any others that he may have known, present Jesus' death as a martyrdom.

For the most part, Irenaeus' insistence on the historical, nondocetic character of the life and death of Jesus is reflected in his choice of gospels. The Synoptic Gospels clearly affirm Jesus' historicity. The Gospel of John, however, appears to be dominated by an ahistorical character that goes against the grain of Irenaeus' thinking. Perhaps he was so sure about the apostolic origin of this gospel that any judgment about it on the basis of its content was out of the question. We know that Irenaeus insisted that the Fourth Gospel was written by the disciple John.[60]

This analysis of Irenaeus' formal elements has enabled us to discover some of the beliefs that early Catholic Christianity insisted on preserving: the continuity of Christian faith with the Hebrew Scriptures; the historicity of Christian faith; the historicity and humanity of the martyr Jesus; the unity of God; the historical value of the prophets; the universality and unity of the church; and the creation of the world by the one God. The most notable characteristic of this form of Christianity is its historical awareness. It adopts a history of salvation—a message predicted by the prophets, proclaimed by Jesus, preserved by the apostles and their successors.

In relation to contemporary varieties of Christianity, early Catholicism was a product of exclusion and assimilation. It accepted the late Jewish-Christian feeling for historical continuity but rejected its ethnic identity. It accepted from Gnosticism the basic human desire for salvation but rejected the entire Gnostic mythic structure and its understanding of divine nature. It also picked up and formalized elements from earlier Christian traditions. It claimed to be continuous with early Jewish Christianity but de-emphasized its eschatological expectation. With Paul, it rejected the demands of Torah but suppressed his emphasis on freedom in the Christian life and virtually ignored the more subtle aspects of his treatment of the relation of Torah and Sin. In large measure it accepted the Johannine Christology and sacramentalism, but it rejected its ahistorical tendency and de-emphasized those points that may have seemed conducive to Gnostic interpretations.

Early Catholic Christianity is a synthetic form made necessary by the historical contingencies of the second century. It was chiefly a reaction and response to the Gnostic and Marcionite challenges. But it had also been

[59] Ibid., p. 209.
[60] Cf. Irenaeus, op. cit., III, 1:1.

growing alongside other forms. It is not simply a synthesis but a retention and elaboration of older views. Once we have seen what this form of thought meant to a person such a Irenaeus, it is possible to look back and see important similarities, which in other contexts served as anticipations for the more developed thought. The late Pauline letters had drawn from Paul but moved surely in the direction of early Catholic thought. The epistle to the Ephesians put a great deal of stress on the unity of the church, and the pastoral letters underscored the authority of church officials. 1 Clement called for obedience to the constituted officers of the church, and Ignatius made the bishop the visible and present representative of Jesus Christ. The author of 2 and 3 John, who called himself a presbyter, felt no reluctance about interfering in distant churches and expecting them to respect his authority. The author of Luke-Acts, in presenting a history of salvation, paved the way for an understanding of historical continuity and for a doctrine of the church as part of the work of God. Luke took special pains to relate all of the early apostles to one another, so that even an independent Paul receives authorization from the Jerusalem apostles. Luke's narrative of the apostles easily led to the doctrine of apostolic succession. Documents such as Jude, 2 Peter, and 1 John show as much concern for the danger of deviant thought as does Irenaeus. Finally, we must call attention to the contribution of the synoptic writers. They do not seem to react in any conscious way against Docetism, but it is significant that they found it appropriate, even necessary, to present their faith in terms of the deeds and sayings of the historical Jesus. Because Christians of all stripes were able to proclaim their faith without any detailed information on the historical Jesus, the effort of the synoptic writers (and to a lesser extent John) stands out in bold relief. In so doing, they gave to early Catholic Christianity a heritage of preserved tradition that armed it to renounce Docetism.

A historical judgment to the effect that the dominance of early Catholic Christianity was inevitable is unwarranted. But because the church moved in this direction, it is possible to see that it made explicit a number of implicit ideas and forms. It is true that it claimed to be in perfect harmony with the religion of early Jewish Christianity, and there is a good deal of merit in the claim. But early Jewish Christianity had the seeds of a number of developments, and late Jewish Christianity made the same claim with equally good justification. The dominance of early Catholic Christianity eventually brought to an end the period of increasing diversity. But that earlier freedom of thought did not completely disappear. The church retained such writings as the letters of Paul and the Gospel of John, in which from time to time people have been able to find grounds for freedom in faith. People will remember that the Johannine Jesus said, "The truth will make you free" (John 8:32). People will remember the battles of Paul against his opponents and will draw analogies to their own battles against what they perceive to be an oppressive church. Ernst Käsemann, a German NT scholar, has dramatically expressed the paradox that, in preserving the letters of Paul, the church preserved the seeds of "her own permanent crisis." "She cannot get away from him who for the most part only disturbs her. For he remains even for her the Apostle to the heathen; the pious still hardly know what to make of him."[61]

DIVERSITY AND UNITY IN EARLY CHRISTIANITY

Now that we have looked at examples of diversity and efforts to achieve unity in early Christianity, it is necessary to see if some answer can be given to the question: What was the nature of early Christianity as a whole (from 30–185 CE)? The question should allow for a reasonable distinction between basic issues and particular approaches.

If we concentrate on the particular approaches, it is clear that early Christianity was an amalgam of changeable and diverse phenomena. It was certainly no one thing, as we have seen. So it is impossible to give a simple answer to the question: What was it like to be a Christian in the early days? The character of one's religion would have depended in part on the precise time and place in which one lived, for Christianity in Judea during the earliest period was not the same as that in Gaul toward the end of the second century. Furthermore, the movement was profoundly affected by the culture of those who embraced it. It mattered a great deal whether one had been a Jew or a Gentile before he or she became a Christian, or whether he or she had been exposed to a body of Gnostic thought. It also mattered a great deal that certain creative thinkers had left the impress of their own personalities and thought on the religion. The NT and early Christianity would have been very different without the writings of Paul, or John, or the anonymous author of Hebrews, or the synoptic writers. It is significant that, in the formation of the NT canon, there was no attempt to eliminate the diversity that is to be seen in these authors.

These observations are important because it is usually assumed that an analysis of the early Christian movement will produce a unified body of ideas that can serve as a means of distinguishing between Christian and non-Christian ideas. But that is not the case, for the ideas must always be classified as Johannine, Pauline, Gnostic, or one of the others. This fact itself reveals a great deal about the character of early Christianity. It was the kind of religion that was subject to change. If our analysis of early Christianity can point to any one thing as characteristic of the movement as a whole, it is that of adaptability. It showed itself to be responsive to the

---

[61] Ernst Käsemann, "Paul and Nascent Catholicism," trans. by Wilfred R. Bunge, in *Distinctive Protestant and Catholic Themes Reconsidered* (New York: Harper, 1967), p. 26.

challenges of changing times, diverse thinkers, and cultural differences. To be sure, the movement finally became dominated by early Catholic Christianity, a response to the same stimuli, but one that insisted on the perpetuation of a particular content. But this was not the whole, as we have seen.

If adaptability is accepted as a chief characteristic of the particular approaches in early Christianity, we must yet ask about the basic issues in the movement. The character of a movement is illuminated by the issues to which it addresses itself. Although early Christians produced a variety of answers to the questions, there is yet a kind of unity in the questions themselves. The importance of the questions lies in the fact that they reveal certain underlying concerns. These concerns provide a measure of unity in early Christianity and in the NT. The concerns are two in number: a concern for the relationship between the divine and the human and a concern for the centrality of the Christ.

From earliest days Christians addressed themselves to the problem of the relationship beween the divine and the human. Early Jewish Christians came out of a background that assumed that the relationship had been once and for all proclaimed in terms of Torah, but they came to feel that something more had to be said about the relationship. Other Christians differed widely in their definition of the divine-human relationship, but they agreed that it had suffered some disruption. Paul felt that people were in slavery to Sin and that Torah could not liberate them. Gnostic Christians also talked about human slavery, but they expressed it in a more metaphysical and less historical sense. Amid the diversity, early Christianity showed itself to be concerned with the problem of our relationship to God.

Christians also saw in the Christ the solution to the human problem. All varieties accepted the belief that in the Christ a process of salvation was either beginning or had been completed. It is true that here we come upon an amazing variety of interpretations. Early Jewish Christians emphasized the future as the time of final salvation. Paul looked to the future also, but he felt that the death of Jesus was the central event in which God's justification, reconciliation, and redemption took place. Late Jewish Christians saw the chief significance of Jesus in his abolition of the sacrificial practices of the Jews. Johannine Christianity saw the solution to the human problem in the revelation of the Father granted by the divine-human Jesus, who had been with the Father from the beginning. Gnostic and Marcionite Christians tended to see the solution as a release from the creator-God accomplished by the Christ. Although their portraits were materially different from one another, the variant Christian groups tended to unite under the proposition that the Christ is the solution to the problematical relationship between us and God.

These issues seem to form the framework on which early Christianity operated and on which the NT canon was formed: a recognition of the problematical aspect of human life and a confidence that, in the Christ, God was solving the problem.

BIBLIOGRAPHY

Christians and Persecution
Christian Responses to Persecution

Eusebius. *The Ecclesiastical History*. Trans. by Kirsopp Lake and J. E. L. Oulton. Loeb Classical Library. Cambridge, Mass.: Harvard University Press, 1926, 1932. 2 volumes

Eusebius. *The History of the Church from Christ to Constantine*. Trans. by G. A. Williamson. Minneapolis, Minn.: Augsburg Publishing House, 1965.

Frend, W. H. C. *Martyrdom and Persecution in the Early Church*. New York: Doubleday & Company, Inc., 1967.

Grant, Robert M., ed. *The Apostolic Fathers*, Volume IV. New York: Thomas Nelson Inc., 1966.

Lietzmann, Hans. *The Beginnings of the Christian Church*. 2nd ed. Trans. by Bertram Lee Woolf. New York: Meridian Books, 1949.

Richardson, Cyril C., ed. *Early Christian Fathers*. Library of Christian Classics, Volume I. Philadelphia: Westminster Press, 1953.

Schoedel, William R., ed. *The Apostolic Fathers*. Volume V. New York: Thomas Nelson Inc., 1967.

Two translations of Eusebius' *Ecclesiastical History* are listed. The one translated by Lake and Oulton contains the Greek text and an English translation. The Williamson translation has only the English. The volume of *The Apostolic Fathers* edited by Robert Grant contains an introduction, commentary, and translation of the letters of Ignatius. The volume by Schoedel contains Polycarp's letter to the Philippians and the Martyrdom of Polycarp. Richardson has Ignatius, Polycarp, and the Martyrdom of Polycarp, as well as the writings of Justin and Athenagoras. Richardson also has extensive excerpts from Irenaeus. Frend deals with the history of conflict involving Christians to the mid-fourth century. Lietzmann's is a more general history of Christianity to the middle of the second century.

The Rise of Early Catholic Christianity

Bonner, Campbell. *The Homily on the Passion by Melito Bishop of Sardis*. Philadelphia: University of Pennsylvania Press, 1940.

Grant, Robert M., and Holt H. Graham, eds. *The Apostolic Fathers*. Volume II. New York: Thomas Nelson Inc., 1965.

Kraft, Robert A., ed. *The Apostolic Fathers*. Volume III. New York: Thomas Nelson Inc., 1965.

Roberts, Alexander, and James Donaldson, eds. *The Ante-Nicene Fathers*. Volume I. Grand Rapids, Mich.: Eerdmans, 1885.

The first volume of *The Ante-Nicene Fathers* contains a translation of the complete text of Irenaeus' *Against Heresies*. This volume also contains translations of 1 Clement, Polycarp, Ignatius, Barnabas, and Justin. The volume by Richardson, listed in the previous section, treats 1 Clement and the Didache, and has selections from Irenaeus. The volume by Kraft contains commentary and translation of the Epistle of Barnabas and the Didache, and it shows clearly the overlapping sections in these two documents. The volume by Grant and Graham treats 1 Clement.

The Character of Early Catholic Christianity

Farmer, William R. *Jesus and the Gospel*. Philadelphia: Fortress Press, 1982.

Grant, Robert M. *The Formation of the New Testament*. New York: Harper & Row, Publishers, 1965.

Kelly, J. N. D. *Early Christian Doctrines*. Rev. ed. New York: Harper & Row, Publishers, 1978.

Lietzmann, Hans. *The Founding of the Church Universal*. 2nd ed. Trans. by Bertram Lee Woolf. New York: Meridian Books, 1949.

Von Campenhausen, Hans. *The Formation of the Christian Bible*. Trans. by J. A. Baker. Philadephia: Fortress Press, 1972.

Lietzmann treats the general history of Christianity in the second and third centuries. Kelly deals with a number of Christian doctrines in topical fashion. Although he covers a more extensive period of time than has been treated here, he shows how second-century concepts relate to the later developments. Grant and Von Campenhausen deal with the development of the canon. Farmer also deals with canon in the last section of his *Jesus and the Gospel*.

Diversity and Unity

Bauer, Walter. *Orthodoxy and Heresy in Earliest Christianity*. Ed. by Robert A. Kraft and Gerhard Krodel. Philadelphia: Fortress Press, 1971.

Dunn, J.D.G. *Unity and Diversity in the New Testament*. Philadelphia: Westminster Press, 1977.

Bauer's is a classic study of the problems of diversity and unity. It first appeared in German in 1934. Dunn, although confining his attention to the NT, shows that the problems are to be found in the foundational documents of the Christian church.

Glossary

Apocalypse. A revelation; a document that represents the apocalyptic viewpoint.

Apocalypticism. A viewpoint in Judaism and Christianity that conceives of the suprahistorical as the realm of reality, believes that historical events are controlled in the suprahistorical realm, and retains a belief that history will come to an end.

Apocrypha. Documents contained in some versions of the Hebrew Scriptures, recognized as canonical by early Christians, rejected in modern times by Protestant Christians.

Apology. A defense of Christianity, usually addressed to a government official.

Bar. Aramaic word, used in names, meaning "son of."

Ben. Hebrew word, used in names, meaning "son of."

Bishop. A church officer in Christianity.

Canon. A standard for religious belief; a set of documents recognized as sacred and authoritative by a religious community.

Christology. Christian belief about the nature and function of Jesus.

Christology, Adoptionistic. Christian belief that God adopted Jesus as the Messiah.

Covenant. An agreement or contract between one or more Gods and a group of people who are regarded as chosen by the God or Gods.

Deacon. A church officer in Christianity.

Demiurge. In some forms of Gnostic Christianity, the name of the creator of the universe.

Diaspora. Jewish communities outside the traditional Jewish areas.

Docetism. A belief, frequently associated with Gnostic Christianity, that affirms that Jesus was never a human being.

Episcopacy. A system in Christianity by which the church is governed by bishops.

439

Episcopate, Monarchical.   A system in Christianity in which one bishop holds supreme authority in a particular city and the surrounding region.

Eschatology.   A belief that history will come to an end.

Essenes.   A Jewish sect in Hellenistic times, probably associated with the Dead Sea Scrolls.

Eucharist.   A thanksgiving; a Christian practice in observance of the last supper of Jesus, involving the use of bread and wine, and specifically commemorating Jesus' death.

Evangelist.   One who preaches the Christian message; an author of a Christian gospel.

Form Criticism.   A study of oral traditions that attempts to discover the early form of a narrative or a saying.

Gentile.   A non-Jew.

Glossolalia.   The ability to speak in an unknown tongue.

Gnosis.   Greek word meaning "knowledge."

Gospel.   A formulation of the Christian message in terms of sayings and actions of Jesus.

Gospel, Fourth.   The Gospel of John.

Gospels, Apocryphal.   Christian gospels that were not included in the NT canon when it was finally formulated.

Gospels, Canonical.   Matthew, Mark, Luke, and John.

Gospels, Synoptic.   Christian gospels that are similar to one another in perspective and content; Matthew, Mark, and Luke.

Hellenistic.   Greeklike; a historical period from 336–31 BCE; the dominant culture in the eastern Mediterranean during that historical period and during the Roman period (31 BCE–306 CE).

Homily.   A sermon.

Kerygma.   Greek word meaning "preaching."

Logos.   Greek word with multiple meanings, usually translated "word." It often has religious meanings and stands for a being who is a mediator between God and humans.

Messiah.   Hebrew word meaning "anointed." It frequently is used in apocalyptic literature as a title for the agent God is expected to use in bringing history to a close; equivalent to the title "Christ."

Mishnah.   A written collection of Jewish laws that had formerly been oral; the best known is that by Judah ha-Nasi in c. 200 CE.

Monotheism.   Belief in the existence of one and only one God.

Parable.   A form of teaching found in the Christian oral tradition; a metaphor told as a story.

Parousia.   A Christian belief in the return, or second coming, of Jesus after his death and resurrection.

Pentecost.   Greek name for the Jewish observance (Shavuot) that probably commemorated the making of the Hebrew covenant; in Christianity, the observance of the occasion on which Jesus' followers first received the Holy Spirit.

Pericope. A small literary unit, such as a narrative or a form of teaching.

Pharisees. A Jewish sect in the Hellenistic period that believed in a two-fold law, one part written, one part oral.

Pleroma. Greek word meaning "fullness;" in Gnostic Christianity, the name of the divine realm.

Presbyter. A church officer in Christianity; same as "elder."

Pronouncement Story. A form of teaching found in the Christian oral tradition; a saying with a narrative introduction that concludes with a pronouncement of Jesus.

Pseudepigrapha. Literally "false writings"; writings that claim to have been written by authors who lived earlier; a group of books revered by some Jews and Christians in the Hellenistic period.

Redaction Criticsm. A form of study that concentrates on the editorial work of the authors of the Christian gospels.

Sadducees. A Jewish sect in the Hellenistic period that accepted only the written Torah as authoritative.

Tanach. The Hebrew Scriptures.

Terminus a Quo. Latin phrase meaning "time from which;" the earliest time at which a document could have been written.

Terminus ad Quem. Latin phrase meaning "time toward which;" the latest time at which a document could have been written.

Typology. A form of interpretation that understands narratives and teachings in the OT as patterns for what Jesus was later to do and say.

Yahweh. Hebrew name for the God of the covenant.

Zealots. A name for several Jewish sects that, in the Roman period, opposed the Roman occupation and control of Judea.

Index

Note: Page numbers in *italics* refer to pages on which figures and illustrations appear.